MBA Managerial Economics–Macroeconomics Component

A Custom Edition for The University of Texas at Austin McCombs School of Business

Taken from:

Money, the Financial System, and the Economy, Sixth Edition
by R. Glenn Hubbard

Published by Addison-Wesley
75 Arlington Street, Suite 300
Boston, MA 02116

Macroeconomics, Third Edition
by Stephen D. Williamson

Published by Addison-Wesley

International Economics, Fourth Edition
by James Gerber

Published by Addison-Wesley

International Economics, Seventh Edition
by Steven Husted, Michael Melvin

Published by Addison-Wesley

Custom Publishing

New York Boston San Francisco
London Toronto Sydney Tokyo Singapore Madrid
Mexico City Munich Paris Cape Town Hong Kong Montreal

Cover Art: Courtesy of PhotoDisc, EyeWire/Getty Images, brandXpictures

Taken from:

Money, the Financial System, and the Economy, Sixth Edition
by R. Glenn Hubbard

Published by Addison-Wesley
75 Arlington Street, Suite 300
Boston, MA 02116

Macroeconomics, Third Edition
by Stephen D. Williamson

Published by Addison-Wesley

International Economics, Fourth Edition
by James Gerber

Published by Addison-Wesley

International Economics, Seventh Edition
by Steven Husted and Michael Melvin

Published by Addison-Wesley

This special edition published in cooperation with Pearson Custom Publishing.

Printed in the United States of America

10 9 8 7 6 5 4 3 2 1

2008400110

JL

Pearson
Custom Publishing
is a division of

www.pearsonhighered.com

ISBN 10: 0-558-04660-6
ISBN 13: 978-0-558-04660-6

Brief Contents

CONTENTS

CHAPTER 1

Introduction

THIS CHAPTER FRAMES THE APPROACH TO MACROECONOMICS THAT WE TAKE IN THIS BOOK, AND IT foreshadows the basic macroeconomic ideas and issues that we develop in later chapters. We first discuss what macroeconomics is, and we then go on to look at the two phenomena that are of primary interest to macroeconomists, economic growth and business cycles, in terms of post-1900 U.S. economic history. Then, we explain the approach this book takes—building macroeconomic models with microeconomic principles as a foundation—and discuss the issue of disagreement in macroeconomics. Finally, we explore the key lessons that we learn from macroeconomic theory, and we discuss how macroeconomics helps us understand recent and current issues.

What Is Macroeconomics?

Macroeconomists are motivated by large questions and by issues that affect many people and many nations of the world. Why are some countries exceedingly rich while others are exceedingly poor? Why are most Americans so much better off than their parents and grandparents? Why are there fluctuations in aggregate economic activity? What causes inflation? Why is there unemployment?

Macroeconomics is the study of the behavior of large collections of economic agents. It focuses on the aggregate behavior of consumers and firms, the behavior of governments, the overall level of economic activity in individual countries, the economic interactions among nations, and the effects of fiscal and monetary policy. Macroeconomics is distinct from microeconomics in that it deals with the overall effects on economies of the choices that all economic agents make, rather than on the choices of individual consumers or firms. Since the 1970s, however, the distinction between microeconomics and macroeconomics has blurred in that microeconomists and macroeconomists now use very similar tools. That is, the **economic models** that macroeconomists use, consisting of descriptions of consumers and firms, their objectives and constraints, and how they interact, are built up from microeconomic principles, and these models are typically analyzed and fit to data using methods similar to those used by microeconomists. What continues to make macroeconomics distinct, though, is the issues it focuses on, particularly **long-run growth** and **business cycles.** Long-run growth refers to the increase in a nation's productive capacity and average standard of living that occurs over a long period of time, whereas business cycles are the short-run ups and downs, or booms and recessions, in aggregate economic activity.

The approach in this book is consistently to build up macroeconomic analysis from microeconomic principles. There is some effort required in taking this type of approach, but the effort is well worth it. The result is that you will understand better how the economy works and how to improve it.

Gross Domestic Product, Economic Growth, and Business Cycles

To begin our study of macroeconomic phenomena, we must first understand what facts we are trying to explain. The most basic set of facts in macroeconomics has to do with the behavior of aggregate economic activity over time. One measure of aggregate economic activity is **gross domestic product (GDP)**, which is the quantity of goods and services produced within a country's borders during some specified period of time. GDP also represents the quantity of income earned by those contributing to domestic output. In Figure 1.1 we show real GDP per capita for the United States for the period 1900–2005. This is a measure of aggregate output that adjusts for inflation and population growth, and the unit of measure is thousands of 2000 dollars per person.

The first observation we can make concerning Figure 1.1 is that there has been sustained growth in per capita GDP during the period 1900–2005. In 1900, the average income for an American was \$4,232 (2000 dollars), and this grew to \$37,773 (2000 dollars) in 2005. Thus, the average American became about nine times richer in real terms over the course of 105 years, which is quite remarkable! The second important observation from Figure 1.1 is that, while growth in per capita real GDP was sustained over long periods of time in the United States during the period 1900–2005, this growth was certainly not steady. Growth was higher at some times than at others, and there were periods over which per capita real GDP declined. These fluctuations in economic growth are business cycles.

Two key, though unusual, business cycle events in U.S. economic history that show up in Figure 1.1 are the Great Depression and World War II, and these events dwarf any other twentieth-century business cycle events in the United States in terms of the magnitude of the short-run change in economic growth. During the Great Depression, real GDP per capita dropped from a peak of \$7,105 (2000 dollars) per person in 1929 to a low of \$5,056 (2000 dollars) per person in 1933, a decline of about 29%. At the peak of war production in 1944, GDP had risen to \$13,053 (2000 dollars) per person, an increase of 158% from 1933. These wild gyrations in aggregate economic activity over a 15-year period are as phenomenal, and certainly every bit as interesting, as the long-run sustained growth in per capita GDP that occurred from 1900 to 2005. In addition to the Great Depression and World War II, Figure 1.1 shows other business cycle upturns and downturns in the growth of per capita real GDP in the United States that, though less dramatic than the Great Depression or World War II, represent important macroeconomic events in U.S. history.

Figure 1.1 thus raises the following fundamental macroeconomic questions, which motivate much of the material in this book:

1. What causes sustained economic growth?
2. Could economic growth continue indefinitely, or is there some limit to growth?

Figure 1.1 **Per Capita Real GDP (in 2000 dollars) for the United States, 1900–2005.**
Per capita real GDP is a measure of the average level of income for a U.S. resident. Two unusual, though key, events in the figure are the Great Depression, when there was a large reduction in living standards for the average American, and World War II, when per capita output increased greatly.

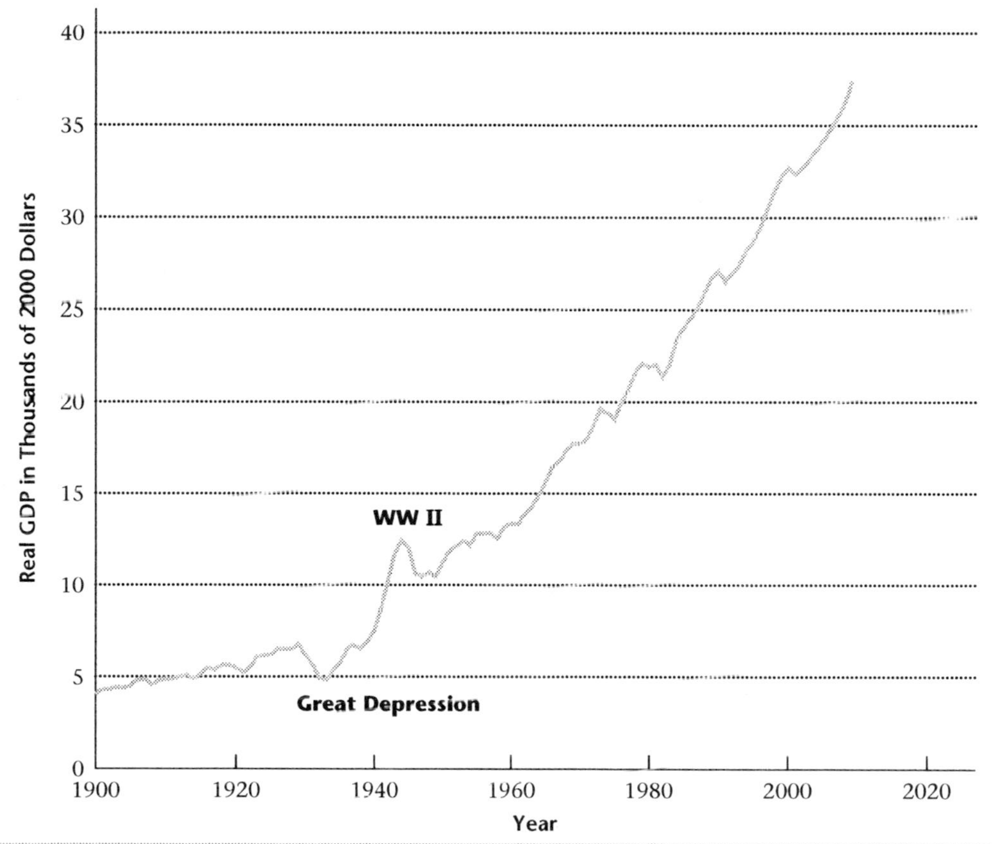

3. Is there anything that governments can or should do to alter the rate of economic growth?
4. What causes business cycles?
5. Could the dramatic decreases and increases in economic growth that occurred during the Great Depression and World War II be repeated?
6. Should governments act to smooth business cycles?

In analyzing economic data to study economic growth and business cycles, it often proves useful to transform the data in various ways, so as to obtain sharper insights. For economic time series that exhibit growth, such as per capita real GDP in Figure 1.1, a useful transformation is to take the natural logarithm of the time series. To show why this is useful, suppose that y_t is an observation on an economic time series in period t; for example, y_t could represent per capita real GDP in year t, where $t = 1900, 1901, 1902$, etc. Then, the growth rate from period $t-1$ to period t in y_t can be denoted by g_t, where

$$g_t = \frac{y_t}{y_{t-1}} - 1.$$

Now, if x is a small number, then $\ln(1+x) \approx x$, that is, the natural logarithm of $1+x$ is approximately equal to x. Therefore, if g_t is small,

$$\ln(1+g_t) \approx g_t,$$

or

$$\ln\left(\frac{y_t}{y_{t-1}}\right) \approx g_t,$$

or

$$\ln y_t - \ln y_{t-1} \approx g_t.$$

Because $\ln y_t - \ln y_{t-1}$ is the slope of the graph of the natural logarithm of y_t between periods $t-1$ and t, then the slope of the graph of the natural logarithm of a time series y_t is a good approximation to the growth rate of y_t when the growth rate is small.

In Figure 1.2 we graph the natural logarithm of real per capita GDP in the United States for the period 1900–2005. As explained above, the slope of the graph is a good approximation to the growth rate of real per capita GDP, so that changes in the slope (e.g., when there is a slight increase in the slope of the graph in the 1950s and 1960s) represent changes in the growth rate of real per capita GDP. It is striking that in Figure 1.2, except for the Great Depression and World War II, a straight line would fit the graph quite well. That is, over the period 1900–2005 (again, except for the Great Depression and World War II), growth in per capita real GDP has been "roughly" constant at about 2.1% per year.

A second useful transformation to carry out on an economic time series is to separate the series into two components: the growth or **trend** component, and the business cycle component. For example, the business cycle component of real per capita GDP can be captured as the deviations of real per capita GDP from a smooth trend fit to the data. In Figure 1.3 we show the trend in the natural log of real per capita GDP as a colored line,[1] while the natural log of actual real per capita GDP is the black line. We then define the business cycle component of the natural log of real per capita GDP to be the difference between the black line and the colored line in Figure 1.3. The logic behind this decomposition of real per capita GDP into trend and business cycle components is that it is often simpler and more productive to consider separately the theory that explains trend growth and the theory that explains business cycles, which are the deviations from trend.

In Figure 1.4 we show only the percentage deviations from trend in real per capita GDP. The Great Depression and World War II represent enormous deviations from trend in real per capita GDP relative to anything else during the time period in the

[1] Trend GDP was computed using a Hodrick–Prescott filter, as in E. Prescott, 1986. "Theory Ahead of Business Cycle Measurement," *Federal Reserve Bank of Minneapolis Quarterly Review*, Fall.

Figure 1.2 **Natural Logarithm of Per Capita Real GDP.**

Here, the slope of the graph is approximately equal to the growth rate of per capita real GDP. Excluding the Great Depression and World War II, the growth rate of per capita real GDP is remarkably close to being constant for the period 1900–2005. That is, a straight line would fit the graph fairly well.

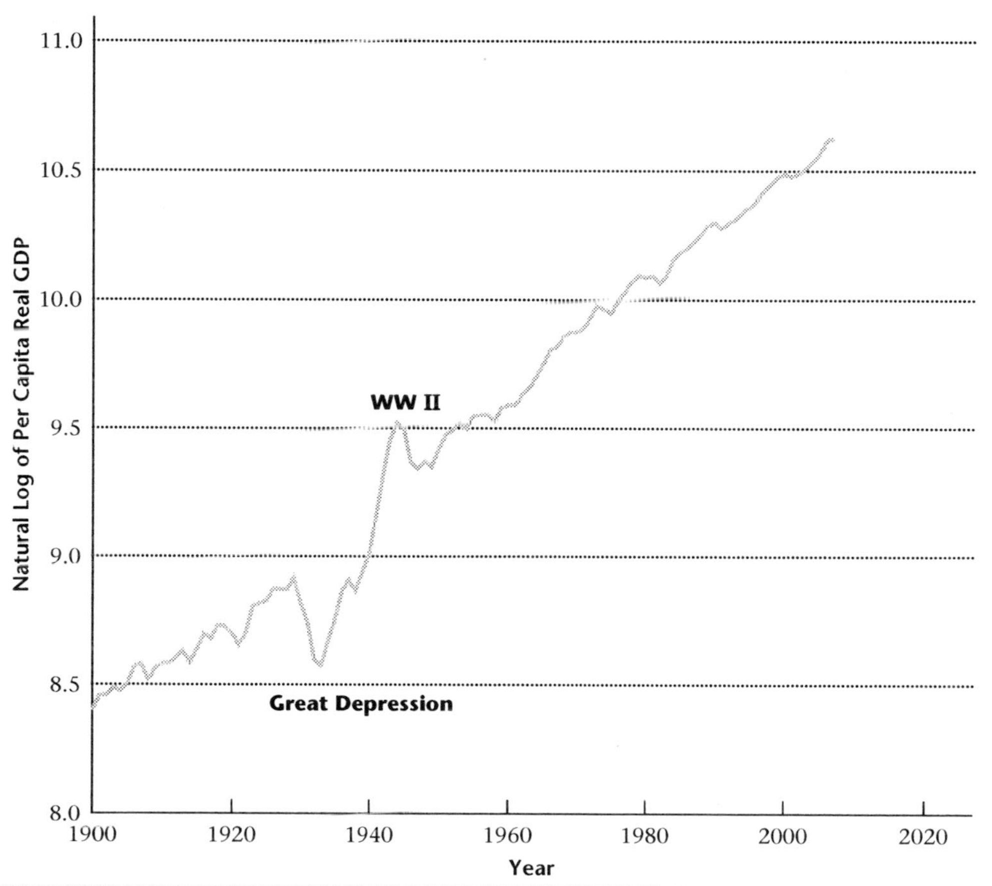

figure. During the Great Depression the percentage deviation from trend in real per capita GDP was close to −20%, whereas the percentage deviation from trend was about 20% during World War II. In the period after World War II, which is the focus of most business cycle analysis, the deviations from trend in real per capita GDP are at most about ±5%.[2]

[2]The extremely large deviation from trend in real per capita GNP in the late 1920s is principally a statistical artifact of the particular detrending procedure used here, which is akin to drawing a smooth curve through the time series. The presence of the Great Depression forces the growth rate in the trend to decrease long before the Great Depression actually occurs.

Figure 1.3 **Natural Logarithm of Per Capita Real GDP and Trend.**
Sometimes it is useful to separate long-run growth from business cycle fluctuations. In the figure, the black line is the natural log of per capita real GDP, while the colored line denotes a smooth growth trend fit to the data. The deviations from the smooth trend then represent business cycles.

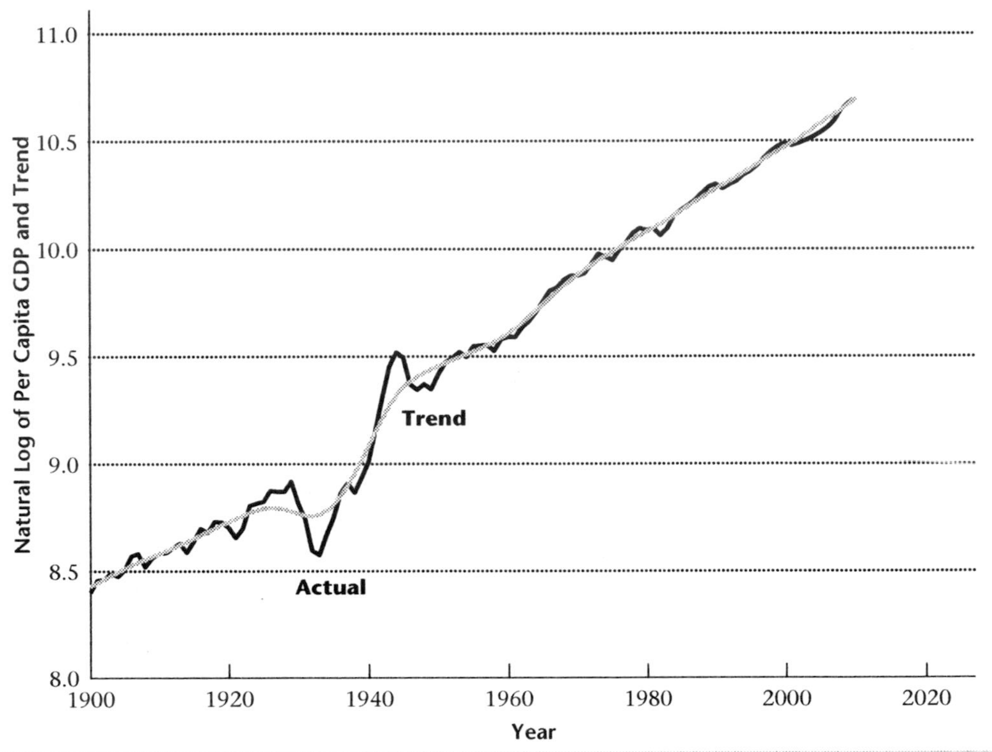

Macroeconomic Models

Economics is a scientific pursuit involving the formulation and refinement of theories that can help us better understand how economies work and how they can be improved. In some sciences, such as chemistry and physics, theories are tested through laboratory experimentation. In economics, experimentation is a new and growing activity, but for most economic theories experimental verification is simply impossible. For example, suppose an economist constructs a theory that implies that U.S. output would drop by half if there were no banks in the United States. To evaluate this theory, we could shut down all U.S. banks for a year to see what would happen. Of course, we know in advance that banks play a very important role in helping the U.S. economy function efficiently and that shutting them down for a year would likely cause significant irreparable damage. It is extremely unlikely, therefore, that the experiment would be carried out. In macroeconomics, most experiments that could be informative are simply too costly to carry out, and in this respect macroeconomics is

Figure 1.4 **Percentage Deviations from Trend in Per Capita Real GDP.**
The Great Depression and World War II represent extremely large deviations from trend relative to post–World War II business cycle activity and business cycles before the Great Depression.

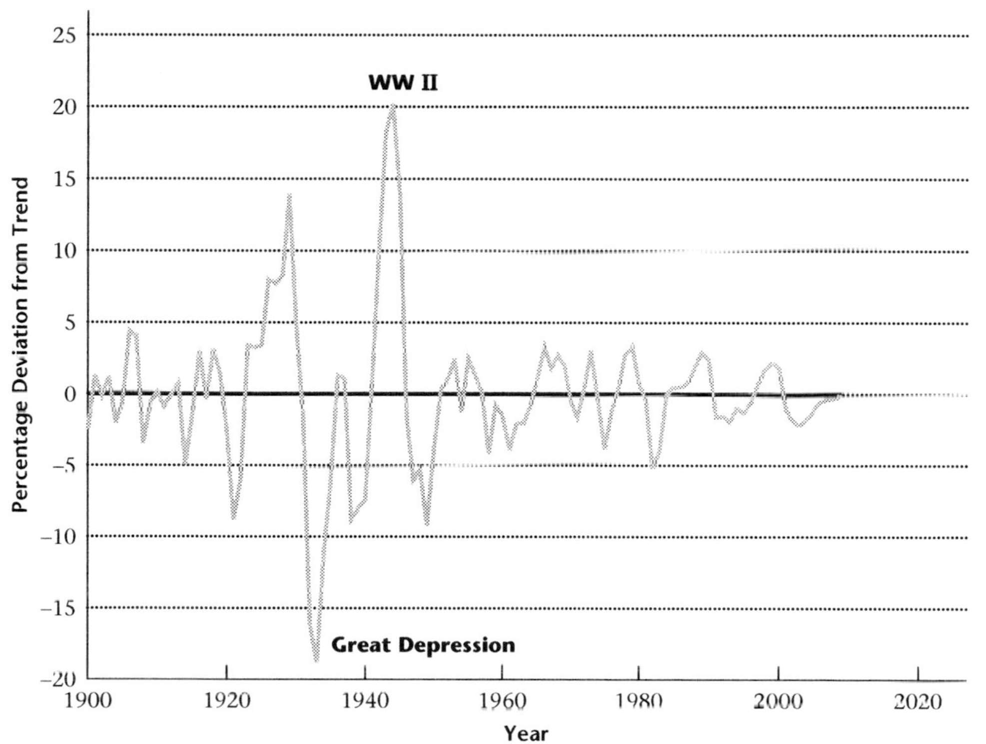

much like meteorology or astronomy. In predicting the weather or how planets move in space, meteorologists and astronomers rely on **models,** which are artificial devices that can replicate the behavior of real weather systems or planetary systems, as the case may be.

Just like researchers in meteorology or astronomy, macroeconomists use models, which in our case are organized structures to explain long-run economic growth, why there are business cycles, and what role economic policy should play in the macroeconomy. All economic models are abstractions. They are not completely accurate descriptions of the world, nor are they intended to be. The purpose of an economic model is to capture the essential features of the world needed for analyzing a particular economic problem. To be useful then, a model must be simple, and simplicity requires that we leave out some "realistic" features of actual economies. For example, a roadmap is a model of a part of the earth's surface, and it is constructed with a particular purpose in mind, to help motorists guide themselves through the road system from one point to another. A roadmap is hardly a realistic depiction of the earth's surface, as it does not capture the curvature of the earth, and it does not typically include a great deal of information on topography, climate, and vegetation. However, this does not limit the map's usefulness; a roadmap serves the purpose for which it was constructed, and it does so without a lot of extraneous information.

To be specific, the basic structure of a macroeconomic model is a description of the following features:

1. The consumers and firms that interact in the economy.
2. The set of goods that consumers wish to consume.
3. Consumers' preferences over goods.
4. The technology available to firms for producing goods.
5. The resources available.

In this book, the descriptions of the above five features of any particular macroeconomic model are provided in mathematical and graphical terms.

Once we have a description of the main economic actors in a model economy (the consumers and firms), the goods consumers want, and the technology available to firms for producing goods from available resources, we want to then use the model to make predictions. This step requires that we specify two additional features of the model. First, we need to know what the goals of the consumers and firms in the model are. How do consumers and firms behave given the environment they live in? In all the models we use in this book, we assume that consumers and firms **optimize,** that is, they do the best they can given the constraints they face. Second, we must specify how consistency is achieved in terms of the actions of consumers and firms. In economic models, this means that the economy must be in **equilibrium.** Several different concepts of equilibrium are used in economic models, but the one that we use almost universally in this book is **competitive equilibrium.** In a competitive equilibrium, we assume that goods are bought and sold on markets in which consumers and firms are price-takers; they behave as if their actions have no effect on market prices. The economy is in equilibrium when market prices are such that the quantity of each good offered for sale (quantity supplied) is equal to the quantity that economic agents want to buy (quantity demanded) in each market.

Once we have a working economic model, with a specification of the economic environment, optimizing firms and consumers, and a notion of equilibrium, we can then begin to ask the model questions.[3] One way to think of this process is that the economic model is an experimental apparatus, and we want to attempt to run experiments using this apparatus. Typically, we begin by running experiments for which we know the answers. For example, suppose that we build an economic model so that we can study economic growth. The first experiment we might like to run is to determine, by working through the mathematics of the model, using graphical analysis, or running the model on a computer, whether in fact the model economy will grow. Further, will it grow in a manner that comes close to matching the data? If

[3]The following description of macroeconomic science is similar to that provided by Robert Lucas in "Methods and Problems in Business Cycle Theory," reprinted in *Studies in Business Cycle Theory,* 1981, MIT Press, pp. 271–296.

it does not, then we want to ask why and to determine whether it would be a good idea to refine the model in some way or to abandon it altogether and start over.

Ultimately, once we are satisfied that a model reasonably and accurately captures the economic phenomenon in which we are interested, we can start running experiments on the model for which we do not know the answers. An experiment we might want to conduct with the economic growth model is to ask, for example, how historical growth performance would have differed in the United States had the level of government spending been higher. Would aggregate economic activity have grown at a higher or a lower rate? How would this have affected the consumption of goods? Would economic welfare have been higher or lower?

In keeping with the principle that models should be simple and designed specifically for the problem at hand, we do not stick to a single all-purpose model in this book. Instead, we use an array of different models for different purposes, although these models share a common approach and some of the same principal building blocks. For example, sometimes it proves useful to build models that do not include international trade, macroeconomic growth, or the use of money in economic exchange, whereas at other times it is crucially important for the issue at hand that we explicitly model one, two, or perhaps all of these features.

Generally, macroeconomic research is a process whereby we continually attempt to develop better models, along with better methods for analyzing those models. Economic models continue to evolve in a way that helps us better understand the economic forces that shape the world in which we live, so that we can promote economic policies that make society better off.

Microeconomic Principles

This book emphasizes building macroeconomic models on sound microeconomic principles. Because the macroeconomy consists of many consumers and firms, each making decisions at the micro level, macroeconomic behavior is the sum of many microeconomic decisions. It is not immediately obvious, however, that the best way to construct a macroeconomic model is to work our way up from decision making at the microeconomic level. In physics, for example, there is often no loss in ignoring micro behavior. If I throw a brick from the top of a five-story building, and if I know the force that I exert on the brick and the force of gravity on the brick, then Newtonian physics does a very accurate job of predicting when and where the brick lands. However, Newtonian physics ignores micro behavior, which in this case is the behavior of the molecules in the brick.

Why is it that there may be no loss in ignoring the behavior of molecules in a brick, but that ignoring the microeconomic behavior of consumers and firms when doing macroeconomics could be devastating? Throwing a brick from a building does not affect the behavior of the molecules within the brick in any way that would significantly change the trajectory of the brick. Changes in government policy, however, generally alter the behavior of consumers and firms in ways that significantly affect the behavior of the economy as a whole. Any change in government policy effectively alters the features of the economic environment in which consumers and firms must make their decisions. To confidently predict the effects of a policy change in terms of aggregate behavior, we must analyze how the change in policy affects individual consumers and firms. For example, if the federal government changes the income tax rate, and we are interested in the macroeconomic effects of this policy change, the most productive approach is first to use microeconomic principles to determine how a change in the tax rate affects an individual consumer's labor supply and consumption decisions, based on optimizing behavior. Then, we can aggregate these decisions to arrive at a conclusion that is consistent with how the individuals in the economy behave.

Macroeconomists were not always sympathetic to the notion that macro models should be microeconomically sound. Indeed, before the **rational expectations revolution** in the 1970s, which generally introduced more microeconomics into macroeconomics, most macroeconomists worked with models that did not have solid microeconomic foundations, though there were some exceptions.[4] The argument that macroeconomic policy analysis could be done in a sensible way only if microeconomic behavior is taken seriously was persuasively expressed by Robert E. Lucas, Jr. in a journal article published in 1976.[5] This argument is often referred to as the **Lucas critique.**

Disagreement in Macroeconomics

There is little disagreement in macroeconomics concerning the general approach to be taken to construct models of economic growth. The Solow growth model,[6] studied in Chapters 6 and 7, is a widely accepted framework for understanding the economic growth process, and newer **endogenous growth models,** which model the economic mechanism determining the rate of economic growth (covered in Chapter 7), have been well received by most macroeconomists. This is not to say that disagreement has been absent from discussions of economic growth in macroeconomics, only that the disagreement has not generally been over basic approaches to modeling growth.

The study of business cycles in macroeconomics, however, is another story. As it turns out, there is much controversy among macroeconomists concerning business cycle theory and the role of the government in smoothing business cycles over time. In Chapters 11 and 12 we study four competing theories of the business cycle.

The first theory is **real business cycle theory,** initiated by Edward Prescott and Finn Kydland in the early 1980s.[7] Real business cycle theory implies that government policy aimed at smoothing business cycles is at best ineffective and at worst detrimental to the economy's performance. Real business cycle theorists argue that business cycles are caused primarily by shocks to the economy's technological ability to produce goods and services. The second approach is the **market segmentation theory.** Early

---

[4]See M. Friedman, 1968. "The Role of Monetary Policy," *American Economic Review* 58, 1–17.

[5]See R.E. Lucas, 1976. "Econometric Policy Evaluation: A Critique," *Carnegie-Rochester Conference Series on Public Policy* 1, 19–46.

[6]See R. Solow, 1956. "A Contribution to the Theory of Economic Growth," *Quarterly Journal of Economics* 70, 65–94.

[7]F. Kydland and E. Prescott, 1982. "Time to Build and Aggregate Fluctuations," *Econometrica* 50, 1345–1370.

work on segmented markets models of money was done by Sanford Grossman and Laurence Weiss,[8] and by Julio Rotemberg,[9] with later important breakthroughs by Robert Lucas and Timothy Fuerst.[10] In the market segmentation theory, shocks to the money supply have their first-round effects in financial markets, in part acting to relax financial constraints faced by firms, inducing them to hire more labor. The market segmentation theory implies that monetary policy can cause the aggregate economy to fluctuate in undesirable ways, but the theory also implies some potential benefits from active monetary policy. The third business cycle theory we study is the **Keynesian coordination failure theory,** which is a modern approach to **Keynesian** ideas. Keynesian macroeconomists are influenced by a line of work dating back to J. M. Keynes's *General Theory of Employment, Interest, and Money* published in 1936. Keynesians argue that the government can and should play an active role in smoothing out business cycles. In the coordination failure approach, business cycles can be caused by waves of self-fulfilling optimism and pessimism, and government policy may be effective in smoothing out business cycles.

All three of the aforementioned business cycle theories, covered in Chapter 11, are equilibrium models, that is, all prices and wages are perfectly flexible and move so that the quantity supplied equals the quantity demanded in each market. In the fourth theory we study, in Chapter 12, business cycles arise because wages are sufficiently inflexible that supply is not always equal to demand in the labor market. This is a traditional Keynesian sticky wage model, and it is consistent with the original ideas of Keynes in his *General Theory*. In Chapter 12 we also study a Keynesian sticky price model, which has much in common with the sticky wage model, but with some important differences as well.

This book seeks to take an objective view of all these competing theories of the business cycle. In Chapters 11 and 12, we study the key features of each of the above four theories of the business cycle, and we evaluate the theories in terms of how their predictions match the data.

What Do We Learn from Macroeconomic Analysis?

At this stage, it is useful to map out some of the basic insights that can be learned from macroeconomic analysis and which we develop in the remainder of this book. These are the following:

1. *What is produced and consumed in the economy is determined jointly by the economy's productive capacity and the preferences of consumers.* In Chapters 4 and 5, we develop a one-period model of the economy, which specifies the technology for producing goods from available resources, the preferences of consumers over goods, and

[8]Grossman, S. and Weiss, L. 1983. "A Transactions-Based Model of the Monetary Transmission Mechanism," *American Economic Review* 73, 871–880.

[9]Rotemberg, J. 1984. "A Monetary Equilibrium Model with Transactions Costs," *Journal of Political Economy* 92, 40–58.

[10]See Lucas, R. 1990. "Liquidity and Interest Rates," *Journal of Economic Theory* 50, 237–264 and Fuerst, T. 1992. "Liquidity, Loanable Funds, and Real Activity," *Journal of Monetary Economics* 29, 3–24.

how optimizing consumers and firms come together in competitive markets to determine what is produced and consumed.

2. *In free market economies, there are strong forces that tend to produce socially efficient economic outcomes.* Social inefficiencies can arise, but they should be considered unusual. The notion that an unregulated economy peopled by selfish individuals could result in a socially efficient state of affairs is surprising, and this idea goes back at least as far as Adam Smith's *Wealth of Nations,* written in the eighteenth century. In Chapter 5, we show this result in our one-period model, and we explain the circumstances under which social inefficiencies can arise in practice.
3. *Improvements in a country's standard of living are brought about in the long run by technological progress.* In Chapters 6 and 7, we study the Solow growth model (along with the Malthusian model of economic growth and an endogenous growth model), which gives us a framework for understanding the forces that account for growth. This model shows that growth in aggregate output can be produced by growth in a country's capital stock, growth in the labor force, and technological progress. In the long run, however, growth in the standard of living of the average person comes to a stop unless there are continuous technological improvements. Thus, economic well-being ultimately cannot be improved simply by constructing more machines and buildings; economic progress depends on continuing advances in knowledge.
4. *A tax cut is not a free lunch.* When the government reduces taxes, this increases current incomes in the private sector, and it may seem that this implies that people are wealthier and may want to spend more. However, if the government reduces taxes and holds its spending constant, it must borrow more, and the government will have to increase taxes in the future to pay off this higher debt. Thus, future incomes in the private sector must fall. In Chapter 8, we show that there are circumstances in which a current tax cut has no effects whatsoever; the private sector is no wealthier, and there is no change in aggregate economic activity.
5. *What consumers and firms anticipate for the future has an important bearing on current macroeconomic events.* In Chapters 8 and 9, we consider two-period models in which consumers and firms make dynamic decisions; consumers save for future consumption needs, and firms invest in plant and equipment so as to produce more in the future. If consumers anticipate, for example, that their future incomes will be high, they want to save less in the present and consume more, and this has important implications for current aggregate production, employment, and interest rates. If firms anticipate that a new technological innovation will come on line in the future, this makes them more inclined to invest today in new plant and equipment, and this in turn also affects aggregate production, employment, and interest rates. Consumers and firms are forward-looking in ways that matter for current aggregate economic activity and for government policy.
6. *Money takes many forms, and having it is much better than not having it. Once we have it, however, changing its quantity ultimately does not matter.* What differentiates money from other assets is its value as a medium of exchange, and having a medium of exchange makes economic transactions much easier in developed economies.

Currently in the United States, there are several assets that act as a medium of exchange, including U.S. Federal Reserve notes, transactions deposits at banks, and travelers' checks. In Chapters 10 and 15, we explore the role of money and banking in the economy. One important result in Chapter 10 is that a one-time increase in the money supply, brought about by the central bank, has no long-run effect on any real economic magnitudes in the economy; it only increases all prices in the same proportion.

7. *Business cycles are similar, but they can have many causes.* In Chapter 3, we show that there are strong regularities in how aggregate macroeconomic variables fluctuate over the business cycle. In Chapters 11 and 12, we also study several theories that can potentially explain business cycles. The fact that there are several business cycle theories to choose from does not mean that only one can be right and all the others are wrong, although some may be more right than others. Potentially, all of these theories shed some light on why we have business cycles and what can be done about them.
8. *Countries gain from trading goods and assets with each other, but trade is also a source of shocks to the domestic economy.* Economists tend to support the lifting of trade restrictions, as free trade allows a country to exploit its comparative advantage in production and, thus, make its citizens better off. However, the integration of world financial and goods markets implies that events in other countries can cause domestic business cycles. In Chapters 13 and 14, we explore how changes in goods prices and interest rates on world markets affect the domestic economy.
9. *In the long run, inflation is caused by growth in the money supply.* **Inflation,** the rate of growth in the average level of prices, can vary over the short run for many reasons. Over the long run, however, the rate at which the central bank (the **Federal Reserve System** in the United States) causes the stock of money to grow determines what the inflation rate is. We study this process in Chapter 15.
10. *Unemployment is painful for individuals, but it is a necessary evil in modern economies.* There will always be unemployment in a well-functioning economy. Unemployment is measured as the number of people who are not employed and are actively seeking work. Because all of these people are looking for something they do not have, unemployment might seem undesirable, but the time unemployed people spend searching for jobs is typically well spent from a social point of view. It is economically efficient for workers to be well matched with jobs, in terms of their skills, and if an individual spends a longer time searching for work, this increases the chances of a good match. In Chapter 16, we explore the determinants of the aggregate unemployment rate, in terms of two theories of unemployment, **search theory** and **efficiency wage theory.** Search theory explains unemployment in terms of the costs and benefits of searching for job offers, while efficiency wage theory posits that workers are unemployed because of an excess supply of labor brought about when firms pay high wages to induce their workers not to shirk.
11. *There may be a significant short-run trade-off between aggregate output and inflation, but aside from the inefficiencies caused by long-run inflation, there is no long-run trade-off.* In some countries and for some historical periods, a positive relationship appears

to exist between the deviation of aggregate output from trend and the inflation rate. This relationship is called the **Phillips curve,** and in general the Phillips curve appears to be a quite unstable empirical relationship. The Friedman–Lucas money surprise model, discussed in Chapter 17, provides an explanation for the observed Phillips curve relationship. It also explains why the Phillips curve is unstable and does not represent a long-run trade-off between output and inflation that can be exploited by government policymakers. In Chapter 17, we explore the importance of commitment on the part of central bank policymakers in explaining recent inflation experience in the United States.

Understanding Recent and Current Macroeconomic Events

Part of the excitement of studying macroeconomics is that it can make sense of recent and currently unfolding economic events. In this section, we give an overview of some recent and current issues and how we can understand them better using macroeconomic tools.

Aggregate Productivity

A measure of productivity in the aggregate economy is **average labor productivity,** $\frac{Y}{N}$, where Y denotes aggregate output and N denotes employment. That is, we can measure aggregate productivity as the total quantity of output produced per worker. Aggregate productivity is important, as economic growth theory tells us that growth in aggregate productivity is what determines growth in living standards in the long run. In Figure 1.5 we plot the log of average labor productivity for the United States, measured as the log of real gross domestic product per worker. Here, we show the log of average labor productivity (the blue line), because then the slope of the graph denotes the growth rate in average labor productivity. The key features of Figure 1.5 are that average labor productivity grew at a high rate during the 1950s and most of the 1960s, growth slowed down from the late 1960s until the early 1980s, and then productivity growth increased beginning in the mid-1980s and remained high through the 1990s and into the early twenty-first century. The period from the late 1960s until the early 1980s is referred to as the **productivity slowdown.**

What caused the productivity slowdown, and what led to the resurgence in productivity growth after 1980? If we can understand this recent behavior of aggregate productivity, we might be able to avoid productivity slowdowns in the future and to bring about larger future increases in our standard of living. One potential explanation for the productivity slowdown is that it simply reflects a measurement problem. Estimates of economic growth during the productivity slowdown period could have been biased downward for various reasons, which would also cause productivity growth to be biased downward. This explanation seems quite unexciting, but economic measurement generally is imperfect. Economists have to be very careful in tempering their conclusions with a thorough knowledge of the data they are studying. A more exciting potential explanation for the productivity slowdown, and the subsequent increase in productivity growth, is that

Figure 1.5 **Natural Logarithm of Average Labor Productivity.**

Average labor productivity is the quantity of aggregate output produced per worker. Because the graph is of the log of average labor productivity (the blue line), the slope of the graph is approximately the growth rate in average labor productivity. A key feature in the figure is the productivity slowdown, which we see as a decrease in the slope of the graph beginning in the late 1960s and continuing into the early 1980s.

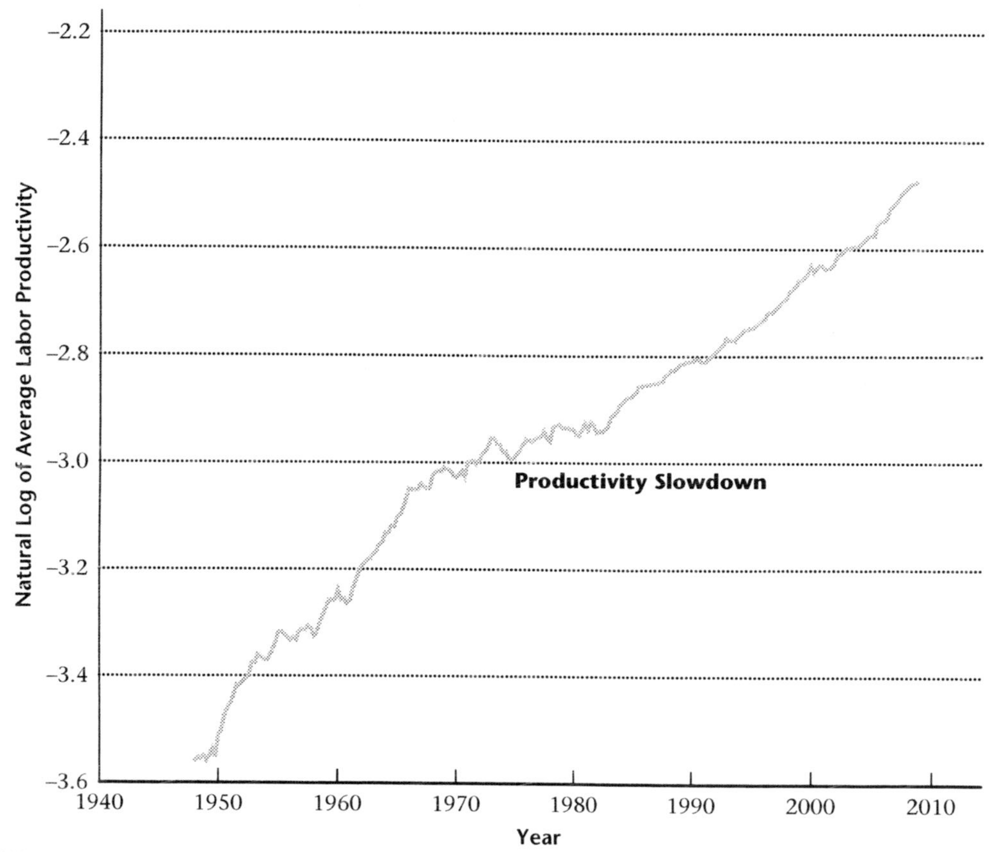

this is symptomatic of the adoption of new technology. Modern information technology began to be introduced in the late 1960s with the wide use of high-speed computers. In learning to use computer technology, there was a temporary adjustment period, which could have slowed down productivity growth from the late 1960s to the early 1980s. By the early 1980s, however, according to this story, people discovered how to embody new information technology in personal computers, and the 1990s saw further uses for computer technology via the Internet. Thus, the productivity slowdown could have been caused by the costs of adjusting to new technology, with productivity growth rebounding as information technology became widely diffused through the economy. We explore these issues further in Chapters 6 and 7.

Taxes, Government Spending, and the Government Deficit

In Figure 1.6 we show total taxes (the black line) and government spending (the colored line) by all levels of government (federal, state, and local) in the United States from 1960 to 2006, as percentages of total gross domestic product. Note the broad upward trend in both taxes and spending. Total taxes were about 25% of GDP in 1960, and they increased to near 32% of GDP in 2000, while total spending rose from about 22% of GDP in 1960 to a high of close to 34% of GDP in the early 1990s. These trends generally reflect an increase in the size of government in the United States relative to the aggregate economy over this period.

What ramifications does a larger government have for the economy as a whole? How does higher government spending and taxation affect private economic activity? We show in Chapters 5 and 9 that increased government activity in general causes a **crowding out** of private economic activity. That is, the government competes for resources with the rest of the economy. If the size of the government increases, then through several economic mechanisms there is a reduction in the quantity of spending by private firms on new plant and equipment, and there is a reduction in private consumption expenditures.

Figure 1.6 **Total Taxes (black line) and Total Government Spending (colored line) in the United States, as Percentages of GDP.**

Taxes and spending both increased on trend from 1947 until the 1990s, indicating growth in the size of government in the United States.

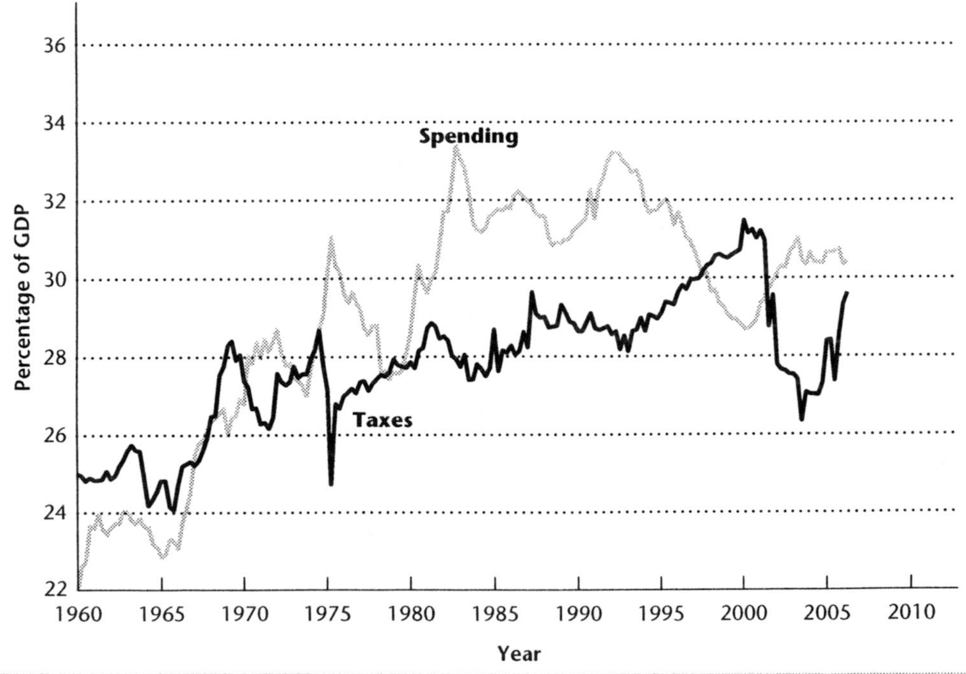

Figure 1.7 **The Total Government Surplus in the United States as a Percentage of GDP.** The government surplus declines on trend until the early 1990s, increases, and then decreases again in 2000 before increasing somewhat. Except for a brief period in the late 1990s, the government surplus has been negative since 1980.

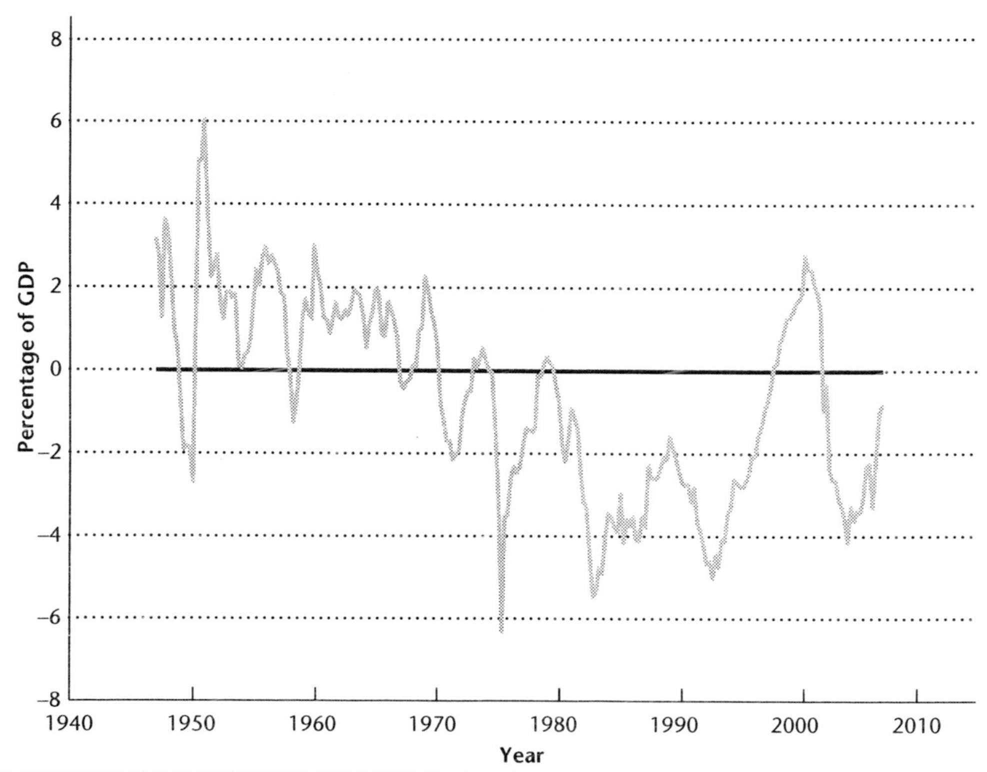

An interesting feature of Figure 1.6 is that governments in the United States sometimes spent more than they received in the form of taxes, and sometimes the reverse was true. Just as is the case for private consumers, the government can in principle spend more than it earns by borrowing and accumulating debt, and it can earn more than it spends and save the difference, thus reducing its debt. Figure 1.7 shows the total **government surplus** or total **government saving,** which is the difference between taxes and spending, for the period 1947–2006. From Figure 1.7, the government surplus was positive for most of the period from 1948 until 1970, but from 1970 until the late 1990s the surplus was usually negative. When there is a negative government surplus, we say that the government is running a deficit; the **government deficit** is the negative of the government surplus. The largest government deficit over this period was more than 6% of GDP, in 1975. It was not until the late 1990s that there was again a positive government surplus; in 1999, the government surplus had reached more than 2% of GDP. However, the surplus declined dramatically after 1999, reaching −4% of GDP in 2003 before increasing again.

What are the consequences of government deficits? We might think, in a manner similar to popular conceptions of household finance, that accumulating debt (running a deficit) is bad, whereas reducing debt (running a surplus) is good, but at the aggregate level the issue is not so simple. One principal difference between an individual and the government is that when the government accumulates debt by borrowing from its citizens, then this is debt that we as a nation owe to ourselves. Then, it turns out that the effects of a government deficit depend on what the source of the deficit is. Is the government running a deficit because taxes have decreased or because government spending has increased? If the deficit is the result of a decrease in taxes, then the government debt that is issued to finance the deficit will have to be paid off ultimately by higher future taxes. Thus, running a deficit in this case implies that there is a redistribution of the tax burden from one group to another; one group has its current taxes reduced while another has its future taxes increased. Under some circumstances, these two groups might essentially be the same, in which case there would be no consequences of having the government run a deficit. This idea, that government deficits do not matter under some conditions, is called the **Ricardian equivalence theorem,** and we study it in Chapter 8. In the case of a government deficit resulting from higher government spending, then there are always implications for aggregate economic activity, as discussed earlier in terms of the crowding out of private spending. We examine the effects of government spending in Chapters 5 and 9.

Interest Rates

Interest rates are important, as they affect many private economic decisions, particularly the decisions of consumers as to how much they borrow and lend, and the decisions of firms concerning how much to invest in new plant and equipment. Further, movements in interest rates are an important element in the economic mechanism by which monetary policy affects real magnitudes in the short run. In Figure 1.8 we show the behavior of the short-term **nominal interest rate** (the blue line) in the United States over the period 1934–2006. This is the interest rate in money terms on 91-day U.S. Treasury bills, which are essentially riskless short-term government securities. In the 1930s and 1940s the short-term nominal interest rate was quite low and did not vary much, but it rose on trend through the 1950s, 1960s, and 1970s, reaching a high of more than 15% early in 1980. Since then, the nominal interest rate has declined on trend, and it was below 1% in late 2003 before increasing again.

What explains the level of the nominal interest rate? In the figure we have plotted the inflation rate as the black line, which is measured here by the rate of increase in the consumer price index. The consumer price index is a measure of the price level, the average level of prices across goods in the economy. In the figure the inflation rate tracks the nominal interest rate reasonably closely. Also, several of the peaks in inflation, around 1970, in the mid-1970s, around 1980, around 1990, and in 2001, are coupled with peaks in the nominal interest rate. Thus, the nominal interest rate tends to rise and fall with the inflation rate. Why is this? Economic decisions are based on real rather than nominal interest rates. The **real interest rate,** roughly speaking, is the nominal interest rate minus the expected rate of inflation. That is, the real interest rate is the rate that a borrower expects to have to repay,

Figure 1.8 **The Nominal Interest Rate and the Inflation Rate.**

Macroeconomic theory tells us that the nominal interest rate and the inflation rate are positively related. After 1950, the nominal interest rate tends to track the ups and downs in the inflation rate.

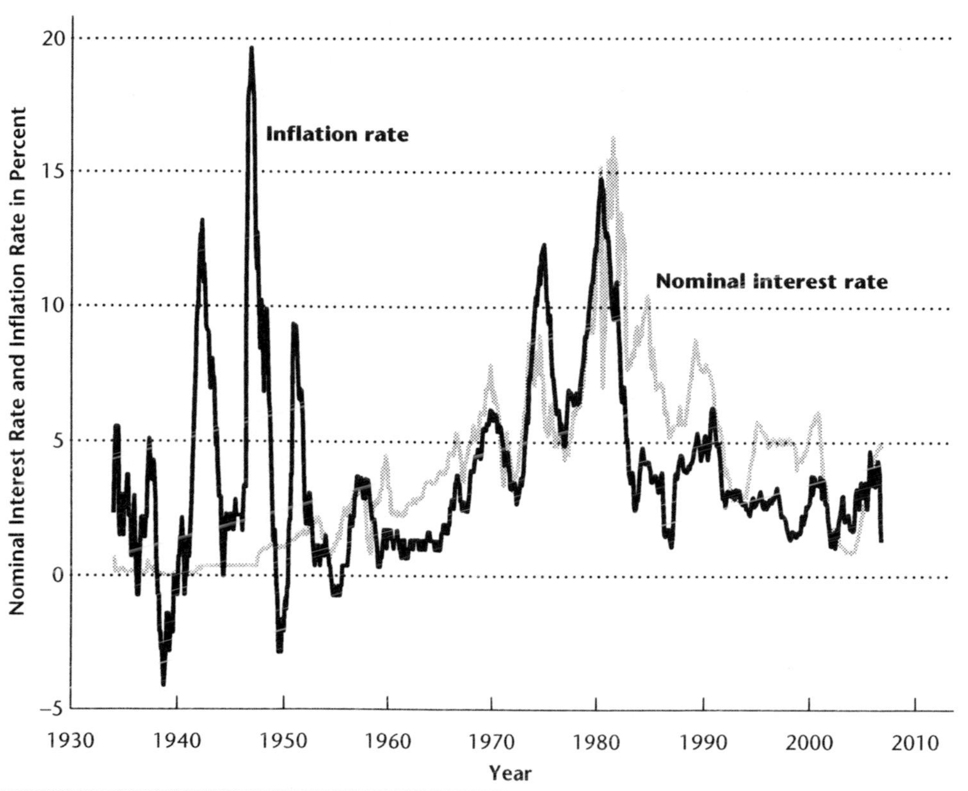

adjusting for the inflation that is expected to occur over the period of time until the borrower's debt is repaid. If Allen obtains a one-year car loan at an interest rate of 9%, and he expects the inflation rate to be 3% over the next year, then he faces a real interest rate on the car loan of 6%. Now, because economic decisions are based on real interest rates rather than nominal interest rates, market forces tend to determine the real interest rate. Therefore, as the inflation rate rises, the nominal interest rate tends to rise along with it. In Chapters 7 and 9, we study the determination of real and nominal interest rates in the long run, and the relationship between real and nominal rates.

In Figure 1.9 we plot an estimate of the real interest rate, which is the nominal interest rate minus the actual rate of inflation. Thus, this would be the actual real interest rate if consumers and firms could correctly anticipate inflation, so that actual inflation is equal to expected inflation. Consumers and firms cannot correctly anticipate the actual inflation rate. However, given that inflation does not change too much from quarter to quarter, their forecasts are fairly accurate, and our estimate of the real interest rate has a reasonably small measurement error. The real interest rate fluctuates

Figure 1.9 **Real Interest Rate.**

The figure shows a measure of the real interest rate, which here is the short-term nominal interest rate minus the actual rate of inflation. Monetary policy can have a short-run effect on the real interest rate; for example, the high real interest rates in the early 1980s and the low real interest rates during 1990–91 and 2001 recessions are often attributed to monetary policy actions.

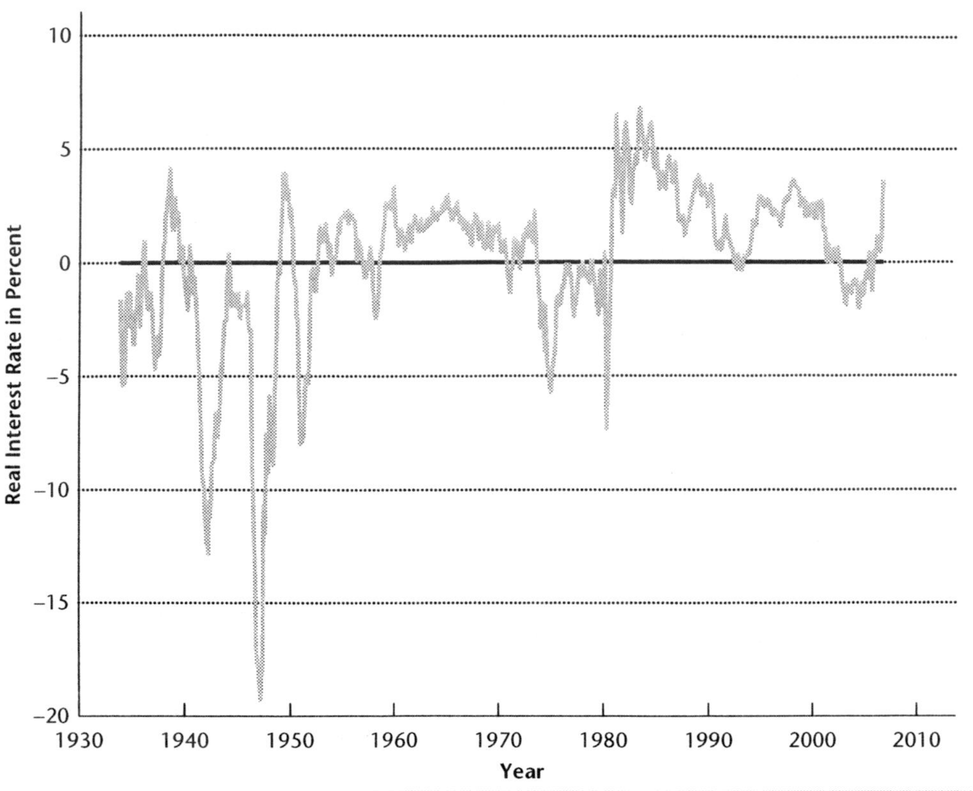

a great deal over time. The real rate has sometimes been negative, falling to almost −20% in the late 1940s, to −8% in the early 1950s, and to −6% in 1980. For most of the period since the early 1980s, the real interest rate has been positive, but it fell below zero early in the 1990s and in 2003.

In the short run, the real interest rate is affected by monetary policy, though there is some disagreement among macroeconomists concerning why the central bank can control the real interest rate, and for how long it can do so. We can give the following interpretation to the path of the real interest rate from the mid-1970s to 2006 in Figure 1.9. First, the real interest rate was low in the mid to late 1970s because the Federal Reserve (the Fed) was causing the money supply to grow at a high rate, that is, monetary policy was expansionary and accommodating. As a result of the high inflation caused by this high money growth, the Fed embarked on a contractionary course in the early 1980s, reducing money supply growth and causing the real interest rate to rise. Since the mid-1980s, the Fed has remained seriously concerned about the possibility that high inflation could reemerge, and it has for the most part maintained a nonaccommodating monetary policy stance, which has caused the real interest rate to be historically high. During the business cycle downturn in the early 1990s, the Fed temporarily relaxed, causing the real interest rate to dip to close to 0%. Then, in 2001, the Fed acted to reduce the real interest rate again, in response to a slowdown in aggregate economic activity. As there appeared to be no threat of serious inflation and economic activity had not picked up significantly, the real interest rate continued to fall through late 2003. Then, when the economy was growing at a high rate, and there was a greater threat from inflation, the real interest rate increased, through 2006. In Chapters 11 and 12, we study some theories of the business cycle that explain how the central bank can influence the real interest rate in the short run. While the rate of money growth may affect real interest rates in the long run, monetary policy is aimed not at setting the long-run real interest rate but at determining long-run inflation while staying in tune with the short-run effects of monetary policy.

Business Cycles in the United States

As was mentioned above, individual business cycle events may have many causes, and the causes that are important in one business cycle event may be very unimportant in others. For example, a particular recession might be attributed to monetary policy actions, while another recession may have been caused primarily by a downturn in aggregate productivity.

As above, we define business cycles to be the deviations from trend in aggregate economic activity. In Figure 1.10, we show the percentage deviations from trend in GDP for the period 1947–2006. Recessions in the figure are negative deviations from trend, and the significant recent recessions in the United States were those of 1974–1975, 1981–1982, 1990–1991, and 2001. What were the causes of these recessions?

Before the 1974–1975 recession, there was a particularly sharp rise in the price of energy on world markets, caused by a restriction of oil output by the Organization of Petroleum Exporting Countries (OPEC). In Chapters 4, 5, and 9, we explain how an increase in the price of energy acts to reduce productivity and leads to a decrease in aggregate output, which occurred in 1974–1975, as we see in Figure 1.10. Other features of the 1974–1975 recession, including a reduction in measured productivity, a fall in employment, and a decrease in consumption and investment expenditures, are all consistent with this recession having been caused by the increase in the price of energy.

The recession of 1981–1982, like the recession of 1974–1975, was preceded by a large increase in the price of energy, which in this case occurred in 1979–1980. For this second recession, the energy price increase perhaps happened too soon before the recession to have been its principal cause. As well, other evidence seems to point to monetary policy as the primary cause of the 1981–1982 recession. As we see later in this section, inflation had become relatively high in the 1970s in the United States, and by the early 1980s the Fed, under then-Chairman Paul Volcker, took dramatic steps to reduce inflation by restricting growth in the supply of money and driving up interest rates. This produced the side effect of a recession. While there is much controversy among macroeconomists concerning the short run effects of monetary policy, and the

Figure 1.10 **Percentage Deviation from Trend in Real GDP, 1947–2006.**

The key recent recessions in the United States, indicated in the figure by negative deviations of real GDP from trend, occurred in 1974–75, 1981–82, 1990–91, and 2001.

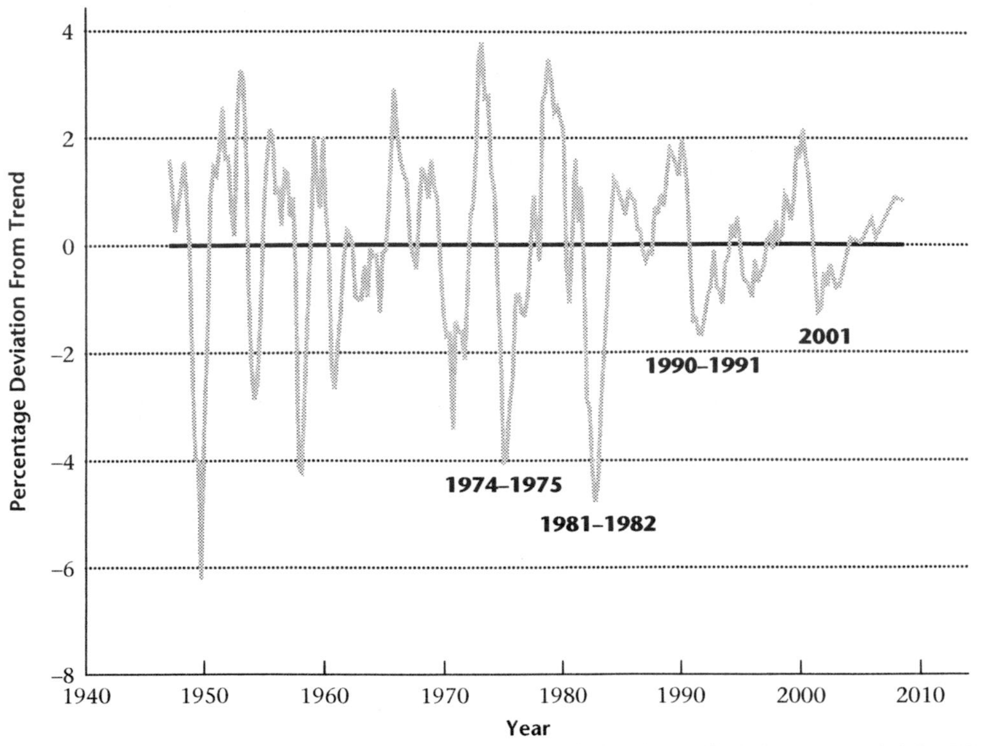

role of money in the business cycle, most macroeconomists are inclined to view the 1981–1982 recession as being caused primarily by monetary policy.

The 1991–1992 recession was mild compared to the previous two major recessions (the negative deviation from trend in Figure 1.10 is smaller), and it was the only interruption in sustained economic growth over a roughly 19-year period from 1982 to 2001 in the United States. For this recession, it is difficult to pinpoint a single cause. Possibly an increase in energy prices during the Persian Gulf War was an important contributing factor, although this price increase was temporary.

The most recent recession of 2001, though even milder than the 1991–1992 recession (see Figure 1.10), appears to have been the result of a collapse in optimism in the United States. During the 1990s, there was a boom in investment expenditures—spending on new plants, equipment, and housing—fed in part by great optimism concerning the revolution in information technology and its implications for future productivity. This optimism was also reflected in a large increase in the average price of stocks in the 1990s. In about 2000, optimism faded rapidly, investment expenditures and the stock market crashed, and the result was the recession of

2001. Also contributing to the 2001 recession were the terrorist attacks of September 2001, which acted to reduce aggregate output through several mechanisms that we study in Chapter 9.

The Current Account Surplus and the Government Surplus

As the technology for transporting goods and information across countries has advanced and government-imposed impediments to trade have been reduced in the post–World War II period, the United States has become a more open economy. That is, trade in goods and in assets between the United States and the rest of the world has increased. The change in the flow of goods and services between the United States and the rest of the world is shown in Figure 1.11, where we plot U.S. exports (the black line) and imports (the colored line) as percentages of GDP from 1947 to 2006. U.S. exports increased from about 5% of GDP in 1947 to somewhat more than 12% of GDP in 2006, while imports increased from somewhat

Figure 1.11 **Exports and Imports of Goods and Services for the United States as Percentages of GDP.**

The increase in both imports and exports after World War II reflects a general increase in world trade. Exports have been lower than imports for most of this period.

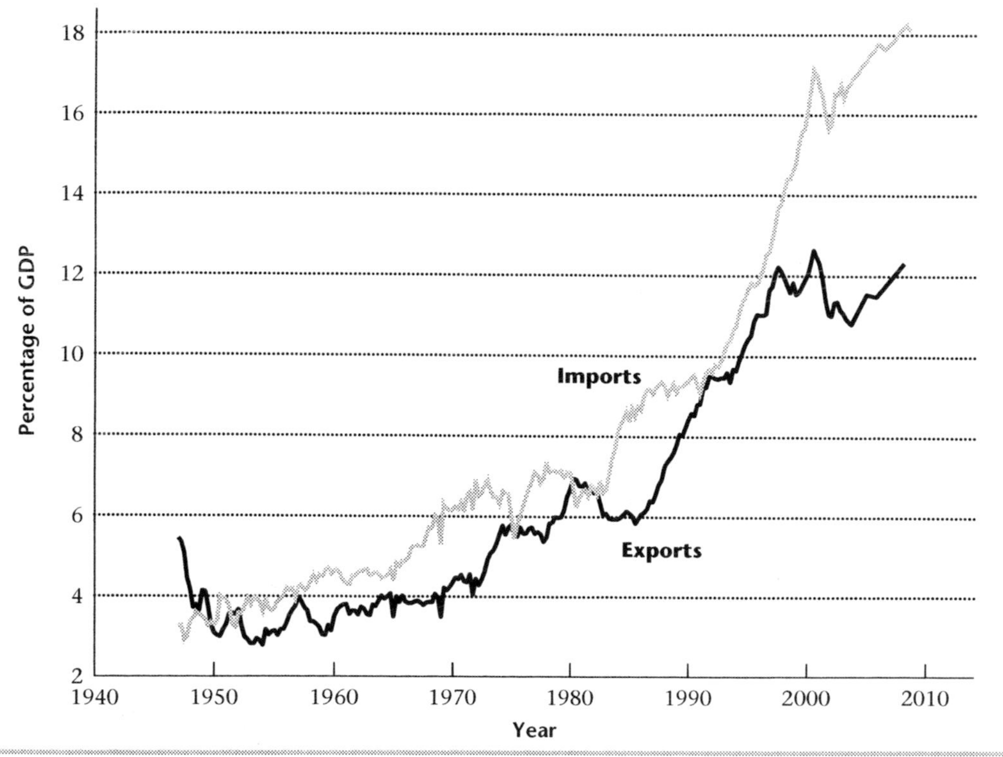

more than 3% in 1947 to about 18% in 2006. As mentioned in the previous section, more trade has a positive effect on general economic welfare, as it allows countries to specialize in production and exploit their comparative advantages. However, more trade could also expose a given country to the transmission of business cycle fluctuations from abroad, although this need not necessarily be the case.

While the level of trade with the outside world is important in terms of aggregate economic activity and how it fluctuates, the balance of trade also plays an important role in macroeconomic activity and macroeconomic policymaking. One measure of the balance of trade is the **current account surplus,** which is **net exports** of goods and services (exports minus imports) plus **net factor payments** (net income from abroad). In Figure 1.12 we have graphed the current account surplus for the period

Figure 1.12 **The Current Account Surplus and the Government Surplus, 1960–2006.**
There was a trend decrease in the current account surplus from 1960 until 2003. During the 1980s, the current account surplus and the government surplus tended to move in the same direction, but they moved in opposite directions during the 1990s.

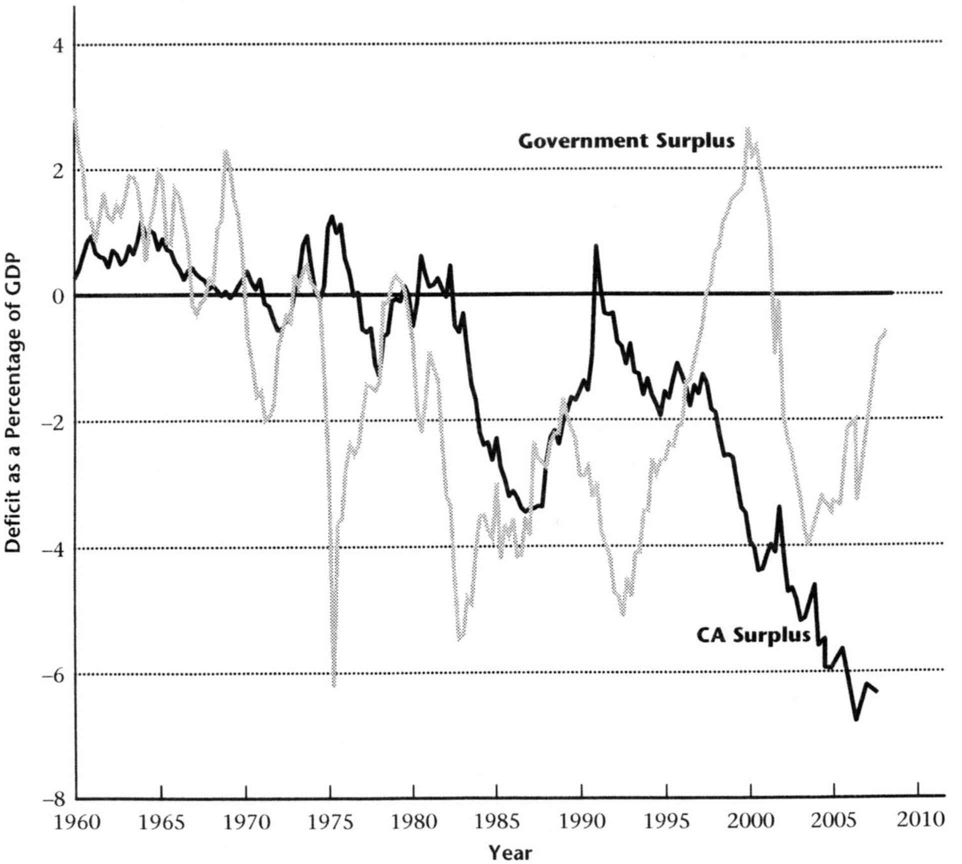

1960 to 2006. In the figure the current account surplus was positive for most of the period 1960–1985, and it has been negative for most of the period 1985–2006.

Why is the current account surplus important? When the current account surplus in the United States is negative, there is a **current account deficit,** and the quantity of goods and services purchased abroad by domestic residents is smaller than the quantity of domestic goods and services purchased by foreigners. To finance this current account deficit, residents of the United States and/or the U.S. government must be borrowing abroad. Is it a bad idea for a country to run a current account deficit? This need not be the case, for two reasons. First, just as it may make sense for an individual to borrow so as to smooth his or her flow of consumption over time, it may also be beneficial for a country to borrow in the short run by running a current account deficit so as to smooth aggregate consumption over time. Second, persistent current account deficits may make sense if the associated foreign borrowing is used to finance additions to the nation's productive capacity that will allow for higher future living standards.

What accounts for movements over time in the current account surplus? One important influence on the current account surplus is government spending. When the government increases its spending, holding taxes constant, this increases the government deficit, which needs to be financed by increased government borrowing. If the private sector does not save more, so as to increase its lending to the government, then the increased government borrowing is done abroad, and it shows up as an increase in the current account deficit. Thus, an increase in the government deficit can be coupled with an increase in the current account deficit. This is exactly what appears to have occurred in the United States in the mid-to-late 1980s. In Figure 1.12, we see a sharp decrease during this period in the current account surplus. As well, we have shown the government surplus in the figure, and this also decreases sharply in the 1980s (though the decline in the government surplus precedes the decline in the current account surplus). This phenomenon is referred to as the **twin deficits.**

The government surplus need not always be the primary influence on the current account surplus. For example, from the early 1990s until 2000, the current account surplus was decreasing while the government surplus was increasing, which is inconsistent with the twin deficits phenomenon, where the two surpluses moved in the same direction. During the 1990s, the current account surplus was primarily influenced by a boom in U.S. investment spending that was essentially financed through borrowing from the rest of the world, which caused a large current account deficit. From 2000–2004, the government surplus and the current account surplus both decrease, which is consistent with the twin deficits phenomenon.

We study international trade, the determinants of the current account surplus, and other issues associated with international business cycles and international financial relations in Chapters 13 and 14.

Inflation

Inflation, as mentioned earlier, is the rate of change in the average level of prices. The average level of prices is referred to as the price level. In Figure 1.13 we show the inflation rate, the black line in the figure, as the percentage rate of increase in

Figure 1.13 **The Inflation Rate and the Money Growth Rate.**

Money growth and inflation show a trend increase from 1960 until the 1980s, and then the inflation rate falls on trend. After 1980, the money growth rate is quite erratic and the relationship between money growth and inflation is loose.

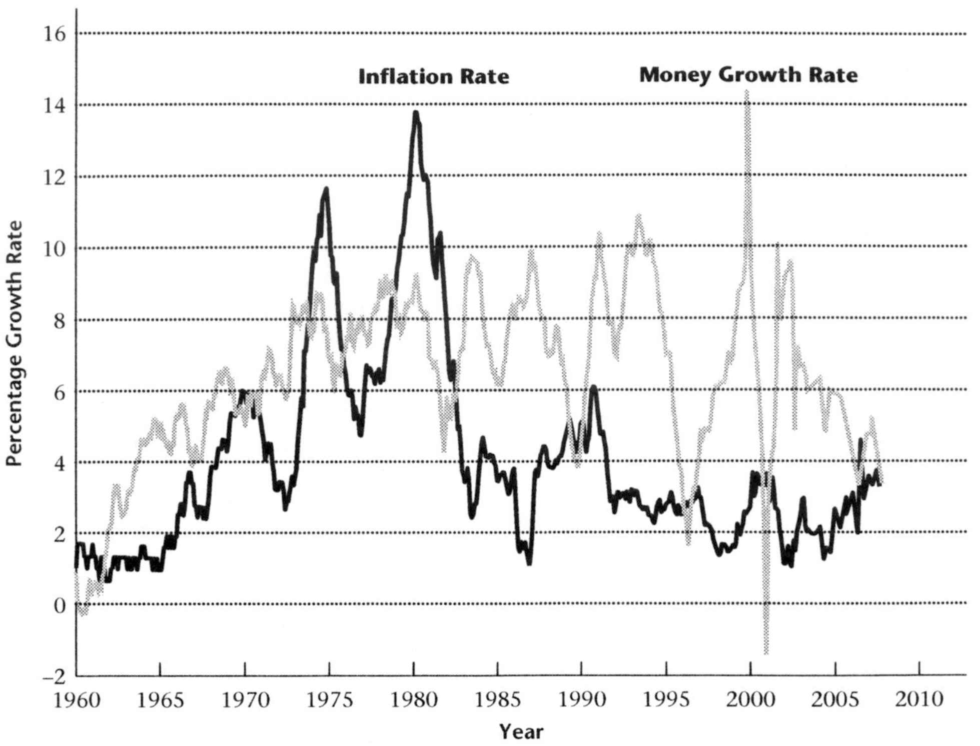

the consumer price index over the period 1960–2006. The inflation rate was quite low in the early 1960s and then began climbing in the late 1960s, reaching peaks of about 12% per year in 1975 and about 14% per year in 1980. The inflation rate then declined steadily, reaching rates of 2% and below in the late 1990s.

Inflation is economically costly, but the low recent rates of inflation we are experiencing are certainly not viewed by the public or by policymakers as being worthy of much attention. However, it is certainly useful to understand the causes of inflation, its costs, and why and how inflation was reduced in the United States. There are good reasons to think that the inflation experience of the 1970s and early 1980s, or worse, could be repeated. The inflation rate is explained in the long run by the rate of growth in the supply of money. Without money supply growth, prices cannot continue to increase, and higher money supply growth implies that there is more and more money chasing a given quantity of goods. This will ultimately cause prices to be bid up at a higher rate. In Figure 1.13 we show the rate of money growth (measured as the percentage rate of growth in M0, a narrow monetary aggregate) as the colored line.

Here, it is clear that the short-run relationship between the rate of inflation and the rate of money growth is not a tight one; there are many short-run ups and downs in the rate of money growth that are not reflected in similar movements in the inflation rate and vice versa. Thus, there must be other factors that explain short-run movements in the rate of inflation in addition to changes in the money growth rate. However, the broad trends in money growth in Figure 1.13 match the broad trends in the inflation rate. Money growth increases, on trend, until the 1980s, and then falls, as does the inflation rate, though money growth behavior is quite erratic from the mid-1980s on. We study the short-run effects of nonmonetary factors on the price level in Chapters 10, 11, and 12, and in Chapter 15 the long-run effects of money growth on inflation are explored.

Long-run inflation is costly, in that it tends to reduce employment, output, and consumption, as we show in Chapter 15. However, because inflation is caused in the long run by money growth, the central bank determines the long-run inflation rate through its control of the rate at which the money supply grows. Why would the central bank want to generate inflation if it is costly? In Chapter 17, we explore the answer to this question, with recent experience in the United States as a backdrop. Surprise increases in the rate of inflation can cause short-run increases in employment and output, and the central bank might be tempted to generate these short-run surprises, either because it has not learned the consequences of long-run inflation, or because there is a failure of the central bank to commit itself to long-run actions. In Chapter 17, we study the importance of central bank learning and commitment for the behavior of inflation.

Unemployment

In the previous section we explained how the phenomenon of unemployment need not represent a problem, because unemployment is in general a socially useful search activity that is necessary, though painful to the individuals involved. As macroeconomists, we are interested in what explains the level of unemployment and what the reasons are for fluctuations in unemployment over time. If we can understand these features, we can then go on to determine how macroeconomic policy can be formulated so that labor markets work as efficiently as possible.

In Figure 1.14 we show the unemployment rate in the United States for the period 1948–2006. There are three important features that can be observed in Figure 1.14. First, the average unemployment rate in the period after 1970 is much higher than the average unemployment rate before 1970. Second, the unemployment rate fluctuates significantly; it is not unusual for it to move up or down by four or five percentage points within a year or two. Third, since 1970 there was a trend increase in the unemployment rate until about the mid-1980s and then a trend decrease; in 1999 the unemployment rate was lower than it had been at any point since 1970. What explains these features of the data?

There are four factors affecting unemployment that can explain essentially all of the observed behavior of the unemployment rate in Figure 1.14. These four factors are aggregate economic activity, the structure of the population, government intervention, and sectoral shifts. First, in general the unemployment rate fluctuates inversely along

Figure 1.14 **The Unemployment Rate in the United States, 1948–2006.**
The unemployment rate is affected by aggregate economic activity, the structure of the population, government intervention, and sectoral shifts.

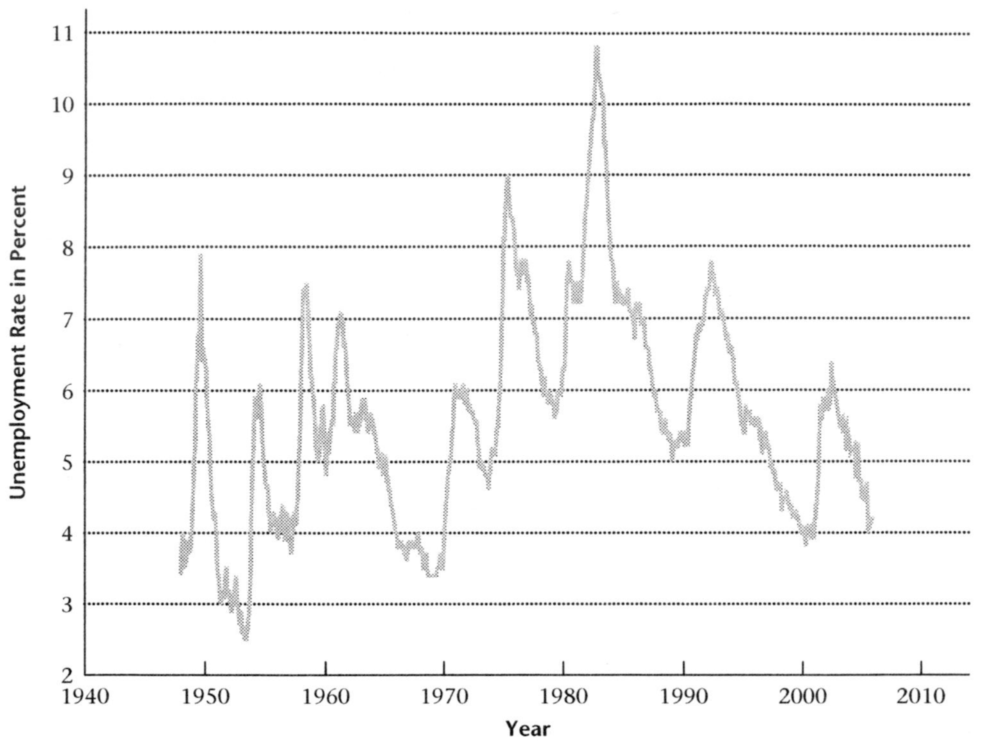

with aggregate economic activity; when aggregate output is above trend, then the unemployment rate tends to be low. Second, the population structure affects the unemployment rate, as workers in different age cohorts tend to behave differently in the labor market. For example, younger workers have a weaker attachment to jobs than older workers, and they tend to experience more frequent episodes of unemployment as they change jobs early in their careers. Third, government intervention affects the unemployment rate, particularly through the unemployment insurance system. For example, more generous unemployment compensation implies that the cost of searching for a job is reduced, and unemployed workers then tend to search longer, increasing the unemployment rate. Fourth, sectoral shifts are long-run changes that occur in the sectoral structure of production. For example, in the United States there has been a shift from the manufacturing sector of the economy to the services sector. This kind of sectoral shift tends to displace workers from the declining sector, and they need to acquire new skills and to spend time searching to find jobs in the expanding sector of the economy. Therefore, the greater the extent of sectoral shifts occurring in the economy, the higher the unemployment rate is.

The fact that the unemployment rate is on average higher after 1970 than before, as observed in Figure 1.14, is probably mainly the result of changes in the population structure. The postwar baby boom generation entered the labor force mostly between the late 1960s and 1980, so that the working-age population became more youthful through the 1970s, which would tend to push the unemployment rate up. Sectoral shifts may have also played a role in pushing up the unemployment rate after 1970. The unemployment rate fluctuated from 1948 to 2006 mainly because of fluctuations in aggregate economic activity. In Figure 1.15 we show deviations from trend in real GDP (in percentage terms) as the colored line and deviations from trend in the unemployment rate (in percentage points) as the black line. Clearly, when GDP is above (below) trend, the unemployment rate tends to be below (above) trend. Finally, the pattern in the unemployment rate since 1970 can be explained in part by the population structure and in part by the influence of aggregate economic activity. As the postwar baby boom generation began to age in the 1980s and 1990s, the unemployment rate fell as this large group of workers entered a phase in their careers

Figure 1.15 **Deviations from Trend in the Unemployment Rate (black line) and Percentage Deviations from Trend in Real GDP (colored line).**

The unemployment rate tends to be high (low) relative to trend when real GDP is low (high) relative to trend.

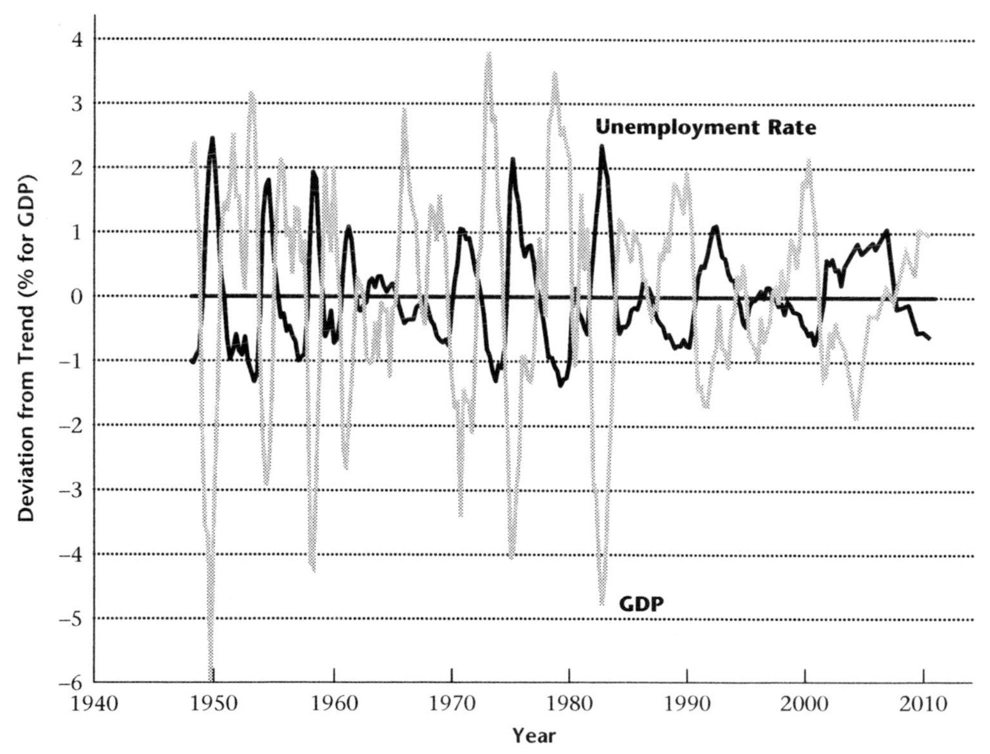

when unemployment spells were less frequent. Also, the sustained growth in the U.S. economy since the early 1980s, interrupted only by the mild recessions in the early 1990s and 2001, contributed to a decrease in the unemployment rate.

We study determinants of the unemployment rate and theories of unemployment in Chapter 16.

Chapter Summary

- Modern macroeconomics analyzes issues associated with long-run growth and business cycles, using models that are built up from microeconomic principles.
- During the twentieth century, the United States experienced long-run sustained growth in per capita gross domestic product; we also observed that gross domestic product exhibits business cycle fluctuations about a smooth long-run trend.
- Two unusual but important events in twentieth-century U.S. economic history were the Great Depression and World War II.
- The primary questions of interest to macroeconomists involve the causes of long-run growth and business cycles and the appropriate role for government policy in influencing the performance of the economy.
- Macroeconomists rely mainly on abstract models to draw conclusions about how the world works, because it is usually very costly or impossible to experiment with the real economy. A good macroeconomic model is simple, while retaining all of the features essential for addressing the macroeconomic issue for which the model was intended.
- The models we construct and use in this book are ones in which price-taking consumers and firms optimize given the constraints they face and in which the actions of consumers and firms are consistent in a competitive equilibrium.
- Building models from microeconomic principles is important, because this will more often give us the correct answers to questions regarding the effects of changes in economic policy.
- There is relatively little disagreement among macroeconomists concerning approaches to modeling growth, but there are contentious issues in business cycle modeling, between Keynesian macroeconomists and those who argue for non-Keynesian alternative explanations for business cycles.
- The issues discussed in this chapter, to be addressed later in the book, are the productivity slowdown; taxes, government spending, and the government deficit; interest rates; business cycles in the United States; the current account surplus and the government surplus; inflation; and unemployment.

Key Terms

Economic models A description of consumers and firms, their objectives and constraints, and how they interact.

Long-run growth The increase in a nation's productive capacity and average standard of living that occurs over a long period of time.

Business cycles Short-run ups and downs, or booms and recessions, in aggregate economic activity.

Gross domestic product The quantity of goods and services produced within a country's borders during some specified period of time.
Trend The smooth growth path around which an economic variable cycles.
Models Artificial devices that can replicate the behavior of real systems.
Optimize The process by which economic agents (firms and consumers) do the best they can given the constraints they face.
Equilibrium The situation in an economy when the actions of all the consumers and firms are consistent.
Competitive equilibrium Equilibrium in which firms and households are assumed to be price-takers, and market prices are such that the quantity supplied equals the quantity demanded in each market in the economy.
Rational expectations revolution Macroeconomics movement that occurred in the 1970s, introducing more microeconomics into macroeconomics.
Lucas critique The idea that macroeconomic policy analysis can be done in a sensible way only if microeconomic behavior is taken seriously.
Endogenous growth models Models that describe the economic mechanism determining the rate of economic growth.
Real business cycle theory Initiated by Finn Kydland and Edward Prescott, this theory implies that business cycles are caused primarily by shocks to technology and that the government should play a passive role over the business cycle.
Market segmentation theory A theory of how changes in the money supply can cause changes in real output and employment in the short run. The theory implies that monetary policy can contribute to undesirable fluctuations in the economy, but there is also potentially a role for active monetary policy.
Keynesian coordination failure theory A modern incarnation of Keynesian business cycle theory positing that business cycles are caused by self-fulfilling waves of optimism and pessimism, which may be countered with government policy.
Keynesian Describes macroeconomists who are followers of J. M. Keynes and who see an active role for government in smoothing business cycles.
Inflation The rate of change in the average level of prices over time.
Federal Reserve System (Fed) The central bank of the United States.
Search theory Theory that explains unemployment in terms of the costs and benefits of searching for job offers.
Efficiency wage theory Theory positing that workers are unemployed because of an excess supply of labor brought about when firms pay high wages to induce their workers not to shirk.
Phillips curve A positive relationship between the deviation of aggregate output from trend and the inflation rate.
Average labor productivity The quantity of aggregate output produced per worker.
Productivity slowdown The period of low productivity growth occurring from the late 1960s until the early 1980s.
Crowding out The process by which government spending reduces private sector expenditures on investment and consumption.
Government surplus The difference between taxes and government spending.
Government saving Identical to the government surplus.
Government deficit The negative of the government surplus.
Ricardian equivalence theorem Theory asserting that a change in taxation by the government has no effect.

Nominal interest rate The interest rate in money terms.
Real interest rate Approximately equal to the nominal interest rate minus the expected rate of inflation.
Current account surplus Exports minus imports plus net factor payments to domestic residents from abroad.
Net exports Exports of goods and services minus imports of goods and services.
Net factor payments Payments received by domestic factors of production from abroad minus the payments to foreign factors of production from domestic sources.
Current account deficit Situation in which the current account surplus is negative.
Twin deficits The phenomenon during the late 1980s when the U.S. government was running a deficit at the same time that the United States was running a current account deficit.

Questions for Review

1. What are the primary defining characteristics of macroeconomics?
2. What makes macroeconomics different from microeconomics? What do they have in common?
3. How much richer was the average American in 2003 than in 1900?
4. What are two striking business cycle events in the United States during the last 105 years?
5. List six fundamental macroeconomic questions.
6. In a graph of the natural logarithm of an economic time series, what does the slope of the graph represent?
7. What is the difference between the trend and the business cycle component of an economic time series?
8. Explain why experimentation is difficult in macroeconomics.
9. Why should a macroeconomic model be simple?
10. Should a macroeconomic model be an exact description of the world? Explain why or why not.
11. What are the five elements that make up the basic structure of a macroeconomic model?
12. Why can macroeconomic models be useful? How do we determine whether they are useful?
13. Explain why a macroeconomic model should be built from microeconomic principles.
14. What are the four theories of the business cycle that we study?
15. What are two possible causes of the productivity slowdown?
16. What is the principal effect of an increase in government spending?
17. Why might a decrease in taxes have no effect?
18. What is the cause of inflation in the long run?
19. Explain the difference between the nominal interest rate and the real interest rate.
20. When did the four most recent recessions occur in the United States?
21. How are the government surplus and the current account surplus connected?
22. What are four factors that determine the quantity of unemployment?

Problems

1. Consider the following data on real GDP per capita in the United States:

Year	*U.S. Real GDP Per Capita (2000 dollars)*
1950	\$11,745
1960	\$13,951
1970	\$18,561
1980	\$22,784
1990	\$28,598
1995	\$30,525
1996	\$31,396
1997	\$32,520
1998	\$33,544
1999	\$34,367
2000	\$35,265
2001	\$35,165
2002	\$35,368
2003	\$35,895
2004	\$36,939
2005	\$37,773

(a) Calculate the percentage growth rates in real GDP per capita in each of the years 1996 through 2005 from the previous year.

(b) Now, instead of calculating the annual percentage growth rates in the years 1996 through 2005 directly, use as an approximation $100 \times (\ln y_t - \ln y_{t-1})$, where y_t is real per capita GDP in year t. How close does this approximation come to the actual growth rates you calculated in part (a)?

(c) Repeat parts (a) and (b), but now calculate the percentage rates of growth in real per capita GDP from 1950 to 1960, from 1960 to 1970, from 1970 to 1980, 1980 to 1990, and 1990 to 2000. In this case, how large an error do you make by approximating the growth rate by the change in the natural log? Why is there a difference here relative to parts (a) and (b)?

(d) During what decade from 1950 to 2000 was growth in real per capita GDP the highest? When was it the lowest?

2. Suppose that you had the special power to travel in time and to carry out any experiment you wanted on the economy. If you could turn back the clock to the time of the Great Depression, what experiment would you like to run on the U.S. economy? Why?

3. Give an example of a model that is used in some area other than economics, other than the roadmap example explained in this chapter. What is unrealistic about this model? How well does the model perform its intended function?

4. Why do you think taxes would fall during a recession, as happened in the mid-1970s (see Figure 1.6)?

5. Explain why the total government surplus became positive in the United States in the late 1990s, in terms of the behavior of taxes and government spending.

6. Does Figure 1.13 make you suspicious of the claim that a high rate of inflation is caused by a higher rate of money growth? Why or why not?
7. Why do you think the real interest rate was low during the recession in the mid-1970s?
8. How do the behavior of imports and exports help to explain the decrease in the current account surplus beginning in the early 1990s?
9. Why do you think the unemployment rate in the United States was very low at the end of the 1960s?

Working with the Data

1. Graph gross domestic product (GDP) and gross national product (GNP) in 2000 dollars for 1947 and thereafter. Is there much difference in these two measures of aggregate economic activity for the United States?
2. Total government expenditures consist of expenditures by the federal government and by state and local governments. Calculate and graph the ratio of federal government expenditures to total government expenditures. Has the federal government become larger or smaller relative to state and local governments over time?
3. Using the consumer price index as a measure of the price level, calculate and graph the annual inflation rate for 1960 to 2006. Calculate this as the percentage increase in the CPI from December to December (the annual inflation rate for 1999 would be the percentage increase in the CPI from December 1998 to December 1999). In addition, calculate and graph on the same chart the percentage annual increase in M2 (a measure of the money supply) for the same years. How does your picture differ from Figure 1.13?

CHAPTER 2

Measurement

ECONOMICS IS BUILT ON THE TWIN PILLARS OF MEASUREMENT AND THEORY. MEASUREMENTS OF THE performance of the economy motivate macroeconomists to build simple models that can organize our thinking about how the economy works. For example, surveys of consumer prices done every year can tell us something about how prices change over time and, coupled with observations on other economic variables, can help us to develop theories that explain why prices change over time. Meanwhile, economic theory can better inform us about the most efficient ways to carry out economic measurement. For example, theories of consumer behavior can tell us something about the appropriate way to use the prices of consumer goods to derive a price index that is a good measure of the price level.

Our goal in this chapter is to understand the basic issues concerning how key macroeconomic variables are measured. These key macroeconomic variables play important roles in the economic models that we construct and study in the remainder of this book. In particular, in the rest of this chapter we examine the measurement of GDP and its components, and the measurement of prices, savings, wealth, capital, and labor market variables.

Measuring GDP: The National Income and Product Accounts

The chief aim of national income accounting is to obtain a measure of the total quantity of goods and services produced for the market in a given country over a given period of time. For many issues in macroeconomics (although by no means for all), the measure of aggregate economic activity we are interested in is **gross domestic product (GDP),** which is the dollar value of final output produced during a given period of time within the borders of the United States. GDP is published on a quarterly basis as part of the **National Income and Product Accounts (NIPA),** one source for which is the Survey of Current Business, published by the U.S. Department of Commerce.

There are three approaches to measuring GDP, each of which is incorporated in some way in NIPA. All three approaches give exactly the same measure of GDP, provided there are no errors of measurement in using any of these approaches. The three approaches are the **product approach,** the **expenditure approach,** and the **income approach.** We discuss each in turn, using an example.

In our running example, we consider a simple fictional economy that captures the essentials of national income accounting. This is an island economy where there is a coconut producer, a restaurant, consumers, and a government. The coconut producer owns all of the coconut trees on the island, harvests the coconuts that grow on the trees, and in the current year produces 10 million coconuts, which are sold for $2 each, yielding total revenue of $20 million. The coconut producer pays wages of $5 million to its workers (who are some of the consumers in this economy), $0.5 million in interest on a loan to some consumers, and $1.5 million in taxes to the government. The relevant data for the coconut producer are shown in Table 2.1.

Of the 10 million coconuts produced, 6 million go to the restaurant, which specializes in innovative ways of serving coconuts—for example "shredded coconut in its own milk," "coconut soup," and "coconut in the half-shell." The remaining 4 million coconuts are bought by the consumers. Again, all coconuts are $2 each. Coconuts serve two roles in this economy. First, a coconut is an **intermediate good,** a good that is produced and then used as an input to another production process—here, the production of restaurant food. Second, it is a final consumption good, in that coconuts are purchased by consumers. The restaurant sells $30 million in meals during the year (this is a rather large restaurant). The total cost of coconuts for the restaurant is $12 million, and the restaurant pays its workers $4 million in wages and the government $3 million in taxes. Data for the restaurant are provided in Table 2.2.

Next, we need to calculate after-tax profits for each of the producers (the coconut producer and the restaurant). After-tax profits in this example are simply

$$\text{After-tax profits} = \text{Total Revenue} - \text{Wages} - \text{Interest} - \text{Cost of Intermediate Inputs} - \text{Taxes}.$$

Therefore, from Tables 2.1 and 2.2 above, we calculate after-tax profits in Table 2.3.

The government's role in this economy is to provide protection from attacks from other islands. In the past, foreign invaders have destroyed coconut trees and made off with coconuts. The government collects taxes to provide national defense. That is, it uses all of its tax revenue to pay wages to the army. Total taxes collected are $5.5

Table 2.1 **Coconut Producer**

Total Revenue	$20 million
Wages	$ 5 million
Interest on Loan	$ 0.5 million
Taxes	$ 1.5 million

Table 2.2 **Restaurant**

Total Revenue	$30 million
Cost of Coconuts	$12 million
Wages	$ 4 million
Taxes	$ 3 million

Table 2.3 **After-Tax Profits**	
Coconut Producer	$13 million
Restaurant	$11 million

Table 2.4 **Government**	
Tax Revenue	$5.5 million
Wages	$5.5 million

Table 2.5 **Consumers**	
Wage Income	$14.5 million
Interest Income	$ 0.5 million
Taxes	$ 1 million
Profits Distributed from Producers	$24 million

million ($4.5 million from producers and $1 million from consumers), and so the data for the government are as shown in Table 2.4.

Consumers work for the producers and for the government, earning total wages of $14.5 million. They receive $0.5 million in interest from the coconut producer, pay $1 million in taxes to the government, and receive after-tax profits of $24 million from the producers, because some of the consumers own the coconut firm and the restaurant. Data for the consumers are shown in Table 2.5.

Now, given the abovementioned data for this simple economy, we examine how GDP would be calculated using the three different national income accounting approaches.

The Product Approach

The product approach to NIPA is also called the **value-added** approach because the main principle in this approach is that GDP is calculated as the sum of value added to goods and services across all productive units in the economy. To calculate GDP using the product approach, we add the value of all goods and services produced in the economy and then subtract the value of all intermediate goods used in production to obtain total value added. If we did not subtract the value of intermediate goods used in production, then we would be double-counting. In our example, we do not want to count the value of the coconuts used in the production of restaurant services as part of GDP.

In the example, the coconut producer does not use any intermediate goods in production, so value added in producing coconuts, which is the coconut producer's total revenue, is $20 million. For the restaurant, however, value added is total revenue minus the value of the coconuts used in production; thus, total value added for the restaurant is $18 million. For government production, we have a problem, because the

Table 2.6 **GDP Using the Product Approach**	
Value added—coconuts	$20 million
Value added—restaurant food	$18 million
Value added—government	$ 5.5 million
GDP	$43.5 million

national defense services provided by the government are not sold at market prices. Standard practice here is to value national defense services at the cost of the inputs to production. Here, the only input to production was labor, so the total value added for the government is $5.5 million. Total value added, or GDP, therefore, is $43.5 million. The GDP calculation using the product approach is summarized in Table 2.6.

The Expenditure Approach

In the expenditure approach, we calculate GDP as *total spending on all final goods and services production in the economy*. Note again that we do not count spending on intermediate goods. In the NIPA, total expenditure is calculated as:

$$\text{Total expenditure} = C + I + G + NX,$$

where C denotes expenditures on consumption, I is investment expenditure, G is government expenditure, and NX is net exports—that is, total exports of U.S. goods and services minus total imports into the United States. We add exports because this includes goods and services produced within the United States. Imports are subtracted because, in general, each of C, I, and G includes some goods and services that were produced abroad, and we do not want to include these in U.S. GDP.

In our example, there is no investment, no exports, and no imports, so that $I = NX = 0$. Consumers spend $8 million on coconuts and $30 million at the restaurant, so that $C =$ $38 million. For government expenditures, again we count the $5.5 million in wages spent by the government as if national defense services had been purchased as a final good at $5.5 million, and so $G =$ $5.5 million. Therefore, calculating GDP using the expenditure approach, we get

$$\text{GDP} = C + I + G + NX = \$43.5 \text{ million}.$$

The GDP calculation using the expenditure approach is shown in Table 2.7. Note that we obtain the same answer calculating GDP this way as using the product approach, as we should.

The Income Approach

To calculate GDP using the income approach, we *add up all income received by economic agents contributing to production*. Income includes the profits made by firms. In the NIPA, income includes compensation of employees (wages, salaries, and benefits), proprietors' income (self-employed firm owners), rental income, corporate profits, net interest, indirect business taxes (sales and excise taxes paid by businesses), and

Table 2.7 **GDP Using the Expenditure Approach**	
Consumption	$38 million
Investment	0
Government Expenditures	$ 5.5 million
Net Exports	0
GDP	$43.5 million

depreciation (consumption of fixed capital). Depreciation represents the value of productive capital (plant and equipment) that wears out during the period we are considering. Depreciation is taken out when we calculate profits, so it needs to be added in again when we compute GDP.

In the example, we need to include the wage income of consumers, $14.5 million, as a component of GDP. In addition, we need to count the profits of producers. If we do this on an after-tax basis, total profits for the two producers are $24 million. Next, we add the interest income of consumers (this is net interest), which is $0.5 million. Finally, we need to add the taxes paid by producers to the government, which are essentially government income. This amount is $4.5 million. Total GDP is then $43.5 million, which of course is the same answer that we obtained for the other two approaches. The calculation of GDP using the income approach is summarized in Table 2.8.

Why do the product approach, the expenditure approach, and the income approach yield the same GDP measure? This is because the total quantity of output, or value added, in the economy is ultimately sold, thus showing up as expenditure, and what is spent on all output produced is income, in some form or other, for someone in the economy. If we let Y denote total GDP in the economy, then Y is total aggregate output, and it is also aggregate income. Further, it is also true as an identity that aggregate income equals aggregate expenditure, or

$$Y = C + I + G + NX.$$

This relationship is sometimes referred to as the **income–expenditure identity,** as the quantity on the left-hand side of the identity is aggregate income, and the right-hand side is the sum of the components of aggregate expenditure.

Table 2.8 **GDP Using the Income Approach**	
Wage Income	$14.5 million
After-tax profits	$24 million
Interest Income	$ 0.5 million
Taxes	$ 4.5 million
GDP	$43.5 million

An Example with Inventory Investment

One component of investment expenditures is inventory investment, which consists of any goods that are produced during the current period but are not consumed. Stocks of inventories consist of inventories of finished goods (for example, automobiles that are stored on the lot), goods in process (for example, automobiles still on the assembly line), and raw materials.

Suppose in our running example that everything is identical to the above, except that the coconut producer produces 13 million coconuts instead of 10 million, and that the extra 3 million coconuts are not sold but are stored as inventory. In terms of the value-added approach, GDP is the total value of coconuts produced, which is now \$26 million, plus the value of restaurant food produced, \$30 million, minus the value of intermediate goods used up in the production of restaurant food, \$12 million, plus value added by the government, \$5.5 million, for total GDP of \$49.5 million. Note that we value the coconut inventory at the market price of coconuts in the example. In practice, this need not be the case; sometimes the book value of inventories carried by firms is not the same as market value, although sound economics says it should be.

Now, for the expenditure approach, $C = \$38$ million, $NX = 0$, and $G = \$5.5$ million as before, but now $I = \$6$ million, so $\text{GDP} = C + I + G + NX = \$49.5$ million. It may seem odd that the inventory investment of \$6 million is counted as expenditure, because this does not appear to be expenditure on a final good or service. The convention, however, is to treat the inventory investment here as if the coconut producer bought \$6 million in coconuts from itself.

Finally, in terms of the income approach, wage income to consumers is \$14.5 million, interest income to consumers is \$0.5 million, taxes are \$4.5 million, as before, and total profits after taxes for the two producers are now \$30 million, for total GDP of \$49.5 million. Here, we add the \$6 million in inventories to the coconut producer's profits, because this is an addition to the firm's assets.

An Example with International Trade

To show what can happen when international trade in goods comes into the picture, we take our original example and alter it slightly. Suppose that the restaurant imports 2 million coconuts from other islands at \$2 each, in addition to the coconuts purchased from the domestic coconut producer, and that all of these coconuts are used in the restaurant. The restaurant still sells \$30 million in restaurant food to domestic consumers.

Here, following the value-added approach, the value added by the domestic coconut producer is \$20 million as before. For the restaurant, value added is the value of food produced, \$30 million, minus the value of intermediate inputs, which is \$16 million, including the cost of imported coconuts. As before, total value added for the government is \$5.5 million. Therefore, GDP is total value added for the two producers and the government, or \$39.5 million.

Next, using the expenditure approach, consumption of coconuts by consumers is \$8 million and restaurant service consumption is \$30 million, so that $C = \$38$ million. Government expenditures are the same as in the initial example, with

$G = \$5.5$ million, and we have $I = 0$. Total exports are 0, while imports (of coconuts) are \$4 million, so that net exports are $NX = -\$4$ million. We then have GDP $= C + I + G + NX = \$39.5$ million.

Finally, following the income approach, the wage income of consumers is \$14.5 million, interest income of consumers is \$0.5 million, and taxes are \$4.5 million, as in the initial example. The after-tax profits of the coconut producer are \$13 million, also as before. The change here is in the after-tax profits of the restaurant, which are reduced by \$4 million, the value of the imported coconuts, so that after-tax restaurant profits are \$7 million. Total GDP is then \$39.5 million.

Gross National Product

Before 1991, **gross national product (GNP)** was used in the United States as the official measure of aggregate production. In line with international practice, however, the official measure became GDP in December 1991. In practice, there is little difference between GDP and GNP in the United States, but in principle the difference could matter significantly. GNP measures the value of output produced by domestic factors of production, regardless of whether the production takes place (as is the case for GDP) inside U.S. borders. For example, if a Nike plant in Southeast Asia is owned and managed by U.S. residents, then the incomes accruing to U.S. factors of production include the managerial income and profits of this plant, and this is included in U.S. GNP, but not in U.S. GDP. Similarly, if a Honda plant in Ohio has Japanese owners, the profits of the plant would not be included in GNP, as these profits are not income for U.S. residents, but the profits would be included in GDP.

Gross national product is the sum of GDP and net factor payments (NFP) from abroad to domestic residents or

$$GNP = GDP + NFP,$$

where NFP denotes net factor payments from abroad. For 2005, GDP for the United States was \$12,455.8 billion, and GNP was \$12,487.7 billion, so NFP was \$31.9 billion. Thus, for this typical year, the difference between GDP and GNP for the United States was 0.256% of GDP, which is small. For some countries, however, there is a significant difference between GDP and GNP, particularly for those countries where a large fraction of national productive capacity is foreign-owned, in which case NFP is significant.

What Does GDP Leave Out?

GDP is intended simply as a measure of the quantity of output produced and exchanged in the economy as a whole. Sometimes GDP, or GDP per person, however, is used as a measure of aggregate economic welfare. There are at least two problems with this approach. The first is that aggregate GDP does not take into account how income is distributed across the individuals in the population. At the extreme, if one person in the economy has all the income and the rest of the people have no income, the average level of economic welfare in the economy would be very low. Second, GDP leaves out all nonmarket activity, with work in the home being an example. If people eat restaurant meals rather than eating at home, then GDP rises, because there are now more services produced in the market than before. People should be better off as a result, because they had the option of eating at home but chose to go out. However, the increase in GDP exaggerates the increase in economic welfare, as GDP does not measure the value added when food is cooked at home.

GDP may be an inaccurate measure of welfare, but there are also some problems with GDP as a measure of aggregate output. First, economic activities in the so-called **underground economy** are, by definition, not counted in GDP. The underground economy includes any unreported economic activity. A high-profile example of underground activity is trade in illegal drugs; a low-profile example is the exchange of babysitting services for cash. Economic activity goes underground so as to avoid legal penalties and taxation, and underground activity often involves cash transactions. The size of the underground economy may indeed be significant in the United States, as evidenced by the fact that the quantity of U.S. currency held per U.S. resident was approximately $2,474 in July 2006.[1] Clearly, most individuals engaged in standard market transactions do not hold this much currency. This large quantity of currency in circulation can in part be explained by the large amount of U.S. currency held outside the country, but it still reflects the fact that the underground economy matters for the measurement of GDP in the United States.

A second problem in measuring GDP, which we encountered in our example, involves how government expenditures are counted. Most of what the government produces is not sold at market prices. For example, how are we to value roads, bridges, and national defense services? The solution in the NIPA, as in our example, is to value government expenditures at cost, that is, the payments to all of the factors of production that went into producing the good or service. In some cases this could overvalue what is produced; for example, if the government produced something that nobody wanted, such as a bridge to nowhere. In other cases, government production could be undervalued; for example, we may be willing to pay much more for national defense than what it costs in terms of wages, salaries, materials, and so forth.

The Components of Aggregate Expenditure

Typically, particularly in constructing economic models to understand how the economy works, we are interested mainly in the expenditure side of the NIPA. Here, we consider each of the expenditure components in more detail. Table 2.9 gives the GDP components for 2005.

Consumption

Consumption expenditures are the largest expenditure component of GDP, accounting for 70.2% of GDP in 2005 (see Table 2.9). **Consumption** is expenditure on consumer goods and services during the current period, and the components of consumption are durable goods, nondurable goods, and services. Durable goods include items like new automobiles, appliances, and furniture. Nondurables include food and clothing. Services are nontangible items like haircuts and hotel stays. Clearly, the division between durables and nondurables is somewhat imprecise because, for

[1] *Source:* U.S. Department of Commerce and Board of Governors of the Federal Reserve System.

Table 2.9 **Gross Domestic Product for 2005**

Component of GDP	$Billions	% of GDP
GDP	12,455.8	100.0
Consumption	8,742.4	70.2
Durables	1,033.1	8.3
Nondurables	2,539.3	20.4
Services	5,170.0	41.5
Investment	2,057.4	16.5
Fixed Investment	2,036.2	16.3
Nonresidential	1,265.7	10.2
Residential	770.4	6.2
Inventory Investment	21.3	0.2
Net Exports	−613.2	−4.9
Exports	1,303.1	10.5
Imports	2,019.9	16.2
Government Expenditures	2,372.8	19.1
Federal Defense	589.3	4.7
Federal Nondefense	289.0	2.3
State and Local	1,494.4	12.0

example, shoes (a nondurable) could be viewed as being as durable as washing machines (a durable). Further, some items included in consumption are clearly not consumed within the period. For example, if the period is one year, an automobile may provide services to the buyer for ten years or more and is, therefore, not a consumption good. However, it might economically be more appropriately considered an investment expenditure when it is bought. The purchase of a used car or other used durable good is not included in GDP, but the services provided (for example, by a dealer) in selling a used car would be included.

Investment In Table 2.9, investment expenditures were 16.5% of GDP in 2005. **Investment** is expenditure on goods that are produced during the current period, but are not consumed during the current period. There are two types of investment. **Fixed investment** is production of capital, such as plant, equipment, and housing, and **inventory investment** consists of goods that are essentially put into storage. The components of fixed investment are nonresidential investment and residential investment. Nonresidential investment adds to the plant, equipment, and software that make up the capital stock for producing goods and services. Residential investment—housing—is also productive in that it produces housing services.

Though investment is a much smaller fraction of GDP than is consumption, investment plays a very important role in business cycles. Investment is much more variable than GDP or consumption, and some components of investment also tend to lead the business cycle. For example, an upward or downward blip in housing investment tends to precede an upward or downward blip in GDP. We study this phenomenon further in Chapter 3.

Net Exports As exports were less than imports in 2005, the United States ran a trade deficit in goods and services with the rest of the world—that is, **net exports** were negative (see Table 2.9). Exports were 10.5% of GDP in 2005 while imports were 16.2% of GDP. Trade with the rest of the world in goods and services, therefore, is quite important to the U.S. economy, as we noted in Chapter 1.

Government Expenditures **Government expenditures,** which consist of expenditures by federal, state, and local governments on final goods and services, were 19.1% of GDP in 2005, as seen in Table 2.9. The main components of government expenditures are federal defense spending (4.7% of GDP in 2005), federal nondefense spending (2.3% of GDP in 2005), and state and local spending (12.0% of GDP in 2005). The NIPA also makes the important distinction between government consumption and government gross investment, just as we distinguish between private consumption and private investment. An important point is that the government spending included in the NIPA is only the expenditures on final goods and services. This does not include **transfers,** which are very important in the government budget. These outlays essentially transfer purchasing power from one group of economic agents to another, and they include such items as Social Security payments and unemployment insurance payments. Transfers are not included in GDP, as they are simply money transfers from one group of people to another, or income redistribution rather than income creation.

Nominal and Real GDP and Price Indices

While the components of GDP for any specific time period give us the total dollar value of goods and services produced in the economy during that period, for many purposes we would like to make comparisons between GDP data in different time periods. This might tell us something about growth in the productive capacity of the economy over time and about growth in our standard of living. A problem, however, is that the average level of prices changes over time, so that generally part of the increase in GDP that we observe is the result of inflation. In this section, we show how to adjust for this effect of inflation on the growth in GDP and, in so doing, arrive at a measure of the price level and the inflation rate.

A **price index** is a weighted average of the prices of a set of the goods and services produced in the economy over a period of time. If the price index includes prices of all goods and services, then that price index is a measure of the general **price level,** or the average level of prices across goods and services. We use price indices to measure the **inflation rate,** which is the rate of change in the price level from one period of time to another. If we can measure the inflation rate, we can also determine how much of a change in GDP from one period to another is purely **nominal** and how much is **real.** A nominal change in GDP is a change in GDP that occurred only because the price level changed, whereas a real change in GDP is an increase in the actual quantity

Table 2.10 Data for Real GDP Example

	Apples	Oranges
Quantity in Year 1	$Q_1^a = 50$	$Q_1^o = 100$
Price in Year 1	$P_1^a = \$1.00$	$P_1^o = \$0.80$
Quantity in Year 2	$Q_2^a = 80$	$Q_2^o = 120$
Price in Year 2	$P_2^a = \$1.25$	$P_2^o = \$1.60$

of goods and services (including, for example, the numbers of apples and oranges sold during a period of time), which is what ultimately matters for consumers.

Real GDP

To see how real GDP is calculated in the NIPA, it helps to consider an example. Imagine an economy in which the only goods produced are apples and oranges. In year 1, 50 apples and 100 oranges are produced, and the prices of apples and oranges are \$1.00 and \$0.80, respectively. In year 2, 80 apples and 120 oranges are produced, and the prices of apples and oranges are \$1.25 and \$1.60, respectively. These data are displayed in Table 2.10. For convenience in expressing the formulas for real GDP calculations, we let the quantities of apples and oranges, respectively, in year 1 be denoted by Q_1^a and Q_1^o with respective prices denoted by P_1^a and P_1^o. Quantities and prices in year 2 are represented similarly (see Table 2.10).

The calculation of nominal GDP in each year is straightforward here, as there are no intermediate goods. Year 1 nominal GDP is

$$GDP_1 = P_1^a Q_1^a + P_1^o Q_1^o = (\$1.00 \times 50) + (\$0.80 \times 100) = \$130.$$

Similarly, year 2 nominal GDP is

$$GDP_2 = P_2^a Q_2^a + P_2^o Q_2^o = (\$1.25 \times 80) + (\$1.60 \times 120) = \$292,$$

so the percentage increase in nominal GDP from year 1 to year 2 is equal to

$$\left(\frac{GDP_2}{GDP_1} - 1\right) \times 100\% = \left(\frac{292}{130} - 1\right) \times 100\% = 125\%.$$

That is, nominal GDP more than doubled from year 1 to year 2.

Now, the question is, how much of this increase in nominal GDP is accounted for by inflation, and how much by an increase in the real quantity of aggregate output produced? Until 1996, the practice in the U.S. NIPA was first to choose a base year and then to calculate real GDP using these base year prices. That is, rather than multiplying the quantities produced in a given year by current year prices (which is what we do when calculating nominal GDP), we multiply by base year prices to obtain real GDP. In the example, suppose that we use year 1 as the base year, and let $RGDP_1^1$ and $RGDP_2^1$ denote real GDP in years 1 and 2, respectively, calculated using year 1 as the base year. Then, real GDP in year 1 is the same as nominal GDP for that year, because year 1 is the base year, so we have

$$RGDP_1^1 = GDP_1 = \$130$$

Now, for year 2 real GDP, we use year 2 quantities and year 1 prices to obtain

$$RGDP_2^1 = P_1^a Q_2^a + P_1^o Q_2^o = (\$1.00 \times 80) + (\$0.80 \times 120) = \$176.$$

Therefore, the ratio of real GDP in year 2 to real GDP in year 1, using year 1 as the base year is

$$g_1 = \frac{RGDP_2^1}{RGDP_1^1} = \frac{176}{130} = 1.354,$$

so the percentage increase in real GDP using this approach is $(1.354 - 1) \times 100\% = 35.4\%$. Alternatively, suppose that we use year 2 as the base year and let $RGDP_1^2$ and $RGDP_2^2$ denote real GDP in years 1 and 2, respectively, calculated using this approach. Then, year 2 real GDP is the same as year 2 nominal GDP, that is

$$RGDP_2^2 = GDP_2 = \$292$$

Year 1 GDP, using year 1 quantities and year 2 prices, is

$$RGDP_1^2 = P_2^a Q_1^a + P_2^o Q_1^o = (\$1.25 \times 50) + (\$1.60 \times 100) = \$222.50.$$

Then, the ratio of real GDP in year 2 to real GDP in year 1, using year 2 as the base year, is

$$g_2 = \frac{RGDP_2^2}{RGDP_1^2} = \frac{292}{222.5} = 1.312,$$

and the percentage increase in real GDP from year 1 to year 2 is $(1.312 - 1) \times 100\% = 31.2\%$.

A key message from the example is that the choice of the base year matters for the calculation of GDP. If year 1 is used as the base year, then the increase in real GDP is 35.4%; if year 2 is the base year, real GDP is calculated to increase by 31.2%. The reason the choice of the base year matters in the example, and in reality, is that the relative prices of goods change over time. That is, the relative price of apples to oranges is $\frac{\$1.00}{\$0.80} = 1.25$ in year 1, and this relative price is $\frac{\$1.25}{\$1.60} = 0.78$ in year 2. Therefore, apples became cheaper relative to oranges from year 1 to year 2. If relative prices had remained the same between year 1 and year 2, then the choice of the base year would not matter. In calculating real GDP, the problem of changing relative prices would not be too great in calculating GDP close to the base year (say, 2005 or 2006 relative to a base year in 2004), because relative prices would typically not change much over a short period of time. Over many years, however, the problem could be severe, for example, in calculating real GDP in 2006 relative to a base year in 1982. The solution to this problem, adopted in the NIPA, is to use a **chain-weighting** scheme for calculating real GDP.

With the chain-weighting approach, a Fisher index is used, and the approach is essentially like using a rolling base period. The chain-weighted ratio of real GDP in year 2 to real GDP in year 1 is

$$g_c = \sqrt{g_1 \times g_2} = \sqrt{1.354 \times 1.312} = 1.333,$$

so that the chain-weighted ratio of real GDP in the two years is a geometric average of the ratios calculated using each of years 1 and 2 as base years.[2] In the example, we calculate the percentage growth rate in real GDP from year 1 to year 2 using the chain-weighting method to be $(1.333 - 1) \times 100\% = 33.3\%$. The growth rate in this case falls between the growth rates we calculated using the other two approaches, which is of course what we should get given that chain-weighting effectively averages (geometrically) the growth rates calculated using years 1 and 2 as base years.

Now, once we have the chain-weighted ratio of real GDP in one year relative to another (g_c in this case), we can calculate real GDP in terms of the dollars of any year we choose. For example, in our example, if we want real GDP in year 1 dollars, then real GDP in year 1 is the same as nominal GDP or $GDP_1 = \$130$, and real GDP in year 2 is equal to $GDP_1 \times g_c = \$130 \times 1.333 = \$173.29$. Alternatively, if we want real GDP in year 2 dollars, then real GDP in year 2 is $GDP_2 = \$292$, and real GDP in year 1 is $\frac{GDP_2}{g_c} = \frac{\$292}{1.333} = \$219.05$.

In practice, the growth rates in real GDP in adjacent years are calculated just as we have done it here, and then real GDP is "chained" together from one year to the next. Chain-weighting should in principle give a more accurate measure of the year-to-year, or quarter-to-quarter, changes in real GDP. In Figure 2.1 we show nominal GDP and real GDP, calculated using the chain-weighting approach, for the United States over the period 1947–2006. Real GDP is measured here in 2000 dollars, so that real GDP is equal to nominal GDP in 2000. Because the inflation rate was generally positive over the period 1947–2006 and was particularly high in the 1970s, real GDP grows in Figure 2.1 at a lower rate than does nominal GDP.

Measures of the Price Level

There are two commonly used measures of the price level. The first is the **implicit GDP price deflator,** and the second is the **consumer price index (CPI).** The implicit GDP price deflator is measured as

$$\text{Implicit GDP Price deflator} = \frac{\text{Nominal GDP}}{\text{Real GDP}} \times 100.$$

Here, multiplying by 100 just normalizes the price deflator to 100 in the year we are choosing nominal GDP to be equal to real GDP. For the example above, the price deflator we calculate would depend on whether we use year 1 or year 2 as a base year or compute chain-weighted real GDP. We give the results in Table 2.11, and arbitrarily choose chain-weighted real GDP to be in year 1 dollars. Note in Table 2.11 that the answers we get for the percentage rate of inflation between year 1 and year 2 depend critically on how we measure real GDP.

The alternative measure of the price level, the CPI, is not as broadly based as the implicit GDP price deflator, because it includes only goods and services that are purchased by consumers. Further, the CPI is a fixed-weight price index, which takes the quantities in some base year as being the typical goods bought by the average

[2] For more detail on the calculation of real GDP using the chain-weighting method, see *A Guide to the NIPA's*, available from the Bureau of Economic Analysis at http://www.bea.doc.gov/bea/an/nipaguid.htm.

Figure 2.1 **Nominal GDP (black line) and Chain-Weighted Real GDP (colored line) for the Period 1947–2006.**

Note that the two time series cross in 2000 because real GDP is measured in year 2000 dollars. The growth rate in real GDP is smaller than the growth rate for nominal GDP because of positive inflation over this period.

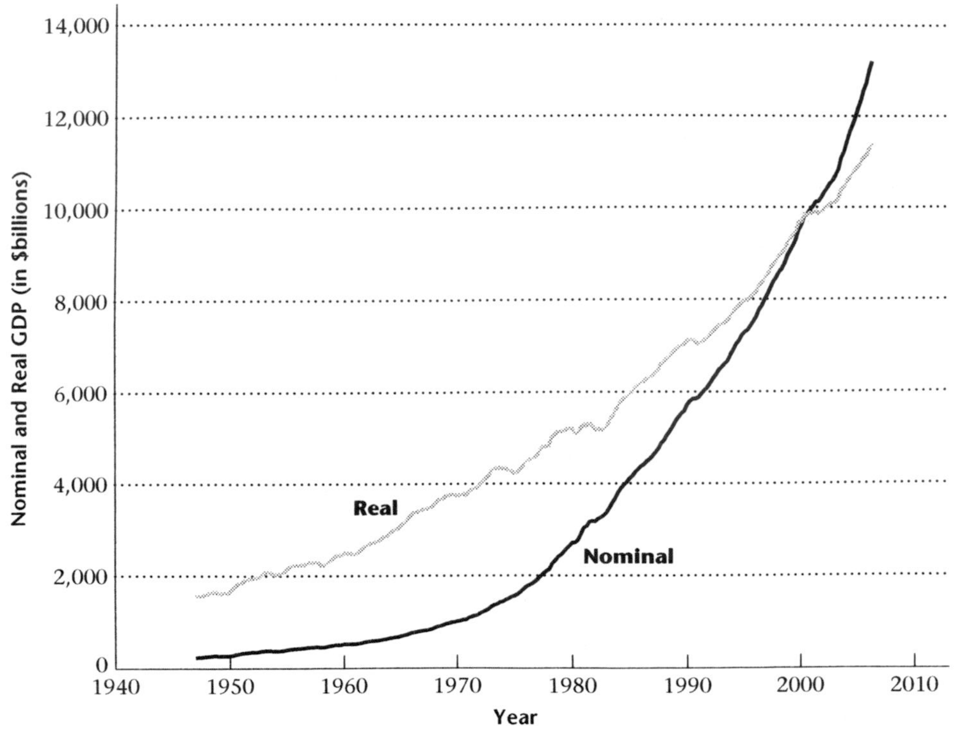

Source: U.S. Department of Commerce, Bureau of Economic Analysis.

Table 2.11 **Implicit GDP Price Deflators, Example**

	Year 1	Year 2	% Increase
Year 1 = base year	100	165.9	65.9
Year 2 = base year	58.4	100	71.2
Chain-weighting	100	168.5	68.5

consumer during that base year, and then uses those quantities as weights to calculate the index in each year. Thus, the CPI in the current year would be

$$\text{Current year CPI} = \frac{\text{Cost of base year quantities at current prices}}{\text{Cost of base year quantities at base year prices}} \times 100.$$

In the example, if we take year 1 as the base year, then the year 1 (base year) CPI is 100, and the year 2 CPI is $\frac{222.5}{130} \times 100 = 171.2$, so that the percentage increase in the CPI from year 1 to year 2 is 71.2%.

In practice, there can be substantial differences between the inflation rates calculated using the implicit GDP price deflator and those calculated using the CPI. Figure 2.2 shows the GDP deflator inflation rate (the black line) and CPI inflation rate (the gray line), calculated quarter by quarter, for the United States over the period 1947–2006. The two measures of the inflation rate track each other broadly, but the CPI inflation rate tends to be more volatile than the GDP deflator inflation rate. At times, there can be large differences between the two measures. For example,

Figure 2.2 **Inflation Rate Calculated from the CPI (gray line), and Calculated from the Implicit GDP Price Deflator (black line).**

These measures are broadly similar, but at times there can be substantial differences. In particular, note the spikes in the CPI inflation rate occurring in the late 1970s, the 1980s, and the early 1990s, which are not replicated in the GDP deflator inflation rate series.

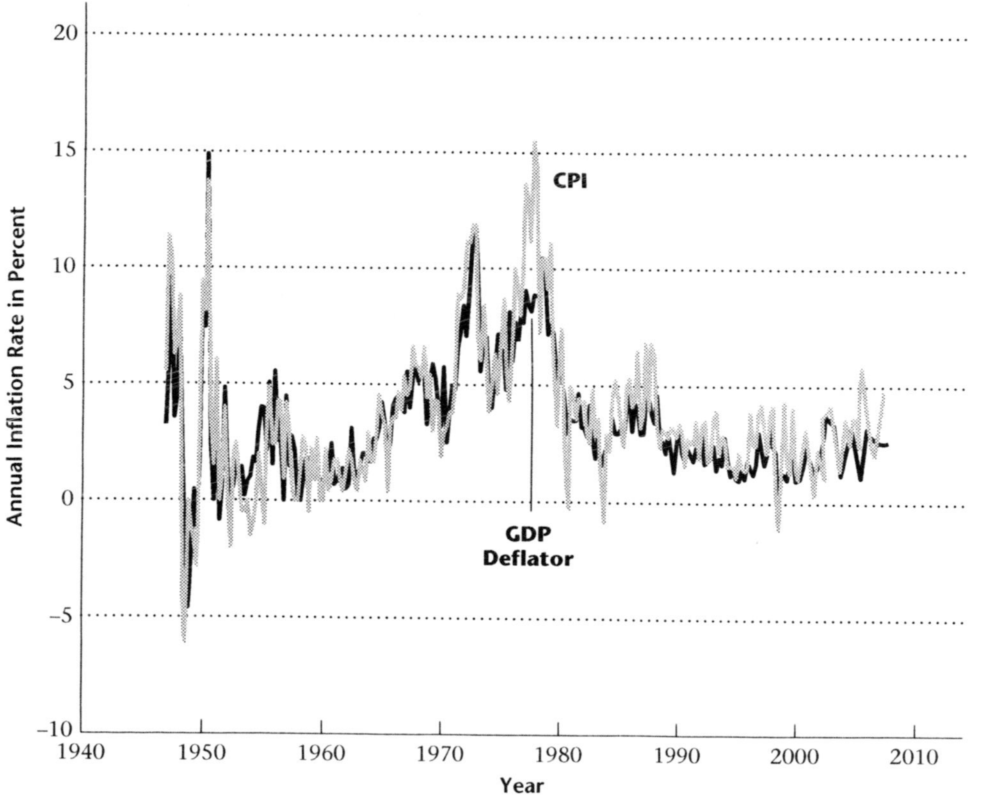

Source: U.S. Department of Commerce, Bureau of Economic Analysis, and Bureau of Labor Statistics.

in late 1979, the CPI inflation rate exceeded 15%, while the GDP deflator inflation rate was about 8%. These differences in inflation rate measures could matter greatly for contracts (for example, labor contracts) that are geared to the inflation rate or for the formulation of monetary policy, where close attention is paid to inflation performance.

Figure 2.2 shows the differences we can observe in measured inflation rates, depending on whether we use the CPI or the implicit GDP price deflator as a measure of the price level. As well, over long periods of time there can be very large differences in the rates of inflation calculated using the two alternative price level measures. To see this, in Figure 2.3 we show the CPI and GDP price deflator in levels for the period 1947–2006, normalizing by setting each measure equal to 100 in the first quarter of

Figure 2.3 **The Price Level as Measured by the CPI and Implicit GDP Price Deflator, 1947–2006.** In this figure, each price level measure is set to 100 in the first quarter of 1947. The CPI increases by a factor of 9.3 over the whole period, while the implicit GDP price deflator increases by a factor of 7.7.

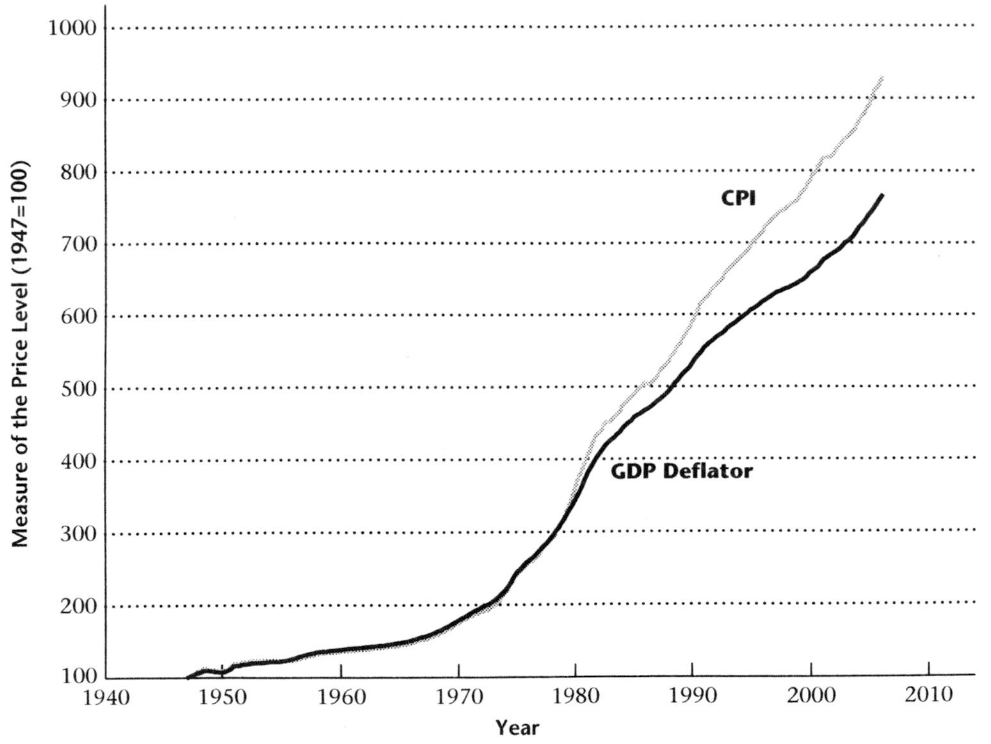

Source: The U.S. Department of Commerce and the Bureau of Labor Statistics.

1947. What the picture tells us is that, if we accept the CPI as a good measure of the price level, then the cost of living increased by a factor of 9.3 over 59 years. However, the GDP price deflator indicates an increase in the cost of living by a factor of only 7.7. Put another way, the average annual inflation rate between 1947 and 2006 was 3.76% as measured by the CPI, and 3.44% as measured by the implicit GDP price deflator. These differences reflect a well-known upward bias in the CPI measure of inflation (for more details, see Macroeconomics in Action: The Boskin Commission and the Consumer Price Index on page 56).

The GDP price deflator tends to yield a better measure of the inflation rate than does the CPI. However, in some cases there are alternatives to either the GDP price deflator or the CPI that serve the purpose better. For example, if we are interested only in measuring the cost of living for consumers living in the United States, then it may be preferable to use the implicit consumption deflator rather than the implicit GDP price deflator as a measure of the price level. The implicit consumption deflator is a price index including only the goods and services that are included in consumption expenditures. The GDP price deflator includes the prices of investment goods, exports, and goods and services sold to the government, none of which would matter directly for consumers. However, if we are looking for a price index reflecting the price of aggregate output produced in the United States, then the GDP price deflator is the appropriate measure.

MACROECONOMICS IN ACTION

Comparing Real GDP across Countries and the Penn Effect

Just as it is useful to obtain a measure of real GDP for a given country so that we can study the growth of output over time in that country, it is also important to be able to make comparisons between real GDPs, or GDPs per person, in different countries. For example, if we can compare real GDP across all countries in the world, we can potentially learn the reasons for differences in the standard of living across countries. This is one of the issues that will concern us when we study economic growth, particularly in Chapter 7.

Coming up with comparable measures of GDP is potentially a daunting task. First, although international organizations have worked to standardize the national income and product accounts across countries, there can still be significant differences in how key data are collected in different countries. For example, poor countries may have limited resources available to devote to data collection. However, even if the prices and quantities of final goods and services were measured without error in all countries, there would still be a problem in making international real GDP comparisons. This is because the prices of identical goods sold in different countries typically vary significantly, even after we express prices in units of the same currency.

To understand the measurement problem, suppose that P denotes the price of goods and services in the United States (in U.S. dollars), and P^* is the price of goods and services in Mexico (in Mexican pesos). Also, suppose that e is the exchange rate of U.S. dollars for Mexican pesos, that is e is the price of a peso in dollars. Then, eP^* would be the cost of Mexican goods and services for an American, or the price in dollars of Mexican goods and services. If we observed that $P = eP^*$, then we would say that we observed the *law of one price* or *purchasing power parity*, in that prices of goods and services would be the same in the United States and Mexico, correcting for exchange rates. In fact, what we tend to observe is that $P > eP^*$ for the United States and Mexico, that is goods and services prices in U.S. dollars tend to be higher in the United States than in Mexico. This difference is particularly large for services, such as auto repairs, which are difficult to trade across international borders.

The *Penn effect* refers to the regularity in data on prices and exchange rates across countries—that prices tend to be higher, correcting for currency exchange rates, in high-income countries than in low-income countries. The problem is that, if we made real GDP comparisons across countries by just expressing all prices in the same currencies, then we would exaggerate the differences in income between rich and poor countries. For example, for the United States and Mexico, if the same quantity of a given good were produced in each country, we would tend to measure this as a smaller contribution to real GDP in Mexico than in the United States if we expressed the quantity produced in terms of its value in U.S. dollars.

An approach to correcting for the Penn effect is to make international real GDP comparisons based on purchasing power parity. For example, for the United States and Mexico, if P is the U.S. price level (in U.S. dollars), and P^* is the Mexican price level (in Mexican pesos), then to compare GDP in the United States with GDP in Mexico, we would multiply nominal quantities for Mexico by P/P^* rather than by e. This is the approach taken in the *Penn World Tables*, a comprehensive set of international data developed by Alan Heston, Robert Summers, and Bettina Aten at the University of Pennsylvania.[3] We will make use of the Penn World Tables when we study economic growth in Chapters 6 and 7.

[3]Heston, A., Sumers, R., & Aten, B., September 2006, Penn World Table Version 6.2, Center for International Comparisons of Production, Income, and Prices at the University of Pennsylvania.

Problems with Measuring Real GDP and the Price Level

As we saw above, particularly in how the implicit GDP price deflator is derived, the measurement of real GDP and the measurement of the price level are intimately related. If a particular measure of real GDP underestimates growth in real GDP, then the rate of inflation is overestimated. In practice, there are three important problems with measuring real GDP and the price level.

The first problem was mentioned above, which is that relative prices change over time. We showed how chain-weighting corrects for this problem in the measurement of real GDP and, therefore, corrects for the bias that relative price changes would introduce in the measurement of inflation using the implicit GDP price deflator. Changes in relative prices can also introduce severe bias in how the CPI measures inflation. When there is a relative price change, consumers typically purchase less of the goods that have become more expensive and more of those that have become relatively cheap. In the previous example, apples became cheaper relative to oranges in year 2, and the ratio of apples consumed to oranges consumed increased. In computing the CPI, the implicit assumption is that consumers do not change their buying habits when relative price changes occur, which is clearly false. As a result, goods that become relatively more expensive receive a higher weight than they should in the CPI, and, therefore, the CPI-based measure of the rate of inflation is biased upward. This is a serious policy issue (see the box on the Boskin Commission on page 56), because some federal transfer payments, including Social Security, are indexed to the CPI, and, therefore, an upward bias in CPI inflation would also commit the federal government to higher transfer payments, which in turn would increase the size of the federal budget deficit. Also, federal income tax brackets are geared to CPI inflation. Upward bias in CPI inflation causes tax revenues to fall, increasing the government deficit. Rather than the rate of increase in the CPI, a more accurate measure of the rate of inflation in consumer goods is the implicit consumption price deflator, which is the price deflator associated with chain-weighted real consumption expenditures.

A second problem in measuring real GDP is changes in the quality of goods over time. Consider the case of 2006 cars versus 1950 cars. Clearly, the price of a new car in 2006 was much higher than the price of a new car in 1950, but the 2006 car is very different from the 1950 car. In 2006, most cars sold in the United States had computerized devices to monitor engine performance, automatic transmissions, power windows, air bags, seat belts, and CD players, none of which were standard equipment (or in some cases even invented) in 1950. In a sense, the 2006 car is "more car," because its quality is higher; therefore, some of the increase in price from 1950 to 2006 simply represents the fact that the buyer is receiving more in exchange for his or her money. To the extent that NIPA does not compensate for changes in quality over time, growth in real GDP is biased downward and inflation is biased upward.

A third problem is how measured GDP takes account of new goods. For example, personal computers were introduced in the early 1980s, and they did not exist in the NIPA before then. Clearly, we cannot make a straightforward calculation of real GDP growth from the 1970s to the 1980s, as there were no prices existing for personal computers in the 1970s. If the NIPA does not correctly take account of the fact that the new personal computers that were introduced (initially at very high prices) were a huge quality advance over old-fashioned calculators and slide rules, then this could bias downward the measure of real GDP growth and bias upward the measure of the inflation rate.

MACROECONOMICS IN ACTION

The Boskin Commission and the Consumer Price Index

The Boskin Commission, or more formally, the Advisory Commission to Study the Consumer Price Index, was appointed by the Senate Finance Committee in June 1995 to review CPI measurement and come up with recommendations for improvement. The Commission's report, authored by a group of well-known economists and published in 1996,[4] came to some perhaps startling conclusions. Given the biases in the inflation rate computed from the CPI, as discussed in the text, the Commission estimated that the upward bias in the CPI inflation rate was a substantial 1.1 percentage points per year. It was estimated that this upward bias in CPI inflation would contribute an extra $202 billion to government spending and $1.07 trillion to the government debt by 2008, primarily as a result of the indexing of Social Security benefits and federal income taxes. Government spending as a result of the CPI inflation bias would then be the fourth largest component of federal spending, behind Social Security, health care, and defense!

The Boskin Commission recommended that the Bureau of Labor Statistics refine its measurement procedures so as to reduce or eliminate the CPI inflation bias, but not everyone greeted the Commission's recommendations with adulation. Given that the elimination of the CPI inflation bias would substantially reduce the future income of senior citizens from Social Security, lobby groups representing seniors put considerable effort into casting doubt on the Commission's findings. Many of the Boskin Commission's recommendations, however, were implemented by the Bureau of Labor Statistics, and Robert Gordon estimated that these changes had eliminated about half of the CPI inflation bias.[5]

[4]Boskin, E. Deulberger, R. Gordon, Z. Griliches, and D. Jorgensen, 1997, "The CPI Commission: Findings and Recommendations," *American Economic Review* 87, 78–83.

[5]See Gordon, R., December 1999, "The Boskin Commission Report and Its Aftermath," in *Monetary and Economic Studies*, Tokyo, Japan: Bank of Japan; also available on the web at http://www.imes.boj.or.jp/japanese/all99/abst/me17-3-2.html

Savings, Wealth, and Capital

While the components of GDP in the NIPA measure aggregate activity that takes place within the current period, another key aspect of the economy that is of interest to macroeconomists is aggregate productive capacity and how aggregate savings adds to this productive capacity. In this section we explore, by way of several accounting identities, the relationships among savings, wealth, and capital.

An important distinction in economics is between **flows** and **stocks.** A flow is a rate per unit time, while a stock is the quantity in existence of some object at a point in time. In the NIPA, GDP, consumption, investment, government spending, and net exports are all flows. For example, GDP is measured in dollars spent per period. In contrast, the quantity of housing in existence in the United States at the end of a given year is a stock. In the following, we see that national saving is a flow, while the nation's wealth is a stock. In this case, national saving is the flow that is added to the stock of the nation's wealth in each year. A classic analogy is the example of water flowing into a bathtub, where the quantity of water coming out of the faucet per minute is a flow, while the quantity of water in the bathtub at any point in time is a stock.

Savings can mean very different things, depending on whether we are referring to the private (nongovernment) sector, the government, or the nation as a whole. For the private sector, to determine savings we first need to start with what the private sector has available to spend, which is **private disposable income,** denoted Y^d. We have

$$Y^{\mathrm{d}} = Y + NFP + TR + INT - T,$$

where Y is GDP, NFP is net factor payments from abroad to U.S. residents, TR is transfers from the government to the private sector, INT is interest on the government debt, and T is taxes. Recall that GNP is $Y + NFP$. What the private sector saves is simply what it has available to spend minus what it consumes, and so letting S^p denote **private sector saving,** we have

$$S^{\mathrm{p}} = Y^{\mathrm{d}} - C = Y + NFP + TR + INT - T - C.$$

What the government has available to spend is its tax revenue, T, minus TR, minus INT, and what it consumes is government expenditures, G. Thus, **government saving** S^g is given by

$$S^{\mathrm{g}} = T - TR - INT - G.$$

Government saving is simply the **government surplus,** and the government surplus is the negative of the **government deficit,** denoted D, or

$$D = -S^{\mathrm{g}} = -T + TR + INT + G,$$

which is just government outlays minus government receipts. If we add private saving and government saving, we obtain **national saving,**

$$S = S^{\mathrm{p}} + S^{\mathrm{g}} = Y + NFP - C - G,$$

which is GNP minus private consumption, minus government consumption. Because the income–expenditure identity gives $Y = C + I + G + NX$, we can substitute for Y in the previous equation to obtain

$$\begin{aligned} S &= Y + NFP - C - G \\ &= C + I + G + NX + NFP - C - G \\ &= I + NX + NFP \end{aligned}$$

Thus, national saving must equal investment plus net exports plus net factor payments from abroad. The quantity $NX + NFP$ is the **current account surplus** with the rest of the world, which we denote CA; thus, we have

$$S = I + CA.$$

The current account surplus is a measure of the balance of trade in goods and services with the rest of the world. The above identity reflects the fact that any domestic savings not absorbed by domestic investment must be shipped outside the country in the form of goods and services.

As a flow, national saving represents additions to the nation's wealth. Because $S = I + CA$, wealth is accumulated in two ways. First, wealth is accumulated through investment, I, which is additions to the nation's **capital stock.** The capital stock is the quantity of plants, equipment, housing, and inventories in existence in an economy at a point in time. Second, wealth is accumulated through current account surpluses, CA, because a current account surplus implies that U.S. residents are accumulating claims on foreigners. The current account surplus, CA, represents increases in claims on foreigners because if goods are flowing from the United States to other countries, then these goods must be paid for with a transfer of wealth from outside the United States to U.S. residents. The current account surplus is then a flow, while the quantity of claims on foreigners in existence in the United States is a stock.

Labor Market Measurement

The labor market variables we focus on here are those measured in the monthly household survey, carried out by the Bureau of Labor Statistics. In this survey, people are divided into three groups: the **employed**—those who worked part-time or full-time during the past week; the **unemployed**—those who were not employed during the past week but actively searched for work at some time during the last four weeks; and **not in the labor force**—those who are neither employed or unemployed. Thus, the labor force is the employed plus the unemployed.

Of key interest in analyzing the results of the household survey are the **unemployment rate,** measured as

$$\text{Unemployment rate} = \frac{\text{Number unemployed}}{\text{Labor force}},$$

and the **participation rate,** measured as

$$\text{Participation rate} = \frac{\text{Labor Force}}{\text{Total working age population}}$$

The unemployment rate is potentially useful as a measure of **labor market tightness,** which is the degree of difficulty firms face in hiring workers.[6] However, there are two ways in which the unemployment rate might mismeasure labor market tightness (see Macroeconomics in Action: Measuring Unemployment and Labor Force Attachment on page 59). First, some people, referred to as **discouraged workers,** are not counted in the labor force and have stopped searching for work but actually wish to be employed. Thus, during a long recession, when the level of aggregate economic activity

[6]Another measure of labor market tightness is the the number of unemployed divided by the number of job vacancies, where vacancies are the number of job openings in the economy that firms are trying to fill. Unfortunately, the measures that exist of vacancies in the U.S. economy are notoriously poor, at least going back more than a few years from the present.

is depressed for an extended duration, the unemployment rate possibly might fall only because some unemployed people have become discouraged and stopped looking for work. In this circumstance, labor market tightness would not really have increased with the decrease in the unemployment rate, but we might be fooled into thinking so.

The second factor that could cause the unemployment rate to be a bad measure of labor market tightness is that the unemployment rate does not adjust for how intensively the unemployed are searching for work. When the unemployment rate is high, the unemployed might not search very hard for work—for example, each worker might spend one or two hours per day trying to find work. When the unemployment rate is low, however, the unemployed might all be searching very hard—for example, they might each search eight or ten hours per day. If this were the case, then the unemployment rate would be a biased measure of labor market tightness, since it would actually be harder for a firm to hire a worker in a recession and easier for a firm to hire a worker during a boom in economic activity than what the unemployment rate reflects on its own.

Partly because of problems in interpreting what movements in the unemployment rate mean, macroeconomists often focus attention on the level and growth rate of employment when they analyze the implications of labor market activity. Indeed, many of the models we analyze in this book do not explain the behavior of unemployment; however, we study some explanations for unemployment in Chapters 12 and 15.

So far, we have learned how aggregate economic activity is measured in the NIPA, how nominal GDP can be decomposed to obtain measures of real GDP and the price level, what the relationships are among savings, wealth, and capital, and what the key measurement issues in the labor market are. Before we begin our study of macroeconomic theory in Chapter 4, in Chapter 3 we deal with business cycle measurement, deriving a set of key business cycle facts that focus our theoretical discussion in the following chapters.

MACROECONOMICS IN ACTION

Measuring Unemployment and Labor Force Attachment

The traditional approach to labor market measurement is to divide the working age population into three groups, the employed (E), the unemployed (U), and those not in the labor force (N). This approach is useful because the economic behavior of the three groups is in principle distinct. Those in group E are engaged in the production of goods and services for the market, those in group U are engaged in search activity with the goal of joining group E, and those in group N are engaged in home production (childcare and home maintenance, for example) and leisure. Once labor market measurement is done in this way, we can then use the data in conjunction with economic theory to understand better why people choose to be in each of the three groups and to understand the implications for government policy.

Some recent research casts doubt on the traditional approach to labor market measurement. Leaving aside the issue of who should be counted as employed (rules about how many hours of work constitute employment are clearly arbitrary), there are varying degrees of search activity and separation from the labor force in the groups U and N, respectively. Stephen Jones and Craig Riddell[7] find that these differences among people in groups U and N appear to matter sufficiently that we should change how people are categorized in the labor force survey.

The first issue addressed by Jones and Riddell is related to the behavior of discouraged workers, or what they call the "marginally attached." This group of people expresses a desire to be employed, but they are not engaged in any of the activities constituting search behavior. A possibility is that the marginally attached are just engaged in wishful thinking and that they are appropriately included in N. However, Jones and Riddell's statistical analysis shows that the behavior of the marginally attached is distinct from the remainder of the people in group N, as well as from those included in U. Further, the marginally attached constitute a significant fraction of the population. This finding points to the need for distinguishing the marginally attached from U and N in the labor force survey.

A second issue studied by Jones and Riddell is the behavior of the subgroup of marginally attached people who are "waiting." This group is not actively searching for work but is waiting for a recall from a layoff period, waiting for replies from potential employers, etc. Jones and Riddell find that it would be appropriate to categorize the waiting as U rather than N. In fact, the waiting are more likely to be employed in the future than are those in group U.

Finally, Jones and Riddell examine the differing behavior of those who are currently classified as U. There is some question as to whether those who simply look at job postings in newspapers, for example, should be classified as U rather than N, as such persons may be uninterested in actually contacting potential employers. However, the general behavior of those engaged in low-level search activity shares more with the remainder of the U group than with the N group.

Ultimately, the primary recommendation coming from the work of Jones and Riddell is that labor market measurement and research should be conducted based on the notion of four distinct groups. Adding a group of discouraged workers (the marginally attached) to the three traditional labor market groups appears to be a sound approach.

[7]See Jones, S.R.G., & Riddell, W.C., 1999. "The Measurement of Unemployment: An Empirical Approach," *Econometrica* 67, 147–162.

Chapter Summary

- Gross Domestic Product (GDP) is measured in the National Income and Product Accounts (NIPA) of the United States. GDP can be measured via the product approach, the expenditure approach, or the income approach, which each yield the same quantity of GDP in a given period if there is no measurement error.
- GDP must be used carefully as a measure of aggregate welfare, because it leaves out home production. Further, there are problems with GDP as a measure of aggregate output, because of the existence of the underground economy and because government output is difficult to measure.

- It is useful to take account of how much of nominal GDP growth is accounted for by inflation and how much is growth in real GDP. Two approaches to measuring real GDP are choosing a base year and chain-weighting. The latter is the current method used in the NIPA. Chain-weighting corrects for the bias that arises in real GDP calculations when a base year is used and there are changes in relative prices over time. Problems with real GDP measurement arise because it is difficult to account for changes in the quality of goods over time and because new goods are introduced and others become obsolete.
- Private saving is private disposable income minus consumption, while government saving is government receipts minus government spending and transfers. The government surplus is equal to government saving. National saving is the sum of private and government saving and is equal to investment expenditures plus the current account surplus. National saving is just the accumulation of national wealth, which comes in the form of additions to the capital stock (investment) and additions to domestic claims on foreigners (the current account surplus).
- The labor market variables we focus on are those measured in the household survey of the Bureau of Labor Statistics. The working age population consists of the employed, the unemployed (those searching for work), and those not in the labor force. Two key labor market variables are the unemployment rate and the participation rate. The unemployment rate is sometimes used as a measure of labor market tightness, but care must be taken in how the unemployment rate is interpreted in this respect.

Key Terms

Gross domestic product (GDP) The dollar value of final output produced during a given period of time within a country's borders.

National Income and Product Accounts (NIPA) The official U.S. accounts of aggregate economic activity, which include GDP measurements.

Product approach The approach to GDP measurement that determines GDP as the sum of value added to goods and services in production across all productive units in the economy.

Expenditure approach The approach to GDP measurement that determines GDP as total spending on all final goods and services production in the economy.

Income approach The approach to GDP measurement that determines GDP as the sum of all incomes received by economic agents contributing to production.

Intermediate good A good that is produced and then used as an input in another production process.

Value-added The value of goods produced minus the value of intermediate goods used in production.

Income–expenditure identity $Y = C + I + G + NX$, where Y is aggregate income (output), C is consumption expenditures, I is investment expenditures, G is government expenditures, and NX is net exports.

Gross national product (GNP) $GNP = GDP$ plus net factor payments to U.S. residents from abroad.

Underground economy All unreported economic activity.

Consumption Goods and services produced and consumed during the current period.

Investment Goods produced in the current period but not consumed in the current period.

Fixed investment Investment in plant, equipment, and housing.

Inventory investment Goods produced in the current period that are set aside for future periods.

Net exports Expenditures on domestically produced goods and services by foreigners (exports) minus expenditures on foreign-produced goods and services by domestic residents (imports).
Government expenditures Expenditures by federal, state, and local governments on final goods and services.
Transfers Government outlays that are transfers of purchasing power from one group of private economic agents to another.
Price index A weighted average of prices of some set of goods produced in the economy during a particular period.
Price level The average level of prices across all goods and services in the economy.
Inflation rate The rate of change in the price level from one period to another.
Nominal change The change in the dollar value of a good, service, or asset.
Real change The change in the quantity of a good, service, or asset.
Chain-weighting An approach to calculating real GDP that uses a rolling base year.
Implicit GDP price deflator Nominal GDP divided by real GDP, all multiplied by 100.
Consumer price index (CPI) Expenditures on base year quantities at current year prices divided by total expenditures on base year quantities at base year prices, all multiplied by 100.
Flow A rate per unit time.
Stock Quantity in existence of some object at a point in time.
Private disposable income GDP plus net factor payments, plus transfers from the government, plus interest on the government debt, minus taxes.
Private sector saving Private disposable income minus consumption expenditures.
Government saving Taxes minus transfers, minus interest on the government debt, minus government expenditures.
Government surplus Identical to government saving.
Government deficit The negative of the government surplus.
National saving Private sector saving plus government saving.
Current account surplus Net exports plus net factor payments from abroad.
Capital stock The quantity of plant, equipment, housing, and inventories in existence in an economy at a point in time.
Employed In the Bureau of Labor Statistics household survey, those who worked part-time or full-time during the past week.
Unemployed In the Bureau of Labor Statistics household survey, those who were not employed during the past week but actively searched for work at some time during the last four weeks.
Not in the labor force In the Bureau of Labor Statistics household survey, those who are neither employed or unemployed.
Unemployment rate The number of unemployed divided by the number in the labor force.
Participation rate The number in the labor force divided by the working age population.
Labor market tightness The degree of difficulty firms face in hiring workers.
Discouraged workers Those who are not counted in the labor force and have stopped searching for work but actually wish to be employed.

Questions for Review

1. What are the three approaches to measuring GDP?
2. Explain the concept of value added.
3. Why is the income–expenditure identity important?
4. What is the difference between GDP and GNP?
5. Is GDP a good measure of economic welfare? Why or why not?

6. What are two difficulties in the measurement of aggregate output using GDP?
7. What is the largest expenditure component of GDP?
8. What is investment?
9. Is national defense a large fraction of government spending?
10. Why does the base year matter in calculating real GDP?
11. Explain what chain-weighting is.
12. Explain three problems in the measurement of real GDP.
13. What are the differences and similarities among private sector saving, government saving, and national saving?
14. What are the two ways in which national wealth is accumulated?
15. Give two reasons that the unemployment rate may mismeasure the degree of labor market tightness.

Problems

1. Assume an economy where there are two producers: a wheat producer and a bread producer. In a given year, the wheat producer grows 30 million bushels of wheat of which 25 million bushels are sold to the bread producer at $3 per bushel, and 5 million bushels are stored by the wheat producer to use as seed for next year's crop. The bread producer produces and sells 100 million loaves of bread to consumers for $3.50 per loaf. Determine GDP in this economy during this year using the product and expenditure approaches.
2. Assume an economy with a coal producer, a steel producer, and some consumers (there is no government). In a given year, the coal producer produces 15 million tons of coal and sells it for $5 per ton. The coal producer pays $50 million in wages to consumers. The steel producer uses 25 million tons of coal as an input into steel production, all purchased at $5 per ton. Of this, 15 million tons of coal comes from the domestic coal producer and 10 million tons is imported. The steel producer produces 10 million tons of steel and sells it for $20 per ton. Domestic consumers buy 8 million tons of steel, and 2 million tons are exported. The steel producer pays consumers $40 million in wages. All profits made by domestic producers are distributed to domestic consumers.
   (a) Determine GDP using (i) the product approach, (ii) the expenditure approach, and (iii) the income approach.
   (b) Determine the current account surplus.
   (c) What is GNP in this economy? Determine GNP and GDP in the case where the coal producer is owned by foreigners, so that the profits of the domestic coal producer go to foreigners and are not distributed to domestic consumers.
3. Assume an economy with two firms. Firm A produces wheat and firm B produces bread. In a given year, firm A produces 50,000 bushels of wheat, sells 20,000 bushels of wheat to firm B at $3 per bushel, exports 25,000 bushels of wheat at $3 per bushel, and stores 5,000 bushels as inventory. Firm A pays $50,000 in wages to consumers. Firm B produces 50,000 loaves of bread, and sells all of it to domestic consumers at $2 per loaf. Firm B pays consumers $20,000 in wages. In addition to the 50,000 loaves of bread consumers buy from firm B, consumers import and consume 15,000 loaves of bread, and they pay $1 per loaf for this imported bread. Calculate gross domestic product for the year using (a) the product approach, (b) the expenditure approach, and (c) the income approach.

4. In year 1 and year 2, two products are produced in a given economy, computers and bread. Suppose that there are no intermediate goods. In year 1, 20 computers are produced and sold at $1,000 each, and in year 2, 25 computers are sold at $1,500 each. In year 1, 10,000 loaves of bread are sold for $1.00 each, and in year 2, 12,000 loaves of bread are sold for $1.10 each.
   (a) Calculate nominal GDP in each year.
   (b) Calculate real GDP in each year, and the percentage increase in real GDP from year 1 to year 2 using year 1 as the base year. Next, do the same calculations using the chain-weighting method.
   (c) Calculate the implicit GDP price deflator and the percentage inflation rate from year 1 to year 2 using year 1 as the base year. Next, do the same calculations using the chain-weighting method.
   (d) Suppose that computers in year 2 are twice as productive as computers in year 1. That is, computers are of higher quality in year 2 in the sense that one computer in year 2 is equivalent to two computers in year 1. How does this change your calculations in parts (a) to (c)? Explain any differences.

5. Assume an economy in which only broccoli and cauliflower are produced. In year 1, 500 million pounds of broccoli are produced and consumed, and its price is $0.50 per pound, while 300 million pounds of cauliflower are produced and consumed and its price is $0.80 per pound. In year 2, 400 million pounds of broccoli are produced and consumed and its price is $0.60 per pound, while 350 million pounds of cauliflower are produced and its price is $0.85 per pound.
   (a) Using year 1 as the base year, calculate the GDP price deflator in years 1 and 2, and calculate the rate of inflation between years 1 and 2 from the GDP price deflator.
   (b) Using year 1 as the base year, calculate the CPI in years 1 and 2, and calculate the CPI rate of inflation. Explain any differences in your results between parts (a) and (b).

6. Consider an economy with a corn producer, some consumers, and a government. In a given year, the corn producer grows 30 million bushels of corn and the market price for corn is $5 per bushel. Of the 30 million bushels produced, 20 million bushels are sold to consumers, 5 million are stored in inventory, and 5 million are sold to the government to feed the army. The corn producer pays $60 million in wages to consumers and $20 million in taxes to the government. Consumers pay $10 million in taxes to the government, receive $10 million in interest on the government debt, and receive $5 million in Social Security payments from the government. The profits of the corn producer are distributed to consumers.
   (a) Calculate GDP using (i) the product approach, (ii) the expenditure approach, and (iii) the income approach.
   (b) Calculate private disposable income, private sector saving, government saving, national saving, and the government deficit. Is the government budget in deficit or surplus?

7. In some countries, price controls exist on some goods, which set maximum prices at which these goods can be sold. Indeed, the United States experienced a period of wage and price controls when the Nixon administration introduced them in 1971. Sometimes the existence of price controls leads to the growth of black markets, where goods are exchanged at prices above the legal maximums. Carefully explain how price controls present a problem for measuring GDP and for measuring the price level and inflation.

8. In this chapter, we learned that the quantity of U.S. currency outstanding was $2,474 per U.S. resident in July 2006. Suppose that we were to try to use this number to estimate the amount of output produced in the underground economy in the United States during 2006.

Discuss how we would use this information on the quantity of currency in circulation, and what additional information you would want to have to come up with a good estimate. In your answer, you will need to consider how underground transactions might take place by other means in the United States than through the use of U.S. currency, and how some of U.S. currency is not being used for underground transactions in the United States.

9. Consider the identity

$$S^p - I = CA + D,$$

where S^p is private sector saving, I is investment, CA is the current account surplus, and D is the government deficit.
   (a) Show that the above identity holds.
   (b) Explain what the above identity means.

10. Let K_t denote the quantity of capital a country has at the beginning of period t. Also, suppose that capital depreciates at a constant rate d, so that dK_t of the capital stock wears out during period t. If investment during period t is denoted by I_t, and the country does not trade with the rest of the world (the current account surplus is always zero), then we can say that the quantity of capital at the beginning of period $t+1$ is given by

$$K_{t+1} = (1-d)K_t + I_t.$$

Suppose at the beginning of year 0 that this country has 80 units of capital. Investment expenditures are 10 units in each of years 0, 1, 2, 3, 4, . . ., 10. The capital stock depreciates by 10% per year.
   (a) Calculate the quantity of capital at the beginning of years 0, 1, 2, 3, 4, . . ., 10.
   (b) Repeat part (a), except assume now that the country begins year 0 with 100 units of capital. Explain what happens now and discuss your results in parts (a) and (b).

11. Suppose that the government deficit is 10, interest on the government debt is 5, taxes are 40, government expenditures are 30, consumption expenditures are 80, net factor payments are 10, the current account surplus is −5, and national saving is 20. Calculate the following (not necessarily in the order given):
   (a) Private disposable income
   (b) Transfers from the government to the private sector
   (c) Gross national product
   (d) Gross domestic product
   (e) The government surplus
   (f) Net exports
   (g) Investment expenditures

12. Suppose that the unemployment rate is 5%, the total working age population is 100 million, and the number of unemployed is 2.5 million. Determine: (i) the participation rate; (ii) the labor force; (iii) the number of employed workers.

Working with the Data

1. Calculate consumption of durables, consumption of nondurables, and consumption of services as percentages of total consumption, and plot these time series. Comment on the changes that have taken place over time in the consumption of services relative to durables and nondurables.

2. Macroeconomists sometimes study the behavior of the consumer price index, leaving out food and energy prices. Calculate the year-to-year inflation rate (December to December), in percentage terms, using the consumer price index (all items) and using the consumer price index less food and energy. Plot the two inflation rates, and comment on the differences. Why would we want to neglect food and energy in our calculation of the CPI? Why would we not want to neglect these items?
3. Plot the stocks of capital, private nonresidential capital, private residential capital, government capital, and consumer durable goods over time. Comment on the movements in these time series and the proportion that each component of capital takes up in the total.

CHAPTER 3

Business Cycle Measurement

BEFORE WE GO ON TO BUILD MODELS OF AGGREGATE ECONOMIC ACTIVITY THAT CAN EXPLAIN why business cycles exist and what, if anything, should be done about them, we must understand the key features that we observe in economic data that define a business cycle. In this chapter, we move beyond the study of the measurement of gross domestic product (GDP), the price level, savings, and wealth, which we covered in Chapter 2, to an examination of the regularities in the relationships among aggregate economic variables as they fluctuate over time.

We show that business cycles are quite irregular, in that they are unpredictable; macroeconomic forecasters often have a difficult time predicting the timing of a business cycle upturn or downturn. Business cycles are quite regular, however, in terms of comovements, which is to say that macroeconomic variables move together in highly predictable ways. We focus separately on the components of real GDP, nominal variables, and labor market variables.

This chapter describes a set of key business cycle facts concerning comovements in U.S. macroeconomic data. In Chapters 4, 5, 8 and 9, we use these facts to show how our models can make sense of what we observe in the data. Then, in Chapters 11 and 12, we use the key business cycle facts to help us evaluate alternative theories of the business cycle.

Regularities in GDP Fluctuations

The primary defining feature of **business cycles** is that they are *fluctuations about trend in real GDP.* Recall from Chapter 1 that we represent the trend in real GDP with a smooth curve that closely fits actual real GDP, with the trend representing that part of real GDP that can be explained by long-run growth factors. What is left over, the deviations from trend, we take to represent business cycle activity.

In Figure 3.1 we show idealized business cycle activity in real GDP, with fluctuations about a long-run trend. In the figure, real GDP is represented by the black line, while the trend is represented by the colored line. There are **peaks** and **troughs** in real GDP, a peak being a relatively large positive deviation from trend, and a trough a relatively large negative deviation from trend. Peaks and troughs in the deviations from trend in real GDP are referred to as **turning points.** In a manner analogous to wave motion in the physical sciences, we can think of the maximum deviation from trend in Figure 3.1 as the **amplitude** of the business cycle, and the number of peaks in real GDP that occur per year as the **frequency** of the business cycle.

Figure 3.1 **Idealized Business Cycles.**
The black curve is an idealized path for real GDP over time, while the colored line is the growth trend in real GDP. Real GDP cycles around the trend over time, with the maximum negative deviation from trend being a trough and the maximum positive deviation from trend being a peak. The amplitude is the size of the maximum deviation from trend, and the frequency is the number of peaks that occur within a year's time.

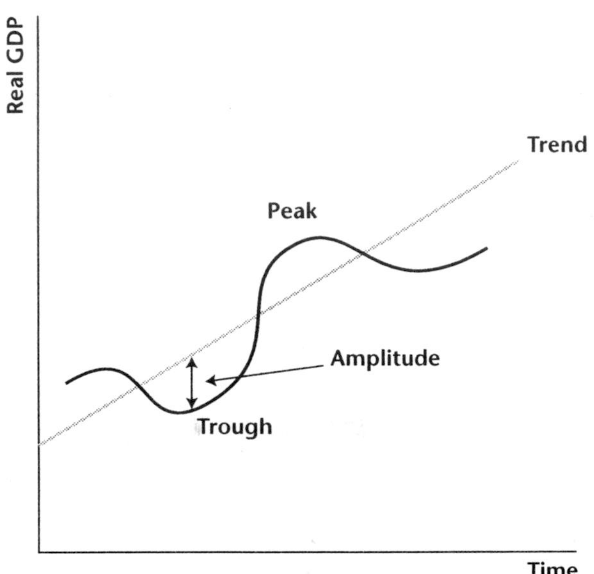

Next, in Figure 3.2 we show the actual percentage deviations from trend in real GDP for the United States over the period 1947–2006. A series of positive deviations from trend culminating in a peak represents a **boom,** whereas a series of negative deviations from trend culminating in a trough represents a **recession.** In Figure 3.2, we have marked four important recessions, which occurred in 1974–1975, 1981–1982, 1990–1991, and 2001. The first two of these recessions were quite significant, with the deviation from trend in real GDP exceeding 4%, whereas the last two were relatively mild, with deviations from trend of between 1% and 2%. In fact, since the 1981–1982 recession real GDP has been remarkably stable in the United States, in that it has stayed much closer to trend than in the period from World War II to 1982.

An examination of Figure 3.2 indicates a striking regularity, which is that the deviations from trend in real GDP are **persistent.** That is, when real GDP is above trend, it tends to stay above trend, and when it is below trend, it tends to stay below trend. This feature is quite important in terms of economic forecasting over the short run; persistence implies that we can fairly confidently predict that if real GDP is currently below (above) trend, then it will be below (above) trend several months from

Figure 3.2 **Percentage Deviations from Trend in Real GDP from 1947–2006.**
Of particular note are the four most recent recessions, in 1974–1975, 1981–1982, 1990–1991, and 2001. Since the 1981–1982 recession, real GDP has stayed quite close to trend, relative to the entire post–World War II history.

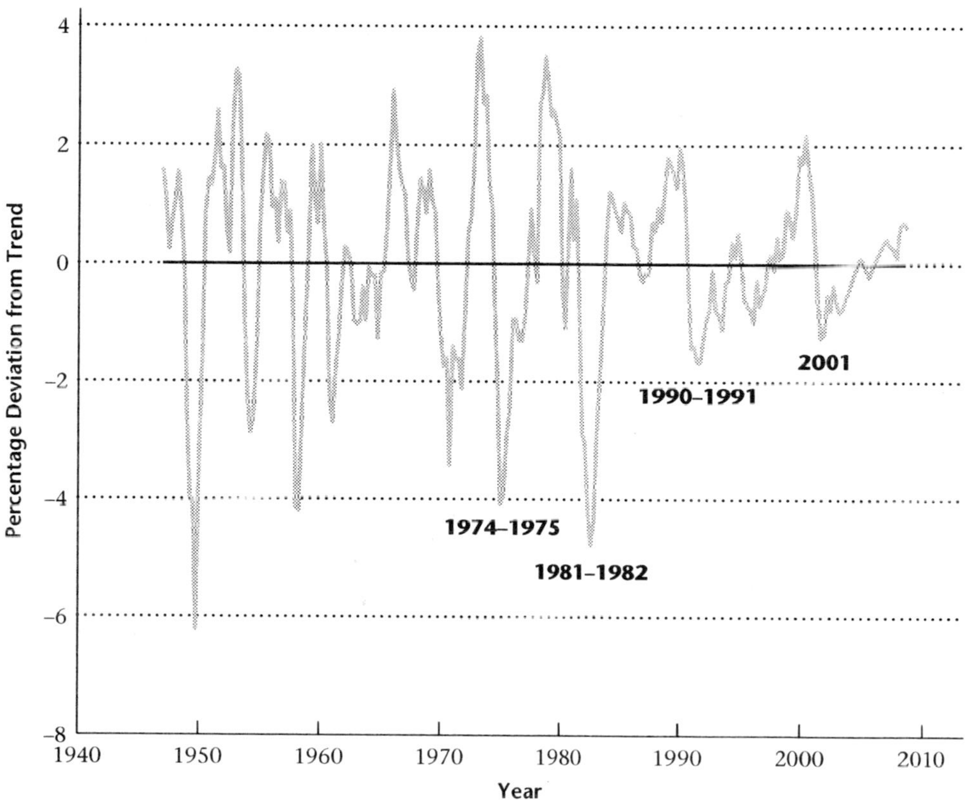

Source: U.S. Department of Commerce.

now. Other than being persistent, however, the deviations from trend in real GDP are actually quite irregular. There are three other features to note in Figure 3.2:

1. The time series of deviations from trend in real GDP is quite choppy.
2. There is no regularity in the amplitude of fluctuations in real GDP about trend. Some of the peaks and troughs represent large deviations from trend, whereas other peaks and troughs represent small deviations from trend.
3. There is no regularity in the frequency of fluctuations in real GDP about trend. The length of time between peaks and troughs in real GDP varies considerably.

Though deviations from trend in real GDP are persistent, which makes short-term forecasting relatively easy, the above three features imply that longer-term forecasting is difficult. The choppiness of fluctuations in real GDP make these fluctuations difficult to predict, while the lack of regularity in the amplitude and frequency of fluctuations implies that it is difficult to predict the severity and length of recessions and booms. Therefore, predicting future fluctuations in real GDP by looking only at past real GDP is much like attempting to forecast the weather by looking out the window. If it is sunny today, it is likely that it will be sunny tomorrow (weather is persistent), but the fact that it is sunny today may give us very little information on whether it will be sunny one week from today.

MACROECONOMICS IN ACTION

The Pitfalls of Macroeconomic Forecasting

In the United States, macroeconomic forecasting is done by government agencies such as the Congressional Budget Office and the Federal Reserve System and by private firms, such as the Conference Board, which sell forecasts to government and businesses. There are essentially three approaches to macroeconomic forecasting: judgmental forecasting, model forecasting, and statistical forecasting.

Judgmental forecasters gather various kinds of information and data from official and unofficial sources, and then they forecast future macroeconomic activity based on their own informal judgment about how the economy works. A judgmental forecaster does not use sophisticated statistical methods or macroeconomic theory in a rigorous way but instead relies on his or her "gut feelings" about where the economy is headed.

Model forecasting is done using an explicit macroeconomic model that is constructed using macroeconomic theory. The types of models used vary considerably, but those developed in the 1960s and 1970s, some of which are still in use at central banks, in governments, and at private forecasting firms, consist of several hundred equations that capture the relationships among several hundred macroeconomic variables. A forecast using one of these models can involve work by a team of people who fine-tune the model before the forecast, and then generate a forecast that is a computer simulation of the model's predictions for future macroeconomic activity.

Statistical forecasting is a reaction to model forecasting, in that some macroeconomists argue that forecasting models had simply got out of hand. These macroeconomists argue that typical macroeconomic forecasting models are so large and complicated that no one actually understands how they work. Further, as they argue, a forecasting exercise with a large team of forecasters typically degenerates into an exercise where members of the team supply "add factors" to the model to make the forecast results conform to their own judgment concerning how the forecast should look. At worst then, the model is not allowed to make predictions but is simply a device for enforcing national income accounting identities (like the income–expenditure identity). As critics argued, the forecast is then judgmental and not a model forecast at all.

An example of a statistical model is the Bayesian Vector Autoregression (or BVAR) model developed at the Federal Reserve Bank of Minneapolis in the 1970s and 1980s. This is a model that is quite small and simple, and, once up and running, it can generate a forecast using the time of one person, who need not be a trained economist.

No matter what the forecasting method used, macroeconomic forecasters can often be wrong, particularly in predicting turning points and in making predictions over a long horizon. A case in point occurred during the 2001 recession. In January 2001, the Congressional Budget Office (CBO) forecast that there would be a mild slowdown in real GDP growth from 3.8% in 2000 to 2.4% in 2001, with a recovery to robust growth of 3.4% in real GDP in 2002.[1] This forecast turned out to be exceedingly optimistic, particularly for 2001, as real GDP ultimately grew by 0.3% in 2001 and 2.4% in 2002. The CBO failed to predict the 2001 recession, which included negative growth in real GDP in the first, second, and third quarters of 2001. Perhaps surprisingly, the events of September 11, 2001, cannot receive much of the blame for the large forecast error for 2001, as real GDP actually grew by 2.7% in the fourth quarter of 2001 at a time when the airlines and the travel industry were suffering from the negative effects of the terrorist attacks.

Were the economists at the CBO in January 2001 an especially bad group of forecasters? Apparently not, as the Blue Chip consensus forecast (an average of 50 private-sector forecasts) in January 2001 was if anything slightly more optimistic than the CBO forecast, predicting growth in real GDP of 2.6% and 3.4% for 2001 and 2002, respectively.[2] The evidence would seem to indicate that the large error in the CBO forecast was not because of incompetence. This is simply an example illustrating that macroeconomic forecasters are often wrong because forecasting the course of the macroeconomy can be extremely difficult.

[1]See "The Budget and Economic Outlook: Fiscal Years 2002–2011, January 2001," at http://www.cbo.gov/showdoc.cfm?index=2727\&sequence=3

[2]See "The Budget and Economic Outlook: Fiscal Years 2002–2011, January 2001," at http://www.cbo.gov/showdoc.cfm?index=2727\&sequence=3

Comovement

While real GDP fluctuates in irregular patterns, macroeconomic variables fluctuate together in patterns that exhibit strong regularities. We refer to these patterns in fluctuations as **comovement.** Robert Lucas once remarked that "with respect to qualitative behavior of comovements among [economic time] series, business cycles are all alike."[3]

Macroeconomic variables are measured as **time series**; for example, real GDP is measured in a series of quarterly observations over time. When we examine comovements in macroeconomic time series, typically we look at these time series two at a time, and a good starting point is to plot the data. Suppose, for example, that we have two macroeconomic time series and we would like to study their comovement.

[3]See Lucas, R., "Understanding Business Cycles," in *Studies in Business Cycle Theory,* MIT Press, p. 218.

Figure 3.3 **Time Series Plots of x and y.**

(a) Two time series that are positively correlated. When x is high (low), y tends to be high (low) as well. (b) Two time series that are negatively correlated. In this case, when x is high (low), y tends to be low (high).

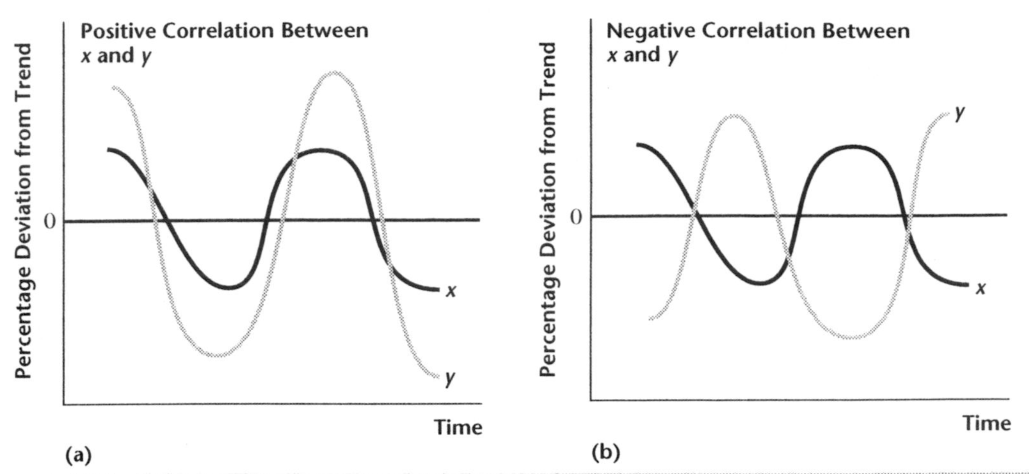

We first transform these two time series by removing trends, and we let x and y denote the percentage deviations from trend in the two time series. One way to plot x and y is in time series form, as in Figure 3.3. What we want to look for first in the time series plot is a pattern of **positive correlation** or **negative correlation** in x and y. In Figure 3.3(a), there is positive correlation between x and y: x is high when y is high, and x is low when y is low. That is, one economic time series tends to be above (below) trend when the other economic time series is above (below) trend. In Figure 3.3(b) x and y are negatively correlated: x is high (low) when y is low (high).

Another way to plot the data is as a **scatter plot**, with x on the horizontal axis and y on the vertical axis. In Figure 3.4, each point in the scatter plot is an observation on x and y for a particular time period. Here, whether x and y are positively or negatively correlated is determined by the slope of a straight line that best fits the points in the scatter plot. Figure 3.4(a) shows a positive correlation between x and y, (b) a negative correlation, and (c) a zero correlation. For example, if for each of the fifty states in the United States we plotted cigarettes smoked per person per year against the incidence of lung cancer in a scatter plot, we would observe a positive correlation.

Macroeconomists are often primarily interested in how an individual macroeconomic variable comoves with real GDP. An economic variable is said to be **procyclical** if its deviations from trend are positively correlated with the deviations from trend in real GDP, **countercyclical** if its deviations from trend are negatively correlated with the deviations from trend in real GDP, and **acyclical** if it is neither procyclical nor countercyclical. As an example of comovement between two macroeconomic time

Figure 3.4 **Correlations Between Variables y and x.**

(a) A scatter plot of two variables, x and y, that are positively correlated. (b) x and y are negatively correlated. (c) x and y are uncorrelated.

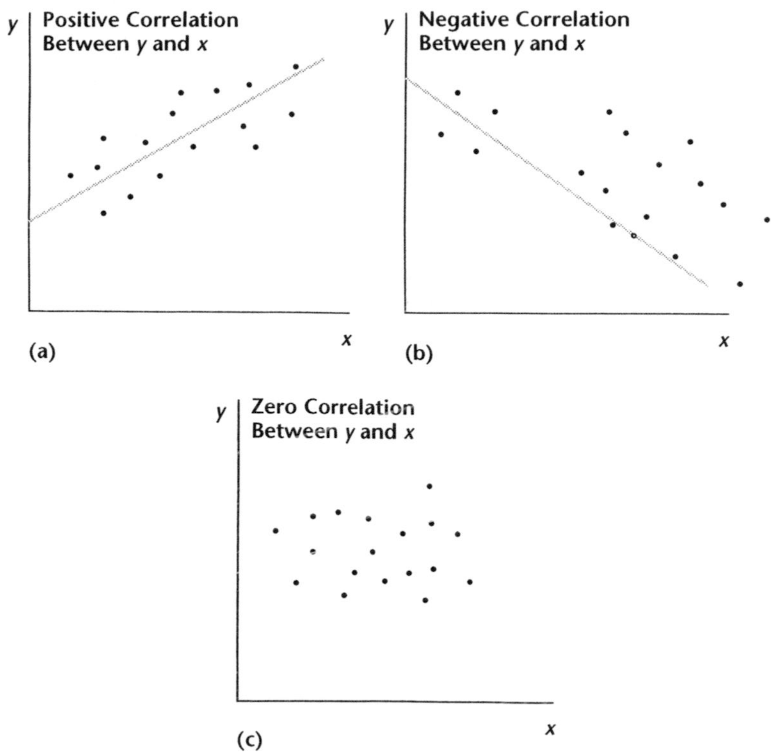

series, we consider real GDP and real imports for the United States over the period 1947–2006. In Figure 3.5 we plot the percentage deviations from trend in real GDP (the colored line) and real imports (the black line) in time series form. There is a distinct pattern of positive correlation in Figure 3.5; when GDP is high (low) relative to trend, imports tend to be high (low) relative to trend. This positive correlation also shows up in the scatter plot in Figure 3.6, where we show a graph of observations of percentage deviations from trend in imports versus percentage deviations from trend in GDP. Note that a straight line fit to the points in Figure 3.6 would have a positive slope.

A measure of the degree of correlation between two variables is the **correlation coefficient.** The correlation coefficient between two variables, x and y, takes on values between -1 and 1. If the correlation coefficient is 1, then x and y are **perfectly positively correlated** and a scatter plot of observations on x and y falls on a positively sloped straight line. If the correlation coefficient is -1, then x and y are **perfectly negatively correlated** and a scatter plot would consist of points on a negatively sloped

Figure 3.5 **Imports and GDP.**

The figure, as an example, shows the time series of percentage deviations from trend in real imports (black line) and real GDP (colored line) for the United States for the period 1947–2006. Imports and GDP are clearly positively correlated, so imports are procyclical.

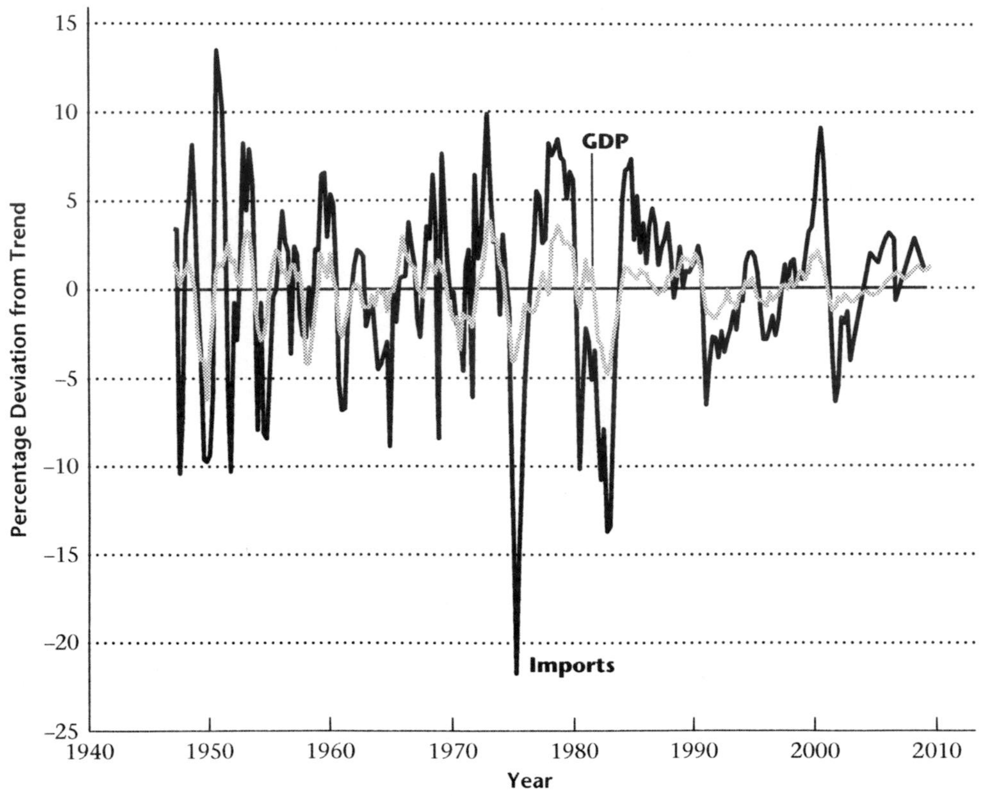

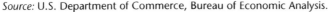

Source: U.S. Department of Commerce, Bureau of Economic Analysis.

straight line. If the correlation coefficient is 0, then x and y are uncorrelated. In the example above, the percentage deviations from trend in real GDP and real imports have a correlation coefficient of 0.69, indicating positive correlation.

An important element of comovement is the leading and lagging relationships that exist in macroeconomic data. If a macroeconomic variable tends to aid in predicting the future path of real GDP, we say that it is a **leading variable**, whereas if real GDP helps to predict the future path of a particular macroeconomic variable, then that variable is said to be a **lagging variable.** In Figure 3.7 we show idealized time series plots of the percentage deviations from trend in real GDP and two variables, x and y. In Figure 3.7(a), variable x is a leading variable, whereas variable y is a lagging variable in Figure 3.7(b). A **coincident variable** is one which neither leads nor lags real GDP.

Figure 3.6 **Scatter Plot of Imports and GDP.**

The figure shows the same data as in Figure 3.5 but in a scatter plot rather than in time series form. Here, we again observe the positive correlation between imports and GDP, as a positively sloped straight line would best fit the scatter plot. Again, imports are procyclical.

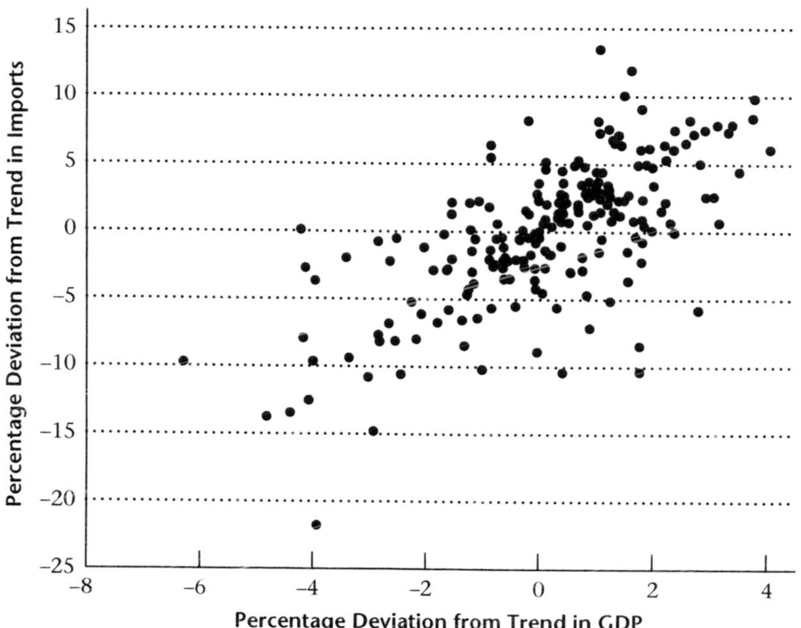

Source: U.S. Department of Commerce, Bureau of Economic Analysis.

If it is known that some set of macroeconomic variables all tend to be leading variables, this information can be very useful in macroeconomic forecasting, because timely information on leading variables can then be used to forecast real GDP. One way to use this information is to construct a macroeconomic model, grounded in economic theory, that incorporates the relationships between leading variables and real GDP and that can then be used for forecasting. Some economists, however, argue that forecasting can be done simply by exploiting past statistical relationships among macroeconomic variables to project into the future. A very simple form of this approach is the construction and use of the Conference Board's **index of leading economic indicators.** This index is a weighted average of macroeconomic variables that have been found to do a good job of predicting future real GDP. Watching the index of leading economic indicators can sometimes provide useful information for forecasters, particularly with respect to the turning points in aggregate economic activity. In Figure 3.8 we show a plot of the percentage deviations from trend in real GDP (the colored line) and in the index of leading economic indicators (the black line). The index of leading economic indicators tends to track real GDP fairly closely but with

Figure 3.7 **Leading and Lagging Variables.**

In (a), *x* is a leading variable, as its peaks and troughs tend to precede those of real GDP. In (b), *y* is a lagging variable, as the peaks and troughs in real GDP tend to lead those in *y*.

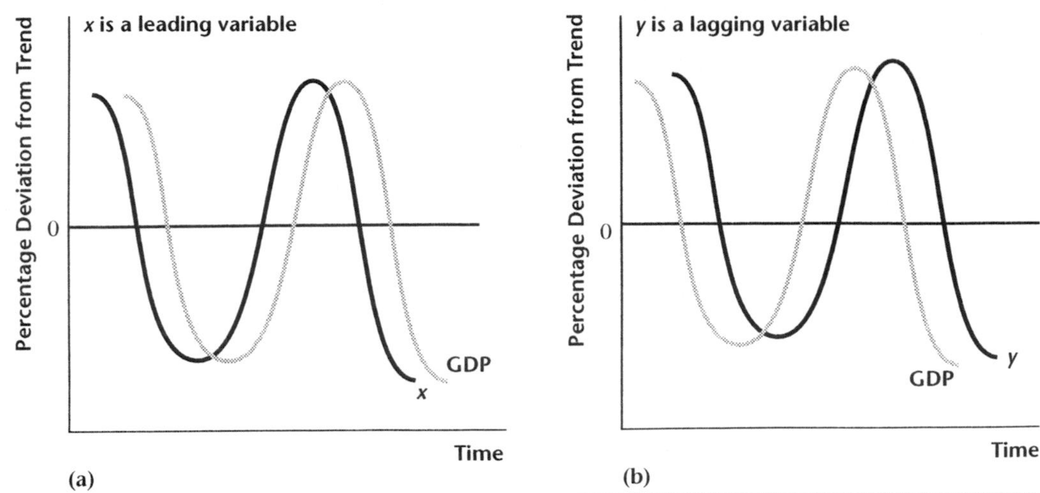

a lead. In particular, turning points in the index of leading economic indicators in Figure 3.8 tend to fall before turning points in real GDP.

Finally, there are key regularities in terms of the variability of economic variables over the business cycle. As we will see, some macroeconomic variables are highly volatile, while others behave in a very smooth way relative to trend. These patterns in variability are an important part of business cycle behavior that we would like to understand. A measure of cyclical variability is the **standard deviation** of the percentage deviations from trend. For example, in Figure 3.5, imports are much more variable than GDP. The standard deviation of the percentage deviations from trend in imports is more than twice that for GDP.

Next we examine some key macroeconomic variables, and we evaluate for each whether it is (1) procyclical or countercyclical, (2) leading or lagging, and (3) more or less variable relative to real GDP. These facts then make up the set of important business cycle regularities that we explain using macroeconomic theory.

The Components of GDP

In Figure 3.9 we show the percentage deviations from trend in real aggregate consumption (the black line) and real GDP (the colored line). Clearly, the deviations from trend in consumption and in GDP are highly positively correlated, in that consumption tends to be above (below) trend when GDP is above (below) trend; these two time series move very closely together. The correlation coefficient between the percentage deviation from trend in real consumption and the percentage deviation from

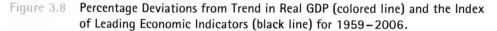

Figure 3.8 **Percentage Deviations from Trend in Real GDP (colored line) and the Index of Leading Economic Indicators (black line) for 1959–2006.**

The index is a weighted average of leading variables and so, not surprisingly, it tends to lead real GDP.

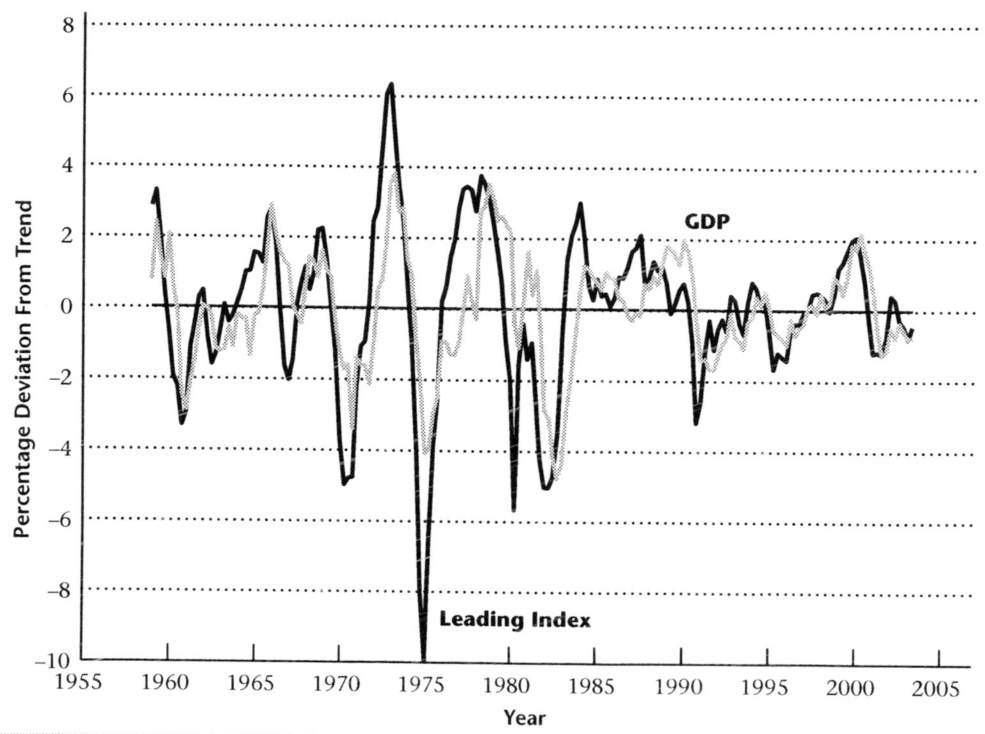

trend in real GDP is 0.76, which is greater than zero, so consumption is procyclical. There appears to be no discernible lead lag relationship between real consumption and real GDP in Figure 3.9—the turning points in consumption do not appear to lead or lag the turning points in real GDP. Consumption, therefore, is a coincident variable.

From Figure 3.9, note that consumption is less variable than GDP, in that the deviations from trend in consumption tend to be smaller than those in GDP. In Chapter 8 we study the theory of consumption decisions over time, and this theory explains why consumption tends to be smoother than GDP. For the data displayed in Figure 3.9, the standard deviation of the percentage deviations in real consumption is 75.0% of that for real GDP. This is a more precise measure of what our eyes tell us about Figure 3.9, which is that consumption is smoother than GDP.

The percentage deviations from trend in real investment (the black line) and real GDP (the colored line) are plotted in Figure 3.10. As with consumption, investment is procyclical, because it tends to be above (below) trend when GDP is above (below)

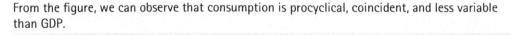

Figure 3.9 **Percentage Deviations from Trend in Real Consumption (black line) and Real GDP (colored line) 1947–2006.**

From the figure, we can observe that consumption is procyclical, coincident, and less variable than GDP.

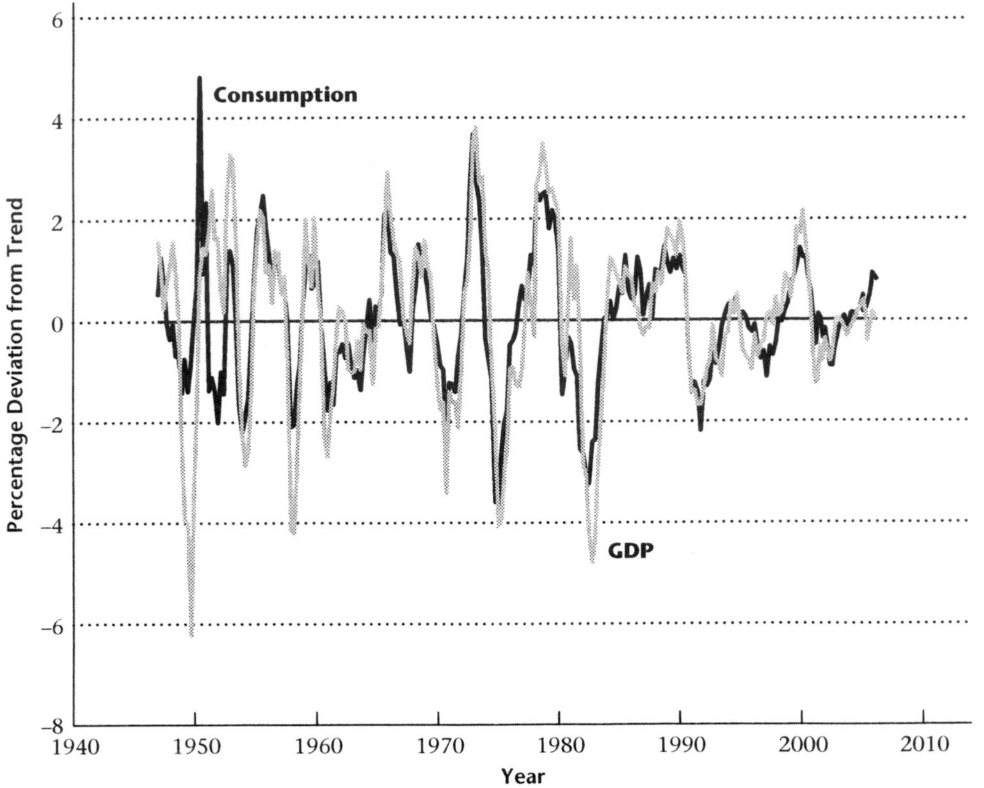

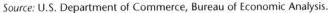

Source: U.S. Department of Commerce, Bureau of Economic Analysis.

trend. The correlation coefficient between the percentage deviations from trend in investment and those in GDP is 0.83. There is no tendency for investment to lead or lag GDP from Figure 3.10, and so investment is a coincident variable. However, some components of investment, in particular residential investment and inventory investment, tend to lead the business cycle. In contrast to consumption, investment is much more volatile than is GDP. This is indicated in Figure 3.10, where the deviations from trend in investment tend to be much larger than those for GDP. The standard deviation of the percentage deviations from trend in investment is 472.6% of what it is for GDP. Given that some components of investment lead GDP and that it is highly volatile, investment can play a very important role over the business cycle.

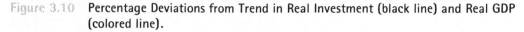

Figure 3.10 **Percentage Deviations from Trend in Real Investment (black line) and Real GDP (colored line).**

We can observe from the figure that investment is procyclical, coincident, and more variable than GDP.

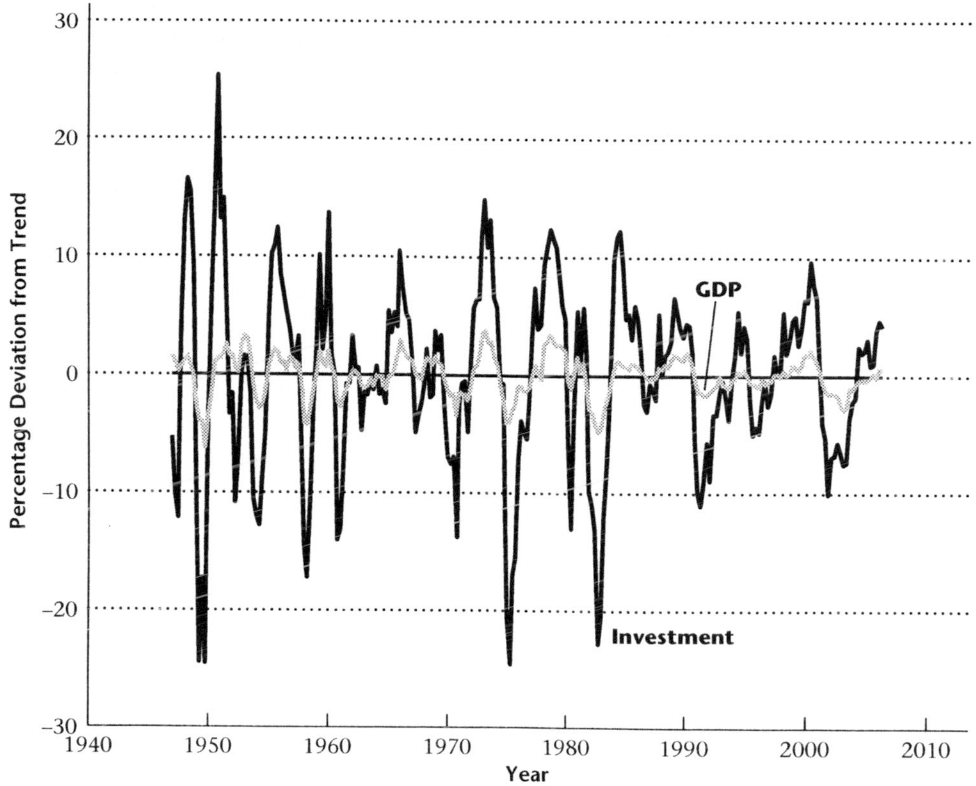

Source: U.S. Department of Commerce, Bureau of Economic Analysis.

Nominal Variables

The correlation between money prices and aggregate economic activity has long been of interest to macroeconomists. In the 1950s, A. W. Phillips observed that there was a negative relationship between the rate of change in money wages and the unemployment rate in the United Kingdom, a relationship that came to be known as the **Phillips curve.**[4] If we take the unemployment rate to be a measure of aggregate economic activity (as we see in Chapter 16, the unemployment rate is a strongly countercyclical variable; when real GDP is above trend, the unemployment rate is

[4]See Phillips, A., 1958, "The Relationship Between Unemployment and the Rate of Change of Money Wages in the United Kingdom, 1861–1957," *Econometrica* 25, 283–299.

low), then the Phillips curve captures a positive relationship between the rate of change in a money price (the money wage) and the level of aggregate economic activity. Since Phillips made his initial observation, "Phillips curve" has come to be applied to any positive relationship between the rate of change in money prices or wages, or the deviation from trend in money prices or wages, and the deviation from trend in aggregate economic activity. As we see in Chapter 16, observed Phillips curves are notoriously unstable—that is, they tend to shift over time—and there are sound theories to explain this instability. However, a regularity in the 1947–2006 period in the United States is the negative correlation between deviations of the price level from trend and deviations of GDP from trend, observed in the scatter plot in Figure 3.11. We might think of this as a **reverse Phillips curve**, as there is a negative rather than a positive correlation between the price level and real GDP, with the correlation coefficient for the data in Figure 3.11 being −0.28. Over the period 1947–2006, therefore, the price level is a countercyclical variable.

In Figure 3.12 the price level (black line) is quite smooth relative to real GDP (colored line); the standard deviation of the percentage deviations from trend in the

Figure 3.11 **Scatter Plot for the Percentage Deviations from Trend in the Price Level (the Implicit GDP Price Deflator) and Real GDP.**

The figure shows a negative correlation between the two for 1947–2006; therefore, the price level is countercyclical for this period. The figure captures a reverse Phillips curve relationship.

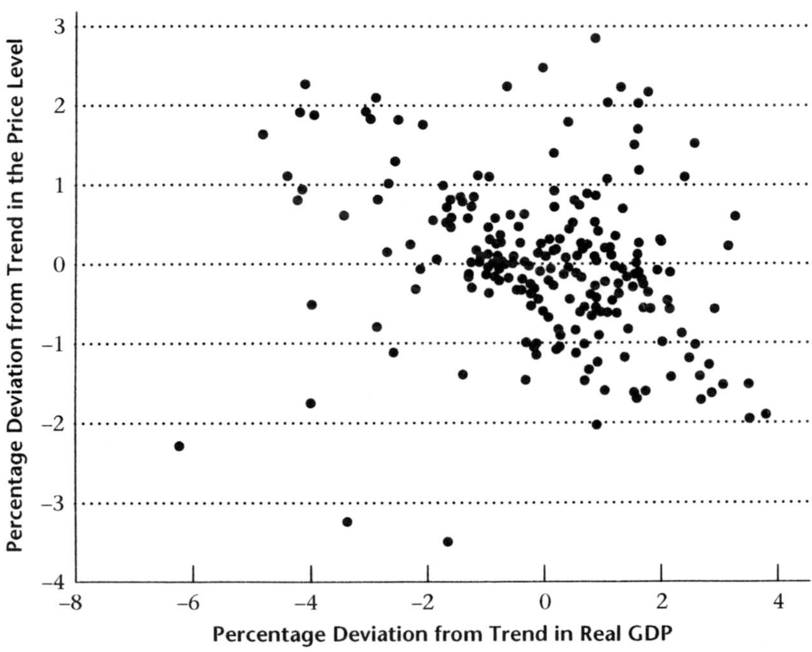

Source: U.S. Department of Commerce, Bureau of Economic Analysis.

Figure 3.12 **Price Level and GDP.**

This figure shows the time series plot of the same data as in Figure 3.11 Here, we see that the price level (black line) is countercyclical, coincident, and less variable than real GDP (colored line).

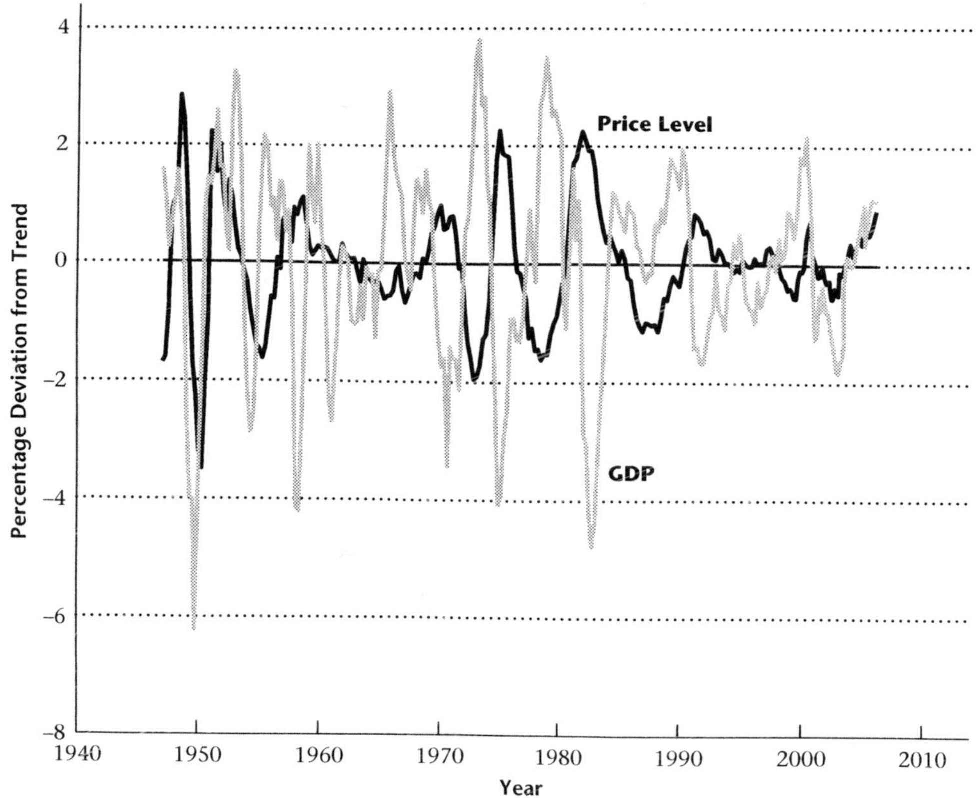

Source: U.S. Department of Commerce, Bureau of Economic Analysis.

price level is 57.1% of that for GDP. The price level tends to be much smoother than most asset prices. For example, the average price of shares traded on the stock market is highly variable relative to the money prices of goods and services. In Figure 3.12 there appears to be no tendency for the price level to lead or lag real GDP, so that the price level appears to be coincident.

Whether the price level is procyclical or countercyclical, and whether it is a leading or a lagging variable, can play an important role in resolving debates concerning the causes of business cycles, as we see in Chapters 11 and 12. In contrast to the 1947–2006 U.S. data examined previously, it appears that the price level was a procyclical variable over some periods of history in some countries, for example, during the period between the World Wars in the United States. An alternative interpretation of Figure 3.12 is that the price level is a procyclical and lagging variable.

That is, when real GDP is above (below) trend, the price level tends to be above (below) trend about two years later. Without other evidence to guide us, however, we stick to the interpretation that the price level is a countercyclical coincident variable in the post–World War II U.S. data.

In addition to Phillips curve relationships and reverse Phillips curve relationships, a key element of the comovement between nominal variables and aggregate economic activity is the positive correlation between deviations from trend in the nominal money supply and deviations from trend in real GDP. The money supply is a measure of the nominal quantity of assets used in making transactions in the economy. In the United States, the money supply includes U.S. currency and checking accounts at banks and other depository institutions. In Figure 3.13 we show the percentage deviations from

Figure 3.13 **Percentage Deviations from Trend in the Money Supply (black line) and Real GDP (colored line) for the Period 1959–2006.**

Money is a procyclical and leading variable, and it is less variable than real GDP.

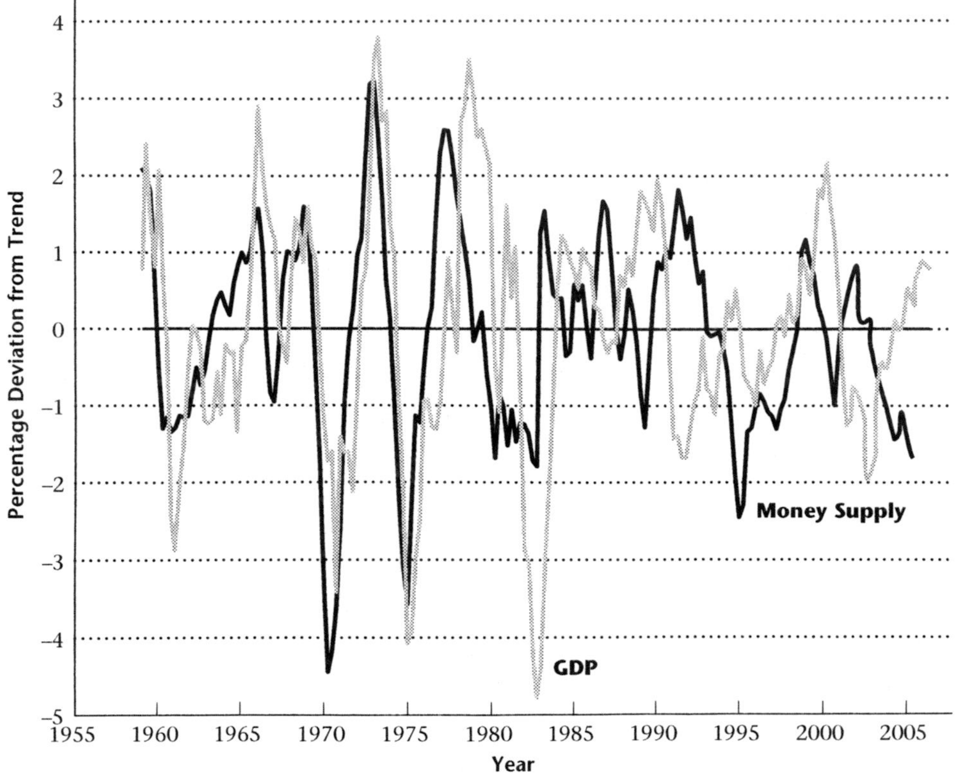

Source: U.S. Department of Commerce, Bureau of Economic Analysis, and Board of Governors of the Federal Reserve System.

trend in a measure of the money supply (black line) and in real GDP (colored line) over the period 1959–2006.[5] The procyclical nature of the money supply is quite pronounced until about 1980, after which the link between the money supply and real GDP weakens. The correlation coefficient for the data in Figure 3.13 is 0.32. Another important observation concerning the nominal money supply and real GDP is that money tends to be a leading variable, which we observe as a tendency for turning points in the money supply to lead turning points in GDP in Figure 3.13. This observation was emphasized by Milton Friedman and Anna Schwartz,[6] who studied the behavior of the money supply and real GDP in the United States over the period 1867–1960 (see Macroeconomics in Action: The Money Supply and Aggregate Economic Activity on page xx).

The money supply is somewhat smoother than GDP, with the standard deviation of the percentage deviations from trend in the money supply being 80.4% of what it is for GDP. This can also be observed in Figure 3.13.

MACROECONOMICS IN ACTION

The Correlation Between the Price Level and Aggregate Output Across Countries and Over Time

In Chapters 9 through 12 we will study how the comovements among macroeconomic variables can be affected by the types of shocks that are hitting the economy, the relative severity of those shocks, and the manner in which macroeconomic policy reacts to shocks. One interesting way in which this is reflected in the data is in the correlation we see between the price level and aggregate output. For example, in the United States an increase in the price of oil on world markets will tend to increase the price level and reduce aggregate output, producing a negative correlation between these two variables, or a countercyclical price level. However, an increase in the money supply, engineered by the Federal Reserve System, will tend to increase the price level and increase aggregate output, producing a procyclical price level. Whether the price level is countercyclical or procyclical in the data might then be determined by which is more important, shocks to the world price of oil or money supply shocks.

David Backus and Patrick Kehoe have studied the properties of business cycles across countries and over long periods of

[5]The money supply measure used here is M2. In Chapters 9 and 15, we discuss the measurement of the money supply in more detail.

[6]See Friedman, M., & Schwartz, A., 1963, *A Monetary History of the United States: 1867–1960,* Princeton University Press, Princeton, NJ.

time.[7] A finding of theirs is that the correlations among real variables are remarkably similar across countries and over time. However, the correlation between the price level and aggregate output is not. After World War II, the price level was countercyclical in most of the countries that Backus and Kehoe study,[8] just as we saw for the United States in the data from 1947–2006. However, before World War I and between the World Wars, the price level was procyclical in most of the countries in this set. This is an important piece of information that will be useful for us in evaluating theories of the business cycle in Chapters 11 and 12.

[7]See Backus, D., & Kehoe, P., 1992, "International Evidence on the Historical Properties of Business Cycles," *American Economic Review* 82, 864–888.

[8]Australia, Canada, Denmark, Germany, Italy, Japan, Norway, Sweden, the UK, and the United States.

Labor Market Variables

The last business cycle regularities we examine are those in labor markets, relating to the variables we determine in the business cycle models in Chapters 9 through 12. First, in Figure 3.14 we show percentage deviations from trend in employment (black line) and in real GDP (colored line) for the period 1948–2006. Clearly, the deviations from trend in employment closely track those in real GDP, so employment is a procyclical variable. The correlation coefficient for the data in Figure 3.14 is 0.80. In terms of lead/lag relationships, we can observe a tendency in Figure 3.14 for turning points in employment to lag turning points in GDP, thus employment is a lagging variable. Employment is less variable than GDP, with the standard deviation of the percentage deviation from trend for employment being 59.9% of that for real GDP in Figure 3.14.

In the macroeconomic models we analyze, a key variable is the market **real wage,** which is the purchasing power of the wage earned per hour worked. This is measured from the data as the average money wage for all workers, divided by the price level. The cyclical behavior of the real wage proves to be crucial in helping us discriminate among different theories of the business cycle in Chapters 11 and 12. The weight of empirical evidence indicates that the real wage is procyclical.[9] We do not show data on the aggregate real wage, because it is difficult to measure the relationship between real wages and real GDP by examining aggregate data. The key problem is that the composition of the labor force tends to change over the business cycle, which tends to bias the correlation between the real wage and real GDP. There is no strong evidence on whether the real wage is a leading or a lagging variable.

Productivity plays a key role in the economy, as was mentioned in Chapter 1, and in later chapters productivity is an important element in our study of business cycles and economic growth. One measure of productivity is **average labor productivity,** $\frac{Y}{N}$, where Y is aggregate output and N is total labor input. For our purposes Y is GDP and N is total employment, so we are measuring average labor productivity as

[9]See Solon, G., Barsky, R., & Parker, J., February 1994, "Measuring the Cyclicality of Real Wages: How Important Is Composition Bias?" *Quarterly Journal of Economics*, 1–25.

Figure 3.14 **Percentage Deviations from Trend in Employment (black line) and Real GDP (colored line).**

Employment is procyclical, it is a lagging variable, and it is less variable than real GDP.

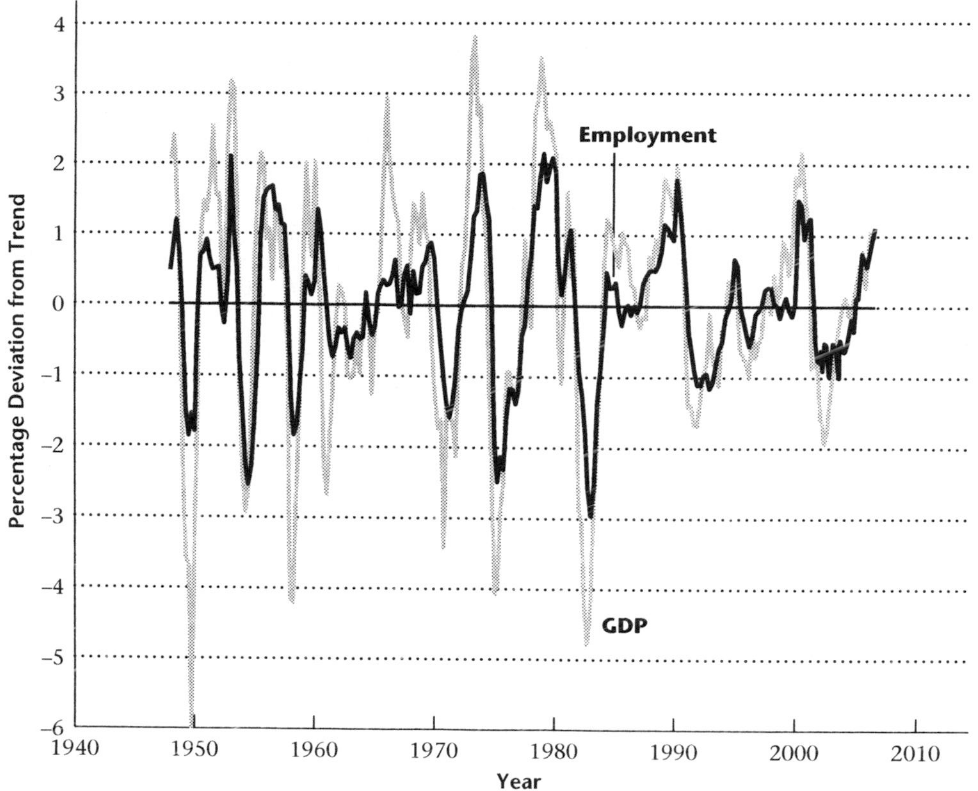

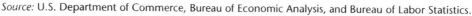

Source: U.S. Department of Commerce, Bureau of Economic Analysis, and Bureau of Labor Statistics.

output per worker. In Figure 3.15 we show the percentage deviations from trend in real GDP (colored line) and average labor productivity (black line). From the figure, average labor productivity is clearly a procyclical variable. The correlation coefficient for percentage deviations from trend in real GDP and average labor productivity is 0.82. Average labor productivity is less volatile than GDP; the standard deviation of the percentage deviations from trend in average labor productivity is 62.7% of that for real GDP. Further, there is no apparent tendency for average labor productivity to lead or lag real GDP in Figure 3.15, so average labor productivity is a coincident variable. In Chapters 11 and 12, the predictions of different business cycle theories for the comovements between average labor productivity and real GDP are important in helping us to evaluate and compare these theories.

Figure 3.15 **Percentage Deviations from Trend in Average Labor Productivity (black line) and Real GDP (colored line) for 1948–2006.**

Average labor productivity is procyclical and coincident, and it is less variable than is real GDP.

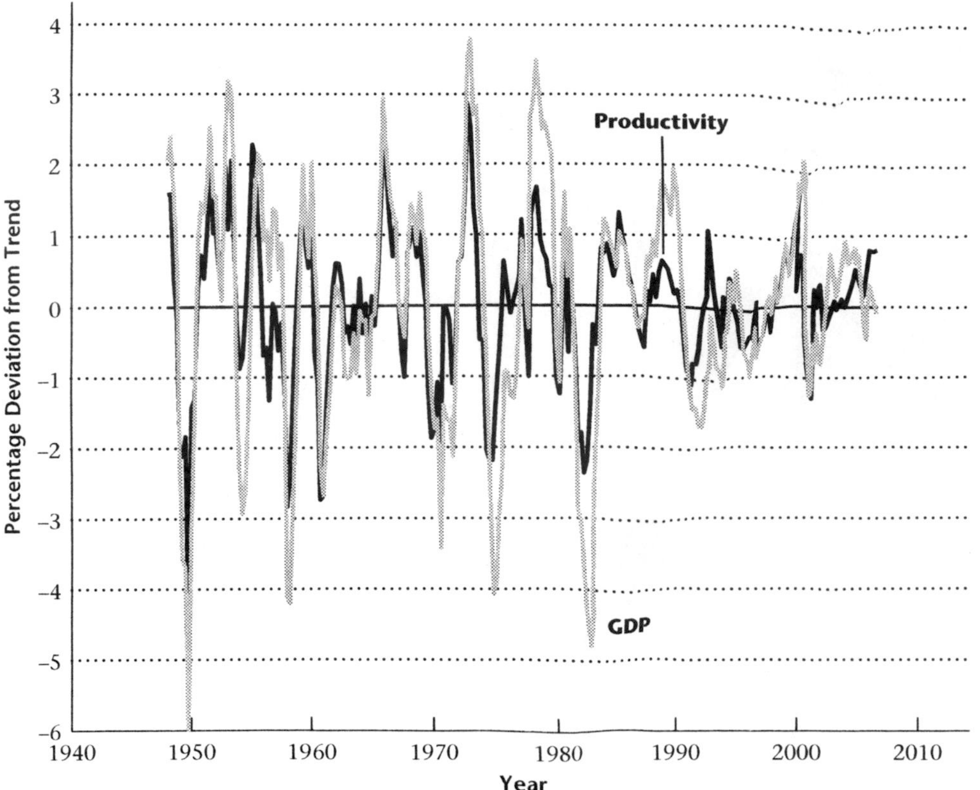

Source: U.S. Department of Commerce, Bureau of Economic Analysis, and Bureau of Labor Statistics.

Seasonal Adjustment

The economic data we are studying in this chapter, and most data that is used in macroeconomic research and in formulating macroeconomic policy, is **seasonally adjusted.** That is, in most macroeconomic time series, there exists a predictable seasonal component. For example, GDP tends to be low during the summer months when workers are on vacation, investment expenditure tends to be low in the winter months when building roads, bridges, and some types of structures is more difficult, and the money supply tends to be high during the December holiday season, when the quantity of retail transactions is high.

There are various methods for seasonally adjusting data, but the basic idea is to observe historical seasonal patterns and then take out the extra amount that we tend to see on average during a particular week, month, or quarter, simply because of the time of year. For example, to seasonally adjust the money supply, we would want to subtract some quantity in December which is just due to the extra spending over the holiday season. To see what seasonal adjustment can do, in Figure 3.16 we show the seasonally adjusted money supply (M1 in this case) and seasonally unadjusted money supply. As can be seen in the figure, seasonal adjustment tends to smooth out a time series that has a seasonal component.

Working with seasonally adjusted data can often be the appropriate thing to do, but one has to be careful that the process of seasonal adjustment is not masking important phenomena that might interest us. For example, there may be economic factors that cause the nature of seasonality to change over time. For example, technological developments may make it less costly to do road construction in the winter and thus reduce the seasonal fluctuations we see in investment expenditure. If we confine our attention to only seasonally adjusted data, we might not be aware that this process is occurring.

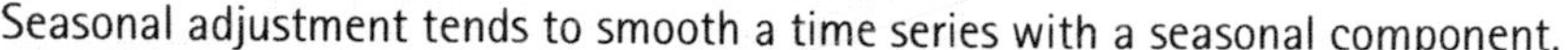

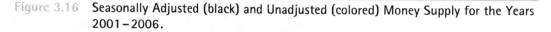

Figure 3.16 **Seasonally Adjusted (black) and Unadjusted (colored) Money Supply for the Years 2001–2006.**

Seasonal adjustment tends to smooth a time series with a seasonal component.

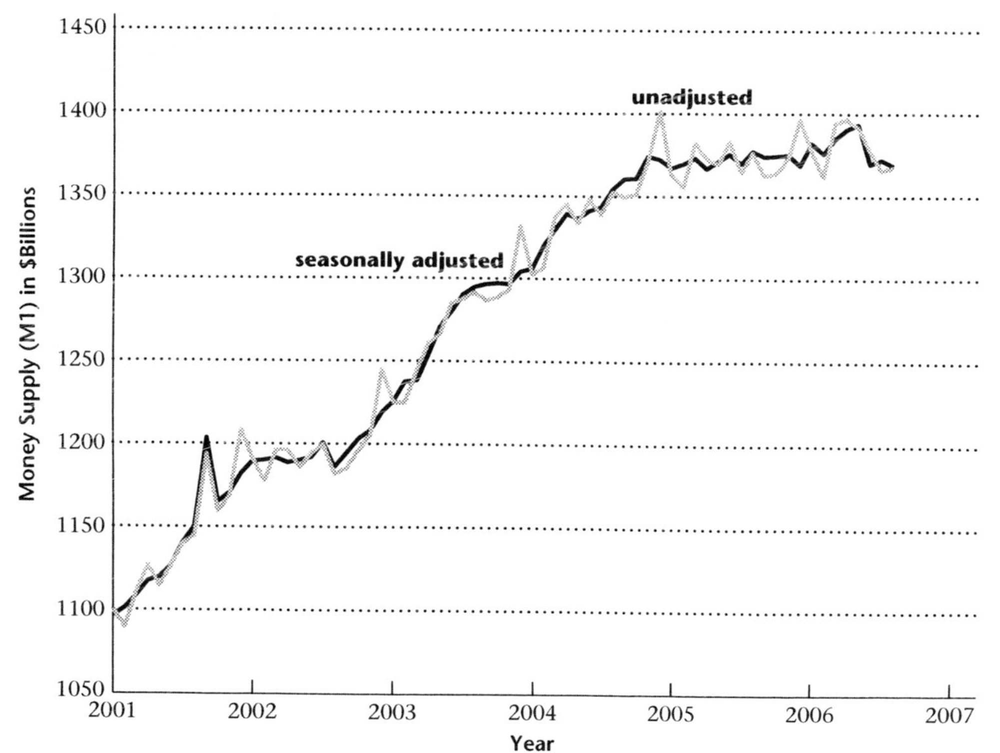

Source: Federal Reserve Board.

Table 3.1 **Correlation Coefficients and Variability of Percentage Deviations from Trend**

	Correlation Coefficient (with GDP)	Standard Deviation (% of S.D. of GDP)
Consumption	0.76	75.0
Investment	0.83	472.6
Price Level	−0.28	57.1
Money Supply	0.32	80.4
Employment	0.80	59.9
Average Labor Productivity	0.82	62.7

Table 3.2 **Summary of Business Cycle Facts**

	Cyclicality	Lead/Lag	Variability Relative to GDP
Consumption	Procyclical	Coincident	Smaller
Investment	Procyclical	Coincident	Larger
Price Level	Countercyclical	Coincident	Smaller
Money Supply	Procyclical	Leading	Smaller
Employment	Procyclical	Lagging	Smaller
Real Wage	Procyclical	?	?
Average Labor Productivity	Procyclical	Coincident	Smaller

Comovement Summary

To summarize the business cycle facts discussed above, we present Tables 3.1 and 3.2. These two tables, particularly Table 3.2, prove very useful, particularly when we discuss the predictions of different theories of the business cycle in Chapters 11 and 12. A first test of the usefulness of macroeconomic theories is their ability to match what we see in macroeconomic data.

We have concluded our study of measurement issues, in that we now know the basics of national income accounting, basic macroeconomic accounting identities, price measurement, labor market facts, and business cycle facts. In the next chapters, we proceed to build useful macroeconomic models, starting with some basic microeconomic principles concerning the behavior of consumers and firms.

Chapter Summary

- The key business cycle facts relate to the deviations of important macroeconomic variables from their trends and the comovements in these deviations from trend.
- The most important business cycle fact is that real GDP fluctuates about trend in an irregular fashion. Though deviations from trend in real GDP are persistent, there is no observed regularity in the amplitude or frequency of fluctuations in real GDP about trend.

- Business cycles are similar mainly in terms of the comovements among macroeconomic time series. Comovement can be discerned by plotting the percentage deviations from trend in two economic variables in a time series or in a scatter plot or by calculating the correlation coefficient between the percentage deviations from trend.
- We are interested principally in how a particular variable moves about trend relative to real GDP (whether it is procyclical, countercyclical, or acyclical), whether it is a leading, lagging, or coincident variable (relative to real GDP), and how variable it is relative to real GDP.
- Consumption is procyclical, coincident, and less variable than real GDP.
- Investment is procyclical, coincident, and more variable than real GDP.
- In the data set we examined here, the price level is a countercyclical variable (there is a reverse Phillips curve), it is coincident, and it is less variable than GDP.
- The money supply is procyclical, leading, and about as variable as real GDP. The fact that the money supply tends to lead real GDP was assigned much importance by Milton Friedman.
- In the labor market, employment is procyclical, lagging, and less variable than real GDP. The real wage, too, is procyclical. There is, however, no consensus among macroeconomists on whether the real wage is a leading or lagging variable. Average labor productivity is procyclical, coincident, and less variable than real GDP.

Key Terms

Business cycles Fluctuations about trend in real GDP.
Peak A relatively large positive deviation from trend in real GDP.
Trough A relatively large negative deviation from trend in real GDP.
Turning points Peaks and troughs in real GDP.
Amplitude The maximum deviation from trend in an economic time series.
Frequency The number of peaks in an economic time series that occur per year.
Boom A series of positive deviations from trend in real GDP, culminating in a peak.
Recession A series of negative deviations from trend in real GDP, culminating in a trough.
Persistent Describes an economic time series that tends to stay above (below) trend when it has been above (below) trend during the recent past.
Comovement How aggregate economic variables move together over the business cycle.
Time series Sequential measurements of an economic variable over time.
Positive correlation Relationship between two economic time series when a straight line fit to a scatter plot of the two variables has a positive slope.
Negative correlation Relationship between two economic time series when a straight line fit to a scatter plot of the two variables has a negative slope.
Scatter plot A plot of two variables, x and y, with x measured on the horizontal axis and y measured on the vertical axis.
Procyclical Describes an economic variable that tends to be above (below) trend when real GDP is above (below) trend.
Countercyclical Describes an economic variable that tends to be below (above) trend when real GDP is above (below) trend.
Acyclical Describes an economic variable that is neither procyclical nor countercyclical.
Correlation coefficient A measure of the degree of correlation between two variables.
Perfectly positively correlated Describes two variables that have a correlation coefficient of 1.
Perfectly negatively correlated Describes two variables that have a correlation coefficient of -1.

Leading variable An economic variable that helps to predict future real GDP.
Lagging variable An economic variable that past real GDP helps to predict.
Coincident variable An economic variable that neither leads nor lags real GDP.
Index of leading economic indicators A weighted average of leading macroeconomic variables that is sometimes used to forecast the deviations of real GDP from trend.
Standard deviation A measure of variability. The cyclical variability in an economic time series can be measured by the standard deviation of the percentage deviations from trend.
Phillips curve A positive correlation between a money price or the rate of change in a money price and a measure of aggregate economic activity.
Reverse Phillips curve A negative correlation between a money price or the rate of change in a money price and a measure of aggregate economic activity.
Real wage The purchasing power of the wage earned per hour worked.
Average labor productivity Equal to Y/N where Y is aggregate output and N is total labor input.
Seasonal adjustments The statistical process of removing the predictable seasonal component from an economic time series.

Questions for Review

1. What is the primary defining feature of business cycles?
2. Besides persistence, what are three important features of the deviations from trend in GDP?
3. Explain why forecasting GDP over the long term is difficult.
4. Why are the comovements in aggregate economic variables important?
5. What did Robert Lucas say about the comovements among economic variables?
6. How can we discern positive and negative correlation in a time series plot? In a scatter plot?
7. Give a noneconomic example of two variables that are positively correlated and an example of two variables that are negatively correlated.
8. Why is the index of leading economic indicators useful for forecasting GDP?
9. What are the three features of comovement that macroeconomists are interested in?
10. Describe the key business cycle regularities in consumption and investment expenditures.
11. What are the key business cycle regularities with respect to the price level and the money supply?
12. Does a Phillips curve relationship exist in the data set that was studied in this chapter?
13. What are the key business cycle regularities in the labor market?

Problems

1. Consider the following data, which are observations on x and y over several periods of time.

Period	x	y
1	100	500
2	200	500
3	200	1000
4	100	1000
5	50	500
6	50	250
7	100	250

(a) Construct a scatter plot of y against x. Are y and x positively correlated, negatively correlated, or uncorrelated? Explain your answer.
(b) Now, construct a time series of y and x. Is y a leading, lagging, or coincident variable with respect to x? Explain your answer.
(c) Do x and y exhibit persistence? Explain.

2. From Figure 3.2, determine how many booms and recessions occurred from 1947–1976, and from 1977–2006, and calculate the average strength of booms and the average severity of recessions from 1947–1976 and from 1977–2006. To do this, count as peaks and troughs only those deviations from trend that exceed 1%. As a measure of the strength of a boom or the severity of a recession, use the percentage deviation from trend of real GDP at the peak of trough, respectively.
   (a) When were booms more frequent, from 1947–1976 or from 1976–2006?
   (b) When were recessions more frequent, from 1947–1976 or from 1977–2006?
   (c) When were booms stronger, from 1947–1976 or from 1977–2006?
   (d) When were recessions more severe, from 1947–1976 or from 1977–2006?
3. From Figure 3.5, we determined that real imports and real GDP were positively correlated. Suggest a reason for this and discuss.
4. From Figure 3.8, is the index of leading indicators infallible? That is, do peaks and troughs in the index always predict peaks and troughs in real GDP? Explain.
5. In Figure 3.17 the percentage deviations from trend in GDP (Y) and government expenditures (G) for the period 1947–2006 are plotted. Figure 3.18 is a scatter plot of the same data.

Figure 3.17 Percentage Deviations from Trend in Real GDP and Government Expenditures.

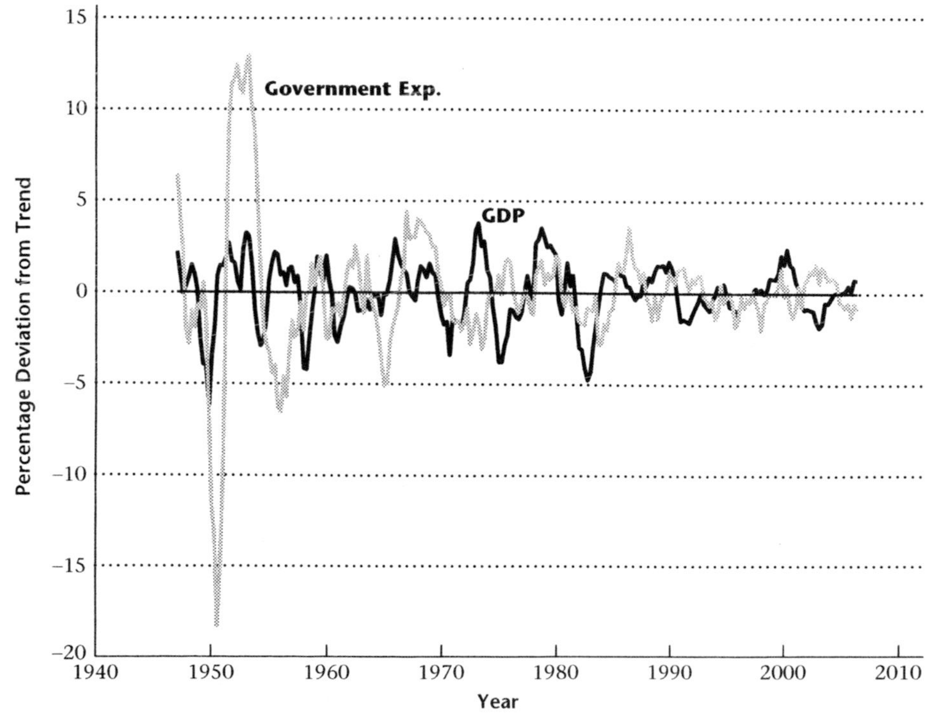

Figure 3.18 Scatter Plot of Government Expenditures Against Real GDP.

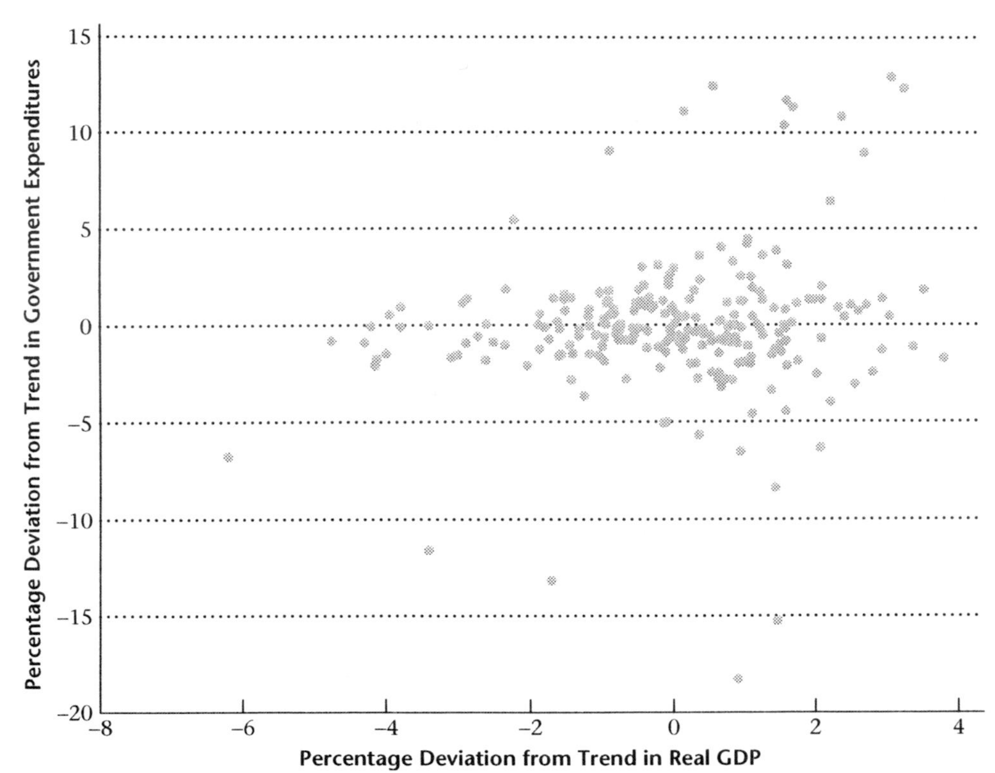

(a) Which is more variable, Y or G?

(b) Is G procyclical, countercylical, or acyclical, and how can you tell? What do you think explains this?

(c) Is there any tendency for G to lead or lag Y, or is G coincident?

6. Figure 3.19 shows the percentage deviations from trend in GDP (Y) and exports, and Figure 3.20 shows the same data in a scatter plot. Repeat parts (a), (b) and (c) of question 5, but for exports instead of G.

7. Figure 3.21 shows time series for two economic variables, X and Z. Does X lead Z, or does Z lead X? Explain.

8. We have measured average labor productivity in this chapter as Y/N, where Y is real GDP and N is employment. The business cycle facts concerning employment relate to how the denominator N comoves with the numerator Y, and those concerning average labor productivity relate to how Y/N comoves with Y. Explain how the business cycle facts concerning employment and average labor productivity in Tables 3.1 and 3.2 are consistent.

9. Consumption of durables is more variable relative to trend than is consumption of nondurables, and consumption of nondurables is more variable relative to trend than is

Figure 3.19 Percentage Deviations from Trend in Real GDP and Exports.

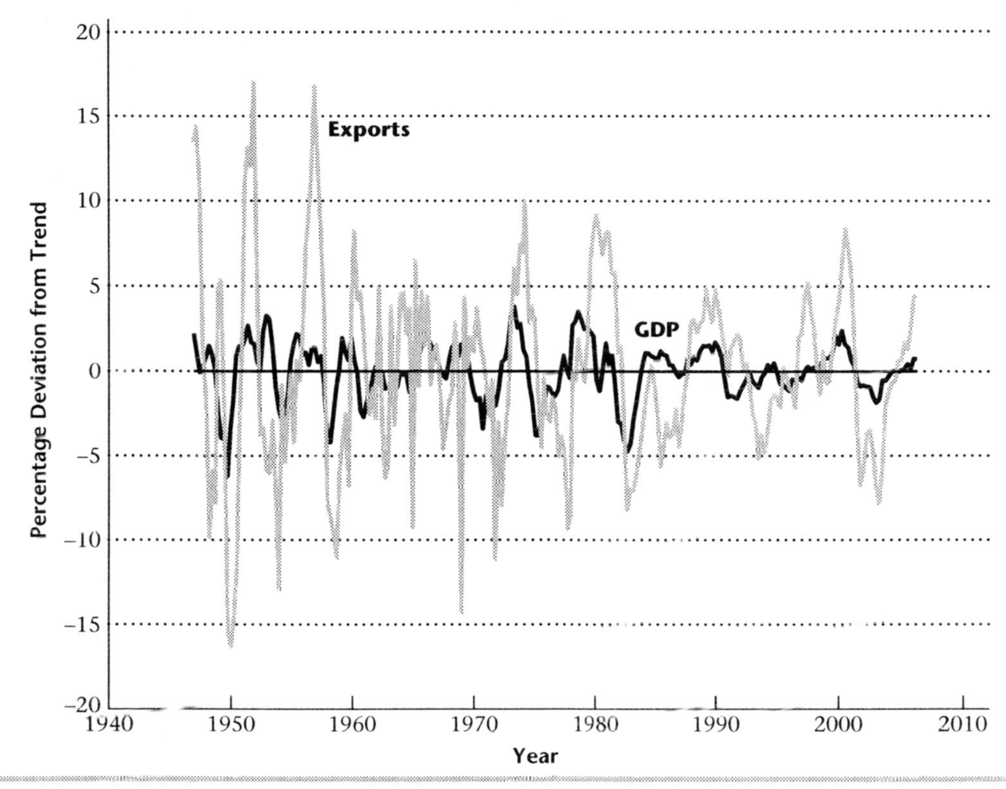

consumption of services. Speculate on why we observe these phenomena and relate this to the key business cycle facts in Tables 3.1 and 3.2.

Working with the Data

1. Calculate the year-to-year (December-to-December) percentage increase in the consumer price index (CPI), and then do a scatter plot of this against the unemployment rate (match the December 1996 unemployment rate with the percentage change in the CPI from December 1995 to December 1996, for example). Do you observe a positive correlation, a negative correlation, or a correlation that is essentially zero? Is there a Phillips curve relationship here or a reverse Phillips curve?
2. The index of industrial production is an output measure that is not as comprehensive as GDP, but it is available on a more timely basis (monthly rather than quarterly). Calculate the percentage year-to-year (December-to-December) growth rates in the index of industrial production and the percentage year-to-year growth rates in the money supply (M2). Graph the growth in industrial production and in the money supply using a time series plot and using a scatter plot.

Figure 3.20 Scatter Plot of Exports vs. GDP.

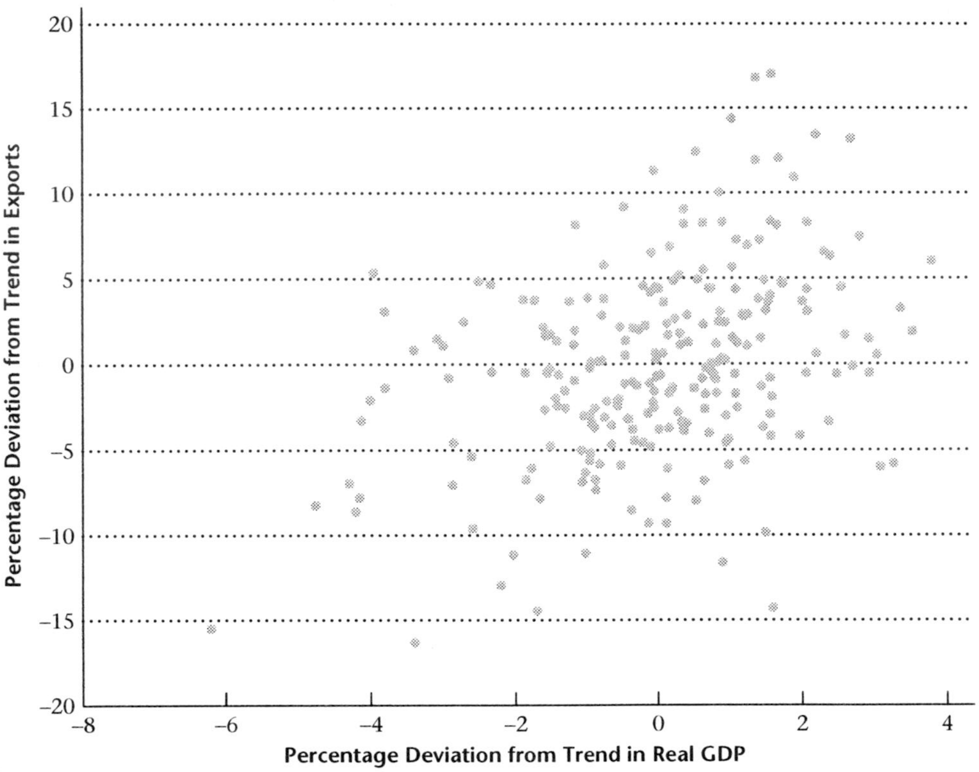

Percentage Deviation from Trend in Exports

Percentage Deviation from Trend in Real GDP

(a) Are growth in industrial production and in the money supply positively correlated or negatively correlated?

(b) Does one time series lead the other, or are they coincident?

(c) Are your answers to (a) and (b) consistent with what we observed in Figure 3.13? Explain.

3. Plot: (i) detrended GDP and detrended consumption of durables; (ii) detrended GDP and detrended consumption of nondurables; (iii) detrended GDP and detrended consumption of services.

   (a) What do you notice in these plots compared to Figure 3.9 for GDP and total consumption and Figure 3.10 for GDP and investment?

   (b) Provide an explanation for the your observations in part (a).

4. Plot detrended GDP along with each of detrended residential investment, detrended nonresidential investment, and inventory investment.

Figure 3.21 X and Z.

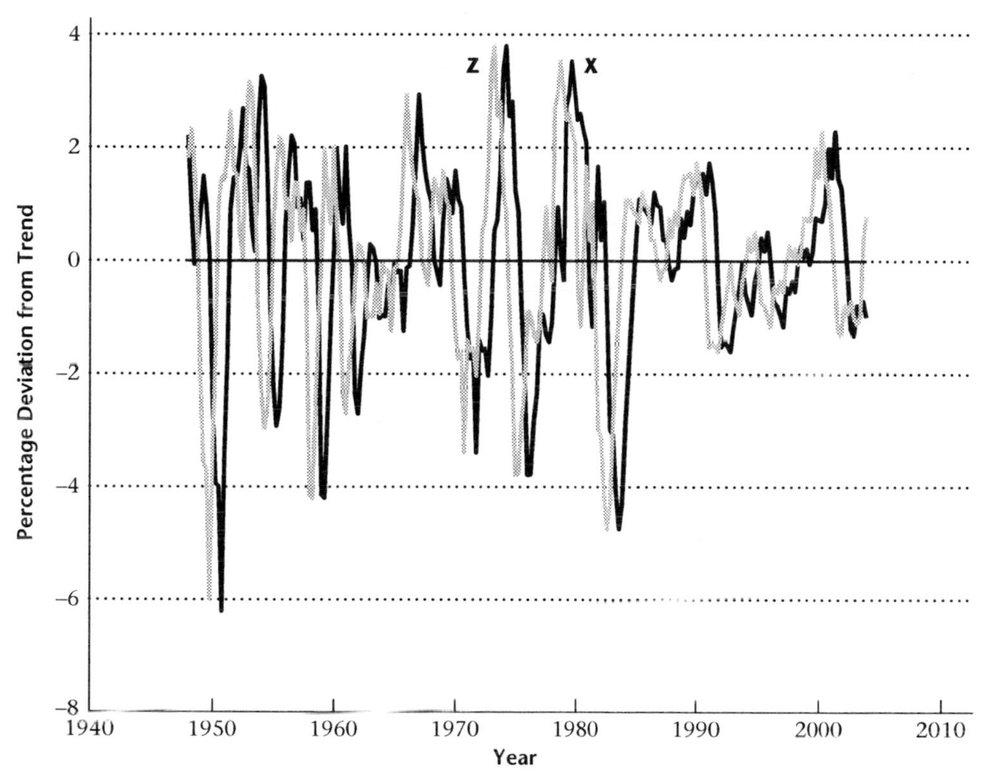

(a) Which of the components of investment shows the most (least) variability relative to GDP?

(b) What lead/lag patterns do you detect in the plots?

(c) Provide possible explanations for the patterns you detected in parts (a) and (b).

CHAPTER 25
AGGREGATE DEMAND AND AGGREGATE SUPPLY

In addition to damaging the nation's psyche, America's participation in the Vietnam conflict left scars on the economy. Economists blamed the persistent increases in the price level that began the late 1960s on the government's decision not to raise taxes to finance the war. After the war, the oil supply shocks that occurred between 1973 and 1975 made matters worse. The term "stagflation"—falling output and rising prices—entered the economic lexicon. Stagflation was a double blow to workers who lost jobs and faced higher prices. These events transformed the way economists, businesspeople, and policymakers thought about how the financial system and the economy interact and about what factors determine the economy's output and price levels.

Fluctuations in output and the price level, such as those in the 1970s, cause problems for individuals and businesses. As a result, many of them pressured policymakers to develop programs to maintain steady output growth and a stable price level. But to design these policies, they need to know what factors cause changes in output and in the price level. We study these determinants in this chapter by building a model that relates output to price level: the *AD-AS* model. Once we build the model, we use it to explain events such as the inflationary consequences of the Vietnam War, the stagflation of the 1970s, and the recessions of the early 1990s and early 2000s. We also use it in subsequent chapters to assess the impact of monetary policies that are designed to promote price stability and steady economic growth.

The Aggregate Demand Curve

To begin, we seek a relationship for the demand for goods and services that we can use to determine how price level changes affect output. We start with an expression for aggregate demand that we can use in our model. **Aggregate demand** for the economy's output equals the sum of demands for (1) goods and services for consumption, C; (2) investment in business plant and equipment, inventories, and housing, I; (3) government purchases of goods and services (not including transfer payments to individuals), G; and (4) net exports (domestic sales of goods and services to foreigners minus domestic purchases of goods and services from foreigners), NX. Hence aggregate demand for current output, Y_d, is

$$Y_d = C + I + G + NX. \tag{25.1}$$

The **aggregate demand (*AD*) curve** illustrates the relationship between the aggregate demand for goods and services (the goods market) and the aggregate price level.

Deriving the Aggregate Demand Curve

The shape and position of the *AD* curve are important in determining the values of output and the price level that exist when the economy is in equilibrium. In the remainder of this section, we describe why the *AD* curve is downward-sloping; then we describe the factors that change its position—that is, cause the *AD* curve to shift.

The *AD* curve is downward-sloping because an increase in the price level reduces the aggregate demand for goods and services if nothing else changes. Although the aggregate demand curve and the demand curves for individual goods and services are all downward-sloping, there are differences between these two types of curves. For example, the quantity of wheat that is demanded depends negatively on the price of wheat, but the demand curve for wheat relates the quantity of wheat that is demanded to the price of wheat relative to prices of substitutes. An increase in the price of wheat relative to the price of corn reduces the quantity of wheat that is demanded. In contrast, the aggregate demand curve relates the aggregate quantity of output demanded, Y_d, to the aggregate price level, P. Therefore, if prices of all goods rise by 5%, the aggregate price level P rises by 5%, but relative prices do not change. Nonetheless, the increase in the price level, P, reduces the aggregate quantity of output demanded, Y_d.

Web Site Suggestions: http://www.bls.gov/data/home.htm Shows information on the U.S. price level and unemployment in the Bureau of Labor Statistics' home page.

An increase in the price level reduces real money balances, changing the equilibrium in the money market. This, in turn, affects aggregate demand. To demonstrate how this happens, we trace the steps that occur when the price level rises:

1. When the price level, P, rises, for any nominal money supply, M, the supply of real money balances, (M/P), falls.
2. For the public to be willing to hold a smaller quantity of real money balances and a larger quantity of nonmoney assets, the real interest rate must rise. A higher real interest rate on nonmoney assets increases the opportunity cost of holding money, so the public is willing to hold the lower level of real money balances.
3. The rise in real interest rates makes firms less willing to invest in plant and equipment, and it gives consumers an incentive to save rather than spend. If we include this behavior in our expression for Y_d, then C and I fall, and Y_d declines as P increases.
4. There is also a change in net exports because of the effect of rising real interest rates on the exchange rate. A higher domestic real interest rate makes returns on domestic financial assets more attractive relative to those on foreign assets, raising the exchange rate. The rise in the exchange rate increases imports and reduces exports, thereby reducing NX and Y_d in Eq. (25.1).

Conversely, a decrease in the price level increases real money balances, leading to a drop in the real interest rate in the money market. The lower real interest rate reduces saving (thereby increasing consumption) and raises investment and net exports. Hence from Eq. (25.1), the quantity of aggregate output demanded rises.

Figure 25.1 shows the *AD* curve, which slopes down and to the right, giving it a shape like any demand curve. But as you can see from our analysis, the reason for the *AD* curve's shape is quite different from that of an individual demand curve. Points along the aggregate demand curve represent combinations of the price level and current output for which the goods market and the asset markets are in equilibrium at the same time. Within asset markets, the money market is in equilibrium because the quantity of real money balances equals the available supply. The nonmoney asset market is in equilibrium because households and businesses are satisfied with their holdings of nonmoney assets. The goods market is in equilibrium because saving equals investment. The simultaneous equilibrium of all three markets that constitute the financial

FIGURE 25.1

The Aggregate Demand Curve

The aggregate demand curve *AD* illustrates the negative relationship between the price level and the aggregate quantity of output demanded. The aggregate demand curve slopes downward. Increases in the price level reduce real money balances, raising the real interest rate and reducing the quantity of output demanded.

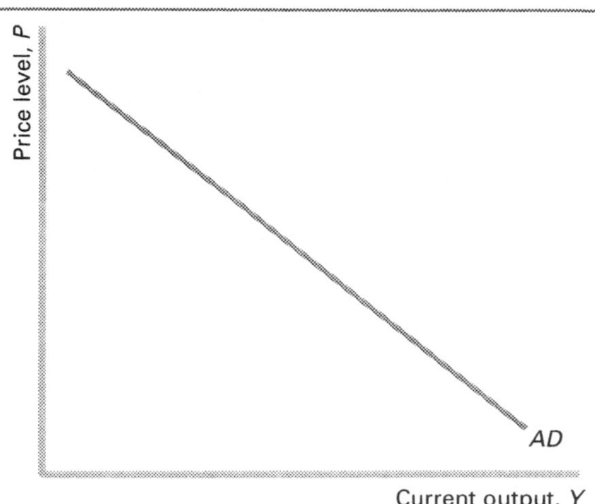

system and the economy is called *general equilibrium*. Each point on the *AD* curve represents a potential equilibrium output and the price level. Which equilibrium point prevails depends on the supply of output, which we discuss later.

Shifts of the Aggregate Demand Curve

In addition to knowing the pattern or shape of the *AD* curve, the placement of the *AD* curve on the graph is crucial to our understanding of the effects of policy measures. Shifts of the aggregate demand curve occur when aggregate demand for the economy's current output increases or decreases at a particular price level. A shift of the aggregate demand curve to the right is *expansionary* because the price level is associated with a higher level of aggregate demand for current output. Expansionary shifts in aggregate demand can be traced to the asset markets or the goods market. A shift of the aggregate demand curve to the left is *contractionary* because the price level is associated with a lower level of aggregate demand for current output. Like expansionary shifts, contractionary shifts in aggregate demand can originate either in the asset markets or in the goods market.

Shifts originating in the asset markets. If the Fed increases the nominal money supply and prices are sticky in the short run, real money balances rise. The real interest rate then falls in the asset markets. To maintain equilibrium in the goods market at the lower interest rate, saving must fall (raising consumption, *C*), and investment, *I*, must rise. As a result, aggregate demand rises, shifting the aggregate demand curve to the right.

Another cause of expansionary shifts originating in the asset markets is a decline in money demand. It can be the result of a drop in the interest paid on money relative to that on other assets or of a change in the payments system that makes money less desirable for use in transactions. At any level of real money supply, the decline in money demand reduces the real interest rate. As in the case of an increase in the nominal money supply, the drop in the real interest rate raises aggregate demand in the goods market and shifts the *AD* curve to the right.

In the asset markets, contractionary shifts result from a decline in the nominal money supply or a rise in money demand at each level of output. If the Fed restricts the nominal

CONSIDER THIS ...

Do Tax Cuts Stimulate Aggregate Demand?

Economists and policymakers have debated vigorously whether reductions in current taxes—holding government spending constant—increase aggregate demand. Those who believe that tax cuts increase aggregate demand reason that consumers spend some of the additional income from the tax cut, raising consumption and thereby increasing aggregate demand. Those who believe that tax cuts don't increase aggregate demand argue that a tax cut today increases the budget deficit. They propose that the public understands that the government's borrowing must eventually be repaid (with interest). In this view—known as the *Ricardian equivalence proposition*[†]—the reduction in taxes doesn't improve consumers' well-being: The increase in current income from a tax cut is offset by higher taxes in the future to pay off the debt.

Economists who hold the view that tax cuts raise aggregate demand make two arguments. The first is that a tax cut gives consumers who may face restrictions on the amount that they can borrow the opportunity to increase their consumption, thereby raising aggregate demand. The second is that consumers may not understand that government borrowing must be repaid by themselves as taxpayers. Therefore they will then try to increase current consumption—and aggregate demand—even though they are no better off.

Which school of thought is correct? Indirect evidence indicates that part of the population faces borrowing constraints on consumption. More directly, consumption rose in the United States following the large deficit-financed tax cuts legislated in 1981. In other cases, however, tax cuts have not significantly increased consumption.

[†] The Ricardian equivalence proposition traces its origin to David Ricardo, an eighteenth-century economist. Robert Barro has argued the proposition most persuasively; see Robert Barro, "The Ricardian Approach to Budget Deficits," *Journal of Economic Perspectives*, 2:37–54, 1989.

money supply, real money balances fall in the short run; the real interest rate rises to restore equilibrium in the asset markets. To maintain equilibrium in the goods market at the higher interest rate, saving must rise (reducing consumption, C), and investment, I, must fall. As a result, aggregate demand falls. A rise in money demand means that at any level of money supply, the real interest rate must rise to restore equilibrium in the money market. The increase in the real interest rate reduces aggregate demand.

Shifts originating in the goods market. Expansionary shifts also can originate in the goods market owing to changes in saving and investment, in government purchases, or in net exports. A decline in saving or an increase in investment at any real interest rate raises aggregate demand. A decline in saving might occur if consumers expect an increase in expected future income or if they feel confident about the future conditions—raising consumption, C. Taxes may also play a role in the behavior of consumers and affect aggregate demand. Some, though not all, economists also believe that increases in current income from tax cuts reduce desired saving and increase consumption. Firms increase investment, I, if they expect the future profitability of capital to rise or business taxes to fall. An increase in government purchases, G, directly adds to aggregate demand. An increase in foreign demand for U.S.-produced goods raises the demand for current output and net exports, NX. Each change in C, I, G, or NX increases aggregate demand in the goods market and shifts the AD curve to the right.

In the goods market, contractionary shifts reflect a decline in desired consumption or investment, in government purchases, or in net exports. A decline in consumption reflects a decrease in expected future income or less confidence about future economic conditions. Firms reduce investment if they expect the future profitability of capital to decline or business taxes to rise. A drop in government purchases directly reduces aggregate demand, as does a decline in foreign demand for U.S.-produced goods. Table 25.1 summarizes factors that shift the aggregate demand curve.

CHECKPOINT

Many businesspeople and policymakers argue that an investment tax credit—giving firms the right to subtract part of the purchase price of new factories and equipment from their income tax bill—is an effective way to stimulate aggregate demand. Why? An investment tax credit reduces the cost of investing, raising the after-tax profitability of building a new factory or installing new equipment. As a result, desired investment rises, shifting the *AD* curve to the right. ♦

TABLE 25.1 Determinants of Shifts in the Aggregate Demand Curve

An Increase in . . .	Shifts the *AD* Curve . . .	Because . . .
the nominal money supply	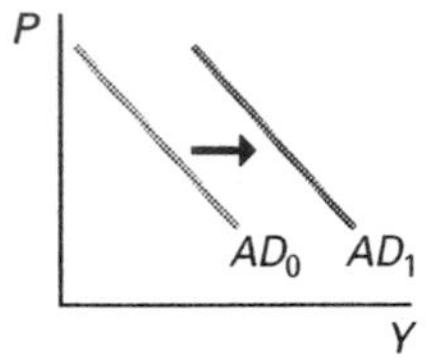 P; AD_0 → AD_1; Y	real money balances rise and the real interest rate falls.
the interest rate on money balances	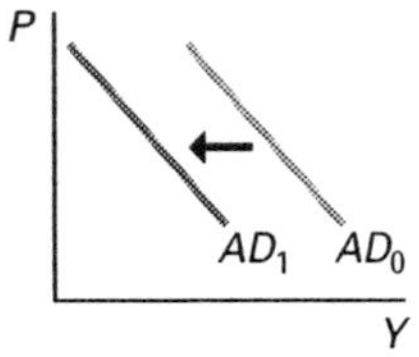 P; AD_1 ← AD_0; Y	money demand rises and the real interest rate rises.
expected future output	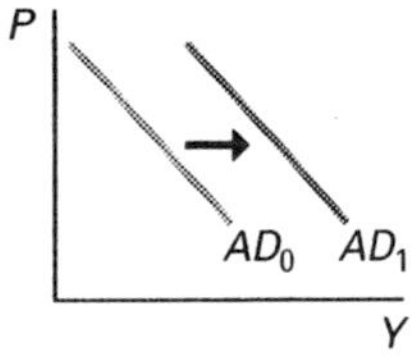 P; AD_0 → AD_1; Y	consumption rises.
government purchases	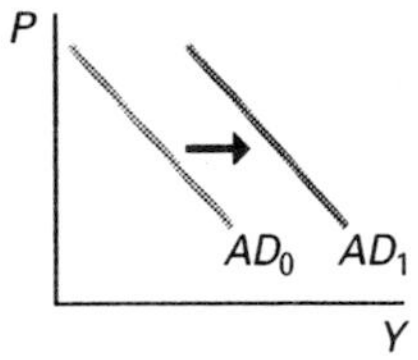 P; AD_0 → AD_1; Y	aggregate demand increases directly.
the expected future profitability of capital	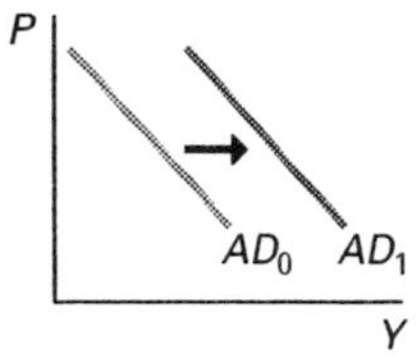 P; AD_0 → AD_1; Y	investment rises.
business taxes	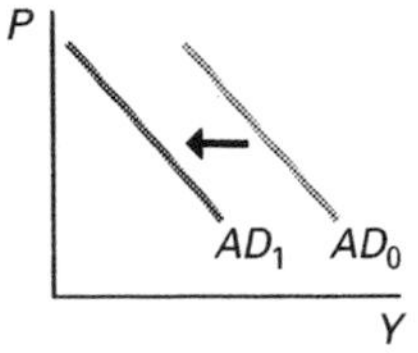 P; AD_1 ← AD_0; Y	investment declines.

The Aggregate Supply Curve

We now proceed to the second step in building the *AD-AS* model. Here we explain **aggregate supply**, the total quantity of output that producers are willing to sell at various price levels. Our goal is to construct an **aggregate supply (*AS*) curve**, which represents levels of output that producers are willing to supply at each price level.

We are interested in the shape and position of the aggregate supply curve, but our analysis is not as simple as it was for aggregate demand. Firms differ in their reaction to changes in the price level in the short run and the long run. For example, firms may adjust factors of production to minimize labor costs or to take advantage of improved technology, but such changes take time to incorporate into the production process. Therefore we divide our analysis of aggregate supply according to the time horizon that firms face. We start by examining the short-run aggregate supply curve and then turn to the long-run aggregate supply curve. In addition, economists are not in complete agreement about the behavior of firms, particularly in the short run. Although most economists believe that the aggregate quantity of output that is supplied in the short run increases as the price level rises and that, in the long run, changes in the price level have no effect on the aggregate quantity of output supplied, they attribute these patterns to different causes. We therefore describe the views of two different schools of thought: the new classical economists and the new Keynesian economists. These interpretations of firms' behavior will allow us to construct short-run and long-run aggregate supply curves. As we discuss in Chapter 26, the two views offer somewhat different answers to the question of whether public policy should be used to stabilize economic fluctuations.

Although the aggregate supply curve (particularly the short-run aggregate supply curve) may look like the supply curve facing an individual firm, it represents different behavior. The quantity of output that an individual firm is willing to supply depends on the price of its output relative to the prices of other goods and services. In contrast, the aggregate supply curve relates the aggregate quantity of output supplied to the price level. The new classical and new Keynesian views offer different explanations of this relationship.

Short-Run Aggregate Supply Curve

Most economists believe that short-run aggregate supply is positively related to the general price level. Therefore the **short-run aggregate supply (*SRAS*) curve** slopes upward.

New classical view and misperception. The **new classical view** of aggregate supply in the short run builds on research by Nobel Laureate Robert E. Lucas, Jr., of the University of Chicago. He studied the effects on aggregate supply of the imperfect information that firms possess. Because Lucas described firms' misperceptions, his explanation is also known as the **misperception theory.** To understand how it works, let's begin with an example.

Consider the supply decisions of Bigplay, a toy manufacturer. Bigplay maximizes profits by increasing the volume of toys it produces when the relative price of toys is high and decreasing production when the relative price of toys is low. Bigplay's managers face an information problem: they care about *relative* prices, so they need to know the price of toys *and* the general price level. Although they know a lot about toy prices, their knowledge of the general price level is not complete because they lack continuous information on all prices outside the toy market.

Suppose that the price of toys increases by 15%. If the general price level doesn't change at the same time, the relative price of toys has increased, and Bigplay should supply more toys. But if all prices in the economy are 15% higher, the relative price of toys is unchanged, and Bigplay would have no incentive to manufacture more toys. Bigplay's managers should separate an observed change in the price of toys into a change in the general price level and a change in the relative price of toys. Lacking complete information about the general price level, Bigplay guesses that a 15% increase in the price of toys reflects an increase in the general price level of 10% and an increase in the relative price of toys of 5%. Because of the increase in the relative price, Bigplay will increase the quantity of toys it produces.

Bigplay is only one producer. Generalizing to include all producers in the economy, we discover why the misperception theory suggests a relationship between aggregate output and the price level. Suppose that all prices in the economy rise by 15% but that relative prices don't change. If individual producers fail to recognize the situation, aggregate output increases. This change in output occurs because producers think that some of the increase in prices represents increases in their products' relative prices, and they increase the quantity of their products supplied.

How do producers distinguish between general and relative price increases? Suppose that, before they observe any price changes, some producers forecast that the general price level will rise by 10%. If those producers observe an increase of 15% in the prices of their goods, they will assume that the relative prices of their products have increased by 5% and will increase the quantities supplied of their goods. That assumption may be incorrect.

According to the new classical view, suppliers that have perfect information about price changes would react in the following way. They would raise the quantity of toys supplied when prices of toys increased only if that increase differed from the expected increase in the general price level in the economy. If all producers expect the price level to increase by 10%, and Bigplay sees the price of toys increase by only 5%, the toy manufacturer will *cut* toy production. If all prices actually increase by only 5%, producers (having expected a 10% increase in the price level) will collectively cut production.

From this ideal behavior, we can write an equation for aggregate output supplied. The new classical view suggests a positive relationship between the aggregate supply of goods and the difference between the actual and expected price level. If P is the actual price level and P^e is the expected price level, the relationship between aggregate output and the price level, according to the new classical view, is

$$Y = Y^* - a(P - P^e), \tag{25.2}$$

where Y is aggregate output, Y^* is **full employment output,** or the output produced by full employment of existing factors of production, and a is a positive number that indicates by how much output responds when the actual price level is greater than the expected price level.

Equation (25.2) states that output supplied, Y, equals full employment output, Y^*, when the actual price level and the expected price level are equal. When the actual price level is greater than the expected price level, firms increase output. When the actual price level is less than the expected price level, output falls. As a result, output can be higher or lower than the full employment level in the short term until firms can distinguish changes in relative prices from changes in the general price level. Thus, in the short run, for an expected price level, an increase in the actual price level raises the aggregate quantity of output supplied. Hence the aggregate supply curve slopes upward.

CHECKPOINT

Chair Lair—your custom-made furniture store—is experiencing its best year ever. Sales are up 25%, and you raise the prices on your popular models. How can you determine whether to increase production or just raise prices? If the increased sales are the result of increased customer demand for your chairs relative to other goods, you should increase your production. If the higher sales are the result of rising prices generally, you should increase prices without changing production. You can check aggregate economic statistics on inflation and sales of goods generally. You can gather information on your prices and sales (and those of other businesses in the furniture industry) based on your own experience more quickly than reliable data for the economy are published. This information allows you to estimate, on average, how much of a given price change reflects general price movements and how much reflects changes in relative prices. ♦

New Keynesian view and sticky prices. John Maynard Keynes and his followers believed that prices failed to adjust in the short run in response to changes in aggregate demand. That is, prices are sticky in the short run. In the most extreme view of price stickiness, we would observe a horizontal *AS* curve; prices would not adjust to increases or decreases in aggregate demand. Contemporary economists who follow Keynes's view of price stickiness have sought reasons for the failure of prices to adjust in the short run. Their work has modified Keynes's view that prices fail to adjust in favor of a slow or gradual adjustment. Economists who embrace the **new Keynesian view** use characteristics of many real-world markets—rigidity of long-term contracts and imperfect competition—to explain price behavior.

One form of rigidity arises from long-term nominal contracts for wages (between firms and workers) or prices (between firms and their suppliers or customers). Under a long-term nominal contract, a wage rate or price is set in advance for several to many periods in nominal terms.† Suppose, for example, that *all* workers agreed to a fixed wage for the next three years. Then, on the basis of this labor cost and other components of expected total production costs, all firms set prices that would remain fixed for the next three years. In this case, firms would not be able to change prices easily in response to changes in demand because their costs of production are fixed.

Although many such long-term arrangements exist in the economy, not all contracts come up for renewal during a particular period; that is, contracts are overlapping or staggered. Hence only some wages and prices can be adjusted in the current period. Contracts ultimately will be adjusted to changes in expected money growth, but they can't all adjust immediately. For example, businesses that expect high current money growth to lead to a rise in the price level in the future can negotiate price changes for the future but not for the period under contract. New Keynesians reject the notion that all prices are flexible in the short run; they believe that the price level adjusts slowly to changes in the nominal money supply.

†If wages or prices in a long-term contract were fully indexed to, say, changes in the general price level, wages or prices could still adjust to aggregate nominal disturbances. An example is *cost of living adjustments* (COLAs) in many wage contracts. Evidence for the United States suggests that such contracts generally are only partially indexed.

New Keynesians also attribute price stickiness to differences in market structure and the price-setting decisions that take place in different types of markets. In markets for wheat or stocks or Treasury bills, the product is standardized, many traders interact, and prices adjust freely and quickly to shifts in demand and supply. In such competitive markets, the purchases and sales of individual traders are small relative to the total market volume. For example, a few wheat farmers can't raise their prices above those of other wheat farmers; in the competitive wheat market, no one would buy their wheat. Individual traders are *price takers*; that is, they take the market price (as reported on the floor of an exchange or in the newspaper) as a given.

However, many markets in the economy—such as the markets for high-fashion clothing, art, and medical care—don't resemble the continuously adjusting price-taking markets of exchanges because their products are not standardized. When products have individual characteristics and there are few sellers of each product, monopolistic competition results. A seller who raises prices might see the quantity demanded fall, but not to zero. In monopolistically competitive markets, sellers do not take prices as a given because they are price setters. New Keynesian economists argue that prices will adjust only gradually in monopolistically competitive markets.

To understand why, consider the market for high-fashion clothing. Firms in this market might have a central meeting place where buyers submit bids and sellers quote asking prices (much as buying and selling in the market for Treasury securities is conducted). If a designer gets favorable reviews, demand increases and the product's price rises, whereas unfavorable reviews by critics reduce the product's price. Individual high-fashion clothing stores do not continuously adjust prices. Instead, they set the price of clothes in nominal terms for periods of time and meet the demand at that price. They may, however, change prices from time to time in response to major changes in demand or costs of production.

New Keynesian economists contend that this pricing behavior can be in firms' interests as long as markets are monopolistically competitive and there are costs to changing prices. The costs of changing prices—informing current and potential customers, remarking prices, and so on—may not seem that large. Why then do new Keynesians think they are so important?

To return to our example of a perfectly competitive market, when a seller of goods or assets traded on exchanges charges a price that is just a bit high, that seller will sell nothing at all. However, a monopolistically competitive firm (such as a clothing boutique) won't lose many of its customers if its prices deviate slightly from the market price. If potential profits are small relative to the cost of changing prices, the firm won't change its price.

Why is a firm willing to meet demand by selling more at the posted price? For a monopolistically competitive firm, the product price is higher than the marginal cost—that is, the cost of producing an extra unit. Hence the firm is happy to sell extra output. As a result of satisfying the level of demand, the firm's output will rise and fall, depending on aggregate demand.

Let's translate this description of price-setting behavior into an equation that will show how changes in the price level affect output. Because new Keynesians show that the behavior of firms with flexible prices differs from that of firms with sticky prices, we must start with an expression that shows the decisions each firm faces in setting its prices. Firms with flexible prices can change their prices freely and continually. The price, p, that an individual firm in this category charges is related to the aggregate price level, P, and output, Y, relative to full employment output, Y^*. An increase in the price level means that the firm's costs are higher and that the firm would like to charge more for its output. An increase in aggregate output implies that higher incomes in the economy are likely to raise the demand for the firm's product. As the marginal cost of producing output tends to rise at higher levels of production (because of, for example, the need to pay overtime wages to workers), the firm's desired price rises with the level of demand. That is,

$$p = P + b(Y - Y^*), \tag{25.3}$$

where b is a parameter with a value greater than zero. Equation (25.3) reveals that a price-setting firm's desired price depends on the price level, P, and the level of aggregate output relative to full employment output, $(Y - Y^*)$.

Firms with sticky prices set their prices in advance on the basis of their expectation of output. If we let the superscript e denote expectation, we can rewrite Eq. (25.3) for price-setting firms as

$$p = P^e + b(Y^e - Y^{*e}),$$

To keep the analysis simple, let's further assume that firms expect output to be at the full employment level. In this case, $b(Y^e - Y^{*e})$ is zero, and

$$p = P^e.$$

Price-setting firms base their prices on their expectations of other firms' prices, as reflected in the expected aggregate price level.

We combine our analysis of pricing decisions by the two types of firms to develop the new Keynesian aggregate supply curve. The aggregate price level, P, is the weighted average of the prices that are charged by the flexible-price and sticky-price firms. If c represents the fraction of firms with sticky prices and $(1 - c)$ represents the fraction of firms with flexible prices, the aggregate price level is

$$P = cP^e + (1 - c)[P + b(Y - Y^*)].$$

Subtracting $(1 - c)P$ from both sides of the equation and dividing both sides by c give the general price level:

$$P = P^e + b\left(\frac{1-c}{c}\right)(Y - Y^*). \tag{25.4}$$

This expression for the aggregate price level is a reminder that (1) an increase in the expected price level raises expected costs and leads firms to raise prices, and (2) an increase in current output raises the demand for an individual firm's products, so flexible-price firms raise their prices.†

The short-run aggregate supply curve that is implied by the new Keynesian view slopes upward: An increase in current output leads to an increase in the price level in

---

†Note that we can rearrange the terms in Eq. (25.4) to yield an expression that is similar to Eq. (25.2):

$$Y = Y^* + \left[\frac{c}{b(1-c)}\right](P - P^e).$$

the short run. The larger the proportion of firms in the economy with sticky prices, the flatter the *SRAS* curve will be. Indeed, if all firms had sticky prices in the short run, the *SRAS* curve would be horizontal.

CHECKPOINT

Amalgamated Industries has two major divisions: one grows fruit in California, and the other manufactures and sells designer sweaters in New York. If aggregate demand rises, which price should rise first? Agricultural products are sold largely in competitive markets with flexible prices. An increase in aggregate demand will raise the price of Amalgamated Industries' fruit because the quantity supplied can't increase in the short run. In the designer sweater market, markups of price over cost are much higher, and Amalgamated's stores are less likely to change the price tags in the short run. Its sweater stores will meet the greater demand at the unchanged price in the short run. ♦

Long-Run Aggregate Supply Curve

The short-run aggregate supply curve, *SRAS*, slopes upward in both the new classical and new Keynesian explanations of aggregate supply, but this relationship doesn't hold in the long run. In the new classical view, firms eventually realize that the price level is changing in response to a change in current output. They adjust their estimates of the expected price level until the actual and expected price level are equal—that is, until $P = P^e$. This relationship shows that current output Y equals full employment output Y^*, so the **long-run aggregate supply (*LRAS*) curve** is vertical at Y^*. In the new Keynesian view, both firms with flexible prices and firms with sticky prices adjust their prices in response to a change in demand in the long run. As with the new classical view, the *LRAS* curve is vertical at the full employment level of output $Y = Y^*$.

Figure 25.2 summarizes the short-run and long-run aggregate supply relationships between price level and current output.

Shifts in the Short-Run Aggregate Supply Curve

Changes in aggregate supply can explain changes in output in the short run. In both the new classical and new Keynesian explanations of short-run aggregate supply, the factors that shift the short-run aggregate supply curve also affect the costs of producing output. These factors are (1) changes in labor costs, (2) changes in other input costs, and (3) changes in the expected price level.

Web Site Suggestions: http://www.census.gov/compendia/statab/ Presents useful statistics on macro variables for the U.S. economy.

Changes in labor costs. Labor typically accounts for most of the costs of producing output. When output, Y, exceeds the full employment level, Y^*, the high volume of output produced raises the demand for labor. The higher labor demand, in turn, bids up wages, increasing firms' labor costs. As a result, the short-run aggregate supply curve shifts up and to the left. When output falls below the full employment level, workers' wages decline. The resulting drop in production costs shifts the short-run aggregate supply curve down and to the right.

Changes in other input costs. Shifts in the price or availability of raw materials or in production technologies affect production costs and the aggregate supply curve. Such changes are commonly called **supply shocks.** Supply shocks include changes in technology, weather, or the prices of oil and other inputs of energy and materials.

FIGURE 25.2

The Short-Run and Long-Run Aggregate Supply Curves

The *SRAS* curve slopes upward: When the price level *P* exceeds the expected price level P^e, the quantity of output supplied rises. In the long run, the actual and expected price levels come together: The *LRAS* curve is vertical at the full employment level of output, Y^*.

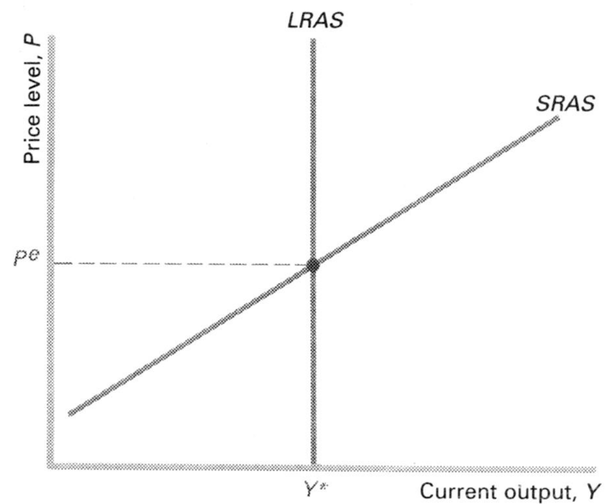

Positive supply shocks, such as the development of labor-saving technologies or lower food prices owing to good growing seasons, shift the aggregate supply curve down and to the right. Negative supply shocks, such as an increase in the price of oil, shift the aggregate supply curve up and to the left.

Changes in the expected price level. When workers bargain for wages, they compare their wages to the costs of goods and services that they buy. When workers expect the price level to rise, they will demand higher nominal wages to preserve their real wages. Similarly, firms make decisions about how much output to supply by comparing the price of their output to the expected prices of other goods and services. When the expected price level rises, firms raise prices to cover higher labor and other costs. An increase in the expected price level shifts the short-run aggregate supply curve up and to the left. A decline in the expected price level shifts the short-run aggregate supply curve down and to the right. This occurs because firms reduce prices as nominal wages and other costs fall.

Shifts in the Long-Run Aggregate Supply Curve

The long-run aggregate supply curve, *LRAS*, indicates the full employment level of output in the economy at a specific time. The *LRAS* curve shifts over time to reflect growth in the full employment level of output. Sources of this economic growth include (1) increases in capital and labor inputs and (2) increases in productivity growth (output produced per unit of input).

Increases in inputs raise the economy's productive capacity. When firms invest in new plant and equipment (excluding replacement of old plant and equipment), they increase the capital stock. Labor inputs increase when the population grows or more people participate in the labor force. Studies of output growth in the United States and other countries show that over long periods of time, the pace of output growth also is influenced significantly by productivity growth. Productivity growth is the improvement in the efficiency with which capital and labor inputs produce output.

The principal sources of change in productivity growth are energy prices, technological advances, worker training and education, and regulation of production. The

OTHER TIMES, OTHER PLACES ...

Shock Therapy and Aggregate Supply in Poland

The close of 1992 brought holiday cheer to the beleaguered Polish economy after three years of shock therapy prescribed by Western economic advisers. Although factory output dropped by nearly 40% in 1990 and 1991 from the levels that had been produced during the communist regime, output was growing and inflation was beginning to decline.

Like other former communist countries in Eastern Europe, Poland had tried to transform its centrally planned economy and remove price controls by pursuing radical economic reforms—but much more rapidly than most of the other countries. Lifting price controls (which had fixed the price level) increased the expected price level, shifting the *SRAS* curve up and to the left. Because reductions in the growth rate of the nominal money supply and elimination of many subsidies decreased aggregate demand, the shift in the *SRAS* curve led to a severe decline in output in the short run.

The immediate result of the shock therapy was a rise in the price level (a result of the shift in the *SRAS* curve) as well as a decline in output. By 1992, falling economic activity in Poland placed downward pressure on inflation.

Polish policymakers were more interested in long-run prospects for economic growth than in the short-run changes in output. Long periods of price control and government allocation had reduced the efficiency with which the Polish economy produced and distributed goods and services. Hence the big question was whether the reforms would improve the outlook for long-run aggregate supply.

While experts maintained that the end of price controls and government allocation would lead to more efficient and competitive firms, it was clear that many individuals would be worse off in the short run. The gamble in Poland was that these short-term costs would be rewarded handsomely in long-term gains in production and consumption possibilities for Polish citizens.

Many economists, notably Jeffrey Sachs of Columbia University, argued that the rebound of the Polish economy in 1992 was the beginning of favorable shifts in long-run aggregate supply in Poland. The removal of central planning and improvements in factory productivity shift the *LRAS* curve to the right, increasing output and dampening inflationary pressures. These long-run developments hold the key to the future growth of Poland's economy, which saw generally stronger economic growth and falling inflation in the remainder of the 1990s and the early 2000s.

huge increases in oil prices in 1973 reduced productivity in heavy energy-using industries and (in the view of many analysts) led to a worldwide slowdown in productivity growth. Technological advances, as in communications technology and computers, raise productivity. Many economists believe that environmental, health, and safety regulations reduce productivity growth, because capital and labor inputs are devoted to these activities instead of to producing goods and services. However, such consequences of regulation do not necessarily mean that they are not in society's interest. For example, society must weigh the benefits of cleaner air or increased workplace safety against the potential costs of reduced productivity.

Table 25.2 summarizes factors that shift the short-run and long-run aggregate supply curves.

Equilibrium in Aggregate Demand and Aggregate Supply

Web Site Suggestions: http://www.whitehouse.gov/fsbr/esbr.html Presents reports and data from the White House economic statistics briefing room.

We now have a model that shows us what level of output is likely to prevail in the economy at a given price level. The relationships for aggregate demand and short-run and long-run aggregate supply are the components of a model that we can use to determine the level of output and the price level in the economy. At that equilibrium, the aggregate demand curve and aggregate supply curve intersect. Because there is a difference in the behavior of firms in supplying output in the short run and the long run, we have two equilibrium values for output and the price level: short-run equilibrium and long-run equilibrium.

TABLE 25.2 Determinants of Shifts in the Aggregate Supply Curve

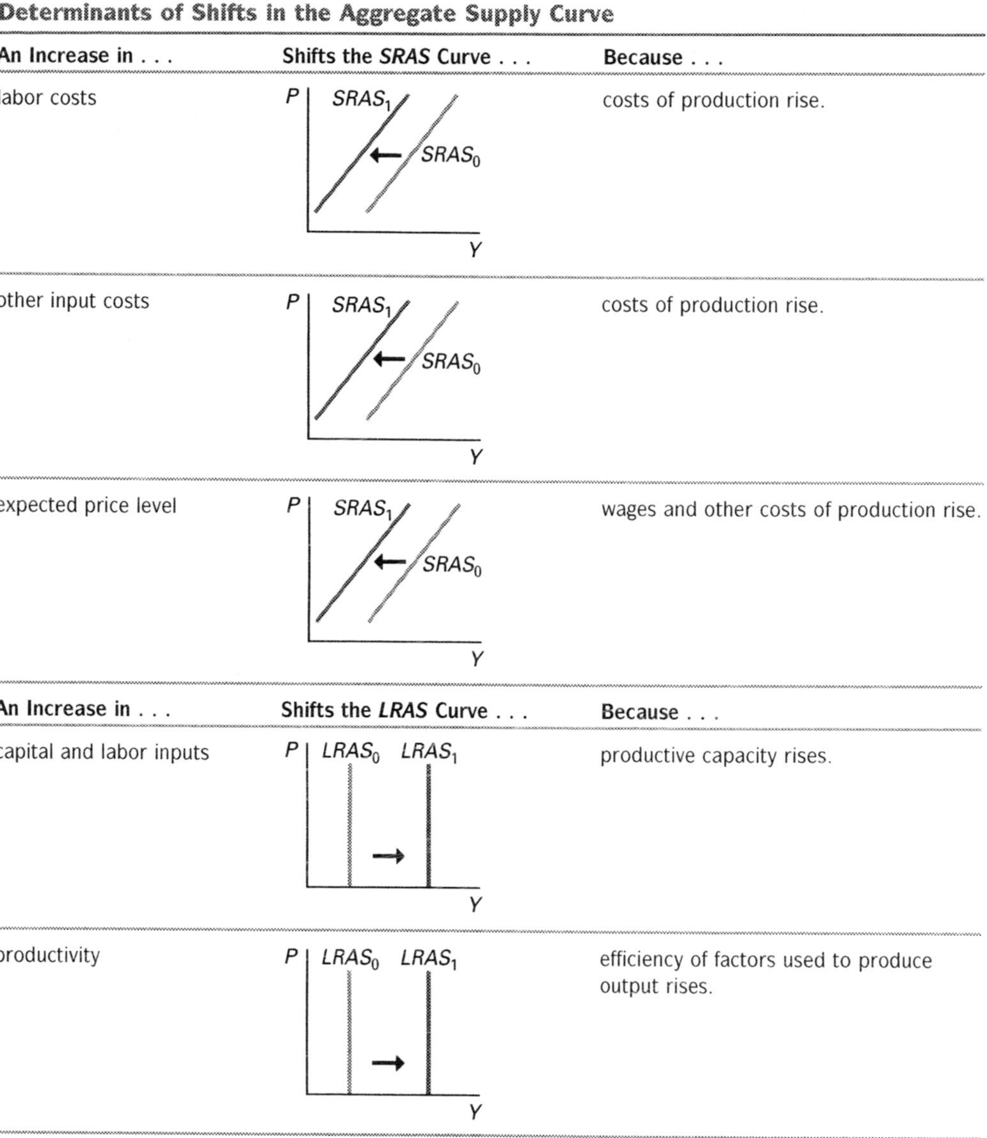

An Increase in . . .	Shifts the *SRAS* Curve . . .	Because . . .
labor costs		costs of production rise.
other input costs		costs of production rise.
expected price level		wages and other costs of production rise.
An Increase in . . .	**Shifts the *LRAS* Curve . . .**	**Because . . .**
capital and labor inputs		productive capacity rises.
productivity		efficiency of factors used to produce output rises.

Short-Run Equilibrium

To determine output and the price level in the short run, we combine the aggregate demand curve, *AD*, and the short-run aggregate supply curve, *SRAS*. Figure 25.3 shows these two curves.

The economy's short-run equilibrium occurs at the intersection, E_0, of the *AD* and *SRAS* curves. No other point represents equilibrium. For example, E_1 is an equilibrium level of aggregate demand, but at price level P_1, firms would supply more output than households and businesses would demand. The price level would fall to restore equilibrium at E_0. Point E_2 lies on the *SRAS* curve. However, at price level P_2, households and businesses would demand more output than firms would be willing to produce. The price level would rise to equate the quantity of output demanded and the quantity of output supplied.

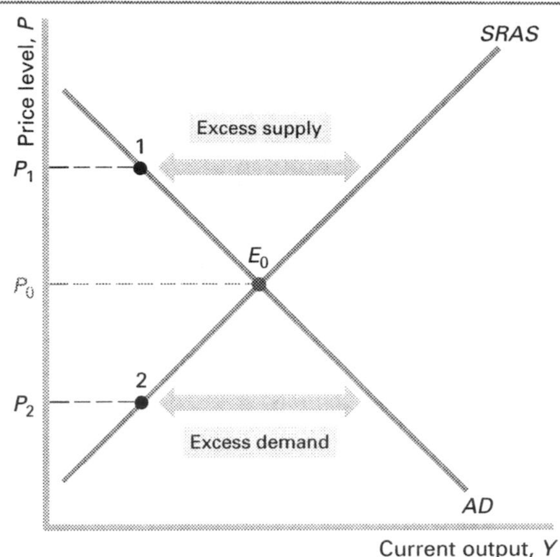

FIGURE 25.3

Short-Run Equilibrium

The economy's short-run equilibrium is represented by the intersection of the *AD* and *SRAS* curves at E_0. The equilibrium price level is P_0. Higher price levels are associated with an excess supply of output (at point 1, for example), and lower price levels are associated with excess demand for output (at point 2, for example).

CHECKPOINT

Does a rising price level indicate good news or bad news about the economy? It depends. If the price level rises because of a shift in the *AD* curve, output rises in the short run. For example, a tax cut to spur business investment increases aggregate demand for current output and the price level. However, if the price level rises because of a shift in the *SRAS* curve, output falls in the short run. For example, a harsh winter during which workers often can't get to their jobs reduces the quantity of output supplied and increases the price level. ♦

Long-Run Equilibrium

Our analysis of the economy's equilibrium in the short run suggests many possible combinations of output and the price level, depending on where the aggregate demand curve and the short-run aggregate supply curve intersect. However, in the long run, the price level adjusts to bring markets for goods and assets into equilibrium at full employment output, Y^*. In Figure 25.4, the aggregate demand curve ADO_0 and the short-run aggregate supply curve $SRAS_0$ intersect at this level of output, with a price level of P_0.

Now suppose that aggregate demand expands unexpectedly, shifting the aggregate demand curve to the right from AD_0 to AD_1. Output and the price level increase in the short run. The new short-run equilibrium, $E_{1'}$, lies at the intersection of the AD_1 and $SRAS_0$ curves. Over time, as firms learn that the general price level has risen, the *SRAS* curve shifts to the left from $SRAS_0$ to $SRAS_1$ because at the new price level, firms are willing to supply less output. In the long run, the *SRAS* curve will have to shift far enough to intersect with AD_1 at Y^*. The long-run equilibrium is at point E_1, with a price level P_1 and full employment output Y^*.

If aggregate demand contracted unexpectedly, so that the *AD* curve shifted to the left, the process would be reversed. Initially, output and the price level will decline. Over time, as firms learn that the price level has fallen, the *SRAS* curve will shift to the right. This process of adjustment is more gradual (owing to sticky prices for many

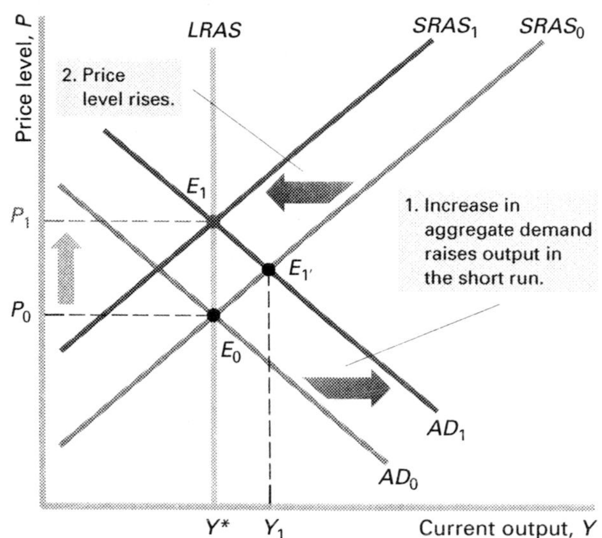

FIGURE 25.4

Adjustment to Long-Run Equilibrium

1. From initial equilibrium at E_0, an increase in aggregate demand shifts the *AD* curve from AD_0 to AD_1, increasing output from Y^* to Y_1.

2. Because $Y_1 > Y^*$, prices rise, shifting the *SRAS* curve from $SRAS_0$ to $SRAS_1$. The economy's new equilibrium is at E_1. Output has returned to Y^*, but the price level has risen to P_1.

The *LRAS* curve is vertical at Y^*, the full employment level of output. Shifts in the *AD* curve affect the level of output only in the short run. This outcome holds in both the new classical and new Keynesian views, although price adjustment is more rapid in the new classical view.

firms) in the new Keynesian view than in the new classical view. At the new long-run equilibrium, output equals Y^*, and the price level is lower than P_0.

In the long run, the *LRAS* curve is vertical at Y^*, the full employment output level. The economy will produce Y^*, and the price level will adjust to shifts in aggregate demand to ensure that all markets for goods and assets are in equilibrium.

CONSIDER THIS . . .

Can Shifts in Aggregate Demand Affect Output in the Long Run?

In general, increases or decreases in aggregate demand have no effect on the full employment level of output. That is, the *LRAS* curve does not shift in response to a shift in the *AD* curve. Some economists believe that large negative shifts in aggregate demand actually reduce the full employment level of output. In that situation, known as *hysteresis*, unemployment rates can be higher than those associated with the full employment level of output for extended periods of time.

Some economists believe that hysteresis is a source of persistent unemployment. If unemployment rates rise, more individuals lose their skills (or are viewed by employers as lacking current skills) and therefore have difficulty being rehired. Furthermore, workers who are unemployed for long periods may become discouraged and drop out of the labor force permanently. Obstacles to locating new jobs extend an individual's job search process and reduce the full employment level of output. Some economists argue that the persistently high unemployment rates in many European countries (particularly in the United Kingdom) in the early 1980s resulted from hysteresis. The government of Prime Minister Margaret Thatcher pursued a contractionary monetary policy in the early 1980s, but effects on output and unemployment lasted for several years. Economists who attribute this decline in full employment to hysteresis believe that expansionary monetary or fiscal policies were needed to restore the economy's initial level of output and employment.

Not all economists accept the proposition that expansionary shifts in aggregate demand are necessary to restore higher output and employment. They note, for example, that generous unemployment insurance systems (that pay workers benefits when they are unemployed) in many European countries might account for persistent unemployment. Evidence for hysteresis is inconclusive. The phenomenon remains a topic of ongoing research because it suggests that economic downturns that are caused by a decline in aggregate demand can impose costs on the economy for long periods of time.

Because the *LRAS* curve is vertical, economists generally agree that changes in aggregate demand affect the price level but not the output level in the long run. This link between shifts in *AD* and the price level is called **monetary neutrality**. It means that money has no effect on output in the long run, because an increase in the nominal money supply raises the price level in the long run but doesn't change equilibrium output. Conversely, a decline in the nominal money supply lowers the price level in the long run but has no effect on output.

The Real Business Cycle View

Although most economists believe that shifts in aggregate demand affect output and the price level, some economists who hold another view believe that changes in aggregate demand have no effect on output, even in the short run. In other words, not only is the long-run aggregate supply curve vertical, but the short-run aggregate supply curve also is vertical. Unlike the new classical view, the alternative **real business cycle view** assumes perfect information. Unlike the new Keynesian explanation of sticky prices, it assumes perfectly flexible prices. The real business cycle model explains short-term changes in output primarily as temporary shocks to productivity. These shocks include changes in the availability of raw materials (food, energy, and minerals, for example), regulatory restrictions on production or markets, and innovations that make the economy more productive.

Shocks to productivity result in increases or decreases in current productivity, which in turn affect the *SRAS* curve, as Figure 25.5 shows. During the Gulf War, for example, the crisis in the Middle East reduced the supply of oil in world markets, increasing somewhat the price of oil. In this case, starting from an initial equilibrium at E_0 in Figure 25.5, the productivity of energy-using producers decreases, and the *SRAS* curve shifts to the left from $SRAS_0$ to $SRAS_1$. If the productivity shock is expected to be temporary, lasting only for the current period, future productivity is unaffected and the *AD* curve doesn't shift. Because the *AD* curve doesn't shift, the new short-run equilibrium lies at the intersection of the *AD* curve and the $SRAS_1$ curve—at E_1 in Figure 25.5. At that point, output is lower and the price level is higher than at the economy's initial equilibrium, E_0.

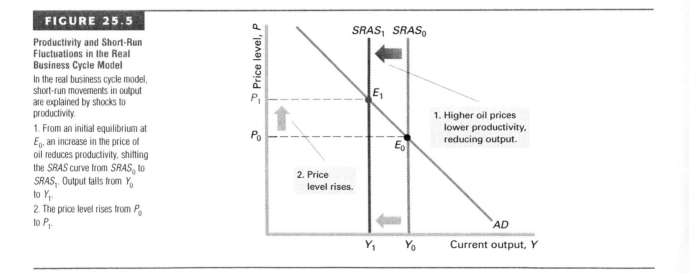

FIGURE 25.5

Productivity and Short-Run Fluctuations in the Real Business Cycle Model

In the real business cycle model, short-run movements in output are explained by shocks to productivity.

1. From an initial equilibrium at E_0, an increase in the price of oil reduces productivity, shifting the *SRAS* curve from $SRAS_0$ to $SRAS_1$. Output falls from Y_0 to Y_1.

2. The price level rises from P_0 to P_1.

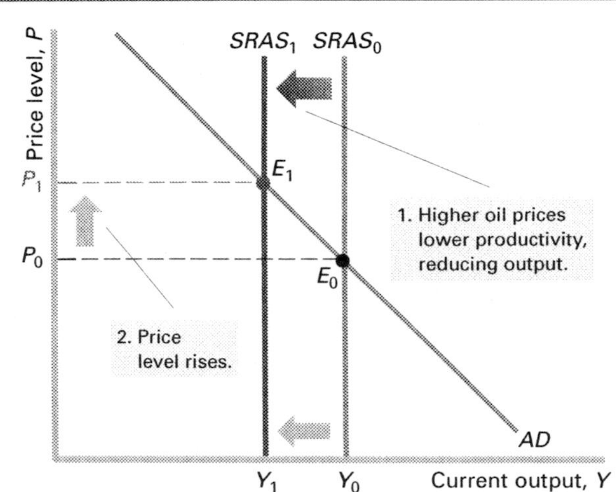

Ongoing research on the real business cycle model focuses on the significance of temporary disturbances to productivity in explaining output fluctuations. As we discuss next (and in Chapter 26), however, evidence from many episodes suggests that increases or decreases in aggregate demand affect output in the short run.

Economic Fluctuations in the United States

We can use economic models to explain past events and to predict future economic developments. Fluctuations in current output can be explained by shifts in the aggregate demand curve or the aggregate supply curve. We now use *AD-AS* analysis to help explain three episodes of economic fluctuations in the United States: (1) shocks to aggregate demand, 1964–1969; (2) supply shocks, 1973–1975 and 1995–2005; and (3) a credit crunch shock to aggregate demand, 1990–1991. Then we use *AD-AS* analysis to predict consequences for output and prices of pro-investment tax reform. In Chapter 26, we apply the *AD-AS* model to predict the outcome of monetary policies on output and the price level.

Shocks to Aggregate Demand, 1964–1969

By 1964, U.S. participation in the conflict in Vietnam had grown to a major war effort, and real government purchases—principally for military equipment and personnel—had expanded by about 9% since 1960. Those expenditures would expand by another 21% from 1964 through 1969. The Fed was alarmed by the prospect of rising interest rates. (If nothing else changed, the rise in aggregate demand from government purchases would increase money demand and the interest rate.) As a result, the Fed pursued an expansionary monetary policy: the annual growth rate of *M1* rose from 3.7% in 1963 to 7.7% in 1964.

The combination of fiscal and monetary expansions led to a series of shifts to the right of the aggregate demand curve. Rising aggregate demand caused output to exceed the full employment level in the mid-1960s, putting upward pressure on production costs and the price level. As we demonstrated in the analysis of short-run and long-run equilibrium with the *AD-AS* diagram, the *SRAS* curve shifts up and to the left, restoring the economy's full employment equilibrium at a higher price level. Because fiscal and monetary expansion continued for several years, the *AD-AS* analysis indicates that output growth and inflation (the rate of change in the price level) should have risen from 1964 through 1969. The demand expansion panel in Figure 25.6 shows that is generally what happened.

Supply Shocks, 1973–1975 and 1995–2005

By the early 1970s, many economists and policymakers believed that output growth and inflation went hand in hand—a sensible conclusion when changes in the economy's equilibrium output and price level are driven by changes in aggregate demand. The United States (and other industrialized countries) experienced negative supply shocks in 1973 and 1974. In 1973, the Organization of Petroleum Exporting Countries (OPEC) sharply reduced the supply of oil in the world oil market in an attempt to punish the United States and other countries for supporting Israel in the 1973 Arab–Israeli conflict. Along with the quadrupling of world oil prices, poor crop harvests around the world caused food prices to rise significantly. In the United States, these two negative supply shocks were reinforced by the lifting of wage and price controls that had been in effect since 1971, which caused a round of catch-up wage and price increases.

In *AD-AS* analysis, this set of negative supply shocks shifts the short-run aggregate supply curve up to the left, raising the price level and reducing output. As Figure 25.6 shows, output growth fell in 1974 and 1975 while inflation rose. This type of inflation causes the economy to stagnate, a result that is known as *stagflation*. The falling output and rising prices indicated that aggregate supply shocks, as well as aggregate demand shocks, could change the economy's short-run equilibrium. A similar pattern occurred in response to adverse oil supply shocks in the 1978–1980 period.

Web Site Suggestions: http://www.gpoaccess.gov/indicators/browse.html Presents data on output growth and inflation in the Council of Economic Advisers *Monthly Economic Indicators*.

We can also examine favorable supply shocks, such as the acceleration in productivity growth experienced in the U.S. economy in the late 1990s and 2000s. In the background, the Federal Reserve had begun to increase interest rates in February 1994 to counteract what it saw as inflationary pressures. The economic boom continued, with high output growth and a decline in inflation toward 2%. This favorable supply shock can be illustrated using *AD-AS* analysis. Some economists feared that adverse productivity shocks from increased regulation after the September 11, 2001, terrorist attacks or after Hurricane Katrina in 2005 would weaken productivity growth, but underlying productivity growth remained strong.

Many economists highlight the role of productivity growth stemming from information-technology-related investments—partially in the "new economy." As a consequence, the aggregate supply curve shifted to the right, increasing output and reducing inflation.

Credit Crunch and Aggregate Demand, 1990–1991

Many analysts believe that a reduction in banks' ability or willingness to lend, called a *credit crunch*, deepened the 1990–1991 recession. The Gulf War provided a negative supply shock early in the recession. Recall that financial institutions such as banks are likely to be important suppliers of funds to borrowers that have few alternative sources of finance from nonmoney markets. Two events may have led to a credit crunch dur-

FIGURE 25.6

Output Growth and Inflation, 1960–2005

The short-run changes in output growth and inflation observable between 1960 and 2005 can be explained by shifts in aggregate demand or aggregate supply that caused output to exceed or fall short of the full employment level.

Source: Council of Economic Advisers, *Economic Report of the President*, see also http://www.gpoaccess.gov/eop/tables06.html.

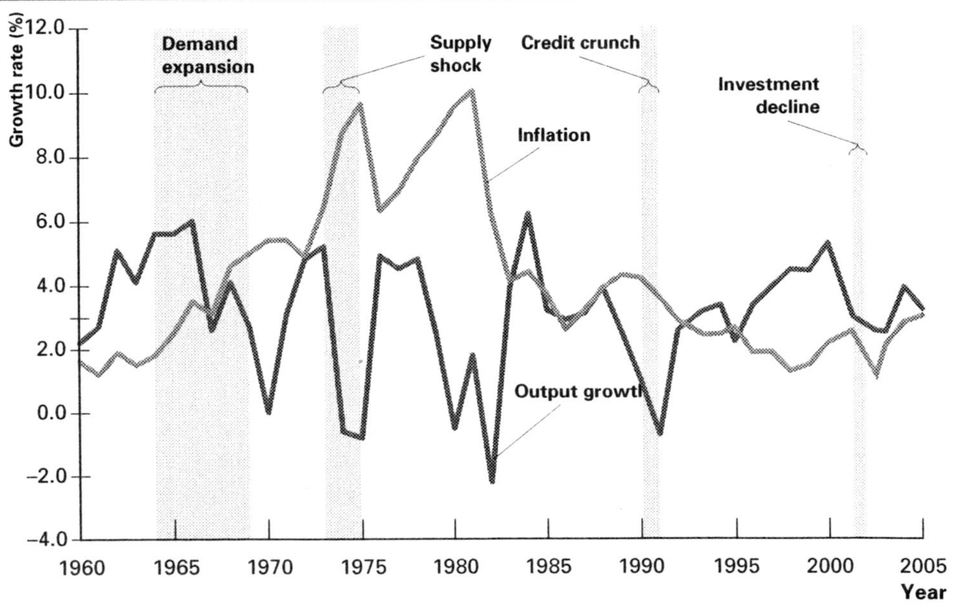

ing this recession. First, more stringent bank regulation reduced banks' ability to lend. Second, declines in real estate values and the large debt burdens of many corporations reduced banks' willingness to lend to borrowers at any expected real interest rate. Because households and small and medium-sized businesses weren't able to replace bank credit with funds from other sources, spending for consumer durable goods and business plant and equipment fell.

In *AD-AS* analysis, the decline in spending translates into a reduction in aggregate demand, shifting the *AD* curve to the left. Over time, the drop in aggregate demand puts downward pressure on prices, shifting the *SRAS* curve down. Figure 25.6 shows that output growth fell during the 1990–1991 recession and that inflation fell from 4.3% in 1989 to 2.9% in 1992. Some economists worried about the reemergence of such a credit crunch pattern in output growth and inflation in late 2000 and early 2001.

Investment and the 2001 Recession

The U.S. economic expansion that began in March 1991 ended exactly a decade later. The 2001 recession ended some time in November of that year, according to the National Bureau of Economic Research, the arbiter of U.S. business cycles. The principal contributing factor precipitating the recession was a decline in business investment. In the late 1990s, with high expected profitability of capital and the rapid growth of information technology investment surrounding Y2K issues, the U.S. economy accumulated more capital than businesspeople desired once expectations of future profitability declined after 2000. (The large decline in U.S. equity values in 2000 and 2001 reflected this drop in expected future profitability.) This excess of actual capital stock over desired capital stock implied that new business investment must fall sharply for a while. In *AD-AS* analysis, the decline in investment shifts the *AD* curve to the left, reducing both output growth and inflation during the recession, as Figure 25.6 shows.

The continued rapid pace of productivity growth during this period, leading to a rightward shift of the *AS* curve, cushioned the decline in output predicted by focusing on the *AD* shift. The *AS* shift also reinforced the disinflationary pressure from the drop in aggregate demand. Indeed, in 2002 and 2003, some economists worried that the United States could experience deflation, a falling general price level, though that did not occur.

Are Investment Incentives Inflationary?

In the late 1990s, many economists and policymakers urged consideration of tax reforms that would stimulate business investment. And in 2002, the Bush administration proposed and won Congressional approval for investment incentives. Such reforms included the introduction of expensing—in which businesses write off the purchase of new plant and equipment all at once, rather than gradually—and cuts in dividend and capital gains taxes that reduce the cost of capital. Many economists argued that such reforms would significantly increase business investment demand and output of capital goods. Would they also increase inflation?

In *AD-AS* analysis, the stimulus in investment translates into an increase in aggregate demand, shifting the *AD* curve to the right. However, as the new plant and equipment are installed, the economy's capacity to produce increases, and the *AS* curve shifts to the right, reducing the inflationary pressure from pro-investment tax reform. Recent evidence suggests that the supply response is potent and investment incentives are unlikely to be inflationary.

MOVING FROM THEORY TO PRACTICE . . .

THE WALL STREET JOURNAL NOVEMBER 29, 2006

Bernanke Warns Inflation Remains A Significant Risk

In a contrast with the widely held view on Wall Street that slower economic growth will lead to interest-rate cuts, Federal Reserve Chairman Ben Bernanke offered an upbeat assessment of the nation's economy, warning that tight labor markets could put more pressure on wages and prices.

a Many investors point to declining housing construction, mixed news on holiday sales and a tame reading on inflation as indications that the economy is weakening, inflation risks are fading and that the next move by the Fed will be to cut interest rates, perhaps as soon as next spring.

However, Mr. Bernanke's hawkish message suggests rate cuts are unlikely in the months to come.

In his first major speech on the economic outlook since his testimony to Congress in July, Mr. Bernanke said growth outside of housing and autos remains "solid," underlying inflation "uncomfortably high" and that the choice before the Fed is whether to raise rates, not whether to cut them. Since June, the central bank has held its target for short-term interest rates steady at 5.25%.

"A failure of inflation to moderate as expected would be especially troublesome," Mr. Bernanke told the National Italian American Foundation in New York yesterday. "Whether further policy action against inflation will be required depends on the incoming data."

b Yesterday, Mr. Bernanke spotlighted the labor market as a potential source of inflation pressure. "It seems clear that labor costs . . . have been rising more quickly of late. Some part of this acceleration no doubt reflects the current tightness in labor markets," he said.

The unemployment rate fell to 4.4% in October, well below the 4.75% to 5% range Fed officials had projected in July.

Charles Plosser, president of the Federal Reserve Bank of Philadelphia, reinforced the Fed's hawkish message yesterday in a speech at the University of Rochester in Rochester, N.Y. "There remains some risk that policy is not yet firm enough to ensure a return to price stability over a reasonable time horizon," he said.

c Economists themselves are divided on the outlook for the economy, with some predicting that a housing-led slowdown will intensify and others saying that low unemployment rates and buoyant financial markets will fuel a pickup in economic activity.

ANALYZING THE NEWS . . .

In the fall of 2006, many economists, businesspeople, and policymakers were concerned over the state of the U.S. economy. While the U.S. economy had been expanding rapidly over the past few years some began to worry as the rate of economic growth began to slow in the second half of 2006. Analysts were worried that increasing interest rates would reduce aggregate demand, pushing the economy into a recession, while others worried that there were growing inflationary pressures. We can use *AD-AS* analysis to explain these developments and see why there was a fear of a recession while at that same time a fear of growing inflation.

a Declining housing construction and weak holiday spending would suggest that overall consumer spending may be decreasing. As consumption falls, the aggregate demand curve shifts backward or toward the origin. If the short-run aggregate supply curve is upward-sloping, these reductions in aggregate demand would bring about reductions in the price level or reducing inflationary pressures.

b As described in the chapter, increases in labor costs result in the short-run aggregate supply curve shifting up and to the left. As producers face higher labor costs, all else equal, total output will fall while the price level will be pushed upward. In the fall of 2006, it appeared labor costs were increasing more rapidly than in earlier periods in part due to a lack of unemployed workers. As firms competed for these relatively scarce workers by offering higher wages, labor costs were pushed upward and the short-run aggregate supply curve shifted up and to the left.

c Economists were uncertain as to the net effects of all of these simultaneous changes. Part of the uncertainty centered on which impact would have a bigger impact. On the one hand, falling housing prices could reduce consumer confidence and thus reduce consumption. On the other hand, reduced unemployment rates and rising stock market prices could increase consumer confidence and thus increase consumption. Economists were uncertain as to the final outcome of these offsetting forces.

For further thought . . .

Suppose inflationary pressures continued to build in the U.S. economy and the Fed was forced to raise interest rates. Discuss the implications for both *AS* and *AD* in the United States.

Source: Excerpted from Greg Ip, Rafael Gerena-Morales, and Michael Corkery, "Bernanke Warns Inflation Remains A Significant Risk," *The Wall Street Journal*, November 29, 2006, p. A1

KEY TERMS AND CONCEPTS

Aggregate demand
Aggregate demand (*AD*) curve
Aggregate supply
Aggregate supply (*AS*) curve
Long-run aggregate supply (*LRAS*) curve
Short-run aggregate supply (*SRAS*) curve
Full employment output
Misperception theory
Monetary neutrality
New classical view
New Keynesian view
Real business cycle view
Supply shocks

SUMMARY

1. Aggregate demand represents the level of current output that households and firms are willing to purchase at a particular price level. Aggregate supply represents the amount of output that producers in the economy are willing to sell at a particular price level.
2. The aggregate demand (*AD*) curve illustrates the quantity of current output that is demanded at each price level. The price level and the aggregate quantity of output demanded are negatively related. Each point along the *AD* curve represents a combination of price level and aggregate output for which the goods and asset markets are in equilibrium. Factors that shift the *AD* curve include increases or decreases in the nominal money supply, money demand, determinants of desired saving, and determinants of desired investment.
3. The aggregate supply (*AS*) curve represents the quantity of output supplied at each price level. The long-run aggregate supply (*LRAS*) curve is vertical at the full employment level of output. Increases or decreases in the current productivity of factors of production shift the *LRAS* curve. The short-run aggregate supply (*SRAS*) curve slopes upward. In the new classical view, an unexpected increase in the aggregate price level increases the quantity of output that firms are willing to supply in the short run. In the new Keynesian view, the *SRAS* curve slopes upward because many firms have sticky prices and are willing to meet the demand for their output over a range from an initially stated price. In both new classical and new Keynesian views, shifts in the *SRAS* curve reflect shifts in the expected price level or costs of production.
4. The economy's short-run equilibrium output and price level occur at the intersection of the *AD* curve and the *SRAS* curve. The economy's long-run equilibrium occurs at the intersection of the *AD* curve and the *LRAS* curve.
5. Changes in the equilibrium price level and output can be explained by shifts in the aggregate demand curve, the aggregate supply curve, or both.

REVIEW QUESTIONS

1. Why is there a negative relationship between the price level and aggregate output along the *AD* curve?
2. Which of the following will shift the *AD* curve to the right?
   a. The Fed carries out an open market sale.
   b. The interest rate on checkable deposits falls.
   c. The federal government launches a massive program to rebuild the nation's highways.
   d. The federal government cuts the corporate profits tax.
3. Why does a rise in the price level increase aggregate output supplied in the short run, according to the new classical view?
4. What is meant by the term *price stickiness* in the new Keynesian view? What elements of the economy lead to price stickiness?
5. What is the slope of the long-run aggregate supply curve? Why does it have this slope?
6. What predictions do the new classical and new Keynesian views yield about monetary neutrality in the long run?
7. According to the new Keynesian view, what is the effect on output in the short run of an increase in government defense purchases?
8. What is a real business cycle? If a winter storm temporarily reduces agricultural output, which curves shift in the *AD-AS* diagram?

ANALYTICAL PROBLEMS

9. The derivation of the *AD* curve presented in the chapter depends on (for an increase in the price level) the impact of a rising real interest rate on the demand for real money balances. Suppose you believe Irving Fisher's formulation of the quantity theory of money and you do not believe that the real interest rate affects the demand for real money balances. Is it possible for you to give another rationale for a downward-sloping *AD* curve?
10. Using the new classical view and the *AD-AS* diagram, describe the effects on the price level and current output of an increase in the price of oil. How would your answer differ if the Fed increased the money supply to stimulate aggregate demand?
11. Suppose that the economy is initially in equilibrium at full employment. Then the government unexpectedly increases income taxes. What are the effects on output and the price level in the short run and the long run, according to the new Keynesian view?
12. The Fed today is often said to see price stability as its most important goal. Back in the 1964–1969 period the Fed increased the rate of growth of the money supply even though federal expenditures were rising rapidly and GDP was already near its full employment level. Why do you believe the Fed acted as it did during the late 1960s? If confronted with the same circumstances today, would the Fed be likely to react in the same way?
13. The chapter describes the aggregate demand shocks of 1964–1969 and the aggregate supply shocks of 1973–1975 and 1995–2006. Draw an *AD-AS* diagram to illustrate what happened during these years.
14. In the mid-1970s and again in the late 1970s, OPEC raised oil prices sharply. The higher cost of oil reduced the productivity of energy-using industries. Show what would happen to output and the price level in the short run according to the new Keynesian view.
15. One way in which misperception of the aggregate price level is thought to affect the economy is through the labor market. Suppose that the unemployment rate u is related to the rate of inflation π and the expected rate of inflation π^e, as follows:

$$\pi = 0.08 - 2u + \pi^e.$$

    a. If there is no misperception of inflation (so $\pi = \pi^e$), what is the unemployment rate (in percent)?
    b. If expected inflation is 8% and actual inflation is 4%, what is the unemployment rate?
    c. If expected inflation is 4% and actual inflation is 8%, what is the unemployment rate?
16. John Maynard Keynes stressed the role played by *animal spirits*—changes in the confidence or optimism of entrepreneurs and managers—in economic fluctuations. Suppose that a wave of optimism hits the U.S. business community. Describe the effects of aggregate demand and the price level in terms of the new Keynesian view.
17. Suppose that as a result of a vigorous "thrift campaign" by U.S. policymakers, the public increases its saving rate. In other words, at any particular combination of income and real interest rate, the public saves more income. Describe the short-run and long-run effects on output in terms of the new Keynesian view.
18. Because of an increase in the expected future productivity of capital, the stock market rises. Describe the effects on investment, current output, and future output in terms of the new classical view.
19. Many economists and policymakers worry that increased government purchases are not expansionary because they crowd out private investment spending. Using the derivation of the *AD* curve, explain the logic of this argument.
20. Suppose that Congress passes a law allowing all taxpayers to subtract \$500 from their tax bill while government spending remains unchanged. Assuming that the Ricardian equivalence proposition holds, describe the effect of this policy on aggregate demand.
21. Suppose that the President and Congress agree on an infrastructure program to raise federal spending on highways, bridges, and airports. Proponents of the program argue that it will increase productivity in the long run. Opponents of the program argue that it will reduce private investment in the short run. Using the *AD-AS* diagram, illustrate these positions.
22. The Fed can use expansionary or contractionary policy to shift the *AD* curve. Using the *AD-AS* diagram, illustrate how monetary policy should be used to return output to its full employment level when
    a. the *AD* curve intersects the *SRAS* curve to the left of the full employment level of output
    b. the *AD* curve intersects the *SRAS* curve to the right of the full employment level of output

23. Throughout the 1980s, the interest rate that banks' customers received on their deposits increased, owing in large part to improvements in computer and communications technologies. What effect did this development have on the *AD* curve? If it is not offset by other factors, what effect did this development have on the price level, assuming a vertical *LRAS* curve?

DATA QUESTIONS

24. Find the latest volume of the *Economic Report of the President* in your library and calculate the annual percentage change in the gross domestic product (in constant dollars) and in the price deflator for the gross domestic product. Using these two series, identify episodes in which shifts in aggregate demand are more important in explaining changes in output as well as episodes in which shifts in aggregate supply are more important.
25. Using data in the *Economic Report of the President*, calculate the growth rate of output per worker in the nonfarm business sector for three time periods: 1960–1969, 1973–1979, 1985–1990, and 1995–2000. Evaluate the implications of the patterns of growth in output per worker for shifts in the *LRAS* curve during the three periods.
26. The U.S. Department of Labor's Bureau of Labor Statistics collects information on the U.S. price level. At its data web site (http://www.bls.gov/data/home.htm) locate the reported inflation rates for all urban consumers ("U.S. All Items"). With the information provided, construct the average inflation rate for each year of the 1970s and then again for each year of the 1990s. Evaluate the probable effects of the reported inflation rate on (i) real interest rates, (ii) firm investment, (iii) the desire to hold real money balances, and (iv) the *AD* curve.
27. The U.S. Department of the Census' *Statistical Abstract* presents many useful statistics on the U.S. economy. Recent issues can be obtained at http://www.census.gov/compendia/statab/. Collect the most recent annual data that pertains to worker earnings and compensation and to employee benefits in the United States. Based on this information, what effect (all else equal) have these data had on the short-run aggregate supply curve?
28. During 2001, nominal U.S. gross domestic product fell. Access a recent issue of *Economic Indicators*, a monthly publication of the Council of Economic Advisers at http://www.gpoaccess.gov/indicators/browse.html that lists quarterly GDP data for that year. Did GDP increase for 2001? Which quarters experienced declines, and could the decline be attributed to changes in aggregate demand or aggregate supply, given the breakdown of GDP presented there? Using the AD-AS analysis, explain why the price level remained low during this time period (all else equal).

CHAPTER 17
THE MONEY SUPPLY PROCESS

In the fall of 1998, Edward Boehne, a Federal Reserve executive, knew the Fed had goofed. When he checked into a hotel in a small town in Pennsylvania, the clerk looked at his title and said, "You didn't do enough." By mid-November 1998, the Fed had intervened three times to expand the money supply. After the third time, investors reacted to the good news of the expansionary policy by buying stock, causing the U.S. stock market to rise. Business executives celebrated falling interest rates, which could stimulate spending for plant and equipment.

The money supply is an economic variable that has an impact on interest rates, exchange rates, inflation, and an economy's output of goods and services. Fluctuations in the money supply can affect returns on investments, the prices of goods and services, and general economic well-being. As a result, the central bank—whether it is the European Central Bank, the Fed in the United States, the Bank of Japan, or the Bank of England—attempts to manage the money supply. How does a central bank like the European Central Bank or the Fed do this? To answer this question, you must know what influences the money supply and how a central bank can increase or decrease the amount of money in circulation. Our goal in this chapter is to construct a model that explains the size and variation in the money supply. Specifically, we look at the **money supply process** in the United States.

We organize our investigation of the money supply process by first describing the monetary base and then identifying the factors that convert the monetary base to the money supply. Then we combine these variables to determine the money supply. Our model includes the behavior of three actors in the money supply process: the Fed, the banks in the banking system, and the nonbank public. The Fed plays the largest role in determining both the monetary base and the money multiplier—but the Fed doesn't have complete control over the money supply. The behavior of banks and the nonbank public is crucial to the quantity of money that circulates in the economy. Figure 17.1 represents the money supply process, the actions that determine the quantity of money in the economy. This figure also shows which actors in the economy primarily influence each variable. In a nutshell, this diagram shows the components of the model and is the backbone of our analysis in this chapter.

In building the model of the money supply process, we work with a very limited definition of money. "Money" is limited to assets that are used as a medium of exchange, specifically currency and checkable deposits in financial institutions. This monetary aggregate, *M1*, is the Fed's narrowest measure of money. The chapter appendix describes the money supply process for the next broadest measure of the money supply, *M2*.

The Fed and the Monetary Base

In addition to acting as a banker's bank, regulating the banking industry, and operating a network to clear checks, the Fed has another function. The Fed is the institution that is responsible for managing the nation's money supply. One way it does that is to

FIGURE 17.1

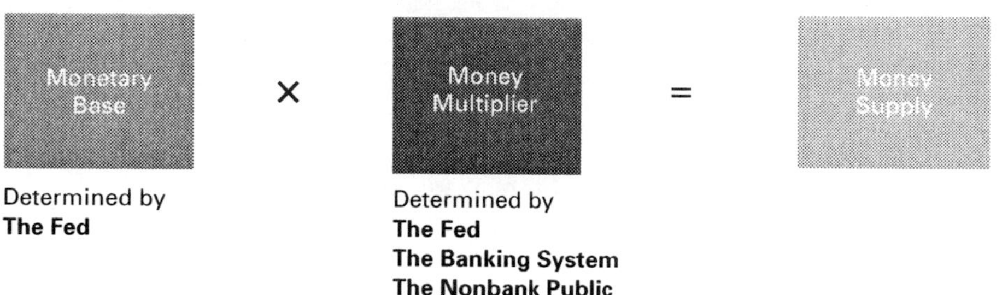

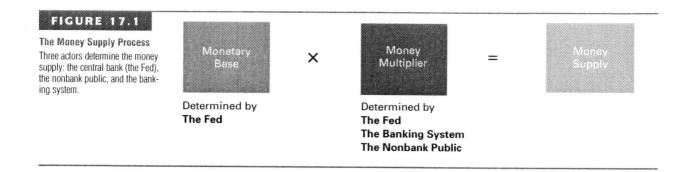

The Money Supply Process
Three actors determine the money supply: the central bank (the Fed), the nonbank public, and the banking system.

control the monetary base. The **monetary base** comprises all currency in circulation and reserves held by banks.

We start our investigation of the monetary base—the first variable in the money supply process—by identifying the assets and liabilities on the Fed's balance sheet that measure components of the monetary base. Then we look at actions of the Fed that cause these assets and liabilities to change, thereby increasing or decreasing the monetary base.

To observe how the Fed manages the monetary base, we work with a simplified balance sheet. Although the Fed's actual balance sheet is more complex than the one we introduce here, the four entries shown in the following balance sheet matter the most in identifying the Fed's actions to increase or decrease the monetary base.

BALANCE SHEET OF THE FEDERAL RESERVE SYSTEM

Assets	Liabilities
U.S. government securities	Currency in circulation
Discount loans to banks	Reserves

The Fed's Liabilities

The Fed's principal liabilities are currency in circulation and reserves (deposits by banks with the Fed and cash held by banks). The sum of these two liabilities, together with the monetary liabilities of the U.S. Treasury (primarily coins in circulation, called *Treasury currency in circulation*), equals the monetary base. We consider the monetary base to be the sum of the Fed's currency in circulation and reserves, because the monetary liabilities of the Treasury are so small:

$$\text{Monetary base} = \text{Currency in circulation} + \text{Reserves}.$$

The dollar bills in your wallet are *Federal Reserve Notes*. They are part of the Fed's currency outstanding, which includes currency in circulation and vault cash. Specifically, **currency in circulation** is the currency held by the nonbank public, and **vault cash** is the currency held by depository financial institutions. Vault cash is still a liability of the Fed, but it is counted as reserves:

$$\text{Currency in circulation} = \text{Currency outstanding} - \text{Vault cash}.$$

At the end of July 2006, currency in circulation equaled $792.6 billion.

Reserves. The second largest liability of the Fed is **bank reserves,** or vault cash in banks and deposits by commercial banks and savings institutions with the Fed. Reserve deposits are assets for financial institutions. They are liabilities for the Fed because the Fed must redeem banks' requests for repayment on demand in Federal Reserve Notes. The total reserves of the banking system are the sum of banks' deposit accounts with the Fed ($12.3 billion as of July 2006) and vault cash ($491.1 billion as of July 2006). Thus

Reserves = Deposits with the Fed by depository institutions + Vault cash.

We can also view reserves from the banks' perspective. Total reserves are made up of amounts that the Fed compels depository institutions to hold, called **required reserves,** and extra amounts that depository institutions elect to hold, called **excess reserves:**

Reserves = Required reserves + Excess reserves.

The Fed specifies a percentage of deposits that banks must hold as reserves, which is known as the **required reserve ratio.** For example, if the required reserve ratio is 10%, a bank would have to set aside 10% of its checkable deposits—combinations of vault cash and deposits with the Fed—as reserves with the Fed. As of July 2006, of the $44.2 billion of bank reserves, only about $1.5 billion was excess reserves. Because the Fed doesn't pay interest on reserves, depository institutions prefer not to hold all their liquid balances as reserves. Instead, they hold some of their balances in marketable securities, on which they can earn interest.

The Fed's Assets

The two principal Fed assets are government securities and discount loans. The levels of these assets held by the Fed are determinants of the monetary base. In addition, the Fed earns income on its portfolio of government securities and interest on its discount loans. The Fed does not pay interest on currency or reserves. Most of the Fed's substantial earnings are returned to the Treasury.

Government securities. The Fed's portfolio of government securities consists principally of holdings of U.S. Treasury obligations: Treasury bills, notes, and bonds. As of July 2006, the Fed held about $765 billion in Treasury securities.

Discount loans. By extending loans to depository institutions to help banks handle liquidity problems, the Fed can increase the level of reserves. It earns a market interest rate on the U.S. government securities that it holds as assets. When the Fed lends to depository institutions, the loans are called **discount loans.** In making such loans, the Fed specifies an interest rate on the loans known as the **discount rate.** As of July 2006, the Fed's outstanding discount loans totaled about $346 million. The discount rate at the same date was 6.25%.

How the Fed Changes the Monetary Base

The Fed increases or decreases the monetary base by manipulating the levels of its assets—that is, the Fed changes the monetary base by buying and selling Treasury securities or by making discount loans to banks. We describe the execution of these transactions in Chapter 20. In the description of the transactions that follows, we show how each changes the monetary base.

Open market operations. The most direct method the Fed uses to change the monetary base is **open market operations**—that is, buying or selling securities, generally U.S. government securities. In an **open market purchase,** which raises the monetary base, the Fed buys government securities. To execute such a transaction (for example, to buy \$1 million in government securities), the Fed draws checks totaling \$1 million on the Federal Reserve Bank of New York and uses them to buy the securities through banks or from the nonbank public. Commercial banks can redeem these checks for currency or, more likely, the banks can deposit the funds with the Fed as reserves. In either case, an open market purchase raises the monetary base, B, because the base is the sum of currency in circulation, C, and bank reserves, R. This relationship is expressed as

Web Site Suggestions: http://www.federalreserve.gov/releases/h3 Presents data on reserves and the monetary base.

$$B = C + R. \tag{17.1}$$

When bank reserves, R, increase, the monetary base, B, increases. The following transactions will illustrate how this change in B takes place.

Suppose that the Fed buys \$1 million in T-bills from Megabank and pays for them with a check for \$1 million. Megabank can either deposit the funds in its account with the Fed or hold them as vault cash. Either action increases the reserves in the banking system by \$1 million. The banking system's balance sheet shows a decrease in security holdings of \$1 million and an increase in reserves of the same amount:

BANKING SYSTEM

Assets		Liabilities	
Securities	−\$1 million		
Reserves	+\$1 million		

The changes in the Fed's balance sheet show an increase in securities (an asset) and an increase in reserves (a liability) by \$1 million:

FEDERAL RESERVE

Assets		Liabilities	
Securities	+\$1 million	Reserves	+\$1 million

The open market purchase from depository institutions increases reserves and thus the monetary base by \$1 million.

If the Fed purchases government securities from the nonbank public, sellers have two options: (1) to hold the proceeds as checkable deposits or (2) to hold the proceeds as currency. If the sellers deposit checks drawn on the Fed in the banking system, checkable deposits increase by \$1 million. When banks deposit the Fed's checks in their account with the Fed, reserves also rise by \$1 million:

NONBANK PUBLIC

Assets		Liabilities	
Securities	−\$1 million		
Checkable deposits	+\$1 million		

BANKING SYSTEM

Assets		Liabilities	
Reserves	+$1 million	Checkable deposits	+$1 million

As a result of the open market purchase, the Fed's portfolio of securities rises by $1 million, and bank reserves rise by the same amount:

FEDERAL RESERVE

Assets		Liabilities	
Securites	+$1 million	Reserves	+$1 million

As in the case of an open market purchase from depository institutions, this open market purchase from the nonbank public increases bank reserves by $1 million, thereby increasing the monetary base by $1 million.

If households and businesses decide to cash the Fed's checks and hold the proceeds as currency, the nonbank public decreases its holdings of securities by $1 million and increases its currency holdings by the same amount. The Fed increases currency in circulation by $1 million to acquire the $1 million of securities in the open market purchase:

NONBANK PUBLIC

Assets		Liabilities	
Securities	−$1 million		
Currency	+$1 million		

FEDERAL RESERVE

Assets		Liabilities	
Securites	+$1 million	Currency in circulation	+$1 million

While the proceeds from the sale of securities to the Fed are held as currency, the monetary base (the sum of currency in circulation and bank reserves) increases by the amount of the open market purchase, or $1 million.

To summarize, an open market purchase increases the monetary base by the amount of the purchase in all cases. The effect of the open market purchase on bank reserves depends on whether the nonbank public chooses to hold some of the proceeds as currency.

Similarly, the Fed can *reduce* the monetary base by an **open market sale** of government securities. Whether the securities are purchased with currency or with checkable deposits, an open market sale decreases the monetary base by the amount of the sale.

For example, suppose the Fed sells $1 million of securities to depository institutions or the nonbank public. If payments to the Fed are entirely in the form of checkable deposits, the Fed receives in payment $1 million in checks drawn on commercial banks. In this case, bank reserves with the Fed (a Fed liability) fall by $1 million, the

Fed's securities holdings (an asset for the Fed) also fall by $1 million, and the monetary base falls by $1 million:

BANKING SYSTEM

Assets		Liabilities	
Securities	+$1 million		
Reserves	−$1 million		

FEDERAL RESERVE

Assets		Liabilities	
Securites	−$1 million	Reserves	−$1 million

Thus, if payments to the Fed are entirely in checkable deposits, reserves (and the monetary base) decline by the amount of the open market sale.

However, if payments to the Fed are entirely in currency, the open market sale won't affect reserves:

NONBANK PUBLIC

Assets		Liabilities	
Securities	+$1 million		
Currency	−$1 million		

FEDERAL RESERVE

Assets		Liabilities	
Securites	−$1 million	Currency in circulation	−$1 million

However, the monetary base (currency in circulation plus reserves) falls by $1 million.

The effects of open market operations on reserves and the monetary base are summarized in Figure 17.2.

Discount loans. Although the Fed uses open market operations most often in managing the monetary base, it can also increase or decrease reserves by making discount loans to depository institutions. This change in bank reserves changes the monetary base.

Let's examine the balance sheets for both the banks and the Fed to see how the monetary base changes if banks obtain $1 million in discount loans from the Fed. For the Fed, assets rise by $1 million from the addition to discount loans, and liabilities rise by $1 million from the addition to bank reserves. Thus the discount loan affects both sides of the Fed's balance sheet:

FEDERAL RESERVE

Assets		Liabilities	
Discount loans	+$1 million	Reserves	+$1 million

Effect of Open Market Operations on Reserves and the Monetary Base

One method that the Fed uses to increase the monetary base is open market purchases of securities from the nonbank public or banks. The nonbank public holds the proceeds of the sale as currency (increasing currency in circulation) or deposits the proceeds in banks. Banks may choose to hold the proceeds as vault cash or deposit the proceeds in a Fed account, increasing reserves in either case. Because increases in currency in circulation or in reserves raise the monetary base, open market purchases increase the monetary base. The process of reducing the monetary base (not shown here) works in reverse.

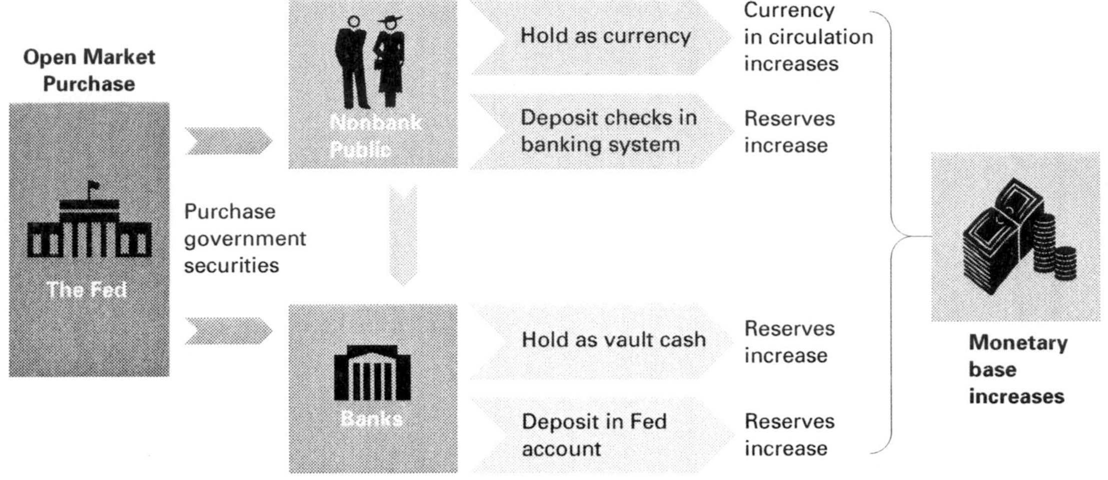

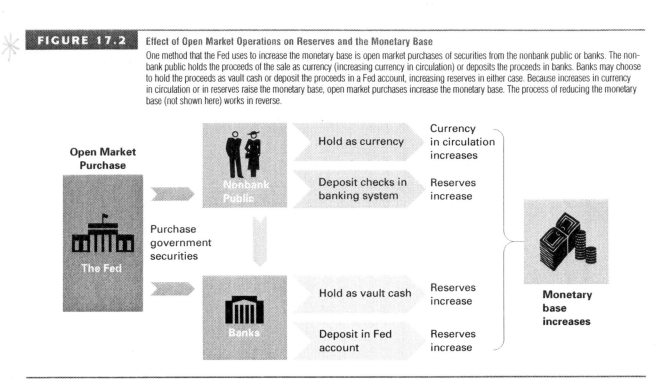

Both sides of the banking system's balance sheet are also affected. Banks acquire $1 million of assets in the form of reserves and $1 million of liabilities in the form of discount loans payable to the Fed:

BANKING SYSTEM

Assets		Liabilities	
Reserves	+$1 million	Discount loans	+$1 million

As a result of the Fed's making $1 million of discount loans, bank reserves and the monetary base increase by $1 million.

However, if banks repay $1 million in discount loans to the Fed, the preceding transactions are reversed. Reserves fall by $1 million, as do the Fed's discount loans (assets) and the banking system's discount loans (liabilities):

FEDERAL RESERVE

Assets		Liabilities	
Discount loans	−$1 million	Reserves	−$1 million

BANKING SYSTEM

Assets		Liabilities	
Reserves	−$1 million	Discount loans	−$1 million

The effects of discount loans on reserves and the monetary base are summarized in Figure 17.3.

FIGURE 17.3 **Effect of Discount Loans on Reserves and the Monetary Base**

A second method for the Fed to increase the monetary base is through discount loans. The Fed does not control completely the volume of discount loans; it can reduce the discount rate, but banks must decide whether to borrow from the Fed. If banks choose to borrow from the Fed, reserves increase, increasing the monetary base. The process of reducing the monetary base using discount loans (not shown here) works in reverse.

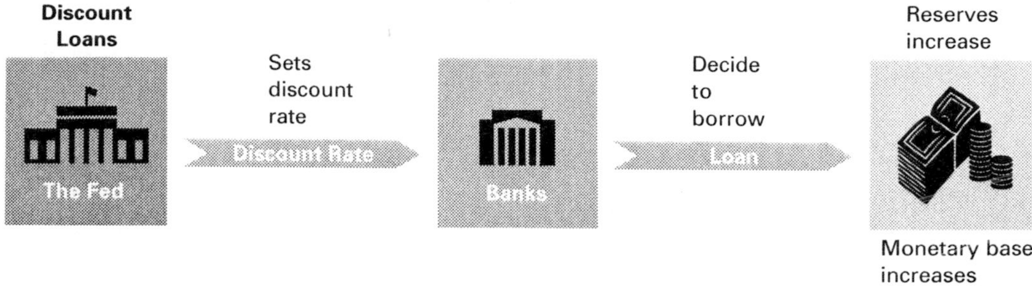

Comparing Open Market Operations and Discount Loans

Although open market operations and discount loans both change the monetary base, the Fed has greater control over open market operations than over discount loans. The Fed completely controls the volume of open market operations because it initiates purchases or sales of securities by placing orders with dealers in the government securities markets. Of course, if the Fed wants to sell a T-bill, someone must buy it or there is no open market operation. The Fed can sell securities at whatever price it takes to accomplish its goal, however.

The Fed's control over discount lending is much less complete than its control over open market operations because banks decide whether to borrow from the Fed. The Fed has some control over discount loans because it sets the discount rate. In fact, the discount rate differs from most interest rates because it is set by the Fed, whereas most interest rates are determined by market forces. An increase in the discount rate makes borrowing from the Fed more expensive for banks. If nothing else changes, banks then decrease their discount borrowing, which in turn reduces the monetary base. Hence decisions by both banks and the Fed determine the volume of discount loans.

Historically, the discount rate typically was lower than other short-term market interest rates, such as the federal funds rate or the rate on three-month T-bills. (The federal funds rate is the rate that banks charge each other on overnight loans.) Thus banks had a profit opportunity in that they can borrow from the Fed at the discount rate and lend the funds at higher rates. However, the Fed discourages banks from borrowing from it too often. Now, the discount rate exceeds the federal funds rate.

As a result of the difference in the Fed's control over open market operations and discount loans, we think of the monetary base as having two components: the *nonborrowed monetary base*, B_{non}, and *borrowed reserves*, BR, or discount loans. We can express the monetary base, B, as

$$B = B_{non} + BR. \tag{17.2}$$

Although decisions by both the Fed and depository institutions determine the volume of discount loans, the Fed has greater control over the nonborrowed monetary base. In Chapter 18, we discuss in more detail the components of the monetary base and the Fed's ability to control each component.

CHECKPOINT

Which has a greater impact on the monetary base: an open market purchase of $10 million or a discount loan of $10 million? How do bank reserves change in each case? In each case, the monetary base rises by $10 million. The effect on bank reserves of an open market operation depends on how much currency the public chooses to hold. In the case of a discount loan, reserves rise by the amount of the loan. ♦

The Simple Deposit Multiplier

We now turn to the money multiplier in our quest to determine the factors that contribute to the money supply. The analysis proceeds in three steps because the money multiplier is determined not only by the Fed, but also by the actions of the nonbank public and banks in the banking system. The first step, which we describe in this section, shows how the money supply can be increased or decreased through multiple deposit creation. In this part of the analysis, we determine the simple deposit multiplier—a factor that converts the monetary base into a portion of the money supply. The second step adds the actions of the nonbank public on the money multiplier, and the third includes the actions of banks. In the sections that follow, we describe those steps and refine the simple deposit multiplier to find the money multiplier.

Multiple Deposit Expansion

What happens when the Fed increases bank reserves through open market operations or discount loans? To answer this question, we trace the changes that occur in a single bank and in the banking system.

How a bank responds to an increase in reserves. Suppose that the Fed purchases $100,000 in T-bills from Megabank, increasing Megabank's reserves by $100,000. After this transaction, Megabank's balance sheet changes to reflect these transactions:

MEGABANK

Assets		Liabilities
Securities	−$100,000	
Reserves	+$100,000	

The Fed's purchase of Megabank's T-bills increases Megabank's excess reserves, not its required reserves. The reason is that required reserves are determined as a percentage of the bank's checkable deposits. Because this transaction has no effect on Megabank's checkable deposits, it doesn't change the amount of reserves that Megabank is required to hold. Megabank earns no interest on the additional reserves obtained from the T-bill sale and will therefore try to use them to earn a return.

Suppose that Megabank loans $100,000 to Amalgamated Industries, thereby acquiring an asset on which it earns interest. Megabank extends the loan by creating a checking account for Amalgamated and depositing the loan proceeds in it. Both the asset and liability sides of Megabank's balance sheet increase by $100,000:

MEGABANK

Assets		Liabilities	
Securities	−$100,000	Checkable deposits	+$100,000
Reserves	+$100,000		
Loans	+$100,000		

Recall that the money supply equals currency in circulation plus checkable deposits (the definition of *M1*). By lending money to Amalgamated, Megabank creates checkable deposits. As a result of Megabank's actions, the money supply increases because checkable deposits have increased. Money is created because something that becomes money—namely, funds in the hands of the borrower—is exchanged for something that is not money—namely, a loan note in the hands of the lender.

Suppose that the required reserve ratio established by the Fed is 10%. That is, 10% of Megabank's checkable deposits must be held in cash reserves either at the Fed or as vault cash. Because Megabank increased its reserves by $100,000 and its deposits by $100,000, it must hold ($100,000)(0.10) = $10,000 as reserves. It now has additional excess reserves of $100,000 − (0.10)(100,000) = $90,000. However, the bank can't lend this amount because Amalgamated will be withdrawing its loan proceeds to buy goods and services supplied by other businesses and individuals. When Amalgamated has withdrawn the entire proceeds of the loan, Megabank will have lost $100,000 of reserves and checkable deposits:

MEGABANK

Assets		Liabilities	
Securities	−$100,000	Checkable deposits	$0
Loans	+$100,000		
Reserves	$0		

How the banking system responds to an increase in reserves. When Amalgamated writes checks to other businesses and individuals, these recipients deposit the proceeds in other banks—and those banks, in turn, make new loans. Thus the $100,000 increase in reserves from the Fed's purchase of securities from a single bank has expanded the volume of checkable deposits in the banking system. This process is called **multiple deposit expansion.** How much can other banks lend from an increase in their reserves? Because borrowers are likely to withdraw loan proceeds, banks cannot lend a greater amount than their total excess reserves. Nevertheless, multiple deposit expansion extends the monetary base and increases the money supply, as we describe in the following examples.

Suppose that Amalgamated uses the $100,000 it borrowed from Megabank to buy $100,000 of equipment from Toolco. Toolco deposits the $100,000 in its bank, Onebank. After this transaction, Onebank's balance sheet changes as follows:

ONEBANK

Assets		Liabilities	
Reserves	+$100,000	Checkable deposits	+$100,000

CONSIDER THIS . . .

What Are the Origins of Multiple Deposit Expansion?

Multiple deposit expansion increased the money supply long before the founding of the Federal Reserve System. Indeed, we trace the safekeeping of money (say, gold or silver) using a deposit contract to Greek and Roman times. However, the earliest banks served only as warehouses for funds; that is, bankers did not make loans from deposits.

By the thirteenth and fourteenth centuries, deposit banking was well established in Italy and Spain, countries that were heavily engaged in trade and commerce. Merchant bankers there loaned money to businesses and maintained reserves to cover depositors' withdrawals. In Barcelona, for example, banks typically held reserves in gold of less than 30% of deposits. This system of banking, known as *fractional reserve banking*, was a significant step toward a more sophisticated financial system.

Although the Roman Catholic Church objected to charging interest on loans financed by deposits, a practice it called *usury*, the importance of deposit banking for commerce overcame those objections. Indeed, "a banker's social standing in thirteenth-century Florence was probably at least as good as in twentieth-century New York."† Deposit expansion, then and now, enables a greater volume of loans and deposits to be supported by a given level of bank reserves.

† Sidney Homer and Richard Sylla, *A History of Interest Rates*. New Brunswick, N.J.: Rutgers University Press, 1991, pp. 76–77.

Onebank's reserves have increased by $100,000. If the required reserve ratio is 10%, Onebank now has additional excess reserves of $90,000. Because Onebank can safely lend only this amount of excess reserves, it makes a $90,000 loan to Midtown Hardware to purchase new office equipment. Initially, Onebank's assets (loans) and liabilities (checkable deposits) rise by $90,000; but when Midtown spends the loan proceeds, Onebank's balance sheet changes as follows:

ONEBANK

Assets		Liabilities	
Reserves	+$10,000	Checkable deposits	+$100,000
Loans	+$90,000		

Midtown Hardware withdraws $90,000 to buy office equipment from Computer Universe. Computer Universe deposits the $90,000 in its bank, Twobank:

TWOBANK

Assets		Liabilities	
Reserves	+$90,000	Checkable deposits	+$90,000

Now, checkable deposits in the banking system have risen by another $90,000. In total, the volume of deposits has risen by $100,000 at Onebank and $90,000 at Twobank, for a total of $190,000.

Twobank faces the same decisions that confronted Megabank and Onebank. It wants to use the increase in reserves to expand its loans, but it can prudently lend only the increase in excess reserves. With a required reserve ratio of 10%, Twobank must add ($90,000)(0.10) = $9000 to its required reserves and can lend only $81,000. Twobank lends the $81,000 to Howard's Barber Shop for remodeling. Initially, Twobank's assets (loans) and liabilities (checkable deposits) rise by $81,000; but when Howard's spends the loan proceeds, Twobank's balance sheet changes as follows:

TWOBANK

Assets		Liabilities	
Reserves	+\$9,000	Checkable deposits	+\$90,000
Loans	+\$81,000		

If the proceeds of the loan to Howard's Barber Shop are deposited in another bank, checkable deposits in the banking system will have risen by another \$81,000. The \$100,000 increase in reserves supplied by the Fed has increased the level of checkable deposits by \$100,000 + \$90,000 + \$81,000 = \$271,000. The money supply is growing with each loan. The initial increase of the monetary base changes the money supply by a multiple of that amount.

The process still isn't complete. The recipient of the \$81,000 check from Howard's Barber Shop will redeposit it, and checkable deposits at other banks expand. The process continues to ripple through the banking system and the economy, as Table 17.1 shows. Note that new checkable deposits continue to be created each time money is redeposited and loaned but that the increment gets smaller each time. The reason is that part of the money at each step cannot be lent; banks must hold it as reserves. As long as each bank lends the full amount of its excess reserves, we can calculate the amount of money created by the Fed's initial \$100,000 purchase of securities. The change in deposits, ΔD, is related to the initial change in reserves, ΔR, as follows:

$$\begin{aligned}\text{Change in deposits} &= \text{Loan to Amalgamated} + \text{Loan to Midtown}\\ &\quad + \text{Loan to Howard's} + \cdots\end{aligned}$$

or

$$\begin{aligned}\Delta D &= \Delta R + \Delta R[1 - (\overline{R/D})] + \Delta R[1 - (\overline{R/D})]^2 + \cdots\\ &= \$100{,}000 + \$100{,}000(1 - 0.10) + \$100{,}000(1 - 0.10)^2 + \cdots\end{aligned}$$

where

$$\begin{aligned}D &= \text{deposits}\\ R &= \text{reserves, and}\\ \overline{R/D} &= \text{the required reserve ratio.}\end{aligned}$$

TABLE 17.1 **Multiple Deposit Expansion for the Fed's Purchase of \$100,000 in Government Securities from Megabank and a Required Reserve Ratio of 10%**

Bank	Increase in deposits	Increase in loans	Increase in reserves
Onebank	\$ 100,000	\$ 90,000	\$ 10,000
Twobank	90,000	81,000	9,000
Nextbank3	81,000	72,900	8,100
Nextbank4	72,900	65,610	7,290
Nextbank5	65,610	59,049	6,561
.	.	.	.
.	.	.	.
.	.	.	.
	\$1,000,000	\$900,000	\$100,000

We can restate the relationship between the change in the level of checkable deposits and the change in the level of reserves by simplifying the preceding equation. The change in checkable deposits equals the change in reserves multiplied by the **simple deposit multiplier,** which is the reciprocal of the required reserve ratio:

$$\Delta D = \Delta R\left\{\frac{1}{1 - [1 - (\overline{R/D})]}\right\} = \Delta R\left(\frac{1}{\overline{R/D}}\right), \tag{17.3}$$

or, in our example,

$$\Delta D = 100{,}000\left(\frac{1}{0.10}\right) = \$1{,}000{,}000.$$

Eventually, the increase in reserves of $100,000 leads to a tenfold expansion of checkable deposits. Thus the volume of checkable deposits expands by a factor equal to the reciprocal of the required reserve ratio, in this case 1/0.10 = 10.

If a depository institution decides to invest all or some of its excess reserves in marketable securities, deposit expansion still results in the same relationship between the change in reserves and the change in deposits. Suppose that Onebank had decided to purchase $90,000 worth of Treasury bills instead of extending the $90,000 loan to Midtown. Onebank would write a check to the owner of the securities in the amount of $90,000, which the seller would deposit in the banking system, and so on. Thus the effect on multiple deposit expansion is the same whether banks use excess reserves to make loans or buy securities.

At first you might think that individual banks are creating money. However, an individual bank can lend only the amount of its reserves that exceeds the amount it wants (or is required) to maintain. Deposits are expanded or created when borrowers do not hold the proceeds of loans as currency. If funds are redeposited, money flows back into the banking system as reserves. If banks do not want to hold excess reserves, the multiple deposit expansion process ends only when all excess reserves have been eliminated. Multiple deposit expansion refers to the banking system as a whole, not to the action of an individual bank.

CHECKPOINT

Suppose that, in Nationia, bank reserves equal $10 million and the required reserve ratio is 10%. If citizens of Nationia do not hold currency, how large is the stock of checkable deposits (if banks hold no excess reserves)?

$$D = \frac{R}{\overline{R/D}}$$

$$= \frac{\$10 \text{ million}}{0.10} = \$100 \text{ million}.$$

What will happen to the level of checkable deposits if the central bank of Nationia increases the level of bank reserves by $500,000?

$$\Delta D = \Delta R\left(\frac{1}{R/D}\right)$$

$$= \frac{\$500{,}000}{0.10} = \$5 \text{ million.}$$

The level of checkable deposits rises by $5 million. ◆

Multiple Deposit Contraction

The Fed expands the volume of checkable deposits in the banking system by increasing reserves. Similarly, it can *contract* the volume of such deposits in the banking system by reducing reserves. The Fed does so by selling government securities in an open market operation. This action has a ripple effect that is similar to deposit expansion in the banking system, but in the opposite direction. The result of the open market sale is **multiple deposit contraction.**

Suppose that the Fed sells $100,000 in Treasury securities to Megabank, thereby reducing Megabank's reserves by $100,000. If Megabank has not maintained any excess reserves, it cannot now meet its reserve requirement. Megabank continually makes loans, and loans continually come due. Megabank can, if it has to, call some loans—that is, not renew them. By doing so, Megabank replenishes its reserves and can thus meet withdrawals. To raise reserves, then, Megabank could demand repayment of $100,000 of loans but could also sell $100,000 of securities. In either case, Megabank gains the needed $100,000 of reserves. In the process, however, another bank loses reserves and checkable deposits. For example, if a depositor at Onebank buys $100,000 of securities from Megabank, Onebank's reserves and checkable deposits fall by $100,000.

When it loses $100,000 in checkable deposits to Megabank (with a required reserve ratio of 10%), Onebank's required reserves decline by $10,000. Hence it must increase its reserves by $100,000 − $10,000 = $90,000. Onebank now faces the problem that Megabank experienced. If it has no excess reserves, it will have $90,000 less reserves than it needs to satisfy the reserve requirement. As a result, Onebank must sell securities or demand repayment of loans to raise its reserves by $90,000.

ONEBANK

Assets		Liabilities	
Reserves	−$10,000	Checkable deposits	−$100,000
Securities } Loans	−$90,000		

Onebank's contraction will ripple through the banking system to other banks. Suppose that the $90,000 that Onebank receives for its securities (or from loan repayments) is a check drawn on Twobank. Remember that Onebank faced a required reserves shortfall as a result of the loss of reserves to Megabank. The same problem now confronts

Twobank. Twobank's required reserves are insufficient by \$90,000 − (0.10)(\$90,000), or \$81,000.

Our examination of multiple deposit expansion showed that an increase in reserves is multiplied in the banking system. Similarly, a decrease in reserves is multiplied in the banking system, resulting in multiple deposit contraction. If we assume that banks hold only required reserves, the reduction in deposits in the banking system because of the decrease in reserves is equal to the change in reserves multiplied by the reciprocal of the required reserve ratio:

$$\Delta D = \Delta R\left(\frac{1}{R/D}\right)$$

This is the same formula that we developed for multiple deposit expansion.

Multiple deposit expansion and multiple deposit contraction result from the actions of many banks in the banking system, not from the actions of one bank. As you can see from the examples, banks are a link between the Fed and the nonbank public, taking the increase in reserves from the central bank and funneling them to the nonbank public—and, in the process, increasing the money supply.

The Money Multiplier and Decisions of the Nonbank Public

The simple deposit multiplier illustrates how a change in the monetary base results in a change in the money supply—but it is not the complete story. In deriving the simple deposit multiplier, we made an assumption that individuals and businesses held all their money as checkable deposits and that all excess reserves are loaned out. But everyone holds some money in cash, and banks do not always lend out their excess reserves. The behavior of individuals, the nonbank public, and banks changes the prediction of how the monetary base is multiplied to become the money supply. In this section, we look at the decisions that the nonbank public make that influence the money multiplier; in the next section, we look at the decisions of banks. You may read in the financial press that "the Fed controls the money supply." This statement is not quite correct, as you will soon see. The Fed acts to set the monetary base, but the behavior of the nonbank public and banks also influences the money supply.

The money supply equals currency in circulation and checkable deposits, which we represent by the now familiar equation:

$$M = C + D.$$

The amounts held as checkable deposits, D, are subject to multiple deposit creation; the amounts held as currency, C, are not. Therefore the money supply is likely to expand at a greater rate if the nonbank public has large holdings of D relative to C. We can express the proportion of cash to checkable deposits in a measure called the **currency–deposit ratio** (C/D). However, before demonstrating that a low value of the currency–deposit ratio increases the money supply, we examine how and why the currency–deposit ratio has changed over time. The ratio generally declined from the late nineteenth century through the mid-1960s, except during World War I, the early 1930s, and World War II. Beginning in the late 1960s, C/D began to rise steadily.

Determinants of Portfolio Choice

The decision the nonbank public makes on how to allocate liquid deposits between currency and checkable deposits is an example of portfolio allocation. As in our analysis in Chapter 5, we can predict how individuals make this decision according to their wealth as well as characteristics of each asset.

Wealth. One decision that the nonbank public makes is how much of its wealth to hold in the form of currency. Currency is a *necessity* asset. The proportion of wealth held in currency doesn't increase as a person gets richer. In other words, a typical wealthy individual will hold more currency than a not-so-wealthy individual will, but the wealthy person will not hold proportionately more. The reason is that checkable deposits are safer and more efficient for payment than holding larger amounts of currency. Hence an individual's currency–deposit ratio declines with increases in income and wealth. Moreover, for the economy as a whole, as the economy grows and national wealth increases, the currency–deposit ratio, *C/D*, declines. This change in national wealth explains the pattern of declining *C/D* before World War I, between the two world wars (except for the early 1930s), and after World War II until the early 1960s. These were periods of relatively steady economic growth, and therefore *C/D* decreased.

Expected returns. In choosing to hold currency or checkable deposits, the nonbank public compares the expected returns on these assets. The demand for an asset (in this case, currency or checkable deposits) depends on its expected return relative to expected returns on assets with similar risk, liquidity, and information characteristics. Because holding currency yields no interest, an increase in the interest paid on checkable deposits decreases the demand for currency relative to checkable deposits, decreasing *C/D*. A decrease in interest rates paid on checkable deposits increases *C/D*. Between 1933 and 1980, banking regulations prohibited banks from paying interest on checkable deposits; since 1980, regulations have allowed interest-bearing checkable deposits. As a result, the nonbank public is more likely to hold checkable deposits than cash.

Risk. Most often, there is little difference in the default risk of holding currency and checkable deposits. During a banking panic, however, there is a difference in the risk of currency versus checkable deposits. The return from holding currency is 0% in nominal terms, whereas holding checkable deposits in a failed bank can lead to a negative return. Therefore in times of crisis in the banking industry, we would expect to find an increased currency–deposit ratio. Indeed, in the early 1930s, when the public lost confidence in the banking system, depositors converted checkable deposits into currency, increasing *C/D*. Since the 1930s, most bank deposits have been covered (within limits) by federal deposit insurance. Reassured that their checkable deposits are safe, the nonbank public is less likely to include default risk in comparing currency with checkable deposits.

Liquidity. Currency is the most liquid asset possible because Federal Reserve Notes are definitive money in the United States. Checkable deposits by definition are convertible on demand into currency. Therefore the nonbank public doesn't generally consider liquidity differences when allocating how much currency to hold relative to checkable deposits.

Information cost. At first, the costs of obtaining information about currency and checkable deposits might seem to be identical. After all, no information is required to assess the value of currency, and with federal deposit insurance and bank supervision, individual depositors need little information to assess the value of checkable deposits. Nevertheless, there is an important difference between the two assets: currency holdings are anonymous, whereas checkable deposits aren't. In other words, when you hold your money as checkable deposits, you leave a trail of information, but how much currency you hold would be very difficult for someone to discover. Currency thus carries an *anonymity premium*, meaning that it has a higher value than checkable deposits for its usefulness in illegal activities, such as drug transactions, black-market sales, and tax avoidance. The anonymity premium can help to explain two patterns observed during the twentieth century. First, the increase in *C/D* during wars, such as World Wars I and II, reflects the use of currency in black-market activities and high income tax rates during the war years. Second, from the late 1960s until the present, there has been a steady increase in *C/D*. Economists point to high marginal income tax rates during the 1960s—providing an incentive for individuals to accept untaxed cash—and the apparent increase in illegal activity in the drug trade during the 1980s and 1990s as reasons for this reversal. Analysts refer to economic activity and income earned but not reported to taxing authorities as the *underground economy.*

There is good reason to estimate a sizable underground economy in the United States because the amount of currency outstanding for every person in the country is more than $1000. Few individuals hold that much cash at any time, so it seems plausible that large amounts of cash are circulating in the underground economy to finance illicit activities or to avoid taxes. In fact, some experts estimate that the underground economy may account for more than 10% of total U.S. economic activity. In a $12 trillion U.S. economy, this amount would be more than $1 trillion. Collecting tax revenue from underground economic activity would sharply reduce the federal budget deficit. Significant amounts of U.S. currency also circulate as low-information-cost assets abroad—in Russia, for example.

If the underground economy, by definition, isn't measured, how can we estimate its size? Using what we know about the determinants of currency holdings by the nonbank public, we can trace movements in *C/D* to the underground economy. For example, an increase in marginal tax rates or the imposition of rationing (as in wartime) would increase the anonymity value of currency and hence *C/D*. Conversely, legalization of drugs, prostitution, or gambling would decrease the need for currency for underground transactions, reducing *C/D*.

Concluding Remarks

Table 17.2 summarizes the decisions the nonbank public makes in choosing currency over checkable deposits, and it shows the impact of these decisions on the currency–deposit ratio. The currency–deposit ratio represents a portfolio allocation decision by the nonbank public. Currency holdings relative to checkable deposits are influenced by the determinants of portfolio choice: wealth and expected returns adjusted for risk, liquidity, and information-cost characteristics.

TABLE 17.2 Determinants of the Currency–Deposit Ratio

An increase in . . .	Causes *C/D* to . . .	Because . . .
wealth	fall	in general, *C/D* decreases with rising income and wealth in the economy.
expected returns on deposits	fall	an increase in interest rates offered on checkable deposits increases the public's demand for those deposits relative to currency and decreases *C/D*.
riskiness of deposits	rise	under normal circumstances, default risk does not affect *C/D*. During banking panics, an increase in the perceived riskiness of deposits increases *C/D*.
liquidity of deposits	no change	under normal circumstances, there is little difference in the liquidity of currency and checkable deposits and thus little or no effect on *C/D*.
information or anonymity value of cash	rise	an increase in the demand for anonymity, owing to black-market, tax evasion, other illegal activities, or desirability abroad increases *C/D*.

CHECKPOINT

In each of the following cases, what would you expect to happen to the currency–deposit ratio?

(a) Interest rates on checkable deposits rise.

(b) Higher tax rates prompt increased underground activity.

(c) A tremendous wave of counterfeit bills hits the United States.

Answers:

(a) Expected return on deposits rises, so *C/D* falls.

(b) Increased underground activity raises demand for currency, so *C/D* rises.

(c) Increased risk of currency reduces demand for currency, so *C/D* falls. ♦

Bank Behavior: Excess Reserves and Discount Loans

In addition to assuming that the nonbank public holds all its currency in checkable deposits when constructing the simple deposit multiplier, we assumed that banks held no excess reserves. (Excess reserves, you will recall, are reserves greater than those required by the Fed.) But banks sometimes hold excess reserves in vault cash or deposits with the Fed. When banks hold reserves, the size of the money multiplier is less than the simple deposit multiplier would suggest. Like the nonbank public, banks make portfolio allocation decisions that determine whether they will hold excess reserves or use them to make loans or investments. In addition, banks must decide whether to borrow from the Fed, and their decisions to incur discount loans also affect the amount of the monetary base that the Fed controls.

Excess Reserves

How do banks determine how much excess reserves to hold relative to their deposits? The principal determinant is the expected return from holding excess reserves as compared to the return on alternative uses of the funds. Because reserves deposited with the Fed pay no interest, the opportunity cost of holding excess reserves is the market interest rate—the rate that the bank could obtain by lending or investing its funds.

Figure 17.4 shows that banks hold generally small levels of excess reserves, but the amount of excess reserves fluctuates over time. In the early 1980s, when market interest rates were high, banks decreased their excess reserves. An increase in market interest rates, all else being equal, decreases excess reserves; a decrease in the market interest rate increases excess reserves. In other words, holdings of excess reserves by banks are inversely related to the market interest rate.

The reason banks hold excess reserves despite the opportunity cost has to do with Fed–bank relationships. The Fed stipulates certain reserve requirements, but it discourages banks from frequent borrowing at the discount rate to satisfy reserve requirements. When a bank's reserve holdings are insufficient, the Fed may impose penalties. Such penalties include a penalty rate on discount loans needed to satisfy the reserve requirement and a "stern discussion." To avoid relying on discount borrowing to satisfy reserve requirements, banks hold small amounts of excess reserves. In addition, when banks overestimate withdrawals expected from depositors, they end up with reserves in excess of those required.

An even more important reason for banks to hold excess reserves is that they serve as a cushion against high expected deposit outflows or significant variability in deposit outflows. Without this cushion, if deposit withdrawals exceeded reserves, a bank would be forced to bear the costs in one of three ways: (1) by selling securities, (2) by calling in loans, or (3) by borrowing from the Fed or in the open market. In extreme cases, the bank could fail. Hence the benefit of excess reserves as a cushion against

FIGURE 17.4

Excess Reserves and Discount Loans (1959–2006)

Banks hold some reserves in excess of their required reserves. Discount loans represent reserves borrowed by banks from the Fed.

Source: Federal Reserve Bulletin, various issues. See also http://research.stlouisfed.org/fred2/series/BORROW, and http://research.stlouisfed.org/fred2/series/EXCRESNS?7cid=45.

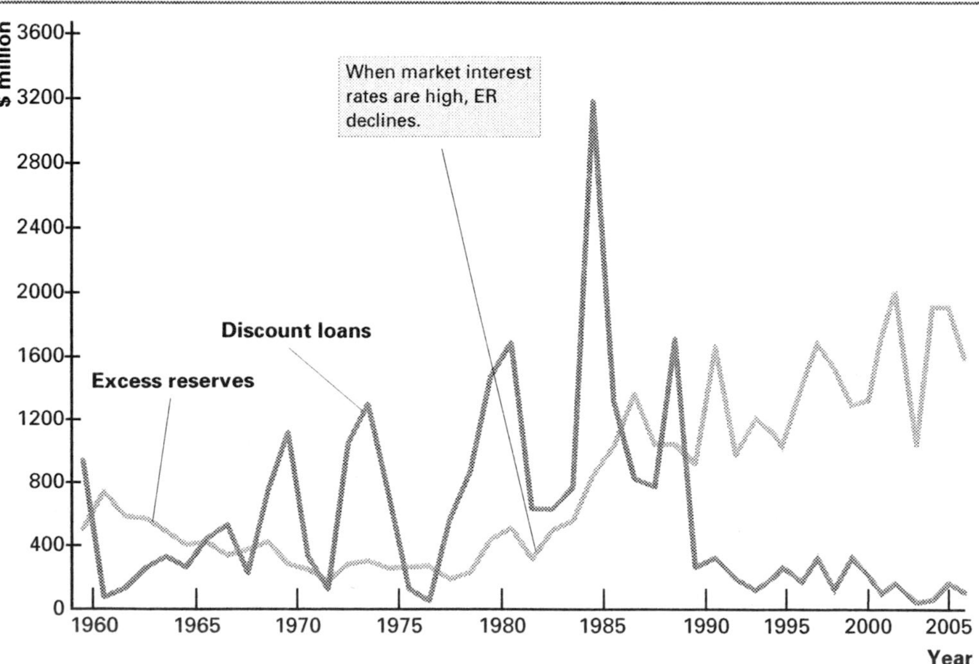

deposit outflows can outweigh the opportunity cost of other uses of those funds. As an example, banks maintained high excess reserve holdings during the early 1930s to ensure that they could satisfy future deposit withdrawals. The theory of portfolio allocation predicts that an increase in the expected level or variability of deposit outflows increases excess reserves. Conversely, a decrease in the expected level or variability of deposit outflows decreases excess reserves. Thus the level of excess reserves in the banking system is positively related to the expected level or variability of deposit outflows.

Discount Loans

The Fed makes discount loans available to banks, but the level of loans is determined by the banks themselves. Banks are more inclined to borrow from the Fed when the market interest rate they can earn on their loans and investments is greater than the discount rate. Banks are less likely to borrow from the Fed when the spread between the market interest rate and the discount rate is small. Hence discount borrowing by banks is positively related to the market interest rate and negatively related to the discount rate. When market interest rates are high relative to discount rates, as in the early 1980s in Figure 17.4, banks have an incentive to seek discount loans.

Economists have documented that when the spread between the rates on three-month T-bills and discount loans increases, so does the volume of discount lending. In addition, the Fed's willingness to lend to banks influences the volume of discount loans made to banks. The Fed generally discourages routine discount borrowing, but on occasion it has strongly encouraged banks to borrow from it. For example, it did so during the October 1987 stock market crash.

Table 17.3 summarizes the determinants of banks' decisions regarding excess reserves and discount loans. Banks' portfolio allocation decisions about excess reserves and discount loans—decisions based on expected returns—influence the money multiplier and the money supply.

Before going on to the conclusion of the money supply process, it is worth reflecting on the Fed's actions and the behavior of banks and the nonbank public. We now have all the pieces we need to calculate an accurate **money multiplier**—an expression that converts the monetary base to the money supply. This expression is a modification of the simple deposit multiplier that includes the nonbank public's decisions on holding currency versus checkable deposits and banks' decisions on holding reserves and taking discount loans. You also can see why we say that the Fed doesn't "control" the money supply. Although it influences the amount of checkable deposits in the economy by determining in large part the monetary base, it cannot completely control the actions of other players in the economy. Therefore it is more accurate to say that the Fed manages the money supply or guides monetary policy—but it does not wave a magic wand and establish a particular amount of money in the economy.

TABLE 17.3 **Determinants of Excess Reserves and Discount Loans**

An increase in . . .	Causes . . .	Because . . .
market interest rates	excess reserves to fall	the opportunity cost of holding excess reserves rises.
average level or variability of deposit outflows	excess reserves to rise	banks require a greater cushion against outflows.
market interest rates relative to the discount rate	discount loans to rise	banks' profits from discount borrowing increase.

Deriving the Money Multiplier and the Money Supply

We can synthesize the information presented about the monetary base and the modification of the simple deposit multiplier into an equation that predicts what the money supply will be. The conclusion of our efforts requires two steps: First, we must calculate the money multiplier; then we can use this expression to find the money supply.

We build on our analysis of decisions by the Fed, the nonbank public, and banks to derive the money multiplier. In particular, we take into account (1) the effects of Fed decisions on the level of reserves; (2) the effects of portfolio allocation decisions by the nonbank public, assuming that the ratio of currency to checkable deposits, C/D, is constant; and (3) the effects of decisions by banks about excess reserves, ER, assuming that banks hold a constant proportion of deposits as excess reserves, ER/D.

Let's begin by considering how the Fed affects the money multiplier m by setting the required reserve ratio. Total reserves, R, equal the sum of required reserves, RR, and excess reserves, ER:

$$R = RR + ER. \tag{17.4}$$

The Fed sets the level of required reserves by requiring banks to hold a certain percentage of checkable deposits as reserves. Thus required reserves equal the required reserve ratio, R/D, multiplied by the level of checkable deposits, D:

$$RR = (\overline{R/D})(D). \tag{17.5}$$

Substituting this expression for required reserves into Eq. (17.4) for total reserves, we get

$$R = (\overline{R/D})(D) + ER. \tag{17.6}$$

Recall that we started our discussion of the money supply process by noting that the money supply can be thought of as the product of the monetary base and the money multiplier. Hence we need to move from reserves to the monetary base. The monetary base, B, equals the sum of currency, C, and reserves, R, so we use Eq. (17.6) to obtain

$$\begin{aligned} B &= C + R \\ &= C + (\overline{R/D})(D) + ER. \end{aligned} \tag{17.7}$$

Suppose, for example, that checkable deposits total \$1 billion and that currency totals \$300 million. Suppose also that the Fed requires banks to hold 10% of their checkable deposits as reserves and that banks hold no excess reserves. How large is the monetary base? It is the sum of currency (\$300 million) and reserves (the required reserve ratio, 0.10, times the level of deposits, \$1 billion):

$$B = \$300 \text{ million} + (0.10)(\$1 \text{ billion}) = \$400 \text{ million}.$$

Now we incorporate the nonbank public's and banks' portfolio allocation decisions into the equation for the monetary base. If currency holdings by the nonbank public are a constant fraction of checkable deposits, then

$$C = (C/D)(D).$$

If banks' holdings of excess reserves are a constant fraction of checkable deposits, then

$$ER = (ER/D)(D).$$

Substituting these two expressions into Eq. (17.7), we obtain the following equation for the monetary base:

$$\begin{aligned} B &= (C/D)(D) + (\overline{R/D})(D) + (ER/D)(D) \\ &= [(C/D) + (\overline{R/D}) + (ER/D)](D). \end{aligned} \tag{17.8}$$

If we divide both sides of Eq. (17.8) by the term in the brackets and rearrange, we can express the relationship of checkable deposits to the monetary base as

$$D = \left[\frac{1}{(C/D) + (\overline{R/D}) + (ER/D)}\right](B). \tag{17.9}$$

Returning to our example, we can verify that checkable deposits are equal to $1 billion. The monetary base is $400 million; banks hold no excess reserves, so $ER/D = 0$; and the required reserve ratio is 0.10. The currency–deposit ratio is $300 million/$1 billion, or 0.30. Hence

$$D = \left(\frac{1}{0.30 + 0.10 + 0}\right)(\$400 \text{ million}) = \$1 \text{ billion}.$$

Finally, we are ready to complete the process by moving from deposits to the money supply, M, which is equal to currency, C, plus deposits, D. Then, substituting $(C/D)(D)$ for C, we get

$$\begin{aligned} M &= C + D \\ &= [(C/D)D] + D \\ &= D[1 + (C/D)]. \end{aligned}$$

Substituting for D and using Eq. (17.9) gives an expression relating the money supply, M, to the monetary base, B:

Money supply = (Money multiplier) (Monetary base),

or

$$M = \left[\frac{1 + (C/D)}{(C/D) + (\overline{R/D}) + (ER/D)}\right](B). \tag{17.10}$$

The expression in brackets in Eq. (17.10) is equal to the money multiplier, m. The money supply equals the monetary base times the money multiplier. The money multiplier conveys by how much the money supply responds to a given change in the monetary base.

For example, suppose that Nationia's monetary base is $10 billion, the required reserve ratio is 0.15, the currency–deposit ratio is 0.35, and banks hold no excess reserves. How large is the stock of checkable deposits? How large is the total money supply? The money multiplier in this case is

$$m = \frac{1 + (C/D)}{(C/D) + (\overline{R/D})} = \frac{1.35}{0.35 + 0.15} = 2.7.$$

OTHER TIMES, OTHER PLACES . . .

The Money Multiplier and Money Supply During the Early 1930s

During the depths of the Great Depression in the United States (1930–1933), the money multiplier was extremely unstable. Why did this happen? What insights can we gain from that experience for predicting the multiplier in the future?

The most severe banking crisis in U.S. history occurred in the early 1930s. Problems originated in the late 1920s, as falling farm prices caused farmers to default on agricultural bank loans. Other sources of the crisis were the failures of some prominent U.S. and European financial institutions in 1930 and 1931 and Britain's abandonment of the gold standard in September 1931, which led international investors to question whether the dollar would continue to be tied to gold. By 1933, more than one-third of the commercial banks in the United States had failed or had been taken over by other banks.

The banking crisis significantly changed the money multiplier by affecting the portfolio allocation decisions of the nonbank public and banks. First, because of the perceived increase in riskiness of bank loan portfolios, wary depositors converted (or tried to convert) deposits into currency. The currency–deposit ratio, C/D, increased steadily after 1931 and dramatically in early 1933, more than doubling. Currency holdings by the public represent a leakage from the deposit creation process, so the multiplier and money supply fell while the monetary base was relatively stable.

Because of the wave of bank runs, by 1932 banks had to anticipate greater deposit outflows and increased their holdings of excess reserves. As a result, the ratio of excess reserves to deposits, ER/D, increased, further reducing the money multiplier.

The Fed did not aggressively increase its discount lending during the banking panic of 1931–1933, worsening the problems of the banking system and prompting the public to convert checkable deposits to currency and banks to convert loans to reserves. As a result of these portfolio allocation decisions by banks and the nonbank public, the money multiplier fell from 3.8 in March 1930 to 2.3 in March 1933. Although the monetary base *increased* by about 20% over the same period, the money supply actually *fell* by 28%.

Note: Figures are based on data from Milton Friedman and Anna J. Schwartz, *A Monetary History of the United States, 1867–1960.* Princeton, N.J.: Princeton University Press, 1963, pp. 299–419.

The money supply is equal to the money multiplier times the monetary base, so

$$\text{Money supply} = 2.75(\$10 \text{ billion}) = \$27 \text{ billion}.$$

Checkable deposits, D, are

$$D = M - C = M - (C/D)(D),$$

so

$$D = \frac{M}{1 + (C/D)} = \frac{\$27 \text{ billion}}{1.35} = \$20 \text{ billion}.$$

We now have a complete description of the money supply process:

1. The money supply equals the monetary base times the money multiplier.
2. The monetary base comprises the nonborrowed base, determined primarily by the Fed through open market operations, and discount loans, determined jointly by the banks and the Fed.
3. The money multiplier depends on the required reserve ratio (determined by the Fed), excess reserves relative to deposits (determined by banks), and the currency–deposit ratio (determined by the nonbank public).

Table 17.4 summarizes the variables determining the money supply. As we show below, understanding these variables helps us to account for actions of the Fed, banks, and the public in the short run and in the long run.

TABLE 17.4 Variables in the Money Supply Process

An increase in the . . .	Based on the actions of . . .	Causes the money supply to . . .	Because . . .
nonborrowed base, B_{non}	the Fed (open market operations)	rise	the monetary base rises, and more reserves are available for deposit expansion.
reserve requirements, $\overline{R/D}$	the Fed (reserve requirements)	fall	fewer reserves can be lent out, and the money multiplier falls.
discount rate	the Fed (discount policy)	fall	discount loans become more expensive, reducing borrowed reserves and the monetary base.
currency–deposit ratio, C/D	the nonbank public (portfolio decisions)	fall	the money multiplier falls, reducing deposit expansion.
excess reserves relative to deposits, ER/D	banks (portfolio decisions)	fall	the money multiplier falls, reducing deposit expansion.
expected deposit outflows	the nonbank public (transactions considerations)	fall	excess reserves rise relative to deposits, reducing the money multiplier and deposit expansion.
variability of deposit outflows	the nonbank public (transactions and portfolio considerations)	fall	excess reserves rise relative to deposits, reducing the money multiplier and deposit expansion.

Read This!!

CASE STUDY

Using the Money Supply Equation to Predict Money Growth

The money supply equation allows us to forecast growth of the money supply. We analyze the determinants of changes in the money supply, M (measured by $M1$), first by examining changes in the money multiplier, m, and then by examining changes in the monetary base, B. Recall that the monetary base, B, equals the sum of the nonborrowed base, B_{non}, and borrowed reserves, BR (discount loans). Thus we can express the money supply as

$$M = m(B_{non} + BR).$$

The money multiplier, m, depends on the required reserve ratio, the currency–deposit ratio, and the ratio of excess reserves to checkable deposits.

To focus on growth rates of the money supply, we need an expression for the percentage change in M: $\%\Delta M$. The percentage change in M is approximately equal to the sum of the percentage change in the money multiplier, $\%\Delta m$, and the percentage change in the monetary base, $\%\Delta(B_{non} + BR)$.

$$\%\Delta M \cong \%\Delta m + \%\Delta(B_{non} + BR).$$

(continued)

FIGURE 17.5 **Accounting for Changes in the Money Supply (*M1*), 1979–2006**

Over long periods of time, fluctuations in the monetary base primarily determine changes in the money supply. Over short periods of time, fluctuations in the money multiplier magnify or dampen the effects of changes in the monetary base on the money supply.

Source: http://www.federalreserve.gov/releases

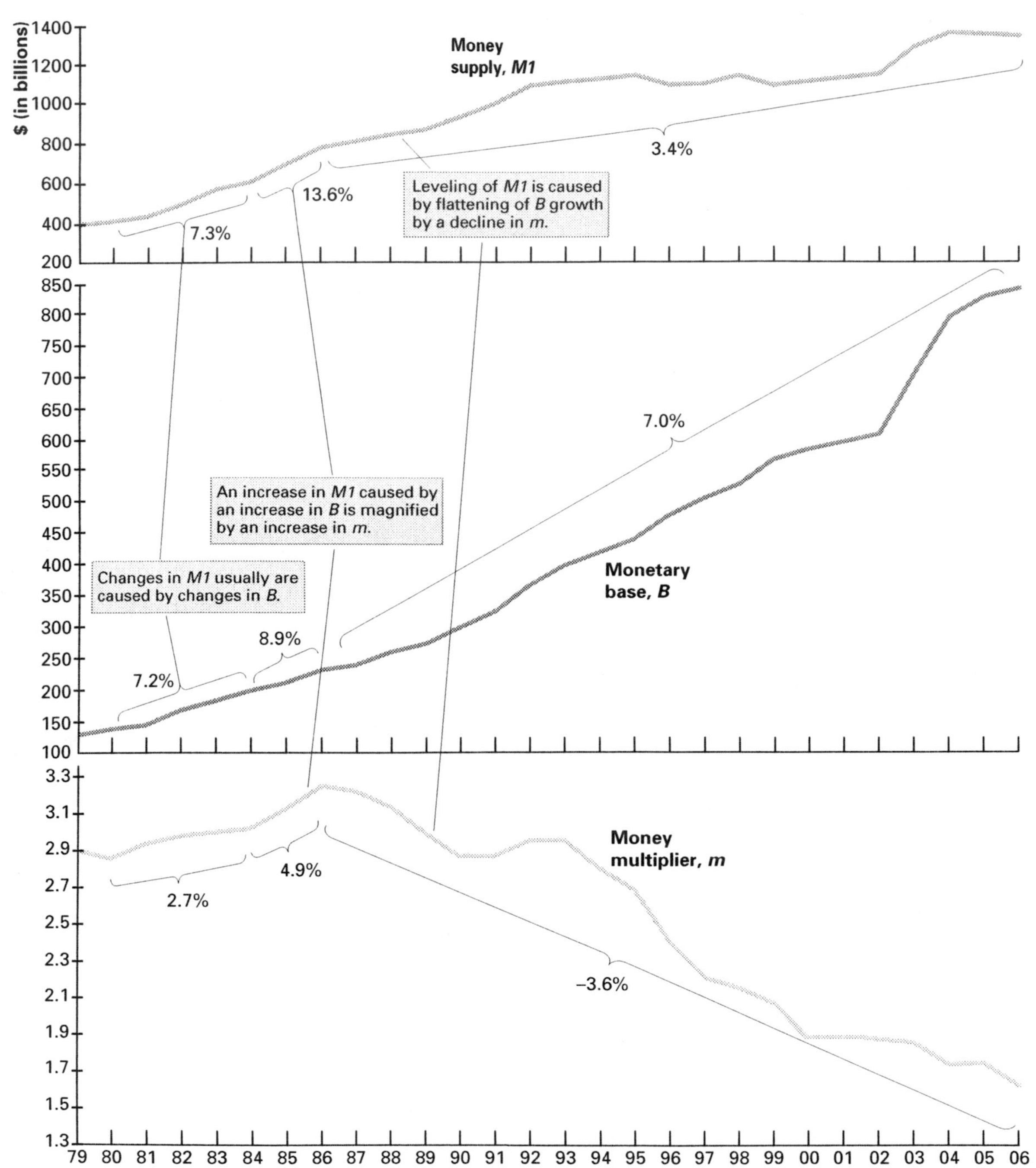

CASE STUDY *(continued)*

Let's begin with a simple example and assume that the money multiplier is constant so that $\%\Delta m = 0$. We can then express the percentage change in the money supply as $\%\Delta M = \%\Delta(B_{non} + BR)$. To forecast the growth rate of the money supply, we need to predict the growth rate of the monetary base. To do so, we study Fed decisions about open market operations that affected the nonborrowed base, B_{non}, and bank and Fed decisions about discount loans, BR. As we noted earlier, BR is small relative to B_{non}, so, not surprisingly, most analysts studying the money supply are Fed watchers, or careful observers of the Fed's actions and intentions. As long as the percentage change in the money multiplier is zero or very small, careful forecasting of changes in discount loans and especially in the nonborrowed base will produce a good prediction of the growth of the money supply.

We can use some actual data to translate changes in the money supply into changes in the monetary base and the money multiplier. Figure 17.5 presents data on percentage changes in the money supply, the monetary base, and the money multiplier from 1979 through 2006. During this period, the money supply grew at an average annual rate of about 5.3%. This growth was fueled mainly by increases in the monetary base, which averaged 7.4% overall. From beginning to end, the money multiplier declined. Figure 17.5 shows that virtually all the average annual rate of growth in the money supply (7.3%) from 1980 through 1984 can be explained by growth in the monetary base (7.2%); the money multiplier grew by only 0.1% per year. Virtually all the growth in the monetary base represented growth in the nonborrowed base from the Federal Reserve System's open market operations. The only significant exception during the 1980s and early 1990s came in 1984, when the Fed provided discount loans of about $5 billion to the distressed Continental Illinois Bank. Over periods of several years, the primary determinant of changes in the money supply is changes in the nonborrowed portion of the monetary base, B_{non}, which is controlled by the Federal Reserve System through open market operations.

Many forecasters in the financial community try to predict *short-term* movements in the money supply. Over short periods of time, however, the correlation between the Fed's actions to change the monetary base and actual changes in the money supply are much less precise. Short-run disturbances in the components of the money multiplier disrupt the relationship, as the second and third periods in Figure 17.5 indicate.

Note that over short periods of time, the money multiplier may change significantly. For example, in 1985 and 1986, the money multiplier grew at a rate of 4.7% per year. Over the same period, the monetary base grew by 8.9% per year, and the *M1* money supply grew by 4.7% + 8.9% = 13.6% per year. To account for the change in the money multiplier, we must analyze changes in its components. The culprit turned out to be the currency–deposit ratio, C/D. Not shown in Figure 17.5, C/D declined by about 17% over these two years, increasing the money multiplier. This effect was reversed after 1986, and since then, the declining money multiplier has generally reflected an increase in the currency–deposit ratio.

Our analysis of this description of changes in the money supply during the 1980s, 1990s, and 2000s, shows that changes in the money multiplier may lead to a significant change in the money supply in a short period of time. Nonetheless, over long periods of time, in periods in which households' demand for money is stable, the majority of changes in the money supply can be explained by changes in the monetary base. By far the most important determinant of changes in the monetary base is the Fed's actions to change the nonborrowed base through open market operations.

KEY TERMS AND CONCEPTS

- Bank reserves
  - Excess reserves
  - Required reserve ratio
  - Required reserves
- Currency–deposit ratio
- Currency in circulation
- Discount loans
- Discount rate
- Money supply process
  - Monetary base
  - Money multiplier
- Multiple deposit contraction
- Multiple deposit expansion
- Open market operations
  - Open market purchase
  - Open market sale
- Simple deposit multiplier
- Vault cash

MOVING FROM THEORY TO PRACTICE . . .

THE WASHINGTON POST JUNE 30, 2006

The Fed and the Monetary Base: Cooling Inflationary Pressures

Federal Reserve policymakers raised a key interest rate yesterday to the highest level in more than five years and signaled that they may lift it further to combat rising inflation.

a Consumer price inflation "has been elevated in recent months," the Federal Open Market Committee, the central bank's top policymaking group, said in a statement after announcing its decision to raise its benchmark interest rate to 5.25% from 5%, the 17th consecutive quarter-percentage-point increase since June 2004.

The Fed has been tightening credit to cool the economy and keep inflation under control. The rate increases have succeeded in slowing economic growth from its rapid pace of earlier this year, primarily by letting some air out of the housing market, the committee noted in its statement.

But the economy did not slow down enough to prevent inflation from edging up in the spring, in part because energy costs soared and more businesses were able to pass them on to consumers by raising retail prices. Fed policymakers said the slowdown "should help to limit inflation pressures over time" but suggested that may not be enough by itself to force inflation back down . . .

The benchmark federal funds rate, which is charged on overnight loans between banks, influences many other borrowing costs. Major banks followed the Fed's action by raising their prime rate on business loans to 8.25% from 8%. b Interest rates charged on credit cards, home equity loans, and mortgages are likely to rise as well, but savers should benefit as financial institutions pay out higher rates on money-market funds and certificates of deposit.

Interest rates on long-term loans have been rising in recent months, although more slowly than short-term rates. c The average rate on a 30-year fixed-rate mortgage, for example, was 6.71% last week, not much higher than its 6.29% level in June 2004, just before the Fed started raising the federal funds rate.

The Fed uses its influence over interest rates to promote economic growth while keeping inflation contained. Higher interest rates cause consumers and businesses to spend less, slowing economic growth and dampening inflation pressures. Lower rates do the opposite.

ANALYZING THE NEWS . . .

On June 29, 2006, the Federal Reserve raised short-term interest rates by one-quarter of a percentage point, from 5% to 5.25%. To accomplish this, the Fed used open-market sales of short-term Treasury securities to decrease bank reserves and the monetary base. The open-market sales put downward pressure on the price of Treasury securities and upward pressure on yields—the Fed's great goal—as the monetary base contracted.

a During 2003, before the Fed started raising interest rates, the growth rate of *M1*, the Fed's measure of money in the form of currency and checkable deposits, grew rapidly; *M2* growth rates also increased. Some economists and policymakers worried that the increase in the money supply growth rates increased the potential for growing inflationary pressures. This worry was not lost on Fed officials, who remembered that the increasing money supply growth in 1998 and 1999 forced the Fed to raise interest rates in 2000, which helped to trip the economy into a recession. Thus, the Fed started raising interest rates gradually in June 2004.

Throughout 2004, the year-on-year growth rate of *M1* was increasing. During the first part of 2005, the year-on-year growth rate of *M1* remained relatively high. In 2006, the rate of growth of *M1* again increased. All during this time, the Fed was continuously increasing short-term interest rates.

b Recall from the analysis of the term structure of interest rates that long-term interest rates reflect in large part expectations of future short-term rates. Thus, as the Fed signaled that it might continue to raise short-term interest rates to keep inflation under control, long-term interest rates also increased.

c Also recall from the analysis of the term structure of interest rates that long-term interest rates do not necessarily always move in lockstep with short-term interest rates. During 2005 and 2006, while the Fed was increasing short-term interest rates, long-term interest rates moved upward very slowly and to a much lesser degree.

For further thought . . .

In recent years, some financial practitioners suspected that changes in *M1* were due to the reallocation of financial portfolios. As returns in both the stock market and the bond market decreased, how might this explain changes in the growth rate of *M1*?

Source: Excerpted from "Key Fed Rate Raised to 5.25%, A 5-Year High," *The Washington Post*, June 30, 2006, p. D01. © 2006 The Washington Post Company.

SUMMARY

1. The basic measure of the money supply we model is *M1*, the sum of currency in the hands of the nonbank public and checkable deposits at depository institutions. The three participants in the money supply process are the Federal Reserve System, depository institutions (banks), and the nonbank public.
2. The money supply process has two parts. First, actions by the Fed largely determine the monetary base. Then the money multiplier measures the amount by which the money supply changes in response to a change in the monetary base.
3. The Fed influences the monetary base primarily by buying and selling government securities (open market operations). Purchases of securities by the Fed increase the monetary base. Sales of securities by the Fed decrease the monetary base. The Fed also can change the monetary base by making discount loans to banks. An increase in discount lending increases the monetary base; a decrease in discount lending decreases the monetary base.
4. The process by which an increase in bank reserves increases the level of checkable deposits is called multiple deposit expansion. The Fed can add to reserves in the banking system by buying government securities or making discount loans. The increase in reserves allows banks to make additional loans, which lead to additional deposits in banks. As a result, the money supply increases. In the simplest case—in which currency holdings do not change and banks do not hold excess reserves—multiple deposit expansion is limited only by the Fed's reserve requirements. An increase in the level of bank reserves raises the level of checkable deposits by a multiple of the change in the reserves. This multiple, the simple deposit multiplier, is equal to the reciprocal of the required reserve ratio.
5. The money multiplier represents the link between the monetary base and the money supply. If the multiplier is constant, the change in the money supply equals the multiplier times the change in the monetary base. An increase in currency or reserve holdings relative to checkable deposits reduces the money multiplier.
6. Despite the Fed's important role in the money supply process through open market operations, discount lending, and reserve requirements, the Fed doesn't completely control the money supply. Portfolio allocation decisions by banks and the nonbank public also affect the monetary base and the money multiplier. The nonbank public decides how to allocate its holdings between checkable deposits and currency. An increase in the nonbank public's demand for currency relative to deposits increases the currency–deposit ratio, reducing the money multiplier. Banks must decide what proportion of checkable deposits to hold as excess reserves (above those required by regulation). Holdings of excess reserves raise the ratio of effective reserves to deposits and reduce the money multiplier. These portfolio allocation decisions by the nonbank public and banks are determined by the principal factors governing asset demand: wealth, expected returns, risk, liquidity, and information. Finally, the Fed doesn't control discount lending. The Fed sets the discount rate (the interest rate charged on discount loans), but the decision to borrow is made by banks.
7. Putting it all together, the money supply process involves important roles for the Fed, banks, and the nonbank public. We can express the money supply (represented by *M1*, the sum of currency and checkable deposits) as

   Money supply = (Money multiplier) × (Nonborrowed base + Discount loans).

REVIEW QUESTIONS

1. What are the major assets and liabilities of the Federal Reserve System? Describe each briefly.
2. What are the components of the monetary base? Why is the monetary base a useful concept?
3. What is the difference between currency in circulation and currency outstanding? Which is added to reserves to get the monetary base?
4. What are excess reserves and how are they calculated? What determines the amount of required reserves?
5. If the Fed wants to increase the money supply, should it make an open market purchase or sale? Should it make more discount loans or fewer? If the Fed wants to decrease the money supply, what should it do?
6. If a bank has \$10,000 in excess reserves, what is the most new lending that it should do? Why shouldn't it do more than that amount?
7. A student remarks, "If any one bank can safely loan only an amount equal to its excess reserves, I don't

understand how the banking system as a whole can loan out an amount equal to several times the initial excess reserves in the system." Resolve the seeming paradox.

8. If the discount rate is usually below the federal funds rate, why don't banks borrow from the Fed at the discount rate and lend the money out at the federal funds rate to profit from the difference in the interest rates?

9. Wealth in the United States has grown steadily. If wealth were the only factor affecting currency demand, what do you expect would have happened to the currency–deposit ratio over time?

10. What happens to the simple deposit multiplier when the Fed makes more discount loans?

11. Suppose that the Fed wanted to increase the money supply (*M1*) by 10% next year. It predicts that the money multiplier will increase by 2%. How much should it increase the monetary base?

12. What happened to the value of the money multiplier between 1979 and 1986? What has happened to its value since 1986? What may have caused these movements in the size of the money multiplier? What consequences do these movements have for forecasters in the financial community who attempt to predict short-term movements in the money supply?

ANALYTICAL PROBLEMS

13. Suppose that Bank Five lends $100,000 to the Monkey Wrench Company. Using T-accounts, show how this transaction is recorded on the bank's balance sheet. If Monkey Wrench spends the money to buy materials from Scrap Steel, Inc., which does its banking at Wonder Bank, show the effect on Bank Five's balance sheet. What is the total change in Bank Five's assets and liabilities?

14. Suppose that a bank currently has assets of $24,000 in reserves and $176,000 in loans and liabilities of $200,000 in deposits. If the required reserve ratio is 10%, what are the bank's required and excess reserves? What is the bank likely to do?

Questions 15 and 16 require the use of the following bank balance sheet (amounts are in millions of dollars).

Assets		Liabilities	
Reserves	48	Checkable deposits	300
Loans	280	Time deposits	200
Securities	182	Net worth	10
	510		510

15. Calculate the bank's excess reserves when the required reserve ratio on checkable deposits is 14% and the required reserve ratio on time deposits is 3%. Now suppose that the required reserve ratios are changed to 16% on checkable deposits and 0% on time deposits. Again, calculate the bank's excess reserves.

16. Suppose that the bank sells $3 million in securities on the open market. Calculate the change in the bank's excess reserves when the required reserve ratio on checkable deposits is 14%.

17. Explain why you agree or disagree with the following observation: "If deposit insurance were eliminated, the Fed's control over the money supply would be reduced."

18. Consider the following data (all values are in billions of dollars):

	June 1930	June 1931	June 1932
Currency	$3.681	$3.995	$4.959
Checkable deposits	21.612	19.888	15.490
Bank reserves	3.227	3.307	2.829

Calculate the values for each period for the currency–deposit ratio, the ratio of total reserves to deposits, the monetary base, the money multiplier, and the *M1* money supply. Can you explain why the currency–deposit ratio and the ratio of total reserves to deposits moved as they did between 1930 and 1932?

19. In the following bank balance sheet, amounts are in millions of dollars. The required reserve ratio is 3% on the first $30 million of checkable deposits and 12% on any checkable deposits over $30 million.

Assets		Liabilities	
Reserves	18.9	Checkable deposits	180.0
Loans	150.0	Net worth	20.0
Securities	31.1		200.0
	200.0		

a. Calculate the bank's excess reserves.
b. Suppose that the bank sells $5 million in securities to get new cash. Show the bank's balance sheet after this transaction. What are the bank's new excess reserves?

c. Suppose that the bank loans its excess reserves in part (b) to a business. Show the bank's balance sheet after the loan has been made but before the business has spent the proceeds of the loan. Now what are the bank's excess reserves?
d. Suppose that the business spends the proceeds of the loan. Revise the bank's balance sheet and calculate its excess reserves.

20. If the required reserve ratio is 25%, banks hold no excess reserves, and the public holds currency equal to 25% of deposits, what is the value of the *M1* money multiplier?

21. Suppose that the statistics for the economy as a whole (in billions of dollars) are as follows:

Currency held by the public	100
Reserves held by banks	200
Checkable deposits held at banks	800
Time deposits held at banks	1200
Excess reserves held by banks	40

If the required reserve ratio on checkable deposits is 20%, what is the value of the *M1* money multiplier?

22. What would the money multiplier be if banks held no excess reserves, the currency–deposit ratio was 1, and the reserve requirement for checkable deposits was 100%?

23. Analysts have noted that at times, a substantial increase in demand for U.S. currency corresponds to a crisis in some foreign country. Is this a coincidence? Explain.

24. Suppose that First Bank discovered that its computer had been programmed incorrectly and that it suddenly was short of reserves by $100 million. What would you expect to happen to the federal funds rate, the number of discount loans made by the Fed, and the amount of excess reserves held by other banks?

25. Suppose that banks were so risk-averse that they would gladly sell securities so as to hold excess reserves. In other words, if the Fed engaged in open market purchases, banks would hold the entire amount of the increase in the monetary base in the form of excess reserves. What would be the money multiplier in such a case? Could the Fed increase the money supply if it wanted to?

Questions 26 and 27 pertain to the chapter appendix.

26. What would happen to *M1* and *M2* if the public decided to hold less currency and more time deposits, so *C/D* fell by 1% and *N/D* rose by 1% (assuming that the ratio of reserves to deposits is less than 100%)?

27. Consider Bank A's balance sheet (all amounts are in millions of dollars).

Assets		Liabilities	
Reserves, *R*	48	Checkable deposits, *D*	300
Loans, *L*	280	Time deposits, *N*	200
Securities, *S*	182	Net worth, *NW*	10
	510		510

For the economy as a whole, the initial level of checkable deposits, *D*, is $2 trillion. Relevant ratios are as follows:

Currency–deposit ratio, *C/D*	0.2
Time deposit–checkable deposit ratio, *N/D*	1.5
Money market account–deposit ratio, *MM/D*	0.5
Excess reserve–deposit ratio, *ER/D*	0.06
Required reserve ratio, $\overline{R/D}$	0.14

a. Calculate the monetary base *B*, *M1* (= *C* + *D*), and *M2* (= *M1* + *N* + *MM*). Does Bank A have any excess reserves? Are there any excess reserves in the economy as a whole?
b. Calculate the multipliers (the respective *m* values) for *M1* and *M2*.
c. Suppose that the Fed changes the required reserve ratio to 16%, or 0.16. In response, banks as a whole reduce their excess reserves to zero. What happens to Bank A's balance sheet? Calculate its required reserves. What are Bank A's excess reserves? Calculate the new *M1* and *M2* multipliers.
d. Suppose that, instead of taking the actions in part (c), the Fed buys $88.888 billion in securities on the open market, including $1.5 million from Bank A. What happens to Bank A's balance sheet? Calculate its required and excess reserves. Calculate the new size of the monetary base.

DATA QUESTIONS

28. Look up the following data in the latest issue of the *Federal Reserve Bulletin* in your library: currency holdings, C; checkable deposits, D; required reserves, RR; excess reserves, ER; and the $M1$ money supply. From these data, calculate the ratios C/D, ER/D, and $\overline{R/D}$. Calculate the $M1$ money multiplier using the multiplier formula. Alternatively, calculate the $M1$ money multiplier using the equation $M1 = (m)(B)$. Compare these multipliers. How do they compare with the simple deposit multiplier, $1/(\overline{R/D})$?

29. The Federal Reserve closely monitors the reserve positions of monetary institutions. Locate the aggregate required reserves held by depository institutions, reported on a monthly basis by the Federal Reserve's Statistical Releases Web site, at http://www.federalreserve.gov/releases (category H3). Compare the required reserves that were reported during the months prior to and then during the most recent recession of 2001. How do reported reserves move with business cycle performance during this time? Do the changes in required reserves seem to have the predicted effect on the monetary base? Why or why not?

APPENDIX

The Money Supply Process for *M2*

In the aftermath of financial innovation during the 1980s and 1990s (much of which we discussed in Chapter 15), many analysts and policymakers became concerned that $M1$ no longer adequately represented assets functioning as the medium of exchange. As a result, they focused more attention on $M2$. It is a broader monetary aggregate than $M1$, including not only currency, C, and checkable deposits, D, but also the nontransaction accounts. These accounts consist of savings and small-time deposits, N, and certain money market accounts, MM. Money market items in $M2$ include money market deposit accounts at commercial banks, general-purpose and broker-dealer money market mutual funds, overnight repurchase agreements issued by banks, and overnight Eurodollars issued to U.S. residents by foreign branches of U.S. banks. As a sum of its components, $M2$ is

$$M2 = C + D + N + MM. \qquad (17A.1)$$

The $M2$ measure of the money supply is less sensitive than $M1$ to shifts in the nonbank public's portfolio preferences. Suppose that, because of financial innovation, the nonbank public wants to switch from checkable and nontransaction deposits to money market–type accounts. In that case, D and N would fall, and MM would rise by the same amount, leaving $M2$ *unchanged.* However, $M1$, the sum of currency and checkable deposits, would fall.

If we make assumptions similar to those used in deriving the $M1$ multiplier, namely, that C/D, N/D, and MM/D are constant, we can express $M2$ as

$$\text{Broader money supply} = (M2\ \text{multiplier})(\text{Base}),$$

or

$$M2 = \left[\frac{1 + (C/D) + (N/D) + (MM/D)}{(C/D) + (\overline{R/D}) + (ER/D)}\right](B). \qquad (17A.2)$$

The *M2* multiplier is significantly larger than the *M1* multiplier. The reason is that the terms *N/D* and *MM/D* are added to the numerator. Because the volume of both nontransaction accounts and money market–type accounts is greater than the volume of checkable deposits, *N/D* and *MM/D* are greater than 1. With no reserve requirements for these measures, *M2* money expansion from a change in the monetary base is greater than that for *M1*. Indeed, the *M2* multiplier has been more stable than the *M1* multiplier during the 1980s and 1990s.

Components of the *M2* multiplier affect the size of the multiplier in a manner similar to that for *M1*. Increases in the required reserve ratio and the currency–deposit ratio reduce the extent of deposit expansion, thereby reducing the multiplier. However, an increase in the nonbank public's preference for nontransaction or money market–type accounts relative to checkable deposits increases the multiplier.

Fed watchers predict the growth of *M2* in much the same way as they do for *M1*. They forecast changes in the monetary base—particularly in the nonborrowed base—and in the components of the *M2* multiplier.

CHAPTER 19

Organization of Central Banks

In October 2005, President George W. Bush announced that economist Ben Bernanke would replace the soon-to-retire, legendary Federal Reserve Chairman Alan Greenspan. Financial markets and economists applauded the choice, fearing that a more politically inspired choice would bode ill for the Fed's strong independence. Such a political tug-of-war had been playing out around the world, as Chairman Greenspan, Bank of Japan Governor Fukui, and European Central Bank President Trichet struggled to balance monetary policy objectives and political pressures.

Why should the choice of a central bank chairman be the subject of political controversy and an event that can trouble financial markets? You know from earlier chapters that the Fed plays an active role in the money supply process. But in learning about the money supply process, we viewed the Fed as a "black box." That is, we observed the results of the Fed's actions in managing the monetary base, setting reserve requirements, and making discount loans, but we didn't look inside the Fed to see *why* those decisions were made and implemented. That is our mission in this chapter and the next two chapters. In this chapter, we begin our study of the way the Fed conducts monetary policy by looking at the structure of the Fed. The Federal Reserve chairman has often been called the second most important person in the nation. The reason is that the Fed is in control of monetary policy—a set of decisions that affect the well-being of individuals and firms during economic downturns and upturns. It is little wonder, then, that speculation on Greenspan's appointment caused some jitters on Wall Street.

Our specific objectives in this chapter are to learn about the Fed's organization and structure and its role as an economic policymaking body. We also describe the political arena in which the Fed operates and the debate over the independence of the central bank. We then examine the organization and independence of central banks outside the United States, including the European Central Bank.

Power Sharing in the Federal Reserve System

Few countries have as complex a structure for their central bank as the United States has in its Federal Reserve System. The Fed's organization was shaped by the same political struggle that gave the United States a fragmented banking system: advocates of strong economic institutions versus those who feared large, powerful economic interests. To understand why the Fed is organized as it is, we need to look back in history at the nation's earlier attempts to create a central bank.

Creation of the System

Not long after the United States won its independence, Treasury Secretary Alexander Hamilton organized the Bank of the United States, which was meant to function as a central bank but had both government and private shareholders. Distrust of the Bank of the United States by Southern and Western agrarian and small-business interests resulted in the bank's demise in 1811. In 1816, the Second Bank of the United States was formed, but populist President Andrew Jackson did not renew its national charter when it expired in 1836. (The bank survived for a time as a state-chartered bank in Pennsylvania.)

Abolition of the Second Bank of the United States left the nation without an official lender of last resort for banks. The void was filled by private institutions such as the New York Clearing House, but severe nationwide financial panics in 1873, 1884, 1893, and 1907—and accompanying economic downturns—raised fears in Congress that the U.S. financial system was unstable. After the 1907 panic and economic recession, Congress considered options for government intervention. Many officials worried that bankers such as New York financier J. P. Morgan, who had served as a de facto lender of last resort, would be unable to manage future crises. Congress appointed a National Monetary Commission to begin formal studies leading to the design of a central bank. With the support of President Woodrow Wilson, the Federal Reserve Act became law in 1913.

The Federal Reserve Act of 1913 created a central bank for the United States, the **Federal Reserve System.** The act provided for checks and balances that were designed to diffuse economic power in three ways: among bankers and business interests, among states and regions, and between government and the private sector. The act and subsequent legislation created four groups within the system, each empowered in theory to perform separate duties: the Federal Reserve banks, member banks, the Board of Governors, and the Federal Open Market Committee (FOMC). The responsibilities that were assigned to each reflected the original intent of the 1913 act to give the central bank control over the amount of currency outstanding and the volume of discount loans to member banks (the lender-of-last-resort function). In theory, the President and Congress didn't envision that the Fed would control monetary policy, broadly defined. In practice, however, over time, the Fed has assumed the lead role in making monetary policy. In the rest of this section, we describe the roles of the principal groups within the Federal Reserve System in conducting open market operations, setting reserve requirements, and making discount loans.

Federal Reserve Banks

The Federal Reserve Act divided the United States into 12 Federal Reserve districts, each of which has a **Federal Reserve bank** in one city (and, in most cases, additional branches in other cities in the district) to conduct discount lending. Figure 19.1 shows the Federal Reserve districts and locations of the Federal Reserve banks. The map may appear strange at first glance: no state (not even California or New York) is a single Federal Reserve district. Some states are split by district boundaries, and economically dissimilar states are grouped in the same district. Most Federal Reserve districts contain a mixture of urban and rural areas, as well as manufacturing, agriculture, and service business interests. This arrangement is intentional, to prevent any one interest group or one state from obtaining preferential treatment from the district Federal Reserve bank. Nor can a district easily have its way at the expense of other districts, owing to supervision by the Board of Governors and the Federal Open Market Committee. If one district is suffering from a recession, it cannot singlehandedly alter Fed money and credit policies to meet its needs. Some cities (New York, Chicago, and San Francisco) clearly were population centers in 1914 and so were chosen as locations for Federal Reserve banks. Other cities were chosen because of political pressure during the

> Web Site Suggestions: http://www.federalreserve.gov/otherfrb.htm
> Offers contact numbers and e-links to the reserve banks.

FIGURE 19.1

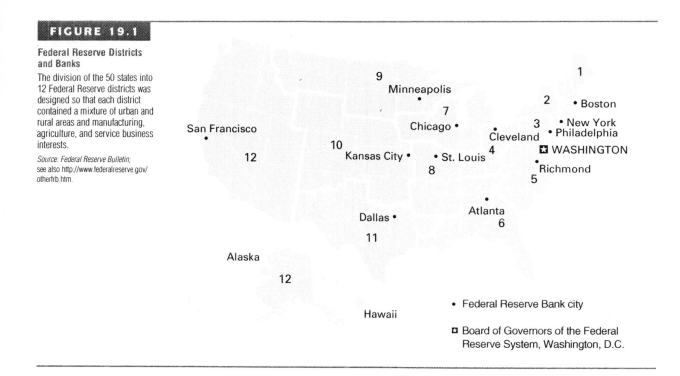

Federal Reserve Districts and Banks

The division of the 50 states into 12 Federal Reserve districts was designed so that each district contained a mixture of urban and rural areas and manufacturing, agriculture, and service business interests.

Source: Federal Reserve Bulletin; see also http://www.federalreserve.gov/otherfrb.htm.

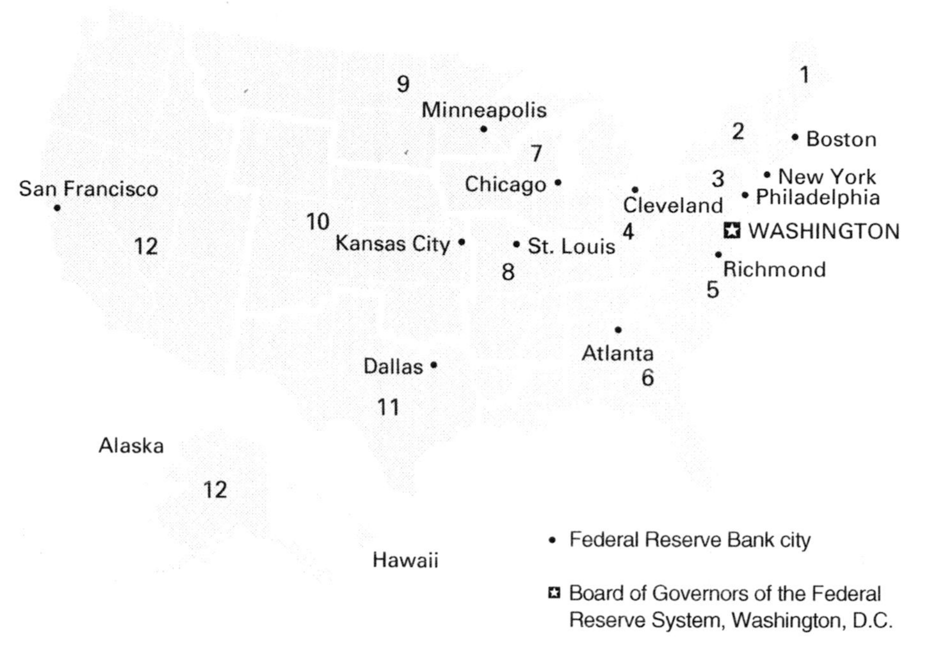

debate over the Federal Reserve Act. (For example, Richmond, Virginia, was the home of Carter Glass, one of the legislative architects of the Federal Reserve System.)

Who owns the Federal Reserve banks? In principle, the private commercial banks in each district that are members of the Federal Reserve System own the district bank. In fact, each Federal Reserve bank is a private–government joint venture. Member banks receive dividends (limited to 6%) on the shares of stock they own in the district bank.

A guiding principle of the 1913 Federal Reserve Act was that one constituency (for example, finance, industry, commerce, or agriculture) would not be able to exploit the central bank's economic power at the expense of another constituency. Therefore Congress restricted the composition of the boards of directors of the Federal Reserve banks. The directors represent the interests of three groups: banks, businesses, and the general public. Member banks elect three bankers (*Class A directors*) and three leaders in industry, commerce, and agriculture (*Class B directors*). The Fed's Board of Governors appoints three public interest directors (*Class C directors*). Subject to the board's approval, the nine directors of a Federal Reserve bank elect the president of that bank.

The 12 Federal Reserve banks carry out duties related to the Fed's roles in the payments system, monetary control, and financial regulation. Specifically, the district banks

- manage check clearing in the payments system;
- manage currency in circulation by issuing new Federal Reserve Notes and withdrawing damaged notes from circulation;
- conduct discount lending by making and administering discount loans to banks within the district;
- perform supervisory and regulatory functions such as examining state member banks and evaluating merger applications; and

- provide services to businesses by collecting and making available data on district business activities and by publishing articles on monetary and banking topics written by professional economists employed by the banks.

The Federal Reserve district banks engage in monetary policy both directly (through discount lending) and indirectly (through membership in Federal Reserve committees). In theory, Federal Reserve banks establish the discount rate and determine the amounts that individual (member and nonmember) banks are allowed to borrow.† The district banks indirectly influence policy through their representatives on the Federal Open Market Committee, which sets guidelines for open market operations (purchases and sales of securities by the Fed to affect the monetary base), and the Federal Advisory Council, a consultative body composed of district bankers.

Member Banks

The Federal Reserve Act required all national banks to become **member banks** of the Federal Reserve System. State banks may elect to become members; currently, only about one in seven state banks is a member. About one-third of all banks in the United States now belong to the Federal Reserve System. These member banks hold a substantial majority of all bank deposits.

Historically, one reason for the low voluntary membership rate was the cost. The Fed's reserve requirements compel banks to keep part of their deposits as idle funds, effectively imposing a tax on bank intermediation. In contrast, when banks are chartered by states rather than the federal government, their reserves can earn interest. As nominal interest rates rose during the 1960s and 1970s, the opportunity cost of Fed membership increased, and fewer state banks elected to become or remain members. During the 1970s, the Fed argued that the so-called reserve tax on member banks placed them at a competitive disadvantage relative to nonmember banks. It claimed that declining bank membership eroded its ability to influence the money supply and urged Congress to compel all commercial banks to join the Federal Reserve System. Although Congress has not yet legislated such a requirement, the Depository Institutions Deregulation and Monetary Control Act (DIDMCA) of 1980 required that all banks (by 1987) maintain reserve deposits with the Fed on the same terms. This legislation gave member and nonmember banks equivalent access to discount loans and to payments system (check-clearing) services. It effectively blurred the distinction between member and nonmember banks and halted the decline in Fed membership. Today, about 3000 banks are Federal Reserve System members.

CHECKPOINT

Suppose that City National Bank pays a 7% annual interest rate on checkable deposits, subject to a reserve requirement of 10%. What is City National's effective cost of funds? Against $100 of deposits, City National must hold $10 in reserves (in vault cash or deposits with the Fed), leaving $90 to invest. The bank must pay depositors (0.07)($100) = $7 to obtain $90 in funds to invest in loans or securities, so its effective cost of funds is not 7%, but 7/90 = 7.8%. Thus reserve requirements impose a tax on bank intermediation, raising City National's cost of funds from 7% to 7.8%. ♦

†In practice, the discount rate is reviewed and approved for each Federal Reserve district by the Board of Governors in Washington, D.C.

Board of Governors

The **Board of Governors** is headquartered in Washington, D.C. Its seven members are appointed by the president of the United States and confirmed by the U.S. Senate. To provide for central bank independence, the terms of board members were set so that one U.S. president generally cannot appoint a full Board of Governors. Governors serve a nonrenewable term of 14 years; their terms are staggered so that one term expires every other January.† Geographical restrictions ensure that no one Federal Reserve district is overrepresented.

Currently, many board members are professional economists from business, government, or academia. Chairmen of the Board of Governors since World War II have come from various backgrounds, including Wall Street (William McChesney Martin), academia (Arthur Burns and Ben Bernanke), business (G. William Miller), public service (Paul Volcker), and economic forecasting (Alan Greenspan). The chairman serves a four-year term and may be reappointed or serve out the balance of a 14-year member's term.

The Board of Governors administers monetary policy to influence the nation's money supply through open market operations, reserve requirements, and discount lending. Since 1935, it has had the authority to determine reserve requirements within limits set by Congress. The Board of Governors also effectively sets the discount rate (which is in principle established by the Federal Reserve banks) through its review and determination procedure. It holds seven of the 12 seats on the Federal Open Market Committee and therefore influences the setting of guidelines for open market operations. In addition to its formal responsibilities relating to monetary control, it informally influences national and international economic policy decisions. The chairman of the Board of Governors advises the president and testifies before Congress on economic matters.

The Board of Governors has certain responsibilities relating to financial regulation. Before the elimination of Regulation Q in 1986, the board administered interest rate regulations. It also sets *margin requirements*, or the proportion of the purchase price of securities that an investor must pay in cash rather than buying on credit. In addition, it determines permissible activities for bank holding companies and approves bank mergers. Finally, it exercises certain administrative controls over individual Federal Reserve banks, reviewing their budgets and setting the salaries of their presidents and officers.

Federal Open Market Committee

Web Site Suggestions: http://www.federalreserve.gov/fomc Describes the FOMC and its members and statements.

The 12-member **Federal Open Market Committee (FOMC)** gives direction to the Fed's open market operations. Members of the FOMC are the chairman of the Board of Governors, the other Fed governors, the president of the Federal Reserve Bank of New York, and the presidents of four of the other 11 Federal Reserve Banks (who serve on a rotating basis). Only five Federal Reserve bank presidents are voting members of the FOMC, but all 12 attend meetings and participate in discussions. The committee meets eight times each year.

The Fed influences the monetary base primarily through open market operations. Therefore, in practice, the FOMC is the centerpiece of Fed policymaking. Prior to the meeting, the FOMC members receive a national economic forecast for the next two years prepared by the Board staff in the "green book." The public "beige book"

†Technically, a governor could resign before the term expired and then be reappointed, thereby lengthening the term. Since 1970, this practice has been rare.

prepared by reserve banks is also available, as is the "blue book" with projections for monetary aggregates from the Board staff. The FOMC doesn't literally buy or sell securities for the Fed's account. Instead, it summarizes its views in a public statement of the *balance of risks* (between higher inflation or a weaker economy) and a directive issued to the Fed's trading desk at the Federal Reserve Bank of New York. There, the manager for domestic open market operations communicates each day with members of the FOMC (and their staffs) about execution of the directive.

Power and Authority Within the Fed

Because Congress configured the Federal Reserve System with many formal checks and balances to ensure that no one group could effectively control it, central (or national) control of the system was virtually nonexistent during the Fed's first 20 years. After the severe banking crisis of the early 1930s, many analysts concluded that the decentralized district bank system could not adequately respond to national economic and financial disturbances. The Banking Acts of 1933 and 1935 gave the Board of Governors authority to set reserve requirements and the FOMC the authority to direct open market operations. The Banking Act of 1935 also centralized the Fed's participation in the money supply process, giving the Board of Governors a majority (seven of 12) of seats on the FOMC and thereby great influence in implementing monetary policy.

The Board of Governors and the FOMC exert most of the Fed's formal influence on monetary policy. However, many Fed watchers believe that the informal authority of the chairman, the staff of the Board, and the FOMC predominates. In other words, the informal power structure within the Fed may be more concentrated and influential than the formal power structure. Because the Federal Reserve Bank of New York always occupies a seat on the FOMC, the president of that bank also can be quite influential. Figure 19.2 shows the organizational and power-sharing arrangements within the Fed, both in theory and in practice.

Member banks, the nominal owners of Federal Reserve banks, have little actual influence within the system. The distinction between *ownership* and *control* within the Federal Reserve System is clear. Member banks own shares of stock in the Federal Reserve banks, but shareholding confers none of the rights that are typically granted to shareholders of private corporations. Member banks receive at most a 6% annual dividend, regardless of the Fed's earnings, and so do not have the residual claim that is normally granted to equity. Moreover, member banks have virtually no control over how their stakes in the system are used because the Board of Governors in Washington formulates policy directives. Although member banks elect the six Class A and Class B directors, there is generally only one candidate per position, whom the Federal Reserve bank or Board of Governors suggests.

Although there is no direct evidence as to who actually holds power in the Fed, the impressions of experienced insiders are revealing. On the basis of his personal experience as a Fed official, economist Sherman Maisel estimated the relative influence of groups within the Fed in setting monetary policy: the chairman of the Board of Governors, 45%; the staff of the Board and the FOMC, 25%; and other governors and the Federal Reserve banks, not particularly powerful.[†] Those impressions were recorded in the 1970s, but current actions support them. Some board members and district bank presidents on the FOMC may challenge the chairman's agenda, but the chairman's influence still dominates.

[†]Sherman J. Maisel, *Managing the Dollar.* New York: W. W. Norton, 1973.

FIGURE 19.2 **Organization and Authority of the Federal Reserve System**

The Federal Reserve Act of 1913 established the Federal Reserve System but incorporated a series of checks and balances into the system. Part (a) shows that in theory, its economic power is diffuse. Part (b) shows that informal power within the Fed is more concentrated in the hands of the chairman of the Board of Governors than the formal structure suggests.

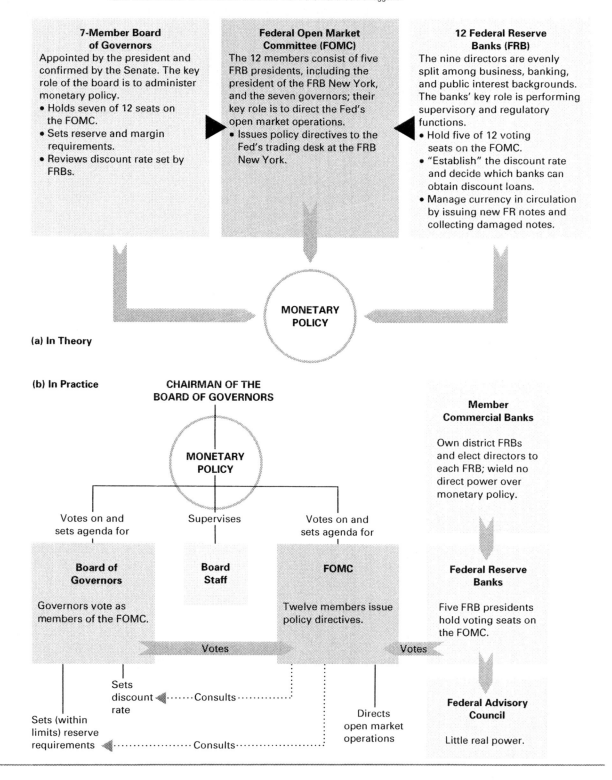

7-Member Board of Governors

Appointed by the president and confirmed by the Senate. The key role of the board is to administer monetary policy.

- Holds seven of 12 seats on the FOMC.
- Sets reserve and margin requirements.
- Reviews discount rate set by FRBs.

Federal Open Market Committee (FOMC)

The 12 members consist of five FRB presidents, including the president of the FRB New York, and the seven governors; their key role is to direct the Fed's open market operations.

- Issues policy directives to the Fed's trading desk at the FRB New York.

12 Federal Reserve Banks (FRB)

The nine directors are evenly split among business, banking, and public interest backgrounds. The banks' key role is performing supervisory and regulatory functions.

- Hold five of 12 voting seats on the FOMC.
- "Establish" the discount rate and decide which banks can obtain discount loans.
- Manage currency in circulation by issuing new FR notes and collecting damaged notes.

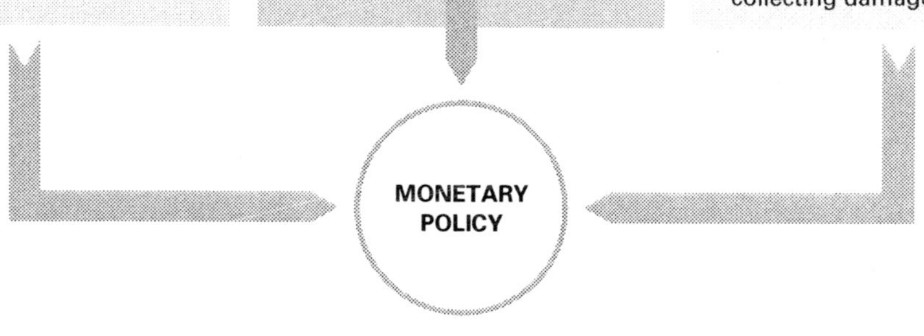

(a) In Theory

(b) In Practice

CHAIRMAN OF THE BOARD OF GOVERNORS

MONETARY POLICY

Votes on and sets agenda for

Supervises

Votes on and sets agenda for

Board of Governors

Governors vote as members of the FOMC.

Board Staff

FOMC

Twelve members issue policy directives.

Votes

Votes

Sets discount rate

Consults

Sets (within limits) reserve requirements

Consults

Directs open market operations

Member Commercial Banks

Own district FRBs and elect directors to each FRB; wield no direct power over monetary policy.

Federal Reserve Banks

Five FRB presidents hold voting seats on the FOMC.

Federal Advisory Council

Little real power.

How the Fed Operates

The government created the Fed to manage the banking system and the money supply. Lacking a constitutional mandate, the Fed operates in a political arena, and it is subject to pressure by legislators and officials. The central bank also exerts power in economic policymaking because of its role in the money supply process. In this section we describe how the Fed operates in the political environment, and we discuss the debate over the independence of the central bank.

Handling External Pressure

Congress intended the Federal Reserve System generally to operate independently of external pressures (for example, from the president, Congress, the banking industry, or business groups). Board members are appointed for long, nonrenewable terms of office, reducing any one president's influence on the Board's composition and the temptation for governors to take actions merely to please the president and Congress.

The Fed's financial independence allows it to combat external pressure. Generally, federal agencies are subject to the annual appropriations process, during which Congress scrutinizes budgetary requests, authorizes funds, and then appropriates the funds. Not only is the Fed exempt from this process, but it is also a profitable organization, contributing funds to the Treasury rather than receiving funds from it. Most of the Fed's earnings come from interest on the securities it holds; smaller amounts come from interest on discount loans and fees that are received from financial institutions for check-clearing and other services. In recent years, the Fed's net income has exceeded $25 billion annually—substantial profits when compared even to the largest U.S. corporations.

Despite the attempt to give the Fed independence, it isn't completely insulated from external pressure. First, the president can exercise control over the membership of the Board of Governors. Often, governors do not serve their full 14-year terms, because they can earn higher incomes in private business. Therefore a president who serves two terms in office may be able to appoint several governors. Additionally, the president may appoint a new chairman every four years—an appointment that can sometimes make or break his presidency. A chairman who is not reappointed may serve the remainder of his or her term as a governor but traditionally resigns, thereby giving the president another vacancy to fill.

Second, although the Fed's significant net income exempts it from the appropriations process (Congress's "power of the purse"), the Fed remains a creation of Congress. The U.S. Constitution does not specifically mandate a central bank, so Congress can amend the Fed's charter and powers or even abolish it entirely. Members of Congress usually are not shy about reminding the Fed of this fact. Nor is Congressional oversight merely rhetoric. In the middle and late 1970s, Congress forced the Fed to explain its goals and procedures. Passed in 1975, House Concurrent Resolution 133 requires the Fed to announce targets for the growth of monetary aggregates. In addition, the Humphrey-Hawkins Act (officially the Full Employment and Balanced Growth Act of 1978) requires the Fed to explain how these targets are consistent with the president's economic objectives. Nevertheless, in practice, the Congress has not often successfully challenged the Fed's policies.

Examples of Treasury–Fed Conflict

Elected officials lack formal control of monetary policy, and this lack of control at times has resulted in conflicts between the Fed and the president, who is often represented by the Secretary of the Treasury. During World War II, the administration increased its control over the Fed. To help finance wartime budget deficits, the Fed agreed to hold interest rates on Treasury securities at low levels. It could do so by buying bonds that were not purchased by private investors, thereby predetermining (pegging) the rates. After the war, the Treasury wanted to continue this policy, but the Fed didn't agree. The Fed's concern was inflation: larger purchases of Treasury securities by the Fed increased the monetary base, potentially increasing the money supply growth rate and inflation. Price controls that had restrained inflation during the war were lifted after the war ended.

Chairman of the Board of Governors Marriner Eccles particularly objected to the rate-fixing policy. His opposition to the desires of the Truman administration cost him the Fed chairmanship in 1948, although he continued to fight for Fed independence during the remainder of his term as a governor. On March 4, 1951, the wartime policy of fixing the interest rates on Treasury securities was formally abandoned with the Treasury–Federal Reserve Accord.

Conflicts between the Treasury and the Fed didn't end with that accord, however. For example, President Ronald Reagan and Federal Reserve Chairman Paul Volcker argued over who was at fault for the severe business recession of the early 1980s. Reagan blamed the Fed's contractionary monetary policy. Volcker held that the Fed could not expand money supply growth until the budget deficit—which results from policy actions of the president and Congress—was reduced.

Early in the George H. W. Bush administration, the conflict was less severe, even though the Treasury typically argued for a more expansionary monetary policy than the Fed wanted. During the debate in 1991 over reforms of U.S. banking regulations, the Treasury and the Fed argued over which would have greater responsibility in overseeing the banking system. Finally, in late 1991 and early 1992, the Treasury pressured the Fed to reduce short-term interest rates. Although the Fed did reduce the discount rate, there is no way of knowing whether Treasury pressure influenced its decision. In early 1993, the Clinton Treasury argued that the Fed should not raise short-term interest rates in the face of the administration's budget package; and in 1994, the administration challenged the Fed's repeated increases in the federal funds rate. In 1996, some members of Congress questioned whether the Fed was sufficiently stringent in its operating budget in light of cutbacks in government budgets. In the George W. Bush administration in 2003, some commentators worried about a conflict between the Treasury and the Fed over the administration's tax policy.

Factors That Motivate the Fed

We have shown that the Fed has considerable power over monetary policy. Let's now examine alternative explanations of how the Fed decides to use its power. We consider two views of Fed motivation: the public interest view and the principal-agent view.

The public interest view. The usual starting point for explaining the motivation of business managers is that they act in the interest of the constituency they serve: the shareholders. The **public interest view** of Fed motivation holds that the Fed, too, acts in the interest of its primary constituency (the general public) and that it seeks to achieve economic goals that are in the public interest. Examples of such goals are price and employment stability and economic growth.

Does the evidence support the public interest view? It doesn't appear to with regard to price stability. The record of persistent inflation since World War II undercuts the claim that the Fed has emphasized price stability. Similarly, some economists dispute the Fed's contributions to the stability of other economic indicators.

CONSIDER THIS ...

Importance of Selecting a Fed Chairman

In the summer of 1979, President Jimmy Carter perceived the failure of his economic policies to roll back inflation as a huge stumbling block in his quest for reelection. Inflation was accelerating, and the value of the dollar was declining sharply on foreign-exchange markets. To try to turn the economy around before the election, Carter sought to replace Federal Reserve Chairman G. William Miller (who was leaving to become Secretary of the Treasury) with a champion of price stability. On July 24, 1979, Carter offered the Fed chairmanship to Paul Volcker, the president of the Federal Reserve Bank of New York and former undersecretary of the Treasury for monetary affairs. Volcker's views on Fed policies were well known. Earlier in 1979, he had argued for a contractionary monetary policy, with a significant increase in the federal funds rate, to fight inflation. The inflation challenge led Volcker to accept the new post (despite having to take a pay cut from $116,000 to $57,500).

In October 1979, the Volcker Fed began a restrictive policy of significantly lower money supply growth that resulted in a dramatic increase in the federal funds rate. High interest rates and a sagging economy were major factors in President Carter's campaign woes. By 1982, the rate of inflation had declined significantly, but the decline came too late for Jimmy Carter. Carter had appointed Federal Reserve Chairman Volcker, but the short-term effects of his policies had helped to hand the 1980 presidential election to Republican Ronald Reagan.

The principal-agent view. Many economists view organizations as having conflicting goals. Although they are created to serve the public and perform a public service, government organizations also have internal goals that might not match their stated mission. In effect, public organizations face the agency problem just as private corporations do. In this section, we describe goals other than those outlined in the Federal Reserve Act that might influence the Fed's decisions and the way in which it exerts its economic power.

Recall that when managers (agents) have little stake in their businesses, their incentives to maximize the value of shareholders' (principals') claims may be weak; in that situation, the agents don't always act in the interest of the principals. James Buchanan and Gordon Tullock of George Mason University formulated a **principal-agent view** of motivation in bureaucratic organizations such as the Fed. They contend that bureaucrats' objective is to maximize their personal well-being—power, influence, and prestige—rather than the well-being of the general public. Hence the principal-agent view of Fed motivation predicts that the Fed acts to increase its power, influence, and prestige as an organization, subject to constraints placed on it by principals such as the president and Congress.

How can we determine whether the principal-agent view accurately explains the Fed's motivation? If it does, we might conclude that the Fed would fight to maintain its autonomy. Unquestionably, it does so; the Fed has resisted congressional attempts to control its budget many times. In fact, the Fed is one of the most successful bureaucratic organizations in mobilizing constituents (such as bankers and business executives) in its own defense.

Proponents of the principal-agent view also think that the Fed would avoid conflicts with groups that could limit its power, influence, and prestige. For example, the Fed could manage monetary policy to assist the reelection efforts of presidential incumbents who are unlikely to limit its power. The result would be a **political business cycle,** in which the Fed would try to lower interest rates to stimulate credit demand and economic activity before an election to make the Fed look good. After the election, the economy would pay the piper when the Fed contracted economic activity to reduce the inflationary pressure caused by its earlier expansion—but, by then, the president who was sympathetic to the Fed would have been reelected. The facts for the United States don't generally support the political business cycle theory, however. For example, expansion of money supply growth preceded President Nixon's reelection in 1972, but contraction of money supply growth preceded President Carter's and President Bush's unsuccessful bids for reelection in 1980 and 1992, respectively.

Nevertheless, the president's desires may subtly influence Fed policy. One study of the influence of politics on changes in monetary policy from 1979 through 1984 measured the number of signals of desired policy from the administration in articles appearing in *The Wall Street Journal.* The author found a close correlation between changes in monetary policy and the number of administration signals.†

One criticism of the principal-agent view addresses the need to separate the Fed's intentions from external pressure: the Fed itself might want to act in one way, whereas Congress and the president might try to get the Fed to pursue other goals. The principal-agent view also fails to explain why Congress allows the Fed to be relatively independent through self-financing. Some economists suggest that the Fed may provide Congress with long-run benefits through self-financing. If self-financing gives the Fed an incentive to conduct more open market purchases, thereby expanding the money supply, more residual revenue will accrue to the Treasury for appropriation by Congress.

Fed Independence

Usually, the political issue of Fed independence arises not because of academic disagreement over monetary policy or even the role of the Fed in managing monetary policy, but because of the public's negative reaction to Fed policy. For example, legislation introduced in Congress in 1982 to decrease the Fed's autonomy stemmed from public reaction to high interest rates. We now analyze the arguments for and against Fed independence.

Arguments for independence. The main argument for Fed independence is that monetary policy—which affects inflation, interest rates, exchange rates, and economic growth—is too important and technical to be determined by politicians. Because of the frequency of elections, politicians may be myopic, concerned with short-term benefits without regard to potential long-term costs. Short-term and long-term interests often clash after inflation. Supporters argue that monetary policy tends to be too expansionary if it is left to policymakers with short horizons, leading to inflation. Therefore the Fed cannot assume that politicians' objectives reflect public sentiment. The public may well prefer that the experts at the Fed, rather than politicians, make monetary policy decisions.

Another argument for Fed independence is that complete control of the Fed by elected officials increases the likelihood of political business cycle fluctuations in the money supply. For example, those officials might pressure the Fed to assist the Treasury's borrowing efforts by buying government bonds, increasing the money supply and fueling inflation.

Arguments against independence. The importance of monetary policy for the economy is also the main argument against central bank independence. Supporters

†Thomas Havrilesky, "Monetary Policy Signaling from the Administration to the Federal Reserve," *Journal of Money, Credit, and Banking*, 20:83–101, February 1988.

OTHER TIMES, OTHER PLACES . . .

Conflicts Between the Treasury and the Central Bank in Japan over Independence

The United States isn't the only country in which tensions between the Treasury and the central bank influence monetary policy. Japanese monetary policy during the late 1980s and early 1990s provides another good example. During the mid-1980s, Bank of Japan Governor Satoshi Sumita conducted an expansionary monetary policy. Mr. Sumita, a former vice minister of finance (the Ministry of Finance is akin to the U.S. Treasury), favored low interest rates. Yasushi Mieno, appointed to head the Bank of Japan in 1989, pursued a more contractionary policy. *The Wall Street Journal* reported that "Mr. Mieno took away the *sake* bowl just as the party started getting rambunctious."† That is, Japanese money growth would be reduced, leading to concerns that the runup in Japanese stock prices would end.

During 1990, increases in the Bank of Japan's discount rate sent Japanese stock market prices plunging and threatened some highly leveraged firms with financial distress. The surprise decision by the Bank of Japan to reduce its discount rate from 6% to 5.5% on July 1, 1991, caused Japanese central bank watchers to worry that Mieno was currying favor with Finance Minister Ryutaro Hashimoto. The finance minister was a strong candidate to be the Japanese prime minister, and Mieno's actions seemed to create a political business cycle.

Like Federal Reserve actions in the United States, the Bank of Japan's actions can be viewed as reflecting responsible, independent behavior: The bank may have tried to ease the likelihood of a financial crisis in Japan induced by high interest rates, even though it could attempt relatively contractionary policies over the medium term. In more recent years, the Bank of Japan became formally independent of the government.

† Marcus W. Brauchli and Clay Chandler, "Financial Shift: In a Major Reversal, the Bank of Japan Cuts Its Key Interest Rate," *The Wall Street Journal*, July 2, 1991.

claim that in a democracy, elected officials should make public policy. Because the public holds elected officials responsible for perceived monetary policy problems, some analysts advocate giving the president and Congress more control over monetary policy. The counterargument to the view that monetary policy is too technical for elected officials is that national security and foreign policy also require sophisticated analysis and a long-term horizon, and these functions are entrusted to elected officials. In addition, critics of Fed independence argue that placing the central bank under the control of elected officials could confer benefits by coordinating and integrating monetary policy with government taxing and spending policies.

Those who argue for greater congressional control make the case that the Fed has not always used its independence well. For example, some critics note that the Fed, because of its deflationary bias, failed to assist the banking system during the economic contraction of the early 1930s. Another example that many economists cite is that Fed policies were too inflationary in the 1960s and 1970s. Finally, some analysts believe that the Fed acted too slowly in addressing credit problems during the recession of the early 1990s.

Concluding remarks. Economists and politicians don't universally agree on the merits of Fed independence. Under the present system, however, the Fed's independence is not absolute, and so it sometimes satisfies one or the other group of critics. In practice, debates center on proposals to limit Fed independence in some respects, not to eliminate its formal independence. Some recent proposals include shortening the term of office of governors, making the chairman's term coincide more closely with that of the president, and placing the Secretary of the Treasury on the FOMC. Enacting any of these proposals would tend to make the Fed's economic policies more consistent with the president's.

Central Bank Independence Outside the United States

The degree of central bank independence varies greatly from country to country. When we compare the structure of the Fed with that of central banks in Canada, Europe, and Japan, four patterns emerge. First, in countries where central bank board members serve fixed terms of office, none is as long as the 14-year term for Federal Reserve governors, implying nominally greater independence for the Fed. Second, in those countries, the head of the central bank has a longer term of office than the four-year term of office of the chairman of the Board of Governors in the United States. Third, of these countries, only Germany has had a federal structure for the central bank (we discuss the European Central Bank below).

Finally, the overall degree of independence of the central bank varies. An independent central bank is free to pursue its goals without direct interference from other government officials and legislators. Most economists believe that an independent central bank can more freely focus on keeping inflation low (we discuss this goal in more detail in Chapter 21). The European Central Bank is, in principle, extremely independent, whereas the central banks of Japan and the United Kingdom traditionally have been less independent, though by 1998, both had become more independent and more focused on price stability.

Web Site Suggestions: http://www.bankofengland.co.uk Presents the Bank of England's Web site.

The Bank of England, the world's oldest central bank (founded in 1694), obtained the power to set interest rates independent of the government in 1997. While the government can overrule the Bank in "extreme circumstances," such deviation is unlikely. The Bank of England's inflation target is set by the Chancellor of the Exchequer. Interest rate determination falls to the Monetary Policy Committee, whose members are the Governor, two Deputy Governors, two members appointed by the Governor (after consulting with the Chancellor of the Exchequer), and four external economic experts named by the Chancellor.

Web Site Suggestions: http://www.boj.or.jp/en/ Presents the Bank of Japan's Web site.

The Bank of Japan Law, in force since April 1998, gives the Policy Board more autonomy to pursue price stability. Policy board members include the Governor, two Deputy Governors, and six outside members named by the cabinet and confirmed by the Diet. While the government may send representatives to meetings of the policy board, it lacks a vote. The Ministry of Finance does, however, retain control over parts of the Bank of Japan's budget unrelated to monetary policy.

Web Site Suggestions: http://www.bank-banque-canada.ca Presents the Bank of Canada's Web site.

The Bank of Canada has an inflation target as a goal for monetary policy, but that target is set jointly by the Bank of Canada and the government. While the government has had since 1967 the final responsibility for monetary policy, the Bank has generally controlled monetary policy. While the finance minister can direct the bank's action, such direction must be written and public, and none has been issued up to this time.

The push for central bank independence to pursue a goal of low inflation has increased in recent years. Indeed, in most of the industrialized world, central bank independence from the political process is gaining ground as the way to organize monetary authorities. In practice, the degree of actual independence in the conduct of monetary policy varies across countries. What conclusions should we draw from differences in central bank structure? Many analysts believe that an independent central bank improves the economy's performance by lowering inflation without raising output or employment fluctuations. Calculations by Alberto Alesina and Lawrence Summers of Harvard University indicate that the countries that have the most independent central banks (Germany and Switzerland) had the lowest average rates of inflation during the

1970s and 1980s. New Zealand, Italy, and Spain, with much less independent central banks, had significantly higher rates of inflation.

What constitutes meaningful central bank independence? Economists emphasize that declarations of independence are insufficient. The central bank must be able to conduct policy without direct interference from the government. The central bank also must be able to set nonconflicting goals for which it can be held accountable. The leading example of such a goal is a target for inflation. Central banks in Canada, Finland, New Zealand, Sweden, and the United Kingdom have official inflation targets. A number of European countries, including France and Germany, had informal inflation targets (prior to the emergence of the European Central Bank), and the European Central Bank does now. Many economists urge that the U.S. Fed adopt an inflation target.

Web Site Suggestions: http://www.ecb.int Provides information on and data from the European Central Bank.

As part of the move toward economic integration in Europe, the *European Central Bank (ECB)* is charged with conducting monetary policy for Europe (that is, for the 11 countries participating in European Monetary Union). Representatives of many European nations signed an important agreement in Maastricht, the Netherlands, in December 1991. This agreement detailed a gradual approach to monetary union to be completed between 1994 and 1999. Although the monetary union became effective only on January 1, 1999, groundwork for the ECB had been laid in advance. Indeed, European nations coordinated an expansionary monetary policy in late 1998.

The ECB's organization is in some respects similar to that of the U.S. Fed. The ECB's executive board, chaired by Jean Claude Trichet, has six members who work exclusively for the bank. Board members (a vice president and four others) are appointed by the heads of state and government, based on the recommendation of the Council of Ministers of Economics and Finance, after consulting the European Parliament and the Governing Council of the ECB. Executive board members serve nonrenewable eight-year terms. Also participating in the governance of the ECB are the governors of each of the member national central banks, each of whom will have a term of at least five years. The long terms of office are designed to increase the political independence of the ECB.

In principle, the ECB has a high degree of overall independence, with a clear mandate to emphasize price stability, following the lead of the Bundesbank (Germany's central bank), and it is free from European Union and national governments in the conduct of policy. Moreover, the ECB's charter can only be accomplished by changing the Maastricht Treaty, which would require the assent of all countries signing the original treaty. Whether legal independence will translate into actual independence is difficult to say, however. Such a translation requires observing the new institution for a period of time.

Based on the historical experience of the Federal Reserve, there may be cause for concern. The decentralized central banking system envisioned in the original Federal Reserve Act of 1913 led to power struggles within the system and offered no mechanism to achieve consensus during the financial crisis of the early 1930s. National central banks have considerable power in the ECB. The governors of the European System of Central Banks (ESCB) hold a majority of votes in the ECB's governing council. And national central banks collectively have a much larger staff than the ECB.

Where might conflict arise? While the ECB statute emphasizes price stability, countries have argued—and likely will continue to argue—over the merits of expansionary or contractionary monetary policy. Also, no consensus has been reached on the way the ECB will function as the lender of last resort in dealing with domestic financial crises. Optimists believe that the united ECB and monetary union forces Europe to confront key structural economic weaknesses, such as an oversized public sector and inflexible labor markets. Pessimists argue that monetary unions generally require a broader political union (the case for the Fed, but not for the ECB) to be successful. One thing is clear—all eyes are still on the ECB.

KEY TERMS AND CONCEPTS

Federal Reserve System
- Board of Governors
- Federal Open Market Committee (FOMC)

Federal Reserve bank
Member banks
Political business cycle
Principal-agent view
Public interest view

SUMMARY

1. The Federal Reserve Act of 1913 created the U.S. Federal Reserve System (the Fed). Its three principal components are the Federal Reserve banks, the Board of Governors, and the Federal Open Market Committee (FOMC).
2. The Fed's formal activities are conducting open market operations, setting reserve requirements, and making discount loans. The FOMC issues guidelines for open market operations. The Board of Governors sets reserve requirements. Depository institutions obtain discount loans through district Federal Reserve banks, although the Board of Governors essentially determines the discount rate (the interest rate charged on discount loans).
3. In practice, power within the Federal Reserve System is more centralized than is apparent from the official structure. The Board of Governors, especially its chairman, typically dominates monetary policy decisions.
4. The Fed is relatively independent of the political process, owing to the long-term appointments of members of the Board of Governors and to the Fed's financial independence. However, because the Federal Reserve System was created by legislation, not by the Constitution, Congress could enact legislation to reduce its power (or even to eliminate it).
5. The public interest view of Fed motivation argues that the Fed pursues monetary policies and financial regulation in the broad national interest. Alternatively, the principal-agent view stresses that the Fed is more interested in enhancing its own well-being as an organization than in the national interest.
6. Should the Fed be independent? Some argue that it should because its longer time horizon (relative to those of elected officials) enables it to pursue monetary policies in the long-term interest of the nation. Critics of central bank independence note that monetary policy is an important part of the national policy agenda and hence should be controlled by elected officials.
7. The degree of independence from the political process and the general procedures for appointing governors vary for central banks of other industrialized countries. Countries having relatively independent central banks generally have lower inflation rates than do countries having less independent central banks.

REVIEW QUESTIONS

1. Why did Congress pass the Federal Reserve Act in 1913 when the United States had gotten along without a central bank since 1836?
2. What are the Board of Governors' duties and responsibilities with regard to monetary policy?
3. Who are the voting members of the Federal Open Market Committee?
4. Where does most of the Fed's income come from?
5. What features of the Fed help to make it independent of political pressure? How does the U.S. Constitution protect the Fed?
6. How many district Federal Reserve banks are there? Where are they located?
7. Who guides the open market operations of the Fed?
8. Why do Federal Reserve districts cut across some state lines, and why do the directors of the district banks represent business, banking, and the general public?

MOVING FROM THEORY TO PRACTICE . . .

FINANCIAL TIMES JULY 3, 2006

Bernanke's Fed Communicates with the Markets

During Alan Greenspan's time at the Federal Reserve, traders made fortunes interpreting and trading on his exquisitely crafted hints about the likely future path of US interest rates.

Under Ben Bernanke, the game is changing . . .

a The new chairman has long been frustrated by what he sees as the market's over-reliance on linguistic guidance from the Fed.

Bruce Kasman, chief US economist at JPMorgan Chase, says the Fed is saying to investors: "I don't want to hold your hand."

He says Mr Bernanke and his colleagues want "to shift the focus of policy biases to the Fed's assessment of the macroeconomic outlook."

b In 2003, when the Fed cut interest rates to 1% in an attempt to ward off a deflation scare, the Greenspan Fed set out to convince the markets that rates would stay low for some time, declaring "the committee believes that policy accommodation can be maintained for a considerable period." When it started raising rates, it swapped that phrase for "policy accommodation can be removed at a pace that is likely to be measured."

From December 2005 until March 2006, it said "some further measured policy firming is likely to be needed" and in May it tweaked that sentence to read "some further policy firming may yet be needed." That three-year period of hand-holding is now over. From Mr. Bernanke's perspective, this is probably not a moment too soon. While he supported the decision to provide explicit guidance in 2003, he saw this as an emergency measure . . .

Mr. Bernanke believes the Fed should explain its own forecasts and encourage market participants to make their own assessment of where the economy and interest rates are heading. This would be bad news for the legion of highly paid Fed watchers, whose job it is to parse every word the Fed issues for hints about its intentions . . .

Mr. Bernanke, under fire for allegedly confusing messages, has to proceed incrementally so as not to un-settle the market. More far-reaching changes will await the conclusion of a review of communications strategy by Fed vice-chairman Don Kohn, a stalwart of the Greenspan era.

Moreover, Mr. Bernanke could backtrack, as he arguably did on June 5, with a hard-hitting speech apparently aimed as much at shoring up the Fed's credibility as explaining the Fed's forecasts. c

ANALYZING THE NEWS ...

On February 1, 2006, Ben Bernanke was sworn in as the new chairman of the Federal Reserve. Bernanke took over the leadership of the U.S. central bank from Alan Greenspan, who retired after having served for over 10 years as Federal Reserve chairman. While Greenspan was widely respected by financial market participants around the world, he was also well known for his difficult-to-follow sentence prose. Some analysts would expend large amounts of effort pouring over every word the Fed Chairman spoke in an attempt to draw conclusions as to where financial markets were headed. As described in the chapter, the Federal Reserve chairman is typically very powerful in the setting of monetary policy.

a Some economists, including Mr. Bernanke, believed that financial market participants were placing far too much emphasis on the chairman's written and spoken words. Instead, these economists believed that financial market participants should spend more time and effort in analyzing the actual economic conditions in forming expectations about the Fed's next change in monetary policy.

b In 2003, the Federal Reserve had to switch from controlling inflation to the opposite problem of controlling fears of growing deflationary pressures. Deflation is dangerous because if market participants believe that prices will fall in the future, they will be reluctant to buy or produce goods and services and, instead, wait for prices to fall. Thus deflationary expectations can quickly lead to an economic slowdown. To counter these deflationary pressures, a central bank can pursue expansionary monetary policy actions (these are described in more detail in Chapter 20). For the central bank to reverse the deflationary beliefs, the central bank must have credibility. The financial market participants must believe that the central bank and the head of the central bank will be successful in their actions to fend off deflation.

c When central bankers give speeches, write articles, and give interviews, they are often trying to achieve two goals: (1) reduce uncertainty in financial markets and (2) strengthen the credibility of the central bank. The authors of the article suggest that Chairman Bernanke wants to reduce uncertainty by communicating more clearly how the Fed arrives at its forecasts.

For further thought . . .

Under what circumstances would the communication abilities of the Federal Reserve chairman be less important? Explain.

Source: Excerpted from "Bernanke Redefines How Fed Communicates with Markets," *Financial Times*, July 3, 2006, p. 2.

9. Is speculation in shares of stock of the Federal Reserve banks possible? Why or why not?
10. What are the duties of Federal Reserve banks?
11. "It is impossible to know where the true power and authority in an organization lie just from examining the formal structure of the organization." Does this observation apply to the Federal Reserve System? Explain.
12. *Evaluate:* The Federal Reserve System is independent of the political process in the United States.
13. *Evaluate:* To conduct monetary policy in the national interest, the Federal Reserve System should be independent of the political process in the United States.
14. *Evaluate:* The Fed's independence from the government's appropriations process necessarily rules out the principal-agent view of Fed motivation.

ANALYTICAL PROBLEMS

15. Is it easier for a central bank to be independent in a modern, industrial country or in a less developed country? What implications does your answer have for what the average inflation rate is likely to be in modern, industrial countries as opposed to less developed countries?
16. Suppose that you are the president of the country Moolah and that you are writing a new constitution for it. Would you give monetary policymakers complete independence from your government? Why or why not?
17. Research shows that 9 to 18 months after the Fed eases monetary policy, the economy shows increased real growth. Suppose that 18 months before a presidential election, the Fed announces a reduction of the discount rate by 1 percentage point. What would you conclude about the Fed's motivation? Would your conclusion change if, six months earlier, real output growth had been forecast to be 3% but the economy weakened and real output grew by only 1%?
18. Why might the president not want to appoint a tough-minded, independent chairman of the Federal Reserve Board of Governors but prefer someone with whom he or she had previous political ties?
19. Are the high rates of inflation that the United States experienced during the 1970s consistent with the public interest view of the Fed's motivation?
20. Is the principal-agent view of the Fed's motivation believable if Fed policymakers routinely turn down jobs on Wall Street that would double or triple their salaries?
21. A recent proposal would remove the presidents of the Federal Reserve banks from the FOMC and add the Secretary of the Treasury and the chairperson of the President's Council of Economic Advisers to the FOMC. What would such a proposal do to the Fed's independence? Would it make the Fed more accountable for its actions? How would regional concerns and information be communicated to the Fed?
22. Suppose that economic conditions worsen and the Fed considers easing monetary policy. But before the Fed can act, the president's chief economic advisor holds a press conference and states that the Fed should ease its policy to stimulate the economy. Does this statement make easing the policy less or more difficult for the Fed? Why?
23. According to an article in *The Wall Street Journal*, early in 1999: "Germany's determined finance minister, Oskar Lafontaine, urged the new European Central Bank to cut interest rates to boost corporate profits and, most important of all, create jobs." What impact do you believe the fact that the European Central Bank had been newly created would have on the likelihood of its accepting the advice of the German finance minister?
24. In Japan, the central bank is not formally independent. Yet Japan's inflation rate is much lower than that of the United States. Does this condition suggest that low inflation doesn't really depend on central bank independence? Why or why not?
25. *Evaluate:* The Fed's occasional mobilization of banking interests to defend itself against legislative attacks is inconsistent with the public interest view of Fed motivation.
26. During the debate in 1991 over reform of U.S. banking regulations, the Treasury advocated the removal of barriers between banking and commerce (for example, allowing nonfinancial firms to own depository institutions), but the Fed opposed such a move. Offer an explanation of the Fed's response in terms of (a) the public interest view of Fed motivation and (b) the principal-agent view of Fed motivation.

DATA QUESTIONS

27. In the *Federal Reserve Bulletin,* the Federal Reserve Open Market Transactions table lists the changes in the Fed's holdings of U.S. government and other securities in the System Open Market Account. Determine how much its holdings have changed during the past three years. In which year was monetary policy the "easiest"? In which year was it the "tightest"?

28. In the latest *Annual Report of the Board of Governors of the Federal Reserve System,* look up the table that reports historical data on "Income and Expenses" of Federal Reserve banks. Find the column that lists payments to the U.S. Treasury—the Fed's profits that are returned to the government. What is the total amount of the Fed's profits for the past three years? Now determine the total amount of U.S. federal government revenue for the past three years from the *Economic Report of the President.* What proportion of the government's total revenue was the Fed's income?

29. Look for articles in *The Wall Street Journal* in which the president or the Treasury Department (or another arm of the administration) delivers strong policy suggestions to the Fed, and then watch for the Fed's response.

30. One of the claims for central bank independence is that it reduces the likelihood of inflationary policies. One well-known study of this issue, by Harvard University economists Alberto Alesina and Lawrence Summers, strongly supports this contention. Consider a graph depicting the results of their research from a paper published by the Federal Reserve Bank of St. Louis, "Central Bank Independence and Economic Performance" (by Patricia S. Pollard) found at http://research.stlouisfed.org/publications/review/93/07/Bank_Jul_Aug1993.pdf. (The graph is on page 23 of the document.) Based solely on the graph, does there appear to be an inverse relationship between inflation and independence? Which countries appear to have high inflation and low independence? Which appear to have low inflation and high independence?

31. The Federal Reserve presents an annual report of its activities on an annual basis to Congress. Find the most recent issue (from http://www.federalreserve.gov/boarddocs/rptcongress/) and find the total amount of the Fed's profits over the last three years (under the heading for payments to the Treasury). Compare your answers with the amount of U.S. federal government revenue over the last three years (from the most recent issue of the *Economic Report of the President*—http://origin.www.gpoaccess.gov/eop/download.html). What proportion of the U.S. government's revenue is made up of the Fed's income?

CHAPTER 20
Monetary Policy Tools

In the fall of 2001, the Federal Reserve made headlines again and again. In the immediate aftermath of the terrorist attacks on September 11, 2001, the Fed's expanded discount lending ensured the smooth operation of commercial banks in affected areas. The $45 *billion* in discount loans outstanding on September 12 dwarfed the $59 *million* average for the prior 10 weeks. On September 17, the Fed cut the federal funds rate by one-half percentage point just before the New York Stock Exchange reopened, boosting confidence. The Fed reacts to the economic environment in setting monetary policy, and changes in monetary policy (implemented with open market operations, discount lending, or setting reserve requirements) affect interest rates, output, and inflation.

In this chapter, we describe the implementation of the Fed's monetary policy tools and see how they can be used to affect short-term interest rates. This chapter extends our study of monetary policy tools from Chapters 17 and 18, in which we described how those tools could change the monetary base and the money supply. As you might expect, the Fed's actions and uses of its policy tools are not without their critics. We also include some of the controversy about the Fed's use of monetary policy tools and alternatives that economists have proposed to improve monetary decisions.

Another theme of this chapter is *Fed watching*: many individuals and organizations scrutinize the actions of the Fed to forecast changes in interest rates and to predict economic changes. Leading banks and Wall Street firms rely on in-house analysis of the Fed's intentions and actions in guiding lending and investment decisions. Individuals watch the Fed's moves to guide decisions about buying a home or making investments. As you will see, understanding how the Fed uses its policy tools is an important component of Fed watching.

Open Market Operations

Open market operations, the purchases and sales of securities in financial markets by the Fed, are the dominant means by which the Fed changes the monetary base. Recall from Chapter 17 that an open market purchase increases the monetary base (generally by increasing bank reserves) and that an open market sale decreases the monetary base. If the money multiplier is relatively stable, the Fed can use open market operations to regulate the money supply by changing the monetary base.

The original Federal Reserve Act didn't specifically mention open market operations, because they weren't well understood in financial markets at that time. The Fed began to use open market purchases as a policy tool during the 1920s when it acquired World War I Liberty Bonds from banks, enabling banks to finance more business loans. Before 1935, district Federal Reserve banks conducted limited open market operations in securities markets, but these transactions lacked central coordination to achieve a monetary policy goal. The lack of concerted intervention by the Fed during the banking crisis of the early 1930s led Congress to establish the Federal Open Market Committee (FOMC) to guide open market operations.

Web Site Suggestions: http://www.federalreserve.gov/fomc/ Describes the work of the FOMC and lists its current members.

The Fed generally conducts open market operations in liquid Treasury securities markets, affecting interest rates in those markets. An open market purchase of Treasury securities increases their price, all else being equal, thereby decreasing their yield and expanding the money supply. An open market sale decreases the price of Treasury securities, thereby increasing their yield and contracting the money supply. Open market purchases tend to reduce interest rates and so are viewed as *expansionary*; open market sales tend to increase interest rates and so are viewed as *contractionary*.

The Fed's actions influence interest rates on other securities. Although the differences in yields on different assets depend on their risk, liquidity, and information costs, the change in the interest rate on Treasury securities has an immediate impact on their yield and return. When the news media say that the Fed sets interest rates, they are implicitly summarizing this process.

We now turn to actions that the FOMC takes to carry out open market transactions.

Implementing Open Market Operations

How does the FOMC guide open market operations? It meets eight times per year (roughly every six weeks) and issues a **general directive** stating its overall objectives for interest rates. The directive also describes instructions for open market operations. These directives are less precise than reserve requirement and discount rate policies. Lacking perfect foresight, the FOMC can't determine in advance the exact actions that are needed to achieve its objectives for changes in interest rates and monetary aggregates.

The Federal Reserve System's account manager (a vice president of the Federal Reserve Bank of New York) is responsible for carrying out open market operations that fulfill the FOMC's objectives. The **Open Market Trading Desk,** a group of traders at the Federal Reserve Bank of New York, trades government securities over the counter electronically with primary dealers. *Primary dealers* are private securities firms selected by the Fed that trade government securities and are permitted to trade directly with the Fed. Before making transactions, the trading desk notifies all the dealers at the same time, asks them to submit offers, and gives them a deadline. The Fed's account manager goes over the list, accepts the best offers, and then has the trading desk buy or sell the securities until the volume of reserves reaches the Fed's desired goal. These securities are either added to or subtracted from the portfolios of the various Federal Reserve banks according to their shares of total assets in the system.

How does the account manager know what to do? The manager interprets the FOMC's most recent directive, holds daily conferences with two members of the FOMC, and personally analyzes financial market conditions. Then the manager compares the level of reserves in the banking system with the desired level recommended by the directive. If the level that the directive suggests is greater than actual bank reserves, the account manager purchases securities to raise the level of bank reserves toward the desired level. If the level that the directive suggests is less than actual reserves, the account manager sells securities to lower reserves toward the desired level. The desk is connected to its trading partners through an electronic system called the Trading Room Automated Processing System, or TRAPS.

One way the account manager conducts open market operations is through **outright purchases and sales** of Treasury securities of various maturities by the trading desk—that is, by buying from or selling to dealers. More commonly, the manager uses **Federal Reserve repurchase agreements** (analogous to commercial bank repos, discussed in Chapter 13). Through these agreements, the Fed buys securities from a dealer in the government securities market, and the dealer agrees to buy them back at a given price at a specified future date, usually within one week. In effect, the government securities serve as collateral for a short-term loan. For open market sales, the trading desk often engages in **matched sale-purchase transactions** (sometimes called *reverse repos*), in which the Fed sells securities to dealers in the government securities market and the dealers agree to sell them back to the Fed in the near future.

In conducting the Fed's open market operations, the trading desk makes both dynamic and defensive transactions. Open market operations that are intended to change monetary policy as desired by the FOMC are known as **dynamic transactions.** A much greater volume of open market transactions are **defensive transactions,** which the Fed's traders use to offset fluctuations in the monetary base arising from portfolio allocation preferences of banks and the nonbank public, financial markets, and the economy. In other words, the Fed uses defensive transactions to offset the effects of disturbances to the monetary base, not to change monetary policy.

Defensive open market operations may be used to compensate for either predictable or unexpected events that change the monetary base. For example, the nonbank public predictably increases its demand for currency before Christmas and other holidays and in response to seasonal preferences for travel. The Fed can also predict certain types of borrowing: borrowing within the banking system occurs periodically to satisfy reserve requirements; and the U.S. Treasury, foreign governments, and large corporations often sell or buy blocks of securities at announced intervals. Other, less predictable, disturbances come from the Treasury or the Fed. Although the Treasury attempts to synchronize withdrawals from its bank accounts with its bill paying (to avoid large shifts in the currency or reserves), it doesn't always succeed. Disruptions in the Fed's own balance sheet caused by Federal Reserve float or changes in discount loans, the amount of Treasury coins outstanding, or the Treasury's holdings of Federal Reserve Notes also produce short-term fluctuations in the monetary base. Fluctuations in Treasury deposits with the Fed and in Federal Reserve float are the most important of the unexpected disturbances to the monetary base.

There are other reasons for defensive transactions besides those needed to correct fluctuations in the monetary base. Even if the monetary base remains constant, movements of currency between the nonbank public and bank reserves affect the volume of bank deposits. Multiple deposit expansion or contraction then causes fluctuations in monetary base. Economic disturbances, such as major strikes or natural disasters, also cause unexpected fluctuations in the demand for currency and bank reserves. The Fed's account manager must respond to unintended increases or decreases in the monetary base and sell or buy securities to maintain the monetary policy indicated by the FOMC's guidelines.

Open Market Operations Versus Other Policy Tools

Open market operations have several benefits that other policy tools lack: control, flexibility, and ease of implementation.

Control. Because the Fed initiates open market purchases and sales, it completely controls their volume. Discount loans also increase or decrease the monetary base, but discount loans enable the Fed to influence the direction of the change in the monetary base rather than to control the volume of reserves added to or taken from the monetary base.

CONSIDER THIS . . .

A Day's Work at the Open Market Trading Desk

9:00 a.m.

The account manager begins informal discussions with market participants to assess conditions in the government securities market. From these discussions and from data supplied by the staff of the FOMC, the account manager estimates how the prices of government securities will change during the trading day.

10:00 a.m.

The account manager's staff compares forecasts on Treasury deposits and information on the timing of future Treasury sales of securities with the staff of the Office of Government Finance in the Treasury Department.

10:15 a.m.

The account manager reads staff reports on forecasted shifts in the monetary base arising from temporary portfolio shifts, fluctuations in financial markets or the economy, or weather-related disturbances (for example, events that might extend the time for checks to clear).

11:15 a.m.

After reviewing the information from the various staffs, the account manager studies the FOMC's directive. This directive identifies the ranges for growth rates of the monetary aggregates and the level of the federal funds rate desired. The account manager must design *dynamic* open market operations to implement changes requested by the FOMC and *defensive* open market operations to offset temporary disturbances in the monetary base predicted by the staff. The account manager places the daily conference call to at least two members of the FOMC to discuss trading strategy.

11:30 a.m.

On approval of the trading strategy, the traders at the Federal Reserve Bank of New York notify the primary dealers in the government securities market of the Fed's desired transactions. If traders plan to make open market purchases, they request quotations for asked prices. If traders plan to make open market sales, they request quotations for bid prices. (Recall that government securities are traded over the counter.) The traders select the lowest prices offered when making purchases and accept the highest bids when making sales.

12:30 p.m.

Soliciting quotes and trading take about 45 minutes, so by about 12:30 p.m., the trading room at the Federal Reserve Bank of New York is less hectic. No three-martini lunch for the account manager and staff, though; they spend the afternoon monitoring conditions in the federal funds market and the level of bank reserves to get ready for the next day of trading.

Flexibility. The Fed can make both large and small open market operations. Often, dynamic transactions require large purchases or sales, whereas defensive transactions call for small securities purchases or sales. Other policy tools lack this flexibility. Reversing open market operations is simple for the Fed. For example, if it decides that its open market sales have made the money supply grow too slowly, it can quickly authorize open market purchases. Discount loans and reserve requirement changes are more difficult to reverse quickly.

Ease of implementation. The Fed can implement its securities transactions rapidly, with no administrative delays. All that is required is for the trading desk to place buy and sell orders with dealers in the government securities markets. Changing the discount rate or reserve requirements requires lengthier deliberation.

Fed Watching and FOMC Directives

Merely observing the Fed's trading activity doesn't necessarily provide reliable information regarding the Fed's *intentions* for monetary policy. For example, the Fed could acquire securities one day and dispose of securities the next day while pursuing the same overall monetary policy.

To discern the Fed's intentions, Fed watchers read carefully the directives issued by the Fed. They do this to try to discern the Fed's policy goals. As of February 1994, the

CONSIDER THIS . . .

How Do You Decode FOMC Statements?

Since February 2000, the essence of the FOMC's policy decisions has been expressed in its statement issued at the end of each meeting. Prior to this time, substantive statements were released only in the event of a policy action or to clarify the FOMC's view about prospective developments in the economy. Under the earlier procedures, the Fed's statements and its domestic policy directive described a "policy bias" toward increasing or decreasing the federal funds rate. The new procedures are designed to make more transparent the Fed's communication with the public. In December 2004, the FOMC decided to move up the publication of its minutes to three weeks after the end of each meeting.

Under these procedures, the statement will point out the FOMC's view of the "balance of risks," described in the context of the Fed's goals as follows:

> Against the background of its long-run goals of price stability and sustainable economic growth and of the information currently available, the Committee believes that the risks are [balanced with respect to prospects for both goals] [weighted mainly toward conditions that may generate heightened inflation pressures] [weighted mainly toward conditions that may generate economic weakness] in the foreseeable future.

In 2002 and 2003, the FOMC struggled with the balance of risks, as the U.S. economy's recovery from the 2001 recession came in fits and starts. The Iraq conflict and the Fed's concern over the chance of deflation (a falling price level) further complicated the assessment of the balance of risks. For example, in its statement on January 29, 2003, the FOMC argued that "the risks are balanced with respect to the prospects for both goals [low inflation and maximum sustainable economic growth] for the foreseeable future." Yet, on March 18, the committee opined that geopolitical uncertainties surrounding the conflict in Iraq made a risk assessment too difficult: "[T]he Committee does not believe it can usefully characterize the current balance of risks with respect to the prospects for its long-term goals of price stability and economic growth."

By May 6 (and similarly on June 25), the FOMC actually split its balance of risk assessment for output growth and inflation: "[T]he Committee perceives that over the next few quarters the upside and downside risks to the attainment of sustainable growth are roughly equal. In contrast, over the same period, the probability of an unwelcome substantial fall in inflation, though minor, exceeds that of a pickup in inflation from its already low level. The Committee believes that, taken together, the balance of risks to achieving its goals is weighted toward weakness over the foreseeable future."

While over the five-month period the FOMC left the federal funds rate unchanged at 1.25%, it sent increasingly strong signals that it was prepared to cut the federal funds rate in the face of deflationary pressures. Response to the Fed's statements was mixed; some analysts praised the FOMC's emphasis on deflation, while others argued that the statements gave too few clues about the direction of monetary policy.

Fed began announcing policy changes made by the FOMC at the time they are made; analysts still read directives carefully for clues about the likely future course of monetary policy. In February 2000, the Fed began to discuss the future "balance of risks" in its FOMC statement, giving its opinion about the relative risk toward economic weakness or higher inflation.

Open Market Operations in Other Countries

Although the Fed relies most heavily on open market operations to change the money supply, central banks in some other countries favor different policy tools. Often, the choice of policy tools depends on the organization of a country's financial markets and institutions. The Fed uses open market operations because the markets for U.S. government securities are highly liquid.

In contrast, historically, the Bank of Japan did not rely on open market operations because a market for government securities didn't exist until the mid-1980s. Japan issued its first six-month treasury bills in 1986 and its first three-month treasury bills in 1989. Until then, the Japanese central bank had used interest rate controls and direct discount lending to banks to influence the money supply in the *Gensaki* market. The Bank of Japan conducts transactions for repurchase agreements in that market; the market is open to financial institutions and nonfinancial corporations and has been free of interest rate regulations since its inception in 1949. Nevertheless, the government treasury bill market in Japan is smaller than that in the United States. Economists studying the Japanese financial system predict that the market for short-term government securities will continue to grow in the new century, providing a better environment for open market operations by the Bank of Japan.

While the European Central Bank commenced operation only in January 1999, it has continued to conduct open market operations principally through fixed-term, fixed-frequency securities repurchase operations, the regular money market tenders through which European central banks have injected liquidity into the financial system. Outright transactions and foreign-exchange repurchase agreements are also used.

Discount Policy

Discount policy, which includes setting the discount rate and terms of discount lending, is the oldest of the Federal Reserve's principal tools for regulating the money supply. Discount policy affects the money supply by influencing the volume of discount loans, which are part of the monetary base. An increase in the volume of discount loans raises the monetary base and the money supply, whereas a decrease in the volume of discount loans reduces the monetary base and the money supply. The discount rate at which the Fed lends funds to depository institutions and its general attitude toward discount lending depend on the effects it wants to have on the money supply. The **discount window** is the means by which the Fed makes discount loans to banks, serving as a channel to meet the liquidity needs of banks.

Before 1980 (except for a brief period during 1966), the Fed made discount loans only to banks that were members of the Federal Reserve System. Indeed, banks perceived the ability to borrow from the Fed through the discount window as an advantage of membership that partially offset the cost of maintaining reserve requirements. Since 1980, all depository institutions have had access to the discount window. Each Federal Reserve bank maintains its own discount window.

Using the Discount Window

The Fed influences the volume of discount loans in two ways: it sets the price of loans (the discount rate) and the terms of its loans.

We can describe the *price effect* on discount loans of a change in the discount rate as follows. Suppose that the Fed increases the discount rate. Banks react to the higher discount rate by reducing their borrowing at the discount window. Hence an increase in the discount rate decreases the volume of discount loans, reducing the monetary base and the money supply. The higher discount rate also exerts upward pressure on other short-term interest rates. As a result, banks find it more expensive to raise funds from other sources, such as by borrowing in the federal funds market or by issuing certificates of deposit. A decrease in the discount rate has the opposite effect: the volume of discount loans rises, increasing the monetary base and the money supply. However, the Fed cannot be sure that banks will borrow from the discount window when the discount rate declines. If profitable lending and investment opportunities aren't available, banks might not increase their discount borrowing.[†]

Web Site Suggestions: http://www.frbdiscountwindow.org Provides details about the Fed's discount lending programs.

Since 2003, the Federal Reserve has reformed its discount lending programs to accomplish better its objectives of ensuring adequate liquidity in the banking system and serving as a backup source of short-term funding for banks. The Fed's discount loans to banks now fall in one of three categories: (1) primary credit, (2) secondary credit, and (3) seasonal credit.

Primary credit is available to healthy banks (generally those with adequate capital and supervisory ratings for safety and soundness). Banks may use primary credit for any purpose and do not have to seek funds from other sources before requesting a discount window loan from the primary credit facility, or *standing lending facility*. The primary credit interest rate is set above the primary credit rate (usually by 1 percentage point). Hence primary credit is only a backup source of funds, as healthy banks choose to borrow less expensively in the federal funds market or from other sources. With few restrictions on its use, primary credit should minimize banks' reluctance to borrow from the discount window, and funds will be available in the event of a temporary shortage in liquidity in the banking system.

Secondary credit is intended for banks that are not eligible for primary credit, and may not be used to fund an expansion of a bank's assets. The secondary credit interest rate is set above the primary credit rate (by 0.5 percentage point), at a penalty rate, because these borrowers are less financially healthy.

Seasonal credit consists of temporary, short-term loans to satisfy seasonal requirements of smaller depository institutions in geographical areas where agriculture or tourism is important. These loans reduce banks' costs of maintaining excess cash or seasonally liquidating loans and investments. The seasonal credit interest rate is tied to the average of rates on certificates of deposit and the federal funds rate. Because of improvements in credit markets, the case that a seasonal credit facility is needed is increasingly difficult to make.

Benefits of Discount Policy

Discount policy offers the Fed certain advantages that the other policy tools do not have. We describe two of these next: (1) contributing to the Fed's role as lender of last resort and (2) signaling the Fed's policy intentions. We then discuss drawbacks of discount policy as a monetary policy tool.

Averting financial crises: lender of last resort. The discount window provides the most direct way for the Fed to act as a lender of last resort to the banking system. Open market operations can change the level of bank reserves and affect short-term interest rates (such as the federal funds rate), but they can't address well the illiquidity problems of individual banks. Hence the Fed relies more on discount lending

[†]Historically, in addition to setting the discount rate, the Fed set the conditions for the availability of loans. One category of loans was made to financial institutions under exceptional circumstances to alleviate severe liquidity problems and restore the bank to financial health. An example is the more than $5 billion in discount loans that was extended to Continental Illinois Bank before its takeover by the FDIC. On January 9, 2003, the Federal Reserve replaced its previous programs, "adjustment" and "extended" credit, with "primary" and "secondary" credit programs. (The "seasonal" credit program was not changed.) In the new regime banks face few, if any, restrictions on their use of primary credit, and interest rates charged are now set above, rather than below, the prevailing rate for federal funds.

in its role as lender of last resort. The Fed's successes in handling the Penn Central crisis in the commercial paper market in 1970 and the stock market crash of 1987 suggest that decisive discount policy can reduce the costs of financial disturbances to the economy.

The Fed historically extended discount loans at its discretion, and an overly generous discount policy during financial crises may have encouraged too much risk taking by banks and the nonfinancial corporations that borrow from them. The reason is that banks, knowing that the Fed historically provided discount loans at favorable terms during business downturns, enforced credit standards less strictly, as happened during the 1980s.

But many analysts praise the Fed's discount window interventions, such as those that took place during the Penn Central crisis of 1970, the Franklin National Bank crisis of 1974, the Hunt brothers' silver manipulation efforts in 1980, the Continental Illinois Bank collapse in 1984, the stock market crash of October 1987, and the aftermath of the September 11 terrorist attacks. They conclude that these cases demonstrate the need for the Fed to continue its use of the discount window to extend credit, case by case, as a lender of last resort during financial crises.

Drawbacks of Discount Policy as a Monetary Policy Tool

Few economists advocate the use of discount policy as a tool of *monetary control*. Fluctuations in the spread between the federal funds rate and the discount rate set by the Fed can cause unintended increases or decreases in the monetary base and the money supply. Moreover, the Fed doesn't control discount policy as completely as it controls open market operations, and changing discount policy is much more difficult than changing open market operations (because banks must decide whether to accept discount loans). Hence the Fed doesn't use discount policy as its principal tool for influencing the money supply.

Discount Policy in Other Countries

Outside the United States, central banks generally use discount lending as a monetary policy tool and as a means of mitigating financial crises. In Japan, for example, the Bank of Japan quotes the *official discount rate* as the cost of its loans to private financial institutions that have accounts at the bank. Changes in the official discount rate are interpreted by financial market participants as reflecting changes in the Bank's basic stance on monetary policy. The European Central Bank uses standing discount facilities to provide and absorb overnight liquidity and signal the stance of monetary policy. As is the case in the United States (where discount loans are made by regional Federal Reserve Banks), the standing facilities are administered in a decentralized manner by national central banks.

CHECKPOINT

When reading *The Wall Street Journal*, you notice that short-term market interest rates (such as the federal funds rate or the yields on three-month Treasury bills) have been declining but that the Fed hasn't reduced its discount rate. Are the Fed's intentions for monetary policy expansionary or contractionary? The Fed may be trying to signal to financial markets that it wants short-term rates to rise. In that case, the Fed would be signaling a contractionary policy. ♦

Reserve Requirements

The Fed mandates that banks hold a certain fraction of their deposits in cash or deposits with the Fed. These **reserve requirements** are the last of the Fed's three principal monetary tools that we examine. In Chapter 17, we showed that the required reserve ratio is a determinant of the money multiplier in the money supply process. Recall that an increase in the required reserve ratio reduces the money multiplier and the money supply, whereas a reduction in the required reserve ratio increases the money multiplier and the money supply. Reserves can be stored as vault cash in banks or as deposits with the Federal Reserve. About 90% of banks meet their reserve requirements with vault cash. The other 10% comprise larger banks whose deposits at Federal Reserve banks account for most of those deposits.

The Board of Governors sets reserve requirements within congressional limits, an authority that was granted by Congress in the Banking Act of 1935. Historically, reserve requirements varied geographically, with member banks in large cities being required to hold more reserves relative to deposits than were banks in smaller cities and towns. This difference dates back to 1864, following the passage of the National Banking Act of 1863, and is another instance of the political compromises between rural and urban interests. Representatives of agricultural states feared abuse by large Eastern banks. To garner these representatives' support for the National Banking Act (1863) and later the Federal Reserve Act (1913), Congress authorized low reserve requirements for rural banks. Between 1966 and 1972, the Fed altered reserve requirements to reflect the size as well as location of depository institutions. In 1980, the Depository Institutions Deregulation and Monetary Control Act established uniform reserve requirements for all depository institutions, regardless of location.

Changes in Reserve Requirements

The Fed changes reserve requirements much more rarely than it conducts open market operations or changes the discount rate. Therefore Fed watchers view the announcement of a change in reserve requirements as a major shift in monetary policy. Because changes in reserve requirements require significant alterations in banks' portfolios, frequent changes would be disruptive. As a result, in the 30 years between 1950 and 1980, the Fed adjusted required reserve ratios gradually (about once a year) and followed changes by open market operations or discount lending to help banks adjust.

During the 1980s, the only changes in reserve requirements were shifts that were mandated by the Depository Institutions Deregulation and Monetary Control Act. Examples were a reduction (from November 1980 through October 1983) in the maturity of nonpersonal time deposits subject to a 3% reserve requirement (from four years to 18 months) and the automatic adjustment of the level of checkable deposits subject to the 3% requirement. In 1990, the Fed lowered reserve requirements on certain other time deposits to zero. In 1992, it reduced the reserve requirement on checkable deposits to 3% on the first $46.8 million and 10% on those in excess of $46.8 million. In 2006, the reserve requirement on checkable deposits was 0% on the first $8.5 million, then 3% up to $45.8 million, and 10% on those in excess of $45.8 million. Eurocurrency liabilities and nonpersonal time deposits currently have no reserve requirement. Over the past several years, lower reserve requirements and the introduction of sweep accounts at banks (which move customer deposits each day from liabilities against which reserves are required to liabilities with no reserve requirement) have reduced required reserve balances.

Measurement and Compliance

Every two weeks, the Fed monitors compliance with its reserve requirements by checking a bank's daily deposits. These two-week *maintenance periods* begin on a Thursday and end on a Wednesday. For each period, the Fed measures the bank's daily deposits with Federal Reserve banks. It calculates the average daily balances in the bank's transactions accounts over a two-week period ending the previous Monday. The Fed also checks the bank's vault cash over a two-week period ending the Monday three days before the maintenance period begins. These built-in accounting lags give the Fed time to analyze the reserve–deposit ratio and give the bank time to adjust its portfolio.

If a bank can't meet its reserve requirements, it can carry up to 4% or $50,000, whichever is greater, of its required reserves to the next two-week maintenance period. If this carryover proves inadequate and the bank still is deficient, the Fed charges interest on the deficit at a rate 2% above the discount rate. This higher rate gives banks an incentive to satisfy reserve requirements. (Similarly, a bank can carry forward up to 4% surplus of required reserves in anticipation of future deficits.) A bank that has inadequate reserves also may borrow funds in the federal funds market or from the Fed through the discount window. The federal funds market can be very active on Wednesdays, when maintenance periods end, as banks try to meet their reserve requirements.

Criticism of Reserve Requirements

Economists and policymakers continue to debate what the Fed's role in setting reserve requirements should be. In the following discussion, we present arguments for and against reserve requirements as a monetary policy tool.

Reserve requirements are costly as a monetary policy tool. Reserves earn no interest, so the use of reserve requirements to control the money supply process effectively places a tax on bank intermediation. In other words, by not being able to lend reserves, banks face a higher cost on funds that they obtain from depositors. For example, suppose that banks pay depositors 5% on deposits and that the required reserve ratio is 10%. On a deposit of $100, the bank must keep $10 in reserves and may loan the remaining $90. It must pay depositors $5 in interest, so its cost of funds to lend $90 is ($5/$90)(100) = 5.6%, rather than 5%.

Large increases in reserve requirements can adversely affect the economy. Increasing the tax on bank intermediation reduces bank lending, which decreases credit availability and the money supply.

Because reserve requirements are a tax on bank deposits and because unwise changes in reserve requirements may have bad economic consequences, economists and policymakers often debate whether the Fed *should* set reserve requirements. Over the years, they have offered two arguments in support of reserve requirements: the liquidity argument and the monetary control argument. To analyze whether the Fed should set reserve requirements, we need to find out how well each argument stands up to close scrutiny.

Liquidity argument. When banks convert liquid deposits to illiquid loans, they incur liquidity risk. As a result, some analysts argue that reserve requirements create a liquid pool of funds to assist illiquid, but solvent, banks during a banking panic. One problem with this view is that, although reserve requirements do produce a pool of liquid funds for the banking system as a whole, they have a limited effect on the liquidity of an individual bank. The decision to hold liquid assets is a portfolio allocation decision that is made by a bank. Reserve requirements limit the funds that a bank has available to invest in loans or securities, but they don't eliminate the need to maintain

OTHER TIMES, OTHER PLACES . . .

An Early Mistake in Setting Reserve Requirements

During the banking crisis of the early 1930s, commercial banks cut back on lending and accumulated excess reserves of about $800 million by the end of 1933. Excess reserves were greater than 40% of required reserves, compared to less than 1% today. By the end of 1935, the level of excess reserves reached more than $3 billion, or about 115% of required reserves. The newly created Federal Open Market Committee worried that significant levels of excess reserves would eliminate its ability to dominate the money supply process. For example, an economic upturn could lead banks to reduce their excess reserves, thereby expanding the money supply.

The Fed needed to find a way to reduce the level of reserves. Large-scale open market sales of securities weren't possible; at about $2.5 billion, the Fed's portfolio of government securities wasn't large enough to eliminate banks' excess reserves. As a result, after it obtained control over the setting of reserve requirements in 1935, the Fed's first significant change was a series of increases in required reserve ratios between August 1936 and May 1937. These effectively doubled the level of required reserves relative to deposits.

This strategy was unsuccessful because bank holdings of excess reserves reflected deliberate portfolio allocation decisions. Hence when the Fed increased reserve requirements, banks maintained their high excess reserves by cutting back on loans. This decline in bank lending made credit unavailable for many borrowers. Many economists blame the large reduction in the growth of the money supply and in the supply of bank credit as important causes of the business recession in 1937 and 1938. As bank lending declined, the Fed was pressured to reduce reserve requirements, which it did.

some portion of these funds in liquid assets. Individual banks still need to hold some of their portfolios in marketable securities as a cushion against unexpected deposit outflows.

Another problem with the liquidity argument is that the likelihood of a liquidity crisis depends not only on the volatility of withdrawals from banks, but also on the volatility of the value of bank assets and the availability to banks of funds from nondeposit sources. However, improvements in markets for loan sales and the growing number of nondeposit sources of funds make liquidity crises less likely, regardless of the volatility of depositors' withdrawals. Moreover, the Fed's ability to intervene directly in a liquidity crisis by making discount loans lessens the danger of such a crisis.

Monetary control argument. A second argument for reserve requirements is that they increase the central bank's control over the money supply process. Recall that the percentage of deposits that are held as reserves is one determinant of the money multiplier and hence of the responsiveness of the money supply to a change in the monetary base. Fed control of the reserve–deposit ratio through reserve requirements makes the money multiplier more stable and the money supply more controllable.

There are two problems with this argument. First, banks would hold reserves even if there were no reserve requirements. Hence reserve requirements need not greatly increase monetary control. Second, there is little evidence that reserve requirements actually improve the stability of the money multiplier.

The late Nobel laureate Milton Friedman proposed an extreme example of the monetary control argument: banks should hold 100% reserves. Under such a system, bank reserves would equal deposits, and the monetary base (the sum of bank reserves and currency in the hands of the nonbank public) would equal the sum of currency and bank deposits, or the *M1* money supply. With 100% reserves, multiple deposit expansion would cease, giving the Fed complete control over currency plus deposits but not over the composition of deposits.

Would complete control of currency and bank deposits translate into control of the *effective* money supply? Probably not. Under a 100% reserve system, banks could not originate or hold loans. Alternative financial intermediaries would emerge to fill this lending vacuum. Because banks have special information advantages in certain types of lending, this shift in financial intermediation could be costly for the economy. Therefore high reserve requirements are not likely to improve monetary control or promote financial intermediaries' role in matching savers and borrowers.

Coping with reserve requirements. One incentive to form bank holding companies (BHCs) was the exemption of such companies' debt from reserve requirements. The Fed responded in 1970 to the growth in this alternative source of funds by imposing a 5% reserve requirement on commercial paper issued by BHCs. In October 1979, in an attempt to increase its control over the money supply, the Fed announced reserve requirements of 8% for several nondeposit sources of bank funds, including repurchase agreements, federal funds borrowing, and asset sales to foreign banks. Since passage of the Depository Institutions Deregulation and Monetary Control Act of 1980, the Fed has applied reserve requirements only to checkable deposits, Eurocurrency accounts, and nonpersonal time deposits with a maturity of less than 18 months. (And since 1992, reserve requirements apply only to checkable deposits.) Hence banks (particularly large banks) can effectively avoid the tax on intermediation as they acquire funds.

Reserve Requirements in Other Countries

Although the reserve requirements imposed by the Bank of Japan do not allow for the payment of interest (consistent with U.S. practice), not all countries follow this practice. In late 1998, for example, the European Central Bank (ECB) inaugurated a system of interest-bearing minimum reserves as a monetary policy tool for the members of European economic and monetary union. The ECB's required reserve ratio varies between 1.5% and 2.5%, and reserve balances are credited with interest at the prevailing repo rate, the ECB's key short-term interest rate. In mid-2006, China raised reserve requirements to curb what was deemed to be excessive growth in bank lending.

Around the world there has been a general trend toward lower reserve requirements. Such requirements were eliminated entirely in the 1990s in Canada, Australia, New Zealand, and Switzerland, for example. One reason for this trend is the acknowledgment of central banks that reserve requirements effectively tax banking and financial intermediation. Such a tax raises the cost of funds and can make banks less competitive in the global financial marketplace. When the Fed announced lower reserve requirements in the United States in 1992, it specifically cited the "tax cut" argument to justify its action.

Because reserve requirements are now very low, some central bankers have worried that at very low levels of required reserves, the central bank has little control over short-term interest rates. Some countries (including Australia, Canada, and New Zealand) have responded to this concern by setting up a *channel* or *corridor system* for conducting monetary policy. Under this system, the central bank establishes a standing lending facility (like that used in the United States) ready to lend any amount to banks at a fixed *lombard rate*, i_l. The central bank then establishes another standing facility that pays a set interest rate i_r on any reserves that banks wish to deposit with the central bank. Hence as the demand curve for reserves shifts, the overnight interest rate always lies between i_r and i_l.

CHECKPOINT

Suppose the Fed reduces the reserve requirement on checkable deposits. How does your bank benefit? Do you and other depositors benefit? In the short run, your bank's profits increase; it can invest the freed funds and earn additional income from loans and investments (reserves pay no interest). In the long run, returns to depositors increase, as the bank becomes willing to pay more to attract deposits. ♦

Fed Watching: Analyzing the Policy Tools

All three of the Fed's principal monetary policy tools influence the monetary base primarily through changes in the demand for or supply of reserves. Hence to develop your skills as a Fed watcher, you need to study carefully the market for reserves, also known as the federal funds market. This section demonstrates how you can predict the outcome of changes in Fed policy on the level of bank reserves, R, and the federal funds rate, i_{ff}. The change in the federal funds rate will be mirrored by other short-term interest rates. Thus being able to predict how the fed funds rate will change will help you to make more informed investment decisions.

The Federal Funds Market

Web Site Suggestions: http://www.newyorkfed.org/aboutthefed/fedpoint/fed15.html Offers a thorough description of the federal funds market.

To analyze the determinants of the federal funds rate, we need to examine the banking system's demand for and the Fed's supply of reserves. We use a graphical analysis of the demand for and supply of reserves to see how the Fed uses its policy tools to influence the federal funds rate and the money supply.

Demand. Reserve demand reflects banks' demand for required and excess reserves. The demand function for federal funds, D, shown in Figure 20.1, includes both required reserves, RR, and excess reserves, ER, for constant reserve requirements and market interest rates other than the federal funds rate. As the federal funds rate, i_{ff}, increases, banks prefer to hold a lower level of reserves; a higher federal funds rate increases the "reserve tax," so required reserves are negatively related to market interest rates. Banks' demand for excess reserves is also sensitive to interest rate changes; at a lower federal funds rate, the opportunity cost of holding excess reserves falls and the quantity of excess reserves demanded rises. Hence the total quantity demanded of reserves is negatively related to the federal funds rate.

Supply. The supply function for reserves, S, also shown in Figure 20.1, represents the supply by the Fed of borrowed reserves (discount loans) and nonborrowed reserves (supplied by open market operations). Note that the supply curve is not a straight line: The vertical portion represents nonborrowed reserves, NBR, supplied by the Fed; that is, regardless of the federal funds rate, reserves equal to NBR are available. The change in the slope of the supply curve occurs at the discount rate, i_d: At a federal funds rate below the discount rate, borrowing from the Fed is zero because banks can borrow more cheaply from other banks. Hence, in this case, reserves equal nonborrowed reserves. When there is demand pressure for the federal funds rate to move above the discount rate, borrowing increases. Specifically, if i_{ff} were greater than i_d, banks would want to borrow as much as they could from the Fed at rate i_d and lend the funds out at the higher rate i_{ff}. Hence the supply curve becomes flat (that is, perfectly elastic), as shown in Figure 20.1.

FIGURE 20.1

Equilibrium in the Federal Funds Market

Equilibrium in the market for reserves is at the intersection of the demand (D) and supply (S) curves. Given nonborrowed reserves, NBR, and the discount rate, i_d, equilibrium reserves equal R^*, and the equilibrium federal funds rate is i^*_{ff}.

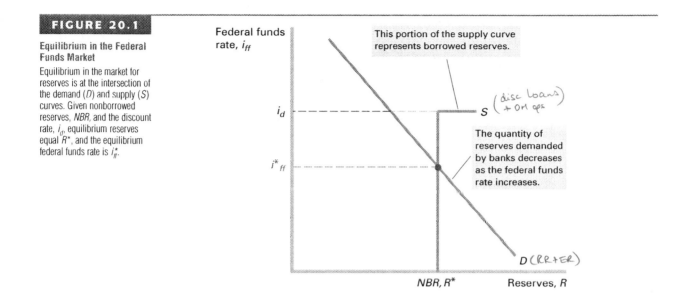

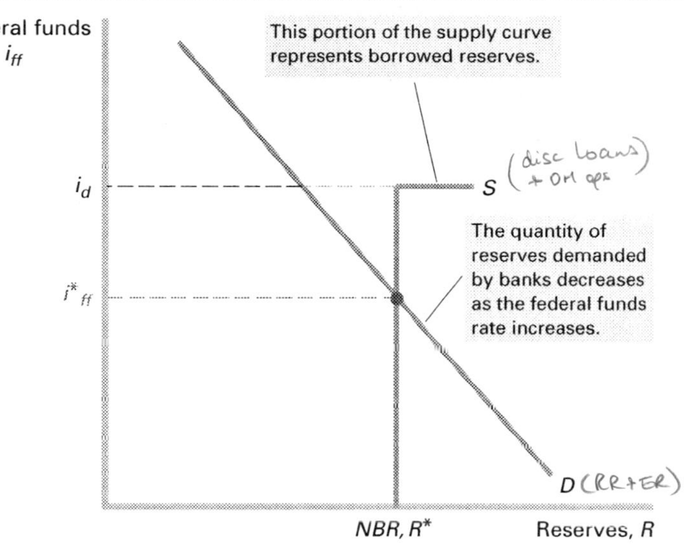

Web Site Suggestions: http://www.federalreserve.gov/fomc/fundsrate.htm Discusses federal funds rate targets.

Equilibrium. The equilibrium federal funds rate and level of reserves occur at the intersection of the demand and supply curves in Figure 20.1. Equilibrium reserves equal R^*, the equilibrium federal funds rate equals i^*_{ff}, and the discount rate is i_d.

Open Market Operations

Suppose that the Fed decides to purchase $1 billion of Treasury securities. If nothing else changes, an open market purchase of securities by the Fed shifts the reserve supply curve to the right, from S_0 to S_1, as in Figure 20.2(a), increasing bank reserves and decreasing the federal funds rate. As a result of the open market purchase, the volume of bank reserves increases from R^*_0 to R^*_1, and the federal funds rate declines from i^*_{ff0} to i^*_{ff1}. Similarly, an open market sale of securities by the Fed shifts the reserve supply curve to the left, from S_0 to S_1, in Figure 20.2(b), decreasing the level of bank reserves from R^*_0 to R^*_1 and increasing the federal funds rate from i^*_{ff0} to i^*_{ff1}. An open market purchase of securities by the Fed decreases the federal funds rate. An open market sale of securities increases the federal funds rate.

Changes in the Discount Rate

Now let's examine the effects of a change in the discount rate on the level of reserves and the federal funds rate. Suppose that the Fed decides to raise the discount rate. An increase in the discount rate means that banks will find borrowing to be less attractive at any federal funds rate. (Assume, as in the figure, that some discount lending is occurring.) Figure 20.3(a) shows that an increase in the discount rate from i_{d0} to i_{d1} shifts the horizontal portion of the supply schedule upward from S_0 to S_1. The equilibrium level of reserves falls from R^*_0 to R^*_1, and the federal funds rate rises from i^*_{ff0} to i^*_{ff1}.

Suppose that the Fed decided to cut the discount rate. In this case, banks now find borrowing more attractive at any federal funds rate. Figure 20.3(b) shows that a decrease in the discount rate from i_{d0} to i_{d1} shifts the horizontal portion of the supply curve downward from S_0 to S_1. The equilibrium level of reserves rises from R^*_0 to R^*_1, and the federal funds rate falls from i^*_{ff0} to i^*_{ff1}.

FIGURE 20.2 **Effects of Open Market Operations on the Federal Funds Market**

As shown in (a):

1. An open market purchase of securities by the Fed increases nonborrowed reserves, shifting the supply curve to the right from S_0 to S_1.
2. Reserves increase from R_0^* to R_1^*, while the federal funds rate falls from i_{ff0}^* to i_{ff1}^*.

As shown in (b):

1. An open market sale of securities by the Fed reduces nonborrowed reserves, shifting the supply curve to the left from S_0 to S_1.
2. Reserves decrease from R_0^* to R_1^*, while the federal funds rate rises from i_{ff0}^* to i_{ff1}^*.

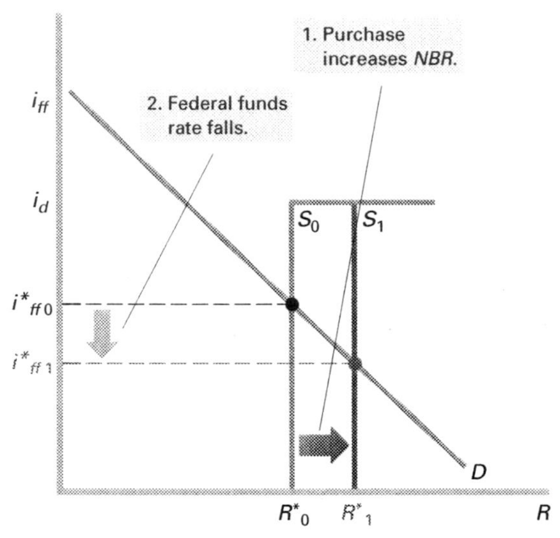

(a) Open Market Purchase of Securities

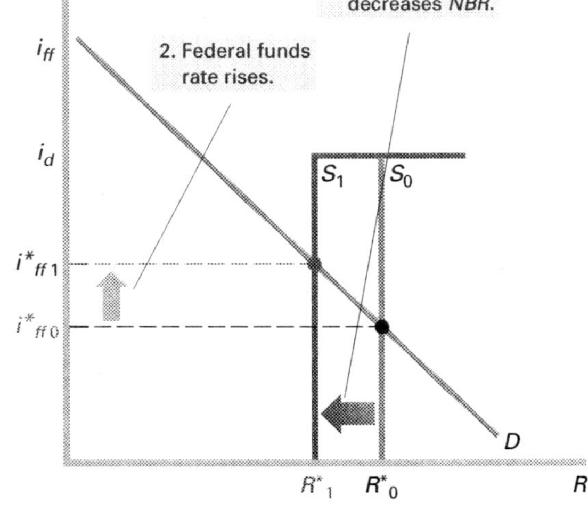

(b) Open Market Sale of Securities

Changes in Reserve Requirements

Finally, suppose that the Fed decides to raise the required reserve ratio. If the other factors underlying the demand and supply curves for reserves are held constant, an increase in the required reserve ratio shifts the demand curve to the right (from D_0 to D_1) because banks have to hold more reserves, as in Figure 20.4(a). As a result, the federal funds rate increases (from i_{ff0}^* to i_{ff1}^*). However, a reduction in the required reserve ratio, as shown in Figure 20.4(b), shifts the demand curve to the left (from D_0 to D_1) because banks demand a smaller amount of reserves, decreasing the federal funds rate (from i_{ff0}^* to i_{ff1}^*). If nothing else changes, an increase in reserve requirements increases the federal funds rate. A decrease in reserve requirements decreases the federal funds rate. Generally, however, the Fed does not use changes in reserve requirements to affect the federal funds rate; instead, the Fed uses changes in nonborrowed reserves to offset effects on the federal funds rate of a change in reserve requirements.

Other Disturbances of the Monetary Base

You can use graphs to analyze other disturbances of the monetary base that might lead the Fed to conduct defensive open market operations. For example, an increase in Federal Reserve float increases nonborrowed reserves (Chapter 18). Hence the supply curve for reserves shifts to the right, leading to higher reserves and a lower federal funds rate than otherwise would occur. As we noted in discussing defensive transactions earlier in

FIGURE 20.3 Effects of Changes in the Discount Rate on the Federal Funds Market

As shown in (a):

1. The Fed raises the discount rate from i_{d0} to i_{d1}.
2. The new supply curve is S_1.
3. The level of reserves falls from R_0^* to R_1^*, and the federal funds rate rises from i^*_{ff0} to i^*_{ff1}.

As shown in (b):

1. The Fed cuts the discount rate from i_{d0} to i_{d1}.
2. The new supply curve is S_1.
3. The level of reserves rises from R_0^* to R_1^*, and the federal funds rate falls from i^*_{ff0} to i^*_{ff1}.

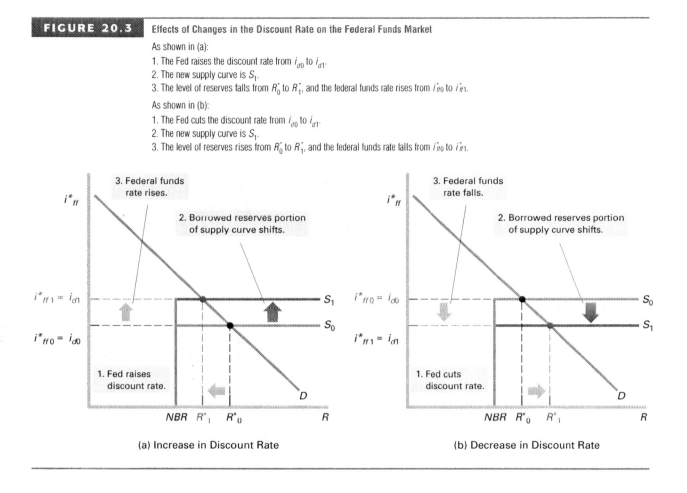

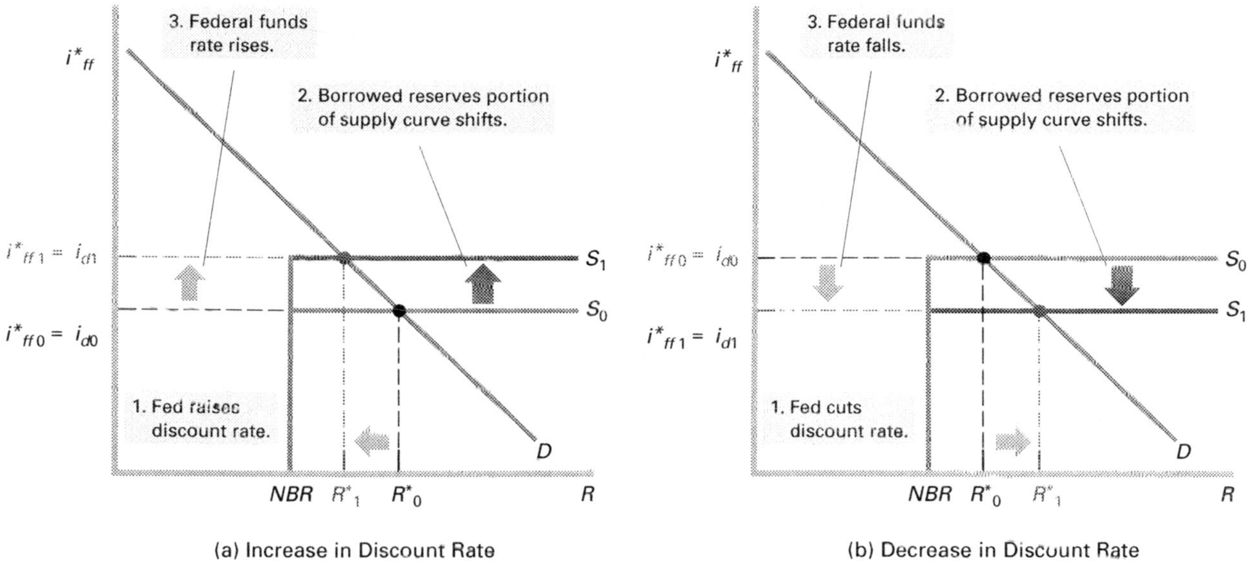

this chapter, the Fed can shift the supply curve for reserves back to the left (by reducing nonborrowed reserves) with an open market sale of securities.

As another example, a large increase in U.S. Treasury deposits with the Fed causes bank deposits to fall. As a result, reserves fall, the supply curve for reserves shifts to the left, and the federal funds rate rises. The Open Market Trading Desk, being in contact with the Treasury, knows about the Treasury action and therefore offsets it with another defensive open market purchase of securities. This action shifts the supply curve back to the right and restores the level of reserves and the federal funds rate to their initial levels.

The Federal Funds Rate and Monetary Policy

Many economists and financial market analysts use changes in the federal funds rate as a summary measure of the Fed's intentions for monetary policy. The reason is that the Fed's substantial control of the level of bank reserves gives it great influence over the level of the federal funds rate. An increase in the federal funds rate relative to other interest rates is interpreted as contractionary, signaling the Fed's intention to raise interest rates and discourage spending in the economy. Conversely, a decrease in the federal funds rate relative to other interest rates is interpreted as expansionary, signaling the Fed's intention to reduce interest rates and encourage spending. The use of short-term

FIGURE 20.4 **Effects of Changes in Required Reserves on the Federal Funds Market**

As shown in (a):

1. An increase in reserve requirements by the Fed increases required reserves, shifting the demand curve from D_0 to D_1.
2. The federal funds rate rises from i^*_{ff0} to i^*_{ff1}.

As shown in (b):

1. A decrease in reserve requirements by the Fed decreases required reserves, shifting the demand curve from D_0 to D_1.
2. The federal funds rate falls from i^*_{ff0} to i^*_{ff1}.

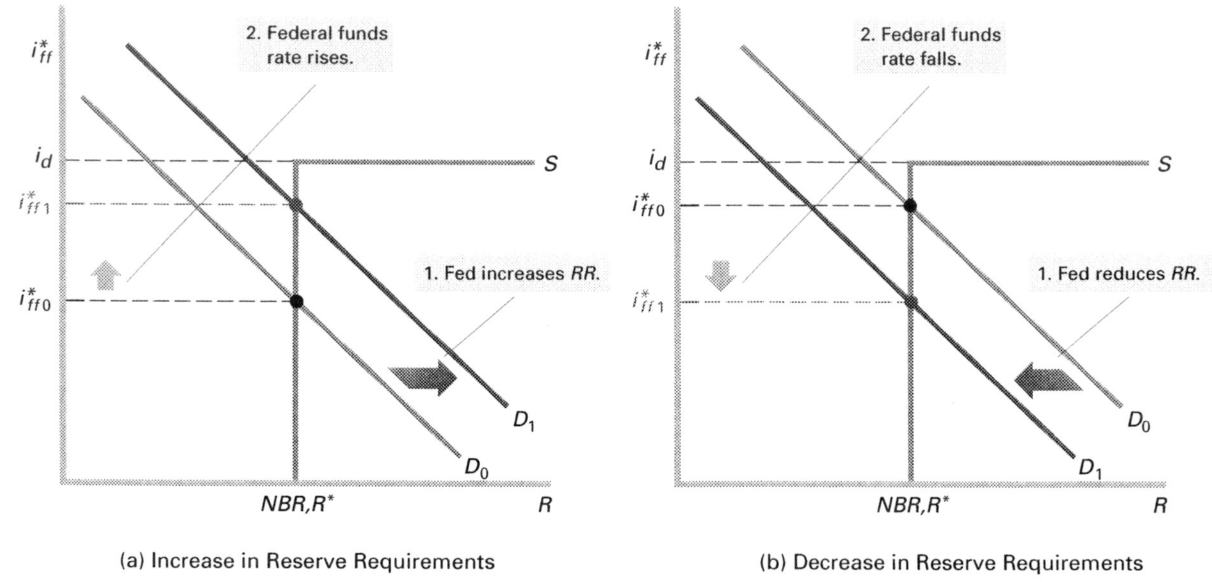

interest rates to signal shifts in monetary policy is also common in countries in the European Monetary Union, the United Kingdom, and Japan.

Our graphical analysis confirms this view and shows how analysts can predict consequences of the Fed's actions for the level of reserves and the federal funds rate. Thus, if nothing else changes, an open market purchase of securities by the Fed reduces the federal funds rate. Purchases are expansionary because they increase the supply of reserves that banks use either to purchase securities or to make loans. As a result, the larger reserves in the banking system lead to lower short-term interest rates. Sales are contractionary because they reduce reserves and increase short-term interest rates. An increase in the discount rate is contractionary when it signals that the Fed wants to raise short-term interest rates. A reduction in the discount rate is expansionary when it signals that the Fed wants to reduce short-term interest rates. If nothing else changes, an increase in reserve requirements with no offsetting changes in the supply of reserves is contractionary and raises the federal funds rate. A decrease in reserve requirements is expansionary and lowers the federal funds rate.

Predicting the outcome of a change in the Fed funds rate. On June 30, 2004, the Federal Open Market Committee voted to increase its federal funds rate target from 1.00% to 1.25%, its first increase after 13 cuts in 2001 and 2002. How does this action affect the federal funds rate? It is a market-determined interest rate, not literally set by the Fed. We can illustrate what happens using the reserves market diagram. As in Figure 20.2(b), the Fed fulfills its intention to increase the federal funds rate by

decreasing the supply of reserves. It conducts open market purchases to increase nonborrowed reserves. This action shifts the supply curve from S_0 to S_1, decreasing reserves from R_0^* to R_1^* and increasing the federal funds rate from i_{ff0}^* to i_{ff1}^*.

The rising cost of funds to lenders leads to higher interest rates charged to private borrowers, as indicated by the increase in loan rates to household and business borrowers. This increase in loan rates decreases demand for business investment and consumer durables.

Concluding Remarks

Fed watchers try to predict the Fed's actions regarding open market operations, discount policy, and reserve requirements so as to forecast changes in the federal funds rate. (Recently, analysts have also begun to consider the role played by uncertainty in bank reserve balances in determining the federal funds rate; for example, on busier days, banks may desire to hold a larger cushion of reserves to protect against penalties for overnight overdrafts.) Predicting Fed changes is the first step toward predicting the effects of monetary policy on other interest rates. However, the Fed's significant control over the federal funds rate does not imply that it can control other interest rates. Recall, for example, that the expectations theory of the term structure of interest rates states that longer-term interest rates reflect, in part, expectations of *future* short-term rates. Therefore *expected future Fed actions*, not just current Fed policy, are important.

CHECKPOINT

Suppose that you read in *The Wall Street Journal* that the Fed raised its target for the federal funds rate by one-half of a percentage point. How would you expect the Fed to achieve its objective? Using the graphical analysis of the federal funds market, you would expect the Fed to use open market sales to reduce nonborrowed reserves, shifting the *NBR* curve to the left and raising the federal funds rate. ♦

KEY TERMS AND CONCEPTS

- Discount policy
  - Discount window
  - Primary credit
  - Seasonal credit
  - Secondary credit
- Open market operations
  - Defensive transactions
  - Dynamic transactions
  - Federal Reserve repurchase agreements
  - General directive
  - Matched sale-purchase transactions
  - Open Market Trading Desk
  - Outright purchases and sales
- Reserve requirements

SUMMARY

1. Open market operations (purchases and sales of securities in financial markets) are the most widely used of the Fed's principal monetary policy tools. The Federal Open Market Committee (FOMC) issues guidelines for open market operations as general directives. Some transactions are dynamic—that is, designed to implement changes in the monetary base suggested by the FOMC. Most transactions are defensive—that is, designed to offset unintended disturbances in the monetary base.
2. The Fed's discount policy sets the discount rate and the terms of discount lending. The Fed fulfills its role as the lender of last resort by providing primary, secondary, and seasonal credit.

MOVING FROM THEORY TO PRACTICE . . .

THE WALL STREET JOURNAL MAY 11, 2006

Fed Raises Rates

a The Federal Reserve, as expected, boosted short-term interest rates to 5% from 4.75%. In its statement, it laid out a rationale for a pause in the series of rate increases that began in mid-2004, while signaling such a brake need not be a halt.

In recent weeks, Fed officials, led by Chairman Ben Bernanke, have tried to signal that they are less certain of where rates are going and that while they may pause soon, they could raise rates again later. But those signals have come while recent data have shown that the economy remains strong and inflationary pressure is growing. Markets have questioned the wisdom of the Fed's game plan by showing greater concern about inflation . . .

All 11 voting members of the 18-member Federal Open Market Committee voted to raise the target for the federal funds rate, charged on overnight loans among banks. (One FOMC seat is vacant.) The Fed also raised the less-important discount rate, charged on central-bank loans to commercial banks, to 6% from 5.75%. Eleven of the Fed's 12 regional banks requested the increase; the board of the Kansas City Fed did not, just as in March. b In response, U.S. commercial banks raised their prime rate, a benchmark for many business and consumer loans, to 8% from 7.75%.

The Fed and its chair are at a delicate juncture. At 5%, short-term rates are now about neutral—neither so low that they stimulate spending, nor so high that they restrain it. And there are signs that, after two years, the Fed is having an impact: long-term rates have started to rise, and home sales prices and price appreciation have slowed.

But the overall economy grew at a robust 4.8% annual rate in the first quarter, and though it's expected to slow to between 3% and 3.5% in the second quarter, the latest data have been strong. Moreover, underlying inflation recently ticked up to the top of the Fed's comfort zone of 1% to 2%. Thus, Mr. Bernanke is caught between the risk of appearing soft on inflation and risks of raising interest rates too much and triggering a serious slowdown . . .

Hank McKinnell, chief executive of Pfizer Inc. and chairman of the Business Roundtable, an association of chief executives, said yesterday: "Interest rates aren't at a point where they've started to bite into financing capability. There's plenty of money around." c

ANALYZING THE NEWS . . .

Analysts first look for effects of the Fed's use of open market operations and discount policy in the federal funds market, the market through which banks lend to each other overnight. Actions by the Federal Reserve to increase the federal funds rate are interpreted as contractionary policies, because interest rates that are charged to households and businesses will also increase, thereby discouraging spending and, it is hoped, reducing inflationary pressures.

a On May 10, 2006, the Federal Open Market Committee voted to increase the federal funds rate target from 4.75% to 5.0%. This represented the sixteenth increase in the target in a little less than two years. How does this action affect the fed funds rate? The fed funds rate is a market-determined interest rate, not literally set by the Fed. We can illustrate what happens using the reserves market diagram. In the graph provided, the Fed fulfills its intention to increase the federal funds rate by decreasing the supply of reserves. It conducts open market sales to decrease nonborrowed reserves. This action shifts the supply curve from S_0 to S_1, decreasing reserves from R_0^* to R_1^* and increasing the federal funds rate from i_{ff0}^* to i_{ff1}^*. As a consequence of the Fed's action, the discount rate (the rate charged on primary credit) also increased from i_{d0} to i_{d1} (in this case from 5.75% to 6%).

b Short-term interest rates are closely linked to the federal funds rate. The increasing cost of funds for lenders leads to higher interest rates charged to private borrowers, as indicated by the increase in rates to households and business borrowers. This increase in loan rates decreases the demand for business investment and consumer durables in an attempt to slow a rapidly expanding economy—and inflation pressures.

c The Federal Reserve's policy to reduce the amount of reserves in the system does not necessarily mean that the economy will slow down significantly. The reduction in reserves (and the corresponding increases in interest rates) may be made in order to remove excess amounts of reserves that are in the system due to previous policy changes in the market.

For further thought . . .

Given the FOMC's concern about inflation and inflationary pressure in the United States, what effect would news that inflationary pressures were building have on the federal funds rate target? On longer-term interest rates? Explain.

Source: Excerpted from Greg Ip, "Fed Raises Rates, Keeps Its Options Open for Future," *The Wall Street Journal*, May 11, 2006, p. A1.

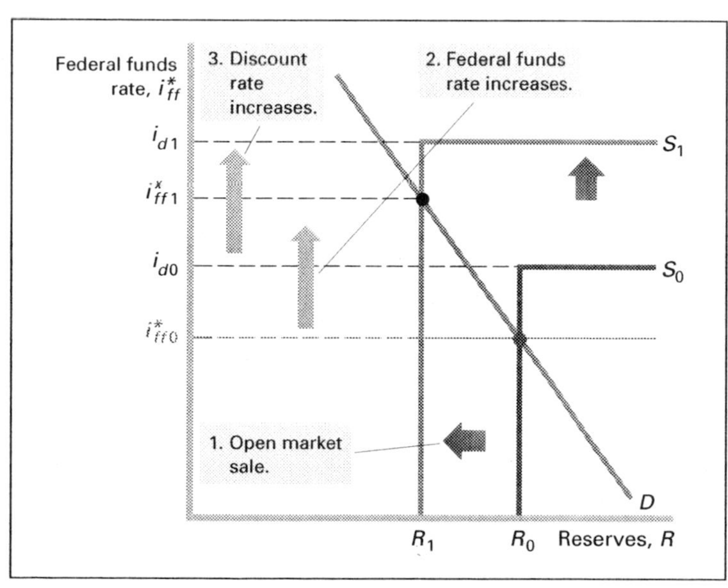

3. Reserve requirements are a potent but drastic way to control the monetary base. Increases in reserve requirements decrease the money multiplier; decreases in reserve requirements increase the money multiplier. Because large changes in reserve requirements can cause costly reallocations of banks' portfolios, the Fed generally avoids them.
4. The federal funds rate is one indicator of monetary policy. A decrease in the federal funds rate relative to other market interest rates is usually associated with an expansionary monetary policy. An increase in the federal funds rate relative to other market interest rates is usually associated with a contractionary monetary policy.

REVIEW QUESTIONS

1. If open market operations are considered the Fed's most important monetary policy tool, why were they not mentioned in the original Federal Reserve Act?
2. Since the 1930s, what has been the Fed's most important tool for monetary policy? What part of the Federal Reserve System determines how this tool is used?
3. What advantages do open market operations have over the other monetary policy tools available to the Fed?
4. *Evaluate:* The Fed was originally established to use discount loans to help put an end to banking panics. Deposit insurance has effectively put an end to banking panics; therefore, we no longer need the Fed. If we allow the Fed to continue to operate we ought, at the very least, to eliminate its ability to grant discount loans.
5. What causes changes in the rate charged on discount loans?
6. *Evaluate:* The Fed changes the reserve requirement frequently because it is such a powerful tool.
7. What is the maintenance period for bank reserves? How does the Fed calculate a bank's required reserves?
8. If a bank is required to hold reserves of $150 million but held only $149 million of reserves over the maintenance period, will the Fed penalize it? Why or why not?
9. What is wrong with the liquidity argument for reserve requirements?
10. How does the Fed police the discount window?
11. *Evaluate:* Because deposit insurance can eliminate the chance of bank lending, discount lending is unnecessary.
12. What type of credit (primary, secondary, or seasonal) does each of the following discount loans represent?
    a. Well-capitalized Bigbank borrows from the Fed because of liquidity problems when one of its major depositors suddenly switches its accounts to another bank.
    b. Weaker Megabank has seen large depositors to withdraw their funds, forcing Megabank to borrow from the Fed.
    c. First Bank borrows $5 million so that it can make loans to farmers for planting, as it does every April.
13. What is a Fed watcher?
14. In daily trading by the Open Market Trading Desk at the Federal Reserve Bank of New York, why does the account manager consult with market participants? With the Treasury Department? With two or more members of the FOMC?
15. What are the differences between dynamic and defensive open market operations?

ANALYTICAL PROBLEMS

16. What interest rate is most directly affected by open market operations? What happens to this interest rate and the money supply when the Fed engages in open market purchases? When the Fed engages in open market sales?
17. If the money multiplier is 8, how large a change in the money supply will result from the sale of $1 billion of bonds by the Fed on the open market? Will the money supply increase or decrease?
18. How could the Fed use its three principal monetary policy tools to decrease the money supply by $100 million if the money multiplier is 10 and the monetary base is $500 million?
19. What is the Fed likely to do near the Christmas holiday season, when the public uses more currency?
20. Which of the following open market operations are defensive and which are dynamic?
    a. The Treasury makes a large payment, which the Fed offsets with an open market purchase.

b. The economy strengthens unexpectedly, to which the Fed responds with open market sales.

c. Bad weather prevents checks from being cleared as quickly as usual, allowing float to increase in the banking system; the Fed responds with open market sales.

d. The dollar's foreign exchange value declines, prompting the Fed to respond with open market sales.

21. The following list contains parts of two different directives to the Open Market Trading Desk from the FOMC. Which is expansionary and which is contractionary?

a. . . . risks are weighted mainly toward conditions that may generate economic weakness in the foreseeable future . . .

b. . . . risks are weighted mainly toward conditions that may generate inflationary pressures in the near future . . .

22. Suppose that the Fed were no longer allowed to grant discount loans. Show the effects on the reserves market diagram. Under these circumstances would an open market purchase have a smaller or a larger effect on the equilibrium federal funds rate? Use a reserves market diagram to illustrate your answer.

23. On the reserves market diagram, show how the Fed can use open market operations to offset an increased demand for reserves by holding the federal funds rate constant.

24. For (a)–(d), use the graphical analysis of equilibrium in the reserves market to predict changes in nonborrowed reserves, borrowed reserves, and the federal funds rate.

a. The Fed conducts open market sales of securities.

b. The Fed more strongly discourages banks' use of the discount window.

c. Banks and the nonbank public become concerned that a banking crisis is imminent and that depositors will prefer to invest in securities in financial markets.

d. The Fed lowers the discount rate and conducts open market purchases of securities.

DATA QUESTIONS

25. Banks complain that reserve requirements hurt their profits because they pay interest to depositors but don't earn anything on their reserves. In the latest *Federal Reserve Bulletin*, find the table that lists reserve requirements. Suppose that a bank has $1 billion in transaction accounts. Calculate the bank's required reserves. In the same publication, look at the average federal funds rate for the past year. Multiply the federal funds rate times the amount of required reserves to determine the cost to the bank of complying with reserve requirements. However, the bank would have held reserves for transaction purposes, even if no reserves were required. Suppose that the bank would hold 5% of its deposits in reserve even if reserves were not required. How much does this holding of nonrequired reserves reduce the bank's profits? What, then, is the true cost of reserve requirements?

26. In carrying out open market operations, the open market desk buys and sells U.S. government securities on a daily basis. What type of securities—short term, intermediate, or long term—do you think it buys and sells the most? Locate the third chapter of the Federal Reserve publication "The Federal Reserve System: Purposes and Functions" at http://www.federalreserve.gov/pf/pf.htm to find out. In terms of liquidity, why does the choice of this security type make sense with respect to the conduct of open market operations?

27. The Federal Reserve's Discount Window Web site (http://www.frbdiscountwindow.org/) maintains information that would be of interest to banks that use the discount market. Consider the historical data listed for the seasonal credit. Does it seem to follow changes in the effective federal funds rate (which can be found at http://research.stlouisfed.org/fred2/data/DFF.txt)? Explain the likely outcome if the Fed kept this rate consistently higher than the federal funds rate. What would happen if it kept this rate consistently lower? Answer verbally and graphically, using a supply and demand diagram for the federal funds market.

28. During a recession, the Federal Reserve's Open Market Committee can be expected to lower its target for the federal funds rate. Consider the federal funds rate targets that existed since 1990 (at http://www.federalreserve.gov/fomc/fundsrate.htm). During the most recent recession, it lowered this rate to 1% (the lowest rate in 45 years). How does this rate compare with the lowest target that resulted in response to the recession of the early 1990s? Compare the length of time that each rate was maintained during each recession. Why do you suppose there is a difference?

CHAPTER 21

The Conduct of Monetary Policy

The 1990s and 2000s witnessed bull then bear markets for central banks as well as for stocks. In the United States, the Fed's influence has grown, and its image in the public's eye has improved. In 1982, a Tennessee construction journal had as its cover a "wanted" poster of then-Fed Chairman Paul Volcker, accusing him of "premeditated and cold-blooded murder of millions of small businesses." By the end of the 1990s, Mr. Volcker's successor, Alan Greenspan, was revered by most investors and citizens. In 1999, investors had high hopes for the success of the newly inaugurated European Central Bank. By the early 2000s, some economists questioned monetary actions in the late 1990s, and urged the Fed to be clearer about its objectives, a goal articulated well by the current Fed Chairman, Ben Bernanke. Bull or bear market, the ways in which central banks conduct monetary policy remains the stuff of headlines.

The Fed uses its monetary policy tools—open market operations, discount policy, and reserve requirements—to change the money supply and short-term interest rates and, ultimately, to achieve its goals for economic performance. In this chapter, we describe how the Fed conducts monetary policy to achieve goals that promote economic well-being. Although it is easy to identify the goals of monetary policy, which we present in the first section, it is not always so simple to enact policies that achieve those goals. In the second section of the chapter, we identify the difficulties in designing effective monetary policies and describe how the Fed can set targets that help it achieve its goals. But as the journal cover of Chairman Volcker demonstrated, the Fed must make choices in selecting its targets. In addition, the outcome of the Fed's policies might not have precisely the economic impact that the theory predicts. We conclude the chapter with an evaluation of the Fed's conduct of monetary policy in achieving its policy goals, and we consider the outlook for future monetary policy in the United States and other industrialized nations.

Goals of Monetary Policy

Web Site Suggestions: http://www.federalreserve.gov/pf/pdf/pf_2.pdf
Describes the Fed's acknowledged objectives.

Most economists and policymakers agree that the overall aim of monetary policy is to advance the economic well-being of the country's citizens. What is *economic well-being*? There are many ways to assess economic well-being, but typically, it is determined by the quantity and quality of goods and services that members of the economy can enjoy. If an economy functions optimally, then citizens allocate limited resources to provide maximum benefits to all. Economic well-being, then, also applies to the efficient employment of labor and capital and to the steady growth in output that arises from the productive use of these factors of production. In addition, stable economic conditions—minimal fluctuations in the business cycle, steady interest rates, and smoothly functioning financial markets—are qualities that enhance economic well-being. The Fed has set six **monetary policy goals** that are intended to promote a well-functioning economy: (1) price stability, (2) high employment, (3) economic growth, (4) financial market and institution stability, (5) interest rate stability, and (6) foreign-exchange market stability. The Fed tries to set monetary policy to achieve these goals, as do most other central banks.

Price Stability

Inflation, or persistently rising prices, erodes the value of money as a medium of exchange and a unit of account. Especially since inflation rose dramatically and unexpectedly during the 1970s, policymakers in most industrial economies have set **price stability** as a policy goal. In a market economy, in which prices communicate information about costs and about demand for goods and services to households and businesses, inflation makes prices less useful as signals for resource allocation. When the overall price level changes, families have trouble deciding how much to save for their children's education or for retirement, and businesses facing uncertain future prices hesitate to enter into long-term contracts with suppliers or customers. Severe inflation causes even greater economic costs. Rates of inflation in the hundreds or thousands of percent per year—known as *hyperinflation*—can severely damage an economy's productive capacity. In extreme cases, money changes value so quickly that it no longer functions as a store of value or medium of exchange. Citizens take cash in wheelbarrows to purchase groceries. During the hyperinflation of the 1920s in Germany, economic activity contracted sharply. The resulting economic instability paved the way for Hitler's fascist regime. The range of problems caused by inflation—from economic uncertainty to devastation—make price stability a desirable monetary policy goal.

High Employment

High employment, or a low rate of unemployment, is another monetary policy goal. Unemployed workers and underused factories and machines lower output (gross domestic product, GDP). Unemployment causes financial distress and decreases self-esteem for workers who lack jobs. Beyond the Fed, branches of the government reinforce the goal of high employment. For example, Congress enacted the Employment Act of 1946 and the Full Employment and Balanced Growth Act of 1978 (the Humphrey-Hawkins Act) to promote high employment and price stability.

Although the Fed is committed to high employment, it does not seek a zero percent rate of unemployment. Even under the best economic conditions, some workers move into or out of the job market or are between jobs. Workers sometimes leave one job to pursue another and might be unemployed in the meantime. Individuals also leave the labor force to obtain more education and training or to raise a family, and reentry may take time. This type of *frictional unemployment* enables workers to search for positions that maximize their well-being.

Although some unemployment always exists, the level of unemployment is determined by the normal working of a healthy economy. When all workers who want jobs have them and the demand for and supply of labor are in equilibrium, economists say that unemployment is at its *natural rate.* In the 1960s, economists thought that the natural rate was 4%, but changes in the economy as a result of technological advances and demographic shifts increased the natural rate somewhat. In the 1990s, many economists believed that the natural rate declined. The unemployment that is caused by changes in the structure of the economy (such as shifts in manufacturing techniques, increased use of computers and electronic machines, and increases in the production of services instead of goods) is called *structural unemployment.*

Economic Growth

Web Site Suggestions: http://www.gpoaccess.gov/indicators/browse.html Presents a range of data on economic activity and growth.

Policymakers also seek steady **economic growth**, increases in the economy's output of goods and services over time, which raises household incomes and thereby increases government revenues. Economic growth depends on high employment. With high employment, businesses are likely to grow by investing in new plant and equipment that raise profits, productivity, and workers' incomes. With high unemployment, businesses have unused productive capacity and are much less likely to invest in capital improvements. Economic growth policies can provide incentives for saving to ensure a large pool of investment funds and direct incentives for business investment. Policymakers attempt to encourage *stable* economic growth, because a stable business environment allows firms and households to plan accurately and encourages the long-term investment that is needed to sustain growth.

Financial Market and Institution Stability

When financial markets and institutions are not efficient in matching savers and borrowers, resources are lost. Firms with the potential to produce high-quality products and services cannot obtain the financing they need to design, develop, and market these products and services. Savers waste resources looking for satisfactory investments. **Financial market and institution stability**—maintaining the viability of financial markets and institutions to channel funds from savers to borrowers—makes possible the efficient matching of savers and borrowers.

The Fed was created after financial panics in the late 1800s and early 1900s. During the past two decades, the Fed's response to problems in the commercial paper, stock, and commodity markets averted financial panics. Of course, the policy goal of financial market and institution stability doesn't guarantee that the Fed's intervention will eliminate panics. For example, federal deposit insurance reduced the severity of banking panics, but the existence of this insurance might have been one cause of the crisis in financial institutions during the late 1980s and early 1990s. The Fed's interventions following the stock market crash of 1987 and the terrorist attacks of September 11, 2001, illustrate its attention to financial stability. Some economists have argued that the Fed should take action to forestall asset price bubbles such as that in U.S. equities in the late 1990s, but most economists argue that the Fed should do so only if its objectives for price stability or economic growth are affected by the bubble.

Interest Rate Stability

Like fluctuations in price levels, fluctuations in interest rates make planning and investment decisions difficult for households and businesses. Increases and decreases in interest rates make it hard for businesses to plan investments in plant and equipment and make households more hesitant about long-term investments in houses. Because people often blame the Fed for increases in interest rates, the Fed's goal of **interest rate stability**, or limited fluctuations in interest rates on bonds, is motivated by political pressure as well as by a desire for a stable saving and investment environment.

Foreign-Exchange Market Stability

In the global economy, **foreign-exchange market stability**, or limited fluctuations in the foreign-exchange value of the dollar, is an important monetary policy goal of the Fed. A stable dollar makes planning for commercial and financial transactions simpler. In addition, fluctuations in the dollar's value change the international competitiveness of

U.S. industry: A rising dollar makes U.S. goods more expensive abroad, reducing exports; a falling dollar makes foreign goods more expensive in the United States.

Can the Fed achieve these monetary policy goals with its policy tools? We next turn to the problems that the Fed faces and the techniques it uses to tackle those problems.

Problems in Achieving Monetary Policy Goals

The central bank's objective in setting monetary policy is to use its policy tools to achieve monetary policy goals. The Fed and other central banks may be successful in pursuing related goals. It might spur both high employment and economic growth because steady economic growth contributes to high employment. Similarly, actions that encourage stability in financial markets and institutions can also promote interest rate stability. But the Fed is not so lucky in achieving all its goals. It faces trade-offs in attempting to reach other goals, particularly high economic growth and low inflation. To demonstrate the problem, suppose the Fed, intending to reduce inflation, uses open market sales to reduce money supply growth. Recall from Chapter 20 that open market sales increase interest rates. Higher interest rates typically reduce consumer and business spending in the short run. Thus a policy that is intended to achieve one monetary policy goal (lower inflation) has an adverse effect on another (economic growth). In 1995, many members of Congress supported a bill that was introduced by then-Senator Connie Mack of Florida that would force the Fed to focus almost entirely on achieving price stability, and many economists support such a focus. Indeed, in 2003, this debate gained force within the Federal Reserve. And in 2006, Fed Chairman Ben Bernanke advocated that the Fed target inflation.

The Fed faces another problem in reaching its monetary policy goals. Although it hopes to encourage economic growth and price stability, it has no direct control over real output or the price level. Interactions among households and businesses determine real output and the price level. The Fed's changes in the money supply have an indirect influence on the behavior of other economic variables. The Fed can influence the price level or output only by using its monetary policy tools—open market operations, discount policy, and reserve requirements. These tools don't permit the Fed to achieve its monetary policy goals directly.

The Fed also faces timing difficulties in using its monetary policy tools. The first obstacle preventing the Fed from acting quickly is *information lag*. This is the Fed's inability to observe instantaneously changes in GDP, inflation, or other economic variables.† If the Fed lacks timely information, it can set policy that doesn't match actual economic conditions, and its actions can actually worsen the problems it is trying to correct. A second timing problem is *impact lag*. This is the time that is required for monetary policy changes to affect output, employment, or inflation. Changes in the monetary base affect the economy over time, not immediately. Because of this lag, the Fed's actions may affect the economy at the wrong time, and the Fed might not be able to recognize its mistakes soon enough to correct them.

†The problem is not limited to monetary policy. One famous instance of information lag in fiscal policy occurred in June 1930, when President Hoover told a group of business leaders that their call for an economic stimulus package was unnecessary: "Gentlemen," he said, "you have come sixty days too late. The depression is over." (Quoted in Arthur M. Schlesinger, Jr., *The Crisis of the Old Order*, Boston: Houghton Mifflin, 1957, p. 331.)

The Fed attempts to solve these problems by using targets to meet its goals. Targets partially solve the Fed's inability to control directly the variables that determine economic performance, and they reduce the timing lags in observing and reacting to economic fluctuations. In the remainder of this section, we describe targets, their benefits and drawbacks, and their use in setting monetary policy. This analysis provides the theoretical background for a review of actual Fed policies in the next section. There we describe the actual success and failure the Fed has experienced in its monetary policy measures in the post–World War II era.

Using Targets to Meet Goals

Targets are variables that the Fed can influence directly and that help achieve monetary policy goals. The Fed relies on two types of targets: intermediate targets and operating targets.

Intermediate targets. **Intermediate targets** are financial variables (such as the money supply or short-term interest rates) that the Fed believes will directly help it to achieve its goals. To understand how intermediate targets work in achieving a goal, imagine the situation facing an archer who is trying to hit a bull's-eye (the goal) that is out of sight on the other side of a hill. The archer would have to guess where the bull's-eye was before shooting. To improve the archer's chance of hitting the bull's-eye, imagine that a ring could be positioned at the top of the hill, in the archer's line of sight, so that going through this intermediate target would make it easier for the arrow to come somewhere near the bull's-eye on the other side of the hill. If the archer makes it through the intermediate target, she knows at once that she has a good chance of hitting the bull's-eye. This target gives immediate feedback and increases the chances of hitting the goal. Intermediate monetary policy targets are like the archery ring at the top of the hill.

When the Fed uses an intermediate target—say, a monetary aggregate like *M1*—it has a better chance of reaching a goal such as price stability or full employment, which is not directly under its control, than it would if it focused solely on the goal. It also knows relatively quickly whether its policy actions are consistent with achieving the goal. From statistical studies, the Fed might estimate that a 3% increase in *M1* would achieve the level of employment and degree of price stability it desired. If the money supply actually grew by 4%, the Fed would know immediately that it was stimulating the economy too much, setting the stage for future inflation. The Fed could then use its monetary policy tools (most likely open market operations) to slow *M1* growth to the target of 3%. Hitting the *M1* intermediate target has no value in and of itself. It simply helps the Fed to achieve its stated goals.

Operating targets. In fact, the Fed controls intermediate target variables, such as interest rates and monetary aggregates, only *indirectly* because private-sector decisions also influence these variables. The Fed seeks targets that are better links between its policy tools, intermediate targets, and goals. These new targets, called **operating targets,** are variables that the Fed controls directly with monetary policy tools and that are closely related to intermediate targets. Examples of operating targets include the federal funds rate and nonborrowed reserves. The federal funds rate is a commonly used interest rate operating target because the market for bank reserves, which the Fed influences heavily, determines the rate. Interest rate operating targets are used by most major central banks.

As Figure 21.1 shows, the Fed selects goals but ultimately controls only policy tools. To sum up our discussions of intermediate and operating targets, the Fed uses

FIGURE 21.1 **Achieving Monetary Policy Goals**

The Federal Reserve establishes goals for such economic variables as output, inflation, and the rate of unemployment. The Fed controls directly only its policy tools. It also uses targets—intermediate targets and operating targets—which are variables that the Fed can influence that help achieve monetary policy goals. To be successful, targets must be measurable and controllable and must have a predictable relationship with the Fed's goals. Targets also provide the Fed with feedback on how well it is achieving its goals.

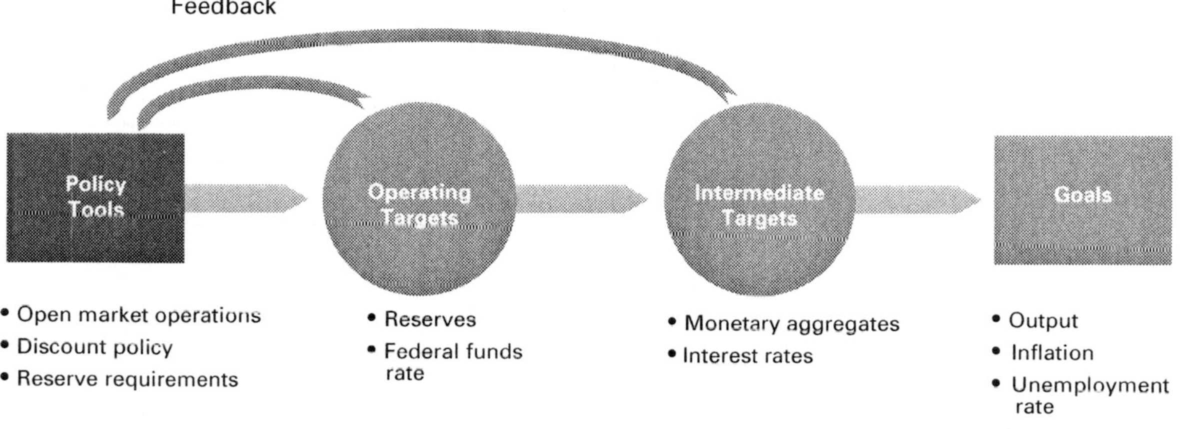

targets to achieve its monetary goals in a two-step process. First, it sets an intermediate target (such as money supply growth) to help achieve goals. Second, it sets an operating target (such as nonborrowed reserves growth) to help it to achieve the intermediate target. An advantage of this two-step targeting procedure is that the Fed can quickly monitor changes in operating targets and determine whether its intervention is having the desired effect. Operating targets provide feedback, enabling the Fed to gauge the effectiveness of its policies and to adjust them rather than waiting to evaluate the ultimate success or failure of efforts to achieve its goals. If this two-step process is to be successful, the Fed must select the appropriate targets with care. We now turn to the types of variables that are candidates for the Fed's targets.

Monetary Aggregates and Interest Rates as Targets

Recall that the Fed cannot generally achieve all of its goals at the same time. Trade-offs among goals force the Fed to select one type of target over another and to favor one goal over another in its policy.

In principle, the Fed has a range of intermediate and operating targets from which to choose, including monetary aggregates (or measures of credit outstanding) and interest rates. The Fed uses either money supply growth targets or interest rate targets. Which should it choose? That is a complicated question, which we will examine shortly. First, however, you need to understand that the Fed can use either money supply growth targets or interest rate targets, but not both. Ultimately, then, the Fed *must* choose.

To understand why, let's turn to a graphical analysis of the demand and supply of money (*M1*). In Figure 21.2, we plot the quantity of money M_d that households and businesses hold depending on the interest rate. We know that currency held pays no interest and that checkable deposits pay less than open market interest rates. Hence the opportunity cost of holding *M1* balances rises with the market interest rate. And as Figure 21.2 shows, in the money market, the demand for *M1* and the market interest rate are negatively related.

FIGURE 21.2 **Money Supply Targeting and Interest Rate Fluctuations**

Setting an intermediate target in terms of a monetary aggregate causes interest rates to fluctuate.

As shown in (a):
1. An increase in money demand from M_{d0} to M_{d1} raises the interest rate from i_0^* to i_1^*.

As shown in (b):
1. A decrease in money demand from M_{d0} to M_{d1} lowers the interest rate from i_0^* to i_1^*.

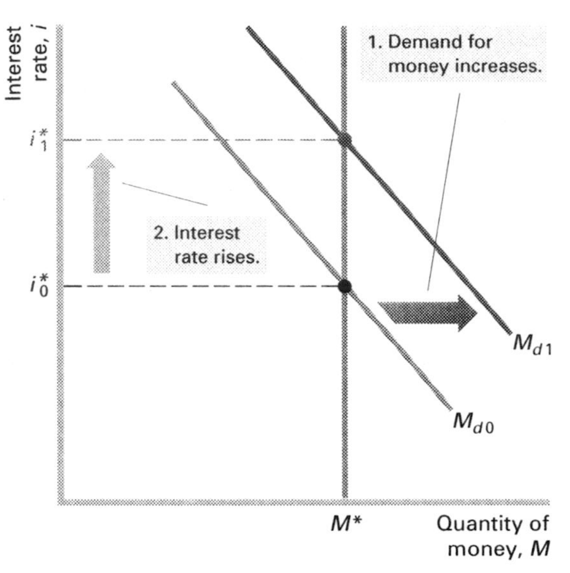

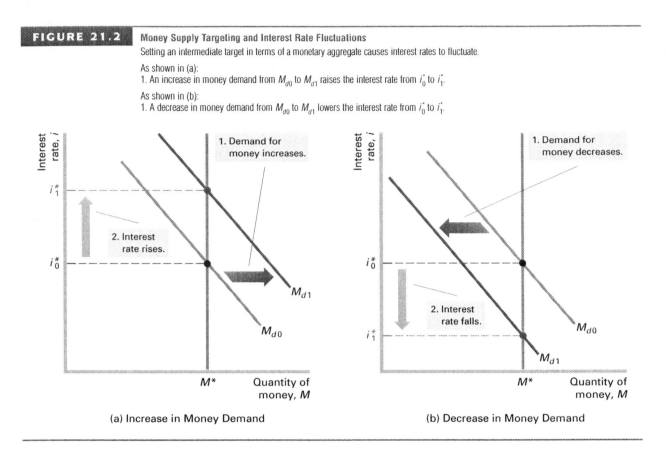

(a) Increase in Money Demand

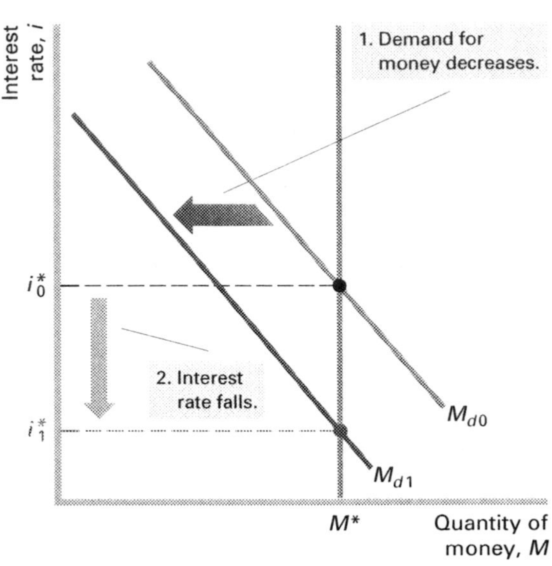

(b) Decrease in Money Demand

Suppose that the Fed decides to use *M1*, the money supply, as an intermediate target, setting it equal to M^*, as in Figure 21.2(a). For the money demand curve M_{d0}, the equilibrium market interest rate equals i_0^*. Any shifts in households' and businesses' demand for currency and bank deposits translate into interest rate movements. In other words, if the demand for money to use in transactions increases at any specific interest rate, the money demand curve shifts to the right from M_{d0} to M_{d1}. With the Fed holding the money supply constant at M^*, the equilibrium market interest rate rises from i_0^* to i_1^*. Suppose instead that the demand for money declines from M_{d0} to M_{d1} at any specific interest rate (Figure 21.2b). In this case, if the money supply remains constant at M^*, the equilibrium market interest rate falls from i_0^* to i_1^*. Using a monetary aggregate for an intermediate target causes interest rates to fluctuate in response to changes in money demand.

Now let's see what happens if the Fed chooses an interest rate as the intermediate target. Let's assume, as in Figure 21.3(a), that the initial money demand and supply curves are M_{d0} and M_0^*, respectively, and that the Fed sets an interest rate target at the equilibrium interest rate, i_0^*. In this case, when the demand for money increases from M_{d0} to M_{d1} at any specific interest rate, the interest rate rises from i_0^* to i_1^*. According to Figure 21.3(a), if the Fed wants to maintain an interest rate of i_0^*, it will have to increase the money supply from M_0^* to M_1^*. Let's suppose instead that the demand for money declines from M_{d0} to M_{d1} at any specific interest rate (Figure 21.3b). In this case, the interest rate falls from i_0^* to i_1^*. If the Fed wants to maintain an interest rate of i_0^*, it will have to reduce the money supply from M_0^* to M_1^*. Note that the money supply curve is, effectively, now horizontal at the targeted interest rate. Setting an inter-

FIGURE 21.3 **Interest Rate Targeting and Money Supply Fluctuations**

Setting an intermediate target in terms of an interest rate causes the quantity of money to fluctuate in response to changes in money demand.

As shown in (a):

1. An increase in money demand from M_{d0} to M_{d1} requires the Fed to increase the money supply from M_0^* to M_1^* to maintain an interest rate of i_0^*.

As shown in (b):

1. A decrease in money demand from M_{d0}^* to M_{d1}^* requires the Fed to reduce the money supply from M_0^* to M_1^* to maintain an interest rate of i_0^*.

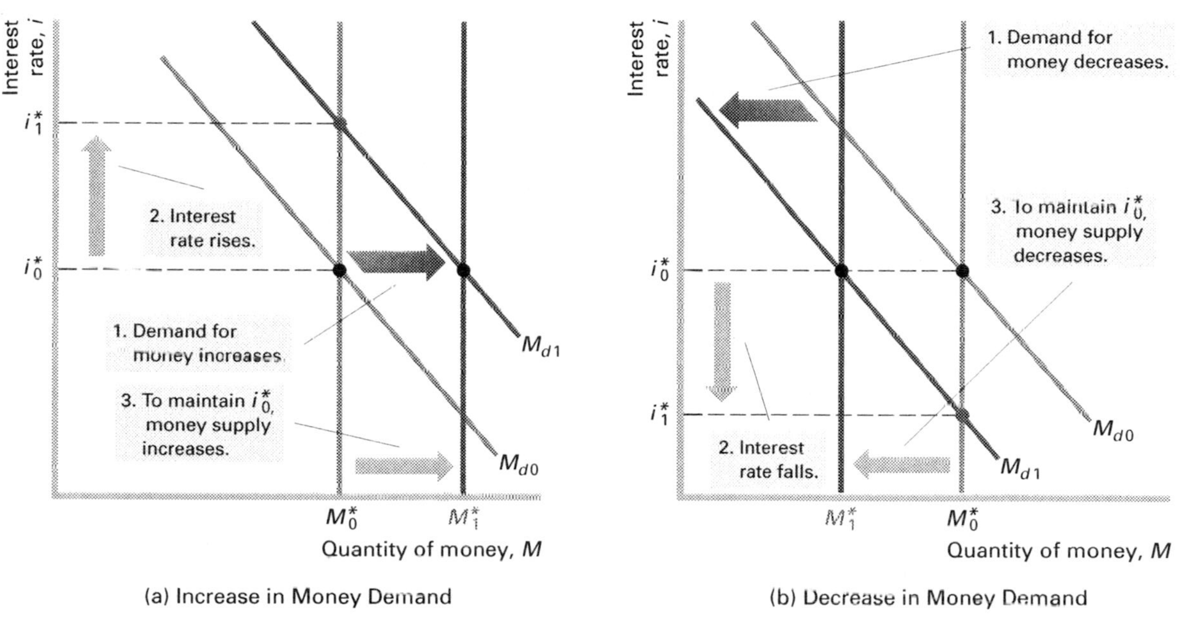

mediate target in terms of the interest rate causes the quantity of money to fluctuate in response to changes in money demand.

This analysis demonstrates the trade-off that the Fed faces in setting targets. The Fed cannot set intermediate targets in terms of both monetary aggregates and interest rates. How, then, does the Fed select targets?

CHECKPOINT

Suppose that households increase their demand for checkable deposits (and hence *M1* rises). Will using *M1* as an intermediate target permit the Fed to accommodate this portfolio allocation shift without affecting interest rates? If the Fed targets the money supply, an increase in the demand for money will, all else being equal, tend to increase short-term interest rates. If the Fed wanted to accommodate the portfolio allocation shift without affecting interest rates, it would conduct open market purchases to increase nonborrowed reserves and the money supply. ♦

Selecting Intermediate Targets

In addition to deciding whether an intermediate target should be a monetary aggregate or an interest rate, the Fed must evaluate the measurability, controllability, and predictability of the variable that is chosen to be the intermediate target. We describe these choices for intermediate targets next and then turn to specific decisions for choosing operating targets.

Measurability. The first criterion for a good target variable is that it must be measurable in a short time frame to overcome information lags. The Fed must be able to measure the target over a short period of time to assess quickly whether its intermediate target is likely to be met. For example, the government compiles data quarterly on a goal variable such as nominal GDP and releases the data after a one-month delay. As potential intermediate targets, both interest rates and monetary aggregates are quickly observable and measurable. With computers, analysts can track interest rates continuously. Money measures are not quite as accessible, although they are reported with at most a two-week lag.

The instantaneous measurability of market interest rates doesn't necessarily make them better intermediate targets than monetary aggregates. The *nominal* interest rate can be measured easily, but assessing the *real* interest rate is more troublesome, owing to the difficulty of measuring market expectations of inflation. Hence, as with monetary aggregates, the Fed can't perfectly measure the relevant interest rates over a short period of time.

Controllability. After identifying the potential targets that are measurable, the Fed must determine whether it can control them to overcome impact lags. An effective intermediate target must be responsive to the Fed's attempts to shift course. For example, during the 1980s and 1990s, some economists began to suggest that the Fed select a broader variable than conventional monetary aggregates, such as the stock of nonfinancial credit outstanding (loans to and bonds issued by nonfinancial corporations) or even nominal GDP. However, the Fed cannot control such variables sufficiently with its policy tools. The Fed's influence over monetary aggregates and short-term interest rates is much greater, and so it prefers to use them as intermediate targets.

By using its monetary policy tools (primarily open market operations), the Fed exerts significant control over the money supply but not complete control. The decisions of banks and the nonbank public also influence the money supply. The Fed can also affect interest rates because open market operations help to determine the supply of bonds. Once again, however, absolute control is impossible, because the Fed cannot control expectations of inflation and hence the real interest rate.

Predictability. We don't observe a preferred type of variable for intermediate targets based on measurability or controllability. The Fed also needs targets that have a predictable impact on the policy goals. How do monetary aggregates and interest rates stack up according to this criterion?

The case for interest rate targets rests on the observation that interest rates influence lending, borrowing, and portfolio allocation decisions. Hence the Fed could increase economic activity by reducing real interest rates to stimulate consumer and business spending. If the Fed wanted to cool off the economy instead, it could discourage consumer and business spending by attempting to increase real interest rates.

There are two problems with interest rates as intermediate targets. First, the Fed's influence over real interest rates is weaker than its influence over nominal interest rates. Second, a Fed policy to stabilize interest rates may be inconsistent with the Fed's goal of maintaining steady economic growth. Suppose businesses and consumers increase their spending because they are optimistic about future economic conditions. As a result, consumers spend more and save less, and businesses increase their investment in plant and equipment. These actions increase interest rates. If the Fed is trying to stabilize interest rates, it will make open market purchases to try to lower interest rates. This fall in interest rates encourages consumers and businesses to spend even more. As a result, the policy of holding interest rates constant is like pouring gasoline on a fire.

The same problem occurs during an economic downturn. A loss of consumer and business optimism reduces spending and depresses interest rates. If the Fed didn't step in, lower interest rates would eventually encourage consumer and business spending, cushioning the downturn and putting the economy back on track. If the Fed were targeting interest rates, it would use open market sales to raise interest rates in the face of the downturn, worsening the economy's problems. In either case, if swings in consumer and business optimism are the major determinants of fluctuations in the economy's output of goods and services, a policy of stabilizing interest rates destabilizes economic growth.

What if the Fed selects a monetary aggregate as an intermediate target instead of an interest rate? In the case of economic expansion, the rising demand for money (to fund a higher level of transactions) increases interest rates, as was shown in Figure 21.2. Higher interest rates help to keep the economy from overheating by reducing consumer and business spending. In the case of an economic downturn, the falling demand for money leads to lower interest rates, as shown in Figure 21.2. The fall in interest rates cushions the downturn.

Do the problems that are encountered with interest rate targets when consumer and business spending fluctuate imply that the Fed should always target monetary aggregates? No. As Figure 21.2 shows, a money supply target means that shifts in the demand for money at any interest rate translate into interest rate changes. An increase in interest rates depresses the level of consumer and business spending, whereas a decrease in interest rates stimulates spending. Hence, if shifts in the money demand relationship occur frequently, money supply targets likely will produce interest rate fluctuations that destabilize the economy.

This analysis demonstrates that no single variable can act as an intermediate target having all the qualities the Fed desires. How, then, does the Fed choose an intermediate target? The answer depends on sources of fluctuations in economic conditions and in the money supply. If the relationship between consumer and business spending and investment decisions and the interest rate is stable, interest rate targets offer the Fed a more predictable way to stabilize economic fluctuations (even though the Fed can't completely control the real interest rate, which is relevant to consumer and business decisions). However, if the relationship between the demand for money and other assets and the interest rate is stable, targeting monetary aggregates offers the Fed a more predictable connection with its goals. The Fed doesn't have the luxury of complete real or financial stability and must cope with disturbances to both sides of the economy.

Selecting Operating Targets

After the Fed selects an appropriate intermediate target, it must decide on the operating target that will best influence the intermediate target. The Fed uses similar criteria when comparing variables for operating targets: the variables should be measurable, controllable, and predictable. In addition, the operating target should be consistent with the intermediate target. The Fed largely controls both reserve aggregates and the federal funds rate and accurately measures them quickly. Hence, if the Fed selects a monetary aggregate as the desired intermediate target, it will select a reserve aggregate (such as the monetary base or nonborrowed reserves) as the operating target because reserve aggregates have a predictable influence on monetary aggregates. But if it picks a market interest rate as the intermediate target, the Fed will select an interest rate such as the federal funds rate as an operating target because the federal funds rate has a predictable impact on market interest rates. Whether the Fed selects a reserve aggregate or the federal funds rate, it uses its three monetary policy tools (principally open market operations) to influence that operating target.

The Monetary Policy Record

Much of the theory that we have described so far about the conduct of monetary policy to achieve economic goals evolved as the Fed designed, implemented, and evaluated economic policy since World War II. In this section, we describe how the Fed has conducted monetary policy—which goals it favored, which targets it used, and whether it was successful in improving economic well-being. Not all of the Fed's efforts have been successful. Using monetary policy tools to control the money supply or interest rates was a new task for the Fed, and it learned what worked and what did not as it attempted to select targets. As part of this learning, the Fed encountered the problem that we identified earlier: constraints imposed by trade-offs among goals and selecting variables that could be evaluated in a timely fashion while still influencing variables that directly affect output, employment, and inflation. In particular, in the postwar period, the Fed has emphasized, at various times, goals of stabilizing economic growth and price stability. Its intermediate and operating targets have at various times included monetary aggregates and short-term interest rates.

Early Interest in Targets: 1951–1970

The Fed's interest in targets began in the early 1950s from its struggle with the U.S. Treasury over the control of monetary policy. During World War II, the Fed agreed to peg interest rates on government securities at their pre-war levels (approximately 3/8% on Treasury bills and 2½% on long-term Treasury bonds) to help the Treasury finance the war effort. The Fed did so by purchasing securities whenever their market prices fell below levels that reflected the pegged rates. The onset of the Korean War in 1950 led to higher levels of government borrowing, causing market interest rates to rise. To maintain its interest rate target, the Fed purchased even larger amounts of government securities. These open market purchases expanded the monetary base, eliminating the Fed's control of the money supply process and causing inflation to rise to 8% by early 1951. The Fed formally abandoned the policy under the Federal Reserve–Treasury Accord in March 1951.

That accord freed the Fed to pursue an independent monetary policy. Believing that fluctuations in consumer and business spending were being managed by government tax and expenditure policy (fiscal policy), the Fed attempted to stabilize fluctuations in the money supply. Under the leadership of Chairman William McChesney Martin, the Fed began to implement a strategy targeted to respond to conditions in the money market. Policies to achieve financial stability set monetary aggregates as intermediate targets. In particular, Fed policy used as intermediate targets short-term interest rates and the level of **free reserves**, or the difference between excess reserves, ER, and borrowed reserves, BR (discount loans), in the banking system.

The Fed believed that free reserves represented slack in the banking system because banks could freely lend (nonborrowed) excess reserves, expanding the money supply through the deposit expansion process. Hence the Fed considered free reserves an indicator of money market conditions. In contrast to a target—which the Fed attempts to control—an **indicator** is a financial variable whose movements reveal information about present or prospective conditions in financial markets or the economy. An increase in free reserves indicates an easing of money market conditions, whereas a decrease in free reserves indicates a tightening of money market conditions. However, during this period, the Fed used free reserves not just as an indicator, but also as an intermediate target, selling securities as free reserves rose and buying securities as free reserves fell.

Interest rates fluctuate during the business cycle. An increase in economic activity during a boom period causes market interest rates to rise. Higher rates increase the opportunity cost of holding excess reserves, so excess reserves decline. At the same time, higher market interest rates raise the incentive for banks to borrow at the discount window (assuming that the discount rate is unchanged), so borrowed reserves (discount loans) increase. These changes cause free reserves to decline. Could the Fed maintain stable interest rates by using free reserves as an intermediate target? Because the Fed is targeting free reserves, the Fed responds with open market purchases that are sufficient to reduce interest rates to a level consistent with previous positions in excess and borrowed reserves—and hence in free reserves.

The process works in reverse during an economic downturn. A decline in national income reduces market interest rates. Hence excess reserves increase and borrowed reserves decrease, so free reserves increase. The Fed responds to the increase in free reserves with open market sales of securities to restore the existing level of free reserves.

Targeting free reserves reduces the Fed's control over the money supply. During a boom, when the demand for money rises, the Fed's actions expand the money supply; in a downturn, when the demand for money falls, the Fed's actions contract the money supply. Hence targeting free reserves also gives the Fed little control over the money supply. In effect, the Fed responds passively to conditions in the economy. Financial economists describe such actions as **procyclical monetary policy**, meaning that the Fed's policy *amplifies* rather than dampens economic fluctuations.

What about the argument that shifts in consumer and business spending could be ignored in favor of a focus on stable interest rates? In fact, government tax and spending policy did not completely stabilize the economy. Rather, the increases in government spending for the Great Society programs and the Vietnam War in the mid- and late 1960s overheated the economy. Procyclical monetary policy failed to promote stable economic growth. *Monetarists*, economists who believe that money supply targets are the best way to conduct monetary policy, were vocal critics of the Fed's targeting procedures.

Similar problems exist with the Fed's use of short-term interest rates as the intermediate target. In this situation, the Fed meets increases in market interest rates during an expansion by making open market purchases, thereby expanding the monetary base and the money supply and loosening interest rates. During an economic downturn, a decline in market interest rates induces the Fed to sell securities, reducing the monetary base and the money supply. Hence interest rate targets fail to promote stable economic growth. This strategy, too, results in procyclical monetary policy.

Because of the experience with procyclical monetary policy during the 1950s and 1960s, increased criticism of its targeting procedures by academic and business economists led the Fed to search for new targets in the late 1960s.

Experimenting with Monetary Targets: 1970–1979

Monetarist critics of the Fed's procyclical monetary policy during the 1950s and 1960s initially welcomed the appointment of Arthur Burns as chairman of the Board of Governors in 1970. Burns stated his belief that the Fed should commit itself to the use of monetary aggregates as targets. However, the Fed's monetary policy during Burns's tenure in the 1970s was as procyclical as the policy during the previous two decades.

Why did the Fed's attempt at monetary targeting fail? Most critics attribute the failure to the Fed's using the federal funds rate as an operating target while using *M1* and *M2* as intermediate targets. The target range for the federal funds rate was narrow; ranges for the monetary aggregates were broad. The Federal Open Market Committee (FOMC) instructed the Open Market Trading Desk to implement policy that would achieve *both* targets. However, as we noted earlier, the Fed can't attain both interest rate and monetary aggregate targets simultaneously. The FOMC gave the federal funds rate top priority, countering departures from the narrow target range with open market purchases or sales, which significantly reduced monetary aggregates. This priority for interest rate targeting made sense if, as the Fed believed, fluctuations in economic growth had been stabilized.

However, fiscal policy did not stabilize fluctuations in economic growth, and procyclical monetary policy reemerged. To counter the increase in the federal funds rate, the Fed made open market purchases, causing faster growth of the monetary base and *M1* than the Fed intended. To solve this problem, the FOMC attempted to put money growth back on course by widening the target range for the federal funds rate. When the economy expanded further, the federal funds rate increased again, bringing additional open market purchases and faster money growth. As a result, both the federal funds rate and the money supply exceeded their target ranges, accompanied by significant inflationary pressures. From late 1972 to early 1973, the federal funds rate virtually doubled from 4½% to 8½%, and *M1* growth exceeded its target level by a wide margin.

The FOMC effectively used the federal funds rate as an operating target for monetary policy. Just as this policy contributes to inflationary pressures during an economic expansion, however, it also reinforces economic contraction. By the end of 1974, the U.S. economy had fallen into its most serious recession since the 1930s. As a result, decreasing credit demand led to a substantial decline in the federal funds rate. The rate was then at the bottom of the target range, so the Trading Desk used open market sales to keep it from falling further. As a result, money supply growth fell. By early 1975, *M1* actually contracted, reinforcing the economic downturn.

The Fed's procyclical monetary policy continued through the 1970s. Burns and his successor, G. William Miller, publicly announced money supply targets while privately targeting the federal funds rate. As long as growth fluctuated, the Fed's desire to control short-term interest rates simply was not consistent with controlling monetary aggregates with an eye toward price stability.

Congress often puts pressure on the Fed to alter the way it conducts monetary policy. The procyclical monetary policy during Burns's tenure angered Congress, which moved to curb the Fed's powers. It passed a concurrent resolution calling for the Fed to be more accountable to Congress. It then passed the Humphrey-Hawkins Act in 1978, which codified those ideas, including the requirement that money and credit targets be set.

De-emphasizing Interest Rates: 1979–1982

In July 1979, President Jimmy Carter appointed Paul Volcker as chairman of the Board of Governors of the Federal Reserve System. Volcker was committed to crushing inflation and chose monetary aggregates as intermediate targets. Under Volcker, the Fed shifted its policy to emphasize nonborrowed reserves as an operating target. The FOMC reversed the practice of the previous decade by paying less attention to the federal funds rate, expanding its target range more than fivefold. As Figure 21.4 illustrates, the federal funds rate became much more volatile. At the same time, the Fed didn't tighten its control over money growth. Note that fluctuations in the growth rate of *M1* in 1979–1982 were *greater* than fluctuations under Burns and Miller. The actual growth rate of *M1* exceeded the target range in 1980 and 1982 and fell below the range in 1981.

Why did the Fed's shift in targeting in October 1979 fail to produce greater control of monetary aggregates to promote price stability? Many economists believe that the fluctuations in GDP and financial markets added too much uncertainty to make money growth targets attainable. Much of this instability resulted from deregulation of the banking industry. Financial innovation led to new substitutes for conventional demand deposits so that monetary aggregates had to be redefined. In addition, business recessions occurred in 1980 and again in 1981–1982. Finally, the Fed implemented credit controls (controls on bank lending) from March until July 1980.†

Many economists believe that the Fed's intention in 1979 was not to gain control over monetary aggregates, but to reduce the high rate of inflation, which was widely viewed by policymakers and the electorate as unacceptable. These economists speculate that the Fed announced monetary targets to disguise its agenda of using high interest rates to combat inflation. As evidence, they point to the significant increase in the federal funds rate that the Fed tolerated in late 1979 and again in late 1980 and 1981 while inflation remained stubbornly high. Indeed, with the decline in inflation during the 1981–1982 recession, the FOMC permitted the federal funds rate to fall. The volatility of the federal funds rate and the growth rates of monetary aggregates from 1979 to 1982 may say more about the Fed's concern with inflation than about monetary control.

Policy After 1982: Back to Interest Rates

In October 1982, the Fed began to pay more attention to the federal funds rate, emphasizing less the targets for monetary aggregates and ranges of acceptable fluctuations in the money supply. Borrowed reserves became the stated operating target for monetary policy. Rising market interest rates during the boom following the 1981–1982 recession induced the Fed to use borrowed reserves, putting upward pressure on the federal funds rate. To ease this pressure, the Fed purchased securities and increased nonborrowed reserves, which slowed the rise in interest rates and borrowed reserves. As a result, the monetary base increased, in effect returning the Fed to a procyclical monetary policy. Under this approach, in an economic downturn, falling interest rates would slow discount borrowing, leading the Fed to sell securities to offset the drop in borrowed reserves. As a result, the monetary base and the money supply would decline.

Return to Figure 21.4 and note the smaller fluctuations in the federal funds rate after 1982. Since February 1987, the Fed hasn't announced targets for *M1*. Fed officials justify this decision by reasoning that deregulation and financial innovation during the 1980s made *M1* less relevant as a measure of the medium of exchange. During this period, the Fed increased its reliance on targets for *M2*, a broader monetary aggregate with a more stable historical relationship with economic growth. Even this relationship

---

†Reserve requirements added a further complication during this period. Until 1983, required reserves for a given week were based on the deposits that had been made two weeks earlier; this made the nonborrowed reserves target difficult to implement. Since 1984, the Fed has required contemporaneous reserve requirement accounting.

FIGURE 21.4 **Federal Funds Rate and Money Supply Growth Rate, 1970–2006**

The Fed's emphasis on controlling monetary aggregates from October 1979 to October 1982 led to large fluctuations in the federal funds rate, as our graphical analysis suggests. Note, however, that the *M1* growth rate was actually less stable during 1979–1982 than during 1975–1979. The Fed's targeting procedure focused on controlling nonborrowed reserves, but major shifts in the *demand* for money as a result of deregulation and financial innovation made money growth erratic. After October 1982, the Fed's renewed interest in stabilizing the federal funds rate further destabilized money supply growth.

Source: Federal Reserve Bulletin, various issues.

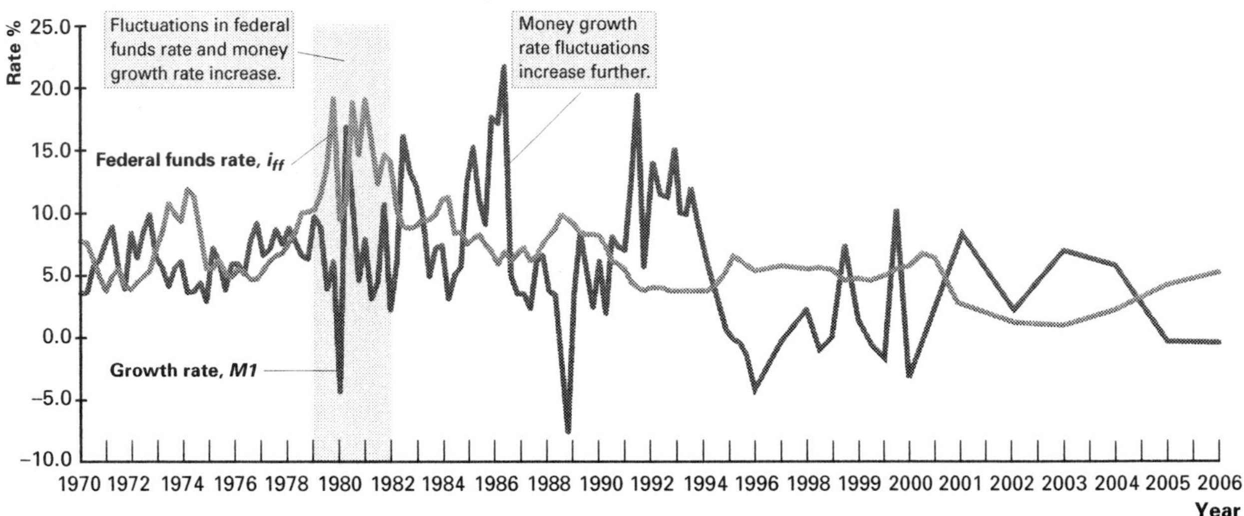

broke down in the early 1990s. By that time, the Fed paid little attention to growth in monetary aggregates in comparison to the attention paid to the federal funds rate. Indeed, in July 1993, then Fed Chairman Alan Greenspan informed the Congress that the Fed would cease its emphasis on using *M1* or *M2* targets to guide the conduct of monetary policy. The Fed has correspondingly increased its reliance on interest rate targets.

In the early 1990s, the Fed became concerned that a *bank credit crunch*, or a severe contraction of the volume of bank lending, was reducing economic growth. In addition to targeting the money supply, the Fed used its monetary policy tools to influence the level of bank lending, including reducing reserve requirements in December 1990 and February 1992.

Increasing International Concerns: The 1980s and 1990s

Web Site Suggestions: http://www.federalreserveonline.org Gives the Fed's links to web pages of other central banks.

Just as the rising importance of international trade changed financial markets and banking, exchange rate movements in international financial markets shaped Fed policymaking more during the 1980s and 1990s than ever before. Foreign-exchange market developments came to the forefront in 1985, when the foreign-exchange value of the dollar rose so high that U.S. businesses faced competitive losses in international markets. The FOMC indicated in its directives that bringing the dollar down would be appropriate. The Fed used an expansionary monetary policy to decrease the value of the dollar in foreign-exchange markets and to reduce short-term interest rates. To decrease the value of the dollar on foreign-exchange markets, the Fed tried to reduce the demand for dollars. By increasing money growth, it tried to lower short-term rates, making investment in dollar-denominated assets less attractive than investment in assets outside the United States, which paid higher interest rates. As investors sold dollars to buy non-U.S. assets, the dollar's value against other currencies declined. Later

OTHER TIMES, OTHER PLACES . . .

Does the Conduct of Monetary Policy Respond to Political Pressure?

Politics may influence the Fed's practices. As the 1980 primary election approached, politicians believed that the high U.S. inflation rate and the low value of the dollar were unacceptable to voters. In part reflecting these pressures, the Fed adopted a strategy of targeting nonborrowed reserves to reduce the growth rate of the money supply and thereby stem inflation. Knowing that this anti-inflation strategy would increase interest rates and wanting to avoid being blamed for the resulting increase, the Fed did not publicly state its objective. Instead, it stated in technical terms its intention to focus on monetary aggregates to deflect political criticism of high interest rates during its battle against inflation.

The intersection of economic policies and political desires appeared again in 1982. Three years after the Fed announced its "policy" of targeting monetary aggregates, Congress criticized the Fed for the volatility of monetary aggregates and the economic downturn in 1981 and 1982. This criticism put the Fed in a bind: if it openly widened target ranges for monetary aggregates to make interest rates less volatile, it would have to admit that it was to some extent using the federal funds rate as an operating target, which it had said before that it wouldn't do. Instead, the Fed chose to claim that it used borrowed reserves as the operating target. By this method of announcing one policy while following another, the Fed tried to balance its economic interest in fighting inflation with its political interest in not being blamed for high interest rates.

in the 1980s, the Fed promoted an increase in short-term rates to raise the value of the dollar. The Fed's actions were joined by coordinated efforts of other central banks through the Plaza Accord (September 1985) and the Louvre Accord (February 1987). In May and June 1994 and on several occasions during 1995, the Fed joined the Treasury in an intervention to support the dollar's value against the Japanese yen; interventions to influence the yen–dollar exchange rate continued later in the 1990s.

In the fall of 1998, Fed concerns about the stability of the international financial system after the Russian financial collapse and continued economic weakness in Asia led it to reduce the federal funds rate by 0.75 percentage points.

Clarifying Objectives and Communication: The 2000s

In the 2000s, a vigorous debate emerged within the Federal Reserve System and among economists about the Fed's policy objectives and how those objectives should be communicated to the public. In part, this discussion reflected a strong interest on the part of some central bank officials and economists in "inflation targeting" (see pages 496–500), under which the Fed would announce more precisely what it views as an acceptable range of inflation. In the view of some, such targets would help anchor inflationary expectations. Also, of particular interest in 2002 and 2003—with actual deflation in Japan and the prospect of deflation in the United States and the Eurozone —was the potential for targets to send signals for expansion.

The large shocks to the U.S. economy in the early 2000s—including a collapse in business investment, economic damage from terrorist attacks, military action in the Middle East, and fears of deflation—led the Fed to articulate a "risk management" approach to monetary policy. That is, policy in some periods might be more aggressive than indicated by the Fed's expectation of economic activity and inflation. In particular, in 2002 and 2003, Fed policy was very accommodative to avoid the chance of the low-probability (but costly) outcome of deflation.

As the Fed added a risk management objective to monetary policy, some economists and financial market participants stressed the need for clearer communication about the conduct of policy. In mid-2003, for example, significant swings in long-term

Treasury yields were associated with confusion about the stance of monetary policy and the Fed's assessment of current economic conditions. Some economists have suggested that the Fed release more information on its economic forecasts. The FOMC already releases a range or a "central tendency" of its projections for real GDP growth and inflation twice each year as part of the semiannual *Monetary Policy Report to the Congress*. These projections could be released more quickly (just after the meetings at which they are compiled) and with the two-year forecasts the FOMC actually considers, though. The release of the forecasts could offer officials an opportunity for communication about the state of the economy and the stance of monetary policy. By 2006, Fed Chairman Bernanke and his colleagues were debating the desirability of releasing more details of the central bank's outlook and forecasts.

Concluding Remarks

The Fed's practices since World War II have not produced very successful intermediate targets. During the 1990s and 2000s, the Fed emphasized a goal of low inflation and used all the tools at its disposal to achieve that goal. The Fed's recent experience suggests that no single target is appropriate. The economy and the financial system experience many different types of disturbances, the relative significance of which changes over time. Hence the Fed's current strategy is a practical one, however imperfect.

Reevaluating Fed Targeting Policy

The underlying assumption behind the use of intermediate targets is that financial variables that the Fed can directly measure and control may influence variables that the Fed can't directly control but that are affected by the target variables in a predictable way. Our discussion of post–World War II monetary policy in the United States illustrates why many economists question the merits of financial variables as *targets* rather than *indicators*. Relationships between measures of money and economic activity appeared to be stable during the 1970s, when many economists and policymakers urged the Fed to use monetary aggregates as intermediate targets. However, the relationship between money and nominal GDP weakened greatly during the 1980s. Critics conclude that, although no measure of money is a perfect intermediate target, owing to short-term instability (and even longer-term drift) in the relationship of the target to goals, other variables might be more useful as indicators.

Alternative Intermediate Targets

Target variables that have recently been suggested to the Fed include nominal GDP, commodity prices, the yield curve, and the foreign-exchange value of the dollar. Let's consider them and then analyze the Fed's current strategy.

Nominal GDP. The collapse in the previously stable relationships between money (or the stock of nonfinancial credit outstanding) and nominal GDP caused some economists in the 1980s to suggest that the Fed use the rate of growth of nominal GDP as a target variable. They reasoned that if real GDP growth is independent of monetary policy in the long run, the use of a nominal GDP target focuses attention on long-run price stability—and the unit-of-account function of money. Critics countered that the Fed's tools don't give it enough control over nominal GDP to achieve accurately any selected target. They proposed that the Fed adjust interest rate operating targets to influence nominal GDP. However, many Fed officials doubted that such a procedure could succeed.

Economists suggested three other variables to the Fed during the 1980s and 1990s: commodity prices, the Treasury yield curve, and the foreign-exchange value of the dollar. They argued that the markets for these assets are *efficient*. In other words, their prices reflect available economic information, including information for the Fed about the current and expected future economic outlook.

Commodity prices. The Fed could influence commodity prices through open market operations in commodity markets. Alternatively, if commodity prices provide advance information about future changes in inflation, the Fed could use price data as a signal of the need to adjust reserve aggregates or the federal funds rate. However, studies of this link show that commodity prices do not predict general inflation well. Hence commodity prices are not likely to be an effective indicator.

Yield curve. Under the expectations theory of the term structure of interest rates, the nominal interest rate on long-term securities indicates the market's expectations of future short-term nominal interest rates. If real interest rates were constant, the yield curve would indicate inflationary expectations, since expected inflation is the difference between the nominal and real interest rates. However, real interest rates aren't constant, so interpreting the slope of the yield curve requires guesses about the relative importance of expected shifts in real rates and inflation. Nevertheless, the slope of the yield curve contains statistically significant predictive power for both real output and inflation, and the Fed and other central banks examine the yield curve when evaluating changes in monetary policy.

Foreign-exchange value of the dollar. Increasing sensitivity of the U.S. economy to international events prompted interest in the information content of changes in the foreign-exchange value of the dollar. Most economists don't advocate the usefulness of exchange rates as targets. However, some evidence suggests that exchange rate movements to a degree do predict future real output and inflation. In spite of this information benefit, analysts generally conclude that exchange rate movements are useful as indicators only in conjunction with such conventional indicators as domestic interest rates.

The Taylor Rule

While the Fed relies on federal funds rate targeting in the context of U.S. monetary policy, the central bank still needs a way to choose the target level of interest rates. Actual Fed deliberations are complex and incorporate many factors about the economy. John Taylor of Stanford University has synthesized these factors in the **Taylor rule** for federal funds rate targeting.[†] The Taylor rule states that the current federal funds rate target should be the sum of the inflation rate, the equilibrium real federal funds rate (defined as the federal funds rate consistent with long-run full employment), and two additional terms. The first of these terms is the "inflation gap"—the difference between current inflation and a target rate; the second is the "output gap"—the percentage difference of real GDP from its estimated full-employment level. That is, the Taylor rule states that

$$\begin{aligned}\text{Federal funds rate target} = {} & \text{Inflation} + \text{Real equilibrium fed funds rate} \\ & + (1/2)\ \text{Inflation gap} + (1/2)\ \text{Output gap}.\end{aligned}$$

[†]John B. Taylor, "Discretion Versus Policy Rules in Practice," *Carnegie-Rochester Conference Series on Public Policy*, 39:195–214, 1993.

In calibrating this rule, Taylor assumed that the equilibrium real fed funds rate is 2% and the target rate of inflation is 2%. Implementing the Taylor rule in practice requires estimating the inflation gap and the output gap. Taylor's incorporation of the inflation gap and the output gap into his monetary policy rule reflects the oft-stated concerns of Fed governors and economists about both inflation and real output fluctuations. If, for example, inflation were 4%—so that the inflation gap is 4% − 2% = 2%—and real GDP were 2% greater than full-employment potential GDP, the Taylor rule recommends a federal funds rate target of 4% inflation + 2% equilibrium real federal funds rate + (1/2) (2% inflation gap) + (1/2) (2% output gap) = 8%.

The Taylor rule also offers a way to analyze the conduct of monetary policy by comparing the federal funds rate target predicted by the rule with the actual federal funds rate target. Under Federal Reserve Chairman Arthur Burns (1970–1979), the federal funds rate target was lower than that recommended by the Taylor rule, offering an explanation for the steady rise in inflation during Burns's oversight. Going the opposite direction, the Fed under Chairman Paul Volcker kept the federal funds rate higher than the Taylor rule level to reduce inflation. During the Greenspan era, the federal funds rate has been much closer to the Taylor rule predictions, consistent with the view that the Fed's conduct of monetary policy has been successful in the 1990s and in the new century. Although the Taylor rule remains silent about changes in the inflation target or the equilibrium interest rate, many economists view the "rule" as a convenient way to analyze the federal funds target, even as Ben Bernanke has succeeded Alan Greenspan as Fed Chairman.

The Future of Targeting

Fed policymaking must strike a balance in its use of intermediate targets: suitable intermediate targets can improve the chances of achieving goals, but evidence from the 1980s and 1990s suggests that suitable variables (those that the Fed can measure and control and that have a predictable impact on goal achievement) are not easy to find. As we pointed out, the Fed deals with this trade-off by compromising. Although it specifies targets for money aggregates, the Fed often defines these targets vaguely and as broad ranges in the FOMC directives. As a result, intermediate targets are less connected to day-to-day or month-to-month operating decisions than the theory of targeting suggests.

The Fed has done a substantial amount of research on the role of intermediate targets in the conduct of monetary policy, and ongoing analysis is likely. However, the practical importance of intermediate targets in the future conduct of monetary policy depends largely on whether controllability and predictability criteria for these targets can be satisfied.

The Fed's targeting efforts for monetary control since World War II haven't been as successful as those of some other countries. Fed watchers believe that the most important reason for continuing to use targets for monetary policy is that a commitment to meeting those targets keeps the money supply process under control. Most economists support the idea that the Fed can significantly control the monetary base and, to the extent that money multipliers remain stable over the long run, can influence the money supply greatly. By the mid-1990s, the Fed began to examine the desirability of **inflation targets,** and announced intentions for inflation to be pursued using the Fed's policy tools.

In practice, several countries have adopted inflation targeting, including New Zealand (1990), Canada (1991), the United Kingdom (1992), Finland (1993), Sweden

CASE STUDY

Is Inflation Targeting a Good Idea?

Over the past decade, many economists and central bankers have expressed significant interest in using *inflation targeting* as a framework for carrying out monetary policy. While the debate over inflation targeting remained at a relatively early stage in the United States in the 2000s, several countries have adopted formal inflation targets. And Ben Bernanke's chairmanship beginning in 2006 focused more attention on inflation targeting, a subject of Bernanke's research. For policymakers in the Fed and the Congress, key elements of the debate over inflation targeting center on how such a policy would work in practice and whether arguments in favor of inflation targeting dominate arguments against such a system.

Economists generally define inflation targeting as a framework for monetary policy in which the central bank commits to conduct policy to satisfy a publicly announced inflation target within a given time frame.† In principle, inflation targeting need not impose an inflexible rule for the central bank; monetary policy could still use discretion in addressing special situations. Nevertheless, monetary policy objectives and operation would focus on inflation and inflation forecasts. If the Fed were to focus explicitly on low inflation, it would have to decide how to reconcile this objective with other objectives—say, output stabilization. For example, an inflation targeting system could accommodate an output stabilization objective by permitting wide inflation target bonds and long inflation target horizons. The central bank must then balance the flexibility of this accommodation with the possibility that financial market participants may question its commitment to price stability.

Arguments in favor of inflation targets focus on four points: First, announcing explicit targets for inflation would draw the public's attention to what the Fed can achieve in practice; most economists believe that over the long run, monetary policy has a greater effect on inflation than the growth of real output. Second, the establishment of transparent inflation targets for the United States would provide an anchor for inflationary expectations. Third, announced inflation targets would help institutionalize good U.S. monetary policy. Finally, inflation targets would promote accountability for the Fed by providing a yardstick against which performance could be measured.

Opponents of inflation targets also make four points: First, rigid numerical targets for inflation diminish the flexibility of monetary policy to address other policy goals. Second, because monetary policy influences inflation with a lag, inflation targeting requires that the Fed depend on forecasts of future inflation, uncertainty about which can create problems for the conduct of policy. Third, holding the Fed accountable only for a goal of low inflation may make it more difficult for elected officials to monitor the Fed's support for good economic policy overall. Finally, uncertainty about future levels of output and employment can impede economic decision making in the presence of an inflation target; that is, inflation targets may obscure this uncertainty by adjusting the amount of time over which deviations from the inflation target are permitted.

Should the Fed adopt inflation targets? On the question of whether inflation targets improve economic policy, the jury is still out. New Zealand, the country with the oldest inflation-targeting regime, had just over a decade of experience by the 2000s. Many economists and central bankers have suggested that gains from transparency and accountability can be achieved without explicit inflation targets, and credibility of monetary policy is better established through experience.†† And an inflation target would require better communication with the public. While an inflation target has the potential for increasing the understanding of policy objectives, the standard for communication becomes more exacting than it would in a world without explicit objectives.

In any case, the debate over the desirability of inflation targeting in the United States remains front and center. In 2003, then Fed governor Ben Bernanke became a public advocate for inflation targeting, while Fed governor Donald Kohn and Fed Chairman Alan Greenspan made the case for continued discretion by the Fed. Chairman Bernanke and Vice Chairman Kohn are directing the analysis of inflation targeting in 2006.

†For broad overviews of issues surrounding inflation targeting, see Guy Debelle, Paul Masson, Miguel Savastano, and Sunil Sharma, *Inflation Targeting as a Framework for Monetary Policy*, Washington, D.C.: International Monetary Fund, 1998; and George A. Kahn and Klara Parrish, "Conducting Monetary Policy with Inflation Targets," *Federal Reserve Bank of Kansas City, Economic Review* (Third Quarter 1998): 5–30.

††See, for example, the interview study of central bank credibility conducted by Alan Blinder of Princeton University. Alan S. Blinder, "Central Bank Credibility: Why Do We Care? How Do We Build It?" Mimeograph, December 1998.

(1993), Australia (1994), and Spain (1994). Variants of inflation targeting have also emerged in newly industrializing economies (such as Chile, Korea, Mexico, and South Africa) and transition economies (such as the Czech Republic, Hungary, and Poland). Generally speaking, the move to inflation targeting has been accompanied by lower inflation (albeit sometimes at the cost of higher unemployment). The question of whether the reductions in inflation are traceable to inflation targeting per se or to the better communication of the central bank's ongoing objectives continues to foster debate.

Federal Reserve performance in the 1980s, 1990s, and the 2000s has generally received high marks from economists, even without a formal inflation target. The 1990s, for example, witnessed low inflation and a substantial economic expansion. The Fed's implicit strategy has been to keep inflation low and steady in the long run. Such a strategy leads Fed policymakers to examine a range of data offering information on future inflationary trends. In addition, the Fed in recent years has acted preemptively when inflation fears have arisen.

The Fed's strategy of an implicit "nominal anchor" has much to recommend it. First, its communication about the importance of low inflation for overall U.S. macroeconomic performance builds public support for the policy. Second, given long and variable lags in the effects of monetary policy on the economy, the Fed's preemptive attacks on incipient inflation are likely to be more successful than waiting to act until actual inflation is rising. This strategy is not without risks, however. The central bank's prestige derives largely from public trust in the anti-inflation statements of Fed officials, particularly former Chairman Alan Greenspan. The fact that Fed leadership changes (though in the 2000 presidential campaign, Arizona Senator John McCain stated that if Chairman Greenspan died, he would prop him in his chair and go on) highlights the need for increasingly formal communication with the public and its elected officials about both the desirability of low inflation and the steps the Fed will take to combat incipient inflation.

International Comparison of Monetary Policy Conduct

Although there are institutional differences in the ways in which central banks conduct monetary policy, there are two important similarities in recent practices. First, most central banks in industrial countries have increasingly used short-term interest rates (such as the federal funds rate in the United States) as the operating target through which goals are pursued. Second, many central banks are focusing more on ultimate goals such as low inflation than on particular intermediate targets. We discuss these practices and institutional settings in the conduct of monetary policy in Canada, Germany, Japan, the United Kingdom, and the European Union.

As in the United States, in *Canada*, the Bank of Canada became increasingly concerned about inflation during the 1970s, and it announced in 1975 a policy of gradually reducing the growth rate of *M1*. By the late 1970s, policy shifted toward an exchange rate target; by late 1982, *M1* targets were no longer used. However, in 1988, the then governor of the Bank of Canada, John Crow, announced the bank's commitment to price stability. In this regime, a series of declining inflation targets are announced. Consistent with the inflation targets, the Bank of Canada sets explicit operational target bands for the overnight rate (analogous to the federal funds rate).

The *German* central bank, the Bundesbank, began experimenting with monetary targets in the late 1970s to combat inflation. The aggregate that it selected, *central bank money*, or *M3*, is defined as a (weighted) sum of currency, checkable deposits, and time and savings deposits. The Bundesbank believed that movements in central bank money had a predictable impact on nominal GDP and that this monetary aggregate was significantly controllable by using central bank tools. Target ranges were set each year during the late 1970s and through the 1980s, during which the Bundesbank lowered its targets for money growth. For the first half of the 1980s, the central bank successfully achieved its targets. Discretionary departures from its targets became more common from 1986 through 1988, as officials wanted to decrease the value of the (then) West German mark relative to the U.S. dollar. To do so, the Bundesbank increased money growth faster than its announced targets.

The reunification of Germany in 1991 posed problems for the Bundesbank's commitment to its announced targets. Two pressures were particularly significant: First, the exchange of West German currency for less valuable East German currency brought inflationary pressures. Second, political objectives for economic growth after reunification raised fears of a weakening of the resolve to keep inflation low. These pressures on the Bundesbank's operating procedures yielded a more flexible indicator approach, similar to that used by the Fed.

Germany, which has had an informal inflation target since 1975, had an inflation goal of 2% per year prior to the inauguration of the European Central Bank in 1999. The Bundesbank believed that adherence to *M3* targeting will keep inflation in check. The central bank used changes in the *lombard rate* (a short-term repurchase agreement rate) to achieve its *M3* target.

The apparent German success in the conduct of monetary policy may be traceable to factors beyond monetary targeting per se. Many analysts note that the Bundesbank has permitted substantial deviation from monetary targets for significant periods of time. The success of German monetary policy may lie more in the clear communication of the central bank's focus on controlling inflation than in a strict emphasis on monetary targeting, a lesson for the current debate over inflation targeting.

In the aftermath of the first OPEC oil shock in 1973, *Japan* experienced an inflation rate in excess of 20%, stimulating a reorientation by the Bank of Japan on money growth targets. In particular, beginning in 1978, the Bank of Japan announced targets for an aggregate corresponding to *M2 + CD*. Following the 1979 oil price shock, the central bank reduced money growth. The gradual decline in money growth over the period from 1978 through 1987 that the Bank of Japan announced and implemented was associated with a faster decline in inflation than that in the U.S. experience. The consistency with which the Bank fulfilled its promises bolstered the public's belief in the bank's commitment to lower money growth and lower inflation. During this period, the Bank of Japan used a short-term interest rate (in the Japanese interbank market, analogous to the U.S. federal funds market) as its operating target.

Like those in the United States, Japanese banks and financial markets experienced a wave of deregulation and financial innovation during the 1980s. As a consequence, the Bank of Japan began to rely less on the *M2 + CD* aggregate in the conduct of monetary policy. After 1987, the bank's concern over the foreign-exchange value of the yen—which had risen significantly against the U.S. dollar—dominated monetary policy until 1989. The rapid rate of money growth during this period led to a boom in Japanese asset prices (particularly in land and stocks). In an attempt to reduce speculation in asset markets during the boom, the Bank of Japan adopted a contractionary monetary policy, which led to a decline in asset prices and ultimately to a drop in Japanese economic growth. Despite the success of the Bank of Japan's fight against inflation during the 1978–1987 period, it has not adopted formal inflation targets (though the Bank emphasizes price stability as an objective). As an operating policy instrument, the central bank uses short-term interest rates and its discount rate. A continuing deflationary Japanese monetary policy in the late 1990s and 2000s is viewed by many financial market commentators to be a significant factor in the weakness of Japanese economic performance during most of that period; a more expansionary monetary policy began to stimulate both economic growth and inflation in the mid-2000s. In 2006, the Bank of Japan began to scale back its expansionary policy. It also adopted a new policy framework focusing on the expected inflation rate one or two years ahead as opposed to the current inflation rate.

In the *United Kingdom*, the Bank of England announced money supply targets in late 1973 in response to inflationary pressures. As was the case in the United States, money targets—in this case a broad aggregate, *M3*—were not pursued aggressively. In response to accelerating inflation in the late 1970s, the Thatcher government formally introduced in 1980 a strategy for gradual deceleration of *M3* growth. Just as achieving the *M1* targets in the United States was made more complicated by financial innovation, the Bank of England had difficulty achieving *M3* targets. Beginning in 1983, it shifted its emphasis toward targeting growth in the monetary base (again with an eye toward a gradual reduction in the rate of growth of the money supply). In 1992, the United Kingdom adopted inflation targets. Consistent with those targets, short-term interest rates have been the primary instrument of monetary policy. Since early 1984, interest rate decisions have been made at monthly meetings between the Governor of the Bank of England and the Chancellor of the Exchequer. When interest rates are changed, a detailed explanation is offered to emphasize that decisions reflect monetary policy's emphasis on inflation goals.

In the *European Union*, following the signing of the Maastricht Treaty, the European System of Central Banks (ESCB), consisting of the European Central Bank (ECB) and the national central banks of all member states of the European Union, commenced operation in January 1999. Modeled on the law governing the German Bundesbank, the primary objective of the ESCB is to maintain price stability. As a secondary objective, the ESCB also has to support the general economic policies in the European Union. The ECB attaches a significant role to monetary aggregates—in particular, the growth rate of the *M3* aggregate. In addition, however, the ECB has emphasized a goal of price stability, defined as an inflation range of 0% to 2%. In practice, the ECB's strategy has not always been clear, as it has not committed to either a monetary-targeting approach or an inflation-targeting approach. In 2006, ECB President Trichet continued to emphasize the relevance of monetary aggregates for monetary policy, while Fed Chairman Bernanke remained skeptical.

KEY TERMS AND CONCEPTS

Free reserves
Indicator
Inflation targets
Monetary policy goals
  Economic growth
  Financial market and institution stability
  Foreign-exchange market stability
  High employment
  Interest rate stability
  Price stability
Procyclical monetary policy
Targets
  Intermediate targets
  Operating targets
Taylor rule

SUMMARY

1. The Fed's broad monetary policy goals are price stability, high employment, economic growth, financial market and institution stability, interest rate stability, and foreign-exchange market stability. These goals are not generally attainable at the same time and, in fact, may conflict at times. Therefore the Fed must make trade-offs among them.

2. The Fed cannot directly control its goals with its tools of monetary policy, so it selects intermediate targets (financial variables that have a predictable impact on the goals). The Fed uses its monetary policy tools to influence operating targets (financial variables that are more directly under its control) that have a predictable impact on intermediate targets.

3. Because financial markets determine interest rates and monetary aggregates together, the Fed must choose between them as intermediate targets. To do so, it uses the criteria of predictability, controllability, and measurability.

4. Since World War II, the Fed's use of targets in the conduct of U.S. monetary policy hasn't led to its control of the money supply. During the 1980s, deregulation and financial innovation made money supply targets more difficult to achieve. Since the mid-1980s, the Fed's policy has responded to direct information about changing conditions in the economy and financial markets.

5. Most economists believe that, as a technical matter, the Fed largely controls the money supply over the long run. Open market operations are a primary determinant of the monetary base. With an appropriately defined monetary aggregate (predictably affected by the monetary base through the money multiplier), monetary control should be possible.

REVIEW QUESTIONS

1. What are the Fed's monetary policy goals?
2. Construct a hypothetical scenario under which the Fed's goals of high employment and foreign-exchange market stability might conflict. In the case of such a conflict, which goal is the Fed likely to emphasize?
3. Suppose that the demand for money becomes less stable (that is, on the money demand–money supply diagram it shifts more frequently). Would this make selecting a monetary aggregate as an intermediate target more or less desirable? Explain.
4. What factors determine the variables that are selected as intermediate targets for monetary policy?
5. What is the difference between a target and an indicator? Is it possible for the Fed to use an indicator as a target?
6. Why is price stability a goal of monetary policy?
7. Should a goal of monetary policy be to reduce the unemployment rate to zero? Why or why not?
8. Why should policymakers care about fluctuations in interest rates or exchange rates?
9. Why do policymakers use a two-step targeting procedure, with both operating and intermediate targets, instead of single-step targeting?
10. Why can't the Fed target both the money supply and interest rates simultaneously?
11. Why was the Fed's pegging of interest rates before 1951 potentially inflationary?
12. Why was using free reserves as an intermediate target in the 1950s a procyclical monetary policy?
13. Why did the federal funds rate become more volatile in 1979? Did the Fed achieve greater monetary control? Why or why not?
14. If the Fed wants to decrease the value of the dollar on foreign-exchange markets, what should it do? What should it do if it wants to increase the foreign-exchange value of the dollar?
15. Why wouldn't commodity prices be useful intermediate targets for monetary policy?
16. How does political pressure influence the Fed's choice of targets? What did the Fed do in 1982 to accommodate these pressures somewhat?
17. Why is the choice of intermediate targets for monetary policy important for the selection of operating targets?

MOVING FROM THEORY TO PRACTICE . . .

THE ECONOMIST MAY 6, 2006

The Weeds of Destruction

If candidates in an economics exam are asked: "What should be the main objective of monetary policy?" the "correct" answer today is price stability: Central banks should single-mindedly reduce inflation and then keep it low; they should also avoid deflation. In that same exam in ten years' time, however, the required answer may be different. Or so implies a new paper by Bill White, the chief economist at the Bank for International Settlements, which asks: "Is price stability enough?"*. . .

a However, stable prices do not guarantee stable economies. The bursting of Japan's bubble in the early 1990s and East Asia's economic crisis in 1997–98 were both preceded by periods of low inflation. Furthermore, recent structural changes in the global economy could mean that a low, positive rate of inflation is not always best. Thanks to the re-emergence of China and India and the productivity gains from information technology, the world is enjoying a terrific positive supply shock, which has reduced the prices of many goods. How should central banks respond? . . .

b Are central banks targeting too high a rate of inflation now that China and India have boosted global capacity so dramatically? With hindsight, some of the deflation that the Fed was fretting about in 2003 was in fact benign deflation due to cheaper goods from China and the IT revolution. But its determination to prevent inflation falling caused it to push interest rates unusually low. This, argues Mr. White, could have long-term costs to the extent that persistently easy money leads to too much borrowing, too little saving and unsustainable asset prices.

c Most central banks base their policy analysis on models derived from Keynesian economics. In these, holding interest rates too low creates excessive aggregate demand and hence inflation. But Mr. White believes that a model based on the Austrian school of economics, at its height between the world wars, may now be more relevant. In Austrian models, the main result of excessively low interest rates is excess credit and an imbalance between saving and investment—rather like the one in America today . . .

Defenders of today's monetary-policy method, focused on consumer-price inflation, may say that it seems to have delivered the goods, in the form of more stable growth. So why change? One reason, suggests Mr. White, is that if monetary policy is concerned solely with price stability, surges in credit will be restrained only if they trigger inflationary pressures. Ever-bigger financial imbalances could thus build up. Even if inflation remains subdued in the short term, low interest rates could either increase the risk of higher inflation in the future or pump up borrowing and asset prices. Should these imbalances eventually correct themselves, there will be a sharp slowdown.

*April 2006: available at www.bis.org/publ/work205.pdf

ANALYZING THE NEWS ...

The Federal Reserve's successful battle against inflation in the 1980s and 1990s has been hailed by many economists and policymakers as a significant achievement in economic policy. There is little disagreement that high rates of inflation are bad for the economy and for society. High rates of inflation reduce economic growth and by distorting movements of relative prices, it leads to a misallocation of resources. It is these negative affects on economic well-being that have led to price stability being one of the major goals of monetary policy.

a Some economists argue that central banks today worry almost exclusively about inflation. Yet, as the author of the article points out, recent economic crises have come about after periods of low inflation. As discussed in the chapter, monetary policy has other goals, such as financial market stability, that also need to be considered.

b In 2002 and 2003, the Fed cut interest rates, in part out of fear that the U.S. economy might be nearing the risk of deflationary pressures. Deflationary pressures, such as those experienced during the Great Depression of the 1930s, are usually associated with significant reductions in borrowing and spending. As borrowing decreases, market interest rates fall, thereby rendering expansionary monetary policy relatively useless. Thus, to stop the onset of deflationary pressures, the Fed cut interest rates to their lowest levels in nearly four decades to ensure increased levels of borrowing and spending.

However, the falling inflation rates in 2002 and 2003 might have been caused by increases in technology and lower-priced imports. If these were the major causes of the moderating inflation, the expansionary monetary policy of the Fed may have been unwarranted.

c The Austrian school of thought, most closely associated with Ludwig von Mises, argues that monetary policy often distorts the financial market ability to set interest rates. The Austrians argue that when central banks or the government intervene in the financial markets to keep interest rates artificially low, excess amounts of borrowing result. As a consequence of this excessive borrowing, excess amounts of credit are supplied, thanks to the expansionary monetary policy. This excessive borrowing and lending can lead to asset bubbles as well as inflation. Therefore, central banks need to watch a wider range of indicators other than consumer price inflation.

For further thought . . .

What other indicators could the Federal Reserve watch to guard against excessive expansionary monetary policy? Why?

ANALYTICAL PROBLEMS

18. *Evaluate:* If the Fed uses the federal funds rate as an operating target, increases (decreases) in the demand for money increase (decrease) the money supply.
19. State whether each of the following variables is most likely to be a goal, an intermediate target, an operating target, or a monetary policy tool.
    a. *M2*
    b. Monetary base
    c. Unemployment rate
    d. Open market purchases
    e. Federal funds rate
    f. Nonborrowed reserves
    g. *M1*
    h. Real GDP growth
    i. Discount rate
20. A recent proposal suggested that the Fed use the monetary base as its operating target to achieve a specified nominal GDP range as its intermediate target. What are the pros and cons of this suggestion?
21. How does using interest rates as an operating or intermediate target lead to procyclical monetary policy? How could policymakers use interest rates in the policy process and avoid procyclical policy?
22. Design a mechanism for monetary policy control of the economy, assuming that the Fed had a good model of the economy that provided accurate forecasts. Why would such a procedure be less useful with less accurate forecasts?
23. When would a simple rule for monetary policy, such as one that makes *M2* rise at a steady rate of 3% each year, be valid? When would problems with such a rule occur?
24. Outline a procedure for Fed control of the federal funds rate. Is this procedure consistent with control of the money supply process? Why or why not?
25. *Evaluate:* If the Fed uses nonborrowed reserves as its operating target, increases (decreases) in the demand for money increase (decrease) the money supply.
26. *Evaluate:* The money supply is inherently procyclical, rising during (and amplifying) economic expansions and declining during (and amplifying) economic contractions.
27. Does it matter for the Fed's conduct of monetary policy whether the federal government's budget is balanced, in surplus, or in deficit? Choose a particular time period in the years since 1945 to illustrate your answer.

Use graphical analysis of the money market to answer Questions 28 and 29.

28. Does using the federal funds rate as an operating target imply that the money supply curve is horizontal? Why or why not?
29. Do interest rate targets help the Fed to soften the impact of economic downturns? Why or why not?

DATA QUESTIONS

30. Look through past issues of the *Federal Reserve Bulletin* to find when the chairman of the Fed's Board of Governors last testified before Congress as required by law under the Humphrey-Hawkins Act. The chairman testifies twice each year, in February and July. Read through the chairman's testimony and identify the variables that the Fed is using as operating targets and intermediate targets. What other variables does the chairman mention as important indicators for the economy? Can you identify the Fed's goals?
31. Locate the most recent monthly issue of *Economic Indicators*, prepared by the Council of Economic Advisers, at http://www.gpoaccess.gov/indicators/index.html. Compare price, employment, and output data in 1999 and in 2003. How would you explain the monetary policies that existed at those times based on the economic data given?

CHAPTER 15

Banking Regulation: Crisis and Response

The economy recovered after the Great Depression, and it prospered during and after World War II. Thanks to the banking regulations enacted in the Depression's aftermath—expansion of the Fed's role as lender of last resort, restrictions on competition for banking services, and federal deposit insurance—which attempted to reduce the chance of a future banking crisis, the environment for banking became very comfortable. During this period, bank managers were said to follow a "3-6-3" rule: borrow at 3%, lend at 6%, and be on the golf course at 3:00.

But this nirvana didn't last long. Other participants in the financial system saw opportunities to serve savers and borrowers in ways that regulated banks could not; the economic forces of the business cycle and episodes of inflation and high market interest rates turned restrictions on the interest that banks could pay into a millstone; deposit insurance gave banks an incentive to act imprudently. The regulations that were designed to keep the banking system healthy contributed in part to problems that began in the 1960s and 1970s, which in turn led to opportunities for innovation. Banking regulators found themselves more like the scientists who attempt to develop a flu vaccine each year than the researchers who were able to prevent smallpox or whooping cough with a single shot. Like the influenza virus, which can mutate each year, the ills that regulations tried to fix occurred with sufficient variety that no single regulation could ensure the profitability of the banking industry. Indeed, bank regulators were aiming at a moving target.

In this chapter we describe the recent history of banking regulation, looking specifically at the crises that fostered the regulation, the effect of the regulations, and the challenges that regulators faced in trying to maintain the banking industry as a conduit of funds from savers to borrowers. As you look at each type of regulation—lender of last resort, restrictions on competition, and deposit insurance—you will notice that a four-stage pattern emerges: (1) crisis, (2) regulation, (3) response by the financial system, and (4) response by regulators. Once you become comfortable with this process of evaluating the regulation of financial institutions, you can use it to interpret future developments in the banking industry and in other financial institutions in the United States and abroad.

The Pattern of Regulation

The first stage in the regulatory pattern is a *crisis* in the banking industry. For example, if savers lost confidence in banks' ability to use their funds wisely, a bank run would result as savers tried to withdraw their funds. When savers lose confidence in them, banks are unable to fulfill their role as intermediaries for many borrowers. Adverse selection and moral hazard can create instability, leading to crises in the banking system.

The second stage occurs when government steps in to end the crisis through *regulation*. The government generally intervenes when it perceives instability in financial institutions and when political pressures make intervention advisable. For example, government regulation in the United States and other countries has responded to banking panics by attempting to maintain banks' profitability or reducing monitoring costs for savers.

The third stage is *response by the financial system*. A major regulatory intervention—deposit insurance, for example—leads to changes and innovation in the activities of financial institutions (borrowing, lending, and provision of risk sharing, liquidity, and information services). As in manufacturing companies or other service businesses, *innovation* (the development of new products or lines of business to serve consumers) gives one company an edge over its competitors. The motivation for financial innovation is the same as that in other businesses: profit.

The fourth stage occurs with *regulatory response*. Regulators observe the impact of regulation on changes in the way that financial institutions do business. In particular, when financial innovations circumvent regulatory restrictions, regulators must adapt their policies or seek new authority as a regulatory response.

Lender of Last Resort

Congress created the Federal Reserve System as the lender of last resort to provide liquidity to banks during banking panics. Essentially, creation of the Fed was a regulatory response to the crisis of bank failures and contractions in bank lending during the late nineteenth and early twentieth centuries. As we will see, however, for a lender of last resort to be effective, its promise to lend to banks during a crisis must be credible and carried out swiftly. The evolution of the Fed's activities illustrates how regulation introduced in response to one crisis can be adapted to respond to future crises.

The Great Depression

The first crucial test for the Federal Reserve System's effectiveness in reducing the costs of financial instability followed the stock market crash of October 1929. In responding to the crash, the Fed performed its role as lender of last resort quickly and decisively by extending credit to the New York banks that made loans to stockbrokers and speculators.

The Fed soon faced a more serious problem: the banking panics that began in late 1930, as a wave of bank failures hit the U.S. economy, caused savers to lose confidence in the banking system. Demand deposits shrank sharply as the public converted them to currency because they perceived bank deposits to be risky. Banks liquidated loans and raised their reserve holdings to 22% of deposits in 1932 (up from 15% of deposits in 1930), but bank intermediation had broken down. In March 1933, President Roosevelt declared a *bank holiday*, forcing all banks to close for a time.

The economic collapse during the early 1930s—the Great Depression—was the most severe financial setback in U.S. history. Many economists consider the bank failures to be a key reason the downturn lasted so long. When banks failed, many borrowers, unable to find substitutes for bank loans (through sales of bonds or shares), couldn't obtain credit. Many small and medium-sized businesses and farms failed as a result. Disruption in the banking system demonstrates how crucial banks are in reducing the information costs of savers in finding creditworthy borrowers. The large number of small, poorly diversified banks—particularly those that held agricultural loans during a period of falling commodity prices—compounded the banking crisis.

During the banking panics, the Fed failed to act decisively as the lender of last resort; it did not lend aggressively enough to struggling banks. Moreover, the Fed actually *raised* the interest rate it charged on loans to member banks in 1931. It is easy to look back and see how the Fed should have acted, but at the time, the Fed shared the view of many economists who believed that the Great Depression would work itself out with no central bank intervention. In addition, the Fed's charter allowed it to lend only to banks that pledged good-quality commercial loans as collateral. The Fed also faced problems because its policy to maintain a fixed exchange rate under the gold standard limited its ability to act. In 1931, when England suspended convertibility of the pound into gold, participants in international financial markets thought that the United States might abandon its fixed exchange rate promise and gold convertibility as well. As a result, foreign investors rushed to convert dollars into gold. To maintain the exchange rate and protect its gold reserves, the Fed increased the interest rate it charged on loans to banks. This increased the exchange rate of the dollar versus other currencies and restored the relative attractiveness of the United States as a place to keep funds. However, higher interest rates made it difficult for struggling banks to borrow from the Fed.

Congressional action after 1932 attempted to solve the problems that had prolonged the banking crisis. Congress amended the Fed's charter to limit convertibility of the U.S. dollar into gold and broadened the definition of permissible collateral for loans from the Fed. Decision making within the Fed was centralized to improve its ability to respond quickly during a crisis. Nonetheless, the financial community remained uncertain as to whether the Fed could be an effective lender of last resort for the banking industry. The Fed's weakness during the calamitous early 1930s motivated the introduction of federal deposit insurance in 1934.

CHECKPOINT

Suppose that banks used checkable deposits to finance commercial loans that could be traded on secondary markets. Would there be a role for a lender of last resort? If banks' loan portfolios were very liquid and sufficient information on their quality were available so that they could be traded, liquidity risk and information costs would be greatly reduced. As a result, there would be less need for a lender of last resort. However, if liquidity and information costs were extremely low, there also would be less need for traditional banking firms. ♦

Success in More Recent Years

Despite its shaky start as a lender of last resort during the Great Depression, the Federal Reserve System has performed well since World War II. The following four episodes show how the Fed can intervene successfully to prevent financial crises.

The Penn Central Railroad crisis. When the Penn Central Railroad, once one of the largest corporations in the United States, filed for bankruptcy in 1970, it defaulted on $200 million of commercial paper. Investors became doubtful about the quality of commercial paper issued by other large companies and wary of supplying funds to that market. Without any intervention by the Fed, raising money in the commercial paper market would become costly because investors would require a large premium to compensate them for the perceived risk. The Fed increased the availability of credit to commercial banks to encourage them to extend short-term credit to make

CONSIDER THIS ...

How Does a Lender of Last Resort Protect the Payments System?

Although Congress created it to act as the lender of last resort for the banking system, the Fed today also engages in a variety of lending activities to maintain the soundness of financial trading mechanisms. One important trading mechanism is the *payments system*, or the means for clearing transactions in the economy by check. The New York–based Clearing House for Interbank Payments and Settlements (CHIPS) settles dollar-denominated transfers among both domestic and foreign-owned banks. If a market participant in CHIPS fails during a business day, all its payments are canceled. These cancellations in turn affect all other participants with which the failed bank was dealing. Hence the failure of a large bank could trigger failures of other institutions. The Fed must wrestle with difficult decisions about how to react, particularly when a crisis develops as the result of failure of a foreign-owned bank.

Another important clearing mechanism is the *Fedwire* system, which is used in clearing securities transactions. Positions are not closed during the day, so if a bank can't settle an overdraft by the end of the day, the Fed effectively must convert it to a (possibly involuntary) discount loan. The role of lender of last resort in maintaining the health of the payments system gets murky when we consider the blurring of distinctions between commercial and investment banking and, in some instances, between finance and commerce. If commercial firms were allowed to conduct banking activities, a crisis in banking could force the Fed to make unsecured, interest-free loans to investment banking firms or even to manufacturing firms.

available the amount of funds that firms would ordinarily borrow in the commercial paper market. It also provided loans to these banks to make the extra lending possible. These actions averted a crisis in the banking system and financial markets.

The Franklin National Bank crisis. When the Franklin National Bank collapsed in 1974, it had issued a large amount of negotiable certificates of deposit. These time deposits could be bought and sold by individuals and institutions with a penalty for early withdrawal but weren't guaranteed by federal deposit insurance. In this instance, investors questioned the quality of other banks' negotiable CDs and cut back their holdings of such deposits. The decline in demand for negotiable CDs worried bankers because they are a significant source of funds to banks. To avert a panic in the negotiable CD market, the Fed reduced investors' information costs by providing discount loans to banks. This action eased investors' fears about the general quality of negotiable CDs.

The Hunt brothers' silver speculation crisis. In the 1980s, Herbert Hunt and Nelson Bunker Hunt, heirs of legendary oil baron H. L. Hunt, used their sizable fortunes and borrowed funds to corner the silver market. Their scheme worked for a while, but the price of silver ultimately tumbled. The collapse of this speculative scheme caused woes not just for the brothers but also for large brokerage houses, including industry giant Merrill Lynch, to which they owed money. The amounts at stake were large enough to threaten the financial stability of the exchange on which the futures contracts were traded. Such a failure would have been costly to savers and borrowers who depended on the exchange to provide information services that are essential to trading in and liquidity of futures contracts. In this case, the Fed worked with a group of banks to provide loans to exchange members, thereby avoiding a rise in information costs and a market panic.

The stock market crash of 1987. The stock market crash on October 19, 1987, raised fears of a repetition of the events that followed the 1929 crash. In particular, investors feared credit squeezes on broker-dealers in the securities industry. Before the stock market opened for trading the following day, Federal Reserve Chairman Alan Greenspan announced to the news media the Fed's readiness to provide liquidity in support of the economic and financial system. At the same time, the Fed, acting as lender of last resort, encouraged banks to lend to securities firms and extended discount credit to banks. This action by the Fed reduced information costs and allowed financial markets to provide risk-sharing and liquidity services to market participants. In addition, the action ensured the soundness of the payments system.

Concluding Remarks

A lender of last resort can help to stabilize the banking system during a crisis. In the United States, the Federal Reserve System has generally performed this role successfully. Indeed, in late 1998, the Fed averted a possible panic from the financial woes of Long-Term Capital Management, a large U.S. hedge fund, by simply using its influence to bring the firm's creditors together. In September 2001, the Fed's swift action bolstered market-makers and commerce after the 9/11 terrorist attacks in New York and at the Pentagon. Figure 15.1 summarizes the evolution of the Fed's role in the cycle of financial crisis, regulation, financial system response, and regulatory response.

Anticompetitive Bank Regulation

A second way in which the federal government sought to maintain banking stability was to limit competition among banks and between banks and other financial institutions. Such intervention was intended to (1) reduce the likelihood of bank runs and (2) reduce the chance of moral hazard in banks' behavior. The argument for limiting competition is that it increases a bank's value, thereby reducing bankers' willingness to make excessively risky investments.

Anticompetitive regulations do not promote banking stability in the long run. Instead, they create an incentive for unregulated financial institutions and markets to

FIGURE 15.1 **Lender of Last Resort: Crisis, Regulation, Financial System Response, and Regulatory Response**

Instability in the banking system reduced the liquidity of bank deposits and raised information costs, leading to a collapse in bank lending and a call for a lender of last resort. After the Fed's early failures to act as a lender of last resort, its powers were broadened, and additional bank regulation was developed.

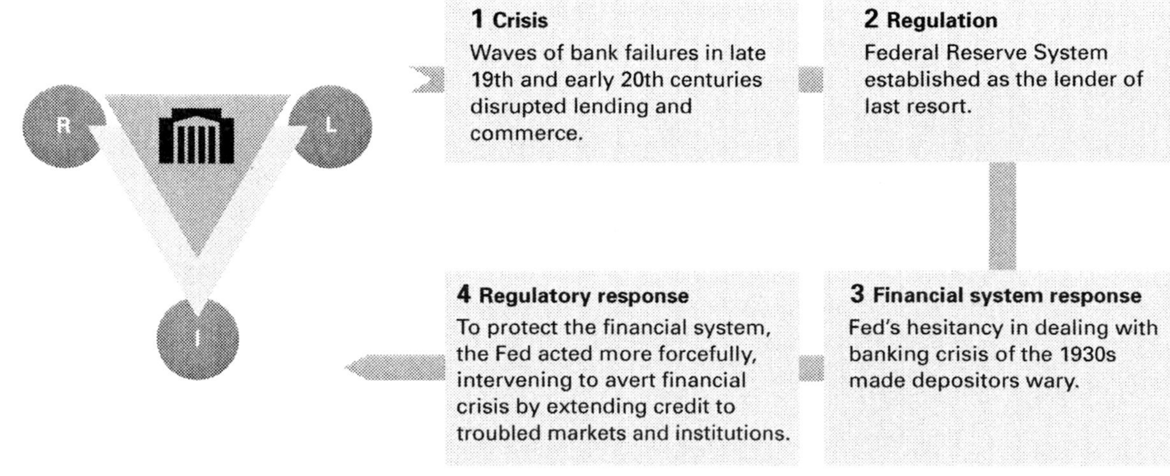
R
L
I
1 Crisis
Waves of bank failures in late 19th and early 20th centuries disrupted lending and commerce.
2 Regulation
Federal Reserve System established as the lender of last resort.
3 Financial system response
Fed's hesitancy in dealing with banking crisis of the 1930s made depositors wary.
4 Regulatory response
To protect the financial system, the Fed acted more forcefully, intervening to avert financial crisis by extending credit to troubled markets and institutions.

compete with banks by offering close substitutes for bank deposits and loans. A dramatic example of how anticompetitive regulation led to competition, financial innovation, and regulatory response occurred in the fight over limits on the interest that banks could pay depositors. The battle began with the Banking Act of 1933, which authorized **Regulation Q.** It placed ceilings on allowable interest rates for time and savings deposits and prohibited the payment of interest on demand deposits (then the only form of checkable deposits). Regulation Q was intended to maintain banks' profitability by limiting competition for funds among banks and guaranteeing a reasonable spread between interest rates on loans and interest rates paid to depositors. In fact, it forced banks to innovate to survive.

The market for short-term credit exists in large part to accommodate firms' demand for working capital, the funds firms use to pay for materials, labor, and inventories before the sale of products can generate revenue. Households and firms hold short-term liquid assets as a buffer against changes in income or spending. Historically, commercial banks dominated the short-term credit market. They specialize in reducing information costs by forming long-term relationships with borrowers and continually reauthorizing short-term loans. Also, by lending through such banks, savers obtain risk-sharing and liquidity benefits.

Setting a ceiling on interest rates that banks could pay depositors was supposed to give banks a competitive advantage in the market for loans. The low cost of funds as a result of interest rate ceilings made banks the leading lenders to households and businesses. But whenever market interest rates rose above that ceiling, large and small savers seeking the highest rates of return had a strong incentive to search for alternatives in the marketplace. This is exactly what happened during the 1960s—and increasingly in the 1970s and 1980s. Large corporations and wealthy households substituted such short-term investments as Treasury bills, commercial paper, and repurchase agreements in place of short-term deposits at banks. The benefits of greater rates of returns from these securities justify the transactions costs of hiring a cash management team or paying brokerage fees to find and manage alternative investments when market interest rates are high.

The financial system responded by introducing money market mutual funds in 1971 as an alternative to bank deposits. This innovation enabled depositors whose bank deposits were paying below-market interest rates (because of Regulation Q) to hold portfolios of government securities and commercial paper. Money market mutual funds gave small and medium-sized depositors an opportunity to earn market rates of return with low transactions costs. They ensured both liquidity and diversification, services that were formerly provided only by banks. These funds grew in popularity in 1978, when market interest rates climbed above the 5.25% ceiling on interest rates for savings accounts and time deposits. Their assets rose from $4 billion in 1977 to $230 billion in 1982 to more than $2014 billion in 2006. The evolution of money market mutual funds in response to regulation is not unique to the United States.

Development of the money market mutual fund market also provided *borrowers* with a new source of funds. Large, well-established firms could raise short-term funds in the commercial paper market, where savers sought higher rates of return than returns on bank deposits and low information costs. This alternative to bank borrowing created new competition between commercial and investment banks and significant loss of loan business for commercial banks. By 2006, total lending in the commercial paper market accounted for about 15% of short-term business financing, compared to 10% in 1980, 7% in 1970, and 2% in 1960. The loss of business that banks suffered was even more damaging than the statistics imply because, as our analysis of the costs of adverse selection predicts, only high-quality borrowers had access to commercial paper, leaving banks with low-quality borrowers.

The exit of savers and borrowers from banks to financial markets is known as **disintermediation,** which costs banks lost revenue from not having savers' funds to loan. In some cases, it also costs borrowers and the economy: although high-quality, established borrowers are able to raise funds in markets such as the commercial paper market, households and less well-established business firms aren't able to do so. As a result, banks aren't able to provide more efficient intermediation than financial markets even when the transactions and information costs of market alternatives are high. Let's look at how the costs of disintermediation can affect the economy.

The Credit Crunch of 1966

In 1966, deposits in commercial banks, savings banks, and savings and loan associations (S&Ls) were subject to interest rate ceilings under Regulation Q. Rising market interest rates caused depositors to shift funds from commercial banks and S&Ls to financial markets. Large commercial banks redirected their investment strategies to raise funds through unregulated sources, such as Eurodollar deposits. Smaller banks and S&Ls had fewer alternative sources of funds and were forced to curtail lending. In the first half of 1966, primarily mutual savings banks and S&Ls were affected by disintermediation, because households' savings deposits were their primary source of funds and their mortgage lending fell dramatically. Commercial banks felt the pinch in the second half of the year when the Fed lowered the interest rate ceiling on bank time deposits, forcing them to cut back on interest paid to depositors.

The blow to mortgage lending and the housing industry caused a **credit crunch,** or a reduction in borrowers' ability to obtain credit at prevailing interest rates. A credit crunch affects small firms the most. In fact, smaller creditworthy firms had to cut back disproportionately on investment because they normally depend on bank loans for external financing.

Banks' Response

As savers and borrowers were lured from banks to financial institutions that offered more attractive interest rates, banks actively countered with their own innovations. To reestablish their ties to borrowers, banks used their information-cost and transactions-cost advantages to enter the commercial paper market through the back door by offering standby letters of credit (Chapter 13). That innovation enabled banks to minimize the damage from anticompetitive regulation by earning fees that compensated them for their information services.

To circumvent the interest rate regulation, banks also developed new financial instruments for savers. Citibank introduced the **negotiable certificate of deposit** (or negotiable CD) as a time deposit with a fixed maturity of, say, six months, to compete with commercial paper. CDs differ from demand deposits in that depositors are penalized with early withdrawal; this feature makes CDs relatively illiquid for the cash management needs of large firms. *Negotiable* CDs circumvent this limitation because they can be sold to someone else even though they cannot be redeemed prior to maturity without penalty. When Citibank created them, negotiable CDs of at least $100,000 were exempt from Regulation Q. Negotiable CDs are now an important source of funds for commercial banks, with a typical denomination of $1 million.

In addition, banks came up with ways to pay interest on depositors' funds. A break for small depositors came when a Massachusetts mutual savings bank created a substitute for checking accounts that was not governed by Regulation Q. Called a **negotiable order of withdrawal (NOW) account,** it required only the introduction of a "withdrawal slip" that the depositor could sign over to someone else. This withdrawal slip functioned like a check; a NOW account is like a checking account. Technically, however, it isn't a demand deposit, so interest can be paid on it. Following a favorable Massachusetts court decision in 1972, NOW accounts spread throughout New England, New Jersey, and New York, effectively offering checking accounts paying 5.25% interest at the time, in contrast to the 0% on traditional demand deposits. (NOW accounts today offer varying interest rates linked to short-term market interest rates.) Small savers holding checking accounts and passbook savings accounts transferred their funds to NOW accounts. In an additional development in 1974, credit unions began issuing share drafts, or checkable deposits paying interest on minimum account balances.

For large depositors, banks used repurchase agreements (RPs), overnight Eurodollars, and automatic transfer system (ATS) accounts. Under a repurchase agreement, the bank regularly converts the balance of a demand deposit into overnight RPs. Recall that in an RP, a corporation purchases Treasury bills from a bank, and the bank commits to repurchase them the next day for a slightly higher price, thereby paying interest to the depositor. In overnight Eurodollar transactions, a customer's demand deposit is automatically withdrawn and deposited in a foreign branch that pays interest. Finally, ATS accounts effectively pay interest on checking accounts by "sweeping" a customer's checking account balance at the end of the day into overnight RPs.

CHECKPOINT

You are an intelligent banker, always looking for ways to increase your bank's profits. You notice that when someone moves money from a demand deposit into a savings account, interest is earned for that day as long as the transfer occurs before midnight. However, there is a law against paying interest on demand deposits. What can you think of to get around this law? You could automatically transfer balances from demand deposits to savings accounts and back by computer each night at midnight. In this way, the demand deposits, in effect, would earn interest, even though technically you are allowed to pay interest only on savings accounts. ♦

Regulatory Response

The breakdown of interest rate regulation in banking came about because of pressure on regulators from small and medium-sized banks. These banks, like large banks, lost deposits to money market mutual funds. Unlike large banks, however, they had limited access to innovations that were not subject to regulation. In response to financial systems' circumvention of Regulation Q, Congress enacted two pieces of legislation: the Depository Institutions Deregulation and Monetary Control Act of 1980 (DIDMCA) and the Garn–St. Germain Act of 1982.

DIDMCA. With passage of the **Depository Institutions Deregulation and Monetary Control Act of 1980,** Congress eased the anticompetitive burden on banks and helped to provide fairness in the financial services industry. The act eliminated interest rate ceilings (known as *usury ceilings*) on mortgage loans and certain types of commercial loans. It also provided for uniform reserve requirements and access to Federal Reserve System services (such as discount loans and check clearing) for all depository institutions. In addition, DIDMCA permitted banks throughout the United States to offer NOW and ATS accounts, thereby allowing banks to compete with money market mutual funds. The effect of this change was dramatic: NOW and ATS deposits rose almost fourfold—from $27 billion to $101 billion—between 1980 and 1982. Also, DIDMCA phased out Regulation Q gradually from 1980 to 1986. As a result, DIDMCA was popular both with banks that were eager to compete and with depositors who were eager to earn interest on deposits.

Other depository institutions received benefits, too (in return for their political support of the legislation). The act allowed S&Ls and mutual savings banks to broaden their lending beyond mortgages. Savings and loan associations were allowed to invest as much as 20% of their assets in corporate bonds, commercial paper, and consumer loans; they also were allowed to expand into credit card lending and trust services. Mutual savings banks were permitted to compete with commercial banks by making commercial loans (for up to 5% of their assets) and accepting checkable deposits in connection with their loans.

However, the DIDMCA phaseout of interest rate ceilings was not a cure-all for financial institutions. Because Regulation Q was eliminated only gradually, money market mutual funds continued to expand at the expense of S&Ls and mutual savings banks; by post–World War II standards, an unprecedented number of S&Ls and mutual savings banks failed (250 in 1982 alone). Regulatory change to address this problem soon followed.

Garn–St. Germain Act. Congress passed the **Garn–St. Germain Act of 1982** to combat problems caused by the gradual demise of Regulation Q under DIDMCA. To give them a more potent weapon against money market mutual funds, the act permitted depository institutions to offer savers federally insured **money market deposit accounts** (MMDAs), which provide services similar to those of money market mutual funds. These accounts were subject neither to reserve requirements nor to Regulation Q ceilings. The combination of market interest rates and the safety and familiarity of banks made the new accounts an instant success.

To solve the special problems facing savings institutions, the Garn–St. Germain Act broadened the ability of federally chartered savings institutions to invest in areas other than mortgages (as much as 30% of their assets in consumer loans and 10% in commercial loans by 1984). Because these changes made savings institutions comparable to banks, the act required that (as of 1984) Regulation Q ceilings be applied uniformly to all depository institutions until the ceilings expired in 1986.

Concluding Remarks

The landmark DIDMCA and Garn–St. Germain legislation placed the banking industry on a more equal footing with its competitors. However, the Garn–St. Germain Act moved savings institutions from the usually calm waters of mortgage lending into the choppy waters of bank lending. Figure 15.2 summarizes the process of financial crisis, regulation, financial system response, and regulatory response as it applies to interest rate ceilings. Liberalization of deposit interest rate ceilings in European countries and Japan also illustrates the interplay between financial innovation and financial regulation.

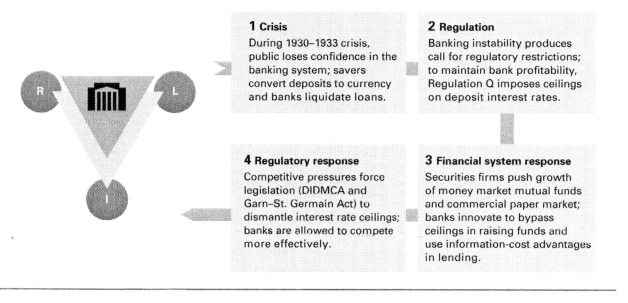

FIGURE 15.2 **Interest Rate Ceilings: Crisis, Regulation, Financial System Response, and Regulatory Response**

Regulation Q imposed interest rate ceilings on bank deposits. Beginning in the late 1960s, nonbank financial firms created innovations that enabled savers to earn higher returns. These innovations allowed nonbanks to gain a competitive advantage in providing liquidity services and lending. Financial innovation by banks and regulatory changes allowed banks to compete more effectively against nonbanks.

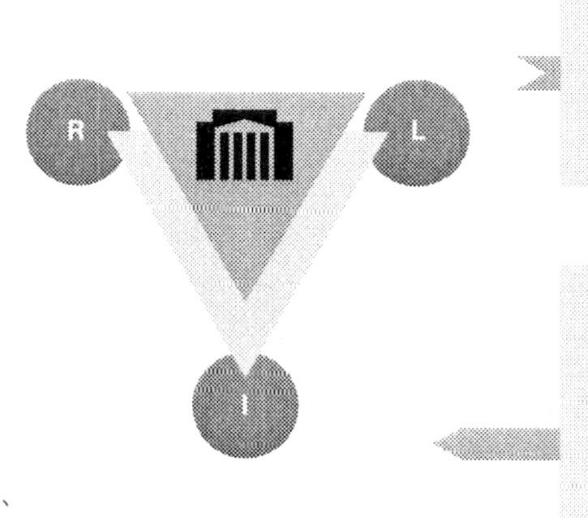

1 Crisis
During 1930–1933 crisis, public loses confidence in the banking system; savers convert deposits to currency and banks liquidate loans.

2 Regulation
Banking instability produces call for regulatory restrictions; to maintain bank profitability, Regulation Q imposes ceilings on deposit interest rates.

3 Financial system response
Securities firms push growth of money market mutual funds and commercial paper market; banks innovate to bypass ceilings in raising funds and use information-cost advantages in lending.

4 Regulatory response
Competitive pressures force legislation (DIDMCA and Garn–St. Germain Act) to dismantle interest rate ceilings; banks are allowed to compete more effectively.

The U.S. Deposit Insurance Crisis of the 1980s

Introduced in response to the banking crises of the 1930s, federal deposit insurance functioned smoothly from its inception in 1934 until the early 1980s. Economists and politicians hoped that bank runs could be consigned to the history books and that the economic costs of a collapsing banking system could be avoided. However, beginning in the 1970s, unnoticed problems were building. The first of the depository institutions to exhibit signs of trouble were S&Ls; next were banks. The lessons of these episodes are currently shaping the activities and regulation of virtually all financial institutions, banks and nonbanks alike.

Beginning of the Crisis: Worsening Conditions in S&Ls

While the origins of federal deposit insurance lie in the 1930s, the stages of crisis and response that we study begin much later. In particular, the story unfolds in two parts. One relates to the outmoded structure of S&Ls (also called *thrifts*), and the other relates to the financial innovation and regulatory changes in the 1970s and early 1980s (discussed in the preceding section).

To promote mortgage lending, banking regulation created S&Ls in the 1930s from the remnants of building and loan societies (many of which had failed). These institutions held long-term, fixed-rate mortgages and financed them with short-term time deposits. As long as interest rates were stable and regulation limited interest payments to depositors (the situation from the 1930s through much of the 1960s), little went wrong. However, the mismatch between the maturities of S&Ls' assets and those of their liabilities created the potential for interest rate risk.

Some episodes of rising market interest rates worried S&Ls in the 1960s and 1970s. However, the real trouble began as U.S. interest rates rose dramatically in late 1979. As a result, the cost of funds for S&Ls escalated, the present value of their existing mortgage assets plummeted, and their net worth declined precipitously. At about the same time, the 1981–1982 recession raised default rates on mortgages, particularly for S&Ls that were located in farm or energy-producing states (such as Texas), where conditions were especially bad. About half the S&Ls had a negative net worth by the end of 1982. Our analysis of moral hazard suggests that this condition should have sounded a warning for deposit insurance. Because savers' deposits (to a regulated amount) were guaranteed by the Federal Savings and Loan Insurance Corporation (FSLIC), managers of S&Ls were strongly tempted to engage in riskier investments.

Financial System Response

Recall, however, that in the early 1980s, Congress tried to help S&Ls by relaxing restrictions on their asset holdings. In making these regulatory changes, Congress intended to allow S&Ls to diversify and combat exposure to interest rate risk by making available new assets, including direct real estate investments, commercial mortgages, and junk bonds. Many S&Ls took advantage of these opportunities. By the early 1990s, S&Ls (originally created to bolster mortgage lending) accounted for fewer than half of U.S. mortgage loans.

In 1980, DIDMCA raised the federal deposit insurance ceiling from $40,000 per account to $100,000 per account, even as the phaseout of Regulation Q increased S&Ls' costs of funds. Now S&Ls could issue insured CDs in larger amounts at high interest rates, with the proceeds invested in risky assets. Our analysis of the costs of adverse selection cautions the *uninsured* saver to be wary of the promise of higher yields (as it brings with it greater risks). Insured depositors flocked to the higher yields because the government guaranteed their deposits. To make matters worse, financial innovators effectively raised the deposit insurance limit many times over by creating **brokered deposits.** In a brokered deposit, a depositor with $1 million goes to a broker, who buys ten $100,000 CDs in ten different banks, giving the depositor ten different bank accounts with insurance on the entire $1 million. Federal authorities banned brokered deposits in 1984, but a federal court decision later reversed the ban.

Moreover, many S&Ls did not manage their assets and liabilities to reduce their exposure to interest rate risk. In principle, savings institutions could have lessened interest rate risk by using variable-rate mortgages, known as *adjustable-rate mortgages* (ARMs). The lender adjusts the mortgage interest rate when market interest rates rise or fall, thereby cushioning the effects of interest rate changes on the institution's net worth. Although ARMs now are popular in mortgage lending, they haven't been a cure-all for at least two reasons. First, the indexes on which they are based are imperfect, and rate adjustment is normally subject to both annual and mortgage term caps. Second, an ARM may increase credit risk. Significant increases in monthly payments may increase the risk of borrower default. That is, payments being held constant, the loan balance could balloon to more than the collateral value of the loan. During the 1980s, S&Ls also made little use of other risk-sharing devices that were available to them. This circumstance isn't really surprising: Moral hazard problems suggest that depository institutions with low net worth have an incentive to increase risky behavior rather than decrease exposure to interest rate risk.

Finally, many analysts blame lax regulatory supervision during the 1980s for encouraging fraud and prolonging the crisis. Some S&L executives used savers' deposits to fund lavish lifestyles or simply embezzled funds. For example, the First Network Savings Bank, whose failure in 1990 cost federal deposit insurance agencies 25 cents on each dollar of deposits, used deposits to build the world's largest "museum of magic" at its headquarters. In another notorious case, S&L entrepreneur Don Dixon was convicted of embezzling bank funds, which he spent on prostitutes, hot tubs, and designer shotguns. Dixon went to jail, but taxpayers paid for the 96% of his S&L's loans that had defaulted.

To avoid bankrupting its reserves, the Federal Home Loan Bank Board (FHLBB) and its deposit insurance subsidiary, the FSLIC, allowed insolvent S&Ls to continue to operate. The cost of closing insolvent S&Ls quickly escalated in the late 1980s and early 1990s. Economists have estimated that the costs to the FSLIC of closing the insolvent S&Ls in 1982 would have been about $20 billion. Although this number is small relative to the costs of the crisis by the 1990s (hundreds of billions of dollars), it was greater than the reserves the FSLIC had built up since 1934. Even so, the FSLIC could have made a credible deposit insurance guarantee based on the implicit backing of the Treasury and the Fed.

To understand the escalation of costs, let's consider how insolvent institutions avoided closure. In the process of evaluating nonfinancial businesses, analysts gauge net worth. To avoid classifying S&Ls as insolvent and depleting deposit insurance funds to reimburse depositors, regulators changed the accounting rules. Instead of estimating economic net worth, they used regulatory accounting principles to allow S&Ls to carry on their books at face value many assets whose value actually had declined because of rising interest rates. In addition, regulators gave S&Ls an inflated value for goodwill, the intangible value of the institution as a going concern. In 1982, total industry net worth was reported at 3.7% of assets under regulatory accounting principles. Had the assets been measured at market value, the industry's net worth would have been −12%. As a result of such calculations, many insolvent or nearly insolvent S&Ls continued to operate, rather than being closed by the FSLIC.

Although deposit insurance reduces the need for individual depositors to monitor banks, the principal-agent problem doesn't disappear. Bank regulators act as agents for the taxpayers who are the principals; taxpayers collectively bear the costs of deposit insurance bailouts. However, as studies by Edward Kane of Boston College have stressed, regulators' incentives differ from those of taxpayers. Regulators hold their positions for relatively short periods of time, so they have an incentive to loosen capital requirements and supervision at the first sign of trouble. They don't want troubled institutions to fail under their supervision. Regulators also have an incentive to pay more attention to elected lawmakers who can influence their careers than to taxpayers.

A good example of the principal-agent problem is the "Keating Five" scandal in 1990. Charles Keating, an S&L entrepreneur, contributed about $1.3 million to the campaigns of five U.S. senators in return for their assistance in getting FHLBB Chairman Edwin Gray to deal lightly with the problems of Keating's Lincoln Savings and Loan in 1987. Lincoln operated with severe financial problems until its failure in 1989, costing taxpayers about $2.5 billion. The senators who should have acted on behalf of the taxpayers instead accepted contributions from Keating. Keating and his son were convicted in 1992 on numerous counts of fraud and betrayal of fiduciary trust by both state and federal courts.

Regulatory Response: The S&L Bailout

By the end of 1986, losses in the S&L industry had wiped out the FSLIC's reserves. President Reagan requested $15 billion for FSLIC, an amount that analysts decried as inadequate. In the Competitive Equality Banking Act of 1987, Congress gave the administration even less than its request. Deprived of funds to resolve the situation, the

FHLBB allowed insolvent institutions to continue operating, paying high interest rates to attract more funds guaranteed by deposit insurance.

Lack of decisive action brought disaster, with actual thrift losses approaching $20 billion by 1989. In January 1989, the FSLIC reported to Congress that 350 federally insured S&Ls were insolvent. Initial estimates of the costs of meeting obligations to insured depositors exceeded $90 billion. Because these estimates referred to costs net of recoveries from asset sales, the initial outlays needed to close insolvent institutions would be much greater. At the same time, William Seidman, then chairman of the FDIC, estimated that ultimately, more than 700 FSLIC-insured S&Ls with combined assets of $400 billion would have to be reorganized or liquidated.

The incoming Bush administration and Congress mandated reform in the **Financial Institutions Reform, Recovery, and Enforcement Act of 1989** (FIRREA), the most comprehensive legislation for the S&L industry since the 1930s. The act eliminated the FSLIC, the separate deposit insurance authority for S&Ls, and formed the Resolution Trust Corporation (RTC) to handle thrift insolvencies and to sell off the more than $456 billion of real estate owned by failed S&Ls. The RTC Oversight Board—made up of the Secretary of the Treasury (as chairperson), the Chairman of the Board of Governors of the Federal Reserve System, the Secretary of Housing and Urban Development, and two other appointees—supervised the RTC; the FDIC managed the RTC. On December 31, 1995, the RTC ceased operations—one year ahead of schedule—having liquidated the assets of failed institutions. The total cost of the thrift cleanup was $145 billion.

The act also created the Resolution Funding Corporation and authorized it to borrow funds to cover insolvencies. The FDIC organized a new deposit insurance fund, the Savings Association Insurance Fund (SAIF), for the S&L industry. Finally, FIRREA mandated uniform capital requirements and accounting and disclosure standards for commercial banks and savings institutions. S&Ls are now supervised and examined by the Office of Thrift Supervision (OTS), an arm of the Treasury Department. Its responsibilities are similar to those the Treasury's Office of the Comptroller of the Currency has for national banks.

To restore SAIF reserves, the FDIC raised the deposit insurance premiums of S&Ls from 20.8 cents per $100 of deposits to 23 cents and then to 32.5 cents. It raised bank deposit insurance premiums from 8.3 cents to 15 cents per $100 of deposits, with an additional increase to 23 cents in 1991 and, depending on bank riskiness, to as high as 31 cents (with an average of 25.4 cents) in 1993; in the summer of 1995, bank premiums were cut to as low as 4 cents per $100 of deposits. In November 1995, bank deposit insurance premiums were replaced for most banks with a flat $2000 annual fee, though savings institutions continued to pay 23 cents per $100 of deposits.

The 1989 legislation also reregulated investment activities of S&Ls, which had been deregulated under DIDMCA in 1980 and the Garn–St. Germain Act in 1982. It mandated that junk bond holdings be sold off by 1994 and tightened rules for other lending activities. It limited loans for commercial real estate to four times the institution's equity capital rather than to 40% of assets (which applied most severely to institutions with capital equal to less than 10% of assets). The act required that housing-related investments be at least 70% (instead of at least 60%) of total assets. Because low net worth was one reason for the onset of the S&L crisis, FIRREA raised capital requirements for S&Ls from 3% to 8% of assets, eventually conforming to risk-based capital standards mandated for commercial banks. Finally, it gave regulators broader authority to issue cease-and-desist orders, impose civil penalties, and fire managers. At the same time, it allocated an extra $75 million each year for three years to the Justice Department to aid regulators and law enforcement officials in investigating and prosecuting fraud.

On the one hand, FIRREA dealt successfully with the S&L crisis by providing substantial resources to close insolvent institutions. On the other hand, many analysts believe that the act imposed severe restrictions on depository institutions without satisfactorily addressing adverse selection and moral hazard arising from federal deposit insurance.

The Congressional Budget Office estimated in the early 1990s that the present value of the cost of the S&L debacle would eventually be as much as $200 billion in 1992 dollars. The vast sums spent in resolving this crisis are transfers from taxpayers to depositors and not a loss of current output for the economy. However, they have caused inefficiency in the economy by diverting the nation's savings in the 1980s from productive investment financed from uninsured sources to less productive investment funded by insured deposits. This large-scale financial inefficiency raises the question: Can the same thing happen in the commercial banking industry?

The Widening Crisis: Commercial Banks

Web Site Suggestions: http://www.fdic.gov Presents information on deposit insurance from the FDIC.

Like S&Ls, commercial banks in the United States prospered greatly between the Great Depression and the mid-1970s. Regulation protected bank profitability. Branching restrictions limited competition faced by local bankers. Regulation Q granted protection against competition by limiting payments to depositors and guaranteed a healthy margin between loan and deposit rates. Thus, owing to regulation, banks were earning above-normal profits, and their markets were protected from entry. The potential for interest rate risk was low.

As in the S&L industry, recall that the pace of financial innovation in commercial banking accelerated in the 1960s and 1970s, owing in large part to the desire to circumvent protective regulation. Increased competition resulting from financial innovation outside the banking industry reduced the value of a key part of banks' net worth: the market power associated with the value of bank charters.

As interest rates rose in the 1970s and early 1980s and the cost of funds to banks climbed, asset portfolios had to earn more income to maintain profitability. The quest for profitability forced banks to accept riskier loans in energy production, real estate, debt issued by developing countries, and agriculture. The two recessions of the early 1980s caused a substantial number of defaults and business failures. Lack of diversification left many groups of banks particularly susceptible (lenders to energy producers in the Southwest and lenders to agriculture and import-sensitive manufacturing in the Midwest, for example). When oil and agricultural commodity prices fell in the 1980s, loans in these sectors declined in value.

Volatile interest rates and exchange rates also took their toll on banks' net worth. Because interest rate risk and exchange rate risk had been small in the past, banks had made few preparations for greater risk. Some bank failures in the 1970s resulted from these risks, however. For example, the Franklin National Bank had tried to increase net worth by speculating in foreign currencies and lengthening the maturity of its assets. Collapse of the dollar and a significant increase in interest rates caused the bank's failure in 1974.

During the late 1980s and early 1990s, banks found themselves exposed to risk through their investment in *highly leveraged transactions* (HLTs), in which banks financed buyouts of firms by their managers or other investors. Some large banks lost heavily on HLT loans to financiers, such as Robert Campeau and Donald Trump, who ran into financial trouble. The fall in commercial real estate prices in New York, Boston, and other large cities bankrupted some prominent real estate developers, leaving banks with overvalued, empty office buildings and property in the midst of the recession.

During the 1980s, FDIC policy was not too successful in dealing with large-bank insolvencies. Tough with small banks, the FDIC relied primarily on the purchase-and-assumption method to make sure that no depositors and creditors lost money when large banks became insolvent.† Examples include the $1.7 billion bailout of Continental Illinois in 1984 and the $3 billion bailout of the First Republic Bank of Dallas in 1988. Many analysts expressed concern that FDIC protection of all deposits at large banks created a belief within large banks that the FDIC considered them *too big to fail*. This belief may have led to increased risk taking by large banks. We return to this problem later.

During the 1980s, branching restrictions limited diversification, which exposed banks to greater credit risk in their loan portfolios. For example, during the oil boom in the 1970s, Texas commercial banks grew significantly and were among the most profitable in the United States. Texas's branching restrictions limited banks to a single full-service location. With limited ability to diversify beyond local energy-related loans, Texas banks suffered greatly when the price of oil plummeted in the 1980s. By 1990, nine of the top ten banks in Texas at the beginning of the decade had gone out of business or had been acquired.

Bank failures remained a problem for the FDIC in the early 1990s as the FDIC, the Treasury Department, and Congress grappled with finding a solution. Although the number of bank failures fell from 205 in 1989 to 104 in 1991, the assets of failed banks in 1991 were $46.7 billion, or 50% more than the figure for 1989. By 1994, bank and thrift failures had become much rarer (none in 2005 and 2006, for example), although some analysts worried about banks' risk-taking ability to cope with increasing competition from nonbank financial institutions.

The United States isn't the only country facing deposit insurance problems. The Japanese banking industry experienced turmoil in the 1990s and early in the new century as well, as several large credit unions failed. In France, taxpayers rescued the state-owned Crédit Lyonnais, whose aggressive lending and weak capital resembled those of the U.S. S&Ls of the 1980s. And China recapitalized its large state-owned banks in the early 2000s.

Options for Regulatory Reform

The principles of insurance management (Chapter 12) suggest several options for banking industry regulatory reform. The options include changes in insurance coverage, insurance pricing, the scope of bank activities, regulatory supervision, and capital requirements.

Insurance coverage. One proposal for reform is to reduce the level of deposit insurance coverage. The lower the amount of deposits covered, the greater is the incentive for depositors to monitor banks. However, the economic rationale for deposit

†Since 1970, only about 25% of bank failures have been resolved by using the payoff method. The banks involved have generally been small, the largest being Penn Square Bank in Oklahoma, which failed in 1982. Between 1985 and 1990—the period with the greatest number of bank failures since the 1930s—full protection by deposit insurance was extended to more than 99% of *uninsured* deposits.

insurance is aimed as much at protecting the economy from the cost of banking panics as at protecting small or large depositors. Indeed, the speed with which uninsured depositors can now move their funds increases the likelihood of a bank run at the first hint of bad news.

This connection between insurance coverage and the likelihood of a run explains the FDIC's handling of large-bank insolvencies. For example, when Continental Illinois became insolvent in 1984, the FDIC guaranteed all deposits—insured and uninsured—and even made sure that no Continental bondholder lost money. Afterward, the Comptroller of the Currency informed Congress that the FDIC maintained a list of banks that it deemed "too big to fail." In these cases, the FDIC would ensure that no depositor or creditor lost money.

The too-big-to-fail policy weakens the desire of large depositors to incur the costs of monitoring a bank. For example, if large deposits were uninsured and large depositors thought that the FDIC would use the payoff method to deal with insolvent banks (closing the bank, paying off insured depositors, and using any remaining funds to pay uninsured depositors), they would monitor banks' lending practices closely. As a result, banks would be less likely to engage in very risky activities. Hence reducing insurance coverage provides a check on bank risk taking.

Moreover, the too-big-to-fail policy is unfair, because it treats small and large banks differently. When the FDIC closed the minority-owned Harlem's Freedom National Bank in 1990 (with less than $100 million of deposits), its large depositors—including such charitable organizations as the United Negro College Fund and the Urban League—received only about 50 cents per dollar of uninsured deposits. Only a few months later, in January 1991, the much larger Bank of New England failed as a result of a collapse in the value of its real estate portfolio. Its large depositors were fully protected by the FDIC, costing taxpayers about $2.3 billion.

FDICIA narrowed significantly the too-big-to-fail distinction to cases in which a failure would generate "serious adverse effects on economic conditions or financial stability." In such a case, two-thirds of the FDIC's directors and the Board of Governors of the Federal Reserve System, joined by the Secretary of the Treasury, would have to approve. The Fed would also be called on to share losses incurred by the FDIC if the Fed's lending to a bank magnified the FDIC's losses.

This improvement notwithstanding, bank regulators are not likely to allow a very large bank to fail; to do so might lead to a banking panic. Regulatory authorities also have been cool to the use of coinsurance, in which depositors have only partial insurance coverage (Chapter 12). Although coinsurance (say, paying off depositors at 85 cents per dollar) would encourage depositors to monitor banks, the problem of bank runs remains. Since the mid-1990s, regulators instead have stressed the need for better ongoing supervision of banks' activities, along with the authority to force banks to stop engaging in certain activities.

Narrow banking. In the late 1980s, some economists proposed **narrow banking**—that is, insuring only deposits in safe assets such as T-bills or high-quality commercial paper, as a method of deposit insurance reform. (Because of the low risk that is inherent in such assets, deposit insurance would be redundant but could promote public confidence.) Banks would make loans from bank equity and raise funds through risky securities. These funds would not be insured, and fewer limits would be placed on the scope of bank activities, sharply reducing moral hazard. However, these proposals would severely curtail the information-gathering and monitoring activities that are essential to bank lending. Because some borrowers have few alternatives to bank deposits, narrow banking could reduce these borrowers' access to the financial system. For a bank to make new loans, old loans would have to be sold or new funds would have to be attracted.

Private deposit insurance. Several economists have suggested that deposit insurance be provided by private insurance companies, at least for deposits greater than the $100,000 ceiling covered by the FDIC. This option would provide an incentive for the private insurer to monitor the banks whose deposits are insured. However, a private insurer probably wouldn't be able to pay off depositors during a general banking crisis. As a result, the problems of bank runs and banking panics remain. Although private insurance alone cannot substitute for federal deposit insurance, economists and policymakers increasingly are offering suggestions that combine private insurance arrangements with a lender-of-last-resort role by the Fed to reduce the chance of a financial crisis.

Risk-based pricing of deposit insurance. Another option for reform is to make deposit insurance premiums reflect risk, as they do in automobile or fire insurance, so that banks would bear more of the risk associated with their lending decisions. A safe bank would pay a low premium, and a risky bank would pay a high premium. However, evaluating risk isn't easy. Assigning market values to some bank loans can be quite difficult. Moreover, risk can be assessed easily after the fact by examining operating income or losses, but risk-based pricing of deposit insurance must be forward-looking to be useful—a much more difficult task.

Risk-based pricing of deposit insurance was mandated in the **Federal Deposit Insurance Corporation Improvement Act of 1991** (FDICIA), which established risk groups according to how well capitalized the bank is. In September 1992, the FDIC voted to implement risk-based premiums for the first time in the history of deposit insurance. These premiums became effective in January 1993, ranging from 23 cents per $100 for well-capitalized banks with no supervisory problems to 31 cents per $100 of deposits for less than adequately capitalized institutions with substantial supervisory problems. Most banks paid the lowest rate, although some large banks (including Citibank) initially paid higher premiums under the new system. Premiums were reduced substantially for all risk classes in late 1995, and remain low in 2006.

Supervision. Passage of FIRREA gave the FDIC more supervisory responsibility. The act requires the FDIC as insurer to monitor the evaluation of a depository institution's federal or state supervisor. It broadens the authority of regulators to intervene in bank management, especially at poorly capitalized banks. New regulatory powers include the ability to set dividend payments and executive pay at poorly capitalized banks and to hire and fire managers in some cases. Proponents say that the new procedures will encourage better management because well-capitalized banks are exempt from the most severe restrictions. Opponents argue that the fear of regulatory intrusion will discourage banks from making commercial loans and encourage them to invest deposits in Treasury securities, thereby diminishing banks' role as intermediaries. How banks, which—after 1999—could participate in a broader range of activities, adjust to the regulations will continue to shape the banking industry during the beginning decade of the new century.

Capital requirements. Moral hazard occurs when banks seek to use their equity capital in risky ventures in an attempt to increase their return on equity. Setting higher minimum capital requirements reduces the potential for moral hazard and the cost to the FDIC of bank failures. As we noted earlier, FIRREA has moved toward reducing moral hazard for S&Ls.

A bank's equity capital is its cushion for paying depositors if its assets decline in value. Minimum capital requirements reduce the likelihood that banks will engage in risky activities. These requirements are set by using *historical cost*, or *book-value*, measures. When assets are valued by using historical cost, changes in the market values of a bank's assets and liabilities (owing to changes in, say, default risk or market interest rates) don't affect the calculation by regulatory authorities of a bank's net worth. This measurement difference is significant because changes in market values of assets and liabilities are precisely what tell depositors and investors when shifts occur in the true value of banks' equity capital. The shifts in market value also set the incentives for moral hazard.

Many economists support the use of *market-value accounting* in calculating minimum capital requirements. Periodically (say, once each quarter), regulators could determine the market value of a bank's assets and liabilities and whether its market-value capital (the difference between the market values of its assets and its liabilities) meets minimum capital requirements. If not, the FDIC would be informed, and the bank would be closed before its market-value net worth became negative. This action would prevent both a loss to the FDIC and excessive risk taking by the bank. Although only an approximation, market-value assessments can highlight a bank's financial condition to bank regulators—and to shareholders and creditors. The push toward more market-value accounting for measuring banks' equity capital has continued during the 1990s, and economists are researching practical ways of implementing market-value accounting.

Another goal of regulators is to assess accurately the risk to which banks are exposed. The 1988 Basel capital standards (Chapter 14) used credit risk to classify bank assets and off-balance-sheet activities. The bank's risk-weighted assets equal the sum of its risk-weighted components. Banks' capital requirements are defined relative to risk-weighted assets. FDICIA authorized the FDIC to use capital-adequacy categories to limit banks' participation in certain activities.

Web Site Suggestions: http://www.bis.org/publ/joint06.htm Presents information on operational risk under Basel II.

These risk-based capital standards assess only credit risk and ignore interest rate risk. For example, if banks reduced their investments in short-term commercial and industrial loans and increased their investments in long-term Treasury securities, they would substitute interest rate risk for credit risk. On April 30, 1993, banking supervisors from industrialized countries agreed in Basel to propose internationally coordinated capital requirements linked to interest rate risk and exchange rate risk. Responding to the fast pace of market developments, in April 1995, that group of supervisors proposed that financial institutions develop their own risk-assessment procedures subject to regulatory review (see also Chapter 14). Further modifications of the Basel—the so-called "Basel II" regime—being implemented in 2006 address capital requirements for banks' operational risks as well.

FDICIA implemented a "prompt corrective action" rule, which mandated that the FDIC and other regulators take action if a bank's capital falls below the required level. For example, regulations require closure or conservatorship within 90 days for the weakest institutions. By directing the FDIC to shut down institutions when their net worth is less than 2% of assets rather than delaying until net worth becomes negative, this requirement decreases potential FDIC (taxpayer) losses and limits the scope for moral hazard. Although the requirement reduces the likelihood of the long delays that were experienced in closing weak institutions in the S&L crisis, regulators must still confront the problem that book-value measures of bank capital do not accurately measure market-value net worth.

Current Issues in Regulatory Reform

In February 1991, the U.S. Treasury Department suggested numerous regulatory reforms for the banking system. These proposals addressed many of the regulations that we have discussed, including anticompetitive restrictions, deposit insurance coverage, and supervision. The department also suggested that banking regulation be more closely linked to bank capital, a proposal that was adopted in part in FDICIA. Many economists believe that the steps taken in FDICIA need to be extended to decrease further the chance of another deposit insurance crisis.

Two major changes in other banking regulations are likely to mitigate future problems in deposit insurance. First, regulations that relax branching restrictions will encourage banks to diversify their assets and reduce the likelihood of a banking crisis. Bank failures during the 1980s were concentrated in states with branching restrictions and in banks that concentrated their loans in particular industries, such as oil (Texas) or agriculture (Kansas). States' liberalization of branching laws and the passage of the federal Riegle-Neal Interstate Banking and Branching Efficiency Act of 1994 have made nationwide banking possible.

Second, some analysts view regulatory overlap as a problem because regulations are complex and regulators duplicate one another's efforts. Currently, four federal agencies share bank supervision. These agencies are the Office of the Comptroller of the Currency, the Federal Reserve, the FDIC, and the Office of Thrift Supervision. In 1994, the Clinton administration unveiled a proposal to create a banking superregulation, combining the supervisory responsibilities of the four federal regulatory agencies. The Fed strongly opposed the proposal, and (then) Fed Chairman Greenspan outlined an alternative: reduce the present four supervisory agencies to two (merge OCC and OTS, and strip the FDIC of all but insurance responsibilities), and expand the Fed's role. The Fed offered a sensible criticism of the Clinton plan: divorced from collecting information from banks, the Fed would find it harder to forestall and address financial crises. In 2006, the Fed, the Treasury, and the Congress were still debating the course of regulatory consolidation in the aftermath of the Gramm-Leach-Bliley Act of 1999.

Concluding Remarks

The deposit insurance crisis and its aftermath illustrate the stages of financial crisis, regulation, financial system response, and regulatory response, as depicted in Figure 15.3. Recent reforms in deposit insurance and likely reforms in other areas of banking regulation generally allow banks to maintain their intermediary role in matching savers and borrowers. The government would permit regulatory intervention when a crisis threatened the entire banking system. Future comprehensive reform of U.S. banking regulation likely will increase the power of the Fed as the lender of last resort and of bank regulators as monitors.

The United States is not unique in relying on its central bank to manage banking crises and in insuring savers' deposits. Although most industrialized countries (and several developing countries) now have deposit insurance systems, deposit insurance authorities resolve bank failures differently. In the United States, the FDIC assumes the

FIGURE 15.3 **Deposit Insurance: Crisis, Regulation, Financial System Response, and Regulatory Response**

Federal deposit insurance was introduced in response to bank runs in the early 1930s. Information problems led to a crisis in deposit insurance in the 1980s, which in turn led to regulatory reform.

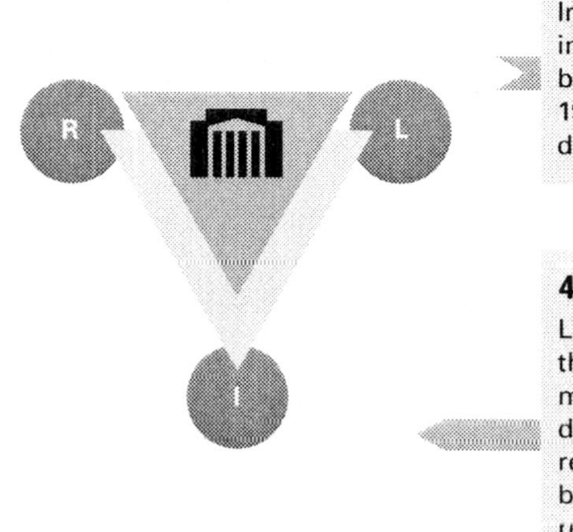

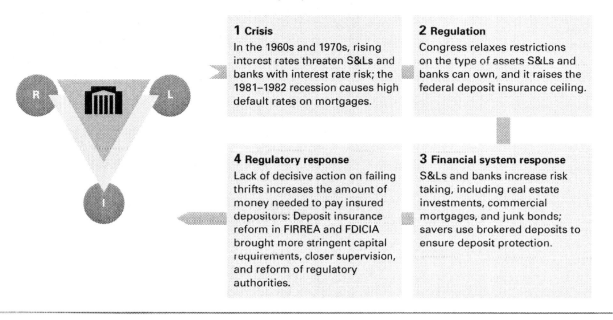

1 Crisis
In the 1960s and 1970s, rising interest rates threaten S&Ls and banks with interest rate risk; the 1981–1982 recession causes high default rates on mortgages.

2 Regulation
Congress relaxes restrictions on the type of assets S&Ls and banks can own, and it raises the federal deposit insurance ceiling.

3 Financial system response
S&Ls and banks increase risk taking, including real estate investments, commercial mortgages, and junk bonds; savers use brokered deposits to ensure deposit protection.

4 Regulatory response
Lack of decisive action on failing thrifts increases the amount of money needed to pay insured depositors: Deposit insurance reform in FIRREA and FDICIA brought more stringent capital requirements, closer supervision, and reform of regulatory authorities.

lead in handling financially distressed banks. In most other countries, private banks bear more of the costs of resolving failures but are backed by the central bank as the lender of last resort in the event of a general banking crisis. Some analysts believe that the relatively small number of banks in other countries allows private banks in those countries to monitor one another more closely in private insurance arrangements.

Lessons from Banking Regulation for Other Institutions

Our analysis of financial crisis, regulation, financial system response, and regulatory response in the banking industry offers lessons that can be extended to other financial institutions. Let's now consider current and likely future developments in the regulation of insurance companies and private pension funds, both of which face problems similar to those of banks.

Insurance Regulation

The distinction between banks and insurance companies for regulatory purposes may be outdated. Like banks, insurance companies are financial institutions that accept funds from individuals in return for promises to repay. Just as banks are connected through interbank money markets and loan sales, insurers are linked through risk-sharing arrangements known as reinsurance. One important difference between banks and insurance companies is that no federal program corresponding to deposit insurance is available to the insurance industry.

Developments in the insurance industry have paralleled those in the banking industry. Property and casualty companies experienced a crisis in the late 1800s by underpricing

OTHER TIMES, OTHER PLACES . . .

The Cycle of Crisis and Response: Russia and Japan

We can use the framework of crisis and response to explain the aftermath of financial crises in other countries, such as Russia and Japan. (Regulatory liberalization and inadequate financial supervision also played a role in the Asian financial crisis of 1997, as we will see in Chapter 22.)

Russia. Prior to the fall of communism in the Soviet Union, banks were owned by the government. When the Russian economy jettisoned communist controls, banks had little experience in addressing adverse selection and moral hazard in private lending markets, and Russian authorities had little expertise in monitoring market-oriented lenders. The seeds of a banking crisis were thus sown. The crisis arrived with full force on August 24, 1995, when fears over banks' solvency led to a collapse of the interbank loan market and government intervention. Three years later, the government restricted repayment of foreign debt to husband resources in the troubled banking sector. By the turn of the century, the Russian central bank noted that a large bailout would be required to compensate stakeholders of the almost half of all banks that were deemed likely to fail. This bailout would be accompanied by substantial regulatory intervention. Whether this intervention heads off the next banking crisis depends on bankers' and investors' incentives to reduce costs of adverse selection and moral hazard.

Japan. In the case of Japan, post–World War II regulations led to a segmented financial system that placed strict limits on activities of banks and securities firms. Financial deregulation in the 1980s, along with lax regulatory oversight, precipitated a boom in risky loans in real estate. The collapse of the Japanese property market in the early 1990s left banks with large loan losses and weak capital positions. The second half of the 1990s witnessed the first bank failures in Japan since World War II, with failures of Cosmo Credit Corporation, Kizu Credit Cooperative, Hanwa Bank, and Hokkaido Takushoku Bank. The megamerger of the Bank of Tokyo and Mitsubishi Bank was designed to shore up the profitability of those institutions.

The regulatory response in Japan largely resembled that of the United States in the 1980s. While capital adequacy standards were nominally in place, Ministry of Finance regulations permitted banks to inflate the value of their assets (by carrying them at historical cost as opposed to current market value) to meet capital standards. Allowing weak banks to continue operating engendered a financial system response of further increases in risk taking.

By 1998, the Japanese government was forced to intervene, and supervisory authority over banks was awarded to the Financial Supervisory Agency (FSA), which reported to the Prime Minister rather than the Ministry of Finance. This change was accompanied by a bailout package of ¥60 trillion (about $500 billion). The jury is still out on future financial system responses, however, because the closure of insolvent banks is not necessarily required. Nonetheless, the government's seizure in late 1998 of the large Long-Term Credit Bank of Japan, which was subsequently sold to a group of U.S. investors, was a promising sign of reform. Financial regulation reforms announced in 2001 were viewed as less promising signs, though in 2002 and 2003 some progress was made in reducing nonperforming loans. By 2006, the health of Japanese banks had improved substantially.

policies and then going broke after several major disasters occurred. Life insurance companies were protected from price competition by restrictions imposed by state regulation in New York (the headquarters of many large insurance companies). In the 1930s and after World War II, Congress attempted to provide stability in the insurance industry. Most notable was the McCarran-Ferguson Act of 1945, which explicitly protected insurers from prosecution under federal antitrust laws. Rapidly rising interest rates in the late 1970s made savers and investors more aware of nonbank opportunities, and financial deregulation broadened their options. Life insurance firms offered higher-yield investment options than banks, but the high yields paid to investors reduced profits significantly. Property and casualty firms competed for premium revenue to invest at record returns, only to discover that even those returns were not enough when record claims came flooding in.

The insurance industry since the 1990s is undergoing change like that in banking. In the aftermath of the catastrophic Executive Life Insurance Company failure early in the decade, which nearly led to a life insurance run, government regulators imposed risk-based capital requirements. The requirements, effective in 1994, were created by the

National Association of Insurance Commissioners, a group of state insurance commissioners that designs uniform standards for the industry. The higher the calculated risk levels, the more capital an insurer must have on its balance sheet to support the risks.

In addition, the insurance industry and the federal government have discussed the consolidation of state "guarantee funds," which are similar to deposit insurance to protect policyholders. The funds do not cover all insurers or products. Nationwide, they would amount to only a few billion dollars per year, a small amount compared to the dollars that were needed to bail out ailing S&Ls. In the aftermath of the multibillion-dollar losses resulting from Hurricane Andrew during September 1992, many analysts questioned the industry's ability to withstand further crises. Some observers believe that any self-regulation should be augmented by a standing national guarantee fund financed by insurance companies or by federal minimum standards for state insurance funds. While the debate over regulation takes place, financial markets are developing new ways to spread catastrophic risks through tradeable securities.

Pension Fund Regulation

Problems arising from deposit insurance protection also apply to pension funds. The Employee Retirement Income Security Act of 1974 (ERISA) created the Pension Benefit Guaranty Corporation (PBGC) to insure defined benefit pensions when companies go bankrupt. (No such need arises for defined contribution plans, which, by definition, are fully funded.) The PBGC is troubled by the hundreds of large underfunded plans that loom as liabilities if the companies offering them fail. In 1992, following the bankruptcies of Eastern Airlines and Pan American Airlines, the PBGC had a deficit of more than $2 billion. The mid-1990s produced better news, though by the 2000s large failures of steel and airline firms and rising unfunded liabilities led policymakers to debate reform.

As in the case of deposit insurance, pension fund managers have incentives to take risks if large profits from such risks accrue to the shareholders of the firm (the residual claimants of the plan) and any losses accrue to the PBGC. As the FDIC did in banking, the PBGC proposed reforms to tie insurance premiums to the riskiness of each pension plan. First, the PBGC increased premiums in 1990 and has proposed additional increases. Second, underfunded plans now pay much higher premiums relative to funded plans than they did under earlier law. Third, the PBGC argued that if a company declares bankruptcy, the PBGC should have a higher-priority claim than other creditors to ensure that participants in pension plans get the benefits promised to them. Some economists have even questioned whether the government's PBGC is preferable to private insurance, which could simply adjust rates to reflect the cost of moral hazard in companies' underfunding of pension liabilities.

CHECKPOINT

Suppose that a financially distressed steel manufacturer with large underfunded pension liabilities is insured by the PBGC, which charges premiums that don't reflect differences in risk. The firm's CEO learns about a new steel-making technology that offers a 10% chance of huge profits and a 90% chance of failure. The investment has a negative present value and would bankrupt the firm if it were unsuccessful. Should the company undertake the project? The prospect might be tempting. If the investment pays off, the CEO and other shareholders profit because they are residual claimants of the company's defined benefit plan. If the investment fails, the PBGC must fulfill the pension promises that the company made to its workers. ♦

MOVING FROM THEORY TO PRACTICE . . .

THE ECONOMIST MAY 20, 2006

China's Growing Banking Problem

Although China likes most of its numbers to be big, it has been trying to reduce one of them: the size of the bad loans burdening its banks. A report this month by Ernst & Young, a big auditing and consulting firm, therefore came as quite a shock. Ernst & Young . . . claimed that **a** China's stock of non-performing loans (NPLs) added up to $911 billion. This is more than five-and-a-half times the latest government estimate of $164 billion, published in March.

The People's Bank of China, the country's central **b** bank, quickly attacked the research as "ridiculous and barely understandable." This week an embarrassed Ernst & Young withdrew it, admitting that it was "factually erroneous" and that it had somehow slipped through the firm's normal checks. Ernst & Young says it plans to publish a revised version in due course.

The authorities' savage reaction is easy to understand. Other commentators and consultants have published estimates of China's NPLs ranging from $300 billion to $500 billion without attracting similar condemnation. Ernst & Young's estimate stood out not only for its size but also for its timing. The central bank's rebuttal came on the very day that Bank of China, the second of the big four to attempt a stockmarket listing in Hong Kong, began its investor roadshow. Bank of China plans to raise $9.9 billion, even more than the $9.2 billion pulled in by China Construction Bank, which was floated last October. A third big bank, Industrial and Commercial Bank of China, hopes for $10 billion in September. Awkwardly, Ernst & Young is this institution's auditor—and as such had subscribed to the official, much lower estimate of bad loans.

Even so, the firm's categorical withdrawal of its research looks like an overreaction. The report was more than a compilation of historic bad debts; drawing on work by other organisations, it also made a stab at estimating the new NPLs that will result from a lending spree between 2002 and 2004. These account for most of the difference between Ernst & Young's figures and the official ones. And they are particularly relevant now that **c** the mainland is in the midst of another credit surge: new loans in April amounted to 317 billion yuan ($40 billion), more than twice as much as in the same month last year. Although China has made progress in shifting bad loans off the banks' balance sheets, there is little sign that the banks themselves have fundamentally changed their behaviour and become rational lenders.

Neither side emerges with much credit from this episode. Ernst & Young seems to have caved in too quickly to Chinese demands, at a cost to the perceived independence that it needs to win respect and clients. The Chinese authorities, meanwhile, look like bullies. Bad loans are almost certainly greater than the official numbers say, even if they are less than Ernst & Young's estimate. To deny this is naive and damages the credibility needed to sell NPLs and shares in its banks to foreign investors. These, indeed, may turn out to be the only winners, if the tale reminds them of the real state of Chinese banks as another one passes round the hat.

ANALYZING THE NEWS ...

In the late 1990s and early 2000s, the Chinese economy grew at astoundingly rapid rates. While many pundits saw this rapid economic growth as a sure sign of China's growing importance in the global economy, many economists worried about the role inefficient bank lending was playing in this "Chinese economic miracle."

As the chapter describes, often bank regulation and financial market reform come about only after a financial collapse. Economic structures and regulations that are designed to spur rapid economic growth often lead to a misallocation of resources, the final result being a financial crisis.

a When banks have high levels of nonperforming loans, these banks can become insolvent. The prudent thing for regulators to do is to close down an insolvent bank. If instead the bank regulators decide to allow the bank to continue in operation, the regulators should take steps to ensure that the bank changes its lending policies to be certain the problem does not arise again.

b As history has shown, one of the worst things regulators can do in the face of insolvent banks is to deny the problem and allow the insolvent banks to continue in operation. As with the savings and loan crisis in the United States, a lack of decisive action can lead to financial disasters when regulators are faced with insolvent banks.

Minxin Pei of the Carnegie Endowment for International Peace in Washington estimates that the Chinese banking system's nonperforming loans equal about 40% of China's gross domestic product. This figure, Pei reports, is after the Chinese government had spent the equivalent of 25% to 30% of the country's gross domestic product on previous bank recapitalizations.

c Despite the need for the Chinese banks to be more conservative in an attempt to rebuild their balance sheets, it appears that Chinese banks are continuing to lend at very rapid rates. This potential excess lending leads to increased levels of total spending, which in turn makes the economy appear to be growing even more rapidly. However, as we have seen, insolvent bank lending often leads to a financial crisis.

For further thought . . .

Many foreign investors see the rapid economic growth in China as a wonderful opportunity for investment. If banks in China fully disclosed their net worth and risk exposures, do you think that required rates of return on foreign investment in China would change?

Source: Excerpted from "A Muffled Report," *The Economist*, May 20, 2006, p. 78.

KEY TERMS AND CONCEPTS

Brokered deposits
Credit crunch
Depository Institutions Deregulation and Monetary Control Act of 1980
Disintermediation
Federal Deposit Insurance Corporation Improvement Act of 1991
Financial Institutions Reform, Recovery, and Enforcement Act of 1989
Garn–St. Germain Act of 1982
Money market deposit accounts
Narrow banking
Negotiable certificate of deposit
Negotiable order of withdrawal (NOW) account
Regulation Q

SUMMARY

1. Bank regulation follows a pattern of financial crisis, regulation, financial system response, and regulatory response. In response to a reduction in banks' ability to provide risk-sharing, liquidity, and information services during banking panics, government has intervened to promote bank stability. Major interventions in the United States include those to (a) create a lender of last resort, (b) restrict competition, and (c) reduce savers' risks through federal deposit insurance. In each case, both regulation and the banking industry were shaped by unintended consequences of intervention.
2. After its failures during the banking collapse in the early 1930s, the Fed emerged as a stabilizing lender of last resort. On many occasions, it has provided emergency liquidity to temporarily weak institutions in the financial system, averting financial crises.
3. Regulation Q restricted interest rates paid on deposits, creating inefficiencies in bank intermediation. To escape the interest rate ceilings, financial institutions introduced alternatives to bank intermediation, including money market mutual funds and the commercial paper market. Two pieces of legislation, the Depository Institutions Deregulation and Monetary Control Act of 1980 and the Garn–St. Germain Act of 1982, effectively removed interest rate ceilings and reduced the likelihood of disintermediation.
4. Federal deposit insurance was introduced in response to the wave of bank failures in the early 1930s. The deposit insurance crisis in the savings and loan industry began in the late 1970s and early 1980s. Deposit insurance provided a valuable source of financial stability, but moral hazard arose as insolvent S&Ls took on substantial risks and incurred large losses. Reforms have centered on changes in deposit insurance pricing and coverage, equity capital requirements, and regulatory supervision.
5. Problems faced by a lender of last resort or deposit insurance authority underscore the need for careful supervision of bank activities. The problems encountered by banking regulatory authorities during the past decade likely will surface in the regulation of insurance companies and pension funds. Federal regulators continue to debate how to safeguard savers' funds without creating unwise incentives for intermediaries.

REVIEW QUESTIONS

1. At the turn of the century, the New York Clearing House performed relatively well in coming to the rescue of individual member banks but did less well in paying off depositors when all its members were in trouble. On the basis of your understanding of that experience, can you suggest guidelines for creating a lender of last resort for banks?
2. What significant errors by the Fed worsened the Great Depression?
3. Some recent lender-of-last-resort actions by the Fed assisted nonbank segments of the financial system (in particular, the commercial paper market and securities exchanges). Suggest some potential information problems in those markets that might justify intervention by the lender of last resort.
4. What are the major costs of disintermediation?
5. What types of innovations did banks develop to get around ceilings on deposit interest rates?
6. How does deposit insurance encourage banks to take too much risk?
7. What initially caused the S&L crisis of the 1980s? What subsequent events caused S&Ls to lose even more money?

8. Why didn't regulators close all the insolvent S&Ls in the early 1980s?
9. Why was the Financial Institutions Reform, Recovery, and Enforcement Act of 1989 passed? What were its key provisions?
10. Why did so many commercial banks fail in the 1980s?
11. What is narrow banking? How would the existence of narrow banks eliminate the need for deposit insurance?
12. How could a run on an insurance company occur? Is there a need for a government guarantee program for the insurance industry similar to that for banking? Why or why not?
13. What is the main problem with underfunded pension plans? Why is this potentially a serious political issue?

ANALYTICAL PROBLEMS

14. Explain the difference between a bank that is illiquid and one that is insolvent. Explain the role this difference played in the Fed's response to the banking panics of the early 1930s.
15. How did the Fed's conflicting responsibilities with respect to maintaining the gold standard and maintaining the health of the banking system explain some of the actions it took in the early 1930s?
16. Describe what happened as interest rates rose above the fixed interest rate ceilings when Regulation Q was in effect.
17. Suppose that, as an innovative banker, you are thinking of ways to increase profits. You note that your bank is required to hold 10% in reserves on deposits held in the United States but that there are no reserve requirements on deposits held outside the country. What innovation does this knowledge suggest?
18. As a smart banker, you are thinking of ways to increase profits. You recognize the time difference between the operating hours of your bank's branches in the United States and Europe. You also note that you can receive interest on loans made for a fraction of a day and that money left in U.S. accounts over a weekend earns nothing. What innovation does this knowledge suggest?
19. Suppose that you manage a small S&L that has a net worth of –$50 million. You fear that within two years, regulators will discover that your firm is insolvent and will shut you down. You have two possible investment strategies: (a) continue to operate as you have been, offering market interest rates on CDs to finance mortgage loans, or (b) offer higher than market interest rates on CDs and use the increased funds to speculate in junk bonds and real estate. Your analysis tells you that strategy (a) has a 10% chance of losing $10 million and a 90% chance of gaining $20 million, with an expected return of $17 million. Strategy (b) has an 80% chance of losing $50 million and a 20% chance of gaining $75 million, with an expected return of –$25 million. What strategy should you follow? Why? What are the consequences of your choice? What should a regulator do in this situation?
20. Suppose that one of the largest banks in the United States defaults on its sales of securitized mortgages, throwing the market into shock. No one wants to buy securitized mortgage loans until they can reevaluate their riskiness, so banks all over the country stop making mortgage loans. As Chairman of the Federal Reserve Board, what could you do?
21. Suppose that terrorists blew up the computers that run the CHIPS system, disrupting all payments nationwide. As a top official of the Federal Reserve System, what would you do?
22. In the late 1990s, the Securities and Exchange Commission became concerned that some banks might be maintaining excessive loan loss reserves (an account that represents banks' best estimates of losses likely on their loan portfolios). The SEC believed some banks were planning to draw down their loan loss reserves to keep their reported earnings high during periods when their reported earnings would otherwise be low. Banks must operate under accounting rules that do not allow this practice. Some banks complained that at the same time that the SEC was investigating whether their loan loss reserves were too high, the Federal Reserve and the Office of Comptroller of the Currency were urging banks to make sure their loan loss reserves were not too low. Discuss how the different responsibilities of the SEC, on the one hand, and the Federal Reserve and the Office of Comptroller of the Currency, on the other, might lead them to send different messages to banks with respect to loan loss reserves.

23. On the basis of what you know about the history of the U.S. banking system, what deposit insurance program and set of regulations do you think would be ideal? What should be the limit on the size of accounts covered by deposit insurance? How can you minimize moral hazard problems? How can you encourage banks to diversify? Should different types of financial institutions exist, each with a different regulator, or should they all be the same? Should narrow banks exist? (*Hint:* There is no single correct answer.)

DATA QUESTIONS

24. In each issue of the *Federal Reserve Bulletin*, you can find consolidated balance sheet information for U.S. commercial banks. Using issues of the *Federal Reserve Bulletin*, calculate the fractions of banks' assets at the end of 1994, 1998, 2002, and 2006 held in the form of (a) U.S. government securities and (b) commercial and industrial loans. Do relative changes in these holdings suggest that banks reduced their exposure to credit risk over this period? Explain. Do these changes indicate that banks may have increased their exposure to other types of risk? Explain. Does your analysis suggest any steps for improving the design of bank capital requirements?
25. As the U.S. provider of deposit insurance for banks and savings and loans, the Federal Deposit Insurance Corporation collects careful records of deposit records at the institutions for which it is responsible. To give you an idea of how carefully these data is collected, locate the "Summary Tables" link at the FDIC's Summary of Deposits Web site, at http://www2.fdic.gov/sod/SODSumReport.asp. What is the ratio of savings institution deposits to commercial bank deposits in your county? How many banks and savings institutions operate in your county?
26. A long-time policy concern is reform of the Pension Benefit Guarantee Corporation, especially as the baby boom generation nears retirement. Consider the table, "Net Financial Position of PBGC's Single-Employer Program" in the most recent issue of the PBGC's Pension Insurance Databook (http://www.pbgc.gov/practitioners/plan-trends-and-statistics/content/page13270.html). For how many years has the system been in surplus? Do the data appear to show a relationship to the business cycle? Explain. Compare these data with those found on the table "PBGC Premium Revenue, Benefit Payments and Expenses, Single-Employer Program" found elsewhere in this report. Is there a relationship between pensions and benefits? Is there any evidence of moral hazard? Explain your answer.

CHAPTER 22

The International Financial System and Monetary Policy

Speculation over the value of the Argentine peso in late 2001 and early 2002 wrought havoc on Argentina's financial system and stoked fears of a broader emerging-markets financial crisis. Hailed positively in the 1990s, Argentina's promise to redeem pesos for U.S. dollars one-for-one put the central bank in a bind. The Argentine government's profligate fiscal policy virtually guaranteed a debt default, inflationary finance, or both. For the central bank, maintaining the convertibility promise became increasingly difficult. Should the central bank continue to intervene as speculators leaned against the peso?

This example demonstrates that central banks participate in international currency markets. In our discussion of the Fed's role in the money supply process, we limited our investigation to the domestic economy. But the Fed and central banks in other countries also attempt to manage the exchange rates of their currencies. In August 1995, the Fed acted aggressively to increase the dollar's foreign-exchange value; in the episode described above, the Fed bid down the value of the dollar against another currency. A central bank's role in the international financial system also influences its ability to conduct domestic monetary policy.

In this chapter we focus on the central bank's participation in the foreign-exchange market. We begin by showing how the Fed's and other central banks' actions influence the monetary base and then describe the effect of these transactions on the exchange rate. We then shift our focus to the interaction of the Fed with other central banks in the international financial system. After describing the Fed's transactions in the international financial system, we explain the relationship between the Fed's transactions and other flows of capital and goods in international markets by analyzing the balance-of-payments accounts. Political forces as well as economic forces influence the Fed's international transactions and monetary policy. In particular, the exchange rate system determines how a central bank must act in influencing the foreign-exchange value of its currency. In the fourth section of the chapter, we describe different exchange rate systems and their effect on domestic monetary policy. As we did for domestic monetary policy in Chapter 21, we also examine the successes and failures of different exchange rate systems.

Foreign-Exchange Intervention and the Money Supply

In our analysis of the money supply process, we described the actions of three participants: the central bank, the banking system, and the nonbank public. However, because international financial markets are linked, *foreign* central banks, banks, and savers and borrowers also can affect the domestic money supply. In particular, international financial transactions affect the money supply when central banks or governments try to influence the foreign-exchange values of their currencies. As a result, such intervention may cause domestic and international monetary policy goals to conflict.

The Federal Reserve and other central banks participate in international markets to control the foreign-exchange value of their currency. The term **foreign-exchange market intervention** describes deliberate actions by a central bank to influence the exchange rate. Foreign-exchange market interventions alter a central bank's holdings of **international reserves,** assets that are denominated in a foreign currency and used in international transactions.

If the Fed wants to increase the value of the dollar, it will sell foreign securities and buy dollars in international currency markets. If the Fed wants to reduce the value of the dollar, it will sell dollars and buy foreign assets. Such transactions affect the domestic monetary base, as you can easily observe by noting the changes in the Fed's balance sheet.

Suppose, for example, that in an effort to reduce the foreign-exchange value of the dollar, the Fed buys foreign assets, say, short-term securities issued by foreign governments, worth a dollar value of $1 billion. This transaction increases the Fed's international reserves by $1 billion—hence the Fed's foreign assets rise by $1 billion. If the Fed pays for the foreign assets by writing a check for $1 billion, it adds $1 billion to banks' deposits at the Fed. Reserves of the banking system, a Fed liability, also rise by $1 billion. We can summarize the effect of this transaction on the Fed's balance sheet as follows:

FEDERAL RESERVE

Assets		Liabilities	
Foreign assets (international reserves)	+$1 billion	Bank deposits at Fed (reserves)	+$1 billion

Alternatively, the Fed could pay for the foreign assets with $1 billion of currency. Because currency in circulation also is a liability for the Fed, its liabilities still rise by $1 billion:

FEDERAL RESERVE

Assets		Liabilities	
Foreign assets (international reserves)	+$1 billion	Currency in circulation	+$1 billion

Because the monetary base equals the sum of currency in circulation and banking system reserves, either transaction causes the monetary base to rise by the amount of the foreign assets (international reserves) acquired. In other words, a purchase of foreign assets by a central bank has the same effect on the monetary base as an open market purchase of government bonds. When a central bank buys foreign assets, its international reserves and the monetary base increase by the amount of foreign assets acquired.

Similarly, if a central bank sells foreign assets to purchase its domestic-currency-denominated assets, its holdings of international reserves and the monetary base fall. Suppose that the Fed sells $1 billion of foreign assets to buy $1 billion of domestic assets. The Fed loses international reserves, causing its foreign assets to fall by $1 billion. At the same time, if the purchasers of the foreign assets sold by the Fed pay with checks drawn on domestic banks, banks' reserves at the Fed, a Fed liability, fall by $1 billion. The transaction affects the Fed's balance sheet as follows:

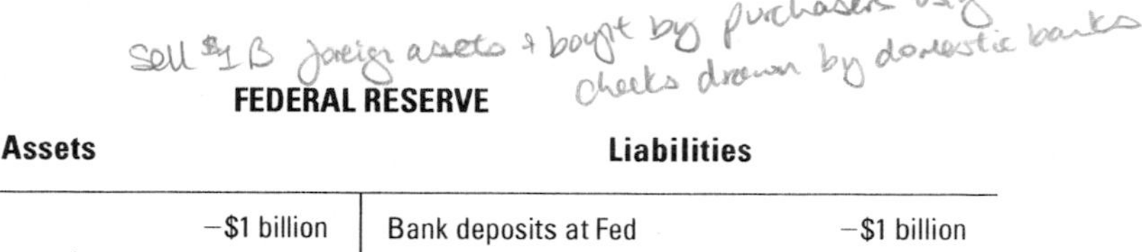

FEDERAL RESERVE

Assets		Liabilities	
Foreign assets (international reserves)	−$1 billion	Bank deposits at Fed (reserves)	−$1 billion

If the Fed had instead purchased domestic currency with the proceeds of its sale of foreign assets, currency in circulation (another Fed liability) would have fallen by the amount of foreign assets sold. Because the monetary base is the sum of currency in circulation and reserves, it falls by the amount of foreign assets (international reserves) sold, regardless of whether the Fed buys domestic bank deposits or currency with the proceeds.

In other words, a sale of foreign assets by a central bank has the same effect on the monetary base as an open market sale of government bonds. Purchases of domestic currency by a central bank financed by sales of foreign assets reduce international reserves and the monetary base by the amount of foreign assets sold.

When a central bank allows the monetary base to respond to the sale or purchase of domestic currency in the foreign-exchange market, the transaction is called an **unsterilized foreign-exchange intervention.** Alternatively, the central bank could use domestic open market operations to offset the change in the monetary base caused by a foreign-exchange intervention. To demonstrate, consider a Fed sale of $1 billion of foreign assets. In the absence of any offsetting interventions, the monetary base falls by $1 billion. At the same time, however, the Fed could conduct an open market purchase of $1 billion of government bonds to eliminate the decrease in the monetary base arising from the foreign-exchange intervention. In this case, the Fed's assets fall by $1 billion when it sells foreign assets. As we showed earlier, the monetary base falls by $1 billion if the Fed does nothing else. However, a Fed purchase of $1 billion of securities on the open market would restore the monetary base to its level prior to the foreign-exchange intervention. The following example illustrates these transactions:

FEDERAL RESERVE

Assets		Liabilities	
Foreign assets (international reserves)	−$1 billion	Monetary base (currency in circulation and reserves)	+$0 billion
Securities	+$1 billion		

A foreign-exchange intervention that is accompanied by offsetting domestic open market operations that leave the monetary base unchanged is called a **sterilized foreign-exchange intervention.**

CHECKPOINT

What is the effect on the Japanese monetary base if the Bank of Japan purchases $5 billion in the foreign-exchange market? The Bank of Japan's holdings of international reserves rise by $5 billion, and the Japanese monetary base increases by the yen equivalent of $5 billion. ♦

Foreign-Exchange Intervention and the Exchange Rate

If foreign-exchange interventions affect the domestic money supply, why do central banks intervene? Central banks and governments seek to minimize changes in exchange rates. A depreciating domestic currency raises the cost of foreign goods and may lead to inflation. Central banks attempt to reduce depreciation by buying their own currencies in the foreign-exchange market. Conversely, an appreciating domestic currency can make a country's goods uncompetitive in world markets. Central banks attempt to reduce appreciation by selling their own currencies in the foreign-exchange market.

In this section, we examine the effects of unsterilized and sterilized foreign-exchange market interventions on the exchange rate, using the graphical analysis of exchange rate determination developed in Chapter 8. Recall from that analysis that traders and investors—individuals, businesses, governments, and central banks—in asset markets determine the exchange rate in the short run. At the equilibrium exchange rate, expected returns on domestic and foreign assets (expressed in domestic currency terms) are equal. Hence at that exchange rate, investors are indifferent between holding domestic and foreign assets.

Unsterilized Intervention

Let's begin with unsterilized intervention. Figure 22.1 shows interventions to increase and decrease the exchange rate. The exchange rate, EX, is expressed in foreign currency per unit of domestic currency. The curve representing the expected rate of return on domestic deposits, R, is vertical (at the domestic interest rate, i). The curve representing the expected rate of return on foreign deposits, R_f, slopes upward to the right. Recall from Chapter 8 that $R_f = i_f - \Delta EX^e/EX$, where i_f is the foreign interest rate and ΔEX^e is the expected appreciation of the domestic currency. Thus, if savers' expectations of the future exchange rate cause EX to rise, the foreign currency is expected to appreciate, which in turn increases R_f. When capital and foreign-exchange markets are in equilibrium, the expected rate of return on domestic assets equals the expected rate of return on foreign assets ($R_0 = R_f$); the equilibrium exchange rate is EX_0^*.

Suppose that the central bank wants to increase the exchange rate from EX_0^* to EX_1^*, as in Figure 22.1(a). To raise the foreign-exchange value of its currency, the central bank must buy domestic currency (or domestic deposits) from foreigners and sell foreign assets. The transaction resembles a domestic open market sale of securities because the foreign-exchange intervention reduces the monetary base. If nothing else changes, the intervention increases the domestic short-term interest rate from i_0 to i_1. As a result, the domestic expected rate of return shifts to the right from R_0 to R_1. Because the expected rate of return on domestic assets has increased relative to the expected rate of return on foreign assets, investors will increase their demand for domestic assets and domestic currency. The exchange rate then rises from EX_0^* to EX_1^*.[†] Thus, if nothing else changes, an unsterilized intervention in which the central bank sells foreign assets to purchase domestic currency leads to a decrease in international reserves and in the money supply and an appreciation of the domestic currency.

[†]The decline in the domestic money supply may increase expected appreciation of the domestic currency, causing R_f to shift to the left, further raising the exchange rate. For simplicity, we ignore this effect here.

FIGURE 22.1 **Unsterilized Foreign-Exchange Market Interventions and the Exchange Rate**

As shown in (a):

1. To raise the exchange rate, the central bank must buy domestic currency, losing international reserves and decreasing the monetary base.
2. Domestic short-term interest rates increase from i_0 to i_1, so the expected rate of return on domestic assets rises from R_0 to R_1. That causes the exchange rate to rise from EX_0^* to EX_1^*.

As shown in (b):

1. To lower the exchange rate, the central bank must sell domestic currency, gaining international reserves and increasing the monetary base.
2. Domestic short-term interest rates decrease from i_0 to i_1, so the expected rate of return on domestic assets falls from R_0 to R_1. This causes the exchange rate to fall from EX_0^* to EX_1^*.

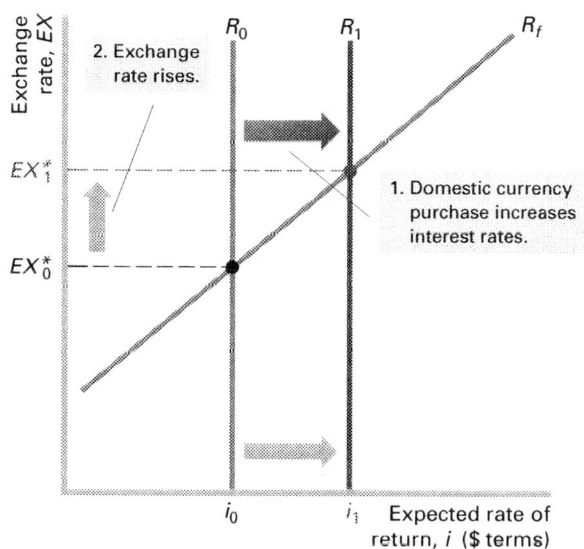

(a) Intervention to Raise the Exchange Rate

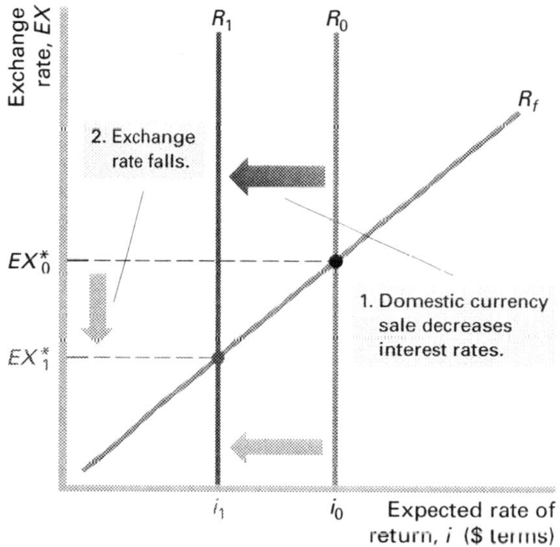

(b) Intervention to Lower the Exchange Rate

Conversely, suppose that the central bank wants to lower the exchange rate with unsterilized foreign-exchange intervention, as represented in Figure 22.1(b). The central bank buys foreign assets, increasing the monetary base and reducing the short-term interest rate from i_0 to i_1. The domestic expected rate of return shifts from R_0 to R_1. The expected rate of return on domestic assets has declined relative to the expected rate of return of foreign assets, so investors will reduce their demand for domestic assets and domestic currency. The exchange rate falls from EX_0^* to EX_1^*. Thus, if nothing else changes, an unsterilized intervention in which the central bank buys foreign assets and sells domestic currency leads to an increase in international reserves and the money supply and depreciation of the domestic currency.

CHECKPOINT

Suppose that the Fed pursues a contractionary monetary policy to increase the short-term interest rate in the United States. What would you predict the consequences for the exchange rate to be? All else being equal, the higher expected rate of return on dollar assets increases the demand for U.S. assets relative to foreign assets, causing the dollar to appreciate. ♦

Sterilized Intervention

In analyzing the effects of an unsterilized foreign-exchange intervention, we assumed that domestic and foreign assets are perfect substitutes. This assumption means that the expected rates of return on domestic and foreign assets are equal in equilibrium. Because a sterilized foreign-exchange intervention doesn't affect the money supply, it will not affect domestic interest rates or expected appreciation of the domestic currency. Hence the domestic expected rate of return, R, and foreign expected rate of return, R_f, do not shift. Thus a sterilized intervention does not affect the exchange rate.

When domestic and foreign assets are not perfect substitutes, an increase in the supply of domestic assets implies greater exchange rate risk, raising the risk premium for the domestic expected rate of return and reducing the exchange rate.† In theory, with a currency risk premium, an increase in the domestic money supply from a sterilized intervention leads to depreciation of the domestic currency, as in the case of an unsterilized intervention. However, most studies by economists have concluded that a sterilized intervention has virtually no effect on the exchange rate. Hence effective central bank interventions that are intended to affect the exchange rate are generally unsterilized.

The currency premium $h_{f,d}$ can be negative; domestic investors may require a higher expected return on foreign assets than on domestic assets. Many economists believe that domestic and foreign assets are imperfect substitutes because investors face difficulties in gathering information about foreign assets or because foreign assets may be exposed to risks of seizure by foreign governments.

Capital Controls

If domestic and foreign assets are not perfect substitutes—that is, if they don't have similar risk, liquidity, and information characteristics—a sterilized intervention can affect the exchange rate. In the past, **capital controls**, or government-imposed barriers to foreign savers investing in domestic assets or to domestic savers investing in foreign assets, caused foreign assets to be less liquid than domestic assets. (Explicit capital controls are now relatively rare in most industrialized countries, though in response to the Asian financial crisis some emerging economies imposed them in 1998.) Capital controls also limit domestic investors' ability to diversify their portfolios internationally, leading those investors to require a higher expected return on domestic assets than on foreign assets.

The major currency crises of the 1990s in Mexico and East Asia were fueled in part by significant changes in capital inflows and capital outflows, leading some economists and politicians to advocate restrictions on capital mobility in emerging market countries. Although capital outflows were, indeed, an element of the financial crises—leading some political leaders such as then Malaysian Prime Minister Mahathir to limit capital outflows—most economists remain skeptical about the effectiveness of such controls. In principle, controls can further weaken confidence in the government and the domestic financial system. (Indeed, Thailand in December 2006 reversed almost

†In this case, the nominal interest rate parity condition in the foreign-exchange market reflects a currency risk premium $h_{f,d}$ [introduced in Chapter 8, Eq. (8.7)]:

$$i = i_f - \frac{\Delta EX^e}{EX} + h_{f,d}.$$

With the addition of a risk premium, a sterilized foreign-exchange market intervention can affect the exchange rate; that is, if a sterilized sale of the domestic currency increases $h_{f,d}$, then, if nothing else changes, EX must fall to satisfy the interest rate parity condition.

immediately its decision to impose capital controls—bowing to pressure from a sharp decline in stock prices.) In practice, they can precipitate evasion by the private sector and corruption of public officials.

Capital inflow restrictions receive more support from economists, in part because such inflows often lead to domestic lending booms and increased risk taking by domestic banks. Other economists point out that this problem could be made less severe by improving bank regulation and supervision in emerging market countries. In this way, capital inflows could still serve as important financial mechanisms for channeling foreign investment to countries with promising investment opportunities.

Recent Interventions

Since the early 1970s, the foreign-exchange value of the dollar has been determined in currency markets. Nonetheless, the Fed and the Treasury have intervened in the foreign-exchange market on several occasions to increase or decrease the exchange rate. U.S. officials carry out intervention through the Exchange Stabilization Fund at the Treasury. The Treasury is the senior authority in organizing foreign-exchange interventions, although it trades through the Federal Reserve Bank of New York. The FOMC has independent authority to conduct foreign-exchange interventions, but in practice, the Treasury and the Fed coordinate their efforts.

During the 1980s, the Reagan administration and the Fed pursued interventions at alternative times to raise or lower the foreign-exchange rate of the dollar. In 1981, the incoming administration announced that it would not intervene in the foreign-exchange market, even though the dollar was appreciating because of high domestic real interest rates. After the dollar's value had almost doubled relative to other major currencies between early 1981 and September 1985, Treasury Secretary James Baker and Federal Reserve Chairman Paul Volcker met in New York with their counterparts from France, Germany, Japan, and the United Kingdom to achieve an agreement to bring down the foreign-exchange value of the dollar. These countries agreed, in the so-called Plaza Accord, to a joint effort to reduce the dollar's value and stabilize the values of the other four currencies against the dollar. Another round of interventions followed in February 1987, the so-called Louvre Accord, which established unofficial trading ranges for currencies. In January 1988, major central banks intervened to halt the dollar's slide and stabilize exchange rates for a time. In the late 1980s and the 1990s, the Treasury and Fed continued to intervene in foreign-exchange markets. In September 2000, the Fed joined the European Central Bank and other central banks to support the euro. Most analysts believe that it is increasingly difficult for governments and central banks to affect the exchange rate by intervening in today's vast foreign-exchange market, in which more than $1 trillion changes hands daily. In the early 2000s, the Bank of Japan intervened frequently to halt a strengthening yen. In early 2001, the Bush administration announced that it would not intervene in the foreign-exchange market to affect the value of the dollar.

Balance of Payments

In describing the foreign-exchange market interventions that the Fed undertakes to manage the exchange rate, we simply noted the increase or decrease in international reserves on the Fed's balance sheet without any mention of why the central bank holds the reserves or what factors account for the size of reserve holdings. Transactions in international reserves are one of several capital flows between the United States and

CASE STUDY

Do Sterilized Interventions Affect the Exchange Rate?

Beginning in the mid-1980s, the G7 countries—the United States, Japan, Germany, Canada, Italy, France, and the United Kingdom—have occasionally pursued coordinated sterilized interventions to influence the dollar's value in world currency markets. According to our theory, sterilized interventions are unlikely to change the exchange rate, but some empirical studies have claimed that concerted interventions by major central banks affect the exchange rate by signaling future changes in monetary policy. In one study, Pietro Catte, Giampoalo Galli, and Salvatore Rebecchini found that all 19 interventions between 1985 and 1991 were successful to some degree.[†] Critics of such studies note that central banks may not intervene at all unless they perceive that they can influence currency markets at that time.

In a later study, Maurice Obstfeld of the University of California, Berkeley, analyzed the ability of interventions between 1993 and 1995 to affect the yen–dollar exchange rate.[††] He found little evidence to support the claim that interventions per se can slow down foreign-exchange market trends and no evidence that they can reverse market trends. The one exception was the intervention of August 14, 1993, which pushed up the dollar's value against the yen. Obstfeld noted, however, that the intervention coincided with a statement by then U.S. Treasury Department Undersecretary Lawrence Summers that the United States did not intend to use dollar depreciation as a means of gaining access to Japanese markets.

To summarize, although coordinated changes in monetary policy are likely to affect the exchange rate, sterilized interventions by themselves are unlikely to have a long-term effect on the exchange rate.

---

†Pietro Catte, Giampoalo Galli, and Salvatore Rebecchini, "Concerted Interventions and the Dollar: An Analysis of Daily Data," in Peter B. Kenen, Francesco Papadia, and Fabrizio Saccomani, eds., *The International Monetary System*. Cambridge, UK: Cambridge University Press, 1995.

††Maurice Obstfeld, "International Currency Experience: New Lessons and Lessons Relearned," *Brookings Papers on Economic Activity* 1:119–220, 1995.

---

other countries. To understand how the Fed amasses international reserves and how much it has available for foreign-exchange market interventions, we must look at the broader flow of funds between the United States and foreign countries. The simplest way to describe these international capital flows is by studying the balance-of-payments accounts. The **balance-of-payments accounts** measure all flows of private and government funds between a domestic economy (in this case, the United States) and all foreign countries.

Web Site Suggestions: http://www.bea.gov/bea/pubs.htm Presents in the *Survey of Current Business* data on the U.S. balance of payments.

The balance of payments for the United States is a bookkeeping procedure similar to one that households or businesses might use to record receipts and payments. In the balance of payments, inflows of funds from foreigners to the United States are *receipts*, which are recorded as positive numbers. Receipts include inflows of funds for purchases of U.S.-produced goods and services (U.S. exports), for acquisition of U.S. assets (capital inflows), and as gifts to U.S. citizens (unilateral transfers).

Outflows of funds from the United States to foreigners are *payments*, which are recorded with a minus sign. Payments include purchases of foreign goods and services (imports), money spent on purchases of foreign assets by U.S. households and businesses (capital outflows), and gifts to foreigners, including foreign aid (unilateral transfers). The principal components of the balance-of-payments accounts summarize transactions for purchases and sales of goods and services (the current account balance, which includes the trade balance) and flows of funds for international lending or borrowing (the financial account balance, which includes official settlements). In exploring which cash flows belong to each component, you will see how the flows of funds generated

USING THE NEWS . . .

The U.S. Balance of Payments

Information on the balance of payments is widely reported in newspapers. The trade balance receives special attention when it is reported near the end of each month. The U.S. Department of Commerce publishes the complete balance-of-payments accounts quarterly in the *Survey of Current Business*. Forecasters, traders, and financial institutions use them to predict changes in exchange rates and interest rates.

Source: Survey of Current Business.

	Transactions, 2005	$ billions
Trade balance	1. Exports of goods, services, and income (2 + 3 + 4)	1749.8
(2) + (6) =	2. Goods	894.6
−772.7 billion	3. Services	380.6
	4. Income receipts on investments	474.6
Current account	5. Imports of goods, services, and income (6 + 7 + 8)	−2455.3
balance	6. Goods	−1667.3
(1) + (5) + (9) =	7. Services	−314.6
−791.5 billion	8. Income payments on investments	−463.3
	9. Unilateral transfers	−86.0
	10. Capital account transactions, net	−4.3
	11. U.S. assets abroad, net [increase of capital inflow (−)] (12 + 13 + 14)	−426.8
	12. U.S. official reserves assets	14.0
Financial account	13. U.S. government assets, other than official reserve assets, net	5.5
balance	14. U.S. private assets, net	−446.4
(10) + (11) + (15) =	15. Foreign assets in the U.S., net [increase of capital inflow (+)] (16 + 17)	1212.2
781.1 billion	16. Foreign official assets, net	199.5
	17. Other foreign assets, net	1012.7
	18. Allocations of Special Drawing Rights	0.0
	19. Statistical discrepancy	10.4

from international transactions influence the economy and the Fed's source of international reserves that are needed to conduct international monetary policy.

Each international transaction represents an exchange of goods, services, or assets among households, businesses, or governments. Therefore the two sides of the exchange must always balance. In other words, the payments and receipts of the balance-of-payments accounts must equal zero, or

$$\text{Current account balance} + \text{Financial account balance} = 0. \tag{22.1}$$

The Current Account

> Web Site Suggestions: http://www.gpoaccess.gov/indicators/browse.html Presents current and historical quarterly information on components of the current account.

The **current account** summarizes transactions between a country and its foreign trading partners for purchases and sales of currently produced goods and services. To begin, the **trade balance** is the difference between goods exports and imports (line 2 plus line 6 in the table above, because imports are entered with a minus sign). The U.S. trade balance in 2005 was a deficit of $772.7 billion, with imports of $1667.3 billion exceeding exports of $894.6 billion. When exports exceed imports, the trade balance is a surplus.

The three other components of the current account are exports and imports of services (lines 3 and 7), net investment income (lines 4 and 8), and unilateral transfers (line 9). In 2005, the United States had a surplus in the sale of services, selling $64 billion more of services to foreigners than U.S. residents purchased abroad. Net investment income was negative for the United States in 2005 by $11.3 billion. That is, U.S. residents paid out less investment income to foreign investors than they received from foreign investments. Finally, the United States contributed, on balance, $86 billion in unilateral transfers. The **current account balance** equals the sum of the trade balance, services balance, net investment income, and unilateral transfers. There was a *deficit* of $791.5 billion in 2005.

If there is a current account surplus (a positive number), United States citizens have funds to lend to foreigners. If there is a negative balance, or deficit, as there was in 2002, the United States must borrow the difference to pay for goods and services purchased abroad. In particular, policymakers have been concerned about U.S. current account deficits in the 1980s, 1990s, and 2000s because those deficits require the

United States to borrow funds from foreign savers to finance the deficits. As in the case of households and businesses, governments' current account surpluses or deficits require offsetting financial transactions. A current account surplus or deficit in the balance of payments must be balanced by international lending or borrowing or by changes in official reserve transactions. Hence the large U.S. current account deficits in the 1980s, 1990s, and 2000s caused the United States to rely heavily on savings from abroad—international borrowing—to finance domestic consumption, investment, and the federal budget deficit. Of particular concern was the growing reliance by the mid-2000s on funds from foreign central banks, as opposed to private investors.

The current account balance also provides information about anticipated movements in exchange rates. If there is a current account deficit, U.S. citizens have a greater demand for foreign goods and services than foreigners have for U.S. goods and services. Therefore U.S. citizens must increase their demand for foreign currencies to buy these foreign goods and services, causing the dollar to decline in value against foreign currencies. Also international lending or borrowing to achieve a balance of payments of zero involves shifts in demand for domestic and foreign assets that can affect domestic and foreign interest rates and the exchange rate (Chapter 8).

Although the balance of payments is a set of accounting relationships, the model of lending and borrowing decisions that was introduced in Chapter 6 helps to explain what factors determine international lending and borrowing. For a large open economy such as that of the United States, factors that tend to increase national saving or international lending lead to a capital outflow and a current account surplus. Factors that tend to decrease national saving or increase international borrowing lead to a capital inflow and a current account deficit.

The Financial Account

The **financial account** measures trade in existing financial or real assets among countries. When someone in a country sells an asset (a skyscraper, a bond, or shares of stock, for example) to a foreign investor, the transaction is recorded in the balance-of-payments accounts as a **capital inflow** because funds flow into the country to buy the asset. When someone in a country buys an asset abroad, the transaction is recorded in the balance-of-payments accounts as a **capital outflow** because funds flow from the country to buy the asset. Thus, when a wealthy Chinese entrepreneur buys a penthouse apartment in New York's Trump Tower, the transaction is recorded as a capital outflow for China and a capital inflow for the United States.

The **financial account balance** is the amount of capital inflows (line 15) minus capital outflows (line 11)—plus the net capital account transactions (line 10), which consist mainly of debt forgiveness and transfers of financial assets by migrants when they enter the United States.† The financial account balance is a surplus if the citizens of the country sell more assets to foreigners than they buy from foreigners. The financial account balance is

†A third, less important, part of the balance of payments is called the *capital account*. The capital account records relatively minor transactions, such as migrants' transfers—which consist of goods and financial assets people take with them when they leave or enter a country—and sales and purchases of nonproduced, nonfinancial assets. A nonproduced, nonfinancial asset is a copyright, patent, trademark, or right to natural resources. The definitions of the financial account and the capital account are often misunderstood because the capital account prior to 1999 recorded all the transactions included now in both the financial account and the capital account. In other words, capital account transactions went from being a very important part of the balance of payments to being a relatively unimportant part. Because the balance on what is now called the capital account is so small, for simplicity we merge it with the financial account here.

a deficit if the citizens of the country buy more assets from foreigners than they sell to foreigners. In 2005, the United States had capital inflows of $1,212.2 billion and capital outflows of $426.8 billion—plus net capital account transactions of −$4.3 billion—for a net capital account balance (an increase in U.S. assets held by foreigners) of $781.1 billion.

Official Settlements

Not all capital flows among countries represent transactions by households and businesses; changes in asset holdings by governments and central banks supplement private capital flows. **Official reserve assets** are assets held by central banks that can be used in making international payments to settle the balance of payments and conduct international monetary policy. Historically, gold was the leading official reserve asset. Official reserves now are primarily government securities of the United States and other industrialized countries, foreign bank deposits, and special assets called Special Drawing Rights created by the International Monetary Fund (an international agency that we discuss later in this chapter). Official settlements equal the net increase (domestic holdings minus foreign holdings) in a country's official reserve assets.

The official settlements balance is often called the *balance-of-payments surplus or deficit*. In 2005, the United States had a significant balance-of-payments deficit. When a country has a balance-of-payments surplus, it gains international reserves because its receipts exceed its payments—foreign central banks provide the country's central bank with international reserves. When a country experiences an official settlements balance deficit, or a balance-of-payments deficit, it loses international reserves. Because U.S. dollars and dollar-denominated assets serve as the largest component of international reserves, a U.S. balance-of-payments deficit can be financed by a reduction in U.S. international reserves and an increase in dollar assets held by foreign central banks. Similarly, a combination of an increase in U.S. international reserves and a decrease in dollar assets held by foreign central banks can offset a U.S. balance-of-payments surplus.

Relationships Among the Accounts

Recall that, in principle, the current account balance and financial account balance sum to zero. In reality, measurement problems keep this relationship from holding exactly. An adjustment for measurement errors, the **statistical discrepancy** (line 19), is reported in the capital account portion of the balance-of-payments accounts. In 2005, it equaled $10.4 billion (a capital inflow). Many analysts believe that large statistical discrepancies in countries' balance-of-payments accounts reflect hidden capital flows (related to illegal activity, tax evasion, or capital flight because of political risk).

To summarize, international goods and financial transactions affect both the current account and the capital account in the balance of payments. To close out a country's international transactions for balance of payments, its central bank and foreign central banks engage in official reserve transactions, which can affect the monetary base.

CHECKPOINT

Using the balance-of-payments accounts, explain what factors determined the shift for the United States from being a net creditor to being a net debtor during the 1980s. Large U.S. trade deficits (a minus sign in the balance of payments) mean that the United States is borrowing from abroad. In the balance of payments, this shows up as an inflow of foreign capital (a plus sign in the balance of payments). Hence large trade deficits are associated with the country's becoming a net debtor to foreign savers. ♦

Exchange Rate Regimes and the International Financial System

The Fed and other central banks engage in foreign-exchange market interventions to maintain the foreign-exchange value of their nations' currencies. Political agreements influence the size and timing of each central bank's purchases and sales of international reserves. Specifically, nations agree to participate in a particular **exchange rate regime**, or system of adjusting exchange rates and flows of goods and capital among countries. At times, countries have agreed to fix exchange rates among their national currencies, and this agreement committed the central banks to act to maintain these exchange rates. At other times, exchange rates have been allowed to fluctuate, but central banks still often acted to limit exchange rate fluctuations. In this section, we describe those exchange rate regimes and their impact on central banks' conduct of monetary policy. In particular, we analyze exchange rate regimes in terms of (1) how the promise holds the system together, (2) how exchange rates adjust to maintain the promise, and (3) how central banks act to maintain equilibrium in the international monetary and financial system. We also evaluate successes and failures of each system.

Fixed Exchange Rates and the Gold Standard

In the past, most exchange rate regimes were **fixed exchange rate systems,** in which exchange rates were set at levels that were determined and maintained by governments. The classical gold standard that supported the international monetary and financial system before World War I illustrates the successes and failures of a fixed exchange rate system. Under a **gold standard,** currencies of participating countries are convertible into an agreed-upon amount of gold. The exchange rates between any two countries' currencies are fixed by their relative gold weights.

For example, if \$1 could be exchanged for $\frac{1}{20}$ of an ounce of gold while FF1 (French franc) could be exchanged for $\frac{1}{80}$ of an ounce of gold, \$1 = FF4 and \$0.25 = FF1. Let's consider an example of trade and capital flows between France and the United States to illustrate the effect of this system of fixed exchange rates. Under a fixed exchange rate system based on a gold standard, a U.S. importer could buy goods from a French exporter by either (1) exchanging dollars for French francs in France and buying goods or (2) exchanging dollars for gold in the United States and shipping gold to France to buy francs and French goods.

Suppose that the demand for French goods rises relative to the demand for U.S. goods, leading to a rising demand for francs and a falling demand for dollars. Hence there is pressure for the exchange rate in francs per dollar to fall in the foreign-exchange market—say, from \$1 = FF4 to \$1 = FF3. In this situation, U.S. importers could make a profit from shipping gold to France to buy francs, as long as the United States and France continue to exchange currencies for gold at the agreed-upon rate.

Therefore, if Sally Sharp, a cloth importer in Philadelphia, wants to buy FF5000 worth of cloth from Deluxe of Paris, she can use either of the two strategies described. First, if she tries to sell dollars for francs in the foreign-exchange market, she will find that she must pay 5000/3 = \$1666.67 for the cloth. Alternatively, she can exchange \$1250 for gold, ship the gold bars to France, and demand that the Bank of France exchange the gold for francs at the fixed exchange rate. At the official exchange rate of \$1 = FF4, she will get FF5000 for her gold, enough to buy the cloth. The second strategy provides the cheaper solution for Sally. Sally's saving on this transaction, $416.67, makes it the best way to buy the cloth, as long as the cost of shipping the gold from Philadelphia to France does not exceed $416.67.

What happens in France as U.S. importers like Sally Sharp ship their gold to Paris? Gold flows into France, expanding that country's international reserves because gold is eventually exchanged for francs. The United States loses an equivalent amount of international reserves because dollars are given to the government in exchange for gold. An increase in a country's international reserves increases its monetary base, whereas a decrease in its international reserves lowers its monetary base. Hence the monetary base rises in France and falls in the United States, putting upward pressure on the price level in France and downward pressure on the price level in the United States. French goods become more expensive relative to U.S. goods. Therefore the relative demand for French goods falls, restoring the trade balance and causing the exchange rate to rise toward the official rate of $1 = FF4.

However, if the relative demand for U.S. goods rises, market forces put upward pressure on the exchange rate. Gold then flows from France to the United States, reducing the French monetary base and increasing the U.S. monetary base. In this case, the accompanying increase in the U.S. price level relative to the French price level makes French goods more attractive, restoring the trade balance. The exchange rate moves back toward the fixed rate of $1 = FF4.

One problem with the economic adjustment process under the gold standard was that countries with trade deficits and gold outflows experienced declines in price levels, or deflation. Periods of unexpected and pronounced deflation caused recessions. During the 1870s, 1880s, and 1890s, several deflation-induced recessions occurred in the United States. A falling price level raised the real value of households' and firms' nominal debt burdens, leading to financial distress for many sectors of the economy.

Another consequence of fixed exchange rates under the gold standard was that countries had little control over their domestic monetary policies. The reason was that gold flows caused changes in the monetary base. As a result, countries faced unexpected inflation or deflation from international trade or financial disturbances. Moreover, gold discoveries and production strongly influenced changes in the world money supply, making the situation worse. For example, in the 1870s and 1880s, few gold discoveries and rapid economic growth contributed to falling prices. In the 1890s, on the other hand, the gold rushes in Alaska and what is now South Africa increased price levels around the world.

In theory, the gold standard required that all countries maintain their promise to convert currencies freely into gold at fixed exchange rates. In practice, England made the exchange rate regime's promise credible. The strength of the British economy, its frequent trade surpluses, and its large gold reserves made England the anchor of the international monetary and financial system.

During World War I, the collapse of the international trading system led countries to abandon their promises to convert currency into gold. The gold standard had a brief revival during the period between the two world wars, but economists generally believe that it deepened the worldwide depression of the early 1930s. The Federal Reserve System's attempts to reduce gold outflows in 1930 and 1931, by increasing the discount rate, contributed to the U.S. financial crisis. Subsequently, the United States suspended the general public's right to convert dollars into gold. Ben Bernanke (now Fed Chairman) and Harold James of Princeton University found that countries that tried to defend the gold standard in the early 1930s suffered more severe deflation and depression than did countries that abandoned the gold standard.†

Adapting Fixed Exchange Rates: The Bretton Woods System

Despite the gold standard's demise, many countries remained interested in the concept of fixed exchange rates. As World War II drew to a close, representatives of the Allied governments gathered at Bretton Woods, New Hampshire, to design a new international monetary and financial system. The resulting agreement, known as the **Bretton Woods system,** lasted from 1945 until 1971. Its framers intended to reinstate a system of fixed exchange rates but to permit smoother short-term economic adjustment than was possible under the gold standard. The promise that was to hold the system together was that foreign central banks would be able to convert U.S. dollars into gold at a price of $35.00 per ounce. Hence agreed-upon exchange rates defined foreign currencies in dollar terms, and dollars were convertible to gold by the United States at the official price of $35.00 per ounce. The United States held this special role because of its dominant position in the global economy at that time and the fact that it held much of the world's gold. Because central banks used dollar assets and gold as international reserves, the dollar was known as the *international reserve currency.*

Under the Bretton Woods system, exchange rates were supposed to adjust only when a country experienced fundamental disequilibrium—that is, persistent deficits or surpluses in its balance of payments at the fixed exchange rate. To help countries make short-run economic adjustment to a balance-of-payments deficit or surplus while maintaining a fixed exchange rate, the Bretton Woods agreement created the **International Monetary Fund (IMF).** Headquartered in Washington, D.C., this multinational organization grew from 30 member countries to more than 150 in 2006. In principle, the IMF was to be a lender of last resort to prevent the short-term economic dislocations that threatened the stability of the gold standard. In practice, the IMF also encourages domestic economic policies that are consistent with exchange rate stability and gathers and standardizes international economic and financial data to use in monitoring member countries.

Not directly related to its establishment of the international monetary system, the Bretton Woods agreement created the **World Bank,** or International Bank for Reconstruction and Development, to make long-term loans to developing countries. These loans were designed to build infrastructure (highways and bridges, power generation and distribution, and water supply, for example) to aid economic development. The World Bank raises funds to lend by selling bonds in the international capital market. Continuation of the traditional roles of both the IMF and the World Bank is currently being debated.

Although the IMF no longer attempts to foster fixed exchange rates (its core Bretton Woods system function), its activities as an international lender of last resort have grown. During the developing world debt crises of the 1980s, the IMF provided credit to such countries to help them repay their loans. IMF lending during the Mexican

†Ben Bernanke and Harold James, "The Gold Standard, Deflation, and Financial Crisis in the Great Depression: An International Comparison," in R. Glenn Hubbard, ed., *Financial Markets and Financial Crises.* Chicago: University of Chicago Press, 1991.

CONSIDER THIS ...

Are the IMF and the World Bank Obsolete?

Some analysts argue for rethinking the purposes of the IMF and the World Bank. These multilateral lending institutions have outlived the Bretton Woods system that created them. In the 1940s and 1950s, the international capital market was small; in the 2000s, the international capital market is the conduit for billions of dollars each day. These analysts ask, why not let the international market make loans to governments?

Proponents of continuing the present system give two arguments. First, the IMF and the World Bank play an important role in gathering and maintaining information and expertise on the economies of many nations, particularly those of developing countries. A loan from one of these institutions can be a better indicator to private lenders of creditworthiness than can a privately rendered credit rating. Second, the IMF and the World Bank can subsidize lending by obtaining funds at a lower cost than the borrower. These reasons, they say, support the conclusion that the IMF and the World Bank should not become obsolete.

During the early 1990s, countries in Eastern Europe, the Commonwealth of Independent States, and Africa placed great demands on the IMF and the World Bank. Some critics have proposed a merger of the two institutions as an intermediate solution for an international monetary and financial system to meet existing demands.

The IMF came under widespread criticism for its handling of the Asian financial crisis and its effects on other emerging economies (particularly Brazil) in 1997 and 1998. The principal concern was that IMF policies led to hardship for many citizens of Thailand, Indonesia, and Malaysia, while not sufficiently punishing speculators with losses, giving rise to moral hazard. While the Clinton administration and the U.S. Congress battled over whether the IMF should receive additional funding, many economists urged wholesale reform of the IMF. In particular, four principles have been urged in the reform discussion: (1) deal expeditiously with insolvent institutions; (2) adopt and enforce capital standards; (3) encourage market discipline; and (4) maintain free flows of capital. The current debate over the IMF affords an opportunity to implement reforms that can curtail the moral hazard associated with international bailouts.

In 2001, the Bush administration assumed a tougher stance on IMF bailouts, urging a greater focus on providing short-term liquidity assistance. Nonetheless, the U.S. Treasury consented to bailouts in Argentina, Brazil, and Turkey.

financial crisis (1994–1995) and the East Asian financial crisis (1997–1998) inspired major controversy over its role in the international financial system.

Advocates of IMF intervention point to the absence of a lender of last resort in emerging market financial crises. Critics of the IMF raise two counterarguments. The first is that the IMF encourages moral hazard in the form of excessive risk taking by bailing out foreign lenders. According to this view, the IMF's bailout of foreign lenders in the Mexican crisis encouraged risky lending to East Asian countries, precipitating that crisis. The second argument is that, in contrast to the IMF's treatment of foreign lenders, the institution's "austerity" programs in developing countries focus on tight macroeconomic policies, leading to unemployment and political risk.

In 1999, a U.S. congressional commission (the International Financial Institutions Advisory Commission), chaired by Allan Meltzer of Carnegie Mellon University, criticized IMF lending operations and argued for more transparency and a greater reliance on microeconomic policies to reform financial regulation. In the aftermath of the Meltzer Commission's report, the IMF remains at the center of controversy both in Washington and in emerging market economies.

The fixed exchange rate system. Central bank interventions in the foreign-exchange market to buy and sell dollar assets maintained the fixed exchange rates of the Bretton Woods system. Exchange rates could vary by 1% above or below the fixed rate before countries were required to intervene to stabilize them. If a foreign currency appreciated relative to the dollar, the central bank of that country would sell its own currency for dollars, thereby driving the exchange rate back to the fixed rate. If a foreign currency depreciated relative to the dollar, the central bank would sell dollar assets from its international reserves and buy its own currency to push the exchange rate back toward the fixed rate.

A central bank can maintain the exchange rate within the acceptable level as long as it is able and willing to buy and sell the amounts of its own currency that are necessary for exchange rate stabilization. When a foreign central bank buys its own currency, it sells dollars (international reserves); when it sells its own currency, it buys dollars. Hence there is an important asymmetry in central banks' adjustments in response to market pressures on the exchange rate. A country with a balance-of-payments surplus has no constraint on its ability to sell its own currency to buy dollars to maintain the exchange rate, although it may be unwilling to do so. However, the ability to buy its own currency (to raise its value relative to the dollar) is limited by the country's stock of international reserves.

As a result, reserve outflows caused by balance-of-payments deficits created problems for central banks that were bound by the Bretton Woods system. When a country's stock of international reserves was exhausted, the central bank and the government would have to implement restrictive economic policies to reduce imports and the trade deficit or abandon the policy of stabilizing the exchange rate against the dollar.

Maintaining the exchange rate: devaluations and revaluations. As an alternative to defending the fixed exchange rate by buying or selling reserves or changing domestic economic policies, a country can change the exchange rate. When its currency is overvalued relative to the dollar, the country can **devalue** its currency—that is, lower the official value of its currency relative to the dollar, thereby resetting the exchange rate. A country whose currency is undervalued relative to the dollar can **revalue** its currency—that is, raise the official value of its currency relative to the dollar.† In the early 2000s, for example, some commentators urged China to revalue its currency, which it had pegged against the U.S. dollar. Maintaining its peg had led China to accumulate very large stocks of U.S. dollar reserves. In 2005, giving in to intense international pressure, the Chinese government began to revalue its currency, though only slightly.

In practice, countries didn't often pursue devaluations or revaluations. Governments preferred to postpone devaluations rather than face political charges that their monetary policies were flawed. Revaluations also were not a popular choice. Domestic producers and their workers complained vigorously when the currency was allowed to rise against the dollar because domestic goods became less competitive in world markets, reducing profits and employment. The political pressures against devaluations and revaluations usually limited government changes in the exchange rate to responses to foreign-exchange market pressures.

Speculative attack. When market participants believe that the government is unable or unwilling to maintain the exchange rate, they may sell a weak currency or purchase a strong currency. These actions, known as a **speculative attack**, force a devaluation or revaluation of the currency. Speculative attacks sometimes produce international financial crises. That happened in 1967, when the British pound was overvalued

†Remember, in a flexible exchange rate system, a falling value of the exchange rate is known as *depreciation*, and a rising value of the exchange rate is known as *appreciation*.

relative to the dollar. To explain the situation, let's use the method of exchange rate determination shown in Figure 22.2. The intersection of the domestic expected rate of return, R_0, and the foreign expected rate of return, R_f, at point *A* gives an exchange rate (in \$/£) that is lower than the fixed exchange rate $\overline{EX}$ of £1 = \$2.80. To defend the overvalued exchange rate, the Bank of England had to sell dollars from its international reserves to buy pounds. The resulting decrease in the money supply increased short-term interest rates from i_0 to i_1, shifting the expected rate of return from R_0 to R_1 and momentarily restoring the exchange rate $\overline{EX}$ of £1 = \$2.80 at point *B*.

As the Bank of England's international reserves shrank, currency traders knew that, at some point, it would have to abandon its stabilization efforts. Speculators responded by selling pounds to the Bank of England (for \$2.80/£1), expecting the pound to fall in value against the dollar. When the pound fell, the speculators used dollars to buy back even more pounds, thus earning a substantial profit. In terms of our graphical analysis, market participants expected the exchange rate (defined from the British perspective in \$/£) to fall, thereby increasing the expected rate of return on non-British assets, R_f, relative to the British expected return *R*. Figure 22.2 shows the effect of this change in expectations in the shift from R_{f0} to R_{f1}. The overvaluation of the pound is even greater at the new intersection of *R* and R_f. This difference between the fixed and market exchange rates forced the Bank of England to buy even more pounds until it ran out of dollars. To defend the exchange rate $\overline{EX}$, the Bank of England would have had to increase short-term interest rates by an amount sufficient to maintain $\overline{EX}$ at point *C*. On November 17, 1967, the Bank of England lost more than \$1 billion of international reserves (on top of earlier losses of several billion dollars). On November 18, it devalued the pound by 14%.

Devaluations are forced by speculative attacks when central banks are *unable* to defend the exchange rate, as in England's 1967 crisis. Revaluations, on the other hand, can be forced by speculative attacks when a central bank is *unwilling* to defend the exchange rate. A speculative attack on the undervalued deutsche mark in 1971 forced a revaluation of the mark against the dollar and hastened the demise of the Bretton Woods system.

FIGURE 22.2

Speculative Attack on the Bretton Woods System: The British Pound, 1967

1. At *A*, the pound is overvalued at the official exchange rate, $\overline{EX}$. The Bank of England sells dollars to buy pounds, increasing short-term interest rates from i_0 to i_1. The domestic expected return shifts from R_0 to R_1, and the exchange rate returns to the fixed rate $\overline{EX}$ of £1 = \$2.80 at *B*.

2. Market participants expect the Bank of England to run out of dollars, and the R_f curve shifts from R_{f0} to R_{f1}. A significant increase in *i* would be required to restore an equilibrium exchange rate of $\overline{EX}$ at *C*. The Bank of England was forced to devalue the pound.

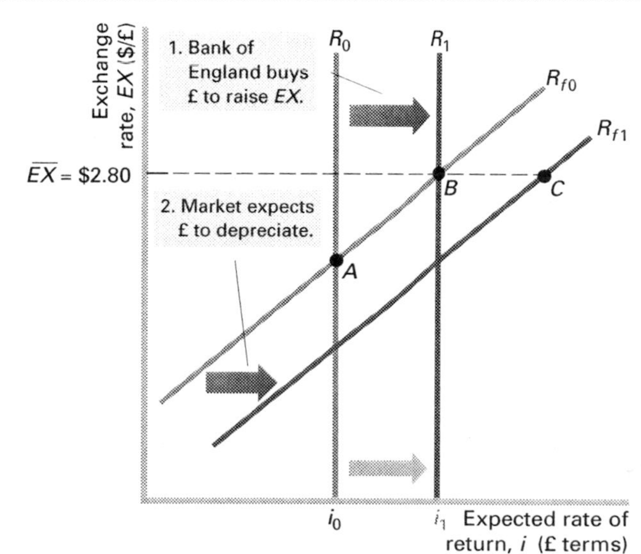

By 1970, the U.S. balance-of-payments deficit had grown significantly. By the first quarter of 1971, the large balance-of-payments surpluses outside the United States were causing fear in international financial markets because many currencies were undervalued relative to the dollar. Worries were greatest in Germany as the Bundesbank (the German central bank) pursued policies to maintain a low inflation rate. The Bundesbank faced a dilemma. If it defended the fixed exchange rate, it would have to sell marks in the foreign-exchange market. By doing so, it would acquire international reserves, increasing the German money supply and putting upward pressure on German prices. If it revalued the mark, it would avoid inflationary pressures but would be breaking its promise under the Bretton Woods system.

This dilemma set the stage for a speculative attack on the mark. In this case, speculators bought marks with dollars, expecting the mark to rise in value against the dollar. When the mark did rise, the speculators used the marks to buy back even more dollars, thus earning a profit.

As Figure 22.3 shows, the intersection of the R_0 and R_f curves at point *A* in early 1971 yielded an exchange rate (from Germany's perspective in \$/DM) that was higher than the fixed rate of \$0.27/DM1. To defend the exchange rate, the Bundesbank had to sell marks. The resulting increase in the money supply lowered short-term interest rates in Germany, shifting the *R* curve from R_0 to R_1 and momentarily restoring the established exchange rate $\overline{EX}$ of DM1 = \$0.27 at point *B*. Because foreign-exchange market participants expected the Bundesbank to revalue the mark to avoid inflationary pressures, they also expected the mark to appreciate. These expectations decreased the expected rate of return on non-German assets relative to German assets, shifting the R_f curve to the left from R_{f0} to R_{f1}. This shift left the mark even more undervalued, and the Bundesbank had

FIGURE 22.3 **Speculative Attack on the Bretton Woods System: The Deutsche Mark, 1971**

1. At *A*, the mark is undervalued at the official exchange rate, $\overline{EX}$. The Bundesbank sells marks to buy dollars, decreasing short-term interest rates from i_0 to i_1. The domestic expected return shifts from R_0 to R_1, and the exchange rate returns to the fixed rate $\overline{EX}$ of DM1 = \$0.27 at *B*.

2. Market participants expect the Bundesbank to resist the money supply increases required to reduce the value of the mark. The expected appreciation shifts the R_f curve from R_{f0} to R_{f1}. A significant increase in the German money supply (to decrease *i*) would be required to restore an equilibrium with an exchange rate of $\overline{EX}$ at *C*. The Bundes-bank revalued the mark.

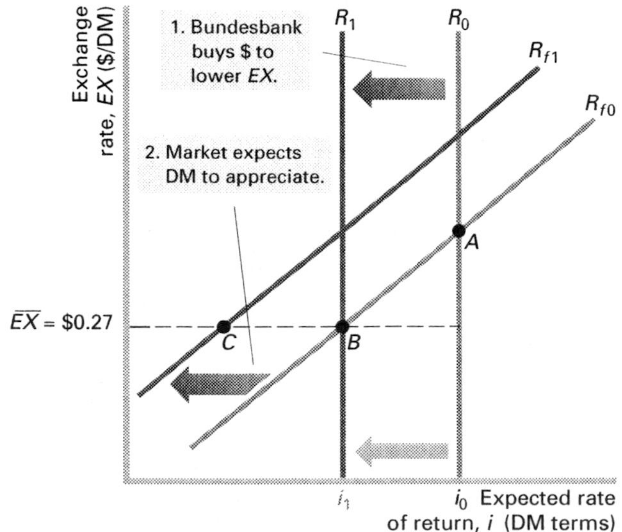

to increase its foreign-exchange intervention to maintain the fixed exchange rate. To defend the exchange rate $\overline{EX}$, the Bundesbank would have had to decrease short-term interest rates by an amount sufficient to maintain $\overline{EX}$ at point C. Having purchased more than 1 billion U.S. dollars early on May 5, 1971 (expanding its monetary base by the same amount), the Bundesbank halted its intervention later that day. The mark, along with the currencies that were tied to it, began to float against the dollar.

United States abandons Bretton Woods. One problem with the Bretton Woods system was that, even though individual currencies could be devalued or revalued against the dollar, changing the *dollar's* value required a coordinated realignment of all other currencies. This requirement was difficult to achieve in practice. As U.S. inflation increased and balance-of-payments deficits mounted in the late 1960s, foreign central banks acquired large amounts of dollar-denominated assets. Recall that the Bretton Woods system was held together by the U.S. promise to exchange foreign central banks' dollars for gold at $35 per ounce. By 1971, however, the dollar assets that were owned by foreign central banks totaled more than three times the official U.S. gold holdings at the $35 per ounce of gold rate. Moreover, U.S. tax policies to encourage exports and discourage imports to reduce its balance-of-payments deficit hadn't worked, and the Fed was unwilling to pursue a contractionary monetary policy. Nor would IMF intervention have worked; the IMF could not force countries such as Germany to pursue expansionary policies, and the United States, as the linchpin of the Bretton Woods system, could ignore the IMF.

On August 15, 1971, the Nixon administration attempted to force revaluations of other currencies against the dollar. The United States suspended the convertibility of dollars into gold and imposed supplementary tariffs on imports that would be reduced only if a country revalued its exchange rate. This process of revaluations against the dollar was completed at the Smithsonian Conference in December 1971. Following the revised agreement, the Fed resumed control of its own domestic monetary policy rather than being guided by pressures under the Bretton Woods system.

The exchange rate conditions that were agreed to at the Smithsonian Conference were not stable in the face of world events. The oil price shocks of 1973 and 1974 had uneven effects on economies. For example, the inflationary effect of these price increases was greater for Japan than for the United States, creating market pressures for depreciation of the yen. Such pressures spread unevenly to other countries because of the global recession of 1974–1975. In practice, many currencies began to float, although central banks intervened to prevent large fluctuations in exchange rates. At its January 1976 conference in Jamaica, the IMF formally agreed to allow currencies to float. At that conference, IMF members also agreed to eliminate gold's official role in the international monetary system.

Even before formal abandonment of the Bretton Woods system, the IMF had begun issuing (in 1970) a paper substitute for gold. The IMF creates these international reserves, known as **Special Drawing Rights (SDRs)**, in its role as lender of last resort. The price of gold is now determined by the forces of demand and supply in the market.

To summarize, the Bretton Woods system was a fixed exchange rate system with a lender of last resort to smooth out short-term economic adjustments in response to balance-of-payments deficits. The lack of commitment of the United States to price stability led to strong market pressures on fixed exchange rates, ultimately causing the market to collapse. Table 22.1 compares the classical gold standard and the Bretton Woods system for fixing exchange rates.

TABLE 22.1 **Comparison of Exchange Rate Regimes**

	Classical Gold Standard	Bretton Woods System
Promise anchoring the system	Currencies convertible into gold at fixed rates.	Currencies convertible into U.S. dollars at fixed rates; dollars convertible into gold at fixed rate.
Exchange rate adjustments	Not permitted.	Devaluation or revaluation permitted in response to fundamental disequilibrium.
Adjustment of economies	Money supply adjustments create inflation or deflation until the fixed exchange rate is restored.	IMF lending could smooth adjustment to short-term overvaluation of exchange rates.
Principal problems	Balance-of-payments deficits lead to deflation and recessions, with no gradual adjustment for short-term problems. Countries with balance-of-payments deficits have an incentive to abandon the promise of convertibility.	Difficult to devalue the U.S. dollar in response to U.S. balance-of-payments deficits.

Central Bank Intervention After Bretton Woods

Since the demise of the Bretton Woods system, the United States officially has followed a **flexible exchange rate system** in which the foreign-exchange value of the dollar is determined in currency markets. Moreover, since 1976, many countries' exchange rates have floated, being determined by demand and supply. However, the Fed and central banks abroad haven't surrendered their right to intervene in the foreign-exchange market to encourage appreciation or depreciation of the domestic currency. That is, the present international financial system can be described as a **managed float regime**, in which central banks do intervene to affect foreign exchange values from time to time. Nonetheless, international efforts to maintain exchange rates continue to affect domestic monetary policy.

Policy trade-offs. Central banks generally lose some control over the domestic money supply when they intervene in the foreign-exchange market. To raise the exchange rate (if nothing else changes), a central bank must sell international reserves and buy the domestic currency, thereby reducing the domestic monetary base and money supply. To lower the exchange rate (if nothing else changes), a central bank must buy international reserves and sell the domestic currency, thereby increasing the domestic monetary base and money supply. Hence a central bank often must decide between actions to achieve its goal for the domestic money supply and actions to achieve its goal for the exchange rate.

The case of the U.S. dollar. Because of the traditional role of the dollar as an international reserve currency, U.S. monetary policy hasn't been severely hampered by foreign-exchange market transactions. After the Bretton Woods system collapsed, the dollar retained its role as a reserve currency in the international monetary and financial system. However, during the 1980s, the Japanese yen and the German mark (as well as SDRs) became more important as additional reserve currencies. By 2006, the dollar still accounted for about 66% of international reserves. Most economists believe that the U.S. dollar isn't likely to lose its position as the dominant reserve currency in the next decade, though the euro is growing in importance (with about 25% of international reserves in 2006).

Many industrial economies have high standards of living without the privilege of their currency being the reserve currency. Nonetheless, because the dollar was less important as a reserve currency in 2006 than it was in 1956 or even 1986, many analysts believe that the United States has something to lose if the dollar is toppled from its reserve currency pedestal.

Why? First, U.S. households and businesses might lose the advantage of being able to trade and borrow around the world in U.S. currency. This advantage translates into lower transactions costs and reduced exposure to exchange rate risk. Second, foreigners' willingness to hold U.S. dollar bills confers a windfall on U.S. citizens because foreigners are essentially providing an interest-free loan. Also, the dollar's reserve currency status makes foreign investors more willing to hold U.S. government bonds, lowering the government's borrowing costs. Finally, New York's leading international role as a financial capital might be jeopardized if the dollar ceased to be the reserve currency.

During the 1980s, 1990s, and 2000s, some business leaders and policymakers pressured the Fed to abandon domestic monetary policy goals and either decrease or increase the value of the exchange rate. The soaring exchange rate in the early 1980s significantly hurt U.S. exports and raised criticism of the Fed for not pursuing a more expansionary monetary policy to cause the dollar to depreciate. The Fed responded by increasing money supply growth and agreed to intervene to reduce the dollar's value after the Plaza Accord in September 1985. By February 1987, the dollar had fallen significantly from its 1985 high, and the United States and other industrialized countries met in Paris to consider interventions to halt the dollar's slide. In April and May 1991, the Fed intervened to halt the dollar's appreciation in response to political tensions in Eastern Europe and strains among the republics of the former Soviet Union. On 18 occasions between April 1993 and August 1995, the Fed sold Japanese yen and bought dollars in an attempt to halt the dollar's plunge against the yen; in June 1998, the Fed intervened again, this time to support the dollar's value against the yen. In September 2000, the Fed joined other central banks in an attempt to raise the foreign-exchange value of the euro. In September 2003 (and on several occasions thereafter), some analysts urged G7 finance ministers to push for a new Plaza Accord to tackle exchange rates of Asian currencies against the U.S. dollar.

Fixed Exchange Rates in Europe

One benefit of fixed exchange rates is that they reduce the costs of uncertainty about exchange rates in international commercial and financial transactions. Because of the large volume of commercial and financial trading among European countries, the governments of many European nations have sought to reduce costs of exchange rate fluctuations. In addition, exchange rate targets can anchor inflation by connecting the inflation rate for traded goods to that in the anchor country. Indeed, in some cases, fixed exchange rates have also been used to constrain inflationary monetary policy.

The exchange rate mechanism and European monetary union. European Economic Community member countries formed the **European Monetary System** in 1979. Eight European countries also agreed at that time to participate in an **exchange rate mechanism (ERM)** to limit fluctuations in the value of their currencies against each other. Specifically, the member countries promised to maintain the values of their currencies within a fixed range set in terms of the *ecu*, the composite European currency unit. They agreed to maintain exchange rates within these limits while allowing these rates to fluctuate jointly against the U.S. dollar and other currencies. The anchor currency of the ERM was the German mark. Both France and the United Kingdom reduced their inflation rates by tying their currencies to the German mark (though, as described on pages 527–528, the United Kingdom was forced to withdraw from the ERM in 1992).

As part of the 1992 single European market initiative, European Community countries drafted plans for the **European Monetary Union,** in which exchange rates would be fixed by using a common currency. Although these plans place severe restrictions on domestic monetary policy for the participants, a monetary union would have important economic benefits for member countries. With a single currency, for example, transactions costs of currency conversion and bearing or hedging exchange rate risks would be eliminated. In addition, the removal of high transactions costs in cross-border trades would increase production efficiency by offering the advantages of economies of scale.

Three conditions are necessary to ensure that monetary union will work in Europe, however. First, there must be either a single currency within the union or multiple currencies with immutable (absolutely unchanging) fixed exchange rates (as is the case for the euro). Second, there must be a single exchange rate (and hence a single exchange rate policy) between the union's currency and other currencies. Third, central banks of member nations must surrender domestic autonomy in conducting open market operations, setting reserve requirements, making discount loans, enforcing capital controls, and intervening in foreign-exchange markets.

How successful is the European monetary union in its objectives? Ongoing success requires overcoming some problems. Within Europe, there is no centralized organization for stabilizing adjustments to balance-of-payments fluctuations by individual countries. As a result, member countries of a monetary union would face greater fluctuations in income and employment from regional shocks to demand, because they wouldn't be able to adjust their exchange rates. Some economists believe that political turmoil over monetary union in Europe arises from controversy about the costs of being unable to conduct independent monetary policy under a fixed exchange rate regime.

European monetary union in practice. In 1989, a report issued by the EC recommended a common central bank, the **European Central Bank (ECB),** to conduct monetary policy and, eventually, to control a single currency. The European Monetary Institute (EMI), set up in Frankfurt on January 1, 1994, was the forerunner of the ECB. In anticipation of monetary union, the EMI coordinated the monetary policies of member countries and monitored the functioning of the ERM. The ECB, which formally commenced operation in January 1999, is structured along the lines of the Federal Reserve System in the United States, with an Executive Board (similar to the Board of Governors) appointed by the European Council and governors from the individual countries in the union (comparable to Federal Reserve Bank presidents). Like the Fed, the ECB is independent of member governments; Executive Board members are to be appointed for nonrenewable eight-year terms to increase their political independence. The ECB's charter states that the ECB's main objective is price stability.

Some analysts believe that the European Central Bank is less politically independent in practice. Member countries occasionally argue the merits of expansionary or contractionary monetary policies. A dominant country—such as Germany—may well prevail in a debate over monetary policy, and some members of the union will be forced

OTHER TIMES, OTHER PLACES ...

Speculative Attack: 1990s Style

In 1991, the German government's budget deficit grew as it financed the unification of East and West Germany. To reduce inflationary pressures from the vast public expenditures that were required, the Bundesbank raised short-term interest rates. As German interest rates rose above those of England, Italy, France, and other European countries, speculators questioned whether those countries would be willing to raise their interest rates or instead would devalue their currencies against the mark. (Sweden, for example, briefly raised short-term interest rates to 500% to deter a speculative attack.)

England was the first test case. As shown in the figure, from point *A*, the Bank of England sold its foreign-exchange reserves of marks to buy large quantities of pounds to support its exchange rate against the mark under the ERM. The purchase shrank the money supply and shifted short-term interest rates from i_0 to i_1. The British domestic expected return shifted from R_0 to R_1, and the exchange rate returned to $\overline{EX}$ at point *B*. In this unstable situation, speculators used pounds to buy marks from the Bank of England, believing that the pound's imminent devaluation would enable them to use the marks to buy back more pounds. The R_f curve shifted from R_{f0} to R_{f1}.

To maintain the fixed exchange rate would require a significant increase in the British exchange rate to restore equilibrium at *C*. Because England was suffering a recession, few analysts believed that it would be willing to tolerate high short-term interest rates to deflect a devaluation of the currency. They were right; after a week, the British government withdrew the pound from the ERM. After the British devaluation, Italy withdrew the lira and Spain devalued the peseta. As the graph shows, this episode is reminiscent of the British devaluation of the pound against the dollar in 1967. However, not all currencies were devalued.

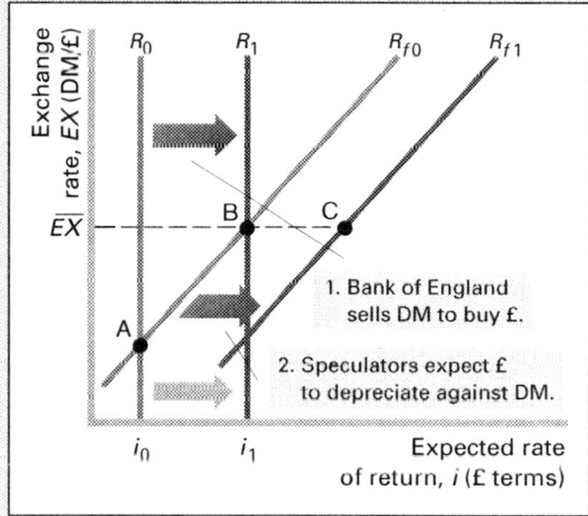

to adopt policies that are inconsistent with their domestic goals. And there are differing views about domestic discretion in lender-of-last-resort roles in dealing with crises in domestic financial markets or institutions.

At Maastricht, the Netherlands, in December 1991, member countries agreed on a gradual approach to monetary union, with a goal of convergent monetary policies by the mid-1990s and completion of monetary union in Europe by January 1, 1999. To have a single currency and monetary policy required more convergence of domestic inflation rates and budget deficits than existed in the mid-1990s. By the time monetary union began in 1999, 11 countries met the conditions for participation (with respect to inflation rates, interest rates, and budget deficits). The United Kingdom declined to participate.

By the late 1990s, some economists suggested that the foreign-exchange market might undermine fixed exchange rates in a speculative attack. The foreign-exchange market handles very large volumes of dollar, yen, euro, and other currency transactions each day, as hedgers transfer risks to speculators betting on the direction of currency markets. Events of September 1992 showed that a market of this size can overwhelm

CASE STUDY

Financial Collapse in Mexico

Less than three weeks after the inauguration of President Ernesto Zedillo in 1994, Mexico abandoned its acclaimed seven-year official connection between the peso and the dollar. In January 1995, the Clinton administration began putting together a financial rescue package of about $40 billion, which was subsequently implemented with a U.S. contribution of about $20 billion. What went wrong?

Though the institutional setting and history are different, the Mexican crisis has parallels to speculative attacks on European countries. In those speculative attacks, currency market participants perceived the lack of a credible commitment to an exchange rate target and forced a realignment of the exchange rate. In Mexico, the lack of a credible commitment figured prominently as well.

Mexico began pegging the peso to the dollar in December 1987; after January 1989, the peso was allowed to depreciate against the dollar, though at a very small rate, given Mexican inflation rates during the 1980s. In 1991, the Mexican government introduced a band within which the exchange rate could fluctuate. These steps were part of an effort by Mexico to demonstrate its commitment to low inflation. Accompanying these monetary policy changes were other economic reforms, including privatization of many state-owned firms, deregulation of capital markets, and a cut in public sector borrowing.

During 1994, financial markets began to doubt Mexico's resolve to defend the peso-dollar exchange rate. After the ruling party's presidential candidate, Luis Donaldo Colosio, was assassinated in March 1994, interest rates on *cetes* (one-year peso-dominated liabilities) rose relative to those on *tesobonos* (the government's three-month dollar-linked bond). This widening differential signaled expectations of a possible devaluation. Feeding this concern was inflationary pressure from a more expansionary Mexican monetary policy during 1994. Indeed, the real appreciation of the peso during 1994 outstripped increases that were plausibly based on fundamentals (such as deregulation and the passage of the North American Free Trade Agreement). With the overvalued peso, Mexico's current account deficit rose to nearly 8% of GDP in 1994, a level of foreign borrowing that was almost impossible to explain.

Investors' fears drained the central bank's foreign-exchange reserves, particularly after Zedillo's inauguration on December 1, 1994. In response to the ensuing speculative attack on the peso, the Mexican government devalued the peso by 15% against the dollar on December 20. Speculative attacks continued, and the sharp drop in the peso's value in currency markets led the government to retreat to a floating rate. A domestic financial crisis followed.

Before the peso's collapse, the Mexican central bank faced a dilemma. The real appreciation of the peso and high nominal interest rates weakened Mexico's economic performance. The adverse consequences for economic performance could be remedied by devaluation, but a devaluation would likely signal a lack of commitment to a low rate of inflation. If Mexican monetary policy had been credibly anti-inflationary, the exchange rate collapse and financial crisis might have been avoided. Financial markets' expectation that short-run domestic concerns would carry the day led to the speculative attacks, just as it did in the European attacks.

---

the foreign-exchange market interventions of central banks and finance ministers, even when governments act in concert. During that month, speculators launched attacks on several currencies as monetary unification was being debated in Europe. Following these speculative attacks, the United Kingdom and Italy withdrew from the ERM.

In the aftermath of the 1992 speculative attacks, the French ratified the Maastricht Treaty in a close vote. The treaty had been rejected by popular vote in Denmark earlier in the year, though the Danes subsequently ratified the treaty in May 1993. Though treaty ratification is now complete, a speculative attack on the French franc in July 1993 and changes in the ERM raised doubts about the viability of monetary union. Nonetheless, even in the aftermath of the Asian financial crisis, the European Monetary Union made its debut in 1999, and has weathered several years.

CASE STUDY

Financial Collapse in Asia

The dizzying pace of currency devaluations and debt defaults that spread from Thailand through Asia to Russia and the emerging economies in Latin America in 1997 and 1998 left everyone from currency speculators to home buyers wondering what went wrong. When Thailand devalued the *baht* in July 1997, a small stone set off an avalanche of devaluations and shrinking output in Thailand, Indonesia, South Korea, and Malaysia—with the shock waves being felt in Japan and China. Russia's debt default in 1998 triggered another round of capital flight from emerging economies and contributed to the spectacular collapse of Long-Term Capital Management, a large U.S. hedge fund. Malaysia responded to the crisis by blaming currency speculators and imposing capital controls, leading many economists to fear a downward spiral of capital controls and trade restrictions in emerging economies.

What went wrong? Prior to the Asian financial crisis, private short-term capital flows swelled the coffers of Asian countries, stimulating substantial domestic borrowing (often in foreign-currency-denominated debt). Indeed, the swing in net private capital flows to Thailand, South Korea, Malaysia, Indonesia, and the Philippines between 1996 and 1998 was about 11% of pre-crisis GDP. In one view, subsequent shifts in market expectations and confidence were the main cause of the initial crisis—a crisis made worse by the harsh policy response of the IMF and the international financial community.

According to another view, the Asian economies entered 1997 with weak economic and financial fundamentals. In these economies, weak banks with lax supervision and poor risk management provided a recipe for moral hazard—excessive risk taking and lending to unprofitable investment projects. The international dimension of the moral hazard problem required moral hazard by international banks, which prior to the crisis loaned large sums to the region's domestic financial intermediaries. (The debt accumulated in this way consisted mainly of foreign-currency-denominated liabilities.) Weaknesses in the undercapitalized financial system led to a buildup of nonperforming loans, a problem exacerbated by the rapid pace of current account liberalization and financial market deregulation in the region, which increased the supply of funds from abroad.

Why did international banks participate? In this view, international lenders assumed that the short-term interbank cross-border loans would be guaranteed by explicit government intervention to bail out debtors or by an indirect bailout by the IMF. Several leading economists, including Paul Krugman of Princeton University, argued that anticipation of a future bailout gave international investors a strong incentive to take on excessive risk in lending to Asian economies.

Which explanation is correct? In all likelihood, both sets of factors played a role. Weak fundamentals in the economies and financial systems of Asia have spawned efforts at reform in countries ranging from Thailand to Japan. While most economists argue against policies to discriminate capital flows, criticisms of the IMF's role have been harsh. In particular, many economists encourage the IMF to conform its international lending to central banking principles—by being a lender of last resort and insisting on strong buffers for domestic banking systems to make a financial crisis less likely.

How Successful Are Fixed Exchange Rates Likely to Be in the Long Run?

Many countries have indicated a desire to stabilize or fix exchange rates. Going forward, how likely are fixed exchange rate arrangements to be successful in the long run? Available evidence does not indicate much hope for success for agreements among major economies.

Many small economies have successfully pegged their exchange rate against the dollar for at least a decade, though these economies generally rely on oil exports (such as Bahrain and the United Arab Emirates) or tourism (such as the Bahamas and Barbados). Other small economies historically pegged their currencies to nondollar currencies (such as Monaco against the French franc and Vatican City against the Italian lira).

CONSIDER THIS . . .

Back to the (Currency) Drawing Board

In some emerging markets, the perception that the central bank is not committed to an exchange rate target may lead the central bank to strengthen its commitment by adopting a *currency board*—that is, by completely backing the currency with reserves of a strong foreign currency (say, U.S. dollars). Under a currency board, the central bank signals its commitment to the exchange rate target by being willing to exchange domestic currency for the foreign currency.

Such a policy offers advantages in terms of both transparency and commitment. The central bank's hands are tied so that it cannot exercise discretion to produce an inflationary monetary policy. That loss of flexibility, however, implies that the central bank will be unable to act as a lender of last resort by creating money during a financial crisis. Concern over the health of the domestic economy can also lead citizens to convert their assets to foreign currencies, contracting the domestic money supply and leading to an economic downturn.

While currency boards have been established in several countries in recent years—Hong Kong (1983), Argentina (1991), Estonia (1992), Lithuania (1994), Bulgaria (1997), and Bosnia (1998)—the Argentine experience is perhaps most illustrative of the strengths and weaknesses. To reduce inflation from stratospheric levels, Argentina implemented a currency board, fixing the exchange rate of the Argentine peso to the U.S. dollar at a one-for-one ratio. Following the introduction of a currency board, annual inflation fell to less than 5% by late 1994, and economic growth was substantial over that period. The Mexican peso crisis led to speculation about the ill health of the Argentine banking system, leading to significant conversions to dollars. The resulting sharp decline in the Argentine money supply was associated with a decline in real GDP of 5% in 1995. Assistance from the IMF and the World Bank in 1995 was required for the currency board's survival. In March 2001, the Argentine government renewed its commitment to the currency board.

An additional fear with a currency board is the risk that participants might abandon it. Some economists argue that a still stronger solution of literally using the foreign currency as the domestic currency—*dollarization*—is the better way to go. Ecuador, for example, adopted dollarization in March 2000 to reduce the chance of a speculative attack. This more extreme version of a currency board suffers from the same drawback as a currency board, plus an additional cost. When a country gives up its currency, it loses *seignorage*, the revenue received because governments do not have to pay interest on currency (which they can invest in bonds). As a result, other taxes must be raised or public spending must be reduced.

Argentina's currency board began experiencing problems in 2001, as market participants questioned the ongoing credibility of the Argentine government's promise to convert pesos into dollars on a one-for-one basis. Because Argentina's budget deficits were large and growing, investors feared that the central bank might resort to inflation, which would ultimately lead to a devaluation of the peso against the dollar. As in Figure 22.2, the lack of credibility led to an increase in the expected return on dollar deposits and a rightward shift of the R_f schedule from R_{f0} to R_{f1}. The new equilibrium exchange rate (at the intersection of the R_0 and R_{f1} curves) was below the peso's pegged value. Eventually, Argentina realized that it lacked enough dollars to maintain the currency board, and the system collapsed. By January 2002, the collapsed currency board and a government debt default caused a banking panic as depositors rushed to convert to dollars. By 2006, Argentina had been recovering for a few years from this crisis.

Postwar evidence suggests that prospects for success among large economies may be slim, however. Among larger economies, historical problems with the stability of the European Monetary System cause some analysts to doubt the ability of European countries to maintain virtually fixed exchange rates for the foreseeable future. Even Hong Kong's commitment, with foreign-exchange reserves in excess of its monetary base, may be questioned. While Hong Kong defended itself during the Asian crisis in 1997 and 1998, some economists have speculated that China, which absorbed Hong Kong on July 1, 1997, might not want to continue to use badly needed foreign-exchange reserves to battle speculators. But it has steadfastly defended the currency in both Hong Kong and mainland China. Some economists in the late 1990s urged key emerging economies to adopt a *currency board*, backing their currency with foreign-exchange reserves to bolster domestic monetary credibility.

KEY TERMS AND CONCEPTS

- Balance-of-payments accounts
  - Capital inflow
  - Capital outflow
  - Current account
  - Current account balance
  - Financial account
  - Financial account balance
  - Official reserve assets
  - Statistical discrepancy
  - Trade balance
- European Central Bank (ECB)
- Exchange rate regime
  - Bretton Woods system
  - Devaluation
  - European Monetary System
  - European Monetary Union
  - Exchange rate mechanism (ERM)
  - Fixed exchange rate systems
  - Flexible exchange rate system
  - Gold standard
  - Managed float regime
  - Revaluation
- Foreign-exchange market intervention
  - Capital controls
  - Sterilized foreign-exchange intervention
  - Unsterilized foreign-exchange intervention
- International Monetary Fund (IMF)
- International reserves
- Special Drawing Rights (SDRs)
- Speculative attack
- World Bank

SUMMARY

1. A central bank's interventions in the foreign-exchange market affect its holdings of international reserves and the domestic monetary base. If nothing else changes, when a central bank buys foreign assets, its international reserves and monetary base increase by the amount of foreign assets acquired. When a central bank sells foreign assets, its international reserves and monetary base fall by the amount of foreign assets sold.
2. The depreciation or appreciation of a country's currency affects the domestic economy. A depreciating domestic currency raises the cost of foreign goods and may lead to inflation. Central banks hope to lessen these problems by buying their own countries' currencies. An appreciating currency may make domestic goods uncompetitive in world markets. Central banks attempt to counter this problem by selling their own countries' currencies in the foreign-exchange market.
3. The balance of payments is an accounting system for keeping track of flows of private and government funds between a country and other countries. The balance-of-payments accounts have two principal parts: the current account and the financial account. The official settlements balance in the financial account represents the net flows of international reserves that must move between countries to finance a balance-of-payments surplus or deficit.
4. Countries have entered into several international agreements to stabilize exchange rates. Before World War I, many countries agreed to convert their currencies into gold at fixed exchange rates. A second major exchange rate system, the Bretton Woods system, was established after World War II. Under the Bretton Woods system, the U.S. dollar was convertible into gold and other currencies were convertible into dollars at fixed exchange rates. Because devaluing the dollar was difficult, despite persistent U.S. balance-of-payments deficits, the Bretton Woods system collapsed in 1971. The present international financial system is best described as one in which exchange rates fluctuate with market forces but central banks intervene in the foreign-exchange market. In Europe, analysts are now observing how successful the fixed exchange rate system through European monetary union is in practice.

REVIEW QUESTIONS

1. If the Fed buys $3 billion worth of foreign assets with dollars, what happens to U.S. international reserves? What happens to the monetary base? Is this a *sterilized* or an *unsterilized* foreign-exchange intervention?
2. Suppose that the Fed sells $1 billion worth of foreign assets in exchange for dollars; at the same time, the Fed engages in a $1 billion open market purchase. What happens to the monetary base? Is this a *sterilized* or an *unsterilized* foreign-exchange intervention?

MOVING FROM THEORY TO PRACTICE . . .

THE ECONOMIST APRIL 29, 2006

Euro Blues

A single currency was the logical completion of the single market, it was said, and would encourage more integration. The end of exchange-rate risk would boost investment and bring economic cycles into line. The reduction in transaction costs would make economies more efficient, boosting growth.

Moreover, a single currency would, it was claimed, foster policy convergence. Because countries **a** could no longer devalue, they would be forced to undergo the hard grind of reform. Since reform would push all countries in a similar direction, the euro would produce convergence. True believers went further, arguing that currency union would, ultimately, bring about political union. Indeed, for them, that was the point. But even short of this, a single currency would still pull economies together. As a result, the perils of a one-size-fits-all monetary policy would not be so worrisome: eventually, one size would, indeed, fit all.

Seven years on, there has been convergence of a kind. The euro area's long-term interest rates are broadly the same: they have converged on Germany's. Some countries, such as Ireland and Spain, have played economic catch-up (convergence in income and wealth), though this may have little to do with the euro as such. Arguably, fiscal policy has converged too.

There has, however, been less convergence of economic performance . . . There are few signs that eco- **b** nomic cycles have become more closely aligned.

The euro, in short, has provided currency stability but has done little to promote growth, jobs or reform. That is a long way from branding the currency a complete failure. But it is clear that what matters most is the "real" side of the economy (growth, jobs, markets), not the nominal indicators of stability (inflation, budget deficits) that are used to decide both whether countries are ready to join, and how they are doing once they are in.

A key lesson is that flexible economies, such as Ireland's and Britain's, **c** thrive, whether in or out of the euro. Inflexible ones can claw back lost competitiveness even inside the euro—but this takes a long time, and can come at a high price because they must keep growth in unit labour costs below average for years.

ANALYZING THE NEWS . . .

Expansion of the European Monetary Union with the launch of the euro in 1999 brought with it expectations for rapid economic growth and prosperity across the eurozone. Many economists warned, however, that the monetary union had both costs and benefits. The costs included loss of country-specific monetary policy and limitations on fiscal policy. The benefits would come from potential gains from increased trade and lower costs of converting currencies, and the reduction of exchange rate risk. However, by the fall of 2006, the euro had a mixed record.

a An additional benefit of the euro, it was argued by many, would be a political convergence in Europe. Because the European countries would have one monetary policy, it was believed it would then be easier for them to agree on one fiscal policy—and, by extension, other political agreements. However, in the summer of 2005, voters in both France and the Netherlands rejected the European Constitution, which would have brought about political convergence to Europe. Many analysts believe the subpar economic performance of France and the Netherlands under the euro was a contributor to the rejection of the European Constitution.

b Many economists argued that the euro would bring one European business cycle since all countries in the eurozone would have the same monetary policy. However, there has been a wide disparity of economic performance among the eurozone economies. Since 1999, exports from Ireland have increased significantly, while exports from Italy have seen only small increases. Economic growth has been strong in Spain, but weak in Portugal. The two biggest economies in the eurozone, France and Germany, have grown slowly, while the major European economy outside of the eurozone, the United Kingdom, has experienced strong economic growth.

c The euro may have reduced exchange rate risk and reduced the costs of converting currencies across the eurozone, but it has done little to alter the underlying structural challenges that face the European economies. While stable exchange rates may be a desirable goal, they should not be seen as a cure-all for all of the economic problems a market may face.

For further thought . . .

How do conditions in the eurozone need to change in order for Great Britain to be enticed to join the euro? Explain.

Source: Excerpted from "Euro Blues: A Solid Currency, Maybe, but a Shame About the Economic Performance," *The Economist*, April 29, 2006, p. 58.

3. Using the exchange rate diagram, show how an unsterilized intervention by Japan can be used to reduce the value of the yen relative to the dollar. Also show how an unsterilized intervention by the United States can be used to reduce the value of the yen relative to the dollar.
4. Under what key assumption does a sterilized intervention have no effect on the exchange rate? If this assumption isn't met, what is the effect on the dollar when the Fed buys foreign assets with dollars in a sterilized intervention? What do the data suggest about this assumption?
5. What are the problems with allowing a currency to appreciate relative to other currencies? What are the problems with allowing it to depreciate?
6. What is the difference between flexible and fixed exchange rate systems?
7. What is the purpose of the U.S. balance-of-payments system?
8. The following appears in a column of business commentary in a newspaper: "In recent years the newly industrializing countries have experienced very large capital inflows as multinational corporations headquartered in Japan, Western Europe, and North America have begun relocating their manufacturing facilities to these countries. With the help of the cutting-edge technology embodied in these factories and the low wages paid to local workers, these newly industrializing countries have been able to run large current account surpluses (exporting more goods and services than they import)." An economist comments on this as follows: "This assertion can be true only if the rules of accounting and arithmetic have been repealed." Discuss.
9. If Japan has a trade surplus, which is larger: its exports or its imports?
10. Why don't countries have control of their money supplies under a gold standard?
11. Why did the United States abandon the Bretton Woods system in 1971?
12. What are the purposes of the IMF and the World Bank?
13. Under a fixed exchange rate system, why do governments often put off devaluation or revaluation? What do markets often do that forces them to devalue or revalue?
14. Why did Europe seek a monetary union in the early 1990s?
15. *Evaluate:* Because the U.S. dollar is the dominant reserve currency, the United States can experience large balance-of-payments deficits indefinitely.
16. *Evaluate:* If exchange rates are flexible, outcomes in the foreign-exchange market have no effect on domestic monetary policy.
17. Compare IMF assistance to halt a speculative attack on an overvalued currency in the Bretton Woods system to the Fed's lender-of-last-resort role for banks.

ANALYTICAL PROBLEMS

18. Suppose that new data show that the United Kingdom is about to head into a recession. Futures contracts on the pound indicate that it is expected to depreciate relative to the mark, yen, and dollar. What do you think financial markets expect the Bank of England to do in the future?
19. If you compared the sum of exports out of every country with the sum of imports into every country, what should be the world's current account balance?
20. If the U.S. current account surplus is \$105 billion and the statistical discrepancy is −\$25 billion, what is the financial account balance? Does this represent a capital outflow or inflow?
21. Under a gold standard, what happens to gold flows if a country runs persistent balance-of-payments deficits?
22. Suppose that a less developed country is running a large government budget deficit and that its central bank is not independent. What problems might this country face in pegging the value of its currency to the dollar?
23. During the fall of 1998 Brazil was attempting to peg the value of its currency against the dollar. In October an article in *The Wall Street Journal* stated: "Brazil will outline today a much-anticipated package of tax increases and budget cuts for 1999, President Fernando Henrique Cardoso said, in a move that should clear the way for the release of emergency funds from the International Monetary Fund." Why would the IMF care whether Brazil balances its budget? Why does Brazil need funds from the IMF?

24. In the spring of 1999 an article in *The Wall Street Journal* stated: "Romania's central bank vowed to intervene to defend the country's currency, the leu. . . . But traders said authorities will have to work quickly to maintain confidence in the currency. . . . With reserves at just $1.59 billion at the end of February, the central bank's arsenal for staving off further speculation is limited." Is it likely that the Romanian central bank was trying to defend an exchange rate that was greater than or less than the exchange rate that would have prevailed in the absence of intervention? Draw a diagram to illustrate your answer. Briefly explain what traders would have to gain by speculating against the leu and what the Romanian central bank's dollar reserves have to do with its ability to defend the Romanian currency.

25. Suppose that the United Kingdom is attempting to maintain its exchange rate with Japan. But you note that Japanese real interest rates are higher than U.K. real interest rates and that inflation is lower in Japan than in the United Kingdom. What is your prediction about the future change in the ¥/£ exchange rate? What actions might you take to try to profit from your knowledge? What would happen if many other people joined you, especially if the United Kingdom had few international reserve assets?

26. If the United States, Japan, and the United Kingdom agree to try to lower the value of the dollar relative to both the yen and the pound while raising the value of the yen relative to the pound, what type of unsterilized interventions should take place?

27. Suppose that the United States has a trade deficit of $45 billion but a current account balance of $20 billion. What is the balance of net services plus investment income plus unilateral transfers?

28. Suppose that a U.S. import company buys 10 Toyota autos from Japan at $20,000 each, and the Japanese company uses the money to buy a $200,000 U.S. Treasury bond at the Treasury auction. How are these two transactions recorded in the balance-of-payments accounts for the United States?

29. Suppose that a Japanese firm donates $1 million of art to a U.S. art center. How is this transaction recorded in the balance-of-payments accounts for the United States? What is the change in the current account balance?

30. Suppose that the U.S. government sells old warships worth $300 million to Japan, and Japan's government pays for them with its official holdings of dollar assets. How is this transaction recorded in the U.S. balance-of-payments accounts?

DATA QUESTIONS

31. Look up exchange rate data in the latest *Economic Report of the President*. In 2005, the Fed reduced money supply growth, increasing short-term interest rates. What happened to the value of the dollar compared to the euro? Compared to the Japanese yen? Compared to the currencies of other countries? Are these results consistent with our theory about what happens to the exchange rate with expansionary monetary policy?

32. During the second half of the 1990s, the U.S. dollar was considered to be strong relative to the other major currencies. Locate the graphs of the major monetary aggregates listed in the most recent issue of the Federal Reserve Bank of St. Louis's *Monetary Trends* (http://research.stlouisfed.org/publications/mt/). Do the general trends of these aggregates during this period of time correlate with a strong dollar? If not, then why can it be said that a strong dollar existed?

33. Locate the annual foreign exchange rate data presented in the most recent issue of the *Economic Report of the President* (found at http://www.gpoaccess.gov/eop/index.html). Throughout 2001, the Fed aggressively increased money supply growth. Is there evidence of this in the exchange rates given for the Canadian dollar, the euro, and the Japanese yen? Why or why not?

34. Compare recent current account balances with the real gross domestic product found in the most recent issue of *Survey of Current Business*, published by the Bureau of Economic Analysis (at http://www.bea.gov/bea/pubs.htm). What is the average value of the current account deficit as a share of real GDP for the most recent four quarters?

19 Alternative International Monetary Standards

TOPICS TO BE COVERED

The Gold Standard: 1880–1914
The Interwar Period: 1918–1939
The Gold Exchange Standard: 1944–1970
The Transition Years: 1971–1973
Floating Exchange Rates: Since 1973
The Choice of an Exchange Rate System
Optimum Currency Areas
The European Monetary System and the Euro
Target Zones
Currency Boards
International Reserve Currencies
Multiple Exchange Rates

KEY WORDS

Gold standard
Commodity money standard
Destabilizing speculation
Seigniorage

Like most areas of public policy, international monetary relations are subject to frequent proposals for change. The international monetary system is the arrangement existing among countries regarding exchange rates and money flows. Fixed exchange rates, floating exchange rates, commodity-backed currency—all have their advocates. Before considering the merits of alternative international monetary systems, we should understand the background of the international monetary system. Although an international monetary system has been in existence since monies have been traded, it is common for most modern discussions of international monetary history to start in the late nineteenth century. It was during this period that the **gold standard** began.

Gold standard
Currencies have fixed values in terms of gold.

THE GOLD STANDARD: 1880–1914

Although an exact date for the beginning of the gold standard cannot be pinpointed, we know that it started during the 1880–1890 period.* Under a gold standard, currencies are valued in terms of a gold equivalent known as the mint parity price (an ounce of gold was worth $20.67 in terms of the U.S. dollar over the gold standard period). Then, because each currency is defined in terms of its gold value, all currencies are linked together in a system of fixed exchange rates. For instance, if 1 unit of currency *A* is worth 0.10 ounce of gold, whereas 1 unit of currency *B* is worth 0.20 ounce of gold, then 1 unit of currency *B* is worth twice as much as *A*, and thus the exchange rate of 1 currency $B = 2$ currency *A* is established.

Maintaining a gold standard requires a commitment from participating countries to be willing to buy and sell gold to anyone at the fixed price. To maintain a price of $20.67 per ounce, the United States had to buy and sell gold at that price. If the government does not stand willing to buy and sell at the mint parity price, then the price will fluctuate with changes in the supply of and demand for money relative to gold. With fluctuating gold prices, currencies would not be linked together at fixed exchange rates.

Gold was used as a monetary standard because it is a homogeneous commodity worldwide (could you have a fish standard?) that is easily storable, portable, and divisible into standardized units, such as ounces. Since gold is costly to produce, it possesses another important attribute—governments cannot easily increase its supply. A gold standard is a **commodity money standard**. Money has a value that is fixed in terms of the commodity gold.

Commodity money standard
The value of money is fixed relative to a commodity.

*Some countries had backed their currency with gold or silver long before 1880. The practice became widespread around 1880. Interesting discussions of the gold standard are found in Robert Triffin, "The Myth and Realities of the So-Called Gold Standard," in *International Finance*, ed. R. N. Cooper (Baltimore: Penguin, 1969); Barry Eichengreen, *The Gold Standard in Theory and History* (London: Methuen, 1985); and Michael David Bordo, "The Classical Gold Standard: Lessons from the Past," in *The International Monetary System: Choices for the Future*, ed. Michael B. Connolly (New York: Praeger, 1982).

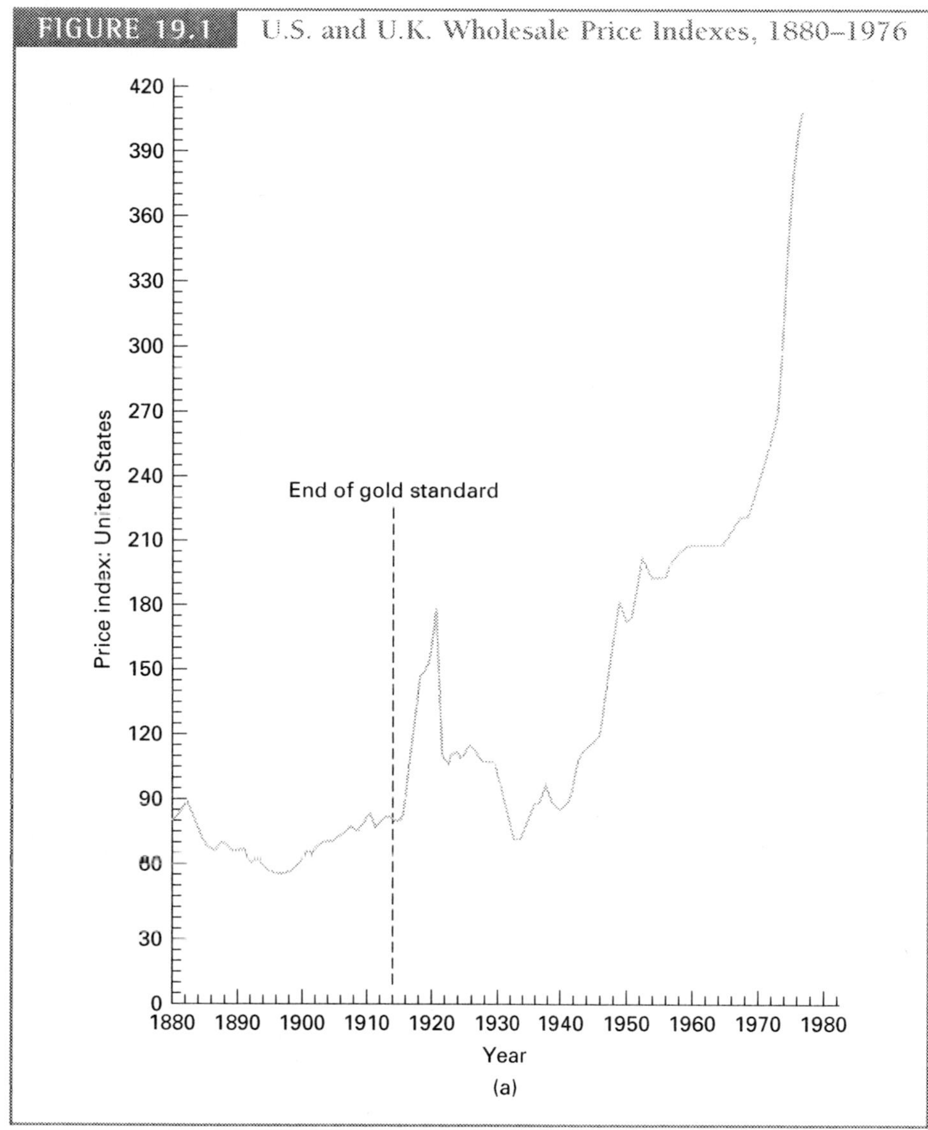

FIGURE 19.1 U.S. and U.K. Wholesale Price Indexes, 1880–1976

SOURCE: Roy W. Jastram, *The Golden Constant* (New York: Wiley & Sons, 1977).

One aspect of a money standard based on a commodity with a relatively fixed supply is long-run price stability. Since governments must maintain a fixed value of their money relative to gold, the supply of money is restricted by the supply of gold. Prices may still rise and fall with swings in gold output and economic growth, but the tendency is to return to a long-run stable level. Figure 19.1 illustrates graphically the relative stability of U.S. and U.K. prices over the gold standard period as compared with later years. Since currencies were convertible into gold, national money

FIGURE 19.1 U.S. and U.K. Wholesale Price Indexes, 1880–1976 (*Continued*)

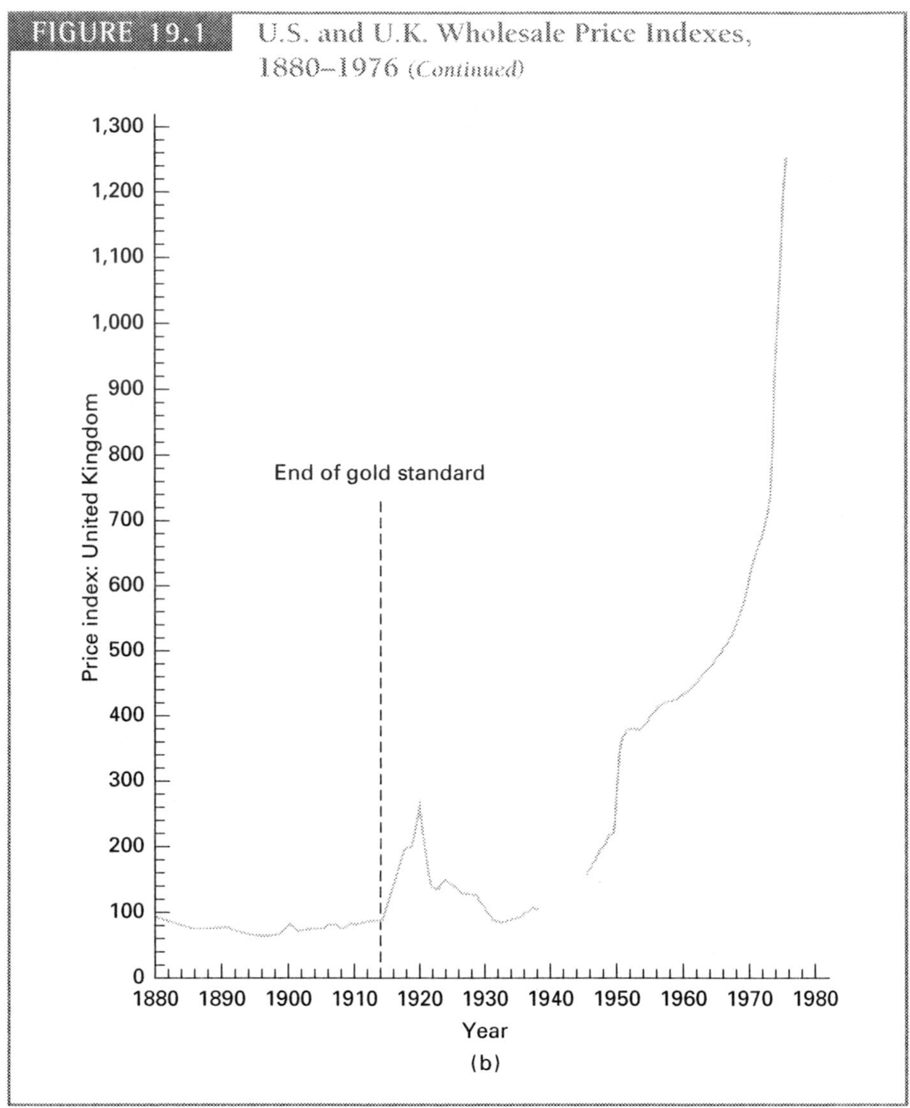

supplies were constrained by the growth of the stock of gold. As long as the gold stock grew at a steady rate, prices would also follow a steady path. New discoveries of gold would generate discontinuous jumps in the price level, but the period of the gold standard was marked by a fairly stable stock of gold.

People today often look back on the gold standard as a "golden era" of economic progress. It is common to hear arguments supporting a return to the gold standard. Such arguments usually cite the stable prices, economic growth, and development of world trade during this period as evidence of the benefits provided by such an orderly international monetary system. Others have suggested that the economic development and stability of the world economy in these years are not necessarily due to the existence of the gold standard, but rather a result of the lack of any significant real shocks, such as war.

Although people may disagree on the merits of returning to a gold standard, it seems fair to say that the development of world trade was encouraged by the systematic linking of national currencies and the price stability of the system.

Because during a gold standard gold is like a world money, we can easily understand how a balance-of-payments disequilibrium may be remedied. A country running a balance-of-payments deficit would find itself with net outflows of gold, thus reducing its money supply and, in turn, its prices. A surplus country would find gold flowing in and expanding its money supply, so that prices would rise. The fall in prices in the deficit country would lead to greater net exports (exports minus imports), and the rise in prices in the surplus country would reduce its net exports, so that balance-of-payments equilibrium would be restored.

In practice, actual flows of gold were not the only, or even necessarily the most important, means of settling international debts during this period. Since London was the financial center of the world and England the world's leading trader and source of financial capital, the pound also served as a world money. International trade was commonly priced in pounds, and trade that never passed through England was often paid for with pounds.

THE INTERWAR PERIOD: 1918–1939

World War I ended the gold standard. International financial relations are greatly strained by war, because merchants and bankers must be concerned about the probability of countries suspending international capital flows. At the beginning of the war, both the patriotic response of each nation's citizens and legal restrictions stopped private gold flows. Because wartime financing required the hostile nations to manage international reserves very carefully, private gold exports were considered unpatriotic. Central governments encouraged (and sometimes mandated) that private holders of gold and foreign exchange sell these holdings to the government. Governments financed wartime expenditures by printing money—the result was that the prewar parities would no longer hold.

Because much of Europe had experienced rapid inflation during the war and the period immediately afterward, it was not possible to restore the gold standard at the old exchange values. However, the United States had experienced little inflation and thus returned to a gold standard by June 1919 at the old parity. The war ended Britain's financial preeminence; the United States had risen to the status of the world's dominant banker country. In the immediate postwar years, the pound fluctuated freely against the dollar in line with purchasing power parity considerations.*

*A good review of the interwar years is given in Ragnar Nurkse, *International Currency Experience* (Geneva: League of Nations, 1944).

In 1925, England returned to a gold standard at the old prewar pound per gold exchange rate even though prices had risen since the prewar period. As John Maynard Keynes had correctly warned, the overvalued pound hurt U.K. exports and led to a deflation of British wages and prices. Due to the low price of gold, the British money supply contracted as citizens exchanged money for government gold. By 1931, the pound was declared inconvertible; the government would no longer exchange gold for pound currency, due to a run on British gold reserves (a large demand to convert pounds into gold), thus ending the brief U.K. return to a gold standard. However, once the pound was no longer convertible into gold, free-market attention centered on the U.S. dollar. The United States now faced a large demand to exchange gold for dollars. This "run" on U.S. gold at the end of 1931 led to a 15 percent drop in U.S. gold holdings. Although this did not lead to an immediate change in U.S. policy, by 1933 the United States raised the official price of gold to $35 an ounce to halt the gold outflow.

The depression years were characterized by international monetary warfare. In trying to stimulate domestic economies by increasing exports, country after country devalued its currency, so that the early to middle 1930s may be characterized as a period of competitive devaluations. Governments also resorted to foreign-exchange controls in the attempt to manipulate net exports in a manner that would increase GDP. Of course, with the onslaught of World War II, the hostile countries utilized foreign-exchange controls to aid the war-financing effort.

THE GOLD EXCHANGE STANDARD: 1944–1970

Memories of the economic warfare of the interwar years led to an international conference at Bretton Woods, New Hampshire, in 1944. At the close of World War II, there was a desire to reform the international monetary system to one based on mutual cooperation and freely convertible currencies. The result of this conference was an agreement to tie the values of all currencies together. The Bretton Woods agreement required that each country fix the value of its currency in terms of gold (this established the "par" value of each currency and was to ensure parity across currencies). The U.S. dollar was the key currency in the system, and $1 was defined as being equal in value to 1/35 ounce of gold. Since every currency had a defined gold value, all currencies were linked in a system of fixed exchange rates.

Nations belonging to the system were committed to maintaining the parity value of the currency within ±1 percent of parity. The various central banks were to achieve this goal by buying and selling their currencies (usually against the dollar) on the foreign-exchange market. When a country was experiencing difficulty maintaining its parity value due to balance-of-payments disequilibrium, it could turn to a new institution created at the Bretton Woods Conference: the *International Monetary Fund (IMF)*. The IMF was created to monitor the operation of the system and provide short-term loans to countries experiencing temporary balance-of-payments difficulties. Item 19.1 describes the operation of the IMF. The IMF's loans were (and still are)

ITEM 19.1 The International Monetary Fund

The IMF was created at the Bretton Woods Conference held July 1–22, 1944, in Bretton Woods, New Hampshire, and began operation on December 27, 1945, with headquarters in Washington, D.C. Country membership in the IMF has grown from 39 countries to 184 countries.

Originally, the IMF was mainly concerned with overseeing members' exchange rate practices to ensure the efficient operation of the system of fixed exchange rates adopted at the Bretton Woods Conference. In the 1950s the IMF began reviewing the balance-of-payments situation of members and macroeconomic policy decisions that might have an impact on the balance of payments. Countries having balance-of-payments problems can borrow from the IMF to finance their deficits. Such borrowing is supposed to be short-term in duration (repayment within three to five years) to ease the burden of temporary problems. More fundamental long-term problems are supposed to require exchange rate devaluations and macroeconomic adjustment policies in consultation with the IMF.

The IMF gains leverage over countries through its "conditionality" requirements. Countries asking for loans from the IMF must agree to conditions set by the IMF to receive their funds. The conditions address recommended exchange rates and domestic policies aimed at improving the countries' international payments imbalance. The IMF's conditions have sometimes become controversial political issues in borrowing countries, as nationalistic pride and domestic-policy goals may be hurt by the policies required by the IMF. For instance, a frequent condition imposed is reducing government subsidies of domestic consumer goods and allowing more free markets. It may be very difficult, politically, for a government to raise the price of bread or milk in a poor country, but such loan conditions are a recognition that the nation's problems arise from excessive government spending.

In 1969, the IMF acquired the power to issue special drawing rights (SDRs). This is a unit of account that functions as a money and may be used to settle debts between member countries. In the late 1960s, there had been a growing concern over the increased use of the U.S. dollar to finance world trade. Many felt that a new kind of international money was required to supplement the use of dollars. The SDR was the response offered by the IMF. However, the SDR has not become a major asset used in world payments as originally envisioned.

In summary, the activities of the IMF generally involve the following areas:

1. Overseeing exchange rate policies.
2. Monitoring international payments imbalances.
3. Providing temporary loans for balance-of-payments financing.

subject to IMF conditions requiring changes in domestic economic policy aimed at restoring balance-of-payments equilibrium. In the case of a fundamental disequilibrium, where the balance-of-payments problems were not of a temporary nature, a country was allowed to devalue its currency, resulting in a permanent change in the parity rate of exchange. Table 19.1 summarizes the history of exchange rate adjustments over the Bretton Woods period for the major industrialized countries.

We note, then, that the Bretton Woods system, although essentially a fixed or pegged exchange rate system, allowed for changes in exchange rates when economic

TABLE 19.1 Exchange Rates of the Major Industrialized Countries over the Period of the Bretton Woods Agreement

Country	Exchange Rates[1]
Canada	Floated until May 2, 1962, then pegged at Can$1.081 = $1. Floated again on June 1, 1970.
France	No official IMF parity value after 1948 (although the actual rate hovered around FF350 + $1) until December 29, 1958, when the rate fixed at FF493.7 = $1 (old francs). One year later, the rate was FF4.937 = $1 when the new franc (1 new franc was equal to 100 old francs) was created. Devaluation to FF5.554 = $1 on August 10, 1969.
Germany	Revalued on March 6, 1961, from DM4.20 = $1 to DM4.0 = $1. Revalued to DM3.66 = $1 on October 26, 1969.
Italy	Pegged at Lit625 = $1 from March 30, 1960, until August 1971.
Japan	Pegged at ¥360 = $1 until 1971.
Netherlands	Pegged at F13.80 = $1 until March 7, 1961, when revalued at F13.62 = $1.
United Kingdom	Devalued from $2.80 = £1 to $2.40 = £1 on November 11, 1967.

[1]Relative to the U.S. dollar.

circumstances warranted such changes. In actuality, the system is best described as an adjustable peg. The system may also be described as a gold exchange standard because the key currency, the dollar, was convertible into gold for official holders of dollars (e.g., central banks and treasuries).

The Bretton Woods system worked well through the 1950s and into the early part of the 1960s. In 1960 there was the first of several dollar crises. The United States had been running large balance-of-payments deficits in the late 1950s. This meant that dollars had been piling up in foreign central banks. Concern over large foreign holdings of dollars led some central bankers to exchange their dollar holdings for U.S. gold reserves, and U.S. gold holdings began to fall. The fall in U.S. gold reserves led to fears that the dollar would be devalued in terms of gold. This fear also led to a higher demand for gold in private gold markets. Central-bank cooperation managed to stabilize gold prices at the official rate, but still, the pressures fermented. Although the problem of chronic U.S. deficits and Japanese and European surpluses could have been remedied by revaluing the undervalued yen, mark, and franc, the surplus countries argued that it was the responsibility of the United States to restore balance-of-payments equilibrium.

The failure to realign currency values in the face of fundamental economic change spelled the beginning of the end for the gold exchange standard of the Bretton Woods agreement. By the late 1960s, the foreign dollar liabilities of the United States were much larger than the U.S. gold stock. The pressures of this "dollar glut" finally culminated in August 1971, when President Nixon declared the dollar to be inconvertible. This action, known as "closing the gold window," ended the Bretton Woods era of fixed exchange rates and convertible currencies.

THE TRANSITION YEARS: 1971–1973

In December 1971, an international monetary conference was held at the Smithsonian Institution in Washington, D.C., to realign the foreign-exchange values of the major currencies. The Smithsonian agreement provided for a change in the dollar per gold exchange value from \$35 to \$38 per ounce of gold. At the same time that the dollar was being devalued by about 8 percent, the surplus countries saw their currencies revalued upward. After the change in official currency values, the system was to operate with fixed exchange rates, whereby the central banks would buy and sell their currencies to maintain the exchange rate within ±2.25 percent of the stated parity.

Although the realignment of currency values provided by the Smithsonian agreement allowed a temporary respite from foreign-exchange crisis, the calm was short-lived. Speculative flows of capital began to put downward pressure on the pound and lira. In June 1972, the British government allowed the pound to float according to supply and demand conditions. Countries experiencing large inflows of speculative capital, such as Germany and Switzerland, applied legal controls to slow further movements of money into their countries.

Although the gold value of the dollar had been officially changed, the dollar was still inconvertible into gold, and thus the major significance of the dollar devaluation was with respect to the foreign-exchange value of the dollar, not with respect to official gold movements. In 1972 and early 1973, currency speculators began selling dollars in massive amounts. This pressure led to a further devaluation of the dollar in February 1973, when the U.S. government raised the official price of an ounce of gold from \$38.00 to \$42.22. Despite the devaluation, speculative capital flows persisted. Country after country announced that it would abandon fixed exchange rates. By March 1973, the major currencies were all floating.

FLOATING EXCHANGE RATES: SINCE 1973

Although we refer to the exchange rate system in existence since 1973 as a floating rate system, exchange rates have not been determined solely by the free-market forces of supply and demand. The system as operated is best described as a managed float, wherein central banks intervene at times to obtain a politically desirable exchange rate apart from that which would be determined by free-market supply and demand. Such managed floating does not apply to all countries and currencies; we observe several different exchange rate policies followed by countries today. Table 19.2 lists the exchange rate practices of the IMF member countries. Some countries, such as the United States, allow their currencies to float freely, whereas others, such as Aruba, choose to maintain a fixed value (or peg) relative to a single currency, such as the dollar or pound, and still others, such as Botswana, choose to peg to a composite or

TABLE 19.2 Exchange Rate Arrangements (as of April 30, 2004)

Crawling pegs (5)	Exchange rates within crawling bands (5)	Managed floating with no preannounced path for exchange rate (51)	Independently floating (35)
Bolivia	Belarus	Afghanistan	Albania
Costa Rica	Honduras	Algeria	Armenia
Nicaragua	Israel	Angola	Australia
Solomon Islands	Romania	Argentina	Brazil
Tunisia	Slovenia	Azerbaijan	Canada
		Bangladesh	Chile
		Burundi	Colombia
		Cambodia	Congo, Dem. Rep. of the
		Croatia	Dominican Rep.
		Czech. Rep.	Guatemala
		Egypt	Iceland
		Ethiopia	Japan
		Gambia, The	Korea
		Georgia	Liberia
		Ghana	Madagascar
		Guyana	Malawi
		Haiti	Mexico
		India	New Zealand
		Indonesia	Norway
		Iran, I.R. of	Papua New Guinea
		Iraq	Philippines
		Jamaica	Poland
		Kazakhstan	Sierra Leone
		Kenya	Somalia
		Kyrgyz Republic	South Africa
		Lao P.D.R.	Sri Lanka
		Mauritania	Sweden
		Mauritius	Switzerland
		Moldova	Tanzania
		Mongolia	Turkey
		Mozambique	Uganda
		Myanmar	United Kingdom
		Nigeria	United States
		Pakistan	Uruguay
		Paraguay	Yemen, Rep. of
		Peru	
		Russian Federation	
		Rwanda	
		São Tomé and Principe	
		Serbia and Montenegro	
		Singapore	
		Slovak Rep.	
		Sudan	
		Tajikistan	
		Thailand	
		Trinidad and Tobago	
		Ukraine	
		Uzbekistan	
		Vietnam	
		Yugoslavia	
		Zambia	

SOURCES: IMF staff reports.

Exchange arrangements with no separate legal tender (41)	Currency board arrangements (7)	Other conventional fixed peg arrangements (including de facto peg arrangements under managed floating) (42)	Exchange rates within horizontal bands (4)
Another currency	Bosnia-Herzegovina	*Against a single currency*	*Within a cooperative*
as legal tender	Brunei Darusalam	Aruba	*arrangement ERM II*
Ecuador	Bulgaria	Bahamas	Denmark
El Salvador	Djibouti	Bahrain	*Other band arrangements*
Kiribati	Estonia	Barbados	Cyprus
Marshall Islands	Hong Kong SAR	Belize	Hungary
Micronesia	Lithuania	Bhutan	Tonga
Palau		Cape Verde	
Panama		China	
San Marino		Comoros	
Timor-Leste		Eritrea	
CFA franc zone		Guinea	
WAEMU		Jordan	
Benin		Kuwait	
Burkina Faso		Lebanon	
Côte d'Ivoire		Lesotho	
Guinea-Bissau		Macedonia, FYR	
Mali		Malaysia	
Niger		Maldives	
Senegal		Namibia	
Togo		Nepal	
CAEMC		Netherlands Antilles	
Cameroon		Oman	
Central African Rep.		Qatar	
Chad		Saudi Arabia	
Congo, Rep. of		Suriname	
Equatorial Guinea		Swaziland	
Gabon		Syrian Arab Republic	
Euro Area		Turkmenistan	
Austria		Ukraine	
Belgium		United Arab Emirates	
Finland		Venezuela	
France		Zimbabwe	
Germany		*Against a composite*	
Greece		Botswana	
Ireland		China	
Italy		Fiji	
Luxembourg		Latvia	
Netherlands		Libya	
Portugal		Malta	
Spain		Morocco	
ECCU		Samoa	
Antigua and Barbuda		Seychelles	
Dominica		Vanuatu	
Grenada			
St. Kitts and Nevis			
St. Lucia			
St. Vincent and the Grenadines			

basket of currencies. There are several reasons for choosing a basket peg. For instance, if trade is not heavily concentrated with one country but is instead diversified across several countries, then it may make more sense to alter the currency value relative to a weighted average of foreign currencies rather than any single currency.

The various headings in Table 19.2 indicate quite a variety of exchange rate arrangements. We provide a brief description of each:

Crawling pegs The exchange rate is adjusted periodically in small amounts at a fixed, preannounced rate or in response to certain indicators (such as inflation differentials against major trading partners).

Crawling bands The exchange rate is maintained within certain fluctuation margins around a central rate that is periodically adjusted at a fixed, preannounced rate or in response to certain indicators.

Managed floating The monetary authority (usually the central bank) influences the exchange rate through active foreign exchange market intervention with no preannounced path for the exchange rate.

Independently floating The exchange rate is market determined, and any intervention is aimed at moderating fluctuations rather than determining the level of the exchange rate.

No separate legal tender Either another country's currency circulates as the legal tender, or the country belongs to a monetary union where the legal tender is shared by the members (like the euro).

Currency board A fixed exchange rate is established by a legislative commitment to exchange domestic currency for a specified foreign currency at a fixed exchange rate. New issues of domestic currency are typically backed in some fixed ratio (like one-to-one) by additional holdings of the key foreign currency.

Fixed peg The exchange rate is fixed against a major currency or some basket of currencies. Active intervention may be required to maintain the target pegged rate.

Horizontal bands The exchange rate fluctuates around a fixed central target rate. Such target zones allow for a moderate amount of exchange rate fluctuation while tying the currency to the target central rate.

THE CHOICE OF AN EXCHANGE RATE SYSTEM

A system of perfectly fixed or pegged exchange rates would work much like a gold standard. All countries would fix their exchange rate in terms of a single currency, say the dollar, and thereby would fix their exchange rate in terms of all other currencies. Under such an arrangement, countries would be required to buy or sell their currency in foreign-exchange markets to keep its price fixed.

Flexible or floating exchange rates occur when the exchange rate is determined by the market forces of supply and demand. As the demand (supply) for a currency increases relative to supply (demand), that currency will appreciate (depreciate). Central banks do not intervene to affect the exchange value of their money.

Economists do not agree on the advantages and disadvantages of a floating versus a pegged exchange rate system. For instance, some would argue that a major advantage of flexible rates is that each country can follow domestic macroeconomic policies independent of the policies of other countries. To maintain fixed exchange rates, countries have to share a common inflation experience, or else purchasing power parity (PPP) becomes increasingly violated. Common inflation rates across countries, in turn, require similar monetary policies. The failure of this condition to hold was often a source of problems under the post–World War II system of fixed exchange rates. For instance, in the late 1960s the U.S. government was following very expansionary policies relative to Japan as it sought to fight two wars: one on poverty, the other in Vietnam. Thus, the existing pegged rate could not be maintained. Yet with flexible rates, each country can choose a desired rate of inflation, and the exchange rate will adjust accordingly. If the United States chooses 8 percent inflation whereas Japan chooses 3 percent, there will be a steady depreciation of the dollar relative to the yen (absent any relative price movements). Given the different political environment and cultural heritage existing in each country, it is reasonable to expect different countries to follow different monetary policies. Floating exchange rates allow for an orderly adjustment to these differing inflation rates.

Still, there are those economists who argue that the ability of each country to choose an inflation rate is an undesirable aspect of floating exchange rates. These proponents of fixed rates indicate that fixed rates are useful in providing an international discipline on the inflationary policies of countries. Fixed rates provide an anchor for countries with inflationary tendencies. By maintaining a fixed rate of exchange to the dollar (or some other currency), each country's inflation rate would be "anchored" to the inflation rate in the United States and thus would follow the policy established for the dollar.

Destabilizing speculation
Speculators increase the variability of exchange rates.

Critics of flexible exchange rates have also argued that flexible exchange rates would be subject to **destabilizing speculation**. By *destabilizing speculation*, we mean that speculators in the foreign-exchange market will cause exchange rate fluctuations to be wider than they would be in the absence of such speculation. The counterargument is that logic suggests that if speculators expect a currency to depreciate, they will take positions in the foreign-exchange market that will cause the depreciation as a sort of self-fulfilling prophecy. But speculators should lose money when they guess wrong, so that only successful speculators will remain in the market, and the latter should serve a useful role by "evening out" swings in the exchange rate. For instance, if a speculator expects a currency to depreciate or decrease in value next month, he or she could sell the currency now, which results in a current depreciation. This will lead to a smaller future depreciation than would otherwise occur. Thus, the speculator spreads the exchange rate change more evenly through time and tends to even out big jumps in the exchange rate. If the speculator had bet on future dollar depreciation by selling the dollar now and holding francs, the speculator will lose if the dollar appreciates instead of depreciates. The francs will be converted back into fewer dollars than originally exchanged, so the speculator loses and will eventually be eliminated from the market if such mistakes are repeated.

Research has shown that there are systematic differences between countries choosing fixed exchange rates and those choosing floating rates.* One important characteristic is country size (measured in terms of economic activity or GDP). Large countries tend to be more independent and less willing to subjugate their own domestic-policy goals to maintain a fixed rate of exchange with foreign currencies. Because foreign trade tends to constitute a smaller fraction of GDP in larger countries, it is perhaps understandable that these countries are less attuned to foreign-exchange rate concerns than smaller countries are.

The openness of an economy is another important factor. By *openness*, we mean the degree to which the country depends on international trade. The greater the fraction of tradable (i.e., internationally tradable) goods in GDP, the more open the economy will be. A country with little or no international trade is referred to as a closed economy. As previously mentioned, openness is related to size. The more open an economy is, the greater will be the importance of tradable-goods prices in the behavior of the overall national price level, and therefore the greater will be the impact of exchange rate changes on the national price level. To minimize such foreign-related shocks to the domestic price level, the more open economy tends to follow a pegged exchange rate.

Remembering the PPP relation, we can understand why countries that choose to allow higher rates of inflation than their trading partners do will have difficulty maintaining fixed exchange rates with those countries. Since prices are rising faster in the high-inflation countries, their currency must depreciate to keep their goods prices comparable to those of other countries. These high-inflation countries will choose floating rates or a crawling-peg type of system wherein the exchange rate is adjusted at short intervals to compensate for the inflation differentials.

Countries that trade largely with a single foreign country tend to peg their exchange rate to the foreign country's currency. For instance, the United States accounts for the majority of Barbadian trade. By pegging its currency, the Barbadian dollar, to the U.S. dollar, Barbados imparts a degree of stability to the prices of its exports and imports that would otherwise be missing. Countries with diversified trading patterns will not find exchange rate pegging so desirable, because only trade with the country to which their currency is pegged would gain price stability, while trade with all other important trading partners would have prices fluctuating.

The evidence from previous studies indicates quite convincingly the systematic differences between peggers and floaters. These characteristics are summarized in Table 19.3. It must be realized that there are exceptions to these generalities because neither all peggers nor all floaters have the same characteristics. We can safely say that, in general, the larger a country is, the more likely it is to float its exchange rate, and the more closed an economy is, the more likely the country will float, and so on. The point is that economic phenomena, and not just political maneuvering, ultimately influence foreign-exchange rate practices.

---

*See Hali Edison and Michael Melvin, "The Determinants and Implications of the Choice of an Exchange Rate System," in *Monetary Policy for a Volatile Global Economy*, ed. W. Haraf and T. Willett (Washington, D.C.: American Enterprise Institute, 1990).

TABLE 19.3 Characteristics Associated with Countries Choosing to Peg or Float

Peggers	Floaters
Small size	Large size
Open economy	Closed economy
Harmonious inflation rate	Divergent inflation rate
Concentrated trade	Diversified trade

There is also concern about how the choice of an exchange rate system will affect the stability of an economy.* If the domestic-policy authorities seek to minimize unexpected fluctuations in the domestic price level, then they will choose an exchange rate system that best minimizes such fluctuations. For instance, the greater foreign tradable-goods price fluctuations are, the more likely it is that authorities will choose to float, since a floating exchange rate helps to insulate the domestic economy from foreign price disturbances.

The greater the domestic money-supply fluctuations are, the more likely it is that there will be a peg, since international money flows serve as a shock absorber that reduces the domestic price impact of domestic money-supply fluctuations. With a fixed exchange rate, an excess supply of domestic money will cause a capital outflow because some of this excess supply is eliminated via a balance-of-payments deficit. With floating rates, the excess supply of money is contained at home and reflected in a higher domestic price level and depreciating domestic currency. Once again, the empirical evidence supports the notion that real-world exchange rate practices are determined by such economic phenomena.

OPTIMUM CURRENCY AREAS

What is the *optimum currency area?* First, a currency area is an area where exchange rates are fixed within the area and floating exchange rates exist against currencies outside the area. The "optimum" currency area is the best grouping of countries to achieve some objective, such as ease of adjustment to real or nominal shocks. How should currency areas be chosen so that exchange rate practices best allow the pursuit of economic goals, such as full employment and price stability?

*See Harvey E. Lapan and Walter Enders, "Random Disturbances and the Choice of Exchange Regimes in an Intergenerational Model," *Journal of International Economics* (May 1980); Michael Melvin, "The Choice of an Exchange Rate System and Macroeconomic Stability," *Journal of Money, Credit, and Banking* (November 1985); and Andreas Savvides, "Real Exchange Rate Variability and the Choice of Exchange Rate Regime by Developing Countries," *Journal of International Money and Finance* (December 1990).

A popular theory suggests that the optimum currency area is the region characterized by relatively costless mobility of the factors of production (labor and capital).* As an illustration of this theory, suppose we have two countries, *A* and *B*, producing computers and cotton, respectively. Now, there is a change in tastes resulting in a shift of demand from computers to cotton. Country *A* will tend to run a trade deficit and have an excess supply of labor and capital because the demand for computers has fallen, whereas country *B* will tend to run a surplus and have an excess demand for labor and capital due to the increase in demand for its cotton. What are the possibilities for international adjustment to these changes?

1. Factors of production (labor and capital) could move from country *A* to country *B* and thereby establish new equilibrium wages and prices in each region.
2. Prices in *A* could fall relative to *B*, and the relative price change will eliminate the balance-of-trade disequilibrium if labor and capital cannot move between the countries. (We are ignoring the capital account now, in order to assume zero capital flows.)
3. The exchange rate could change and bring about the required change in relative prices if *A* and *B* have different currencies.

Now we can understand why the optimum currency area is characterized by mobile factors of production. If factors can freely and cheaply migrate from an area lacking jobs to an area where labor is in demand, then the factor mobility will restore equilibrium because the unemployment in the one area is removed by migration. Thus, fixed exchange rates within the area will be appropriate because relative price movements are not the only means for restoring equilibrium.

When factors are immobile, so that equilibrium is restored solely through relative price change, there is an advantage to flexible exchange rates. If the monetary authorities in each country tend to resist any price changes, then the easiest way to adjust is with flexible exchange rates because the adjustment can go largely through the exchange rate rather than through prices. Looking at the real world, we might suggest that North America and Western Europe appear to be likely currency areas given the geographic position of Canada, Mexico, and the United States as well as the geographic position of the Western European nations. Since exchange rates between the U.S. and Canadian dollars and the Mexican peso seem closely linked (certainly, the peso and the U.S. dollar had a long history of fixed exchange rates), we might expect these three countries to maintain pegged exchange rates with each

*This theory is developed in Robert A. Mundell, "A Theory of Optimum Currency Areas," *American Economic Review* (September 1961). Some additional papers on the topic include Paul De Grauwe, *Economics of Monetary Union,* 4th ed. (Oxford: Oxford University Press, 2000); Kevin Dowd and David Greenaway, "Currency Competition, Network Externalities and Switching Costs: Towards an Alternative View of Optimum Currency Areas," *Economic Journal* (September 1993); Masahiro Kawai, "Optimum Currency Areas," in *The New Palgrave: A Dictionary of Economics* (New York: Stockton Press, 1987); Paul R. Masson and Mark P. Taylor, *Policy Issues in the Operation of Currency Unions* (Cambridge: Cambridge University Press, 1993); Ronald I. McKinnon, "Optimum Currency Areas," *American Economic Review* (September 1963); George Tavlas, "The Theory of Monetary Integration," *Open Economies Review* (March 1994); and Edward Tower and Thomas Willett, *The Theory of Optimum Currency Areas and Exchange Rate Flexibility,* International Finance Section, No. 11 (Princeton University, 1976).

other and to float versus the rest of the world. Western Europeans have, in fact, explicitly adopted such a regional optimum-currency-area arrangement. The adoption of a single currency, the euro, by 12 countries is the ultimate commitment to a fixed exchange rate among the 12.

THE EUROPEAN MONETARY SYSTEM AND THE EURO

The optimum-currency-area literature suggests that in a regional setting like Western Europe a system of fixed exchange rates might be appropriate. While the establishment of the common euro currency may be viewed as a kind of permanently fixed exchange rate, prior to the euro there already had been a system in place to link currencies and limit exchange rate flexibility since the late 1970s. In March 1979, the European Monetary System (EMS) was established to maintain exchange rate stability in Western Europe. The EMS exchange rate mechanism (ERM) required that each nation maintain the value of its currency within 2.25 percent of a fixed value against the currencies of the other member countries (the Italian lira was allowed to fluctuate within a 6 percent band). The exchange rates were to be kept within these narrow bands by central-bank intervention. For instance, if the French franc threatened to fall below the lower bands of its value against the German mark, then the German and French central banks would buy francs to keep the currency within the ERM limits.

While such intervention worked to stabilize exchange rates, sometimes the realities of the market forced a realignment of the ERM values when it became clear that there were fundamental changes in the values of the currencies. For instance, Germany and the Netherlands typically had lower inflation than the other member countries, so realignments were generally aimed at depreciation of the other currencies against the German mark and the Dutch guilder.

The removal of capital controls restricting international financial transactions (including foreign-exchange transactions) played an important role in the breakdown of the system in 1992. Capital controls that helped keep national financial markets insulated from outside pressures made central-bank currency management easier. The removal of such controls, as required by the Single European Act of 1986, allowed for much greater capital mobility among the European nations. In addition, the pursuit of domestic-macroeconomic-policy goals at the expense of exchange rate management put additional pressures on the ERM. In September 1992, as some currencies, particularly the British pound and the Italian lira, neared the bottom of their ERM exchange rate limits, speculators began betting heavily on another realignment that would devalue these currencies. This heavy selling of the pound and lira resulted in the British government pulling the pound out of the ERM on September 16, 1992. A few hours after the British move, the Italian government pulled the lira out of the ERM. The currency crisis resulted in a widening of the ERM bands for exchange rate fluctuations to 15 percent in August 1993.

A major step toward a single European money occurred in December 1991, when the Maastricht Treaty, calling for a single European central bank and single money, was signed. The treaty spelled out the evolution that the EMS followed to approach monetary union. The specific steps taken were as follows:

1. The immediate removal of restrictions on European flows of capital and greater coordination of monetary and fiscal policy.
2. The establishment of a European Monetary Institute (EMI) in January 1994 to coordinate monetary policies of the individual central banks and make technical preparations for a single monetary policy.
3. The irrevocable fixing of exchange rates among all member countries, with a single (euro) currency and a single European Central Bank.

This last step did not occur until January 1999. The countries that moved to this last step of monetary union required their macroeconomic policy to converge to that of the other EMS countries. Convergence was defined as occurring when (1) the country's inflation rate did not exceed the average of the lowest three member country rates by more than 1.5 percentage points; (2) its interest rate on long-term government bonds did not exceed those of the three lowest-inflation members by more than 2 percentage points; and (3) the country's government budget deficit did not exceed 3 percent of GDP, and outstanding government debt did not exceed 60 percent of GDP.

The new European currency, the euro, made its debut on January 1, 1999. The symbol is €, and the ISO code is EUR. Euro notes and coins began to circulate on January 1, 2002. In the transition years of 1999–2001, people used the euro as a unit of account, denominating financial asset values and transactions in euro amounts. Bank accounts were available in euros and credit transactions were denominated in euros. However, actual cash transactions were not made with euros until euro cash started circulating in 2002.

Prior to the beginning of the euro, the value of each of the "legacy currencies" of the euro-area was fixed in terms of the euro. Table 19.4 gives the exchange rates at which each of the old currencies was fixed in terms of euros. For instance, 1 euro is equal to 40.3399 Belgian francs or 1.95583 German marks. Of course, the prior monies of each of the euro-area countries no longer are used, having been replaced by the euro.

One money requires one central bank, and the euro is no exception. The European Central Bank (ECB) began operations on June 1, 1998, in Frankfurt, Germany, and now conducts monetary policy for the euro-area countries. The national central banks such as the Bank of Italy or the German Bundesbank are still operating and perform many of the functions they had prior to the ECB like bank regulation and supervision and facilitating payments systems in each nation. In some sense they are like the regional banks of the Federal Reserve System in the United States. Monetary policy for the euro-area is conducted by the ECB in Frankfurt just as monetary policy for the United States is conducted by the Federal Reserve in Washington, D.C. Yet the national central banks of the euro-area play an important role in each of the respective countries. The entire network of national central banks and the ECB is called the *European System of Central Banks*. Monetary policy for the euro-area is determined by the *Governing Council* of the ECB. This council consists of the heads

TABLE 19.4 Exchange Rates of Old National Currencies Replaced by the Euro

Former Currency	1 Euro =
Belgian franc	BEF40.3399
German mark	DEM1.95583
Spanish peseta	ESP166.386
Finnish markka	FIM5.94753
French franc	FRF6.55957
Greek drachma	GRD340.750
Irish pound	IEP0.787564
Italian lira	ITL1936.27
Luxembourg franc	LUF40.3399
Netherlands guilder	NLG2.20371
Austrian schilling	ATS13.7603
Portuguese escudo	PTE200.482

of the national central banks of the euro-area countries plus the members of the ECB *Executive Board*. The board is made up of the ECB president and vice-president and four others chosen by the heads of the governments of the euro-area nations.

Currently, three member countries of the European Union were eligible to join the euro usage but have not adopted the euro and still maintain their own currencies and monetary policies. The three countries are Denmark, Sweden, and the United Kingdom. It remains to be seen when, and if, these countries become part of "euroland."*

TARGET ZONES

Exchange rate arrangements like the old EMS, where there was limited flexibility around some central fixed value, are sometimes called *target zones*. In this setting, the exchange rate is allowed to change with changes in the fundamental determinants of exchange rates like money supplies, incomes, and prices, but the amount of change allowed is limited by the width of the bands permitted by the target zone arrangement.

*There is a large literature related to the euro. A few useful references include Jay H. Levin, *A Guide to the Euro* (Boston: Houghton Mifflin, 2002); Philipp Hartmann, Michele Manna, and Andres Manzanares, "The Microstructure of the Euro Money Market," *Journal of International Money and Finance* (November 2001); Harald Hau, William P. Killeen, and Michael Moore, "The Euro as an International Currency: Explaining Puzzling First Evidence from the Foreign Exchange Markets," *Journal of International Money and Finance* (June 2002); Hans-Werner Sinn and Frank Westermann, "Why Has the Euro Been Falling?" *CESifo Working Paper No. 493* (May 2001); and Iftekhar Hasan and James Lothian, "The Euro Five Years On," *Journal of International Money and Finance* (November 2004).

FIGURE 19.2 An Exchange Rate Target Zone

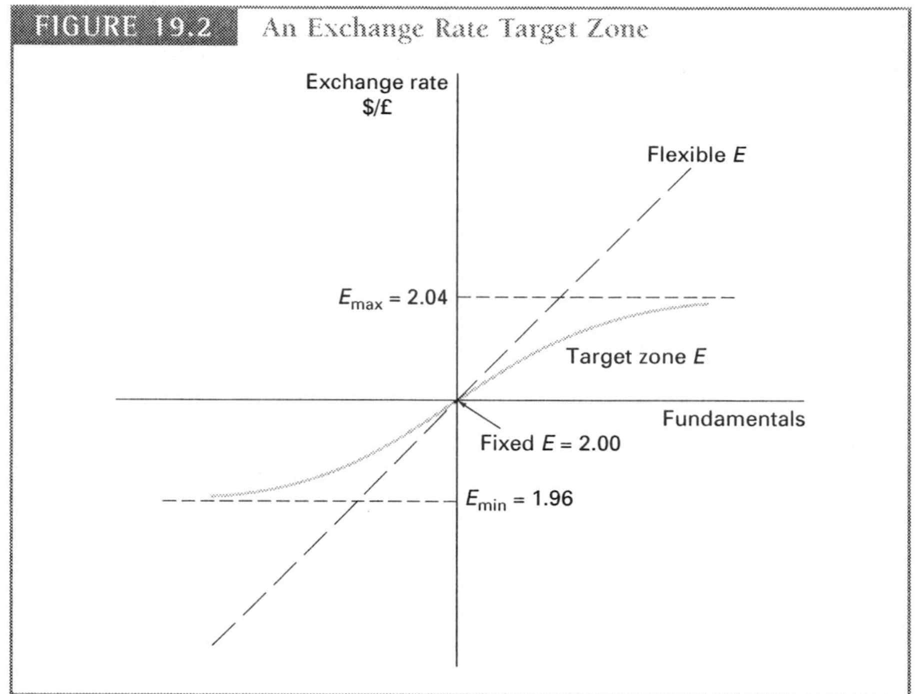

Figure 19.2 illustrates the essentials of a target zone system. For purposes of example, let's assume that the United States and the United Kingdom have agreed on a target zone for the dollar/pound exchange rate where the exchange rate will be kept between 2.04 and 1.96 dollars per pound. The vertical axis of Figure 19.2 measures the exchange rate in dollars per pound. The upper bound of the target zone is shown in the figure as E_{max} = 2.04. The lower bound is shown as E_{min} = 1.96. The horizontal axis measures the value of the "fundamentals" like the net effect of money supply, income, prices, and any other fundamental determinants of exchange rates.

If instead of a target zone there were a fixed exchange rate at $2 per pound, what would that look like in the figure? A fixed exchange rate would be represented by one point in the figure at the origin where $E = 2$. This means that, as other fundamentals change, the central banks change the money supply to offset the effects of the other fundamentals so that the exchange rate is left unchanged.

If instead of a target zone there were a flexible exchange rate system, what would that look like in the figure? A flexible exchange rate would be represented by the 45-degree line. This indicates that the exchange rate changes match changes in the fundamentals as the central banks do not attempt to offset the effects of the fundamentals. Also, note that a flexible exchange rate may rise or fall without bounds if pushed by the fundamentals.

With a target zone system, the central banks are committed to intervening so that the exchange rate rises no higher than $E = 2.04$ and falls no lower than $E = 1.96$.

If people believe that this zone will be enforced by the government authorities, then the exchange rate will lie along the S-shaped line in Figure 19.2.* Note that this line is flatter than the 45-degree line of the flexible exchange rate. This S-shape is due to the fact that the closer the exchange rate gets to the upper or lower limit, the greater the probability of intervention. For instance, suppose the exchange rate is rising and approaches the upper limit of 2.04. The probability of a central-bank intervention is increased so that people will expect a greater probability of the exchange rate dropping with the intervention rather than continuing to rise. As a result, the exchange rate line flattens to give the top of the S-shape. Continued increases in the fundamentals result in smaller and smaller dollar depreciation as the threat increases of central-bank intervention aimed at dollar appreciation. In this sense, a target zone backed by credible government policies helps to stabilize the exchange rate relative to a floating exchange rate.

CURRENCY BOARDS

The discussion of target zones mentioned the *credibility* of the government authorities as a factor in determining the effectiveness of the arrangement. However, it often appears that financial market participants believe that some governments are lacking the credibility required to create confidence in the system. In particular, developing countries with a long history of unstable exchange rates often find it difficult to convince the public that government policy will maintain stable exchange rates in the future. This lack of credibility on the part of a government can be overcome if some sort of constraint is placed on the discretionary policy-making ability of the authorities with control over monetary and exchange rate policy. One such form of constraint is a *currency board*. A currency board is a government institution that exchanges domestic currency for foreign currency at a fixed rate of exchange.

The typical demise of a fixed exchange rate system comes when the central bank runs out of foreign currency to exchange for domestic currency and ends up devaluing the domestic currency. Item 19.2 discusses how international reserve losses can result in *speculative attacks* on the central bank that force a devaluation. Currency boards achieve a credible fixed exchange rate by holding a stock of the foreign currency equal to 100 percent of the outstanding currency supply of the nation. As a result of such foreign currency holdings, people believe that the board will always

*There are technical details of target zone analysis that lie beyond the scope of this text but are discussed in the following sample of the large target zone literature: Paul Krugman, "Target Zones and Exchange Rate Dynamics," *Quarterly Journal of Economics* (August 1991); Lars E. O. Svensson, "An Interpretation of Recent Research on Exchange Rate Target Zones," *Journal of Economic Perspectives* (Fall 1992); Hans Lindberg and Paul Söderlind, "Testing the Basic Target Zone Model on Swedish Data, 1982–1990," *European Economic Review* (August 1994); Marcus Miller and Paul Weller, "Exchange Rate Bands with Price Inertia," *Economic Journal* (November 1991); and Matteo Iannizzotto and Mark P. Taylor, "The Target Zone Model, Non-linearity and Mean Reversion: Is the Honeymoon Really Over?" *Economic Journal* (March 1999).

ITEM 19.2 Speculative Attacks and the Mexican and Asian Financial Crises

The maintenance of fixed exchange rates or target zones of limited flexibility is dependent on government willingness to buy or sell domestic currency for foreign currency at the targeted rate of exchange. The ability to maintain the exchange rate requires the central bank to possess an adequate stock of international reserves in order to meet the demand by the public to sell domestic currency for foreign currency at the fixed exchange rate. If the public believes that the central bank's stock of international reserves has fallen to a point where the ability to meet the demand to exchange domestic currency for foreign currency at a fixed exchange rate is threatened, then a devaluation of the domestic currency is expected. This expectation often leads to a *speculative attack* on the central bank's remaining stock of international reserves. The attack takes the form of massive sales of domestic currency for foreign currency so that the loss of international reserves is hastened and the devaluation is forced by the reserve loss.

In December 1994, the Mexican government faced just such a speculative attack on its U.S. dollar reserves. The result was a peso devaluation followed by a float of the peso /dollar exchange rate. Prior to the period of the attack, the peso/dollar exchange rate was being maintained in a target zone. Following the assassination of the leading presidential candidate, Colosio, the exchange rate stayed near the upper limit of the band. To maintain the exchange rate within the target zone, the central bank (Banco de Mexico) had to exchange dollars for pesos at a rate that created substantial international reserve (dollar) losses in October and November of 1994. Even though the Mexican government did not publicly announce the reserve losses until after the peso devaluation of December 20, 1994, some investors obviously knew there was a problem as there was massive selling of pesos for dollars—the speculative attack—prior to the devaluation. After the 15 percent peso devaluation on December 20, investors continued to attack the government's international reserves with more peso sales, believing that the government lacked the necessary stock of dollars to support the new exchange rate. As a result of the reserve losses, the Mexican peso was allowed to float against the dollar on December 22. The move to a floating exchange rate, combined with a new injection of dollars borrowed from the U.S. Treasury and the IMF, ended the speculative attack.

More recently, the Asian financial crisis of 1997–1998 involved speculative attacks on the Thai baht, Malaysian ringgit, and Indonesian rupiah. In each case, speculators correctly bet that the governments would be unwilling to lose substantial dollar reserves so as to maintain fixed exchange rates. The devaluations of the currencies were followed by much public debate over the merits of fixed versus flexible exchange rates.

have an adequate supply of foreign currency to exchange for domestic currency at the fixed rate of exchange.

For instance, Hong Kong has a currency board where the exchange rate is fixed to the U.S. dollar at 7.8 Hong Kong dollars (HKD) per U.S. dollar (USD). Since the supply of HKD can be increased only if the USD holdings of the currency board increase, and there is guaranteed convertibility of HKD into USD at the fixed exchange rate, a currency board system is quite similar to a gold standard. If Hong Kong runs an official settlements balance-of-payments surplus so that its international reserve holdings increase, it can issue more HKD. If Hong Kong runs a deficit and loses international reserves, the outstanding supply of HKD must shrink. Critics of currency boards point to the requirement of large foreign currency holdings as a cost of operating a currency board. However, since currency boards hold largely interest-bearing short-term securities denominated in foreign currencies rather than non-interest-bearing actual currency, the interest earnings tend to make currency boards profitable.

Countries with currency boards may also have central banks that regulate and provide services to the domestic banking system. However, these central banks have no discretionary authority over the exchange rate. If they did, then the public would likely doubt the credibility of the government in maintaining the fixed exchange rate. As shown in Table 19.2, seven countries maintain currency boards. Clearly, for countries that desire fixed exchange rates but face a problem in creating public confidence in the long-run viability of the fixed rate, a currency board may be a reasonable way to establish a credible exchange rate system.

A recent example of a currency board failure is provided by the case of Argentina. For a decade, Argentina maintained a currency board arrangement that supported an exchange rate of 1 peso per U.S. dollar. However, large fiscal deficits resulted in the essential insolvency of the government. At the same time that the government amassed large debts denominated in U.S. dollars, economic fundamentals were consistent with peso devaluation. The fixed exchange rate of the currency board was no longer consistent with the economic realities created by the expansionary fiscal policy so that an economic crisis erupted in late 2001 and early 2002 that resulted in rioting in the streets, the resignations of two presidents in quick succession, a freeze on bank deposit withdrawals, and a break with the fixed exchange rate. Once the currency board arrangement was ended, the peso quickly fell in value from one-to-one parity with the U.S. dollar to a level of 3 pesos per dollar. The Argentine case serves as a warning that currency boards are not a guarantee of forever-fixed exchange rates. If government policy is inconsistent with the fixed exchange rate, the currency board cannot last.

INTERNATIONAL RESERVE CURRENCIES

In the world economy, there are (almost) as many monies as there are countries. Due to several types of costs, many of these monies are not used in international commerce. Rather, only a few monies (or even one) serve the role of money in the international economy in a fashion similar to the role money plays in a domestic economy. These monies are known as reserve currencies. In domestic monetary theory, economists often identify three roles of money. Money is said to serve as (1) a unit of account, (2) a medium of exchange, and (3) a store of value. Likewise, in an

TABLE 19.5 Roles of a Reserve Currency

Function	Due to	Private Role	Official Role
1. International unit of account	Information costs	Invoicing currency	Pegging currency
2. International medium of exchange	Transaction costs	Vehicle currency	Intervention currency
3. International store of value	Stable value	Banking currency	Reserve currency

international context we can explain the choice of a reserve currency according to criteria relevant for each role.*

Table 19.5 summarizes the roles of a reserve currency. First, the role of the international unit of account is due to information costs. We find that the prices of primary goods, such as coffee, tin, or rubber, are quoted in terms of dollars worldwide. Since these goods are homogeneous, at least relative to manufactured goods, information regarding their value is conveyed more quickly when prices are quoted in terms of one currency. The private use as an invoicing currency in international trade contracts arises from the reserve currency's informational advantage over other currencies. Besides being a unit of account for private contracts, the reserve currency also serves as a base currency to which other currencies peg exchange rates.

The role of a reserve currency as an international medium of exchange is due to transaction costs. In the case of the U.S. dollar, the dollar is so widely traded that it is often cheaper to go from currency *A* to dollars to currency *B* than directly from currency *A* to currency *B*. Thus, it is efficient to use the dollar as an international medium of exchange, and the dollar serves as a "vehicle" for buying and selling nondollar currencies. The private (mainly interbank) role as a vehicle currency means that the dollar (or the dominant reserve currency) will also be used for central-bank foreign-exchange-market intervention aimed at achieving target levels for exchange rates.

The role of a reserve currency as an international store of value is due to its stability of value. In other words, certainty of future value enhances a currency's role as a store of purchasing power. The private-market use of the dollar for denominating international loans and deposits indicates the role of the dominant reserve currency in banking. In addition, countries will choose to hold their official reserves largely in the dominant reserve currency.

As the preceding discussion indicates, market forces, and not government decree, determine a currency's international role. It is important to realize, however, that just as the market chooses to elevate a currency, such as the U.S. dollar, to

*Useful discussions are provided in Paul Krugman, "The International Role of the Dollar: Theory and Prospect," in *Exchange Rate Theory and Practice*, ed. John F. O. Bilson and Richard C. Marston (Chicago: University of Chicago Press, 1984); and Stephen P. Magee and Ramesh K. S. Rao, "Vehicle and Nonvehicle Currencies in International Trade," *American Economic Review* (May 1980).

reserve-currency status, it can also take away some of that status, which happened to the U.K. pound earlier in the twentieth century and which has happened to the dollar to a lesser extent since the 1960s.

International reserves are the means of settling international debts. Under the gold standard, gold was the major component of international reserves. After World War II, we had a gold exchange standard wherein international reserves included both gold and a reserve currency, the U.S. dollar. The reserve-currency country was to hold gold as backing for the outstanding balances of the currency held by foreigners. These foreign holders of the currency were then free to convert the currency into gold if they wished. However, as we observed with the dollar, once the convertibility of the currency becomes suspect, or once large amounts of the currency are presented for gold, the system tends to fall apart.

This appears to describe the dollar after World War II. At the end of the war and throughout the 1950s, the world demanded dollars for use as an international reserve. During this time, U.S. balance-of-payments deficits provided the world with a much-needed source of growth of international reserves. As the rest of the world developed and matured, U.S. liabilities to foreigners continued to grow, eventually reaching a level that greatly exceeded the gold reserves backing these liabilities. Yet as long as the increase in demand for these dollar reserves equaled the supply, the lack of gold backing was irrelevant. Through the late 1960s, U.S. political and economic events began to cause problems for the dollar's international standing. Continuing U.S. deficits were not matched by a growing demand for dollars, so that pressure to convert dollars into gold and a consequent falling gold reserve resulted in the dollar being declared officially no longer exchangeable for gold in August 1971.

The dollar is not the only currency that serves as a reserve currency, although it is the dominant reserve currency. Table 19.6 illustrates the diversification of the currency composition of foreign-exchange reserves since the mid-1980s. There was a period of a falling share devoted to U.S. dollars followed by a rising share. Note also that the advent of the euro has not diminished the role of the dollar as a reserve currency. The euro accounts for only about 20 percent of total international reserves while the dollar accounts for more than 63 percent in the most recent data. Over time, as euro-denominated financial assets grow in popularity, there may be a continued shift away from dollars toward euros.

At first glance, it may appear very desirable to be the issuer of the reserve currency and have other countries accept your balance-of-payments deficits as a necessary means of financing world trade. The difference between the cost to the reserve country of creating new balances and the real resources the reserve country is able to acquire with the new balances is called **seigniorage**. Seigniorage, then, is a financial reward accruing to the reserve currency as a result of its being used as a world money.

Seigniorage
The difference between the exchange value of a money and its cost of production.

Although the dollar has lost some of its reserve-currency market share since the 1970s, the dollar is still, by far, the dominant reserve currency. Inasmuch as the U.S. international position has been somewhat eroded in the past few decades, the question arises: Why have we not seen some other money emerge as the dominant reserve currency? Although the mark, yen, and Swiss franc were popular currencies, the respective governments in each country have resisted a greater international role

TABLE 19.6 Share of National Currencies in Total Identified Official Holdings of Foreign Exchange, End of Year (percentage)

	1987	1989	1991	1993	1995	1997	1999	2001	2003
All Countries									
U.S. dollar	56.0	51.9	50.9	56.2	56.4	62.4	68.4	68.3	63.8
Pound sterling	2.2	2.6	3.4	3.1	3.4	3.7	4.0	4.0	4.4
Deutsche mark	13.4	18.0	15.7	14.1	13.7	12.9	—	—	—
French franc	0.8	1.4	2.8	2.2	1.8	1.4	—	—	—
Swiss franc	1.8	1.4	1.2	1.2	0.9	0.7	0.7	0.7	0.4
Netherlands guilder	1.2	1.1	1.1	0.6	0.4	0.4	—	—	—
Japanese yen	7.0	7.3	8.7	8.0	7.1	5.2	5.5	4.9	4.8
ECU	14.2	10.5	10.0	8.3	6.5	5.0	—	—	—
Euro	—	—	—	—	—	—	12.7	13.0	19.7
Unspecified currencies	3.4	5.7	6.2	6.2	9.7	8.4	8.8	9.0	6.8
Industrial Countries									
U.S. dollar	54.8	48.4	43.8	50.5	52.8	57.9	73.5	74.5	70.8
Pound sterling	1.0	1.2	1.8	2.2	2.1	1.9	2.3	1.8	1.7
Deutsche mark	14.1	20.6	18.3	16.4	15.7	15.9	—	—	—
French franc	0.3	1.1	3.0	2.5	2.1	0.9	—	—	—
Swiss franc	1.5	1.1	0.8	0.3	0.1	0.1	0.1	0.4	0.2
Netherlands guilder	1.1	1.1	1.1	0.4	0.2	0.2	—	—	—
Japanese yen	6.3	7.5	9.7	7.9	6.9	5.8	6.5	5.5	4.0
ECU	19.9	15.0	15.8	14.7	12.3	10.9	—	—	—
Euro	—	—	—	—	—	—	10.7	9.7	20.9
Unspecified currencies	1.0	4.0	5.7	5.2	7.8	6.4	6.9	8.1	2.3
Developing Countries									
U.S. dollar	59.1	60.5	63.3	63.8	60.5	66.2	64.6	64.1	59.3
Pound sterling	5.4	5.8	6.2	4.4	4.9	5.1	5.3	5.5	6.2
Deutsche mark	11.5	11.7	11.0	11.1	11.4	10.3	—	—	—
French franc	2.0	2.1	2.3	1.8	1.5	1.8	—	—	—
Swiss franc	2.7	2.2	2.1	2.4	1.8	1.1	1.1	0.9	0.6
Netherlands guilder	1.3	1.0	1.0	1.0	0.8	0.6	—	—	—
Japanese yen	8.6	6.9	7.0	8.1	7.3	4.7	4.7	4.5	5.2
ECU	—	—	—	—	—	—	—	—	—
Euro	—	—	—	—	—	—	14.2	15.3	18.9
Unspecified currencies	9.5	9.9	7.1	7.6	11.8	10.2	10.2	9.6	9.8

NOTE: Components may not sum to total because of rounding.

for their money. Besides the apparent low seigniorage return to the dominant international money, there is another reason for these countries to resist. The dominant money producer (country) finds that international shifts in the demand for its money may have repercussions on domestic monetary policy. For a country the size of the United States, domestic economic activity overwhelms international activity, so that international capital flows of any given magnitude have a much smaller potential to disrupt U.S. markets than Japanese, German, or Swiss markets, where foreign operations are much more important. In this sense, it is clear why these countries withstood the movement of the yen, mark, and Swiss franc to reserve-currency status. Over time, we may find that the euro emerges as a dominant reserve currency as the combined economies of the euro-member countries provide a very large base of economic activity.

MULTIPLE EXCHANGE RATES

Most countries conduct all varieties of foreign-exchange transactions in terms of a single exchange rate. But some countries maintain multiple exchange rates. A typical arrangement is a dual exchange rate system with a free-market-determined floating exchange rate for capital account transactions and a fixed exchange rate, overvaluing the domestic currency, for current account transactions. Some countries have much more complex arrangements involving three or more exchange rates applied to various transactions.

The IMF has generally sought to unify exchange rates in those countries where multiple rates exist. The argument is that multiple exchange rates harm both the countries that impose them and other countries. With different exchange rates for different types of transactions, domestic relative prices of internationally traded goods tend to differ from international relative prices. This results in distorted decision making in consumption, production, and investment as domestic residents respond to artificial relative prices rather than the true prices set on world markets. Multiple exchange rates are also costly in that people devote resources to finding ways to profit from the tiered exchange rates (e.g., having transactions classified to the most favorable exchange rate category). Finally, the maintenance of a multiple exchange rate system requires a costly administrative structure.

Research has generally found that multiple exchange rates function as a form of protectionism, originally introduced to improve a country's balance of payments.* The elimination of a multiple exchange rate system could simply involve allowing all transactions to occur at the market-determined rate. If a unified fixed exchange rate is desired, the floating rate will suggest an appropriate level for the new fixed rate. Of course, after the fixed rate is established, monetary and fiscal policy must be consistent with the maintenance of the new exchange rate.

---

*Interesting articles on multiple exchange rates include Charles Adams and Jeremy Greenwood, "Dual Exchange Rates and Capital Controls: An Investigation," *Journal of International Economics* (February 1985); Robert P. Flood, "Exchange Rate Expectations in Dual Exchange Markets," *Journal of International Economics* (February 1978); J. Saul Lizondo, "Exchange Rate Differential and Balance of Payments Under Dual Exchange Markets," *Journal of Development Economics* (June 1986); Nancy P. Marion, "Insulation Properties of a Two-Tier Exchange Market in a Portfolio Balance Model," *Economica* (February 1981); and Michael J. Moore, "Dual Exchange Rates, Capital Controls, and Sticky Prices," *Journal of International Money and Finance* (December 1989).

SUMMARY

1. Under a gold standard, currencies are convertible into gold at fixed exchange rates.
2. The IMF and a system of fixed exchange rates were created at the Bretton Woods Conference in 1944.
3. In March 1973, the major developed countries began floating exchange rates.
4. Countries with floating exchange rates tend to be large and closed, with inflation rates that differ from those of their trading partners and trade that is diversified across many countries.
5. The optimum currency area is characterized by mobile factors of production.
6. Target zones have maximum bands for exchange rate fluctuation.
7. A currency board exchanges domestic currency for foreign currency at a fixed rate of exchange.
8. A reserve currency serves as an international unit of account, medium of exchange, and store of value.
9. Multiple exchange rates are used to encourage exports and discourage imports.

EXERCISES

1. An international reserve currency serves several purposes, including being (a) a unit of account, (b) a medium of exchange, and (c) a store of value. What determines which currency (or currencies) will serve these roles?
2. What is seigniorage, and how is it related to competition to become the key reserve currency?
3. Describe the international monetary system known as the Bretton Woods system, or the gold exchange standard, that existed from the mid-1940s to the early 1970s. How did the system work? Why did it eventually break down?
4. Table 19.2 lists the exchange rate practices of IMF members. Examining this table, answer the following questions:
   a. What is the common historical link among those countries that are listed under CFA franc zone (in column 5)? These countries all share a common currency, the Communaute Financiere Africaine franc (or FA franc).
   b. Some countries choose crawling pegs while others choose conventional fixed pegs. What is the difference, and why do you suppose some countries have to choose a crawling peg instead of a fixed peg?

5. Why do you suppose that small countries tend to fix their exchange rate, whereas the largest countries float theirs?

6. In Table 19.2 we see that some countries do not have a unique domestic currency. Some European countries use the euro, some African countries use the CFA franc, and some Caribbean nations use the East Caribbean dollar. What advantage do these countries seek by the use of a common money?

7. Why might multiple exchange rates be undesirable?

8. If a country has a fixed exchange rate for current account transactions and a floating rate for capital account transactions, how can the country determine the correct exchange rate to establish a unified system with one fixed rate for all transactions?

9. List three factors relevant for a country's choice of an exchange rate system. Using the United States as an example, explain how these factors may have affected U.S. policy regarding floating exchange rates.

10. Suppose that the Indonesian rupiah is pegged to a weighted exchange rate index with its three major trading partners. One-fourth of its trade is with Australia, one-fourth is with Japan, and one-half is with the United States. If the rupiah appreciates 10 percent against the yen and depreciates 4 percent against the U.S. dollar, what is the percentage change in the exchange rate index for the rupiah?

11. Carefully explain how a target zone can help create a more stable exchange rate.

12. When did the euro begin? What countries are in the euro-area and which currencies were replaced by the euro?

13. Where is the European Central Bank located? In what way is the European System of Central Banks like the Federal Reserve System?

REFERENCES

Alesina, Alberto, and Robert J. Barro. *Currency Unions*. Stanford: Hoover Institution Press, 2001.

Bordo, Michael David. "The Classical Gold Standard: Lessons from the Past." In *The International Monetary System: Choices for the Future*, edited by Michael B. Connolly. New York: Praeger, 1982.

de Vries, Margaret. "The IMF: 40 Years of Challenge and Change." *Finance and Development* (September 1985).

Edison, Hali J., and Michael Melvin. "The Determinants and Implications of the Choice of an Exchange Rate System." In *Monetary Policy for a Volatile Global Economy*, edited by William S. Haraf and Thomas D. Willett. Washington, D.C.: AEI Press, 1990.

Enoch, Charles, and Anne-Marie Gulde. "Are Currency Boards a Cure for All Monetary Problems?" *Finance and Development* (December 1998).

European Union. *The Euro: Our Currency*, available at http://europa.eu.int/euro.

Levin, Jay H. *A Guide to the Euro.* Boston: Houghton Mifflin, 2002.

Reinhart, Carmen, and Kenneth Rogoff. "The Modern History of Exchange Rate Arrangements: A Reinterpretation." *Quarterly Journal of Economics* (February 2004).

Please visit our Web site at www.aw-bc.com/husted_melvin for more exercises and readings.

chapter

14 The European Union: Many Markets into One

Introduction: The European Union

The European Union is an economic union of 27 nations with over 488 million citizens and more than $13,410 billion in output. It is the largest, oldest, and most integrated of regional agreements. It helped put an end to over a century of wars on the European continent, and its incorporation of new members from Central Europe has reintegrated several countries that had been cut off from their historical and cultural ties to Western Europe. There are a number of lessons to be learned from the struggle of the European Union to expand and deepen the economic ties of its member nations.

Since 2004 12 new members have joined, including three independent nations that were part of the former Soviet Union and seven ex-socialist countries in Central Europe. The rapid accession of many new members is not the first expansion of the European Union. Since its inception in 1957 it has undergone several periods of growth in its numbers and its responsibilities. In 1979 the nine members of what was then called the **European Community (EC)** linked their exchange rates in a system designed to eliminate wide fluctuations among currencies. By 1986 the EC had grown to 12 members, and in 1987, they signed the **Single European Act**, with the intention of creating a single European identity that would form an umbrella over the various national cultures, economies, and political systems. In effect, the Single European Act turned the EC into a common market by allowing for the free movement of labor and capital as complements to the already free movement of goods and services. In 1992 the members signed the **Treaty on European Union**, which led directly to the creation of the common currency, the euro, in 1999.

None of these changes has been easy, or carried out according to a preconceived master plan. Instead, the member states have been forced to act pragmatically as world events called for changes. The shift from fixed to floating exchange rates in the 1970s and 1980s, the fall of the Berlin Wall in 1989, the collapse of communism, the integration of world capital markets and increasing international capital flows, the rise of environmental awareness, and many other forces have shaped the European Union's development. As changes in the world economy have led to new arrangements and new responsibilities for EU institutions, the goal of peaceful political, social, and economic integration has stayed on track. In this regard, the European Union is a truly remarkable achievement, particularly when one considers the bloody history of twentieth-century Europe and the low expectations of most observers when the original documents were signed in 1957.

The European Union is the most ambitious integration agreement in the world today. It has its own revenue and budget, a set of institutions for making laws and regulating areas of common interest, a common currency, and freedom of movement for people, money, goods, and services. Despite this profound integration, it has managed to protect the sovereignty of its member states and to avoid homogenization of cultures and linguistic regions. Indeed, integration in the larger sphere of nation-states has enabled a number of historical national identities to re-emerge and to claim greater autonomy in their political systems. Examples include the Catalans of Spain and the Welsh and Scots of the United Kingdom.

Due to its history and its increasing importance on the world stage, the European Union holds many lessons for other integration areas. Before we move on, however, it is useful to clarify the use of the name **European Union (EU)** The European Union was formerly called the European Community (EC), and before that, the **European Economic Community (EEC)**. When the agreement was implemented in 1958, the six member countries were called the European Economic Community, but as they took on more responsibilities of a social and political nature, they were no longer solely an *economic* community and usage changed to the European Community. In 1993, with the implementation of the Treaty on European Union, also called the **Maastricht Treaty**, the EC became the European Union. This chapter refers to the EC when talking about events before 1993, and to the EU, or European Union for events thereafter.

The Size of the European Market

Before discussing the history or economics of economic integration in Western Europe, let us define the nations and groups that are important to get an idea of the size of the market. In terms of population, the European Union is the largest integrated market in the world. By implication, the European Union is likely to have a major role in determining future international political arrangements, trade patterns and rules, and international economic relations in general. Few countries will be able to grow and prosper without selling their goods in the European market, which is a powerful incentive to accept European leadership on international issues.

Table 14.1 lists the members of the European Union and their population and incomes in 2005. As shown in Table 13.1, income is measured in absolute and per

European Union
Sweden
Finland
Norway
Estonia
Russia
Latvia
Denmark
Lithuania
Ireland
Belarus
Netherlands
Poland
United Kingdom
Germany
Ukraine
Belgium
Czech Republic
Luxembourg
Slovakia
Austria
France
Hungary
Romania
Slovenia
Switzerland
Croatia
Bosnia and Herzegovina
Serbia
Italy
Bulgaria
Portugal
Albania
Spain
Turkey
Greece
Cyprus
Malta
Morocco
Algeria
Tunisia
Egypt
Libya
Lambert Equal Area Projection
0
500
1000 Miles
Map by Dr. Chris Lukinbeal
Revised by Harry D. Johnson

TABLE 14.1 **Population and Income in the European Union, 2005**

	Population (Millions)	GDP (US$, Billions)	GDP per Capita (US$)	GDP per Capita (US$, PPP)
Original members				
Belgium	10.5	365	34,834	32,195
France	60.7	2,110	34,740	30,120
Germany	82.5	2,782	33,726	29,309
Italy	57.5	1,723	29,981	29,019
Luxembourg	0.5	34	73,961	74,573
Netherlands	16.3	595	36,423	32,927
Members, 1973–1995				
Austria	8.2	305	37,086	33,662
Denmark	5.4	254	46,952	33,722
Finland	5.2	193	36,830	31,245
Greece	11.1	214	19,271	23,591
Ireland	4.2	196	47,316	40,942
Portugal	10.6	173	16,396	20,124
Spain	43.4	1,124	25,898	26,125
Sweden	9.0	354	39,241	31,062
United Kingdom	60.2	2,193	36,420	32,005
Members, 2004–2007				
Bulgaria	7.7	27	3,442	8,794
Cyprus	0.8	NA	NA	NA
Czech Republic	10.2	122	11,999	21,317
Estonia	1.3	13	9,745	16,228
Hungary	10.1	109	10,820	18,086
Latvia	2.3	16	6,857	13,631
Lithuania	3.4	25	7,466	14,382
Malta	0.4	6	13,783	19,541
Poland	38.2	299	7,838	13,980
Romania	21.6	99	4,556	9,208
Slovak Republic	5.4	46	8,615	16,459
Slovenia	2.0	34	17,030	22,292
EU-27	488.7	13,410	27,441	26,346

The 27 members of the European Union have income and population totals that are comparable to those for the NAFTA region.

capita terms, and at market exchange rates and purchasing power parity rates. Comparisons at market exchange rates are a less accurate indicator of living standards than comparisons at purchasing power parity rates, but they are a more accurate indicator of the size of each market in terms of its ability to buy goods and services that are imported. Several features of Table 14.1 are worth highlighting. First, not all West European nations are members. Norway, which voted against joining in 1970 and in 1995, and Switzerland are noticeably absent. In addition, a number of the smaller nations, including Iceland, Liechtenstein, San Marino, and Monaco are not members. Second, the majority of nations in the European Union are relatively small. The unification of Germany in the early 1990s created the largest country in the European Union, but only six of the 27 nations (France, Germany, Italy, Spain, Poland, and the United Kingdom) can be considered large, and none are as populous as the United States or Mexico. Third, the combined EU market is very similar to the size of the NAFTA market, in terms of population and GDP. In 2005 the European Union counted 488.7 million people while the NAFTA nations counted 431.9 million; GDP comparisons were $13,410 billion in the European Union and $14,338 billion in NAFTA.

Before the European Union

The European Economic Community was born on March 25, 1957, with the signing of the **Treaty of Rome** by the original six members. The Treaty went into effect about nine months later, on January 1, 1958. The Treaty remains the fundamental agreement while more recent agreements, such as the Single European Act and the Maastricht Agreement were passed as amendments to the original treaty. The six founding members include the Benelux countries (Belgium, Netherlands, and Luxembourg), France, West Germany, and Italy.

The Treaty of Rome

The European Economic Community grew out of the reconstruction of Europe at the end of World War II. The goals of the founders of the EEC were to rebuild their destroyed economies and to prevent the destruction from happening again. The original vision of the founders of the EEC was for a political union that they hoped to create through economic integration. In 1950 the first step was a proposal by Robert Schuman, the foreign minister of France, to pool the European coal and steel industries. Coal and steel were chosen because they were large industrial activities that served as the backbone of military strength. Schuman's plan was to pool the industries of Germany and France, the two largest West European antagonists, but Luxembourg, Belgium, the Netherlands, and Italy signed on as well. The **European Coal and Steel Community (ECSC)** Treaty was signed in 1951 and included provisions for the establishment of the ECSC High Authority, an international agency with regulatory powers. Coal and steel trade between the six members grew by 129 percent in the first five years of the treaty.

The success of the ECSC led to early attempts at integration in political and military areas (the European Defense Community and the European Political Community), but these efforts failed when they were rejected by the French Parliament in 1954. At that point, European leaders decided to focus their efforts on economic integration. In 1955 the six foreign ministers of the ECSC countries launched a round of talks in Messina, Italy, to discuss the creation of the European Economic Community and **European Atomic Energy Community (EAEC** or **Euratom)**. The goal of the former was to create a single, integrated market for goods, services, labor, and capital. The latter sought jointly to develop nuclear energy for peaceful purposes. Two separate treaties were signed in 1957 in Rome, creating the EEC and Euratom.

Institutional Structure of the EEC

The founders of the EEC envisioned a federation in which local, regional, national, and European authorities cooperate and complement each other. The model was similar to the interaction between the cities, counties, states, and federal government in the United States, or local, provincial, and federal governments in Canada.

In EU jargon, **subsidiarity** describes the relationship between national and EU areas of authority, and between national and EU institutions. Subsidiarity is defined as the principle that the Union will only have authority to tackle issues that are more effectively handled through international action than by individual nations acting alone. In some cases, these issues are easily defined, but in others they are not. Current thinking places the responsibility for environmental and regional policy, research and technology development, and economic and monetary union under EU control.

Areas that are less clear-cut and where there continues to be some degree of controversy include the issues of labor market policies, social policies, and competition policies. The presence of controversy, however, has not prevented the European Union from agreeing to a common competition policy and a common set of labor market policies, called the Social Charter. Both areas continue to be sources of significant disagreement and political maneuvering, as national policies reflect fundamental philosophical differences in values and choices. The conflict between policies that reflect national values and the desire to obtain greater gains from trade through economic integration is a pervasive problem in every instance of economic integration. Given that nations rarely speak with a single voice, but are themselves composed of factions and special interests, the struggle over the transfer of sovereignty is all the more contentious.

The European Union is governed by five main institutions and a number of lesser ones. The five most prominent are the **European Commission**, the **Council of the European Union**, the **European Parliament**, the **Court of Justice**, and the **Court of Auditors**. The first three are representative bodies composed of members from each country. Their roles are to initiate and implement laws and regulations for the European Union. Table 14.2 displays the number of votes in each institution, as well as the range of votes granted to each country.

TABLE 14.2 • Votes in the Main EU Institutions

		Votes per Country	
	Total Votes*	Minimum	Maximum
European Commission	25	1	1
Council of the European Union	321	3	29
European Parliament	732	5	99

*Prior to accession of Bulgaria and Romania in 2007.

The European Commission. The executive body of the European Union is the European Commission. Each country has one vote in the commission. Future members will also be given one vote. Commissioners serve five-year terms that are renewable, and they are appointed by national governments with the mutual approval of the member states. The Commission elects one of its own members to serve as its president. Work is divided in a way that gives each commissioner responsibility for one or more policy areas, but all decisions are a collective responsibility.

The Commission's primary responsibility is to act as the guardian of the treaties, ensuring that they are faithfully and legally enforced. This role includes responsibility for creating the rules for implementing treaty articles and for EU budget appropriations. As the executive branch, the Commission has the sole right to initiate EU laws and the same right as the national governments to submit proposals.

The Council of the European Union. The Council is the primary legislative branch of the European Union, a responsibility it shares with the European Parliament. Each country has between 3 (Malta) and 29 (France, Germany, Italy, United Kingdom) votes. The Council is the primary body for enacting laws proposed by the Commission and has more control over the budget than the Parliament or the Commission. Its membership consists of ministers from each nation, with participation varying according to the topic under discussion. For example, labor ministers convene to discuss labor issues, and environmental ministers to discuss environmental legislation. Most legislative decisions require either unanimity among all countries or a **qualified majority**, which is a majority of countries and 232 of 321 votes (72.3 percent).

The Council's presidency rotates among the member states in six-month terms. The chance to serve as President of the Council for six months is an important mechanism for individual member states to bring up their own legislative agendas and has been instrumental in the adoption of key EU regulations.

The European Parliament. The European Parliament has 732 members, directly elected by the people for five-year terms and apportioned among the member states according to population. Members associate by political affiliation rather than national origin. The Parliament has three main responsibilities as follows:

- Passing laws
- Supervising other institutions within the European Union
- Passing the final EU budget

EU laws are usually a co-decision of the Council and Parliament, although the Council alone may make laws in certain areas. The Parliament also provides oversight of the work of the other main bodies, such as the Commission. And finally, passage of the annual budget of the European Union requires approval of the Parliament. Over time, the role of the Parliament has probably changed more than any other institution. In its early years it was primarily an advisory body with little real authority, but as the European Union has grown it has taken on more authority, in part because it provides democratic legitimacy as the only institution directly elected by the citizens of the European Union.

Other Institutions. The final two main institutions are the Court of Justice and the Court of Auditors. The Court of Justice acts as the European Union's Supreme Court, with responsibility for interpreting laws and treaties. The Court's rulings are binding and take precedence over the 27 national courts. The Court of Auditors monitors the finances of the institutions and reports on the use and misuse of funds.

While these five institutions are the main ones, a number of other institutions have had important roles in EU governance. For example, the European Economic and Social Committee offers an institutional voice to civil society, and the Committee of the Regions represents the interests of specific regions, many of which make up areas in more than one country.

The European Constitution. On October 29, 2004, heads of state from the member countries signed the Constitution for Europe. This document will not take effect until it is ratified by each member and a few countries, such as, France and the Netherlands have voted no, leaving its future in doubt. Nevertheless, political and administrative pressures will continue to push for simplification of the many existing treaties by combining them into one main document. A main goal of the constitution was to simplify decision making within the European Union after ten new members joined in 2004 and two more in 2007. The Constitution for Europe is also intended to guarantee civil and human rights, clarify the functions of EU institutions, and define the separation of powers and responsibilities between national governments and the European Union. It would create an EU Foreign Minister, and provide for greater cooperation in the areas of defense, police and judicial affairs, and economic coordination.

Financing the European Union. The total budget of the European Union for 2006 was €111.9 billion ($140 billion). This amounts to slightly more than 1 percent of the gross national income of the member states, and is a relatively small amount of revenue by comparison to that of national governments, which often have total revenue equivalent to 30 to 50 percent or more of the nation's gross national income. The budget is financed through three main sources:

- Tariffs on goods entering the European Union
- An EU share of national value added taxes
- A payment from each member country based on the size of its economy

The latter category is by far the largest, accounting for about 68 percent of the total revenue collected by the European Union.

The two largest expenditure categories of the European Union are for agricultural support, both direct payments in the form of subsidies and indirect payments in the form of rural development, and **cohesion funds**. Agricultural support programs take nearly 40 percent of the budget directly, with another uncertain amount, which is counted as rural development or cohesion expenditures. Cohesion funds take almost 30 percent of the budget and are used to support the less developed regions within the European Union, particularly the new members from Central Europe that have incomes below the EU average. This is accomplished through infrastructure development, particularly environmental projects such as water treatment and transportation projects.

Deepening and Widening the Community in the 1970s and 1980s

When Europeans speak of increasing the level of cooperation between member countries, they use the term *deepening*. Deepening refers to economic and noneconomic activities that cause increased levels of integration of the national economies. For example, the movement from a free market to a customs union, the harmonization of technical standards in industry, or agreements to develop a common security and defense policy are deepening activities that increase interactions between the member states. On the other hand, when Europeans speak about extending the boundaries of the European Union to include new members, they use the term *widening*. Between 1957, when the agreement was signed to create the European Economic Community, and 1995, nine new members were added, bringing the total from six original members to 15. In 2004 10 more members were added and in 2007 Bulgaria and Romania joined. In the next section of this chapter we will look at the various stages of deepening.

Before the Euro

In 1979 the members of the European Economic Community began to link their currencies in an effort to prevent radical fluctuation in currency values. The EC wanted to prevent competitive devaluations, in which one country devalues in order to capture the export markets of another country. **Competitive devaluations** inevitably generate conflict and lead to a breakdown in cooperation, since the devaluing country is viewed as gaining exports and jobs at the expense of others. Nations sometimes find it difficult to resist devaluation, especially during recessions. This tactic is viewed as unfair, however, and in the medium to long term, it is usually ineffective since the nondevaluing countries are obliged to follow suit and retaliate with their own devaluations.

In addition to looking for a mechanism that might discourage competitive devaluations, the EC sought to remove some of the uncertainty and risk from trading and investing across national boundaries. While forward markets can be used to protect against exchange rate risk, they only work about six months into the future.

The goal was to create an environment in which trade and investment throughout the EC was determined by considerations of comparative advantage and efficient resource allocation, rather than by changes in exchange rates. The result was the **European Monetary System (EMS)** and the **exchange rate mechanism (ERM)**. The formation of the EMS in 1979 was a significant deepening of the EC and served to prepare the way for the eventual introduction of a single currency. It was designed to prevent extreme currency fluctuations by tying each currency's value to the weighted average of the others. The group average, the **European currency unit (ECU)**, was used as a unit of account, but not as a means of payment.

The ERM system was an example of an exchange rate band. Each currency in the band was fixed to the ECU, but was allowed to fluctuate several percentage points up or down. If a currency began to move out of the bandwidth of several percentage points around the fixed rate, the central bank of the country was obligated to intervene, by either buying its currency in order to prop it up, or by selling currency in order to push it down in value. In September 1992, for example, the United Kingdom spent an estimated $30 billion in just a few days, in an attempt to protect the British pound from market speculators who had become convinced that it was going to fall in value. In the end, the speculators were right, and the Bank of England lost a lot of money trying to move against the market.

Given the ineffectiveness of market intervention in the face of a strong and determined market movement, most analysts predicted that the ERM would fail as a mechanism for maintaining stable European currency values. An ERM-type arrangement was attempted in 1973, but it soon collapsed as a result of the first oil shortage and its effects on national inflation rates. When the EC proposed a similar arrangement in 1979, many were skeptical that it would survive for very long or that it would effectively stabilize currencies. To most economists' surprise, the ERM effectively linked EC exchange rates for two decades.

The ERM experienced several adjustments, but none of them threatened the functioning of the system until 1992. Oddly enough, it was the reunification of Germany that caused the system to nearly collapse and led to a much weaker linkage between exchange rates. Because German reunification had a profound effect on the ERM, and because it is an interesting lesson in the costs of tying currencies together, it is useful to look at this episode in more detail.

Problems began in 1990 with Germany's decision to speed up its reunification with the German Democratic Republic (East Germany) after the fall of the Berlin Wall in November 1989. Economic conditions in East Germany were worse than expected, and it was soon apparent that the costs of building a productive economy would be enormous. The infrastructure (roads, bridges, ports, utilities, schools, hospitals) was in worse shape than most people realized, and environmental pollution was significant. In order to build a prosperous economy in its eastern region, Germany had to raise the productivity levels of the people living there, which required huge investments in infrastructure and the environment. The unexpectedly large expenditures to raise the productivity of East Germany resulted in a very large fiscal stimulus to the German economy. Such large expenditures by both the government and private sector were also expected to have an inflationary impact, and the Bundesbank (Germany's central bank) acted to counteract the increased probability of future inflation by raising interest rates. An increase in interest rates is expected to slow the economy by increasing the costs of using borrowed capital. Germany, therefore, had an expansionary fiscal policy that was partially offset by a contractionary monetary policy.

High interest rates in Germany made German financial instruments more attractive and caused capital to flow into Germany from the other EC countries. This resulted in the selling of British pounds, French francs, and other currencies in order to buy German marks (and then German bonds) and caused the pound, the franc, and other currencies to fall in value. At first, the movement was within the 2.25 percent bandwidth, and most of the EC hoped that they would somehow muddle through without making any drastic changes in the ERM or the EMS.

One solution would have been for the countries with falling currencies to raise their interest rates to match Germany's. This would have stemmed the outflow of financial capital looking for better rates of return in Germany. Some of the countries—the United Kingdom, for example—were entering recessions in 1990 and 1991 and did not want to raise interest rates just as a recession was taking hold. The likely effect would have been to hasten and deepen the recession, something no policymaker wants to be accused of doing. Other countries, France for example, were not yet entering the recessionary phase of their business cycle, but they had very high unemployment rates, and contractionary monetary policy was not desirable.

The dilemma faced by the EC countries is a good example of a recurring theme in the history of exchange rate systems. By tying their exchange rates to each other, the EC countries gave up a large measure of independence in their monetary policies. Because Germany was the largest country and the one with the most influential central bank, its monetary policy set the tone for the rest of the EC, and, at a time when many of the members wanted expansionary monetary policy, they were forced to adopt contractionary policies. The 1992 episode illustrates the recurrent tension that occurs between the appropriate external policies (exchange rate management) and the appropriate internal policies (full employment, reasonable growth, low inflation) when nations tie their exchange rates together. Since the "right" policy choice for meeting the exchange rate problem was diametrically opposite to meeting the needs of the internal economy, EC members were left with a tough decision. They would have to honor their commitments to the ERM and make their unemployment and growth rates worse, or do the right thing for internal growth and watch the ERM fall apart. In the French case, an interest rate increase threw the country into recession, but France remained within the ERM. In Italy and the United Kingdom, the ERM was abandoned, and their currencies were allowed to freely float against other EC currencies. A third option was chosen by Spain, where the parity, or center of the band, was shifted. In order to lessen the probability of future repeats of this problem, the bandwidth was widened in 1993 from ±2.25 percent to ±15 percent.

The Second Wave of Deepening: The Single European Act

Other than the creation of the European Monetary System in 1979, the changes in the EC were minor through the 1970s and the first half of the 1980s. In the early 1980s most West European countries suffered through a recession that left their unemployment rates high, even as their economic growth recovered in 1984 and 1985. The European economies seemed stale and incapable of new dynamism and many in the United States began to refer to the European situation as "Eurosclerosis," signifying a permanent hardening of the arteries of commerce and industry.

By the late 1980s, people in North America and Europe had stopped using "Eurosclerosis" and begun to speak of "Europhoria." While both terms were exaggerations, dramatic events had reshaped the EC in the intervening years. What was previously dismissed in the early 1980s as a hopeless case of bureaucratic inefficiency was now regarded as a dynamic, forward-looking, integrated regional economy. Europe seemed to be "on the move."

CASE STUDY

The Schengen Agreement

The Schengen Agreement was signed by five countries (Belgium, France, Germany, Luxembourg, and the Netherlands) in the town of Schengen, Luxembourg, in 1985. The purpose of the agreement is to eliminate all passport and customs controls at the common borders of the five nations. Given that they enjoyed free trade, and given the flow of people between the countries, the purpose of examining passports or checking customs paperwork seemed inefficient and unnecessary. Over the next few years, more members of the European Union joined the agreement. When the Single European Act was completely implemented, the idea of a common market allowing free movement of people gave it added logic. By 1995, the agreement was extended to more countries and more areas of activity, including cooperation among police forces, drug enforcement agencies, and the sharing of criminal justice information. Originally, the Schengen Agreement and its subsequent extension were outside the legal framework of the European Union; but in 1999, it was incorporated into EU law. Eventually non-EU countries, among them Iceland and Norway, were allowed to participate.

The dismantling of border-control stations, including passport and customs inspections, undoubtedly has had a positive effect on EU efficiency, because it reduces travel time for both goods and people. It also demonstrates a high degree of social trust among the member nations and contributes to goodwill and better relations. In effect, it shifts customs and passport controls to the perimeter of the European Union, where non-EU citizens and goods first enter the region. While this is beneficial, two main problems have arisen from the shifting of control to the perimeter.

First, Ireland and the United Kingdom have not accepted the dismantling of passport controls at the border because they fear the freedom of movement this will give terrorists. However, as members of the European Union, they must extend the rights of all other EU citizens to travel freely and reside inside their borders, even as they maintain passport checks at the border. Second, the eventual extension of the Schengen Agreement to the 12 new members since 2004 depends on those members' ability to demonstrate control over their own borders to the east, and on the development of a new EU data system for sharing information about individuals and lost or stolen objects. The timetable for extending Schengen beyond its current membership (13 EU members, plus Norway and Iceland) is not set.

The Delors Report

Reshaping the EC got under way with the selection of the former French finance minister, Jacques Delors, to serve a five-year term as president of the European Commission. Delors was a compromise candidate, and no one expected unusual or dramatic changes in the EC under his stewardship. Delors's vision of the EC, however, was of a fully integrated union, and as president of the EC's executive branch, he had a platform from which he could initiate significant change. His vision was shaped in part by the belief that the institutions of the EC could help return individual national economies to economic prosperity and by the desire to complete the task of building an economic and political union.

Delors' first step, and perhaps his most significant one, was to issue a report called "Completing the Internal Market," which detailed 300 specific changes necessary for the EC to move from a quasi-customs union to an economic union. It laid out a timetable for completing the changes and removed the need for unanimous voting in the Council of Ministers. Delors proposed that most measures be allowed to pass with a "qualified majority" and that unanimity be reserved for only the most momentous issues, such as taxes. Although the qualified majority still allowed a minority of countries to block a measure, it prevented any single country from blocking a proposed change.

After some relatively minor changes in the **Delors Report**, it was adopted in its entirety in 1987, as the Single European Act (SEA). Of the 300 steps, or "directives," 279 were included in the SEA. Many of the 21 not included were considered too difficult to accomplish in the time period the EC gave itself, but were taken up as goals of the next round of deepening. For example, monetary union under a single currency was moved forward to the next round of deepening.

The date for implementation of the SEA was January 1, 1993. By the end of 1992, it was expected that the "four freedoms" (freedom of movement for goods, services, capital, and labor) spelled out in the SEA would be instituted and, as a result, the EC would be at the common market level of economic integration. In order to accomplish these goals it was necessary to determine the method of implementation of each of the 279 directives and for each of the 12 member nations to make the necessary changes in their internal laws, standards, and customary practices. While some areas remain incomplete, the vast majority of the directives were put into practice by the end of 1992, and the EC achieved common market status.

The steps taken to implement the SEA can be broadly divided into three areas: (1) the elimination of physical barriers, such as passport and customs controls at the borders between member countries; (2) the elimination of technical barriers, such as differences in product and safety standards; and (3) the elimination of fiscal barriers, such as differences in taxes, subsidies, and public procurement. Each of these poses its own benefits and challenges and will be discussed in more detail. First, we will consider the gains that the EC hoped to reap from the elimination of these barriers.

Forecasts of the Gains from the Single European Act

One of the central reasons for supporting the SEA was to achieve gains in economic efficiency. One set of gains was anticipated to come from the freeing of the movement of goods and services. While the SEA did not mandate the elimination of border inspections, it did grant freedom of movement to people and goods. In many cases, border controls were dismantled, also with support from the Schengen Agreement, but in some cases "tax inspections" replaced customs inspections due to the European Union's inability to establish a common system of value-added taxation. Nevertheless, substantial progress has been made in eliminating long border waits and in speeding up the distribution of goods throughout the EC.

Integration also created economic benefits from greater economies of scale and increased competitiveness. Economies of scale are possible because EC firms are able to produce at one site, or in a fewer number of sites for the entire European market and will not have to duplicate production facilities across national boundaries. This enables some companies to consolidate their operations and to avoid duplication in their production and support services, such as accounting. The increase in competitiveness comes from several sources. For example, the increased pressure of competition will force some firms to make productive investments that they would not otherwise have made. In addition, the openness of the competitive environment will generate a larger, more mobile pool of labor that carries skills from one firm to another. Finally, the free flow of goods and services will generate a greater flow of information and ideas so that firms have easier access to the best new ideas.

Problems in the Implementation of the SEA

One of the most interesting lessons of the Single European Act is that it is still difficult to reduce barriers to trade and investment even when the citizens, businesses, and governments of the involved countries are united in their desire to do so. According to all the polls, the SEA enjoyed very broad support throughout the EC. Still, from the time when it was first proposed in 1985 until its final implementation in 1993, there were very difficult negotiations among the member countries.

The Effects of Restructuring. As we saw in Chapter 3, when a national economy goes from a relatively closed position to a relatively open one, economic restructuring takes place. The less efficient firms are squeezed out, and the more efficient ones grow; overall economic welfare expands as countries concentrate on what they do best, which inevitably means abandoning some industries and expanding others. In the case of the EC, it was forecast that almost all manufacturing industries would see shrinkage in the number of firms. The most extreme case was the footwear industry, which was predicted to lose 207 of its 739 firms. In some cases, the majority of the disappearing firms were concentrated in one or two countries, such as the UK carpet industry, where it was predicted that 31 of 52 manufacturers would go out of business.

The firms that go out of business are part of the economy-wide shift to a more efficient use of labor and capital resources, but it is obvious that there are immediate human costs. In the long run, it is easy to show that the gains in efficiency and the improvement in living standards outweigh the costs of restructuring, but in the short run, individuals and communities can feel acute pain. Due to the inevitable costs from restructuring, many people predicted that adversely affected firms and labor unions, along with the communities and regions that depend on the firms, would fight to prevent the full implementation of the SEA.

The auto industry is the best example of an economic interest that fought to prevent the full realization of the goals of the SEA. Car prices vary throughout the European Union due to a lack of harmonization of national technical standards, documentation requirements, and rates of taxation. Ordinarily, such large price differences would present an opportunity for consumers and distributors to move cars from the low-price countries to the high-price ones and, in the process, bring about a reduction in price differences. The auto industry is covered by a separate set of tax laws, however, that require buyers to pay the tax rate of the country where they register the car, not where they buy the car. This effectively discourages buyers from crossing national borders in order to search out the best deal on car prices and helps maintain the status quo in automobile production.

One significant reason why there have not been more exceptions to the dropping of trade barriers is that the European Union has a broad array of programs to address the problems of structural change. Some of these programs are funded out of the EU budget, and others are national in origin. Programs include the European Union's Regional Development Funds, which can be used to address problems of structural unemployment, and the member nations' income maintenance, education, and retraining funds. The latter vary across the member countries, but, in general, they reduce the costs to individuals and communities of unemployment and structural change by providing a generous social safety net for laid-off workers. The programs can also have positive effects in reducing political opposition to economic change because workers in a factory that is shut down may not fight the closing as much given the economic support system provided for laid-off employees. At the same time, the society-wide perception that workers who have been hurt by restructuring will be taken care of may effectively reduce opposition to change on the grounds of "fairness."

It should be noted that although the generosity of the social safety net in the European Union may be politically instrumental in reducing opposition to economic restructuring, many economists and politicians argue that the generosity created by the social safety net can cause additional problems as well. In particular, many see it as a primary reason for the relatively high unemployment rates since the late 1980s. By providing generous benefits to the unemployed, the European Union has reduced the cost of unemployment and removed some of the incentives to look for work. In addition, taxes for these social programs often fall on employers; therefore, many firms are reluctant to hire new employees during an economic expansion. This is an ongoing debate within the European Union.

Harmonization of Technical Standards. A second major obstacle to the creation of the four freedoms was the problem of harmonizing standards. These include everything from building codes, industrial equipment, consumer safety, and health standards, to university degrees and worker qualifications. The European Union estimated that there were more than 100,000 technical standards that required harmonization in order to realize the benefits of a completely integrated market. Many of the technical standards involved rules that directly touch upon cultural identities. Nowhere was this more true than in the case of food processing. For example, there were discussions around the allowable level of bacteria in French cheese, the type of wheat required to make Italian pasta, the ingredients of German beer, and the oatmeal content of English bangers (breakfast sausages). In the end, the European Union recognized that complete harmonization of standards would generate significant hostility and that the work required to agree on a set of common standards was beyond its capacity. Consequently, a combination of harmonization and mutual recognition of standards was adopted. In particularly sensitive cases, mutual recognition is the rule, but individual nations are allowed to keep their own national production requirements. For example, German beer must be certified as having been made according to the German standards, but Germany must allow all brands of beers to be sold within its borders.

As the discussion in Chapter 8 noted, standards do not have to be the same in order to create a single market, but the gains in economic efficiency that come from sharing the same standard can be significant. Shared standards permit manufacturers to produce to one standard, rather than many, and to capture important economies of scale in the process. These economies also pass outside the European Union, since U.S. or Japanese manufacturers share the benefits of being able to produce to one set of standards as well. Additionally, non-EU-based firms only have to get their product certified once in order to sell in all 27 countries. For this reason, the United States has had a keen interest in the standards-setting process and has looked to create joint U.S.-EU agreements on standards and the procedures by which they are set. The preference of the United States has been to use the procedures of the International Standards Organization (ISO) to streamline the process of harmonization. The ISO is an international organization that provides technical standards and whose ISO-9000 is a set of certifications applying to nearly all types of economic activity.

Value-Added Taxes. A third difficulty standing in the way of completely realizing the four freedoms is the issue of value-added taxes (VAT). These taxes function essentially like sales taxes and are levied by each of the EU members but at a wide variety of rates and coverage. When the SEA was first proposed in 1987, there were significant differences in the dependence of the member governments of the European Union on value-added taxes, ranging from 19 to 35 percent of total government revenue. The European Commission studied the United States to determine the effects of different rates of sales taxation on states sharing common borders and found that once the difference in sales taxes exceeded 5 percent, the higher-tax state lost revenues, sales, and jobs to the neighboring lower-tax state. In other words, a 5 percent difference was enough to cause consumers to cross state boundaries to make purchases. The standard VAT rate in the European Union before the SEA varied from 12 percent at the low end (Luxembourg and Spain) to 20 percent in the Netherlands, 22 percent in

Denmark, and 25 percent in Ireland. In addition, there were special rates for sensitive goods, which varied a great deal more than the standard rates.

VAT rates proved impossible to completely harmonize because they go to the heart of national political philosophy. High-tax countries expect the state to play a relatively greater role in national economic life, while low-tax countries are closer to the laissez-faire end of the political economy spectrum. The level of value-added taxes, and the degree to which the national government depends on them are in large part determined by the political philosophy of the nation. In turn, these philosophical attitudes are shaped by economics, as well as complex historical, cultural, and social factors..

The attempt to harmonize value-added taxes created an inability to agree on a single rate. What was accomplished, however, was the creation of minimum and maximum rates that were set at 15 and 25 percent. Since the difference still exceeds the 5 percent differential that is the threshold at which high-tax countries lose revenue and sales, a number of controls were established to prevent revenue loss, even though these controls prevent the complete realization of the four freedoms.

Despite these obstacles, however, there are still significant incentives for cross-border shopping. Although the SEA has not brought a 100 percent free flow of goods and services, it is important to keep the exceptions in perspective. For most goods and services, in most border regions, consumers are free to cross national boundaries to bring back unlimited quantities of goods, and will not be stopped at a border inspection station.

Public Procurement. Public procurement is the purchase of goods and services by governments or government-owned enterprises, such as state-run television companies, utilities, or hospitals. Most nations of the world tend to use procurement processes that discriminate in favor of nationally owned suppliers, although there are limits on their ability to do so if they belong to the WTO.

Since 1970, the European Union has attempted to eliminate discrimination in public procurement but this has proved difficult. It is a problem particularly in the areas of telecommunications, pharmaceuticals, railway equipment, and electrical equipment. In many instances national governments have attempted to create firms that would serve as "national champions" in world competition. One method was to favor those firms in the government procurement process so that they would have a guaranteed market for their output while they were still learning the most efficient methods of production. Needless to say, firms and industries that receive favorable treatment often develop effective lobbying efforts, particularly if there are a large number of jobs in the industry, or if it can make a credible argument that it is essential to the nation's future development or its national security.

Discrimination in public procurement, however, limits the benefits of restructuring and the gains from trade. If the EU countries are able to successfully develop a common security and foreign policy, the national security argument for discrimination in public procurement begins to lose a great deal of its justification.

The Third Wave of Deepening: The Maastricht Treaty

By 1989, planning for the implementation of the Single European Act in January 1993 was well under way. Europe had seen several years of economic expansion, and the excitement of the SEA seemed to signal that the time was right to consider some of the directives proposed in the Delors Report that had been set aside because they were seen as too complex to accomplish by 1993. In 1990 the European Commission convened an Intergovernmental Conference on Economic and Monetary Union. The purpose of the conference was to bring together the leaders of the 12 nations to discuss the steps necessary to create a monetary union under a single currency. There were other issues on the agenda, but this was the one that attracted the most interest inside and outside the European Union.

The Intergovernmental Conference continued through most of 1991. The final draft of the proposed agreement was completed in December in the Dutch town of Maastricht and, ever since, has been known as the Maastricht Treaty. Many of the provisions in the agreement are technical and cover such arcane issues as the tax treatment of holiday homes in Denmark, or the status of the pope in trade disputes with the Vatican. Other issues dealing with basic EU social policy are much more fundamental. For example, the Maastricht Treaty calls for the creation of a "Social Charter" defining a uniform set of labor laws and worker rights. It defines the right of all residents in a community to vote and stand for election in local contests, regardless of the resident's nationality; it puts more control over health, education, cultural, and consumer safety issues in the hands of the European Commission; it calls for a common defense and security policy along with a common military force; and it defines the steps for achieving a common currency under the control of a European Central Bank by 1999, at the latest.

It is the last goal that has attracted the most attention. Achieving a single currency requires each country to give up its ability to set its own monetary policy and to accept whatever contractionary or expansionary policy the European Central Bank chooses. This is the most controversial feature of the Maastricht Treaty, inside and outside of the European Union. The controversy stems from the fact that no group of countries has ever given up their monetary system to create a single currency, there is significant political opposition to its realization, and there are economic risks associated with voluntarily giving up one of the few tools that governments have to counteract recessions. If, for example, Germany is booming, but Spain is in an economic slump, there is no common monetary policy that will be suitable to both countries. Germany would need a contractionary policy to cool off the economy and to prevent the ignition of inflation, while Spain would need an expansionary policy to create employment and growth. These controversies led to a very different public reception for the Maastricht Treaty than that received by the Single European Act. Whereas citizens, businesses, and governments were solidly behind the SEA, support for the Maastricht Treaty has been much more tentative.

Monetary Union and the Euro

The timetable for monetary union under a single currency is scheduled to occur in three separate stages. Stage one began in 1990 with the lifting of controls on the movement of financial capital within the European Union. Stage two began in 1994 with the creation of the European Monetary Institute, based in Frankfurt, Germany. The Institute was charged with the responsibility for coordinating the move to monetary union and gradually took on elements of a supranational central bank. The third stage began in 1999 with the phased-in introduction of the **euro** and the European Central Bank.

During stage one and two, nations were expected to bring their monetary and fiscal policies into harmony so that the introduction of the euro would not happen under wildly different sets of monetary and fiscal policies. In order to judge when individual national policies were in agreement, the European Union developed a set of **convergence criteria**. These were objective measures that signaled whether the national policies were in conflict or in agreement, and whether individual nations were ready for monetary union. Table 14.3 lists the specific monetary and fiscal variables that are required to be coordinated and the target ranges for each.

Initially, nations were expected to meet all five goals for monetary union. The experience of the first half of the 1990s, however, indicated that no nation, except perhaps Luxembourg, could consistently maintain each of these targets and that some countries would never meet them. For example, Italian and Belgian central government debts were well over 100 percent of their annual GDP, and there was no way to change this in the span of a few years. Some economists questioned why these particular criteria were chosen in the first place, since a country that can maintain its interest rates, debts, deficits, inflation, and exchange rates in the target range is already doing what the European Union hopes to

TABLE 14.3 Convergence Criteria for Monetary Union

Goals	Targets
1. Stabilize exchange rates	Maintain currency within the ERM band
2. Control inflation	Reduce it to less than 1.5 percent above the average of the three lowest rates
3. Harmonize long-term interest rates	Bring to within 2 percent of the average of the three lowest rates
4. Government deficits	Reduce to less than 3 percent of national GDP
5. Government debt	Reduce to less than 60 percent of national GDP

These five goals were designed to harmonize fiscal and monetary policies in preparation for the single currency.

achieve with monetary union. In other words, meeting the convergence criteria was an indicator that the nation can do what monetary union does but without actually giving up its currency. Why, then, should countries surrender control over monetary policy, and why should they give up their national currency, particularly since there are hidden costs?

Costs and Benefits of Monetary Union

There is no doubt that there are benefits to having one currency in a market as large as the European Union's. For example, the average cost of currency conversion for travelers is 2.5 percent of the amount converted. A trip from Portugal to Sweden, with stops along the way, can quickly eat up a sizable portion of one's vacation money. Businesses fare much better, however, and if they buy in quantities greater than the equivalent of $U.S. 5 million, then the costs are a much smaller 0.05 percent, or $5,000 to convert $10 million. One estimate combining tourists and businesses puts the total costs of currency conversion at 0.4 percent of the European Union's GDP. This is not a trivial sum, but it is not huge, either. The 0.4 percent figure could be higher, however, given the costs of maintaining separate accounting systems and separate money management processes for the different currencies.

A second reason for desiring monetary union is to reduce the effects of exchange-rate uncertainty on trade and investment. Since orders for goods are often placed long before delivery occurs, traders face a good deal of uncertainty about their earnings (if they export) and their payments (if they import). A single currency eliminates this uncertainty, in the same way, for example, that California manufacturers can always be certain of the value of payments they will receive when they ship goods to New York. Recall from Chapter 10 that traders and investors can protect themselves from currency fluctuations with forward markets. Therefore, it should not be surprising that there is not much evidence that the elimination of currency fluctuations through a monetary union will increase cross-border trade and investment. On the other hand, tests of this idea are difficult because there are few examples of monetary unions. Recently, however, some evidence has emerged that shows large positive effects on trade and investment flows from the creation of a single currency. Ultimately, the European Union's experience will prove to be a valuable case study.

Given these considerations, the benefits of a single currency appear to be uncertain. The same cannot be said for the potential costs. A single currency does not allow individual nations to pursue an independent monetary policy, in the same way that the state of New York cannot have a monetary policy that differs from California's or the rest of the United States. In a single-currency area, there is a "one size fits all" monetary policy. It is optimal to have a single currency, and to eliminate the costs of currency conversion and other transaction costs, as long as the regions in the single currency area have synchronized business cycles and mobile labor forces. Synchronization of business cycles means that there is a single monetary policy—expansionary, neutral, or contractionary—that is appropriate for everybody. A mobile labor force guarantees that if some regions are not well synchronized, labor will move from the shrinking region to the expanding one, making the business cycles move together. If, however, the business cycles are not synchronized and labor is relatively immobile, then the single monetary policy will be right for some areas but wrong for others.

Business cycles in Europe have never been synchronized, although the convergence criteria were partly designed with this goal in mind. In addition, the Single European Act's guarantee of freedom for labor mobility does not seem to have created significantly more continent-wide labor mobility, and Europeans are far less mobile than Americans. Given that most conventional measures show that the European Union fails both criteria for being an optimal currency area, it seems natural to ask why they are taking this momentous step.

The Political Economy of a Single Currency

Most policies that offer uncertain benefits and potentially large costs should be rejected. Why, then, did monetary union push ahead? This is the question that many economists have asked, and the answers are less than clear. The easiest answers are that the leaders of the European Union believe that monetary union will create substantial trade and investment flows, or that the leaders of the European Union are simply swept up in a euphoric rush to greater political and economic unity. The latter explanation suffers from the defect that the European Union has been unable to forge a consensus around a common defense and security policy, as evidenced by the divisions over the conflict in the former Yugoslavia.

The best explanation for the push to monetary union seems to be that it is politically necessary in the wake of the capital market liberalization required under the Single European Act. Prior to 1990, many countries had controls on the movement of foreign exchange into their country. Regulatory measures were common, such as taxes on foreign currency holdings, or on assets denominated in foreign currencies, and limitations on the uses of foreign currencies were widespread. The removal of these controls made it easier to speculate in foreign currency markets. One outcome of the removal of capital controls was the turmoil of 1992, when speculators became convinced that a number of currencies in the ERM would ultimately have to be devalued, prompting them to sell off large quantities of the currencies. During the sell-off, Portugal, Ireland, and Spain all devalued; Italy temporarily suspended participation in the ERM; and the United Kingdom dropped out permanently. Ultimately, the British pound fell by 25 percent from its peak before the speculative attacks. Soon after it left the ERM, there were several cases of firms that announced their intentions to close plants inside EU countries and move to the United Kingdom. Philips Electronics, the giant Dutch firm, for example, closed plants in Holland, and SC Johnson and the Hoover Company closed French plants, all in order to open new plants in the United Kingdom where French and Dutch currencies bought more land, labor, buildings, and machinery.

Political friction increases and cooperation decreases when one country loses jobs to another as a result of currency depreciations. The desire to reduce these types of frictions is the reason why the European Monetary System, with its Exchange Rate Mechanism, was created in 1979. Consequently, it is the reason why a flexible exchange rate system is not an option. Although floating exchange rates have the advantage of permitting the greatest amount of flexibility in a nation's monetary policies, the European Union's economic integration plans have closed the door on the use of flexible exchange rate systems.

Given that flexible rates are ruled out, it seems logical to ask why the European Union did not choose to institute a system of fixed exchange rates. In fact, the ERM acted somewhat like a fixed exchange rate system because it tied each country's currency to a weighted average of the other currencies. Exchange rates were not completely fixed, however, and there were bands that the currencies tried to stay within. The European Union's problem with a fixed exchange rate system is that it lacked the ability to keep the currencies within their bands, let alone to completely fix them. International currency markets know that there are definite limits to the resolve and the resources of member countries trying to defend their currencies. The European Union partially solved this by changing the bandwidths from ±2.25 percent to ±15 percent, which removed the minor short-term speculative pressures against particular currencies by letting them float down more before intervention became required. This, however, did nothing about the serious pressure against a currency that the United Kingdom and Italy experienced in 1992. In other words, the European Union is not willing to defend their fixed rates if the costs grow too high, which means that fixed rates are not really "fixed."

Implementation of the Single Currency

The inability of the European Union to maintain a set of fixed rates, coupled with the political undesirability of floating rates, made the single-currency option an attractive choice. Membership in the monetary union, however, is a subset of the European Union. The United Kingdom has left the ERM and, along with Denmark and Sweden, did not join the move to a single currency. Few, if any, of the countries met the convergence criteria for compliance by the 1998 deadline. Nevertheless, in May of 1998, it was announced that 11 countries (the 15 members of the European Union, minus the United Kingdom, Sweden, Denmark, and Greece) would adopt the single currency on January 1, 1999. Greece adopted the euro one year later.

In the first stage of the implementation process, countries kept their national currencies, but fixed their exchange rates to each other. Until euro coins and notes began to circulate in 2002, each of the euro area countries continued to use its own national money, which was fixed in value to the euro and, therefore, to the money of the other member countries. During the transition period before the introduction of euro coins and notes, national currencies were managed as separate, national manifestations of the euro. The German mark, for example,

FIGURE 14.1 Dollars per Euro

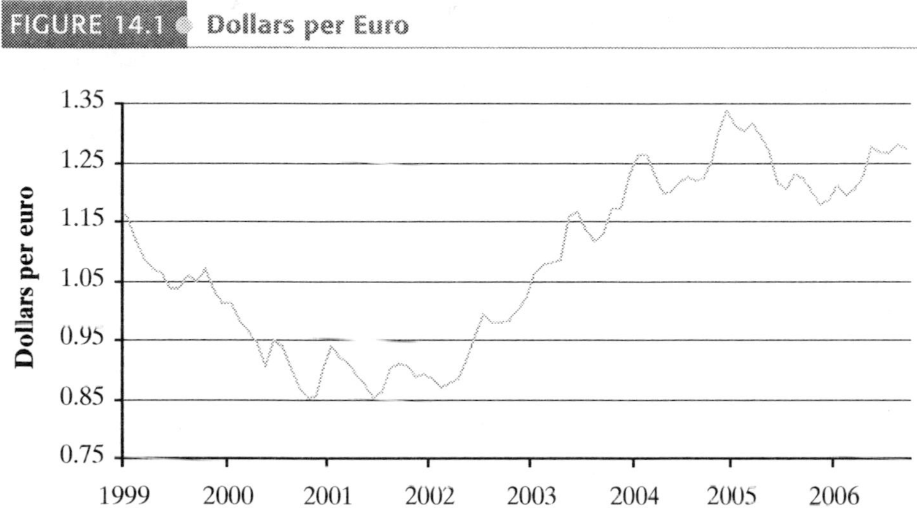

was worth about one-half a euro, just as two quarters are worth one-half a U.S. dollar. Consequently, speculation against any one currency was equivalent to speculating against all of them. The euro itself is on a flexible exchange rate system, so it is free to move up or down against the dollar, the yen, and other currencies. The euro is managed by the European Central Bank (ECB), which also conducts monetary policy in the euro region.

Since its introduction in 1999 at $U.S. 1.18, the euro value has varied significantly (see Figure 14.1). Or, one might say that the dollar's value has fluctuated significantly; either way, the same meaning is implied. The euro lost about one-fourth of its value within the first 18 months and since then has rapidly gained it all back. The decline and the subsequent rise were larger than expected. The decline in 1999 and 2000 was attributed to high—and rising—U.S. interest rates, the high rate of growth in the United States, and the soaring U.S. stock market. The rise in the euro that began in 2002 is perhaps related to the ballooning U.S. trade deficit and the expectation of future declines in the dollar that will be necessary to restore balance, along with the historically low level of U.S. interest rates.

Widening the European Union

After the achievement of monetary union, one of the most pressing problems facing the European Union was the timetable and conditions under which new members would be added to the European Union.

Central and Eastern Europe

Ten countries joined the European Union in 2004 and two more joined in 2007. Ten of the twelve new members are from Central Europe and have undergone profound economic and political transformations as they abandoned relatively closed socialist economies in favor of democratic and capitalist systems.

There are three criteria for membership. First, each of the countries must be stable, functioning democracies. Second, they must have market-based economies, and third, they must formally adopt the EU-wide rules, called the ***acquis communautaire***. These include technical standards, environmental and technical inspections, banking supervision, public accounts, statistical reporting requirements, and other elements of EU law. The *acquis* is sovereign over national laws and must be completely adopted by each new member before it is granted full membership.

In the years leading up to membership, the European Union consults and provides technical assistance to candidate nations. To qualify for admission to the European Union, prospective members must develop the administrative capacity for implementing and enforcing EU rules. Building this capacity requires training legions of professional and technical workers, including judges, lawyers, environmental health and safety inspectors, financial institution supervisors, accountants, and a number of other skilled occupations. The professionals in these areas must become versed in EU law, technical standards, and administrative processes. Failure to demonstrate an ability to enforce the rules can lead to a denial of admission into the European Union.

There are four major problems with the planned expansion. The first is agriculture and agricultural policies. Several of the new members in Central Europe have large agricultural sectors. Poland, for example, is a large country, with a population of 38 million and about 18 percent of its labor force in agriculture. Agriculture is important to several other new members as well, because it generates exports and earns much needed foreign exchange. Large agricultural sectors are a problem for the European Union, however, because of the European Union's agricultural policies, known collectively as the **Common Agricultural Policy (CAP)**. The CAP is the world's most extensive set of farm price supports and farm income maintenance programs. One indicator of the importance of the CAP is that it continues to be the largest item in the EU budget at 40 percent in spite of a number of ongoing reforms to the agricultural support system. In addition, a significant share of expenditures on regional development is agricultural supports that have been reclassified for administrative reasons and to avoid complaints filed through the WTO system.

The CAP sets farm prices, guarantees a market for farm products, and provides direct income payments to farmers. Under a set of reforms passed in 2005, direct payments to farmers will be phased out gradually and decoupled from production. While desirable on their own account, the reforms are necessary in part due to the accession of the new members with large agricultural sectors and low incomes. Agricultural support payments on the same scale as those given to the EU-15 are impossible, given the budget of the European Union. The 12 new members will receive some payments that are phased in gradually over a 10-year period.

The second major issue of expansion is migration. The Single European Act created the right for all EU citizens to move freely and reside wherever they choose. Furthermore, it attempts to create a single labor market that allows workers to search for employment in any member country. Nevertheless, in 2004, when 10 countries joined, only the United Kingdom offered an open labor market, and no countries have shown signs of opening their doors to Romanian and Bulgarian workers when they joined in 2007. Under the rules of accession, countries that were members before 2004 have up to seven years before they must open their labor markets to the new members. New members must also wait for the dismantling of passport controls on their movement (see the Case Study on the Schengen Agreement).

A third issue with expansion is governance. As the original six members of the EEC grew into the 15 members of the European Union, and then added 12 more members, the institutions and governing bodies of the European Union became too complex and cumbersome. The proposed solution, the Constitution for Europe, was intended to simplify decision making processes, among other things, but the proposed document has not been well received by the citizens of the European Union and it is unlikely that it will pass.

Fourth, income difference between the new and existing members is much larger than any previous differences. This creates a variety of tensions, from potential migration pressures, to differences in institutional capacity, and demands on the EU budget for agricultural support payments, cohesion funds, and regional development funds. In the short-to-medium term, the European Union has addressed the migration issue by allowing countries to delay the opening of their labor markets for seven years. It has addressed the institutional gap with a lengthy accession period in which it provided technical assistance and financial support to the new members in order to assist the development of their legal, administrative, and regulatory institutions and to ensure that the new members were capable of enforcing the European Union's body of rules and regulations, or the *aquis communitaire*.

The most serious potential problems associated with the accession of relatively poor members from Central Europe can be ameliorated, if not eliminated completely, by a closing of the income differences between the new and old members. In this regard, the recent experiences of Ireland, Spain, Portugal, and Greece are instructive. Their accession in the 1970s and 1980s led to a similar gap between the richest and poorest members, although not quite as large as the current gap. Recognizing the tensions created by large disparities, the European Union created the Cohesion Fund and expanded its Regional Development Fund. These, and other sources of financing, are now being used to build infrastructure and to connect the new regions to the Western Europe and the global economies.

Turkey

Turkey officially submitted its application for membership in 1987, and in 2004 the European Commission recommended to start negotiations in 2005. Turkey's population of 72.6 million in 2005 would make it the second largest member, although its GDP per capita was only $8,400 at purchasing power parity rates of exchange and $5,004 at market exchange rates. The market rate is less than 20 percent of the EU average, but more than some of the current members, such as Romania and Bulgaria.

The political challenges posed by Turkey's accession are significant. In order to begin negotiations, potential members must demonstrate that they are a stable democracy with respect for human rights, including protections for ethnic minorities, have a functioning market economy, and can implement and enforce the rules and laws of the European Union. Turkey fulfilled these criteria as a precondition for opening negotiations over accession, but it must continue its reforms. In particular, EU officials have warned that the country continues to stifle freedom of speech, that it has not curbed the use of torture in its prisons, and that it has not established civilian control over its military. In addition, Turkey's accession is hampered by the problem of Cyprus, a member of the European Union that is geographically divided into two ethnic regions, a northern half that is Turkish and a southern territory that is ethnically mixed, but largely Greek. Turkey's reluctance to open its ports to Cypriot ships is another barrier to its accession, in part due to the fact that Cyprus can block Turkey's accession under EU rules that grant member countries veto rights over the accession of new members.

It is not certain that Turkey will join the European Union eventually. If it does, the situation will be reminiscent of the situation of Mexico in the NAFTA region. Both are large developing countries with similar per capita income levels. EU pre-accession support programs in financial and technical assistance, and post-accession supports with Cohesion Funds and Regional Development Funds will be critical.

CASE STUDY

Spain's Switch from Emigration to Immigration

Spain's period of highest emigration was from 1881 to 1930, when approximately 4.3 million people left. In 1910 its population was just under 20 million, so a loss of 4.3 million people was significant. The decade with the highest out-migration was 1910 to 1920, when 1.3 million people or well over 5 percent of the population left.

Emigration was slowed by the world depression of the 1930s and World War II, but began again in earnest after 1950. Unlike the earlier migrations, when the majority of migrants went to the Americas, increasing numbers headed for other countries in Central and Western Europe. In particular, France, Germany, and Switzerland were major recipients of Spanish citizens.

By the time Spain joined the European Union in 1986, changes were occurring in the Spanish economy that were reducing the supply-push forces that cause emigration. In 1950 Spain's work force was nearly 50 percent agricultural, but by 1970 agriculture's share of the labor force had fallen to less than 25 percent. With more industry came higher productivity and a shrinking wage gap with France, Germany, and even Switzerland. By the early 1990s, Spain's economic success was turning it into a net attractor of migrants, rather than a net sender. As a result, in the second half of the 1990s, immigration to Spain was accelerating, particularly from North Africa, South America, and western Europe. Well-off Europeans discovered Spain's Mediterranean coast, while Colombians, Ecuadorians, Moroccans, and Mauritanians came for jobs and wages that were significantly higher than what they could earn at home. In 2004 42 percent of the foreign population residing in Spain was from the Americas; they were predominantly Colombians who wished to escape the ongoing violence at home and Ecuadorians looking for work and higher wages. Another 33 percent were Europeans, mostly from western Europe and relatively wealthy and 19 percent were Africans, predominantly from Morocco.

Immigration creates a reaction in most countries where the numbers of immigrants are large. The U.S.–Mexican case is famous but there are numerous others. Mexico itself resists immigration from Guatemalans on its southern border, while Costa Ricans appreciate the hard work of Nicaraguans who come to pick the coffee crop, but they complain about their behavior and use of social services. Germans have a long love-hate relationship with Turks, the French with Algerian immigrants, and so on around the globe. Spain's policy has been relatively accommodating toward immigrants, including six amnesties for undocumented workers since 1990. Its last amnesty occurred in 2005 and offered legal status to more than 700,000 foreigners. At the same time, Spain increased its program of border enforcement, which is primarily aimed at deterring Africans. It also built walls around Ceuta and Melilla, two Spanish territories located inside Morocco, and stepped-up its coastal patrols.

Migration policies are fraught with uncertain side-effects, but one of the most frequent consequences of increased enforcement at the border is a displacement of immigrants to alternative points of entry. In the Spanish case, the walls around Ceuta and Melilla, together with increased vigilance along the coast, resulted in migrants moving their point of departure from Morocco to Western Sahara, a disputed territory on Morocco's southern border. From there, migrants could reach the Canary Islands, which is Spanish territory. When Spain increased its patrols off the coast of Western Sahara, migrants moved their departure points south to Mauritania, and then farther south to Senegal when Spain began to target Mauritania.

It is difficult to name a country that has not gone through a period of high rates of out-migration at some point in its development. Europeans went to the Americas, U.S. citizens went west into what was Mexico and the frontier,

Koreans spread around the globe, and the Japanese went to North and South America. Spain's period of high emigration is over, and it is now one of the desirable target countries where emigrants prefer to settle.

The Demographic Challenge of the Future

As the European Union looks toward the future, a number of challenges are visible. In the short-to-medium run, it must continue to create convergence in income and living standards between its poorest and its most well-off members. Over the medium run, it must also prepare for further widening, in particular for the possible accession of Turkey, a large nation with per capita income levels about one-fifth of the EU average. And finally, in the long run, it must adapt its economies and social support systems to prepare for a much older population.

One of the primary determinants of social spending in virtually all countries is the age structure of the population. As populations age, they need more health care, more pensions, and more long term care. Each of these entails increases in public spending, and given that older citizens regularly vote, democracies usually respond to their demands. A small part of increased spending on services for the elderly will be offset by decreases in educational spending and unemployment benefits, as a smaller share of the total population will need schooling or experience involuntary unemployment. However, these savings will not begin to offset the increases in social spending associated with an aging population. According to estimates carried out by the European Commission, if current policies are left in place, the average EU government will have to increase the public sector by 10 percent simply to maintain its existing programs at their current levels.

Table 14.4 shows a projection of EU population (27 countries) through 2040. By 2040 the percent of the population 65 and over is expected to reach nearly 28 percent of the total, up from below an estimated 18 percent in 2010. The ability of governments to manage a much larger population of retired people will be constrained by the fact that after 2011, the working age population is forecast to begin declining, and after 2018, the total number of people working is projected to start declining as well. Corresponding to the increase in the population over 65, is a nearly equal drop in the working age population, as shown in Table 14.4. Fewer workers means that the rate of economic growth will fall, and that new resources for supporting an aging population will be harder to acquire. At the same time, the number of available workers to support the production of social services needed by the aging population will be both relatively and absolutely smaller.

Migration can play a role at the margin to ameliorate the changes, but it is unlikely that migration alone will have a major impact. Simply to return the estimated 2040 working age population (15–64) to its 2010 estimates would require the immigration of more than 54 million people, or 11 percent of the predicted 2040 population. And this still would not compensate for the absolute increase

TABLE 14.4 Population Forecast, 2010–2040: 27 Members of the European Union

	Population, 2010 (Millions)	Percent, 2010	Population, 2040 (Millions)	Percent, 2040
Total	489.0	100.0	468.6	100.0
By age category				
Ages 0–15	74.6	15.3	63.2	13.5
Ages 15–64	328.7	67.2	274.5	58.6
Ages 65+	85.7	17.5	130.9	27.9

Population in the European Union will stop growing and begin to age rapidly after 2010.

Source: U.S. Census Bureau.

in the number of people 65 and over. Nevertheless, given the potential for EU expansion beyond its current members along with the migration pressures emanating from North Africa and elsewhere, any assumption about the capacity of the European Union to absorb migrants may turn out to be false.

The Commission of the European Union has begun to analyze trends and to recommend changes to pension and health care systems. Several countries have begun to experiment, for example linking pensions to changes in life expectancy, and to encourage workers to postpone retirement. Demographic changes are clearly visible and well understood; whether or not the European Union and the national governments respond will depend on the flexibility and adaptability of their electorates.

Summary

- The 27-member European Union was created in several stages. The earliest stage involved agreements over open trade for coal and steel (ECSC), followed by cooperation over the peaceful development of nuclear energy (Euratom) and a free trade agreement.
- The main institutions of the European Union are the Commission, the Council, the Court of Justice, the Court of Auditors, and the European Parliament. The roles of these institutions have evolved.
- The Treaty of Rome was signed in 1957 and was put into effect in 1958, creating a six-country, free-trade area that was phased in gradually over the next 10 years.
- The next wave of deepening was the creation of the European Monetary System in 1979, linking exchange rates.

- Following the EMS, the Single European Act was passed, creating a common market by 1993. While preparations were taking place for the implementation of the SEA, the Maastricht Treaty, or Treaty on European Union, was signed in 1991 and approved by the national governments in late 1993.
- The Maastricht Treaty created a common currency. In preparation, a set of convergence criteria was developed with targets for interest rates, inflation, government spending, and government debt.
- While the European Union was undergoing its several rounds of deepening integration, it was also widening membership to nearly all of Western Europe. Between 1958 and 1995, it expanded from the original six members to 15. In 2004 10 more countries joined, followed by two more in 2007.
- Eastward expansion of the European Union created problems in the areas of agricultural policy, governance, income differences, and migration.

Vocabulary

acquis communautaire
cohesion funds
Common Agricultural Policy (CAP)
competitive devaluation
convergence criteria
Council of the European Union
Court of Auditors
Court of Justice
Delors Report
euro
European Atomic Energy Community (EAEC or Euratom)
European Coal and Steel Community (ECSC)
European Commission
European Community (EC)
European Currency Unit (ECU)
European Economic Community (EEC)
Monetary System (EMS)
European Parliament
European Union (EU)
exchange rate mechanism (ERM)
Maastricht Treaty
qualified majority
Single European Act (SEA)
subsidiarity
Treaty of Rome
Treaty on European Union

Study Questions

1. What were the three main stages of deepening that occurred in the European Community after the Treaty of Rome was passed?
2. What are the five main institutions of the European Union, and what are their responsibilities?
3. The Single European Act is a case in which it was difficult to create an agreement, despite the fact that there was near unanimity in support of an agreement. If everyone wanted the agreement, why was it hard to negotiate?
4. How did the European Union expect to create gains from trade with the implementation of the Single European Act?
5. A sudden sharp increase in the demand for the German mark almost destroyed the Exchange Rate Mechanism in 1992. Explain how a rise in the demand for a currency can jeopardize a target zone or exchange rate band.
6. Discuss the pros and cons of the single currency.
7. What are the pressures on the European Union to admit new members?
8. What problems arose from the admission of 12 new members between 2004 and 2007?
9. How does the European Union compare and contrast to the NAFTA region in size, institutional structure, and depth of integration?

- Joined 9 other UK territories Federa= of the W.I. but 1961 withdrew

62 - Independence from English but remain member of Commonwealth of Nation

1972 - Socialist policies, under Prime Minister Michael Manley & ↑ relat w/ Cuba

1976 - Start of political violence

1980 - under P.M. Seaga reverse policies of predecessor + ↑ privatiza= + closer ties to US

89 -

90s - heavy emigra= due to ↑ levels of viola, drugs gang warfare

- Econ - HW
- Stats - HW last week
- Econ Reading
-